Our Times

Readings from Recent Periodicals

Our Times

Readings from Recent Periodicals

FIFTH EDITION

Edited by

ROBERT ATWAN

Bedford Books ❧ Boston

For Bedford Books
President and Publisher: Charles H. Christensen
General Manager and Associate Publisher: Joan E. Feinberg
Managing Editor: Elizabeth M. Schaaf
Developmental Editor: Alanya Harter
Editorial Assistants: Amanda J. Bristow and Ellen Thibault
Production Editor: Sherri Frank
Production Assistant: Deborah Baker
Copyeditor: Pamela Thomson
Text Design: Jean Hammond
Cover Design: Hannus Design Associates
Cover Photography: Martin Paul
Composition: Pine Tree Composition, Inc.
Printing and Binding: Haddon Craftsmen, Inc.

Library of Congress Catalog Card Number: 97–74955

Copyright © 1998 by Bedford Books
(A Division of St. Martin's Press, Inc.)

Manufactured in the United States of America.

2 1 0 9 8
f e d c b a

For information, write: Bedford Books, 75 Arlington Street, Boston, MA 02116
(617–426–7440)

ISBN: 0–312–14931–X

Acknowledgments
ABC advertisement: "T.V. is good," *People*, September 15, 1997. Courtesy of ABC Television Network.
Yvonne Abraham, "Lipstick Liberation," *Boston Phoenix*, May 30, 1997. Copyright © The Boston Phoenix Inc.
Adbusters advertisement: "Obsession Fetish" uncommercial, as appeared in *Utne Reader*, January/February 1997. Courtesy of Adbusters, Vancouver, Canada, 1-800-663-1243.
Lylah M. Alphonse, "Race Needs 'Other' Option," *Boston Globe*, October 5, 1996. Reprinted by permission of the publisher.
American Indian College Fund advertisement: "I'll Never Fight for Women's Rights." Print ad developed by Wieden and Kennedy for the American Indian College Fund's public service advertising campaign.

Acknowledgments and copyrights are continued at the back of the book on pages 434–437, which constitute an extension of the copyright page. It is a violation of the law to reproduce these selections by any means whatsoever without the written permission of the copyright holder.

Preface for Instructors

Like its predecessors, the fifth edition of *Our Times* is a collection of contemporary nonfiction intended for use in composition courses. This wealth of very recent writing — half of it published since 1997 and *all* of it since 1994 — is drawn from virtually every important American periodical. In its wide range of timely topics, the collection offers a distinctive and comprehensive view of life in America today.

New to This Edition

All of the selections in this fifth edition are new. They are grouped into fifteen units designed to reflect the dominant themes, issues, and ideas of our time. Several of these units center around the issues of students' everyday lives: self-image, gender differences, racial identity, and our fixation on automobiles. Other units feature a variety of perspectives on some of the nation's most compelling social, cultural, and political issues: immigration, education reform, the "English-only" movement, class and poverty, and same-sex marriage. Included, too, are topics that deal directly with issues of considerable importance to today's colleges: affirmative action, language, the feminist movement, and the changing values of incoming students. In addition, there are new units covering the impending millennium and the enormous influence of mass media and popular culture.

In this edition, issues relating to media and popular culture are not confined to one or two units but surface throughout. Along with all new selections, the fifth edition of *Our Times* contains a wealth of supplementary selections featuring interviews, advertisements, letters, speeches, cartoons, public documents, newspaper clippings, quotations, and commentary. These selections — mainly drawn from popular media, advocacy groups, and the Internet — are clearly identified throughout the table of contents. Taken as a whole, they add a new visual and verbal dimension to the book, one that should appeal to instructors interested in the relationship between media studies and public discourse. This dimension is reinforced by the large number of selections across the chapters that deal with such popular phenomena in our culture as boyfriends who read *Playboy*, lottery tickets, millennialism, automobiles, weddings, celebrity, talk shows, advertising, and situation comedy.

To ensure that this edition leads to even more student interaction with both the material and with each other, a new opening chapter addresses the attitudes, opinions, and values of today's freshman class. Your students are invited to answer a questionnaire designed by UCLA's Cooperative Institutional Research Program, an organization that has studied the American freshman class for over thirty years. After taking the questionnaire, students can then check their results against the survey results to see how they compare to a quarter of a million other American freshmen who took it in 1996: Where do your students stand on such issues as affirmative action, the death penalty, legalization of marijuana, and so on? Besides offering individual students a sense of how the nation's freshman class as a whole thinks, believes, and behaves, the information — more importantly — can help your writing class evaluate its own internal identity: To what extent do your students differ from each other? By using the opening chapter as an orientation to a writing course, your class can begin to appreciate its own cultural and attitudinal diversity, and individual students can be better prepared for subsequent dialogue and debate. To remind students of where they stand in relation to the national norms, statistical data relevant to each topic appear at the beginning of each chapter.

The fifth edition of *Our Times* will easily adapt to the agenda of most composition programs. The units are arranged in a familiar order, starting with topics close to students' personal experiences (for example, physical appearance, gender), and then proceeding to more public topics (for instance, immigration policy, affirmative action). The progression of the topics is reflected in changes in the types of writing assignments in individual units. Though each chapter mixes different kinds of assignments, the apparatus with selections and units generally takes students through personal and expository work and then concentrates on argumentative papers. Instructors who want to focus on all or just some of the rhetorical modes will find them amply represented throughout the collection. In fact, many articles were especially selected to demonstrate rhetorical strategies that will help students shape persuasive arguments — exemplification, classification, and causal reasoning. More so than previous editions, the reading material in this edition of *Our Times* gives instructors the opportunity to introduce first-year students to a wide variety of compositional models.

Instructors who want to approach selections from various compositional perspectives will now find three alternative tables of contents in the back of the book. These alternate arrangements suggest ways the book can be used in courses that cover rhetorical patterns, research techniques, or compositional motive and purpose.

The Units

In contrast to most thematically arranged readers, which contain a small number of broad categories, *Our Times* features a larger number of tightly focused units, most with only three or four selections that speak directly to each other. The advantages of using these smaller units in a composition course should be immediately apparent to instructors: They permit a wider range and variety of topics to be covered in a syllabus; they allow more focused discussion and writing; and they can be adequately handled in one or two class periods.

Like the previous edition, this collection also includes two expanded chapters designed to be used for more extensive assignments and class work. Placed at the end of the book, these "conference chapters" will allow instructors to cover a topic in greater depth and detail. Each conference chapter examines a major cultural issue: the first, America's growing concern with racial identity; and the second, the powerful influence of mass media on American society. Each conference chapter is designed to accommodate extended discussion and debate on topics close to students' lives. In keeping with the spirit of *Our Times*, instructors may want to set up classroom "conferences" around one or both of these chapters. Such conferences would encourage a broad range of discussion and participation; students could form several panels to deal with the various aspects of the issue. Instructors could also use these chapters as a starting point for research papers.

Reading, Discussion, and Writing

With its emphasis on recent issues and ideas, the fifth edition of *Our Times* invites class discussion and debate; in fact, the book is carefully designed to facilitate such student responses. Each unit is prefaced by a contextual note that helps students find their way into the readings and points the way to future discussion. Key biographical information about the authors is unobtrusively included in footnotes. Each unit ends with a section called "Discussing the Unit," which includes three sets of interlocking study questions and tasks that help students prepare for class discussion and then incorporate that discussion into their own writing. First, a "Suggested Topic for Discussion" lets students know beforehand what main topic their class discussion will cover. This topic gives students a common purpose in reading and helps keep the discussion focused. Second, "Preparing for Class Discussion" gives students questions and ideas to think about so they will come to class with something to say about the topic. Included in these preparatory activities are "Prewriting Assignments" that ask the student to do some preliminary writing. Third, "From Discussion to Writing" gives students a writing topic that — without being redundant — draws on and applies the class discussion.

Finally, for instructors who don't want to use the class discussion unit, or who don't want to use it all the time, *Our Times* contains alternate apparatus. Two sets of questions follow each selection: "Responding as a Reader" and "Responding as a Writer." These discussion questions and writing assignments (which require responses ranging from a single sentence to a full essay) can be used by instructors who prefer to concentrate on individual selections. They can also be used, of course, to supplement the unit apparatus.

A basic premise of *Our Times* is that student discussion — often over-looked as a pedagogical resource — can play an important role in composition by stimulating fresh ideas and creating a social context for writing. Instructors interested in using class discussion as a basis for writing (or in simply eliciting more discussion in general) are encouraged to have their students read "Reading, Writing, Research, and Class Discussion," which offers some practical advice on how to prepare for and participate in class discussion. *Our Times* is designed to get students reading, thinking, talking, and writing about the society they live in. Furthermore, the book acquaints students with the diverse viewpoints and controversial contents of America's leading periodicals. In the hope that students will become regular readers of some of these, a subscription list describing the various periodicals represented in the book appears at the back of *Our Times;* and for the first time, we've also included Web addresses for the magazines to give students more options for reading.

The Instructor's Manual

A fuller description of how to generate and direct class discussion can be found in my essay in the instructor's manual, *From Discussion to Writing: Instructional Resources for Our Times.* For teachers interested in using discussion as a basis for composition, the manual features three other relevant essays. In "Forming Forums: Student Presentations to Encourage Research, Discussion, and Better Writing," Liz de Beer of Middlesex County College offers many practical ideas for using *Our Times* in the classroom. In "The Morton Downey Jr. Model: Talk-Show Influence on Classroom Discussion," Judith Rae Davis of Bergen Community College provides a provocative view not only of how talk shows influence student attitudes but also of how they influence classroom discussion in general. Davis's essay, which originally appeared in *Teaching English in the Two-Year College* (October 1989), won the Best Article of the Year Award presented by that journal. And Scott Lloyd DeWitt of Ohio State University in Marion has contributed "Emerging Technologies, Changing Discussions: Using Computer-mediated Discussion in the Writing Classroom." Instructors interested in developing a discussion-based writing agenda within the new electronic technologies will profit from DeWitt's exciting proposals.

Prepared by Shelley Salamensky, the manual is an indispensable component of *Our Times,* built around the idea that the provocative and entertaining work of teaching with *Our Times* is built on proven pedagogic principles — the most important being that talking and writing are related activities. Collaborative work offers students insight into their peers and thus themselves; imaginative exercises let students tap into their own cognitive abilities. Each unit in the manual moves from the personal to the global and from productive and open discussion to lucid, vital writing, opening with a convenient, brief summary of each selection and how the selections relate to each other. Practical advice — called "Teaching this

Unit" — suggests specific strategies for getting students talking about the issues and selections and points out some of the shared rhetorical strategies used by the writers. "Sparking Discussion" questions offer suggestions for prewriting and collaborative activities about the general issues, focusing on what students have brought with them to class; "Encouraging Deeper Analysis" questions give instructors detailed ideas for ways to get students to look carefully at the individual selections in *Our Times* as they talk and write, in and out of class; and "Moving from Discussion to Writing" questions give some possible topics for larger research, writing, and collaborative assignments, encouraging students to take what they've learned from the book and move on from there, on their own.

The Revision Cycle

Why a new edition of *Our Times* after only three years? The reason is simple: to keep the selections as fresh and topical as possible. Any instructor who wants to use reading material that reflects recent controversies and trends knows how quickly issue-oriented anthologies become dated. It always surprises me how broadly most composition readers define "contemporary"; many books in use still contain "contemporary" essays from the sixties. These may be contemporaneous with the experiences of some instructors, but certainly not with those of younger teachers and especially not with their first-year students, who are often being asked to accept as "contemporary" material that was published well before they were born. All of the material reprinted in *Our Times* is truly contemporary with respect to the lives and experiences of students; in fact, most of the material was written during the year or two prior to the book's publication. To keep each edition of *Our Times* as current as possible, the book will be revised every three years. Each edition, moreover, will contain only a small proportion of material from the previous edition.

Acknowledgments

As series editor of the annual *Best American Essays*, I monitor every issue of nearly every major national and regional magazine. I would like to thank the many editors and publishers around the country who generously keep me posted on relevant essays and articles. The selections in the fifth edition of *Our Times* are drawn from fifty-three different magazines and newspapers. These periodicals represent a full spectrum of regions, interests, and points of views — from *People* to the *New York Times*, from *Mademoiselle* to the *New Republic*. New to this edition are webzines, such as *Slate* and *Salon*.

I'd like to thank, too, my students in several writing classes I taught over the past few years at Seton Hall University, where I developed and tried out many of the ideas for this book. I hope some of these students learned as much from me about writing as I learned from them about teaching. A good part of my thinking about the links between writing and discussion grew out of a 1987 conference at Seton Hall, "Redefining the Essay for the Humanities," in which I participated with (among others) the late O. B. Hardison of Georgetown University, Donald McQuade of the University of California at Berkeley, William Howarth of Princeton University, Scott Russell Sanders of Indiana University, George Core of the *Sewanee Review*, Kurt Spellmeyer of Rutgers University, Thomas Recchio of the University of Connecticut, Michael Hall of the National Endowment for the Humanities, Jacqueline Berke of Drew University, and Alexander Butrym (the conference director), Barbara Lukacs, and Nancy Enright of Seton Hall.

For their assistance on the fifth edition of *Our Times*, I'd like to thank a number of friends, colleagues, and reviewers for many helpful suggestions. I especially extend my gratitude to the following people for their extremely helpful in-depth reviews of the previous edition: Michael S. Allen of Ohio State University at Mansfield; Kris Beck of University of Iowa; Christine Berni of Kent State University; Kathryn M. Burton of Miami University at Hamilton; Michele Auriemma Cadigan of Hudson Community College; Mr. Tracy Cave of Pasadena City College; Karen Colpitts of Ohio State University at Mansfield; Susan Elherne of Vermilion Community College; Ken Gilfillan of Rowan College of New Jersey; Catherine Gorge of West Virginia University; Patricia Gott of Southern Illinois University; Joseph Green of Lower Columbia College; Christian A. Hanns of Hudson County Community College; Victor Paul Hitchcock of Southern Illinois University at Carbondale; Nancy Hoffman of Clatsop Community College; William Hunt of Northwestern Connecticut Community Technical College; Martha Kallstrom of Georgia Southern University; Daniel Koen of Colorado State University; Wanda R. Larrier of Rowan Liberal Arts and Science; John Lundquist of Golden West College; Robert M. McIvaine of Slippery Rock University; Kathryn Mapes of University of Louisville; Margaret Dietz Meyer of Ithaca College; Clara Lee R. Moodie of Central Michigan University; Martin Newitz of Golden West College; John Nicholson of University of Iowa; Deanna Odney of Southern Illinois University; Valerie Peterson of University of Iowa; John Robertson of Iowa Central Community College; Elizabeth Rodacker of Merced College; Dr. Jerome L. Rodnitzky of University of Texas at Arlington; Linda L. Schuppener of Kirkwood Community College; Joseph L. Sanders of Lakeland Community College; Roberta Silverman of California State University Dominguez Hills; Timothy Skeen of University of Nebraska; and Elizabeth Tentarelli of Merrimack College.

The four previous editions of *Our Times* profited from the ideas and suggestions of numerous people and, since their influence is still felt in this edition, I would be remiss not to thank them again. Kathleen Shine Cain, Michael Meyer, and Thomas Recchio reviewed the earliest plans for *Our Times* and offered many cogent suggestions. Charles O'Neill and Matthew Kearney provided two enormously useful essay-reviews of the first edition.

Charles O'Neill also prepared — and helped design — the instructor's manual for the first two editions of *Our Times*.

I also receive invaluable help throughout editions from my friend Professor Peter Lushing of the Benjamin N. Cardozo School of Law, who generously advises me on relevant legal issues raised by selections and often supplies me with necessary material.

It is always a pleasure to acknowledge the people at Bedford Books. Bedford's publisher, Charles H. Christensen, brings a Montaignean spirit to these endeavors; he helps fashion and refashion, shape and reshape each book until it reaches a "go-ahead" form. My first editor, Joan E. Feinberg, in the best editorial tradition, not only helped me develop many of my thoughts but contributed many splendid ideas of her own — and continues to do so. Jane Betz and Beth Castrodale, my editors in previous editions, will always remain a presence in the series.

For this fifth edition, I'd like to thank the book's editor Alanya Harter for her many insights and especially for her perceptive views of popular culture and mass media. She also played a leading role in reconceptualizing the book so that it could incorporate a more diverse range of supplementary selections. Aron Keesbury helped with reading and research, as did Amanda Bristow and Ellen Thibault; I'm grateful for their suggestions and their diligence in tracking down some elusive selections and visual material. Arthur Johnson labored behind the scenes with permissions (and remembered what the early Beatles named their mod haircut: "Arthur," of course). Without Bedford's production staff it would be impossible to keep this series on its tight schedule, so very special thanks to Elizabeth Schaaf — and to Sherri Frank, the book's superb production editor — for graciously tolerating once again the panic attacks I regularly inflict on their department as I try to make the collection as up-to-date as book publication allows. Thanks also go to Deborah Baker, production assistant; Pamela Thomson, who expertly copyedited the manuscript, and to Janet Cocker and Cynthia Hastings for reading proof. With its numerous supplemental materials (news clippings, documents, advertisements, and so forth) this edition required an extensive redesign; I am very grateful to Jean Hammond for finding ways of introducing a variety of reading materials into the text clearly and dramatically. I appreciate again the indispensable promotional efforts and creativity of Donna Dennison, Zoe Langosy, and Susan Pace.

Finally, I appreciate the help I received from my son Gregory, whose Internet research skills came in handy throughout the project.

R. A.

Introduction: Reading, Writing, Research, and Class Discussion

Students often begin their college writing courses with a common misconception. They believe that writing is an intensely private activity demanding extraordinary inner resources. They may picture writers sitting alone at their desks, staring at a blank page until inspiration strikes. Indeed, for centuries this romantic image of anxious solitude followed by a burst of creativity has served as a powerful model of how literature is produced. But for the average student, who has little knowledge of how writers work and who has perhaps never observed people writing professionally, this popular image can lead to a distorted view of the writing process and the role it plays in a person's intellectual development.

Most writers work within a lively social environment, one in which issues and ideas are routinely discussed and debated. They often begin writing on topics that grow directly out of specific situations: a journalist covers a murder trial; a professor prepares a paper for a conference; a social worker describes a complex case; an executive reports on an important meeting. Usually, the writer consults with friends and co-workers about the task and solicits their opinions and support. The writer will sometimes ask these friends and colleagues to comment on a draft of the work. If the work is to be published, the writer almost always receives additional advice and criticism in the form of editorial comment, copyediting, proofreading, and independent reviews. By the time the work appears in print, it has probably gone through numerous drafts (some writers do as many as ten or twelve) and has been subjected to a rigorous sequence of editorial efforts, from fact-checking to stylistic fine-tuning.

Nearly all published work has gone through this process. Even the briefest article in a magazine has probably been checked several times by several people. Of course, none of this activity is visible in the final product. Most readers have little knowledge of the various levels of work and collaboration that go into a piece of writing: the author's often extensive reading and research; the time spent traveling, interviewing, and discussing; the organization of information, the composition of several drafts, and the concerted effort of editors and publishers.

Too often, students write in an intellectual and emotional vacuum. You may feel only minimally engaged with an assigned topic — which may seem to have come out of nowhere — and may not know anyone with whom the topic may be seriously and intelligently discussed. Unlike the professional writer, you may feel little personal incentive, encouragement, or support from others. No wonder students often find it hard to begin a paper. Instead of writing for a group of interested people, they often feel that they are only writing for one person — the instructor, who will read not for discussion but for evaluation.

This book is designed to help students fill in the intellectual and emotional vacuum that confronts them when they begin to write. Two of the biggest problems in composition — finding something to say and getting started — most often arise when students lack a vital connection with what other people are saying about an issue or idea. In this sense, the basis of many writing problems is not so much technical or psychological as it is *social*. These problems, at their worst, are reflected in prose that sounds oddly disconnected from current public discourse.

The art of writing and the art of discussion are closely linked. Experienced writers invariably write within a climate of discussion. Their writing often refers to the ideas and opinions of others. Many writers, especially in the academic community, directly respond to other writers: A scientist reexamines the experimental procedures of other scientists; a literary critic takes exception to a prevailing method of interpretation; a sociologist offers an alternate explanation of a colleague's data; a historian disputes the conclusions of another historian. Such people are not writing in a vacuum. Their ideas often originate in discussion, their writing responds to discussion, and their papers will inevitably provoke further discussion.

The Art of Discussion

"Discussion" is one of those commonly used words from speech and rhetoric — like "essay" or "style" — that remains difficult to define precisely. The word has a long and complex history. It derives from the Latin verb *discutere*, meaning to dash, scatter, or to shake out. It gradually took on a legal and, later, a rhetorical sense of "breaking" a case or a topic down into its various parts for investigation. Though the word is ordinarily used today to mean "to talk over" or "to consider carefully," it still retains the rhetorical sense of sifting a topic into separate parts for close examination.

It is easier to say what discussion is not: It is neither conversation nor debate. Unlike conversation, discussion is purposefully conducted around a given topic. Unlike debate, it is not formally organized into two competing points of view. Think of discussion as a speech activity that falls between informal conversation and formal debate. For the purpose of this book, discussion is defined as "the free and open exploration of a specified topic by a small group of prepared people." The goal of such discussion is not to arrive at a group decision or a consensus of opinion, but to investigate as many sides of a topic as possible.

To keep discussion from rigidifying into a debate between two competing sides or from drifting into aimless conversation, a discussion leader or moderator is usually required. The discussion leader may play an active role in discussion (a style we see displayed by many television talk-show hosts) or may choose to remain neutral. But regardless of the extent of the leader's role, he or she will ordinarily introduce the topic, encourage participation, maintain an orderly sequence of responses, and ensure that people stick to the point. If a group desires a greater degree of formality in its discussions, it may also appoint someone to keep notes of the meetings. With its regularly scheduled sessions, diverse members, and clear-cut academic purpose, the typical college composition class of fifteen to twenty-five students is an ideal discussion group.

There are many different kinds of discussion groups and techniques. Anyone who would like to learn more about various discussion groups and methods may want to consult such standard texts as Ernest G. Bormann's *Discussion and Group Methods* (3rd ed., 1989) or Mary A. Bany and Lois V. Johnson's *Classroom Group Behavior: Group Dynamics in Education* (revised edition, 1966). Heidi Hayes Jacobs's *The Discussion Types Model: Reconceptualizing the Discussion to Develop Critical Thought* (1988) is another valuable book on the subject. These and other similar studies can usually be found in the education, psychology, or speech sections of most college libraries.

Participating in Class Discussion

Like writing, discussion is a learned activity. To be adept at group discussion requires the development of a variety of skills — in speaking, listening, thinking, and preparing. By taking an active part in class discussion, college students can help themselves become more intellectually mature and better prepared for professional careers. To help develop these skills, you should keep in mind the following five basic rules:

1. *Be willing to speak in public.* Good discussion depends on the lively participation of all group members, not (as so often happens) on the participation of a vocal few. Many students, however, do not join discussions because they are afraid to speak extemporaneously in a group. This fear is quite common — so common, in fact, that according to a leading communication consultant, Michael T. Motley, psychological surveys "show that what Americans fear most — more than snakes, heights, disease, financial problems, or even death — is speaking before a group." To take an active role in your education you must learn to overcome "speech anxiety." Professor Motley offers the following advice to those who are terrified of speaking before a group: stop thinking of public speaking as a performance and start thinking of it as communication. He believes that people choke up or feel butterflies in their stomachs when starting to speak because they worry more about how people will respond than about what they themselves have to say. "Most audiences," he reminds us, "are more interested in hearing what we have to say than in evaluating our speech skills."

2. *Be willing to listen.* No one can participate in group discussion who doesn't listen attentively. Attentive listening, however, is not passive hearing, the sort of one-way receptivity we habitually experience when we tune in to our radios, cassette players, and television sets. A good listener knows it is important not only to attend closely to what someone is saying but to understand *why* he or she is saying it. Attentive listening also requires that you understand a statement's connection to previous statements and its relation to the discussion as a whole. Perhaps the most valuable result of attentive listening is that it leads to the one element that open and lively group discussion depends on: good questions. An expert on group dynamics claims that most ineffective discussions "are characterized by a large number of answers looking for questions." When the interesting questions start popping up, group discussion has truly begun.

3. *Be willing to examine all sides of a topic.* Good discussion techniques require that you be patient with complexity. Difficult problems rarely have obvious solutions that can be conveniently summarized in popular slogans. Complex topics are multifaceted; they demand to be turned over in your mind so that you can see them from a variety of angles. Group discussion, because it provokes a number of diverse viewpoints, is an excellent way to broaden your perspective and deepen your insight into complex ideas and issues.

4. *Be willing to suspend judgment.* Class discussion is best conducted in an open-minded and tolerant spirit. To explore ideas and issues in a free and open manner, you will need to develop a receptivity to the opinions of others even when they contradict your own. Discussion, remember, is not debate. Its primary purpose is communication, not competition. The goal of group discussion should be to open up a topic so that everyone in the group can hear a wide range of attitudes and opinions. This does not mean that you shouldn't form a strong opinion about an issue; rather, it encourages you to be aware of rival opinions. An opinion formed without awareness of other points of view — that has not been tested against contrary opinions — is not a *strong* opinion but merely a stubborn one.

5. *Be willing to prepare.* Effective discussion is not merely spontaneous conversation. It demands a certain degree of preparation. To participate in class discussion, you must consider assigned topics beforehand and read whatever material is required. You should develop the habit of reading with pen in hand, underlining, noting key points, asking questions of your material, jotting impressions and ideas down in a notebook. The notes you bring to class will be an invaluable aid in group discussion.

To get the most out of your reading and discussion, take careful notes *during* class. You will want to jot down points that give you new insights, information that changes your opinion, positions you take exception to, questions you need to answer, ideas you want to consider more fully. You should think of class discussion as the first step toward your paper, as an opportunity to brainstorm ideas, form an approach, and discover a purpose. When you sit down to write, you will not be starting from scratch. If you've taken careful notes, you've already begun to write.

The art of discussion, as described in these five suggestions, involves speaking, listening, thinking, and preparing. Yet discussion is also closely connected to writing. By learning to participate in serious group discussion, by learning to exchange ideas freely and openly with others, you will also be learning some of the most fundamental principles of good writing.

Discussion and Brainstorming

As you prepare to write for college courses, you may confront difficulties that have less to do with the routine tasks of composition — correcting spelling, punctuation, and grammar — than with the deeper problems of finding something to say and a context in which to say it. It is not uncommon for beginning students to turn in papers that contain few serious mechanical errors, yet lack intellectual substance and a clear orientation. Using group discussion as a basis for composition can help remedy these problems. Group discussion can serve as a stimulus for your ideas and provide a meaningful context in which to express them. Furthermore, as you will see, the art of discussion can function in many ways as an important model for the art of writing.

Finding something to say about a topic always ranks high on lists of student writing problems. This problem is the main reason that the blank sheet of paper (or the blank screen) so often triggers a set of anxious questions: What can I say? Where do I begin? Exploratory discussion offers a way out of this dilemma. Years ago, an advertising executive, Alexander F. Osborne, developed a group method of generating ideas that became enormously popular in many professional fields. With typical advertising savvy, Osborne gave his technique a memorable name — "brainstorming." Osborne's goal was to stimulate creativity by presenting a small group of people with a problem or topic and then encouraging them to toss off as many ideas about it as quickly as possible. Speed, spontaneity, and free-association were essential to his method. But the most important part of the brainstorming technique was its complete absence of criticism. Nobody in the group was allowed to criticize or disagree with any idea, no matter how silly or farfetched it seemed. The absence of criticism, Osborne found, kept ideas flowing, because people were not afraid to sound ill informed or just plain stupid.

This brainstorming technique can clearly be applied to composition as a way to stimulate the flow of ideas. Brainstorming could be done briefly by the whole composition class, or by small groups of students on their own. Moreover, most exploratory discussion — if it is free, open, and relaxed — will contain some degree of spontaneous brainstorming in which ideas can sprout and grow. If you take note of these ideas you will find that when you sit down to write you will not be starting out in a vacuum but will have a context of discussion out of which your composition can take shape.

Another type of brainstorming can also help you move from class discussion to individual writing. In this type of brainstorming (sometimes referred to as "nominal" brainstorming) each person in the class works alone, silently jotting down a brief list of ideas about a topic. Afterward, all the students compare the lists and, after some culling and combining, record their ideas on the blackboard. This brainstorming method can be used at the beginning of class to open up various avenues of discussion. The written list can also serve as a tangible source of ideas for individuals to pursue later in their papers. Since it involves some preliminary writing that can be done in preparation for class, this more focused form of brainstorming is frequently recommended in the instructional material of *Our Times*.

If exploratory discussion can help reduce the anxiety you may feel while trying to develop ideas for papers, it can also alleviate another major writing problem — the feeling of alienation. Thinking and writing alone, with little awareness of an actual audience or of a practical context, it is easy to compose papers that sound disembodied and disengaged. Ideas seem to come out of nowhere; transitions and connections are missing; conclusions that should grow out of the development of an idea are instead little more than blunt, unearned assertions. Though such papers are common, instructors find it difficult to pinpoint precisely what is wrong with them because the problems are vague and difficult to isolate, and therefore hard to identify by the usual marking symbols. The root problem of such essays will not be found in grammar or mechanics, but in the orientation of the writer. The problem is not one of style, structure, or content, but of overall *context*.

Experienced writers, as noted earlier, invariably work with a clear sense of audience and occasion. For example, a literature or composition teacher working on a critical article is writing within a clearly definable context: He or she has a sense of who the audience will be, where the article could be published, and — most important — *why* it is being written. No matter what its subject or point of view, the article will be intellectually oriented to a community of readers presumed to be aware of the topic and attuned to the various points of view involved in its discussion. The fact that so many academic papers are first delivered at professional conferences underscores the vital importance of a concrete audience and occasion.

As you discover the connections between discussion and composition, you will also find your bearings as a writer. Your writing — no matter what the topic — will be oriented toward making a response. Your papers will not only respond to an assigned topic but, more important, will respond within the context of a continuing discussion of that topic. In other words, you will write as an active participant, responding, as you would in group discussion, to the actual or anticipated responses of others. This texture of mutual response is what so often gives professionally written essays and articles their mature tone and clear orientation.

Once you see writing as a form of response, you will also become more conscious of your social and intellectual attitudes as a writer: Are you closed off to other opinions? Are you overbearing? Do you try to see different sides of an issue? Are you patient with complexity? Do you oversimplify difficult problems? These are all values learned in group discussion that directly carry over into composition and all intellectual activities.

As you work through *Our Times*, you will also observe how participation in group discussion is relevant to all types of writing. It is easy to see how an awareness of conflicting opinions can play an important part in critical, analytical, and argumentative papers. Yet personal writing can also profit from exploratory group discussion. By discussing your personal experiences in class, you can begin to view them from broader social and cultural perspectives. *Our Times* starts out with a number of discussion topics and writing assignments that explore the connections between our personal experiences and some of today's dominant themes and issues.

Discussion, Reading, and Research

Learning how to participate effectively in group discussion can help you improve your reading skills as well. In using this book, you are especially encouraged to approach each selection as though you were actively engaged in a discussion with the author: assenting here, disagreeing there; doubting one point, accepting another; rejecting an example, offering a counterexample. You are expected to *listen* to the selection as carefully as you listen to the opinions of others in a group or an opponent in a debate. Although you can't talk directly to the writer, you can still respond to his or her ideas or perspectives in your own writing. This edition of *Our Times* contains numerous examples of how this is done by professional writers. Nearly every selection in the book shows an author directly challenging or confirming the ideas, beliefs, research, and opinions of others. Such interaction is the essence of public discourse.

Good writing, like nature, abhors a vacuum. That is why most experienced writers work within a climate of ideas generated by reading, discussion, and debate. You usually don't have to proceed very far into an essay or article to see how directly the writer is responding to the ideas of others. As you read the selections in *Our Times*, you will certainly notice how often the writers are engaged in a public exchange of ideas, how often they seem to be participating in discussion *as* they write. Throughout this book, you will see how frequently writers begin their essays and articles with the words of other people — quotations from reading, research, and interviews. In fact, many selections open with a direct reference to discussion and debate.

· Note how a leading educator, Amitai Etzioni, begins his essay on the controversial topic of sex education. He situates himself directly in an ongoing discussion. In fact, his opening sentence deals with the way the issue should be discussed: "Instead of approaching the discussion of sex in public schools as a matter of health and safety bereft of moral content or forbidding discussion of sex out of traditional moral concerns (seeking to rely exclusively on the family and religious institutions for this purpose), schools should develop a program of education that provides children with the facts they need to know, within the context of values that responsible and moral persons seek to affirm and embody in their lives." (See "Education for Intimacy," p. 195).

How a topic is customarily discussed and debated (or "framed," as it is often put) may play a large part in a writer's response. For example, you may want to distinguish your own position on a question from the typical ways it has been argued by others. This often occurs when a writer believes a complex issue has been unfairly polarized, forcing everyone to take either one side or another. Such polarization can distort important public issues, as another well-known educator, Richard Weissbourd, suggests in his discussion of the "self-esteem" movement in education. Weissbourd finds himself favoring neither the supporters nor the attackers of "self-esteem": "Plenty of liberals as well as conservatives agree that this attention to self-esteem is not just useless but dangerous. Yet the self-esteem movement has at least tried to deal with serious problems that its critics have ignored. Indeed, the critics' back-to-basics call to teach just reading and writing will also fail large numbers of children." Siding with neither the "self-esteem" nor with the "back-to-basics" movements, Weissbourd refuses to get trapped in an "either/or" position; he proposes a "third path" for educators to follow (see "The Feel-Good Trap" p. 189).

Good discussion demands an exchange of *informed* opinion. Discussion easily deteriorates into empty rhetoric when it consists mainly of an exchange of contending attitudes or mere assertions. Challenging the selections may often demand evidence and support that will require some degree of additional reading or research on your part. To challenge a writer's position on immigration, for example, you might need to check the accuracy of her statistics or the reliability of her sources. A great deal of useful information on current issues can be readily found in a number of popular almanacs and encyclopedias in any library's reference area. Electronic databases and other library tools (such as periodical indexes) can be enormously useful in finding an array of current articles, and in many cases, printing them. And, of course, a vast, practically limitless, expanse of information can be found on the Internet with a few clicks of a mouse. Within minutes, any student should be able to locate by topic a wealth of additional information to challenge, support, or supplement the information collected in this book. The Internet itself, with its many links to periodicals, forums, and chat groups, powerfully reinforces the interconnections among writing, reading, research, and discussion that drive this edition of *Our Times*.

If you think of writing as a form of discussion, you will realize that you are not writing in a vacuum but as part of a group, part of a community. In written work, just as in discussion, someone is always speaking and someone (or some group) is always being addressed. *Our Times* encourages students to view their writing as an extension of group discussion, to see writing as public, not private, behavior, and to see that being a writer is a social, not a solitary, endeavor.

To see writing as an extension of discussion, however, students will need to reimagine themselves as writers. When you sit down to write you should do so not as an isolated individual anxiously awaiting inspiration, but as an active participant in a continuous communication process. You then will not need to wait for ideas to come out of the blue. Rather, you will find your ideas where they are most likely to originate — in your own thoughtful responses to the ideas and opinions of others.

Contents

1 Today's Freshman: How Do *You* Fit the Profile?   1

Over 1.5 million first-time, full-time students enter college each year. Who are they? What characteristics, values, and opinions do they share? How does the latest freshman class differ from those over the past few decades? How do your views and expectations match the general profile? For over thirty years a noted UCLA survey has been providing a comprehensive profile of the American Freshman. If you fill out their "Student Information Form" you will be participating in the annual poll of over a quarter of a million students.... Compare your responses to the UCLA overview ... How do you personally fit the profile with respect to a large number of specific characteristics and issues?.... Do you agree with the *New York Times* that the '90's college freshmen are more conservative than their predecessors?

2 Countdown to the Millennium: What Can We Expect?   28

Is the coming millennium mostly hype or can we expect startling changes? What will happen when the clock strikes midnight on

December 31, 1999? *People* magazine interviews a Boston University history professor who specializes in millennial studies.... A film critic wonders what the next decade should be called.... *Harper's* magazine lists some of the ways manufacturers hope to capitalize on the year 2000. . . . The science and technology of the next century will undoubtedly change, but people won't, argues a *Newsweek* columnist.... A communications researcher says Americans need to wake up "to the fact that the millennium is serious business."

3 Self-Image: How Do We Feel about the Way We Look?   47

What is your self-image? Are you content with the way you look? Are you inclined to fret over physical characteristics others may not even notice? One of the world's most famous cartoonists finds himself stuck with a childhood self-image that no longer reflects his physical appearance .... Fed up with measuring herself against an impossible physical ideal, a young woman fights back .... Why have women over the centuries gone to such dangerous lengths in their quest for beauty? wonders a noted researcher in a comprehensive and thought-provoking essay .... Do you agree with CBS that the advertisement for "Obsession Fetish" violates standards of taste and exploits sex and nudity?

4 Only Words: Does Language Matter?   65

Is the old childhood rhyme true: "Sticks and stones can break my bones, but names will never hurt me"? Or do words have serious consequences? Can they change the way we think about something? Can they cause serious injury? "Having a word for what you're being makes being it easier," suggests a magazine writer as she searches for a label that's more relaxed than "woman" and more grown-up than "girl".... A lawyer and expert on obscenities wonders why the word "squaw" is now offensive whereas some of the dirtiest four-letter words in the English language have grown acceptable .... A leading conservative magazine satirizes a government guide to politically correct speech .... A prominent African American journalist takes a humorous look at the motivation behind the Ebonics movement .... In a brief, official statement, the Linguistics Society of America takes a less humorous look.

5 Automobiles: Do We Need Them?   77

Is America's love affair with the automobile cruising to an end? As more and more environmentally minded and community-oriented people find alternatives to driving, an energetic anti-automobile movement appears to be gaining momentum. The author of a provocative attack on the American automobile explains why she stopped being a hypocrite and finally gave up her car .... Despite the growing hostility toward automobiles, a prominent UCLA public policy specialist finds no transportation alternatives more comfortable, convenient, or so compatible with the American dream .... Social, economic, and environmental issues aside, most people buy cars to fulfill their fantasies, a *Los Angeles Times* column reminds us .... And, when they get inside them, another West Coast periodical suggests, all hell breaks loose.... An advertisement for the Oldsmobile Intrigue capitalizes on the sexy side of our relationship with cars.

6 Gender Differences: How Real Are They?   103

The subject of gender differences is nothing new: The ancient philosophers debated whether men and women were essentially alike or unalike. But with the rise of modern feminism and the advances of neurobiological sciences, the topic has grown into one of the most discussed issues of our time, finding its way incessantly into talk shows, classrooms, and even best-selling books. One of the nation's leading language experts wonders why it's so hard for men to apologize .... A *New York Times* front-page news item shows how significant gender differences have become.... Future ballplayers take note: Throwing styles are not biologically determined, claims a prominent media analyst who investigates what the phrase "throwing like a girl" really means .... Because most men don't live in a state of physical fear, they aren't aware of the "combat-zone" precautions most women must take to get through the day safely, argues an award-winning Native American novelist, as she considers a notable gender difference that is rarely discussed.

7   "I'm a Feminist, But . . .": Where Is the Women's Movement Headed?   125

Today's feminist movement appears to be fragmenting, as different groups of women pursue radically different agendas. What is the future of the women's movement? What is "third-wave" feminism, and what are its main goals? A young controversial essayist confesses that she and many other "independent" women share a forbidden fantasy: They want to find a strong, successful man to take care of them . . . . After printing an opinion piece about a young woman's reluctance to call herself a feminist, the *New York Times* was barraged with angry responses. . . . A Boston journalist examines third-wave feminism and finds that the movement's main problem may no longer be a sexist society but feminism itself . . . . How did anyone — especially Congress — ever get the idea that the American girl represents a genuinely oppressed group? asks one of feminism's prominent female critics . . . . An advertisement shows how contemporary feminism must compete with other claims on a woman's identity . . . . Two well-known feminists exchange combative messages for an on-line magazine.

8   Immigration: Can We Formulate a Policy?   156

Immigration has long been a politically complex and volatile topic, especially in periods of economic uncertainty. Recently, a rising anti-immigration sentiment has been building, as can be seen by the passage of the Illegal Immigration Reform and Immigrant Responsibility

Act of 1996. Does immigration actually contribute to America's economic problems? Is it reinforcing ethnic enclaves and pulling Americans apart into fragmented, hostile groups? To what extent do we expect immigrants to assimilate into American culture and society? An immigration policy expert carefully analyzes the various metaphors we use to describe the assimilation process .... A first-generation South Asian immigrant attacks the implicit racism behind the new immigration law .... Too many legal immigrants wind up on welfare, claims the Texas Congressman who introduced the new immigration reform law .... What is a North American? asks one of America's leading essayists, as he takes a philosophical look at what being an immigrant truly means.

9   America's Schools: What's Wrong with Education?   178

Is America's public school system intellectually bankrupt? Are some 45 million elementary, middle, and high school students being denied a better education because of an entrenched and outdated educational philosophy? A former New York City educator and two-time "Teacher of the Year" award winner has some impassioned and provocative things to say about why our schools don't educate .... If the "self-esteem movement" has led to grade inflation, a dumbing down of the curriculum, and a poor assessment of a student's real needs and capacities, the "back to basics" philosophy hasn't worked very well either, maintains a prominent educator who proposes a third educational strategy .... A cartoonist pokes fun at self-esteem mathematics .... How should schools handle the touchy topic of sex education? The founder of the Communitarian political party offers teachers and parents some ideas.

10 English-Only Laws: Does America Need an Official Language?   204

The United States, unlike some nations, has never established an official language. Many influential politicians think the time has finally come to pass "English-only" legislation. But is an official language a good idea? What will it accomplish? A University of Texas professor specializing in the politics of world languages argues that language poses no threat to American unity and suggests that we simply "relax and luxuriate in our linguistic richness".... Although she can see both sides of the issue, one of the nation's leading political theorists believes that an English-only law would contribute nothing .... If Americans are so eager to have all immigrants speak English, asks an Asian magazine, then why don't they support increased resources for English proficiency courses? ... An advertisment proclaims why an "Immigrant Heads an Organization called U.S English."

11 Class War: Can the Poor Survive?   227

Why is it that in a booming economy so many Americans are living in poverty and hopelessness? Are we rapidly becoming a society made up of the very rich and the very poor? What explains the increasing poverty and misery of America's ghettos? The disappearance of jobs, says a leading sociologist and a professor of social policy at Harvard University .... "What would you do if you won a million dollars?" asks a Chicago writer, who views the lottery — while admitting that it exploits the poor and working class — as "a perfectly rational investment for a person facing a lifetime of drudgery and uncertainty.". . . . A well-known contrarian humorist explains some of the mysteries of money . . . . For too many citizens the "most elementary components of a good life in America," maintains a U.S. Senator, are but "distant and unreachable dreams — more likely to be seen on the television set than in the neighborhood.". . . Poverty is not only a minority issue, a news magazine reminds us in its report on the rapidly growing number of poor whites . . . . Money is what workers are running out of, claims the new President of the AFL-CIO, who sees America becoming "edgier, angrier, and meaner."

12 Same Sex . . . Any Sex: Is Marriage Obsolete?   264

When Hawaii's courts supported the rights of gays and lesbians to marry, the issue of same-sex marriage suddenly became a heated topic of national debate. For many traditionalists, the notion of homosexual marriage is morally repellent and the debate was often acrimonious. For others, the issue led to a larger debate about marriage itself. Is all the fuss about an institution that — given the nation's galloping divorce rate — seems to be dying anyway? Sure, gays and lesbians should be allowed to marry, they say, but why on earth would they want to? Confronting every objection, a Washington essayist carefully constructs a pro-marriage argument — for both gays and straights . . . . A gay and lesbian civil rights organization outlines a few of the hundreds of legal, economic, and practical benefits married couples enjoy but same-sex couples are denied . . . . A progressive magazine editor believes that traditionalists oppose same-sex marriage because they are afraid that "gay people will change what marriage means." . . . A prominent economist and conservative columnist declares that "the gay marriage issue is only a further extension of the notion that a 'family' means whatever anybody wants it to mean." ... An irreverent magazine offers some provocative and entertaining opinions on why people marry: Is it mainly to have a big party? ... In an impassioned speech to the House on same-sex marriage, an Iowa representative comes out of the closet in a surprising manner.

13 Affirmative Action: Do We Still Need It?

Hotly debated in the 1970's, when courts supported college admission policies that would redress the effects of past discrimination, affirmative action is once again at the center of national attention. As campus after campus experiences a backlash against what many now regard as "preferential treatment" or "reverse racism," a large number of the policy's supporters worry about what can be done to prevent the under-enrollment of minority groups and to maintain the academic diversity they fought so hard to implement. A noted English and law professor proposes a new way to think about affirmative action .... Another distinguished professor reminds us that the 1964 Civil Rights Act — the origin of "affirmative action" policy — never authorized quotas, preferences, or timetables .... "Effective January 1, 1997, the University of California shall not use race, religion, sex, color, ethnicity, or national origin as criteria for admission to the University or to any program of study," stated the Board of Regents in a landmark 1995 resolution .... Jesse Jackson comments on what the California resolution will mean for minority students .... A prominent Berkeley law professor and expert on Chicano/Latino policy explains why Latinos, though they far outnumber other disadvantaged minorities in California, have so far remained absent from the affirmative action debate.

CONFERENCE CHAPTERS

14 Understanding Multiracialism: Are Labels Important?   324

As America grows increasingly diverse, racial lines are rapidly becoming harder to define with any precision. Is race, as some social scientists now argue, an obsolete category? Or, given its political significance, is it more important than ever? Can we label individuals as easily as we once thought we could? A University of Michigan anthropology professor explains in an interview why she believes "there is absolutely no such thing as biological race."... Race is no longer as simple as black and white, claims a *Time* magazine cover story on golf sensation Tiger Woods.... A Census Bureau poll finds that few people support a multiracial label .... An Indian-American dislikes being called a "person of color."... "One would think that institutions could come up with a different method of classifying people by now," argues a young woman who is tired of being asked what she is.... In her on-line advice column for the "culturally disgruntled," one of America's most controversial authors comments on the tyranny of racial categories.... How can the racial identity of a 9,000-year-old skeleton be the subject of intense dispute? A *New Yorker* magazine reporter finds out as he confronts the latest conflict between scientific research and religious belief .... Disagreeing with the scientists, a Native American position paper tells why the ancient remains are Indian not Caucasian.... A Chinese American essayist wonders what it would be like to be "white."

15 America's Mass Media and Popular Culture: How Does It Influence Us?   365

Does our popular culture cater to the nation's worst taste and lowest common denominator? Is our vulnerable society morally endangered by movies and television shows that regularly trade on "gratuitous" sex and violence? Are we continually being dumbed down by mindless news programs, talk shows, and infotainment? The *Wall Street Journal* examines how talk shows have affected everyday conversation to the point where everyone wants to talk and nobody cares to listen.... An activist writer who spent several months analyzing dozens of daytime television programs says that the experience "was like being caught in a daylong downpour of fear, hostility, and paranoia."... This experience is shared by a leading African American legal scholar who can't believe the sadism, bigotry, hatred, and anger she routinely hears on popular call-in radio shows .... A media critic vigorously attacks local news programs which in recent years have focused almost exclusively on damage, destruction, and death with barely any attention to significant political or economic coverage.... An advertisement for ABC declares that "T.V. is good." ... A popular culture critic suggests that perhaps sitcoms like Seinfeld come closest to the pulse of our era. . . . If you think the media culture is responsible for America's "dumbing down," a Florida English professor suggests an unusual strategy of fighting back . . . . A libertarian media critic dismisses elitist attitudes toward popular culture and thinks the creative intelligence of the American audience has been vastly underrated.

Our Times

Readings from Recent Periodicals

1

Today's Freshman: How Do *You* Fit the Profile?

Many students begin college unsure of what will be expected of them, uncertain of their career goals, and undecided about their major field of study. In addition to these tensions and uncertainties, most students don't really know much about each other. "Who are my classmates?" "Are they more prepared for college than I am?" "How do their attitudes and values differ from mine?" These questions — and many like them — sometimes keep students from entering freely into class discussion.

Conveniently, some answers to these questions can be found in a comprehensive report issued annually since 1966 by the Higher Education Research Institute (HERI) Based on the responses of over a quarter of a million students at nearly 500 two- and four-year colleges and universities, the 1996 *American Freshman* offers educators, parents, and students themselves a statistically reliable profile of the beliefs, opinions, values, backgrounds, and expectations of the most recent group of college freshmen (as well as proof that the American freshman comes in all educational shapes and political sizes). As can be seen from the *New York Times* selection ("Survey Finds '90's College Freshmen More Conservative Than Predecessors"), the annual release of the data usually receives extended media coverage, as commentators study it for indications of social, cultural, and educational trends.

How do *you* fit the profile? To find out, simply respond to the following Student Information Form, which represents a slightly shorter version of the form actually used by the HERI. (The form has been adapted to cover mainly the topics and issues relevant to *Our Times*.) After you've recorded your responses on a separate piece of paper, compare them to students' responses from across the nation. Immediately following the questionnaire is an overview of trends, which summarizes the profile's results for the class of 2000. We've also included a convenient breakdown of the responses to specific questions and issues if you want to check what company you have on a particular topic. How does your opinion on capital punishment compare to most freshmen? Did you choose a college farther from home than did most first-year students? Are you better or worse informed politically than the average student? How do your financial worries compare with those of other freshmen?

1

Student Information Form

1. Your sex: **a.** Male   **b.** Female

2. How old will you be on December 31st of this year?
   - **a.** 16 or younger
   - **b.** 17
   - **c.** 18
   - **d.** 19
   - **e.** 20
   - **f.** 21–24
   - **g.** 25–29
   - **h.** 30–39
   - **i.** 40–54
   - **j.** 55 or older

3. In what year did you graduate from high school?
   - **a.** 1996
   - **b.** 1995
   - **c.** 1994
   - **d.** 1993 or earlier
   - **e.** did not graduate but passed G.E.D.
   - **f.** never completed high school

4. How many miles is this college from your permanent home?
   - **a.** 5 or less
   - **b.** 6–10
   - **c.** 11–50
   - **d.** 51–100
   - **e.** 101–500
   - **f.** over 500

5. What was your average grade in high school?
   - **a.** A or A+
   - **b.** A–
   - **c.** B+
   - **d.** B
   - **e.** B–
   - **f.** C+
   - **g.** C
   - **h.** D

6. Citizenship status:
   - **a.** U.S. citizen
   - **b.** Permanent resident (green card)
   - **c.** Neither

7. During high school (grades 9–12) how many years did you study each of the following subjects? (none, 1, 2, 3, 4, or 5 or more)
   - **a.** English
   - **b.** Math
   - **c.** Foreign Lang.
   - **d.** Physical Sci.
   - **e.** Biology
   - **f.** History
   - **g.** Computer Sci.
   - **h.** Art/music

8. Where do you plan to live during the fall term?
   - **a.** With parents or relatives
   - **b.** Other private home, apartment, or room
   - **c.** College dormitory
   - **d.** Fraternity or sorority house
   - **e.** Other campus student housing
   - **f.** Other

9. Is this college your: (Mark one)
   - **a.** First choice?
   - **b.** Second choice?
   - **c.** Third choice?
   - **d.** Less than third choice?

10. **To how many colleges other than this one did you apply for admission this year?**
    a. No other   e. 4
    b. 1   f. 5
    c. 2   g. 6 or more
    d. 3

11. **How many other acceptances did you receive this year?**
    a. None   e. 4
    b. 1   f. 5
    c. 2   g. 6 or more
    d. 3

12. **What is the highest academic degree that you intend to obtain?**
    a. None
    b. Vocational certificate
    c. Associate (A.A. or equivalent)
    d. Bachelor's degree (B.A., B.S., etc.)
    e. Master's degree (M.A., M.S., etc.)
    f. Ph.D. or Ed.D.
    g. M.D., D.O., D.D.S., or D.V.M.
    h. L.L.B., or J.D. (Law)
    i. B.D. or M.DIV. (Divinity)
    j. Other

13. **Is English your native language?**
    a. Yes   b. No

14. **Are your parents:**
    a. Both alive and living with each other?
    b. Both alive, divorced or living apart?
    c. One or both deceased?

15. **Are you:** (Choose *all* that apply)
    a. White/Caucasian
    b. African American/Black
    c. American Indian
    d. Asian American/Asian
    e. Mexican American/Chicano
    f. Puerto Rican
    g. Other Latino
    h. Other

16. **Current religious preference:** (Choose *one* for your own, one for your father's, and one for your mother's)
    Baptist   Islamic
    Buddhist   Jewish
    Eastern Orthodox   LDS (Mormon)
    Episcopal   Lutheran

Methodist	United Church of Christ
Presbyterian	Other Christian
Quaker	Other religion
Roman Catholic	None
Seventh Day Adventist	

17. **Do you consider yourself a born-again Christian?**
    a. Yes b.   No

18. **For the activities below, indicate which ones you did during the past year. If you engaged in an activity frequently, choose F. If you engaged in an activity one or more times, but not frequently, choose O (occasionally). Choose N (not at all) if you have not performed the activity during the past year.** (Mark *one* for each item)
    a. Attended a religious service
    b. Was bored in class
    c. Participated in demonstrations
    d. Tutored another student
    e. Studied with other students
    f. Was a guest in a teacher's home
    g. Smoked cigarettes
    h. Drank beer
    i. Drank wine or liquor
    j. Felt overwhelmed by all I had to do
    k. Felt depressed
    l. Performed volunteer work
    m. Played a musical instrument
    n. Asked a teacher for advice after class
    o. Overslept and missed class or appointment
    p. Discussed politics
    q. Worked in a local, state, or national politicalcampaign
    r. Voted in a student election
    s. Socialized with someone of another racial/ethnic group
    t. Missed school due to employment
    u. Lost my temper
    v. Took a prescribed antidepressant
    w. Utilized nontraditional medicine (acupuncture, homeopathy, etc.)
    x. Found it difficult to study at home

19. **Rate yourself on each of the following traits as compared with the average person your age. We want the most accurate estimate of how you see yourself.** (Choose *one* for each category: *H* for Highest 10%, *AA* for Above Average, *A* for Average, *BA* for Below Average, and *L* for Lowest 10%)
    a. Academic ability
    b. Artistic ability
    c. Competitiveness
    d. Cooperativeness
    e. Creativity
    f. Drive to achieve

g. Emotional health
h. Leadership ability
i. Mathematical ability
j. Physical health
k. Popularity
l. Public speaking ability

m. Self-confidence (intellectual)
n. Self-confidence (social)
o. Self-understanding
p. Spirituality
q. Understanding of others
r. Writing ability

20. **What is the highest level of formal education obtained by your parents?** (Mark *one* for your mother, *one* for your father)

Grammar school or less
Some high school
High school graduate
Postsecondary school
    other than college

Some college
College degree
Some graduate school
Graduate degree

21. **What is your best estimate of your parents' total income last year? Consider income from all sources before taxes.** (Mark *one*)

a. Less than $6,000
b. $6,000–9,999
c. $10,000–14,999
d. $15,000–19,999
e. $20,000–24,999
f. $25,000–29,999
g. $30,000–39,999

h. $40,000–49,999
i. $50,000–59,999
j. $60,000–74,999
k. $75,000–99,999
l. $100,000–149,999
m. $150,000–199,999
n. $200,000 or more

22. **Do you have a disability?** (Mark *all* that apply)

a. None
b. Hearing
c. Speech
d. Orthopedic

e. Learning disability
f. Health-related
g. Partially sighted or blind
h. Other

23. **In deciding to go to college, how important to you was each of the following reasons?** (Mark *one* answer for each possible reason: V for Very Important, S for Somewhat Important, and N for Not Important)

a. My parents wanted me to go
b. I could not find a job
c. Wanted to get away from home
d. To be able to get a better job
e. To gain a general education and appreciation of ideas
f. To improve my reading and study skills
g. There was nothing better to do
h. To make me a more cultured person
i. To be able to make more money
j. To learn more about things that interest me
k. A mentor/role model encouraged me to go
l. To prove to others I could succeed

24. **Do you have any concern about your ability to finance your college education?** (Mark *one*)
    a. None (I am confident that I will have sufficient funds)
    b. Some (but I probably will have enough funds)
    c. Major (not sure I will have enough funds to finish college)

25. **How would you characterize your political views?** (Mark *one*)
    a. Far left
    b. Liberal
    c. Middle of the road
    d. Conservative
    e. Far right

26. **During your last year in high school, how much time did you spend during a typical week doing the following activities?** (Choose *one* for each activity, in hours: 0, 0–1, 1–2, 3–5, 6–10, 11–15, 16–20, or more than 20 hours a week)

    Hours per week:
    a. Studying/Homework
    b. Socializing with Friends
    c. Talking with Teachers Outside of Class
    d. Exercising or Sports
    e. Partying
    f. Working (for pay)
    g. Volunteer Work
    h. Student Clubs and Groups
    i. Watching TV
    j. Housework/Child Care
    k. Reading for Pleasure
    l. Playing Video Games
    m. Prayer/Meditation

27. **When considering your future, how important is each of the following objectives?** (Mark *one* answer for each objective: *V* for essential or Very Important, *S* for Somewhat Important, and *N* for Not Important)
    a. Achieving in a performing art
    b. Becoming an authority in my own field
    c. Obtaining recognition from my colleagues
    d. Influencing political structure
    e. Influencing social values
    f. Raising a family
    g. Having administrative responsibility
    h. Being very well off financially
    i. Helping others in difficulty
    j. Making a theoretical contribution to science
    k. Writing original works
    l. Creating artistic works
    m. Being successful in my own business

    n. Being involved in environmental clean-up
    o. Developing a philosophy of life
    p. Participating in community action
    q. Promoting racial understanding
    r. Keeping up-to-date with politics
    s. Being a community leader

28. **Choose one answer for each statement.** (**1** for Disagree Strongly, **2** for Disagree Somewhat, **3** for Agree Somewhat, and **4** for Agree Strongly)
    a. The Federal government is not doing enough to control environmental pollution
    b. The Federal government should raise taxes to reduce the deficit
    c. There is too much concern in the courts for the rights of criminals
    d. Abortion should be legal
    e. The death penalty should be abolished
    f. If two people really like each other, it's all right for them to have sex even if they've known each other for only a very short time
    g. The activities of married women are best confined to the home and family
    h. Marijuana should be legalized
    i. It is important to have laws prohibiting homosexual relations
    j. Employers should be allowed to require drug testing of employees or job applicants
    k. The Federal government should do more to control the sale of handguns
    l. A national health care plan is needed to cover everybody's medical costs
    m. Racial discrimination is no longer a major problem in America
    n. Realistically, an individual can do little to bring about changes in our society
    o. Wealthy people should pay a larger share of taxes than they do now
    p. Colleges should prohibit racist/sexist speech on campus
    q. People should not obey laws which violate their personal values
    r. Affirmative action in college admissions should be abolished
    s. Undocumented immigrants should be denied access to public education
    t. All official federal and state documents should be printed in English only

An Overview of the Class of 2000

[THE AMERICAN FRESHMAN: NATIONAL NORMS FOR FALL 1996]

The 1996 freshman norms are based on the responses of 251,232 students at 494 of the nation's two- and four-year colleges and universities. These data have been statistically adjusted to reflect the responses of the 1.54 million first-time, full-time students entering college as freshmen in Fall 1996. The sections that follow summarize the 1996 results as well as major trends in the survey since Fall 1966.

Students Volunteer in Record Numbers

A record number of entering college freshmen report having performed volunteer work "frequently" or "occasionally" during the past year (71.8 percent, compared to 70.3 percent last year and a low of 62.0 percent in 1989) (see Figure 1). When asked how many hours per week they spend on volunteer work, a record high 38.4 percent of freshmen report spending one or more hours per week volunteering (up from 37.2 percent last year and a low of 26.6 percent when this question was first asked in 1987). Similarly, the percent of freshmen who report tutoring other students "frequently" or "occasionally" during the past year rose to an all-time high of 49.4 percent (up from 47.1 percent last year and a low of 41.6 percent in 1986). Further, a record one in three freshmen consider "becoming a community leader" a "very important" or "essential" life goal (32.1 percent, compared with 29.8 last year and a low of 13.3 in 1971). These trends are especially encouraging

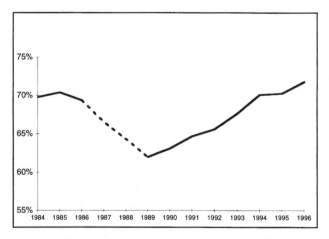

Figure 1. Percent of Freshmen Volunteering in the Last Year.

given recent studies showing that volunteer work has positive effects on students' personal and academic development during and after college.

Financial Concerns Increasingly Influence College Choice

In an era of declining federal and state aid for college students, the student's decision over which college to attend is increasingly driven by financial considerations. In 1996, the percent of freshmen citing "financial assistance" as a "very important" reason for selecting their freshman college increased to an all-time high of 33.1 percent, compared to 31.6 percent last year and a low of 13.6 percent in 1976. Similarly, the percent of freshmen selecting their freshman college because it has "low tuition" rose sharply to its second highest point ever (31.3 percent, from 27.7 percent last year and a low of 16.6 percent in 1979) (see Figure 2). Further, the percent choosing a college because they were not offered aid by their first-choice college reached a high of 5.7 percent, up from 5.2 percent when last asked in 1989 and a low of 4.0 percent in 1984.

Students' college choice decisions are also increasingly influenced by the extent to which graduates of the college are perceived as marketable. The percent of freshmen selecting a college because its "graduates gain admission to top graduate/professional schools" rose to an all-time high of 29.6 percent, compared to 25.5 percent last year and a low of 22.2 percent in 1991. Similarly, the percent choosing a college because "graduates get good jobs" rose to an eight-year high of 46.8 percent, up from 43.1 percent last year and a low of 39.4 percent in 1992.

Two-thirds of college freshmen are at least somewhat concerned that they will not have enough funds to complete college. Perhaps as a result,   5

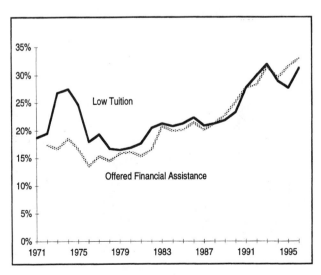

Figure 2. "Very Important" Reasons Noted for Selecting Freshman College.

increasing numbers of freshmen expect to get a job to help pay for college expenses (41.1 percent, compared to 39.5 percent last year and a low of 34.7 percent in 1989). The percent of freshmen who expect to work full-time while attending college rose to 6.4 percent, up from 5.5 percent last year and a low of 3.2 percent when this question was first asked in 1982. Given these trends, it is not surprising that the percent of freshmen who feel frequently "overwhelmed by all I have to do" rose sharply to an all-time high of 29.4 percent, compared to last year's record high 25.3 percent and a low of 16.0 when this question was introduced in 1985.

"Grade Inflation" Continues

In what may be a reaction to the increasingly competitive college admissions process, high school teachers are awarding students higher grades than they did in any previous freshman survey. A full 31.5 percent of freshmen report earning "A" averages in high school, compared to 28.1 percent last year and a low of 12.5 percent in 1969. Conversely, the percent reporting "C" averages or lower dropped to 14.6 percent, from 15.5 percent last year and a high of 32.5 percent in 1969 (see Figure 3).

Competitive college admissions and increasingly stringent entrance requirements may also account for students' taking more college preparatory courses than ever before. Record numbers of students report taking at least three years of math (95.1 percent, up from a low of 83.3 percent when this question was first asked in 1983), two years of foreign language (84.4 percent, compared with a low of 64.2 percent in 1983), and two years of biological science (41.3 percent, compared to a low of 33.1 percent in 1990). Further, increasing numbers of students are taking at least two years of physical science (52.6 percent, compared with a low of 46.8 percent in 1992) and one-half year of computer science (58.3 percent, up from a low of 52.2 percent in 1984).

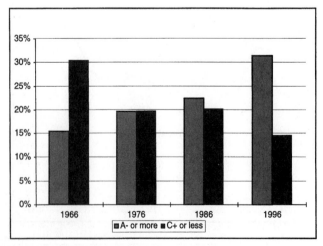

Figure 3. Freshman Trends for "A" and "C" Grades.

Despite these increases in grades and college preparatory courses taken, a high degree of academic disengagement exists among college freshmen. The percent of freshmen reporting being frequently "bored in class" reached an all-time high of 35.6 percent (up from 33.9 percent last year and a low of 26.4 percent in 1985). Also reaching a record high was the percent of students who frequently or occasionally "overslept and missed class or appointment" (34.3 percent, compared to 34.0 percent last year and only 18.8 percent in 1968). Further, the percent of freshmen who report spending six or more hours per week studying remains low at 35.7 percent, compared to a high of 43.7 percent in 1987.

Self-confidence and Aspirations on the Rise

Perhaps as a result of recent movements to build self-esteem among K-12 students, freshmen today report all-time high levels of self-concept. When asked to rate themselves compared to the average person their age, more freshmen than ever rated themselves "above average" or "highest 10%" on academic ability (57.9 percent, compared to 54.8 percent last year and a low of 50.6 percent in 1971), writing ability (41.7 percent, compared to 39.3 percent last year and a low of 27.2 percent in 1966), public speaking ability (30.1 percent, up from 29.0 percent last year and a low of 19.4 percent in 1971), leadership ability (53.6 percent, matching last year's all-time high, compared to a low of 34.9 percent in 1971), and artistic ability (26.1 percent, compared to 24.8 percent last year and a low of 17.7 percent in 1971). Other aspects of self-concept on the rise include mathematical ability (up for the third straight year to 39.0 percent, from a low of 32.0 percent in 1971), intellectual self-confidence (53.6 percent, compared to 51.1 percent last year and a low of 34.8 percent in 1971), and social self-confidence (47.8 percent, compared to 45.4 percent last year and a low of 27.4 percent in 1971).

Increases in self-concept are paralleled by students' growing optimism about their academic future. All-time highs were reached in the percent of freshmen estimating that there is a "very good chance" they will "make at least a 'B' average" in college (49.0 percent, compared to 46.6 percent last year and a low of 32.7 percent in 1972). Record numbers of freshmen also expect to "be elected to an academic honor society" (9.7 percent, compared to 9.0 percent last year and a low of 2.3 percent in 1969). And despite falling retention rates nationwide, increasing numbers of freshmen expect to earn a bachelor's degree (69.0 percent), compared to 65.1 percent last year and a low of 58.7 percent in 1974. Further, a record number of freshmen expect to graduate with honors (17.8 percent), compared to 16.3 percent last year and a low of 3.7 percent in 1968.

Freshman aspirations beyond the baccalaureate are equally high. Among 1996 freshmen, a record 66.3 percent planned to earn graduate or advanced professional degrees, including an all-time high 38.9 percent aspiring to master's degrees and a record 15.1 percent planning to earn Ph.D. or Ed.D. degrees (see Figure 4).

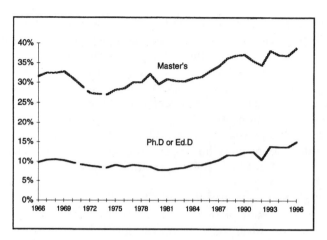

Figure 4. Graduate Degree Aspirations Continue to Rise.

Interest in Teaching Grows; Business and Law Hit New Lows

Freshman interest in elementary and secondary teaching careers rose again to its highest point in 23 years: 10.2 percent (13.7 percent of women; 5.7 percent of men), compared to 9.7 percent last year and a low of 4.9 percent in 1982. Medical careers also remain popular, with 6.4 percent of freshmen (6.9 percent of women; 5.8 percent of men) planning to become medical doctors, matching last year's record high. Interest in business careers hit a twenty-year low at 14.0 percent (11.8 percent of women; 16.8 percent of men), down from 14.6 percent last year and the all-time high of 24.6 percent in 1987. Finally, the percent of freshmen planning to become lawyers hit a new record low of 3.3 percent (3.5 percent of women; 3.1 percent of men), compared to a high of 5.4 percent in 1989.

Political Interest Remains Low in Election Year

Record low political interest observed in recent freshman surveys recovered only slightly in the 1996 election year, remaining far lower than in the 1992 federal election year. Students' commitment to keeping up to date with political affairs as a "very important" or "essential" life goal rose slightly to 29.4 percent, compared to 28.5 last year, 38.8 percent in the 1992 election year, and an all-time high of 57.8 in 1966. Similarly, the percent of freshmen who frequently "discussed politics" during the past year increased to 16.2 percent (from 14.8 percent last year) but remained lower than the 24.6 percent observed in the 1992 election year, and far lower than the all-time high of 29.9 percent reported in the 1968 election year. Further, the percent of students working on a local, state, or national political campaign fell to 6.6 percent, from 7.6 percent last year and a high of 16.4 percent in 1969.

Political and Social Attitudes

After a two-year shift toward "middle-of-the-road" political views, freshmen in 1996 moved in equal numbers to both conservative and liberal categories. The percent of freshmen labeling themselves "middle-of-the-road" fell to 52.7 percent, from 54.3 percent last year. Freshmen describing themselves as "liberal" or "far left" increased from 23.8 to 24.6 percent, while the percent labeling themselves "conservative" or "far right" increased equally from 21.9 to 22.7 percent. And for the second year in a row, both "extreme" categories reached record highs, with the percent of freshmen labeling themselves politically "far left" reaching a twenty-six-year high of 2.9 percent, and the percent considering themselves "far right" reaching an all-time high of 1.7 percent.

The tax cut rhetoric of the 1996 political campaign is reflected in the fact that support for the item, "The federal government should raise taxes to reduce the deficit," has reached its lowest point (23.6 percent) since the question was first asked in 1985. Moreover, the idea that "wealthy people should pay a larger share of taxes than they do now" reached an all-time low of 65.7 percent, down from 67.5 percent last year and a high of 76.2 percent in 1976.

Freshman social attitudes show a continued decline in support for sexual and reproductive freedom. Support for keeping abortion legal declined for the fourth straight year to 56.3 percent, compared to its high point of 64.9 percent in 1990. This decline in support for abortion rights approaches the all-time low of 53.3 percent reported among freshmen in 1979. In a similar trend, support has reached an all-time low for the notion that "If two people like each other, it's all right for them to have sex even if they've known each other for a very short time" (41.6 percent, compared to 42.7 percent last year and a high of 51.9 percent in 1987) (see Figure 5).

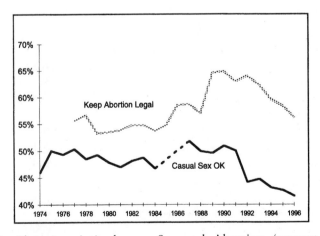

Figure 5. Changing Attitudes on Sex and Abortion (percent agreeing "strongly" or "somewhat").

Selected 1996 Survey Results

[THE AMERICAN FRESHMAN: NATIONAL NORMS FOR FALL 1996]

2. **Age on December 31, 1996**
   a. 16 or younger 0.1
   b. 17 ....2.0
   c. 18 ....65.5
   d. 19 ....27.0
   e. 20 ....2.1
   f. 21 to 24 ....1.7
   g. 25 to 29 ....0.6
   h. 30 to 39 ....0.7
   i. 40 to 54 ....0.3
   j. 55 or older 0.0

3. **Year Graduated from High School**
   a. 1996 ....93.8
   b. 1995 ....2.1
   c. 1994 ....0.7
   d. 1993 or earlier 1.9
   e. H.S. equivalency (G.E.D. test) 1.2
   f. Never completed high school 0.2

4. **Miles from College to Home**
   a. 5 or less 9.2
   b. 6 to 10 ....9.3
   c. 11 to 50 ....28.1
   d. 51 to 100 ....14.3
   e. 101 to 500 ....29.1
   f. More than 500 ....10.0

5. **Average High School Grade**
   a. A or A+ 15.2
   b. A− 16.3
   c. B+ 19.3
   d. B 23.4
   e. B− 11.2
   f. C+ 9.1
   g. C 5.1
   h. D 0.4

6. **Citizenship Status**
   a. U.S. citizen 96.4
   b. Permanent resident (green card) 2.7
   c. Neither 0.9

7. **Met or Exceeded Recommended Years**
   of H.S. Study (2)
   a. English (4 years) 96.1
   b. Mathematics (3 years) 95.1
   c. Foreign language (2 years) 84.4
   d. Physical science (2 years) 52.6
   e. Biological science (2 years) 41.3
   f. History/Am. government (1 year) 98.5
   g. Computer science (1/2 year) 58.3
   h. Arts and/or music (1 year) 73.9

8. **Residence Planned During Fall 1996**
   a. With parents or relatives.......................................30.5
   b. Other private home, apt, room 6.4
   c. College dormitory...59.9
   d. Fraternity or sorority house 0.7
   e. Other campus housing..1.7
   f. Other...0.9

9. **This College Was Student's**
   a. First choice 70.0
   b. Second choice 20.8
   c. Third choice 5.5
   d. Less than third choice 3.6

10. **Number of Other Colleges Applied to for**
    Admissions This Year
    a. None 33.4
    b. 1...14.5
    c. 2...15.5
    d. 3...13.9
    e. 4...9.2
    f. 5...5.7
    g. 6 or more..7.8

11. **Number of Other College Acceptances Received**
    a. No other...13.0
    b. 1...24.2
    c. 2...23.0
    d. 3...18.0
    e. 4...10.4
    f. 5...5.4
    g. 6 or more..6.0

12. Highest Degree Planned
   a. None 0.9
   b. Vocational certificate...............................0.8
   c. Associate (A.A. or equivalent) 3.6
   d. Bachelor's (B.A., B.S.)..........................26.2
   e. Master's (M.A., M.S.)...........................38.9
   f. Ph.D. or Ed.D......................................15.1
   g. M.D., D.O., D.D.S., or D.V.M. 8.7
   h. LL.B. or J.D. (law)................................3.6
   i. B.D. or M.Div. (divinity) 0.4
   j. Other...1.9

13. Student Native English Speaker?
   a. Yes 93.1
   b. No..6.9

14. Status of Parents
   a. Living with each other 69.8
   b. Divorced or separated........................25.5
   c. One or both deceased 4.7

15. Racial Background
   a. White/Caucasian.................................80.4
   b. African American/Black.........................9.7
   c. American Indian 2.3
   d. Asian American/Asian 4.3
   e. Mexican American/Chicano 3.0
   f. Puerto Rican...0.9
   g. Other Latino...1.6
   h. Other...2.4

16. Religious Preference
   Student's
   Baptist 15.3
   Buddhist 0.6
   Eastern Orthodox......................................0.6
   Episcopal 1.8
   Islamic 0.5
   Jewish..1.8
   LDS (Mormon)..0.5
   Lutheran...6.6
   Methodist 7.6
   Presbyterian..3.9
   Quaker 0.2
   Roman Catholic 29.1
   Seventh Day Adventist................................0.4

United Church of Christ 1.6
Other Christian 11.5
Other religion 4.1
None 14.0

Father's
Baptist 14.5
Buddhist 1.0
Eastern Orthodox..0.7
Episcopal 2.0
Islamic 0.7
Jewish...2.3
LDS (Mormon)...0.5
Lutheran..7.5
Methodist...8.4
Presbyterian..4.5
Quaker 0.2
Roman Catholic 31.4
Seventh Day Adventist..0.3
United Church of Christ 1.5
Other Christian 10.5
Other religion 3.3
None 10.7

Mother's
Baptist 14.9
Buddhist 1.0
Eastern Orthodox..0.7
Episcopal 2.3
Islamic 0.5
Jewish...2.1
LDS (Mormon)...0.5
Lutheran..7.6
Methodist...8.7
Presbyterian..4.8
Quaker 0.3
Roman Catholic 32.8
Seventh Day Adventist..0.4
United Church of Christ 1.7
Other Christian 11.5
Other religion 3.5
None 6.7

17. Student Born-Again Christian?
  a. Yes 29.3
  b. No...70.7

18. Activities Engaged in During the Past Year
    a. Attended a religious service 82.1
    b. Felt bored in class 35.6
    c. Participated in demonstrations 41.2
    d. Tutored another student 49.4
    e. Studied with other students 85.5
    f. Was a guest in a teacher's home 27.0
    g. Smoked cigarettes 14.5
    h. Drank beer 52.6
    i. Drank wine or liquor 54.9
    j. Felt overwhelmed 29.4
    k. Felt depressed 10.0
    l. Performed volunteer work 71.8
    m. Played musical instrument 38.2
    n. Asked teacher for advice 21.9
    o. Overslept & missed class/appt 34.3
    p. Discussed politics 16.2
    q. Worked in political campaign 6.6
    r. Voted in student election 23.0
    s. Socialized w/diff ethnic grp 61.8
    t. Missed school due to employment 7.3
    u. Lost my temper 77.4
    v. Took prescribed anti-depress 4.5
    w. Used nontraditional medicine 5.8
    x. Difficult to study at home 57.2

19. Student Rated Self Above Average or Highest 10% in
    a. Academic ability 57.9
    b. Artistic ability 26.1
    c. Competitiveness 53.7
    d. Cooperativeness 69.2
    e. Creativity 49.9
    f. Drive to achieve 65.2
    g. Emotional health 52.7
    h. Leadership ability 53.6
    i. Mathematical ability 39.0
    j. Physical health 54.9
    k. Popularity 37.9
    l. Public speaking ability 30.1
    m. Self-confidence (intellectual) 53.6
    n. Self-confidence (social) 47.8
    o. Self-understanding 54.0
    p. Spirituality 41.7

q. Understanding of others 63.9
r. Writing ability...41.7

20. Education

Father's

Grammar school or less 4.1
Some high school...5.9
High school graduate..25.4
Postsecondary other than college 4.8
Some college 15.4
College degree 24.4
Some graduate school 2.2
Graduate degree 17.8

Mother's

Grammar school or less 3.5
Some high school...4.8
High school graduate..28.7
Postsecondary other than college 6.1
Some college 17.4
College degree 24.6
Some graduate school 2.7
Graduate degree 12.3

21. Estimated Parental Income

a. Less than $6,000...2.7
b. $6,000–   9,999...2.5
c. $10,000– 14,999 ....4.0
d. $15,000– 19,999 ....4.0
e. $20,000– 24,999 ....5.2
f. $25,000– 29,999 ....5.4
g. $30,000– 39,999 ....11.3
h. $40,000– 49,999 ....11.7
i. $50,000– 59,999 ....12.5
j. $60,000– 74,999 ....13.6
k. $75,000– 99,999 ....11.3
l. $100,000–149,999...8.7
m. $150,000–199,999...3.1
n. $200,000 or more 3.8

22. Disabilities

b. Hearing...0.9
c. Speech 0.3
d. Orthopedic..0.9
e. Learning disability..3.1
f. Health-related 1.6

g. Partially sighted or blind...........................2.0
h. Other..1.8

23. **Reasons Noted as Very Important in Deciding to Go to College**
   a. Parents wanted me to go....................37.8
   b. Could not find a job 6.9
   c. Wanted to get away from home...........17.4
   d. Get a better job...................................76.7
   e. Gain general education 62.1
   f. Improve reading and study skills 42.8
   g. Nothing better to do.............................3.4
   h. Become a more cultured person 38.0
   i. Make more money................................72.4
   j. Learn more about things.......................74.3
   k. Role model/mentor encouraged me........14.3
   l. Prove to others I could succeed.............39.5

24. **Concern About Financing College**
   a. None 31.1
   b. Some..50.9
   c. Major 18.0

25. **Political Orientation**
   a. Far left..2.9
   b. Liberal 21.7
   c. Middle of the road..............................52.7
   d. Conservative.....................................21.0
   e. Far right 1.7

26. **Hours per Week in the Last Year Spent on**
   a. **Studying or Doing Homework**
      None 2.4
      Less than one...................................11.2
      1 to 2..21.1
      3 to 5..29.7
      6 to 10..20.5
      11 to 15...8.8
      16 to 20...3.8
      Over 20 ....2.6

   b. **Socializing with Friends**
      None 0.3
      Less than one....................................1.4
      1 to 2...5.1
      3 to 5...15.7
      6 to 10..23.4
      11 to 15..19.0

16 to 20 ....13.2
Over 20 ....21.8

c. **Talking with Teachers Outside of Class**
None 10.5
Less than one...42.2
1 to 2..30.5
3 to 5..11.9
6 to 10...3.2
11 to 15...1.0
16 to 20...0.4
Over 20 ....0.4

d. **Exercising or Sports**
None 5.2
Less than one...9.2
1 to 2..15.9
3 to 5..19.9
6 to 10..17.7
11 to 15..13.8
16 to 20...7.9
Over 20 ....10.3

e. **Partying**
None 18.7
Less than one...13.3
1 to 2..17.1
3 to 5..21.1
6 to 10..14.9
11 to 15..6.9
16 to 20...3.4
Over 20 ....4.6

f. **Working (for pay)**
None 25.8
Less than one...1.9
1 to 2...3.0
3 to 5...6.0
6 to 10..11.0
11 to 15..13.5
16 to 20..17.3
Over 20 ....21.4

g. **Volunteer Work**
None 41.0
Less than one...20.7
1 to 2..19.9
3 to 5..10.7

6 to 10...4.3
11 to 15...1.6
16 to 20...0.7
Over 20 ....1.2

h. **Student Clubs and Groups**
None 32.9
Less than one..13.7
1 to 2...24.0
3 to 5...16.4
6 to 10...7.1
11 to 15...2.9
16 to 20...1.3
Over 20 ....1.7

i. **Watching TV**
None 5.3
Less than one..14.4
1 to 2...23.5
3 to 5...26.8
6 to 10...16.6
11 to 15...6.4
16 to 20...2.9
Over 20 ....4.1

j. **Household/Child Care**
None 21.0
Less than one..21.1
1 to 2...29.2
3 to 5...17.7
6 to 10...6.1
11 to 15...2.2
16 to 20...0.9
Over 20 ....1.9

k. **Reading for Pleasure**
None 25.6
Less than one..26.3
1 to 2...24.2
3 to 5...14.0
6 to 10...5.8
11 to 15...2.2
16 to 20...0.9
Over 20 ....1.0

l. **Playing Video Games**
None 63.4
Less than one..17.2

```
1 to 2 ...............................................................10.0
3 to 5 .................................................................5.5
6 to 10 ..............................................................2.1
11 to 15 ............................................................0.9
16 to 20 ............................................................0.4
Over 20.............................................................0.6
```

m. **Prayer/Meditation (4)**
```
None.................................................................35.5
Less than one ...................................................33.3
1 to 2 ...............................................................20.2
3 to 5 .................................................................6.7
6 to 10 ..............................................................2.3
11 to 15 ............................................................0.8
16 to 20 ............................................................0.4
Over 20.............................................................0.9
```

27. Objectives Considered to Be Essential or Very Important
- a. Achieve in a performing art...............................12.2
- b. Become authority in my own field.....................64.1
- c. Obtain recognition from colleagues...................52.5
- d. Influence political structure 17.7
- e. Influence social values 39.0
- f. Raise a family...72.2
- g. Have administrative responsibility 38.5
- h. Be very well off financially 74.1
- i. Help others in difficulty 62.5
- j. Make theoretical contribution to science...........17.1
- k. Write original works 14.0
- l. Create artistic work..13.4
- m. Be successful in own business...........................39.4
- n. Be involved in environmental clean-up..............20.7
- o. Develop philosophy of life................................42.1
- p. Participate in community action........................23.7
- q. Promote racial understanding............................34.7
- r. Keep up-to-date with politics 29.4
- s. Be a community leader 32.1

28. Agrees Strongly or Somewhat (answered 3 or 4)

	All Institutions	All Black Colleges	Men, All Institutions	Women, All Institutions
a. Govt not controlling pollution	81.9	83.2	78.2	84.9
b. Raise taxes to reduce deficit	23.6	18.1	26.3	21.4
c. Too much concern for criminals	71.6	60.1	73.0	70.4
d. Abortion should be legal	56.3	61.0	55.7	56.7
e. Abolish death penalty	22.2	36.0	19.0	24.8

f. Sex OK if people like each other 41.6	37.1	53.8	31.9
g. Married women best at home.............24.2	30.9	30.8	19.0
h. Marijuana should be legalized............33.0	35.7	37.2	29.6
i. Prohibit homosexual relations............33.5	35.8	45.2	24.1
j. Employers can require drug tests........79.2	83.8	76.4	81.4
k. Fed govt do more handgun control ...81.6	89.3	71.6	89.5
l. National health care plan needed 72.3	84.8	68.0	75.7
m. Racial discrim no longer problem.......16.3	10.7	20.5	12.9
n. Indiv can do little chng society 31.5	32.2	36.7	27.3
o. Wealthy should pay more taxes..........65.7	70.2	65.0	66.3
p. Prohibit racist/sexist speech..............63.8	64.1	59.5	67.3
q. Disobey laws that violate values.........36.2	37.3	40.7	32.7
r. Abolish affirm act in coll admit..........48.9	25.2	56.4	42.8
s. Deny educ acc to undoc immig (4) 55.5	37.3	64.3	48.4
t. All official docs in English (4) 44.3	31.7	54.9	35.9

In the News

Survey Finds '90's College Freshmen More Conservative Than Predecessors

In 1975, when college students were dancing to Donna Summer's suggestive disco hit, "Love to Love You Baby," half of the nation's entering college freshmen said they approved of sex between two people who have known each other only a short time, according to a survey by researchers at the University of California at Los Angeles (UCLA).

These days, according to the 1996 edition of the survey, just over 41 percent endorse casual sex.

That stricter attitude is just one change noted in the 1996 survey. The students say they are smoking more but drinking less, with beer drinking in particular dropping to a record low. And they are more concerned than ever with financing their education.

"Their fears about being able to pay for college have really shot up," said Linda J. Sax, assistant professor

of education at UCLA and associate director of the study, which has been conducted annually for 30 years. "They're dealing with a lot more pressure than students in the past. Feeling overwhelmed is the biggest indicator of this kind of stress."

About 30 percent of the students surveyed said they frequently felt "overwhelmed," nearly double the number in the 1985 edition of the survey.

More than 20 percent said they worked at a job at least twenty hours a week, though that varied among private and public college students: 27 percent of students going to two-year colleges said they worked for that many hours, compared with less than 12 percent of students going to private universities.

And while a good academic reputation continued to be a key factor in choosing a college, many more freshmen cited low tuition and financial aid as "very important" reasons for choosing a school: A third of the students surveyed in 1996 said financial assistance was "very important," compared with 13.6 of students in 1976.

The 1996 study surveyed 354,853 college freshmen in their first week of classes last fall at 494 private and public colleges and universities. The researchers said that they extrapolated the results to reflect the views of the 1.54 million full-time freshmen who entered college in the fall of 1996.

Guzzling beer on campus dropped to a record low: Less than 53 percent said they drank beer occasionally or frequently, about the same as in 1968, compared with about 75 percent in 1981. Wine and liquor consumption also continued to decline steadily, but smoking became increasingly popular. Nearly 15 percent in the 1996 survey said they smoked frequently, compared with less than 9 percent in 1987.

And many more entering freshmen took college-prep courses than in previous years, earned higher grades in their high school classes, and volunteered for community service in their spare time, perhaps to give themselves an edge in college admissions, surmised Alexander Astin, a professor of education at UCLA who directed the study.

"There's tremendous pressure from parents to achieve," Dr. Astin said. "There's a lot more competition in college admissions than there's ever been."

As for campus social life, stricter attitudes toward casual sex, the directors of the study said, were probably because of AIDS awareness. Many more students approved of casual sex in the mid-1970s and '80s, until a record 52 percent endorsed it in 1987.

As college officials began distributing condoms on campus in the late 1980s and spread awareness of AIDS, attitudes about sex began changing, Dr. Sax said. In 1991, the year that Earvin (Magic) Johnson quit his basketball career after announcing that he had contracted the virus that causes AIDS, the students' approval rate of casual sex plummeted.

College freshmen did not, however, banish self-destructive behavior from their routines. In spite of recent public health campaigns against smoking, nearly as many college freshmen in 1996 said they smoke as in 1966.

"It is increasingly becoming trendy for teenagers," Dr. Sax said.

The survey contained other striking statistics: Nearly 30 percent of students surveyed said they were born-again Christians, with black colleges and universities reporting an even higher share, 52.6 percent. Support for abortion declined over the last four years, to 56.3 in 1996, compared with nearly 65 percent in 1992.

About 11 percent of all students said they spent less than one hour a week in their last year of high school studying, though nearly 30 percent said they devoted three to five hours studying.

— From the *New York Times*, January 13, 1997.

Responding as a Reader

1. A leading finding in the survey is a marked increase in the volunteer work that college freshmen said they had performed. Do you think this shows greater community interest and awareness on the part of this incoming class? Are there other ways to interpret this increase?

2. Note the *New York Times* report on the survey. Why do you think they used the headline they did? Are there more conservative students than liberal students? Explain the paper's decision in creating this emphasis. How does the headline predispose your reading of the story? Reexamine the data on political attitudes (p. 24); in light of the figures, critique or justify the *Times* headline.

3. How do you explain the low political interest among students reported by the survey? What cultural factors can account for this? Where do you think most students obtain political information? In what ways might the sources of information be related to low interest?

Responding as a Writer

1. The survey continually refers to first-year college students as "freshmen." Does this traditional label, with its masculine overtones, bother you? Do you find the word biased, or do you regard it as neutral? In an essay, discuss the use of the word "freshmen." After examining its origins and tradition, discuss whether or not you find it acceptable. Explain why or why not. What terms could you substitute if you think the word is sexist?

2. The survey shows over the years that an increasing number of students enter college with A averages. How can you explain this? Are today's students smarter than those of twenty-five years ago? Write an essay in which you discuss this phenomenon.

3. Go through the responses to the questionnaire on pages 14–24. Select one item of data or percentage that surprised you. In an essay, discuss the information and explain why you were surprised by it. To what extent did it deviate from your own response? To what extent did it deviate from what you imagined would be the average response? In your essay, make an attempt to explain why this surprising information may have an effect on your opinions or expectations.

Discussing the Unit

Suggested Topic for Discussion

According to the survey, financial concerns affect both a student's choice of college and the conditions of his or her attendance. Many students believe they will need a job to help pay for school. To many, therefore, a college education represents a considerable sacrifice. Why do you think so many parents and students are willing to make that sacrifice? Why are you making it?

Preparing for Class Discussion

1. The national survey asked numerous questions of first-year students. Do you find the questions to be fair, legitimate, and well expressed? Do you consider any to be too personal, ambiguous, or uninteresting? Did you find that any significant areas were not covered? What questions would you have asked the incoming freshman class?

2. Now that you've seen a comprehensive profile of the recent freshman class, do you think your college has taken this information into account? Do you think, for example, that the experience, backgrounds, and attitudes of your incoming class are reflected in the way your school organizes its educational agenda and conducts its activities? In other words, how well do you think your college understands its own freshmen?

From Discussion to Writing

This national survey of college freshmen has probably made you more aware of your own personal "profile" of characteristics and opinions. Consider these with respect to your generation as a whole. Write a personal essay in which you reflect on how you think a college education will shape your life. Without losing sight of your present expectations, focus your essay on the ways you think college may change your characteristics and opinions. Do you think as a senior your personal "profile" will be the same as it is now?

2

Countdown to the Millennium: What Can We Expect?

As everyone knows, when the clock strikes midnight on December 31, 1999, we will be celebrating not only a new year, new decade, or even new century — we'll be ringing in a new millennium. For a thousand years the first digit of the year has remained unchanged. When "1" is gone forever, what other transformations can we expect? Will the world magically become a different place once we start using "2" in our datebooks and checkbooks? Will the new millennium usher in the fantasies of science fiction as fact? Will human consciousness subtly be altered? Will the calendrical change enhance our collective sense of the future while subtly undermining our sense of the past? Will, for example, some of the major events of the recent past — the assassinations of President Kennedy and Martin Luther King, the Vietnam War, the first moon landing, the dissolution of the Soviet state — suddenly take on the cast of ancient history, an entire millennium away?

For historians, the last years of the waning century are well worth studying. In "Countdown," *People* magazine interviews historian Richard Landes, one of the founders of the Center for Millennial Studies, who has been documenting activities related to the coming millennium. Though reluctant to make predictions, Landes believes that even people who regard themselves as highly rational will increasingly get caught up in a millennial frenzy. Striking a lighter and more practical note, Tim Appelo, in "The Millennium Looms: Do You Know What to Call the New Century?" wonders if we can agree on an appropriate label for the next decade: Should we call it the

"Oughts" or the "Zero Decade"? One term is, of course, golden — "millennium" itself — as *Harper's* magazine demonstrates in their list of some new products and services that hope to capitalize on "The Pending Millennium."

Certainly, the next century will usher in enormous technological change, but will our lives be transformed in the process? In "Back to the Future," *Newsweek* columnist Meg Greenfield argues that no matter how vastly science and technology change the world, we will be "the same old us." Yet, as Stephen D. O'Leary maintains, there's sufficient evidence already to show that lives are being radically altered by the millennium. In the chapter's final selection, "Heaven's Gate and the Culture of Popular Millennialism," O'Leary ponders a recent chain of worldwide tragedies — from Tokyo to Oklahoma City — that should alert us to the catastrophic significance of the year 2000.

And what objectives do today's freshmen — who will be adults in the coming millennium — consider key for the future? The survey results show that three-fourths of the class of 2000 want to have a family and money to spend; one-fourth hope to keep up-to-date with politics and participate in community action.

Selected Survey Results

The Millennium: Objectives Considered to Be Essential or Very Important

- Raising a family: 72.2%
- Being very well off financially: 74.1%
- Helping others in difficulty: 62.5%
- Being involved in environmental cleanup: 20.7%
- Developing philosophy of life: 42.1%
- Participating in community action: 23.7%
- Promoting racial understanding: 34.7%
- Keeping up to date with politics: 29.4%
- Being a community leader: 32.1%

— From The American Freshman: National Norms For Fall 1996.

Q & A

Richard Landes on the Millennium

When the clock strikes midnight on December 31, 1999, Iceland plans to light bonfires, Britain to have church bells pealing from one end of the country to the other, and New York City to stage the most memorable Times Square blowout ever, with an anticipated crowd of one million. But even as revelers ring in the next 1,000 years, some millenarians, anticipating the apocalypse, will be breathless with apprehension and hope — wondering if the world will end in fire or ice, with a bang or a whimper — as the fatal hour is struck.

At least, such is the belief of Dr. Richard Landes, forty-seven, a professor of medieval history at Boston University and one of the founders of the Center for Millennial Studies, a group of some two dozen academics from around the nation who document millennium-related activity. Some historians believe millennial influence is overrated. But Landes, noting, for example, the increasing violence of militia groups and the Heaven's Gate suicides, disagrees. He spoke recently with correspondent Tom Duffy.

Why do some people seem excited, and others unnerved, by the approach of the millennium?

There's something exhilarating about believing that you live at the turning point in human and cosmic history — that God has somehow chosen you to be a key player in the ultimate resolution of good and evil as promised in the Bible. There's also all the resentment people who don't have power feel toward those who do. So there is a certain thrill at thinking that all these bastards are now going to get it in the neck. On top of that, people who believe the end is at hand lose the inhibitions we normally impose on ourselves because of fear of future consequences.

Did the first millennium — the year 1000 — exercise the same hold on the popular imagination?

I think so. Most Christians had been encouraged to see the millennium as the apocalyptic moment. That could mean either it was the time of Armageddon, when the Antichrist was to be unleashed to dominate the world, or that it was the beginning of the millennial kingdom of peace and plenty. The bad guys would get thrown into the lake and the good guys would rule on earth for the next 1,000 years. I think this time around religion will play a less prominent role. On the other hand, with pollution and nuclear weapons, there is scientific reason to be apocalyptic.

What specifically happened around the year 1000?

First, there were the pilgrimages to Jerusalem. They may have started as a trickle, but by the millennium of the Passion — the anniversary of Christ's death, in 1033 — there were thousands, perhaps tens of thousands of Christians going to Jerusalem, where many expected the return of Christ. Then there was the Peace of God movement, particularly in many areas of France, in which thousands of peasants and elites gathered together in open fields for three or four days at a time to worship God in an atmosphere of religious revival. There were numerous "miraculous" healings, most of which we would characterize as psychosomatic — in which the mute, for example, were suddenly able to talk.

Do historians notice similar behavior at the end of centuries?

All the way back to the second century you have Christians who don't plant their crops at the end of the century and who go out collectively in the desert to meet Christ. You get all sorts of groups that announce the end of the world and whose membership shoots up in the period before the end is supposed to happen. You get cults, you get bizarre behavior.

We seem to be getting that now. How will people respond to the coming millennium?

We will see more militia groups coming out of the closet. And, unfortunately, the violence is likely to get worse after the millennium among groups that expect God to intervene on their side. When He fails to appear, they tend to look for scapegoats.

The Pope is calling for a Jubilee, a yearlong celebration of the birth of Christ. And in the year 2000, and again in 2033, I think we'll see once again a wave of pilgrims to Jerusalem. The Israelis are expecting millions of tourists.

I also think we are going to see groups resurface that first took shape in the '60s and early '70s — like the Heaven's Gate cult. But I'm not Jeane Dixon. I'm more like a weatherman saying, "This is hurricane season. Expect a lot of them."

Most people think of themselves as rational and beyond the influence of millennial forces.

A lot of rational people are not nearly as rational as they think. Over the last thousand years we have slowly replaced God with human endeavor as the agent that will bring about the destruction or the redemption of humankind. I think you can be perfectly secular and still be receptive to apocalyptic rhetoric. You don't need to believe in God to think the world can be destroyed.

Is that what will make this millennium different from the last?

Yes. In the year 1000 most people thought the world was coming to an end but that God would do it and that the faithful would be rewarded in the kingdom of heaven. Today, we have the capacity to destroy ourselves in a way we never did before. If we put an end to the world, there will be no redemption.

continued on next page

continued from previous page

Are there any potentially positive developments that could come from the turn of the millennium?

On a basic level optimistic people are saying, "Here's a chance to think big. We can look back over the last millennium and think about the next and try to get people motivated and enthusiastic."

Are you such an optimist?

I'm not expecting the apocalypse, either good or bad. But there will be major changes and it could go either way. In the midst of danger lies opportunity.

— From "Countdown" (*People Magazine,* June 9, 1997).

TIM APPELO

The Millennium Looms: Do You Know What to Call the New Century?

[LOS ANGELES TIMES MAGAZINE/June 23, 1996]

Oh, how we snickered when we learned that most of the nation's computers would think it was 1900 when their internal Dayrunners hit the end of 1999. Red-faced, IBM felt compelled to issue a proclamation that henceforth all its products would be "year-2000 compliant." Silly software

TIM APPELO (b. 1955) was a senior writer for Entertainment Weekly *for five years. He is an outgoing film critic for the* Portland Oregonian *and is soon to be an editor for Amazon.com, a fast-growing, bookselling Web site. Appelo has been a contributor to the* New York Times, Rolling Stone, *the* Washington Post, Premiere, People, *the* Village Voice, *and the* Sciences *magazine and is an Emmy-nominated producer/talent for Seattle's KCTS-TV.*

nerds! They may be zillionaires, but we always knew they were too imprac-
tical to deal with reality.

Well, deal with this, average non-techno-nerd citizen: There is a programming glitch in everyone's head that is going to catch most of us by
surprise in four short years. Until we start getting year-2000 compliant
ourselves, and damn fast, we'd better quit chortling at those myopic pro-
grammers.

The glitch in question is this: How on earth should we refer to the immediately post-fin-de-siècle period? The day it is no longer the '90s; what
will it be?

"I hear it as 'two thousand . . . two thousand and one . . .' and so on,"
says futurist Hazel Henderson, author of *Paradigms in Progress* and *Creating Alternative Futures*.

No way, says forward-looking Ed Doyle, co-founder of a new gallery- 5
cum-emporium called Carnival of Souls, located near the site of the Wood-
stock Festival in Upstate New York. "'Two thousand' is gonna be too
cumbersome. I mean, do you say 'One thousand nine hundred ninety-six'
now? It'll be 'twenty-one . . . twenty-two . . .'." "With respect to the new
millennium — which, against all sense, begins in the year 2001, not in the
year 2000," says University of Washington medieval historian Robert
Stacey, "most people I hear are saying 'twenty-ten' for the year 2010,
etcetera. However, my guess is that 'two thousand two,' etcetera, will win
out over 'twenty oh two' or 'twenty oh three.'" Yet in referring to the last
millennium, scholars sing a different tune. "English-speaking medieval historians generally call the year 1007 'ten oh seven,'" adds Stacey. "And
1096, the date of the first Crusade, is inevitably 'ten ninety-six.'" Perhaps
it's too much to expect history to predict the future on this issue. "A couple of years ago I did some work for the Metropolitan Water District,"
says Pasadena author Bettyann Kevles. "Everything we did was 20, 30
years ahead. It was like living in the future. We always said 'the twenties'
for the first decade and then 'the twenty-tens' . . . 'the twenty-twenties.'"
Still, Kevles is not sure that's how people will be talking in the actual future. "Everything we predicted is already wrong," she jokes.

Novelist Tom Robbins plans to pronounce the year 2004 as "two oh
oh four," lending support to the just-instituted policy of this newspaper,
which shall henceforth refer to the century's first decade as "the '00s," presumably pronounced "the oh-ohs." Carnival of Souls merchant Doyle
loves that idea: "'Uh-oh' is right! Whenever I think about the next decade,
I sure go, 'Uh-oh!' I think we should call that decade 'the Roaring Uh-
Ohs.'"

A few years back, readers participating in an *Orlando Sentinel* poll
suggested that the term "the O-Os" be used for the years 2000–2009. They
also suggested "the Nullies," "the Deuce Decade," "the Two Double-Os,"
"the Zips," and "the Zeros." A major West Coast novelist whose work,
five-zero book advances, and predilection for privacy are akin to Thomas

Pynchon's, addresses the question on the condition of strict anonymity: "I'd go for 'the Zero Decade' and refer to the years as, for instance, 'zero seven' for 2007. The Zeros will be thrust upon us, so your proactive approach is welcome."

Yet purely numerical approaches to the year-2000 compliance miss some of the human drama of the occasion. "Aren't we lucky to be living at the turn of the century?" notes Firesign Theatre co-founder David Ossman, who did a futuristic solo album about the year 2000 in 1973. "It's like having a million miles turn over on your automobile — you want to have your eye on that odometer."

To recognize the epochal nature of the next decade, photographer and music-video director Lance Mercer suggests that we come up with a name evocative of the trippy finale of the film *2001:* "I think we should call it 'the Light Years.'" Neal Karlen, co-author of a rock opera with *1999* composer (let's just say it) Prince, proposes that the first decade should be called "the Oughts" because "it reminds me of Professor Harold Hill in *The Music Man,*[1] who claims to be a graduate of the Gary Conservatory, Class of Ought Five." Television comedy writer Bill Barol agrees in principle, if not in spelling. "I think they should be called 'the Aughts,' as in 'aught one, aught two.'" Ought what the *Los Angeles Times* calls the "'00s" instead be termed "the Oughts"? Miss Manners thinks not.

Or rather, "naught." Judith Martin, author of *Miss Manners' Guide for the Turn-of-the-Millennium,* who describes herself as a professional "etiquetteer," has characteristically pointed notions concerning manners of speech and matters of social grace in the next century. "I think they should be called 'the Naughts' rather than 'the Aughts' because, being in the 'ought' business myself, I know it's an uphill fight, and people would associate the word 'naught' with 'naughty,' which is more enticing."

Mrs. Martin — channeling Miss Manners, as is her wont — believes that vast social consequences will attend the new millennium and that what happened at the turn of this century could happen again four years from now. Indeed, as W.B. Yeats[2] put it: "In 1900, everybody got down off his stilts; henceforth nobody drank absinthe with his black coffee; nobody went mad; nobody committed suicide; nobody joined the Catholic church; or if they did, I have forgotten." In other words, decadence was dead.

"I think people will give in to an uncontrollable urge to behave — for the sheer novelty of it," says Miss Manners. She is not alone in this belief. Back in 1993, Gerald Celente, director of New York's Trends Research Institute, predicted that "one of the hallmarks of the 21st century will be self-responsibility."

[1]*The Music Man* was a popular 1957 Broadway musical, made into a successful movie in 1962.
[2]William Butler Yeats (1865–1939), Irish poet and visionary, wrote one of the best-known apocalyptic poems, "The Second Coming."

In the News

The Pending Millennium

From a list of trademarked brand names and phrases that have recently been registered or are pending with the U.S. Patent and Trademark Office. The list includes applications submitted to the office since January 1, 1995.

Millennium champagne (The Mitten Group)

Millennium vacuum cleaners (White Consolidated Industries, Inc.)

Millenium pest-control products (biosys, Inc.)

Millenium floor wax (G. H. Wood + Wyant)

Millennium slot machines (NSM Aktiengesellschaft)

Millenium gas masks for protection against chemical and biological agents (Mine Safety Appliances Company)

Millenium undergarments (Maidenform)

Millennium Staffing temp agency (Adia Services, Inc.)

Milleniad deodorant (Takred, Inc.)

Millennium Minutes TV history segments (ABC)

Millennium Money scratch-off game cards (Taco Bell Corp.)

Millennium Legacy videos of the deceased for friends and relatives (James M. Oliver)

Millennium Time Capsule plastic long-term storage containers (Bascombe J. Wilson)

Millenniware date-conversion software (Carr Scott Software)

Chateau 2000: The New Millenium recreational vehicles (Thor Tech, Inc.)

Meal of the Millennium culinary events (The Mitten Group)

Living in the 3rd Millennium online services (Time Inc.)

Working Straight Through the Millennium (Time Warner Cable)

The Official Chocolate of the New Millenium (Mars, Inc.)

Official Sponsor of the Millennium (Miller Brewing Company)

Your Home Improvement Store for the Next Millennium (Homer TLC, Inc.)

Billing into the Next Millennium (Bell Atlantic Network Services)

— From *Harper's*, August 1997.

Betsy Borns, a former writer for "Friends," thinks the new century's first decade needs a name, like the '70s Me Decade and the '80s Decade of Greed. "But aside from the fact that all the good decade names are taken," she observes, "it's hard to name a period until you know what's happening — you couldn't call the '50s the 'I Like Ike' decade until you knew there was going to be an Ike. Also, the first decade doesn't have a catchy numerical label, unless you like 'the One Through Ninesies.' So," says Borns, clearly pleased, "I've come up with the 'Perilous Preteens.' It would help, of course, if the first decade decided to cooperate by being a time of insecurity, sexual awakening, and global acne."

Novelist Robbins has a simpler solution — a sort of Zen retort to the whole anxious matter of becoming year-2000 compliant. "I'm hoping for a new Belle Epoque, which is my favorite historical period," he says, referring to the time from the turn of the century to World War I. Still, he certainly isn't about to refer to the postmillennial decade as the Nouvelle Belle Epoque.

"I've just decided," declares Robbins, "I'm going to call it 'Arthur.'"[3]   15

[3]Robbins playfully echoes George Harrison of the Beatles, who in the early '60s was asked by a reporter what the group called their mod haircut. "Arthur," George replied, and his answer was recorded in the movie *A Hard Day's Night*.

Responding as a Reader

1. Appelo is concerned not so much with how we'll refer to the next decade in writing as with how we'll refer to it in speech. Look again at the paragraphs in which Appelo spells out the numbers — the uhs, ohs, zeros, aughts, oughts, and naughts. Say these sentences out loud. In what specific ways is Appelo playing with spelling and pronunciation?

2. Of how much value, on this particular issue, is the perspective of "English-speaking medieval historians" (para. 5)? or that of the woman who worked for the Metropolitan Water District (also para. 5)? Why do you think Appelo put them in the same paragraph? What is the main difference between these people's perspectives and ours?

3. Analyze the quotation from W. B. Yeats (para. 11). How do Yeats' examples lead to Appelo's conclusion that "decadence was dead"? Do you think the turn of the century led to this behavior — or lack of it?

Responding as a Writer

1. How do you think we'll refer to the next decade, in casual conversation? Consider the various options suggested in this article, trying your favorites out in a few sentences (you'll want to pronounce those sen-

tences out loud). Be creative; can you suggest any other millennial terms?

2. Suggest a title for this decade that describes "the Nineties" in a way comparable with names for decades and short historical periods from the past — like the Roaring 20s, the Belle Epoque, the Gilded Age, or the Summer of Love. You might interview a few history majors, American history professors, or even American literature professors to find out what these names were and where they came from.

3. Are we "lucky to be living at the turn of the century" (para. 8) and facing the new millennium? Why or why not? What does this transition signify? Is the shift from December 31, 1999, to January 1, 2000, simply arbitrary or does the shift have real meaning? If so, what gives it that meaning? In an essay, show how a sensible person regards the turning of the millennium.

MEG GREENFIELD

Back to the Future

[NEWSWEEK/January 27, 1997]

We are about to be engulfed in futurist talk: new term, new century, new millennium — what will it all be like? Here's one provisional answer: The science/technology will be different. Its human manipulators, subjects, and beneficiaries won't. Therein lies the enduring story.

Sometimes when I am working my clumsy way through the once inconceivable electronic, cordless present, I think of my own long-departed parents, when they were young and (they no doubt thought) on the cutting edge of modernity. I interrupt their 1920s courtship — the poky car they considered a new-age marvel, the relatively novel telephone and telegram and radio and movie culture in which they were comfortable and their parents were not, the manner of self-presentation and dress their parents denounced as in-

MEG GREENFIELD (b. 1930) is a Washington Post *editorial page editor and writes a weekly national news column. She has won a Pulitzer Prize for editorial writing.*

decent, and the cockiness with which they considered themselves newly secure in their physical health on the basis of medical advances we now consider primitive. I try to tell them about space stations and the Internet and heart and liver transplants and cell phones and laptops. I say: Look, I can sit up here in this airplane, which will get me to Europe in a very few hours, and type a story and file it to an office in Washington and exchange messages and phone calls with people around the world — all right here in my airplane seat. They are agog. But then they make the same mistake social analysts and prophets and visionaries always make. They think that life will have been transformed by these blessings in ways it has not been.

Yes, there is a sense — an important one — in which life *has* been transformed from the past in our age, just as it was transformed from an earlier time in theirs. Illness, ignorance, and want have obviously not been eliminated. But millions upon millions of people living today, who not all that long ago would have been direly afflicted by all three, will never know them in anything like their once common form, if they know them at all. Better, faster, and more are the defining terms of our culture and our condition. I don't see how anyone could doubt that or fail to be awed by the way both physical and intellectual access have been expanded so you can go anywhere and/or learn anything with a speed that only a couple of decades ago, never mind a generation back, would have seemed merely fanciful, sci-fi stuff. And if we know anything, it is that this kind of progression is certain to continue.

Such predictions have always been a pretty safe bet. There were Greeks, there were Renaissance figures (of whom Leonardo was but one), and there were nineteenth-century figures, such as even the poet Tennyson, whose imaginations enabled them to see well beyond the scientific confines of their times. And so of course can we. What is harder to see is a day when human nature and human life on earth will have been commensurately transformed. What I am saying is that the humanists' insights will probably always be more to the point than the imagery of technological marvels yet to be. What Shakespeare uniquely knew about the human mind and heart and the timeless human predicament will be just as apt a millennium or two from now as it is today and was 400 years ago. The uses to which actual, famously fallible people put the newfangled marvels will still be the issue.

I think of this when the lawyer-commentators are taking us through   5
the latest permutations of the O.J. case. All the knowledge about DNA, all the supersensitive means of analyzing microscopic traces of blood and hair and all, do not get you past an ancient kind of drama and an equally familiar set of responses to it by accuser and accused. I think of the dear old Newt mess,[1] entangled as it now is in interception technology, unencrypted cell-phone messages, arguments about which kind of cable connector to

[1]Greenfield alludes to an embarrassing phone call by Speaker of the House Newt Gingrich that was illegally scanned and taped.

which kind of recording device from which kind of scanner went into the notoriously taped phone call.

And, above all, I think of the tremendous conflicts in this country over the uses to which the new technologies will be put. These are conflicts riding on moral choices, and the mathematical principle has not been thought of that can resolve them. We fight about who gets the good of the lifesaving device and technique. This can be a fight among equally needy individuals for a scarce resource or a fight between generations about how much one person must pay to extend another's longevity. We fight about where we should put our pooled resources to get the good of the burgeoning knowledge — in space? in bombs? in basic research? We fight about who owns the new knowledge and its fruits, who has proprietary rights, who is entitled to privacy, who should be able to hook up with whom. We fight about what to do when a new scientific blessing, as is so often the case, comes accompanied by a curse — the pesticide or vehicle or energy source that saves and also, simultaneously, sickens or kills. Decked out in our ever newer skills and abilities and seemingly magical potential, facing the glowing screens of our new life, soaring above the earth, bouncing back from a long dreaded and once mortal disease, guess what? It's the same old us.

I think it is awfully important to remember this as the rhetoric ascends toward the millennial moment, starting this week and gaining verbal altitude as the turn of the century nears. There are not and never can be any scientific rules whereby we can perfect ourselves the way we can perfect certain objects and processes in the physical world. And in this limitation will always reside our potential glory and our potential shame. It will always be easier to do the scientifically impossible thing (as we contemporaneously think of it) than to do the personally possible but difficult thing — the right thing by ourselves and by others and by the technologically amazing world we have concocted to live in. I believe, in other words, that my seemingly quaint, flapper-age parents, once they got the hang of the gadgetry, would be as at home in this world as we all would be in the super-duper one about to come. So far as its human inhabitants are concerned, we would have seen it all before.

Responding as a Reader

1. Why is it a mistake, according to Greenfield, to "think that life will [be] transformed by [the] blessings" of technology (para. 2)? What can we deduce from past technological revolutions?

2. In paragraph 4, Greenfield argues that "humanists' insights will probably always be more to the point than the imagery of technological marvels yet to be." What does she mean? What "point" is she referring to? Do you agree with Greenfield?

3. What is it that Greenfield wants us to remember "as the rhetoric ascends toward the millennial moment" (para. 7)? What is the connection between human fallibility and the turn of the millennium? Why is Greenfield's point especially relevant now?

Responding as a Writer

1. In paragraph 5, Greenfield refers to two stories that were in the news when she wrote this article in January 1997. Try applying her argument to a story that's in the news right now. In a few paragraphs, define the "ancient kind of drama and . . . equally familiar set of responses to it" that are at stake in the issue you choose.

2. Imagine a new technological invention that would solve a particular problem or make a particular process faster or easier and describe your invention in an essay. The invention doesn't have to be realistic; it can be as fantastic as you like. Once you've come up with your invention, describe the social and human complications that would attend it — and these should be in keeping with what you know about how real people actually behave. After evaluating the costs and risks involved, decide if your invention is a boon or a liability in the end.

3. Choose a technology that already exists — like the telephone, the airplane, or the computer — and research public reactions to it when the technology was new. (You can do this by reading newspapers and magazines on microfilm or, if it's a relatively recent technology, interviewing people who were alive at the time.) Compare the early reactions to present-day attitudes toward the technology. Do you see any parallels between these early reactions and present-day attitudes toward cutting-edge technology?

STEPHEN D. O'LEARY

Heaven's Gate and the Culture of Popular Millennialism

[CENTER FOR MILLENNIAL STUDIES / April 1997]

The suicide of the Heaven's Gate sect was timed to coincide with the nearest approach to Earth of the comet Hale-Bopp — a celestial event that, like many comets throughout history, has been greeted in apocalyptic circles as a harbinger of cosmic change. Perhaps coincidentally, it also fell within Holy Week, when millions of Christians around the world celebrate the divine mysteries of death and resurrection. A week and a half after the suicides, groups of millennial activists and partiers around the world celebrated the fact that there are now fewer than 1,000 days until the year 2000. Clearly, we have now entered the "hot zone" of millennial time — the optimum span of one to four years distance for apocalyptic predictions, in which hopes and expectations are raised to a fever pitch and believers sustain a maximum level of missionary and preparatory activity. The work of those who study and measure the millennial zeitgeist will become increasingly crucial in the coming years. At the Center for Millennial Studies (CMS), we hope to provide a useful clearinghouse for information about millennial groups that is being gathered by a network of scholars and to direct the attention of medial and interested publics to sources that will assist in the understanding of millennial trends and events.

*The Center for Millennial Studies can be found on the World Wide Web at http://www.mille.org/OLeary1.html.

STEPHEN D. O'LEARY *is an associate professor at the University of Southern California, Annenberg School for Communication. A research specialist in cults and new religious movements, O'Leary is an active member of the American Academy of Religion and has been awarded grants and research awards from the James H. Zumberge Research and Innovation Fund of University of Southern California (1992–93) and the Speech Communication Association (1992). He has published works in such publications as* Journal of the American Academy of Religion, Philosophy and Rhetoric, *and the* Quarterly Journal of Speech. *In 1994, his book* Arguing the Apocalypse: A Theory of Millennial Rhetoric *was published by Oxford University Press.* A Prescription for Millennium Fever *is expected in 1998.*

The CMS has been sounding the trumpets of alarm for some time, but aside from short bursts of attention from the media in the wake of certain recent tragedies, the full implications of the upcoming millennial crisis have failed to attract the attention of policymakers and the public. The Heaven's Gate tragedy offers an appropriate moment to ponder the approach of the new millennium in light of a series of events over the past few years in Waco, Tokyo, Oklahoma City, Montana, Switzerland, and Canada. If the Branch Davidian deaths, the poison-gas attacks of Aum Shinrikyo, The Oklahoma City bombing, the Freemen standoff, and the Solar Temple suicides were not enough to wake people up to the fact that the millennium is serious business, then perhaps the fate of the most recent deluded messiah and his thirty-eight earnest followers will serve as a grim prophecy of what is to come.

The Heaven's Gate Web pages declare that we are in the "End of the Age" and that the earth is soon to be swept clean of civilization. The disturbing truth about this group's suicide is that the members are far from atypical in their anticipation of end times and catastrophe. They differ from millions of Americans not in the content of their beliefs but in their intensity, and in the extreme action to which these beliefs led them. They blended an eclectic mix of Christian millennial prophecy, UFOs, government conspiracies, and science fiction scenarios straight out of the *X-Files*, *Star Trek*, and *Star Wars*. Much like the Tokyo subway gas attacks of Aum, a doomsday sect with more followers in Russia than in Japan, and the eerily similar suicides of the international Solar Temple, their action may best be explained as an impatient attempt to anticipate the fulfillment of prophecies that receive the attention, if not the full allegiance, of millions of credulous Americans.

Some who fear the power of the Internet are now warning of the dangers of "spiritual predators online." But why should we expect the Internet to be different from the social world it reflects? Certainly, it offers a means of propagating rumors, conspiracy theories, and prophecies to numerous groups whose beliefs may lead to violence and tragedy. However, if one is going to look for technological explanations of the recent events near San Diego, one might as well blame television as the Internet. Heaven's Gate gives a new and terrifying significance to previously innocuous media products that had long enjoyed what are commonly, and unthinkingly, referred to as "cult followings": the *X-Files*, *Star Trek*, and *Star Wars*.

The importance of film and television in the group's belief system is evident from the video suicide notes they left behind, which contain repeated references to science fiction scenarios. The farewell statement by the group's leader referred to Heaven's Gate members as "body snatchers," a reference to a 1956 sci-fi classic remade in the late seventies. One follower's video statement offered these words: "We watch a lot of *Star Trek*, a lot of *Star Wars*, . . . it's just like training on a holodeck . . . it's time to put into practice what we've learned." Most strikingly, the following self-description from the group's Web page, with which they sought to explain and justify their mission, puts the role of the popular media into sharp relief: "To help you understand who we are, we have taken the liberty to express a brief synopsis in the vernacular of a popular 'science fiction' entertainment series. Most readers in the late twentieth century will certainly recognize the intended parallels. It is really quite interesting to see how the context of fiction can often open the mind to advanced possibilities which are, in reality, quite close to fact." The document continues with a theme familiar to science-fiction buffs worldwide: "Extraterrestrials Return with Final Warning."

The members of Heaven's Gate were surely deluded about the existence of alien rescuers and the redemptive value of suicide, but their insight on popular culture is both accurate and profound. The media play a significant role in the social acceptance and growing plausibility of apocalyptic beliefs and millennial scenarios. There is ample evidence that the willing suspension of disbelief demanded in our narrative fictions and our tabloid press now extends to religion and politics in new and distressing ways and that this effect is not confined to suicidal cultists.

Consider these symptoms of our premillennial condition. In Japan, the works of Nostradamus continue to sell in the aftermath of the Aum affair. Closer to home, nearly half of all Americans, according to a 1996 *Newsweek* poll, believe in UFOs; an approximately equal amount believes that our government is concealing the truth about these phenomena. Twenty percent of Americans (more than four million people) believe that the UFOs are piloted by alien life forms from other star systems. Author Whitley Strieber's purported accounts of alien abductions are bought and presumably read by millions, and close observation of the alien abduction movement confirms that this movement is growing increasingly preoccupied with tales of impending planetary catastrophe. Art Bell's radio show, now notorious for having publicized the rumor that an alien spaceship was hidden in the tail of comet Hale-Bopp, is broadcast on more than three hundred stations; his Web page boasts a million and a half visits. "The Celestine Prophecy," a smarmy New Age tale that places dubious insights on personal growth alongside psychic phenomena and predictions of a coming global transformation, has been on the best-seller lists for months. In the last few years, major television networks have run big-budget specials with titles like "Mysteries of the Millennium" and "Ancient Prophecies," which give credence to the catastrophic predictions of New Agers anticipating "Earth Changes" as well as variants of Christian fundamentalist prophecy. The militia movement, galvanized in the aftermath of the Waco tragedy, continues to flourish in urban and rural areas around the country, fueled by rumors of apocalyptic paranoia that read like *X-Files* episodes. This is not surprising, given that the scriptwriters read the newspapers and watch the news shows and the movies as obsessively as any millennial conspiracy theorist.

The significance of the fact that Heaven's Gate derived inspiration from popular science fiction in equal measure with religious scripture has yet to be realized. The media coverage of Heaven's Gate gives ample evidence of the media's tendency to marginalize these groups by emphasizing their differences from the rest of us while neglecting their similarities. One theme that came through in interview after interview with those who had had recent contact with the sect members was the reporters' insistent questioning about signs of mental illness or indication of suicidal tendencies. The interviewers were clearly nonplussed by the responses, which emphasized the friendliness, professionalism, and reliability of the individuals in the group. The profiles of the members and interviews with their families in *People* magazine likewise showed few clues, with their depressing lists of perfectly ordinary disappointments. But confronting the ordinariness of the sect is nearly impossible, for it casts too much else into doubt. Without histories of trauma or mental problems that could be used to explain away their deaths, we can only fall back on the dubious theory of the charismatic and hypnotic cult leader, whose blandishments are so insidious that exposure to the message can cause normal citizens to give up their family lives, surrender critical reason, castrate themselves, and die to demonstrate commitment.

Death and self-castration are not choices that will ever become popular, no matter how much television or how many science fiction movies people watch. But there is precedent for even these extreme actions within the established religious traditions. The Heaven's Gate members compared themselves to the Jews of Masada, who chose death over slaughter and subjugation by the hated Roman power. One of the greatest Christian theologians, Origen, castrated himself at twenty in an attempt to control his sexual desire. And with Easter Sunday following in the immediate wake of the suicides, one could not simply condemn the group's faith in a heaven that awaited them after death. This is not to blame Christianity or any religious body for what happened in Rancho Sante Fe; there will always be those who take ideas to their limit and pass beyond the bounds of orthodoxy. The same is true for the products of popular media. The millennial themes that run as a constant thread through our films and television shows cannot directly cause events such as poison-gas attacks or group suicides. Rather, they provide a sociological Petri dish, a culture in which such virulent strains of apocalyptic as Aum and Heaven's Gate can flourish. In marginalizing these groups, or assisting them as they choose to marginalize themselves, we must remember our own participation in the culture that created them. And this line of analysis leads not to theories of cult brainwashing but back to ourselves. These television shows and films are popular because we flock to see them; it is our own preoccupation with aliens and prophecies that causes Hollywood to pump out product after product to fill the void left by the waning of traditional religion.

As we approach the end of the millennium, we can assume that there   10
will be more bizarre incidents and gruesome deaths, either in anticipation
of prophetic fulfillment or in the aftermath of apocalyptic disappointment.
We would do well to remember two lessons of the recent episodes of millennial madness. First, look closely at the ingredients of whatever religious
snake oil is being sold. (For this, the Web can be a useful tool; the signs of
impending suicide were there for all to see.) Second, don't be quick to dismiss such beliefs as crazy. We may be entering a time when this "insanity"
is being normalized. Millennial prophets today bear little resemblance to
the cartoon caricature of the bearded, white-robed figure with the picket
sign proclaiming that "The End is Near." They can be found in business
suits, at church, at work, on television, and on the Internet. Their followers
are too easily dismissed as hypnotized cultists. They watch the same films
and television shows and read the same newspapers as we do. They are our
children, our parents, our brothers, our sisters, and potentially ourselves.

Responding as a Reader

1. If you do not remember much about the Heaven's Gate story, you'll
   probably want to refresh your memory by looking up one or two substantive articles from March 1997. Does O'Leary seem to be representing the group fairly? Have any comparable stories appeared in the
   news lately? In what ways are these events comparable?

2. Reread the paragraphs in which O'Leary refers to religion (para. 9, especially). Why does O'Leary write that "one could not simply condemn" the faith of the Heaven's Gate members?

3. What seems to be O'Leary's purpose for writing this article? What
   seems to be the role of the Center for Millennial Studies? Is O'Leary a
   journalist who simply reports what he sees and hears or is he an authority on millennial trends?

Responding as a Writer

1. Search for "millennium" on the World Wide Web, looking for Web
   pages for millennial groups such as Heaven's Gate. How many such
   groups can you find? What can you learn about them from their Web
   pages? What do they seem to have in common? Choose one group and
   describe its characteristics to the class.

2. "It is really quite interesting to see how the context of fiction can often
   open the mind to advanced possibilities which are, in reality, quite
   close to fact," said one Heaven's Gate member (para. 5). To what extent do you agree with this statement? Think of examples from fiction
   that might support this argument and compare them to real life. What

(if any) is the connection between your examples and the actions of the Heaven's Gate members?

3. To what extent are the popular media to blame for the growth of these millennial cults? Would the Heaven's Gate story have turned out the way it did were it not for the *X-Files, Star Trek,* and *Star Wars*? Would so many people believe in UFOs if they did not read so much about them in the tabloids? Or does media coverage simply reflect the interests of the public? In an essay, tease apart the causes and effects of this chicken-egg relationship.

Discussing the Unit

Suggested Topic for Discussion

What is the significance of the turn of the millennium? Will the last click of the second hand between December 31, 1999, and January 1, 2000, bring us something different from other new years? Or will *people* — swayed by symbolism — create real change? What sorts of changes will be immediate and what sorts will be long term? Which changes are psychological, which physical, and which imaginary? And how do these three categories of change influence one another?

Preparing for Class Discussion

1. Interview several people about what the turn of the millennium means to them. Do they give it much thought? How do they think life might be different in January 2000?

2. Read the Q & A on page 30. In what ways do you think this millennium shift will be different from the last? In what ways do you think it will be similar?

3. Do you think the next millennium begins with the year 2000 or 2001? What arguments can you offer for your opinion? In a paragraph, explain your reasoning.

From Discussion to Writing

Imagine one day in your life ten years from today — you'll be in the first decade of the next millennium. Write a narrative essay describing its events. It can be an ordinary day or a momentously eventful day, but try to focus on some of the smaller details. What do you eat? What do you wear? What kinds of things do you say?

3

Self-Image: How Do We Feel About the Way We Look?

Every day, millions of Americans go to great lengths to improve their appearance, spending enormous amounts of time and money on diets, exercise, health clubs, spas, makeup, and cosmetic surgery. Some are motivated by the drive toward health and fitness, but for many, the central motivation is dissatisfaction with their bodies, faces, hair. Do most men and women see themselves the way others see them? What are the current standards for good looks and who sets those standards? What do we want to look like — and can we ever achieve better self-images?

In "My Inner Shrimp," Garry Trudeau, the famous creator of "Doonesbury," describes a psychological condition with which many of us are familiar: No matter how much our appearance improves, we continue to see ourselves as we *used* to be. One of the shortest boys in his high school until he was seventeen, Trudeau grew to be over six feet tall, yet he still sees himself as short. How we view ourselves, or course, is complicated by certain "ideal" images not of our own making, like Barbie or Hollywood starlets. Writing for a young woman's magazine, Jennifer Silver in "Caught with a Centerfold" wonders why she feels so threatened when she finds out her boyfriend subscribes to *Playboy* magazine: "Yes, the real reason I hated *Playboy*," she confesses, "was that the models established a standard I could never attain without the help of implants, a personal trainer, soft lighting, a squad of makeup artists and hairdressers, and airbrushing."

Such impossible standards, however, are hardly new to our era. In her comprehensive and well-researched essay, "The Price of Perfection," Robin Marantz Henig reveals that throughout history women have paid a high price for beauty: "Over the centuries, women have mauled and manipulated just about every body part — lips, eyes, ears, waists, skulls, foreheads, feet — that did not quite fit into the cookie-cutter ideal of a particular era's fashion." How dangerous can the quest for beauty be? In "The Beauty Industry Is the Beast," Adbuster's Media Foundation, an organization that creates ads to counterattack noxious mainstream advertising, graphically shows in a TV "uncommercial" what even a model's dissatisfaction with her appearance can lead to.

And how do *you* feel about yourself? The survey results for the Class of 2000 show that freshmen feel *most* confident about their drive to achieve and their understanding of others, and least confident about speaking in public and artistic ability.

Selected Survey Results

Self-Image: Student Rated Self Above Average or Highest 10% in

- Academic ability: 57.9%
- Artistic ability: 26.1%
- Competitiveness: 53.7%
- Drive to achieve: 65.2%
- Emotional health: 52.7%
- Leadership ability: 53.6%
- Mathematical ability: 39.0%
- Physical health: 54.9%
- Popularity: 37.9%
- Public speaking ability: 30.1%
- Self-confidence (intellectual): 53.6%
- Self-confidence (social): 47.8%
- Self-understanding: 54.0%
- Spirituality: 41.7%
- Understanding of others: 63.9%
- Writing ability: 41.7%

— From The American Freshman: National Norms For Fall 1996.

My Inner Shrimp

[THE NEW YORK TIMES MAGAZINE/March 31, 1996]

For the rest of my days, I shall be a recovering short person. Even from my lofty perch of something over six feet (as if I don't know within a micron), I have the soul of a shrimp. I feel the pain of the diminutive, irrespective of whether they feel it themselves, because my visit to the planet of the teenage midgets was harrowing, humiliating, and extended. I even perceive my last-minute escape to have been flukish, somehow unearned — as if the Commissioner of Growth Spurts had been an old classmate of my father.

My most recent reminder of all this came the afternoon I went hunting for a new office. I had noticed a building under construction in my neighborhood — a brick warren of duplexes, with wide, westerly facing windows, promising ideal light for a working studio. When I was ushered into the model unit, my pulse quickened: The soaring, twenty-two-foot living room walls were gloriously aglow with the remains of the day. I bonded immediately.

Almost as an afterthought, I ascended the staircase to inspect the loft, ducking as I entered the bedroom. To my great surprise, I stayed ducked: The room was a little more than six feet in height. While my head technically cleared the ceiling, the effect was excruciatingly oppressive. This certainly wasn't a space I wanted to spend any time in, much less take out a mortgage on.

Puzzled, I wandered down to the sales office and asked if there were any other units to look at. No, replied a resolutely unpleasant receptionist, it was the last one. Besides, they were all exactly alike.

"Are you aware of how low the bedroom ceilings are?" I asked.

She shot me an evil look. "Of course we are," she snapped. "There were some problems with the building codes. The architect knows all about the ceilings.

5

GARRY TRUDEAU (b. 1948), creator of the popular comic strip "Doonesbury," has also contributed articles to such publications as Harper's, Rolling Stone, *and* The New Republic. *A graduate of Yale University, where he received bachelor's and master's degrees, Trudeau won a Pulitzer Prize in 1975 and in 1994 received the award for best comic strip from the National Cartoonists Society.*

"He's not an idiot, you know," she added, perfectly anticipating my next question.

She abruptly turned away, but it was too late. She'd just confirmed that a major New York developer, working with a fully licensed architect, had knowingly created an entire twelve-story apartment building virtually uninhabitable by anyone of even average height. It was an exclusive high-rise for shorties.

Once I knew that, of course, I couldn't stay away. For days thereafter, as I walked to work, some perverse, unreasoning force would draw me back to the building. But it wasn't just the absurdity, the stone silliness of its design that had me in its grip; it was something far more compelling. Like some haunted veteran come again to an ancient battlefield, I was re-visiting my perilous past.

When I was fourteen, I was the third-smallest in a high-school class of   10
one hundred boys, routinely mistaken for a sixth grader. My first week of school, I was drafted into a contingent of students ignominiously dubbed the "Midgets," so grouped by taller boys presumably so they could taunt us with more perfect efficiency. Inexplicably, some of my fellow Midgets refused to be diminished by the experience, but I retreated into self-pity. I sent away for a book on how to grow tall, and committed to memory its tips on overcoming one's genetic destiny — or at least making the most of a regrettable situation. The book cited historical figures who had gone the latter route — Alexander the Great, Caesar, Napoleon (the mind involuntarily added Hitler). Strategies for stretching the limbs were suggested — hanging from door frames, sleeping on your back, doing assorted floor exercises — all of which I incorporated into my daily routine (get up, brush teeth, hang from door frame). I also learned the importance of meeting girls early in the day, when, the book assured me, my rested spine rendered me perceptibly taller.

For six years, my condition persisted; I grew, but at nowhere near the rate of my peers. I perceived other problems as ancillary, and loaded up the stature issue with freight shipped in daily from every corner of my life. Lack of athletic success, all absence of a social life, the inevitable run-ins with bullies — all could be attributed to the missing inches. The night I found myself sobbing in my father's arms was the low point; we both knew it was one problem he couldn't fix.

Of course what we couldn't have known was that he and my mother already had. They had given me a delayed developmental timetable. In my seventeenth year, I miraculously shot up six inches, just in time for graduation and a fresh start. I was, in the space of a few months, reborn — and I made the most of it. Which is to say that thereafter, all of life's disappointments, reversals, and calamities still arrived on schedule — but blissfully free of subtext.

Once you stop being the butt, of course, any problem recedes, if only to give way to a new one. And yet the impact of being literally looked down on, of being *made* to feel small, is forever. It teaches you how to stretch, how to survive the scorn of others for things that are beyond your control. Not growing forces you to grow up fast.

Sometimes I think I'd like to return to a high-school reunion to surprise my classmates. Not that they didn't know me when I finally started catching up. They did, but I doubt they'd remember. Adolescent hierarchies have a way of enduring; I'm sure I am still recalled as the Midget I myself have never really left behind.

Of course, if I'm going to show up, it'll have to be soon. I'm starting to   15
shrink.

Responding as a Reader

1. In the opening sentence, Trudeau claims that he will be a "recovering short person" for the rest of his life. Reread the paragraphs that describe incidents in Trudeau's adult life. How does his "inner shrimp" continue to make himself known?

2. What is the significance of the scene in the apartment building? How does it connect to Trudeau's main point?

3. Consider how Trudeau uses the word "stretch" in paragraph 10 and in paragraph 13. What did the word mean to him when he was young? What does it connote for him now?

Responding as a Writer

1. In what ways does our culture value tallness? Make a list of qualities that you associate with tall people and qualities that you associate with short people. How many of these qualities are directly related to physical stature?

2. During his short years, Trudeau blamed all of his problems on his height (para. 11). Have you ever made one isolated problem the scapegoat for a more complex set of problems? In an essay, describe how you came to recognize this logical error.

3. When he was in high school, Trudeau was labeled a "Midget" (para. 10). For one day, pay attention to the conversations you have with your friends and listen for any unflattering labels that you apply to other people. Has an unflattering label ever been slapped on you? In an essay, analyze why people use such labels and what function they serve in society.

JENNIFER SILVER

Caught with a Centerfold

[MADEMOISELLE/January 1997]

Last year I moved in with my boyfriend, and for a few months we were in that blissful state of fledgling domesticity so sickening to friends and family; sooner or later, there had to be a rude shock. And there was: Like Bluebeard's wife, I found something I wished I hadn't. It *looked* innocuous enough — a piece of scrap paper on the floor — until I picked it up.

You know those subscription cards that flutter out every time you open a magazine? Well, this one had fluttered out of *Playboy*. Gentle reader, I *freaked*.

And thus my true love and I began a battle of truly titanic proportions.

"I thought you were a feminist!" I yelled.

"I can't talk to you when you get this emotional!" he screamed back. 5

It certainly didn't help that, by some diabolical coincidence, the magazine arrived every month while I was in the throes of PMS — which in my book stands for "paranoid and miserable situation."

My boyfriend began to get defensive. "Subscribing to *Playboy* doesn't mean anything," he claimed. "Men are visually stimulated, that's all."

"Oh. *Well.* Then you won't mind if I start going out for coffee with some of the men from my writing class? You know, it won't mean anything — I'm *conversationally* stimulated, that's all."

That gave him pause. But still the damn magazine kept coming, and even I was taken aback by how furious it made me. I've never been uptight about porn. I don't think it's one of the world's graver problems, and I don't believe it needs to be censored unless it has children or violence or degradation in it. So why was I feeling so threatened?

JENNIFER SILVER (b. 1969) was born in Los Angeles, California, and since then, by her latest calculations, she has moved twenty-three times. She has worked as a technical writer, Army officer, legal assistant, omelette chef, ESL instructor, bookkeeper, grocery store cashier, nanny, and unpublished novelist, among other things. She now teaches English in a private girls' school in New York City and hopes to stay there for a good long time.

His Fantasy Was My Nightmare

I started polling my friends, hoping I'd find people to back me up — and I did, in abundance. Many of them agreed they'd be outraged if their boyfriends got *Playboy*.

And yet, like me, my friends were slightly abashed by the vehemence of their feelings about porn. It didn't feel "cool" to get so upset; it felt prudish. Yet we knew we weren't prudish, and our visceral reaction was baffling to us.

Part of the reason had to be political. I'll admit that my feelings about *Playboy* sometimes got mixed in with a general rage about the way women are treated in society. I'd listen to a friend's ongoing problems with sexism in her office, I'd hear some of Pat Robertson's Neanderthal comments on the radio, or I'd see a beer commercial on TV that portrayed women as dumb bimbos — and I'd come home spoiling for a fight. And there was *Playboy*!

But part of my reaction was very definitely personal — and the most obvious explanation, jealousy, just didn't wash. Did I want him to fantasize about no one but me? No. In fact, having a great relationship and still being able to fantasize about others is a natural, eat-your-cake-and-have-it-too kind of pleasure.

How about insecurity, though? Ah.

Measuring Myself Against an Impossible Ideal

Yes, the real reason I hated *Playboy* was that the models established a standard I could never attain without the help of implants, a personal trainer, soft lighting, a squad of makeup artists and hairdressers, and airbrushing. It's a standard that equates sexuality with youth and beauty. I didn't want my boyfriend buying into *Playboy*'s definition of sexuality. I was planning a future with this man, and I wanted to feel secure in the knowledge that, even after two kids and 20 years, he would still find me sexy.

After sorting all this out in my mind, I leveled with my boyfriend. I told him that he wasn't doing something bad, but that it made me *feel* bad. Rational or not, justified or not, I didn't like having *Playboy* in my house. Having to confront my insecurities once a month was not the worst thing in the world, but I could live without it.

When he understood how I felt, he kindly and graciously canceled his subscription. It was a relief not to have to open our mailbox and find that magazine anymore — but, more important, it reminded me that just because my boyfriend got *Playboy* didn't mean he was the enemy. He was willing to look at the world through *my* eyes.

Not Hugh Hefner's.

Responding as a Reader

1. Who is Silver's intended audience? How can you tell? How do you think Silver expects this audience to respond to her dilemma?

2. What reasons does Silver first offer for her discomfort with the *Playboy* subscription? What does she decide is the *real* reason for her discomfort?

3. Silver compares her boyfriend's looking at *Playboy* to her going out for coffee with men from her writing class (para. 8). Is this a fair comparison? Why or why not?

Responding as a Writer

1. "I thought you were a feminist!" Silver shouts in paragraph 4. What argument is Silver invoking here? Sketch out the reasons why feminism and *Playboy* subscriptions are incompatible. Then list the reasons why a subscription to *Playboy* does not necessarily contaminate a belief in feminism.

2. Why do Silver and her friends feel embarrassed by their feelings about pornography? How do they think they *should* feel about it, and why don't they feel that way? In your own words, explain the conflict between the "cool" and the "prudish" schools of thought.

3. Describe a time when your politics came into conflict with your personal life, a time when a real-life situation called one of your strongly held beliefs into question. How did you resolve this conflict?

ROBIN MARANTZ HENIG

The Price of Perfection

[CIVILIZATION / May–June 1996]

Before 1992, when they were taken off the market because of questions about long-term health risks, silicone implants had been inserted into the chests of more than a million American women. A small minority of these were cancer patients undergoing breast reconstruction after mastectomy. But the vast majority were perfectly healthy women who simply wanted to be bustier. Why were these women so willing to undergo risky surgery and endanger their well-being for the sake of a bigger bra size? How had they succumbed to the idea that they had to be beautiful in order to succeed and that there was only one way to be beautiful?

These women were part of a long line of women — and, on occasion, men — who for centuries have undergone mutilating or dangerous procedures in the quest for beauty. Their methods have varied with changing ideals of beauty and new techniques to shift, stretch, and rearrange their bodies. Over the centuries, women have mauled and manipulated just about every body part — lips, eyes, ears, waists, skulls, foreheads, feet — that did not quite fit into the cookie-cutter ideal of a particular era's fashion. In China, almost up until World War II, upper-class girls had their feet bound, crippling them for life but ensuring the three- or four-inch-long feet that were prized as exquisitely feminine. In central Africa, the Mangbettu wrapped the heads of female infants in pieces of giraffe hide to attain the elongated, cone-shaped heads that were taken to be a sign of beauty and intelligence. During the Renaissance, well-born European women plucked out hairs, one by one, from their natural hairlines all the way back to the crowns of their heads, to give themselves the high, rounded foreheads thought beautiful at the time.

ROBIN MARANTZ HENIG (b. 1953) has written about cosmetic surgery as self-mutilation in such publications as the New York Times Magazine, *the* Washington Post, Vogue, Self, *and* Mirabella. *Some of her books include* Being Adopted: The Lifelong Search for Self *(1993) and* A Dancing Matrix: How Science Confronts Emerging Viruses *(1994). She has written extensively about public health and child rearing, the most recent of which is entitled* The People's Health: A Memoir of Public Health and Its Evolution at Harvard *(1996).*

The long history of beauty-by-mutilation makes us rethink today's frenzied search for the ideal female body. The current epidemic of anorexia, face-lifts, and liposuction is often thought of as unique to the late twentieth century. So we tend to blame uniquely modern institutions for these trends, particularly the fashion industry and Hollywood. Fashion magazines tout a single image of beauty, that of a dewy-eyed, slim-hipped 14-year-old dressed to look like a grownup. Movies and TV shows feature actresses who, with the exception of an occasional Roseanne, all look the same. When actress Pamela Lee enhances her curves, when Cher undergoes dozens of cosmetic surgeries, other women tend to assume that they should try to look that way, too. And with the price of many of the most brutal operations now set at about the cost of a 10-day Caribbean cruise, the quest for physical perfection has moved from the salons of Beverly Hills to the living rooms of Middle America.

This dogged pursuit of female beauty, however it is defined and to whatever lengths women go to achieve it, has been with us for so long that it suggests there is some evolutionary advantage to being vain. In the struggle for a male's attention, the woman who dominates may be the one who preens in the right way. She believes that in the state of nature, a male will mate with the female who seems as if she would make the best mother, one who looks youthful and healthy. So in evolutionary terms, the women who come closest to this nubile ideal are the ones who will have the most reproductive success.

The crazed quest for beauty at any cost has led to some bizarre prac-   5
tices along the way. Consider, for instance, the highs and lows of fashions regarding a woman's breasts. In ancient Greece and again in fourteenth-century Europe, breasts were hidden and tightly bound. The ideal torso was a flat torso, an ideal that reemerged for the flappers of the 1920s and the mod models, like Twiggy, of the 1960s. Among the Circassians in the Caucasus region of Asia — reputed to be the most beautiful women in the world because of their symmetrical features and lily-white skin — a young girl was sheathed tightly in leather garments from before puberty until the day she was married. On her wedding night, the bridegroom ritualistically cut apart the leather with his hunting knife. "After that, the breasts were allowed to grow — if, indeed, they were still disposed to," note Arline and John Liggett in *The Tyranny of Beauty.* "What was cheerfully ignored was that many women became anaemic, frequently consumptive, and that a great many died."

By the mid-1800s, Rubenesque[1] curves were back. A well-rounded bosom was something to be proud of — and something to be artfully enhanced with clever undergarments. Breasts were powdered, perfumed, and painted to appear as fair as the face and neck. Middle-aged women even

---

[1] The Flemish artist Peter Paul Rubens (1577–1640) often portrayed large, plump, voluptuous nudes; hence the phrase a "Rubenesque figure."

drew delicate blue veins on their breasts to make their skin look as translucent as a maiden's.

Around this time, falsies first became popular. Originally they were made of wax or stuffed cotton, but these stiff shapes just lay on the chest and failed to move with the wearer. Within a few years, more natural-looking falsies came on the market, made of wire or inflatable rubber, and these, according to one French firm's advertisements, were capable of "following the movements of respiration with mathematical and perfect precision."

In 1903, an iconoclastic Chicago surgeon named Charles Miller opened a cosmetic-surgery practice in which he experimented with new methods of surgical breast enlargement. Miller opened up women's chests and inserted, according to his own account, "braided silk, bits of silk floss, particles of celluloid, vegetable ivory and several other foreign materials." There is no record of how his patients reacted, physically or emotionally, to their stuffed breasts.

When stylish women put their breasts under cover again in the 1920s, they used constricting devices like the one from the Boyish Form Brassière Company of New York, guaranteed to "give you that boy-like flat appearance." Some women actually folded their breasts, squashing them as close as possible against the rib cage and holding them there with elastic binding. Then the pendulum swung once again. By the 1950s, breasts were back. And this time, twentieth-century technological know-how was able to provide far more sophisticated solutions for those who didn't measure up. At first, the only women who surgically enlarged their breasts were professional entertainers. Carol Doda, a topless cocktail waitress from San Francisco, was one of the pioneers. In the late 1950s, she became an instant celebrity when she boosted her bosom to a size 44DD with 20 shots of liquid silicone.

"Enthusiasm for this method waned," notes Kathy Davis in *Reshaping*   10
the Female Body: The Dilemma of Cosmetic Surgery, "when it was discovered that paraffin or silicone injected directly tended to migrate to other parts of the body, causing cysts and necrosis [death] of the skin. Sponges made of terylene wool, polyvinyl or polyethylene were then introduced to replace the injections. These new materials were an improvement, but they often hardened, protruded or caused fluid to accumulate in the breasts, which then had to be drained."

Despite the vagaries of vanity, which changed the notion of ideal breast size every few decades, one factor has held relatively constant: Most cultures, through the centuries, have wanted their women to be slim. Anorexia may seem to be a uniquely late-twentieth-century disease, but the sad truth is that going to great lengths to be thin is nothing new.

In ancient Greece, mothers wrapped their newborn daughters tightly in bands of wool or linen for the first six months or more, in hopes of elongating their proportions to the willowy, slim ideal of the time. And in England in 1665, a health pamphlet titled "To reduce the body that is too fat to a mean and handsome proportion" noted that one handy technique for losing weight was bloodletting. Overweight women, according to this pamphlet, should be bled "largely, twice a year, the right arm in the spring, the left in the autumn" — an eerie precursor to today's binging-and-purging syndrome known as bulimia. For the nether regions that still bulged too much, the pamphlet advised using "ligaments to bind those passages where the member is supplied with nourishment." In the 1930s, desperate women actually swallowed tapeworms to lose weight; the opera diva Maria Callas is said to have been one such reducer.

For those who could not drop all the pounds they wanted to, under-garments came to the rescue. The most notorious — and perplexingly long-lived — of these was the corset. In one form or another, women subjected themselves to wearing corsets for over 500 years, from their introduction during Chaucer's time until far into the Victorian age.

The first corset, or cotte (from the French word côte, meaning "rib"), was made of two pieces of linen fabric stiffened and held together with paste. Later, corsets became far more cumbersome, involving two-inch-wide wooden boards and even heavy lead breastplates. By the nineteenth century, the corset had become a portable torture chamber made of rubber and strips of whalebone, pieces of which might easily protrude from their casings and pierce a woman's skin. It was designed to be worn so tightly that women tended to faint, unable to breathe deeply enough to get sufficient oxygen to their brains.

To many observers, corsets were obviously foolhardy and potentially dangerous. In the British medical journal The Lancet, an 1868 article stated flatly that "the mischief produced by [a corset] can hardly be over-estimated. It tends gradually to displace all the most important organs of the body while by compressing them it must, from the first, interfere with their functions."

Yet the feminine ideal at the time remained a slender "wasp-waisted" figure with an eighteen-inch waist — a size that virtually no woman past puberty could attain without some heavy-duty assistance. This involved not only corseting but also its sadistic extension, tight-lacing. This extreme form of compression is how the servant Mammy squeezed Scarlett O'Hara into her ball gown in Gone with the Wind, pulling and straining at the crisscrossing ribbons that held the corset closed at the back.

No woman could tight-lace herself alone, not only because the laces tied up in the back, but also because the woman's natural instinct for self-preservation would likely prevent her from applying the kind of pressure needed to attain that eighteen-inch ideal. Most required the assistance of their maids (tight-lacing was the madness of the upper classes), their mothers, or at the very least their bedposts. Sometimes the recalcitrant flesh fought back so mightily that it required two helpers, one to tighten the laces while the other held the subject in place with her foot. Tight-lacing, writes Lois W. Banner in American Beauty, "may have been a primary cause of the uterine and spinal disorders widespread among nineteenth-century women." Today, there are surgical alternatives to tight-lacing, including liposuction and tummy tucks. But removing excess fat and skin isn't enough for everyone: Cher even went to the extremes of undergoing an operation to remove two perfectly healthy ribs — and so accentuate her tiny waistline.

Less drastic measures, using laser surgery, are also now allowing women to erase the facial "imperfections" that have troubled them for generations. In the Elizabethan age, many women, in search of skin that looked like porcelain, whitened their faces using ceruse, a potentially lethal combination of vinegar and lead. Queen Elizabeth I used ceruse so consistently that it eventually ate pits into her skin, causing her to pile the paint on in thicker and thicker layers in hopes of camouflaging the growing damage. This, in turn, only led to more corrosion, and the Virgin Queen's face was ultimately so ravaged that she ordered all mirrors banned from the palace. (Arline and John Liggett write that Elizabeth's servants exploited the ban on mirrors in a wickedly mischievous way: Every morning they painted the queen's face white with ceruse, but they painted her nose "a cruel crimson.")

By the mid-1800s, face paint was thought to be cheap and tawdry, so ladies who wanted to achieve the porcelain look "naturally" took to swallowing whitening potions made of vinegar, chalk, or arsenic, the last of which is poisonous even in tiny amounts. Arsenic was also the base for Fowler's Solution, a topical cream prescribed for teenage acne in that period. But like Retin-A a century later, Fowler's not only dried up pimples but also gave a translucent tone to the skin, so some fashionable women used it as a facial cosmetic.

Women unwittingly courted blindness, too, in their beauty quest. The   20 ancient Egyptians, Romans, and Persians tried to make their eyes glitter by using drops of antimony sulfide. The drops often dried up the tear ducts, though, and eventually destroyed vision. In the sixteenth and seventeenth centuries, women used eye drops made of belladonna (also known as deadly nightshade) to dilate their pupils. But while it had the desired effect of making their eyes look dewy, interested, and excited, the drops also robbed these women of the normal pupil-shrinking reflex that keeps bright light away from the delicate retina. Modern experts believe that by continuously dilating their pupils, these women may have predisposed themselves to the potentially blinding eye condition of glaucoma.

Chemicals used to make blondes out of brunettes also proved far more dangerous than their users first suspected. In the nineteenth century, British women used a solution made of poisonous oxalic acid to change their hair color. They believed that dark hair was caused by an excess of iron in the system, and the acid was thought to neutralize iron. They mixed an ounce of oxalic acid in a pint of boiling water, soaked their hair thoroughly, and went out into the sunshine to let it dry. This procedure was repeated, according to one pamphlet of the day, "until it begins to affect the skin when it must be discontinued, otherwise the hair will fall out."

In Venice, the recipe for hair lightening involved a mixture of bisulfate of magnesia and lime. A paste made of these ingredients could be "very effectual in bleaching the hair," wrote one Venetian with tongue firmly in cheek, "and also for burning it away entirely, together with the skin and brains, if there are any, beneath it."

Manipulations of the skeleton proved to be every bit as disfiguring as some of the chemicals applied to the skin and hair. The most notorious and long-lasting practice of bodily mutilation for the sake of beauty was the foot-binding of Chinese girls.

Foot-binding went far beyond wrapping bandages around the feet and hoping they did not grow. It was something more akin to Cinderella's stepsisters cutting off their own heels and toes to fit into the dainty glass slipper. Beginning at about the age of five, a girl's foot was virtually folded in two, and a ten-foot-long bandage was wrapped tightly around it to force the toes down toward the heel as far as possible. The child could not move without doubling over in a graceless and largely futile effort to walk without putting any weight on her feet. Her feet eventually lost all blood supply, which turned the skin blue; portions of the soles and toes might actually drop off. Mercifully, these deadened feet usually — though not always — ended up without any sensation at all. In order to keep the young girls from tearing off the maddening bandages, many families kept their daughter's hands tied to a pole.

Every two weeks, the girl's feet would be squeezed into a new pair of shoes, one-fifth of an inch smaller than the pair before. After several years of this, the girl's bones were sufficiently crippled and deformed to keep the feet stunted at the desired three-inch "golden lotus" length.

"My foot felt very painful at the start," recalled one woman, whose account was related in *The Tyranny of Beauty*. "The heel of my foot became odoriferous and deteriorated. Because of the pain in my foot, my whole body became emaciated. My face colour changed and I couldn't sleep at night." But this woman put up with the agony, because she was convinced that "no one wanted to marry a woman with big feet."

Western cultures, while not going to quite the same extreme as the Chinese, also revered a small female foot; indeed, that is what the Cinderella story is all about. Women wear shoes that are tight, pointy-toed, and high-heeled because they make feet look small, even though they also hurt. High heels are bad not only for the feet but also for the entire body. The woman's torso is not designed to hobble about on its toes; stiletto heels can lead to abnormally shortened calf muscles, stretched spines, and chronic back pain.

Just as painful as stunting the growth of one part of the body is exaggerating the growth of another — a practice that has been widespread in Asia and Africa. Many African peoples have inserted plates into young women's lips to enlarge them or weighed down their earlobes with heavy hoops so that the lobes eventually brush the shoulders. Some contemporary observers think that such practices began as a way to make African women less appealing to the slave traders headed to the New World, but they gradually became accepted as standards of beauty for other members of the tribe.

Among the Padaung people of early-twentieth-century Burma, the ideal of female beauty involved a greatly elongated neck, preferably fifteen inches or more. This was accomplished by fitting girls with a series of brass neck rings. At a very young age, girls began by wearing five rings; by the time they were fully grown, they were wearing as many as twenty-four, piled one on top of another. Even today, Burmese refugees in northern Thailand continue to stretch their daughters' necks, since the bizarre stretching has become something of a tourist attraction. The weight of the ring leads to crushed collarbones and broken ribs, and the vertebrae in the neck become stretched and floppy. Indeed, these women wear the rings round-the-clock because, without them, their stretched-out necks are too weak to support their heads.

What many of these beauty trends have in common is that they forced   30 women into positions of frailty, with their impossibly long necks, impossibly tiny feet, impossibly small waists. And the highest achieving women have tended to be those most susceptible to the lure of the ideal; their perfectionist streak made them want to attain every goal society deemed worthy, no matter how ludicrous it might be. This might explain why Queen Elizabeth I, whose comprehensive classical education was rare for a girl in her day, fretted over her hair and her complexion like a teenager preparing for a ball. And it might explain why Hillary Rodham Clinton, arguably one of the most powerful women in the United States, was willing to jazz up her looks in the 1980s with contact lenses and peroxide for the sake of her husband's political career — and why she careens through hairdos the way other women change their shoes.

One question today, of course, is why women respond to these images in a way that is different from men. How many men take Arnold Schwarzenegger's body personally? While cosmetic surgery is increasing among American males, it is still primarily the province of women, as is the self-loathing that often results in women who fail to look the way they believe they are supposed to look. In surveys that ask men and women, or boys and girls, questions like "What do you think about your body?" females reveal a distorted and inferior body image far more commonly than do males.

There might be an evolutionary explanation for this difference. Sex researchers Masters and Johnson found that while men are highly susceptible to visual cues in their sexual arousal, women respond more to other senses. Evolutionary biologists tell us that men are attracted to women because of the way they look, while what attracts women is not so much a man's looks as evidence of his wealth, status, and power. So maybe it follows that women would be more susceptible to the prevailing idea of what it means to look desirable — they have more at stake.

Aside from trying to look good for men, women have traditionally tried to impress one another, casting sidelong glances to see how they compare

with the other females in the cave, the harem, the secretarial pool, or the executive boardroom. From this perspective, face-lifts and tummy tucks are just another way to keep up with the competition, no more significant than a move from long skirts to short ones. And modern surgical techniques have made changing a bustline almost as easy as adjusting a hemline.

Feminist writer Susan Faludi offers a more political interpretation. She writes in *Backlash: The Undeclared War Against American Women* that as women achieve greater economic power, the prevailing ideal of female beauty becomes more and more passive and childlike. "The beauty standard converges with the social campaign against wayward women," she writes, "allying itself with 'traditional' morality; porcelain and unblemished exterior becomes proof of a woman's internal purity, obedience, and restraint." To Faludi, a change in the prevailing standard of beauty toward a more girlish look — as happened in the 1960s and again in the 1990s — is a sure sign that, politically, women have become too threatening.

Since before Cleopatra's day, women have been judged by the way they look, and they have struggled mightily to make themselves look the way they want to be judged. To expect this to change as women become more powerful is simply naive. Gloria Steinem — a highly accomplished author and publisher, a noted feminist leader, and, not incidentally, a very attractive woman — confessed in her recent autobiography to harboring profound self-doubt about the way she looks. If Steinem feels that way, it is hardly surprising that others do too. Perhaps Elizabeth I was onto something after all. Maybe the only way for women to look ahead is to banish all mirrors from the palace.

35

Responding as a Reader

1. Henig begins with a discussion of the hazards of silicone implants and then puts that problem into historical context. What is the effect of the historical examples? Do they cause you to see the silicone example in a different light?

2. Henig cites examples from many different cultures, considering Western culture in the 1990s alongside ancient Persia and early-twentieth-century Burma. How does this juxtaposition affect readers?

3. In paragraph 4, Henig argues that there might be an evolutionary advantage to "preen[ing] the right way," that more physically attractive women are more likely to have children than less physically attractive women. To what extent is this accurate, in your experience?

Responding as a Writer

1. In an essay, arrive at your own definition of beauty. Do you agree with the epigraph, "One must suffer to be beautiful"?

2. In the opening paragraph, Henig asks, "How had [women] succumbed to the idea that they had to be beautiful in order to succeed and that there was only one way to be beautiful?" What do you think causes women to believe this? Do you believe it?

3. Henig focuses on the sacrifices women have made in an effort to conform to their cultures' definition of beauty. What about men? What sacrifices do they make in order to appear attractive? How, in your experience, do men differ from women in this regard?

Discussing the Unit

Suggested Topic for Discussion

How does physical appearance influence self-image? Do physically attractive people feel better about themselves than unattractive people? What other factors shape a person's self-image? How important is beauty in relation to these?

Preparing for Class Discussion

1. Consider the standards for beauty in contemporary American culture. Who determines these standards? Do they apply to everyone equally? Which characteristics seem most important? Is it possible to acquire these characteristics or is one simply born with or without them?

2. Imagine that you could wave a magic wand and suddenly eliminate all of your physical flaws. How would your life change? What would remain unchanged?

3. *Prewriting Assignment:* Think of the various words people use to describe a good-looking person — "pretty," "attractive," and "handsome," among others. Consider also popular and slang terms — "babe," "hunk," and so on. Make a list of the words and expressions you tend to use. Which terms are the most polite? Which might be offensive? Classify your language. How do the terms differ by gender? Is it possible to rank the terms on a scale of positive value? For example, would "pretty" rank higher than "attractive"?

From Discussion to Writing

The philosopher Schopenhauer wrote that we all proceed with people on the basis of an unspoken rule that everyone *is* as he or she *looks.* In other words, we all seem to think — despite evidence to the contrary — that we can judge people mainly by their physical appearance. Consider your own appearance and how you think it affects other people's assessment of you. In an essay, try to describe yourself as accurately and objectively as you can. In the course of your essay, consider the following questions: Do you think others see you as you see yourself or do you think there is often a disparity between the way you see yourself and how others see you? What mistakes do you think other people make about the way you look and the way you actually view yourself? Do you think the way other people assess your appearance has made a big difference in your life?

4

Only Words:
Does Language Matter?

Do the words we use in our ordinary, daily conversations matter? Does it make any difference whether we say "girl" instead of "woman" or use the expression "colored people" rather than "people of color?" To what extent can the words we use create a climate of respect or of hostility? And what happens when the right word just doesn't seem to exist? M. P. Dunleavy asks in "'Guy' Envy" what women can call themselves besides "woman" — a word that usually sounds too formal or political for casual occasions. In "Unspeakable Names," Richard Dooling finds Americans currently "caught between taboos": "Vulgar sexual terms," he argues, "have become acceptable in the last two decades while all manner of racial or ethnic epithets have become unspeakable." In another blast at "politically correct" speech, *The Weekly Standard* satirizes a White House lexicon advising us on how to refer to the disabled. One of the recent key issues involving language grew out of the Oakland, California, school district's endorsement of Ebonics, also known as "Vernacular Black English." The policy — designed to help teacher-student communication by sensitizing teachers to the language spoken by many black children — failed to gain support, largely as a result of the outrage expressed nationally by both black and white educators, columnists, and intellectuals. In "To Throw in a Lot of 'Bes,' or Not?" the noted African American columnist William Raspberry takes a humorous look at the motivations behind the Ebonics movement. But not all educators and intellectuals resisted Ebonics (the word was coined in the early '70s, combining "ebony," meaning black, with "phonics") as evidenced by the chapter's final document, The Linguistic Society of America's "Resolution on the Oakland 'Ebonics' Issue."

As for the Class of 2000's take on the words we use in daily conversations, the following survey results suggest that how you feel about that question depends in part on what race and sex you are.

Selected Survey Results

Language

- Freshmen who believe that racist/sexist speech should be prohibited: 63.8%
- Men who do: 59.5%
- Women who do: 67.3%
- Freshmen at all black colleges who do: 64.1%

— From The American Freshman: National Norms For Fall 1996.

M. P. DUNLEAVEY

"Guy" Envy

[GLAMOUR / May 1996]

There are still a few reasons to envy men: that 74-cents-to-the-dollar thing, their choke hold on Congress, and the word *"guy."* On the first two fronts — earning power and political clout — women continue to gain ground. But when it comes to calling ourselves something besides "woman,"

M. P. DUNLEAVEY (b. 1965) is a staff writer at Glamour *magazine. Her work has also appeared in the* New York Times, *the* Sunday Times Book Review, *and* New York *magazine. She is also a writer for the critically acclaimed cyberserial "The Couch" (www.thecouch.com).*

something that captures our most laid-back, casual sense of ourselves — our *"guyness,"* if you will — we need a word of our own.

Not that there's anything wrong with *"woman."* Given the umpteen unwonderful alternatives (*"girl," "babe," "chick," "lady," "broad," "dame," "lass"*), it's clear why we fought so hard for this nonpejorative term. Woman is admirable. Woman is honorable. Woman speaks of maturity, motherhood, and busting through barriers. And that's *exactly* why we need a term to give us a break from all that. A word that would let us kick back and not shave for a couple of days. A word like *"guy."*

"Guy" is efficient. Think about it: "There's a new guy in marketing — he's got some great ideas." The focus completely skips over *him* — his gender, his maleness — to the important stuff. That he's a man hardly registers. We females, on the other hand, have no shorthand that unhooks us from the biological and political implications of our sex. "We just hired a woman to run the ad-sales division and she's a dynamo." It's hard to hear that without thinking, Oh, she's a *woman.* Is she young, cute, straight, married? Does she market to women? Did they hire her because she's a woman? Will she fit in with the guys?

A few months ago, Natalie Angier, a science reporter for the *New York Times,* gave in to her own "guy" envy and confessed her longing for "a word that conveys snazziness and style, a casual term for the double-X set . . . a delicious egalitarian word like . . . gal."

Gal? *Gal*? Though Angier insists that "gal has a rich and prismatic   5 quality to it," *The Oxford English Dictionary* strikes closer to the vein, revealing that *"gal"* is nothing more than "a vulgar or dialectal pronunciation" of *girl.* Oh, that's progress. Besides, as a friend from Nevada points out, "Gal is from the heartland. Gal has a warm heart, big hips and a bad dye job."

What women need is a word that will let us slip into a more easygoing side of ourselves the way men can slip into guyhood.

When men take off their uniforms, jackets, and ties, they're guys. When they put them on again, they're men. In part it's an attitude thing: In the Oval Office, Bill Clinton is a man. Jogging down Pennsylvania Avenue, he's a guy. Charles Barkley is a guy, unless he's on the court; then he's a man. Of course, some males favor one side of the man/guy fence. Hawkeye is a guy. Colonel Potter is a man. Humphrey Bogart, Robert De Niro, Ronald Reagan — men. Steve Martin, Jerry Seinfeld, Spike Lee — guys.

But: Mary Tyler Moore, Rita Hayworth, Connie Chung, Hillary Rodham Clinton, Whoopi Goldberg, Julia Louis-Dreyfus, Rosie Perez — all different, all women. Everyone knows that Whoopi is much more of a guy than Hillary is, but we don't have the word to say so. Meanwhile, don't even try plugging female words into classic guy phrases. Whatta *girl*! (Ugh.) She's a great *babe.* (Oh, no.) She's a *woman's woman*? From time to time we do call ourselves "guys" (do any of you guys have a spare tampon?), but let's not kid ourselves. We're on borrowed terminology.

This is not just semantics. Until fairly recently, women could not *be* all that guys were and are. It may seem that we've always lived and worked and dressed as comfortably as one of the fellas, but until 30 years ago women were constrained by a standard of femininity that embraced the word *"lady"* right along with the wearing of gloves. In the 1950s, women didn't require a word like *"guy"* because acting like one wasn't written into their parts. Now our roles have changed, and it's time that language caught up.

The more traditional words that describe women do come in handy; 10 every once in a while you *want* to be a lady, a bitch, or a chick and having a word for what you're being makes being it easier. But how do you describe a woman you hang out with who is cool with herself and others, a woman you can watch the game with and whose shoulder you can cry on, knowing that she knows where you're coming from? There is no womanly translation of *"guy"* and yet most women I know aspire to a certain level of guyhood. Just as our mothers longed to be ladies, this confident, centered, sympathetic yet amusing human being is who we'd like to be.

We'll always be women — no one is advocating giving that up. But we need choices, and unless something better comes along we may just have to stake our own claim to *"guy."* After all, we successfully co-opted the original guy symbol: blue jeans. There *was* a time when women weren't supposed to touch denim unless they were washing it. Funny how things change. Right, guys?

Responding as a Reader

1. Think of the men you know. Which are guys and which are men? What about the women — which are women and which are, well, "guys"?

2. In paragraph 10, Dunleavy writes, "having a word for what you're being makes being it easier." What does she mean by this? Is it harder for women to be "guys" because there is no word for female guyness?

3. According to Dunleavy, what exactly is a guy? Are certain men and boys excluded from guyness, as well as women?

Responding as a Writer

1. Make two lists: words that describe men and words that describe women. Which words correspond fairly closely in meaning ("hunk" and "babe," for example)? Which don't seem to have a counterpart for the other gender? What about the word "fellow" or "dude"? Can these words cross the gender line? What do you suppose this says about the English language?

2. Try to come up with a female counterpart to "guy." You might choose a word that people already use, borrow a word from another language, rediscover a word from the past, combine ideas to make a new word, or invent something new altogether. In a short essay, defend your choice.

3. The English language is rich in synonyms, and no two synonyms mean exactly the same thing. Think of any two words that are close in meaning (like "man" and "guy") — if you're drawing a blank, then use a thesaurus. In an essay, draw a clear distinction between these two words. Be sure to use plenty of examples.

RICHARD DOOLING

Unspeakable Names

[THE NEW YORK TIMES / September 6, 1996]

Minnesota has a rebellious county on its hands. Lake County has refused to comply with a state law, enacted last year, that orders counties to rename any natural geographic place with the word "squaw" in its name.

State officials and American Indian linguists campaigned for the change. According to them, "squaw," a French corruption of the Algonquin words for woman, is an epithet used against American Indians describing female genitals.

But officials in Lake County, Minnesota, citing standard dictionary definitions and complaining about the expense of making new signs and maps, contend that the protest is all so much pointless political correctness. First, Squaw Creek in Lake County and next Squaw Valley, California?

While the citizens of Minnesota are debating whether the word "squaw" is offensive, another word — one almost universally considered

---

RICHARD DOOLING *(b. 1954) was recently nominated for the National Book Award for his second novel,* White Man's Grave. *He is a lawyer specializing in employment-discrimination cases and is the author of* Critical Care *(1992) and* Blue Streak: Swearing, Free Speech and Sexual Harassment.

In the News

Speaking of Disabilities

One would think that the phrase "politically correct" would by now be recognized as self-satirizing. Not so in the case of the Presidential Inauguration Committee that published last January [1997] "a helpful hints reference guide for politically correct speech when interacting with individuals with disabilities." The pamphlet said in part that "in speaking or writing, remember that children or adults with disabilities are like everyone else — except they happen to have a disability." It went on to list negative and positive phrases with respect to the handicapped:

negative

handicapped child
disabled child
retarded
normal
healthy

positive

child with disability
child with disability
person with retardation
non-disabled
non-disabled

— From *The Weekly Standard* (February 10, 1997).

the most offensive word in the English language — can be heard in almost every major motion picture and on any New York City street.

Why is one word being decried, while another is gaining acceptance? We are caught between taboos. Vulgar sexual terms have become acceptable in the last two decades, while all manner of racial or ethnic epithets have become unspeakable. In other words, hatred is finally more dangerous than sex.

When America was founded, a sacrilegious oath — "God's blood!" — was the height of offensiveness. As the country became more secular, dirty words with sexual connotations became more objectionable than sacrilegious oaths.

Of course, four-letter words are still not acceptable in polite company. But we have become more tolerant of their use not only in movies and magazines but also in casual conversation.

This was probably inevitable after the sexual revolution. Premarital sex is now common, its potential risks (new human beings) easily avoided. Sex is less scandalous and doesn't pose a danger to community values. So it's not surprising that the four-letter words have lost some of their power to offend.

Racial epithets, however, have become socially charged. Some lawyers have argued that the O. J. Simpson trial turned on Mark Fuhrman's use of an ugly racial epithet — what Christopher Darden, the deputy district attorney, called "the dirtiest, filthiest, nastiest word in the English language."

Our intolerance for racial epithets is reason for hope. The new taboos are evidence of our collective desire for a new social order. We don't like these words because they are pejorative and we want equality between the races.

But racial tension is evidently so great that we are succumbing to the temptation to censor all sorts of terms — like "squaw" as a name for a place — to give us the illusion that we are resolving these problems. After Minnesota obliterates "squaw" from its maps, road signs, deeds, ledgers, state publications, and history books, will it then remove it from dictionaries?

Instead of creating new laws to ban words or books or speech, why don't we concentrate on fixing the underlying social pathologies instead?

Responding as a Reader

1. Consider the definition of "squaw" given in paragraph 2. How does this make you feel about using the word to describe a woman? To describe a place? Try substituting other names for the female genitals.

2. What word is Dooling referring to in paragraph 4? Is the comparison of this word to "squaw" legitimate? What is the main difference between them, according to Dooling? Why is one acceptable in polite company, while the other isn't? Can you think of other differences?

3. Why does Dooling say that "our intolerance for racial epithets is reason for hope" (para. 10)? Whom does he seem to think he's talking to when he uses the pronoun "our"? What assumptions does Dooling share with the audience he addresses?

4. What is the difference between removing a word from road signs and removing it from the dictionary (para. 11)? Do you believe that the second action is likely to result from the first? Why or why not?

Responding as a Writer

1. Words do change in meaning over time and as they're incorporated into other languages. Has this happened with "squaw" — does it now mean something other than the original Algonquin word? Or does the original meaning still hold a great deal of power? Argue for one point of view or the other.

2. Consider the power of what Dooling calls "four-letter words." What kinds of words do you find most offensive and why? Are your reasons personal, political, cultural? In an essay, explain why you find one category of words particularly offensive.

3. What should be done in this particular case? Should the word "squaw" be removed from "maps, road signs, deeds, ledgers, state publications"? If so, how do you answer the critics? How do we come up with new names, and who should pay the financial cost? If not, what do you say to the people who are offended by the word "squaw"?

WILLIAM RASPBERRY

To Throw in a Lot of "Bes," or Not?

[THE WASHINGTON POST NATIONAL WEEKLY EDITION/January 6,1997]

"'Sup?" the cabbie says.

"No, thanks," I say. After pigging out over Christmas, I was trying to cut back on my caloric intake. "Besides," I point out, "it looks to me like you've only got half a filet of fish and what's left of a small order of fries."

"What you be talking' 'bout, my man?" he says. "I don't be offerin' you my grub; I be sayin' hello. You know, like, what's up?"

Now, I'm a reasonable man, and I don't expect my cab driver to speak like — well, a journalist. But I'd never heard him talk like this. "What's going on?" I ask.

"I'm studying Ebonics," he says, sounding like himself again. "And judging from your response, I'm guessing you don't know the language." 5

"That's not exactly true," I say. "Unless I miss my guess, you're talking about what, until a few weeks ago, was called Black English — and what before that was called Ghettoese. Most African Americans are quite familiar with it. As I recall, it sounds rather like what our mothers used to call Bad English."

"Looks like the man done got to you, my brother," the cabbie says. "Why does what we speak have to be 'bad' anything? If a French dude tells you 'bone jour,' you don't call that bad. If a Hispanic guy says 'que pasta,' you just say 'que pasta' right back. But when I say 'sup,' you pretend you no Nintendo. Why you got to put our language down?"

He is winding up for his self-hating-black-man speech, and I am in no mood for it. "Listen," I tell him. "I know a thing or two about this issue. I'm well aware that some linguists and a growing number of black educators — and not just those in the Oakland school system — are making a deal of the fact that so-called Black English has all the earmarks of a legitimate language, including consistency. They make the further point that there's no basis for declaring one dialect inherently superior to another."

"You're not as dumb as I thought," the cabbie says.

WILLIAM RASPBERRY (b. 1935) is a widely syndicated columnist for the Washington Post. Raspberry won the 1994 Pulitzer Prize for commentary, writing about topics such as crime, AIDS, and urban linguistics. He has been a Knight professor of the practice of journalism in the department of public policy studies in Duke's Trinity College of Arts and Sciences.

"The prestige language within any culture is the language spoken by   10
the prestige class," I continue. "And Black English — Ebonics, if you insist — happens to be the language of the unlettered black masses. Do you
really believe that the Oakland school board can, by making Ebonics an 'official' language, give it — and the children who speak it — more prestige?"

The cabbie is thoughtful for a moment. "Wouldn't you agree," he says
at last, "that if teachers understood the legitimacy of the language spoken
by many young black children, they might stop equating that language
with stupidity? I mean, Hispanic kids might have trouble with English, but
nobody puts down Spanish as a language."

It is a point, I concede. "Do you imagine the teachers will be required
to learn Ebonics in order to qualify as bilingual instructors?"

"And why not?" the cabbie says. "It's not that hard. As I told you, I'm
learning it myself."

"How," I ask. "Tapes? Videos? Berlitz Total Immersion?"

"My brother-in-law," he says. "He says I'm coming on nicely too."   15

"I noticed a couple of errors when you tried your French and Spanish on
me a while back," I say. "Just out of curiosity, who corrects your Ebonics?"

"That's the beautiful part," the cabbie says. "Ebonics gives you a
whole range of options. You can say 'she wish' or 'they goes,' and it's all
perfectly fine. But you can also say 'they go,' and that's all right too. I
don't think you can say 'I does.' I'll have to check on that, but my brother-
in-law tells me you can say pretty much what you please, as long as you're
careful to throw in a lot of 'bes' and leave off final consonants."

As a onetime proofreader, I couldn't believe my ears. "They'll have
teachers learn a language that has no right or wrong expressions, no consistent spellings or pronunciations, and no discernable rules? How will that
help the children learn proper English? What, precisely, is the point?"

"Did you know that the federal government spends serious bucks for
bilingual programs, including the training of bilingual teachers?" the cabbie says. "And don't you see, now that Ebonics is an official language in
Oakland, that we'll finally have a language program the white folks won't
be able to test and poke and certify?

"I mean if this thing catches on, a lot of us could pick up some nice   20
extra cash teaching Ebonics in our spare time."

"Yo!" I say. "Maybe you be onto somethin' dere, my bruvah."

Responding as a Reader

1. Consider the dialogue between Raspberry and the cabbie. Do you
   think this conversation actually took place? How can you tell?

2. Reread the cabbie's speech in para. 7. How is Raspberry characterizing
   the cabbie here? By extension, is Raspberry making a claim about
   those who argue for the legitimacy of Black English?

3. How does Raspberry characterize himself? Consider his style of writing as well as what he says about himself and the Ebonics issue. How do you think Raspberry wants to be perceived by his readers?

Responding as a Writer

1. Read the Oakland resolution reprinted below. Does Raspberry address each of the resolution's four points? Do you believe that he addresses them fairly? Explain.

2. A speech community is a group of people who share a specialized language; that language allows them to discuss the issues that are important to the group in an efficient way and is often incomprehensible to outsiders. Choose one of the speech communities that you belong to — perhaps having to do with work, a sport, or a social group — and write a dialogue in the language of that community.

3. Working from the Oakland resolution, Raspberry's article, and your own experience, take a stand on the Ebonics issue. Should Black English be recognized as a legitimate language? Why or why not?

Document

Linguistics Society of America (LSA) Resolution on the Oakland "Ebonics" Issue

The following resolution was drafted by John R. Rickford, Professor of Linguistics at Stanford University, and approved by the Linguistics Society of America on January 3, 1997.

Whereas there has been a great deal of discussion in the media and among the American public about the 18 December 1996 decision of the Oakland School Board to recognize the language variety spoken by many African American students and to take it into account in teaching Standard English, the Linguistics Society of America, as a society of scholars engaged in the scientific study of language, hereby resolves to make it known that:

a. The variety known as "Ebonics," "African American Vernacular English" (AAVE), and "Vernacular Black English" and by other names is systematic and rule-governed like all natural speech varieties. In fact, all human linguistic systems — spoken, signed, and written — are fundamentally regular. The systematic and expressive nature of the grammar and pronunciation patterns of the African American vernacular has been established by numerous scientific studies over the past thirty years. Characterizations of

Ebonics as "slang," "mutant," "lazy," "defective," "ungrammatical," or "broken English" are incorrect and demeaning.

b. The distinction between "languages" and "dialects" is usually made more on social and political grounds than on purely linguistic ones. For example, different varieties of Chinese are popularly regarded as "dialects," though their speakers cannot understand each other, but speakers of Swedish and Norwegian, which are regarded as separate "languages," generally understand each other. What is important from a linguistic and educational point of view is not whether AAVE is called a "language" or a "dialect" but rather that its systematicity be recognized.

c. As affirmed in the LSA Statement of Language Rights (June 1996), there are individual and group benefits to maintaining vernacular speech varieties and there are scientific and human advantages to linguistic diversity. For those living in the United States there are also benefits in acquiring Standard English and resources should be made available to all who aspire to mastery of Standard English. The Oakland School Board's commitment to helping students master Standard English is commendable.

d. There is evidence from Sweden, the US, and other countries that speakers of other varieties can be aided in their learning of the standard variety by pedagogical approaches which recognize the legitimacy of the other varieties of a language. From this perspective, the Oakland School Board's decision to recognize the vernacular of African American students in teaching them Standard English is linguistically and pedagogically sound.

Chicago, Illinois
January 1997

— From Web site on the Ebonics issue, which can be found at http://www-leland.stanford.edu/~rickford/ebonics.

Discussing the Unit

Suggested Topic for Discussion

"What's in a name?" asks Shakespeare's Juliet — "that which we call a rose / By any other name would smell as sweet." But not everyone agrees with Juliet's widely quoted remark (including the Capulets, the Montagues, and their real-life counterparts). Names — words — often possess vital social, cultural, and political significance. Is it possible to distinguish between a word and its meaning? If we could do away with hurtful words, what effect would that have on the hurtful feelings that those words express? If we could create (or recognize) a language that spoke for a given marginalized group, could that language change the place of that group in society?

Preparing for Class Discussion

1. Consider your personal sensitivity to language. What sort of words do you find offensive — obscenities, insults, racial epithets, sexist terms, and so on? Be prepared to explain why you find certain words inoffensive.

2. Dunleavey focuses on gender differences, and Dooling and Raspberry write on racial issues. Why do you suppose the pieces in this unit on language focus on differences between groups of people?

3. *Prewriting Assignment:* Spend a day (or even an hour or two, if those hours are rich in language) listening carefully to what others say. Write down the phrases that strike you as most meaningful, most powerful. What makes these phrases stand out from all the others?

From Discussion to Writing

Think of a time when you were deeply affected by spoken words — positively or negatively. Describe the incident, and explain why those words were so significant to you. What did the words stand for? What was communicated, besides the simple meaning of the words spoken?

5

Automobiles:
Do We Need Them?

With a giant automobile industry churning out new models every year and an ingenious advertising industry making sure we buy them, it is no surprise that the United States — with only 5 percent of the world's population — uses nearly 50 percent of the world's cars. It is also no surprise that many citizens nationwide are beginning to worry about how our dependence on the automobile is affecting our environment, our communities, and our quality of life. But can Americans give up this dependency? Having argued against the automobile for years, Jane Holtz Kay, a prominent antiautomobile advocate, decided to practice what she preached. In "Without a Car in the World," she explains why she gave up her car and how she manages to live a busy, professional life without one.

"Let us imagine what life would be like in a carless nation," writes James Q. Wilson, a leading public policy analyst, as he confronts Kay's arguments directly. In "Cars and Their Enemies," Wilson sees the war against the automobile as an elitist, urban-oriented attack on the middle class and its suburban way of life. For Wilson, nothing in the foreseeable future will replace the comfort and convenience of the private car. For the advertising industry, moreover, nothing is likely to replace the personal fantasies the American automobile is built to fulfill, as a *Los Angeles Times* news item reminds us. Yet cars can express our unconscious impulses in a number of ways, especially when we're stuck in traffic. In "Automotivational Counseling," William Hamilton examines the psychic side of driving, inviting us to consider the "unreasonably weird emotionality of the traffic experience." And the ad for Oldsmobile's Intrigue capitalizes on the sexy side of our relationship with cars — whether unconscious or not.

JANE HOLTZ KAY

Without a Car in the World

[TECHNOLOGY REVIEW/July 1997]

The trumpet sounded from eighth row center at a Washington University lecture hall in St. Louis five years ago. It was early in my explorations for the book that would become *Asphalt Nation,* and I was happy preaching to the choir. Or, I should say, to fellow passengers; for the students at the architecture school were already on the same trip. They knew intuitively, if not literally, the design formulas that I recited from the podium — for example, that every motor vehicle required building an ancillary seven parking spaces to hold it at rest. They realized that big chunks — some 30 percent — of our cities were hard topped in service to the car's voracious appetite. And they knew how that transformed the built environment into a grim "carchitecture."

The students absorbed my other arguments on the broader compass of America's car costs: financial, social, and environmental. They comprehended the motor vehicle's economic toll — $6,000 a year in personal costs and another $4,000–$5,000 in "invisible" ones borne by the public.

JANE HOLTZ KAY is an architecture/planning critic for The Nation *and has also authored a book entitled* Asphalt Nation: How the Automobile Took Over America and How We Can Take It Back, *which was published by Crown in April of 1997. She has regularly written for* Landscape Architecture, Architecture, Planning, *the* Boston Globe, *the* New York Times, *and many other publications. She has also written two books on the Northeastern landscape and character entitled* Lost Boston *(1980) and* Preserving New England *(1986). In 1991, Kay won the William H. Donaldson Editorial Achievement Award for an environmental cover article and has taught and lectured at Harvard University and Boston University.*

They were startled by the health and environmental hazards of driving, from the more than 120 fatal accidents a day to habitat destruction and global warming. They had experienced the inconveniences of congestion and playing chauffeur, of parking and driving for miles to get a quart of milk. The room darkened and they chuckled at the slides of cartoons and auto-mated mayhem.

Then the questions started pouring forth. Toward the end of the evening came the telling one: "Do you own a car?" And with it my confession: Yes, I did.

Of course I did. With my first child I had bought my first car. In fact, I had recently purchased a new one, my third Saab — the most "environmental" one, I supposed, but a car nonetheless.

With that question, I knew I had to sell my private chariot. I realized   5
that to explore the options or preach the message of car-free living, it was incumbent on me to be carless or, in the vernacular of the activists, "de-vehicularized."

I knew, too, I would assuredly hear the question again from others, believers and skeptics alike. More important, I knew I had to learn the answer firsthand. If I couldn't function without a four-wheeled vehicle, I would have to alter my book's subtitle, *How the Automobile Took Over America and How We Can Take It Back.*

A month later, my car was on the block at the dealer. I was car-free with cash in hand. And damn the consequences.

So what were the consequences?

Since this is a truth walk, I will offer another confession. Much as the image of martyrdom appeals, shedding the car was no ordeal. From the beginning, I had scant trouble adjusting to my nonmotored life. And as the months wore on, the pluses far outweighed the minuses. For me, at least, it was easy to be car-free.

For one reason, I live in a dense, urban neighborhood of Boston. I   10
work downtown. I walk. My office, my friends and family, my entertainment and medical care are reachable by mass transit or on foot. Messenger services are available, and taxis can often fill the breach. My grown daughters have moved away — one overseas, the other to transit-rich New York. The supermarket delivers; the fruits and vegetables I carry home belie the professionalism of my briefcase but fit snugly inside. And because Boston holds many people who walk or take public transportation, services have sprung up to cater to their needs. This isn't Manhattan, with its twenty-four-hour everything, but it is a city. Its neighborhoods and shops ease a hassle-free, less car-dependent life.

At times, it took some doing, I'll concede, and some thinking. I switched tailors. I learned to carry two books or two grapefruits at a time instead of four, to allow extra time to get to the movies or visit my mother. I traded chores for occasional rides and, sometimes, made friends and enriched trips with shared driving. At times, I abandoned a venture to some more distant place or used phone or mail order. Was it a sacrifice to reorganize or reduce my movement? A bit. But it was pure pleasure to forgo trips to the repair shop or the tow lot, or expeditions to the mall encased in a ton of rolling steel. Over all, I simplified my life. I saved time.

One spring day early in my car-free life, a new friend took me on a ride to trace the geography of my childhood and child-rearing days in my home town of Brookline, Mass. In only ten minutes, we traversed the arc of my life . . . by the courtyard apartment where I grew up in an intimate, sidewalk community . . . up a hill to the small house on a dead-end street where I raised my children . . . past the home of my high-school days, paces from my classroom. In short order, we had swung by the library, the corner store, the town swimming pool, my sister's house.

You have lived your life in such a small space, my friend, a planner, said thoughtfully.

"Small," I mused. It had seemed universe enough. Not small at all to a child on foot. Not small to an adolescent or a young mother. Not in the detail, the change, the shifting drift of streets, the palette of tree and vegetation, the variety of architecture, the scale of windows, the ornament adorning facades. Each locale, each corner, each doorway had meaning and actuality. Each segment had a rich and diverse presence as I walked from store to school to playground. To me, the arc was large as life: It was built at a walker's pace, and paced it I had. Its mobility was the pedestrian's — shifting, evolving, engaging eye and mind.

How different from carbound America's hypermobility and its blur of passing faceless places. "Houston is the modern world par excellence," the architect Daniel Solomon writes in his book *ReBuilding*. "The young man who drove me to the airport says he lives thirty miles from school, a one-hour drive each way. His two and a half-year-old truck has 78,000 miles on it and he hasn't been anywhere. Fifty times the Odyssey, eight times the travels of Marco Polo, how many hundreds of times the walks of Leopold Bloom?[1] And with what density of experience, what learned in his 78,000-mile journey?" 15

Not long after my hometown tour, a young German intern in my office gave me a Netherlands Friends of the Earth study of the motorized planet: The environmentalists calculated that to apportion the mileage of drivers in the industrial nations across the global population would allow each planet member only 400 motorized miles a year. A mere 400 miles! The thought was staggering. "How could we move?" I asked a friend. She responded ruefully that her daughter wouldn't be able to live in California. On the other hand, her daughter would be within walking or biking range. My friend's options were at once contracted and enlarged. Mine had been, too.

---

[1]Leopold Bloom is one of the main characters of James Joyce's 1922 novel, *Ulysses;* a modern-day Odysseus, Bloom wanders about the streets of Dublin.

Travails of Travel

For all the conveniences of my home life, I soon found that moving around the wider, car-dependent country took commitment. When I ventured outside of my pedestrian-friendly city to give a speech to conservationists in Yonkers, New York — some 200 miles south of Boston — I understood what deviation from the motorized norm meant.

My trip began with a rocky three-hour Amtrak ride to Stamford, Connecticut, followed by a 45-minute car ride with my host to the venue of the speech. There I met my daughter, who had come a dozen miles by mass transit from Manhattan. None of this was terribly arduous. The worst of it came on the return voyage.

My hosts had assured me that I could take public transportation back to Manhattan. One member of the audience offered to drive us to the nearby train station. Alas, as 11 P.M. approached, the station's bleak environs unnerved her. Instead she drove us to the "safe" bus stop on a lonely Yonkers arterial and dropped us off. Across the street from our perch, a pizza parlor glowed lifelessly in the dark. The sidewalks were mostly deserted. Cars passed; one slowed down ominously. Twenty anxious minutes later, we handed over the $7 fare for a 30-minute bus ride to New York City. Near midnight, we disembarked and caught a cab to my daughter's apartment.

From doorway to doorway, I had spent eight hours transporting my-   20
self.

But whatever the wearisome aspects of walking and mass transit, of being viewed by skeptical friends as an eccentric Mary Poppins wafted by air, I had an easy answer to any predicament in my car-free life. In the back of my brain I carried the mantra of "$6,000," the amount I was saving each year by eliminating the expense of a car. And this figure, now $6,500, according to the Automobile Association of America, continues to rise. A distant doctor's appointment, a delivery charge for groceries or pizza, a cab here or there paled in comparison to the cash benefit of almost $20 a day I got from chucking my car. And, of course, I was practicing what I preached — and learning from the experiment.

Besides my own private gains, I was saving society almost that much in hidden costs, some in the form of pollution and environmental defilement; some in public costs of motor registry services, land consumption, congestion, accidents, and on and on.

In the five years since I began work on *Asphalt Nation*, my car-free lifestyle has begun to look less oddball. Awareness of the automobile's social, economic, environmental, and architectural mischief has risen. Congestion, the most obvious symptom, grows as we travel ever more. So does the realization that our 5 percent of the planet's population owns close to half the world's cars, carrying with that ownership 50 percent of the blame for the automobile's destruction of habitat and contribution to global warming.

Many people want to escape from the ruinous path. Friends now envy my car-free condition, though they remain stubbornly dubious of their own capacity to emulate it. And indeed, after three-quarters of a century of catering to the car, their reluctance is understandable. How *do* people change? How can we reduce the average 11,000 miles per year that Americans drive each of their 200 million motor vehicles? Unquestionably, we can improve our carbound lot. Personally and politically, as I have learned, we can lessen our dependency on the automobile.

Roads to Freedom

What motivated me, and what does and could power others, was an awareness that I would no longer be forced to shuttle a minimum of 2,000 pounds (3,000-plus in a sports utility vehicle) to buy a Popsicle. Most drivers don't realize the hours spent behind the wheel on "shop 'n' drop." They think they use their car mainly to get to work and take vacations. Since two-thirds of all Americans live in metropolitan areas and spend ten forty-hour weeks a year driving to work, that sounds reasonable. But the big picture is sobering. According to the Nationwide Personal Transportation Study done by the U.S. Department of Transportation in the early '90s, only 22 percent of our vehicle miles are used for commuting and only 8 percent for vacation travel. The rest is errands, recreation, chauffeuring unlicensed family members. This realization alone should be enough to envision a better life without a motor vehicle.

A different set of wheels, the bicycle, can often take up the slack or eliminate one of the two or three cars in half our households. Some enthusiasts bike through truck-ridden, traffic-clogged mazes. Others see bicycling as promoting personal and planetary fitness as they perform, say, the forty-mile daily round-trip from Dover, Massachusetts, to downtown Boston taken by Douglas Foy, head of the car-battling Conservation Law Foundation. Pleasure, politics, and the opportunity to save time motivate economist and transportation activist Charles Komanoff, who keeps five bicycles (for different weather and terrain) on hand for family odysseys from Manhattan.

But you don't have to be fanatical to join the 9 percent of the nation's households (largely poor) that don't own a car or the 30 or 40 percent of the population deprived of driving because they are too young, too old, or too disabled. As one pedestrian advocate tells me, most of the time when people dispense with their horseless carriage, it's through happenstance. The buggy gets too old to move another mile. The parking gets too tedious. Money is short. Sometimes there's that other car in the garage. Michael Eberlein, coordinator of nonmotorized travel at Michigan's Department of Transportation in car-locked Lansing, reduced his household to one car for financial reasons. "We were trying to find the extra $6,000 and couldn't," he says.

At first, the newly car-free gripe, and feel guilty about cadging rides. They sometimes learn to rent cars or take cabs, but otherwise frame their days on the human mobility of walking or bicycling. If they are lucky and live in a dense urban or old suburban area, they can take advantage of mass transit. The 80 percent of Manhattanites who do not drive endorse the saying that a car is "more trouble than it's worth." They walk or they ride the omnipresent rail and bus system allowed by places whose land patterns — densely settled, walkable — and commitment to public transportation sustain it. The backpack, the walker's constant companion, doesn't replace a "roomy interior," but it does help.

Opting for homes closer to a core — that is, accepting less house for the money — can save both time and transportation costs and offers the public life of parks, shops, and libraries. Living near a twenty-four-hour store without a car is a money-saving proposition compared with driving to the superstore. Think again: Does the Wal-Mart save you $6,000 a year? Then there are the extra parking spaces — the driveway and the garage — adding to the price of a home. Finally, driving (at $1 a mile, by some estimates) from ever-more-distant suburbs compounds the expense. In the end, the cost equation changes mindsets. In fact, in California, the Bank of America has lowered its mortgage rates for those who cut down on cars and live in nonsprawling communities. The trend to such "location-efficient" mortgages grows.

Even carbound consumers consigned to exurbia by work can find options for becoming less car dependent. Businesses and institutions have begun to supply vehicles for parents to use in emergencies, provide chits for public transportation, organize car pools, and refund money to those who don't use their parking facilities. (The subsidy of free parking, like the subsidy of tax-supported highway infrastructure, tilts the balance to being car dependent.) Paratransit — vans that loop through industrial zones or transport elderly and disabled people — can help. So can messengers and taxi systems; the tighter the land pattern, the greater the possibilities. Communities in Canada and Germany, as well as a few in the United States (including Eugene, Ore., and Boston), have instituted the car-sharing system: pay a fee and you have access to an automobile in a nearby parking lot. Just make a reservation, retrieve a key from a safe-deposit box, take a ride, and return the car.

Work options like telecommuting also stand high on some lists of solutions for lessening autodependency. Telecenters, urban "villages" where telecommuters share facilities and space near their homes, have opened nationwide.

The Personal Becomes Political

Yet futurists who project declining automobile travel as a result of telecommuting fail to reckon how small a number of telecommuters now exists (3 percent of the population), how small a percentage of miles is racked up by the commute, and how large a percentage is needed for errands in sprawling suburbs. The stay-at-homes still pass their days performing the personal trips that run annual mileage into five digits. Only if we solve the land-use issue — designing and preserving compact neighborhoods — can we make telecommuting really count.

Some car-free citizens have worked to such an end by trying to make their communities more walkable, in the process turning the personal into the political. For Chris Bradshaw, president of Otta Walk, a pedestrian advocacy group in Ottawa, staying car-free means fighting to preserve the community center or the blockfronts of small stores, and battling for a public "bare-pavement" policy to keep sidewalks free of snow. Such services and institutions make "trip-chaining" — the traffic engineer's word for performing serial errands — feasible on foot. To Bradshaw, too, staying car-free means coaxing a neighborhood shop to stock a missing item instead of driving to a Big Box store on the periphery.

For others, enhancing a car-free existence may mean stopping a road widening or extension that would bring traffic and threaten the pedestrian. Simple tactics such as widening sidewalks, building speed bumps, and planting trees to slow motorists can reduce the danger to walkers. Providing a safe route for a youngster to walk to school can eliminate two car trips per family per day. Approaching school committees or politicians raises the likelihood of success. Again, the personal becomes political when those who value walkable and bikable neighborhoods participate in zoning decisions to allow mixed commercial and residential development; when they fight to retain or add a streetcar route; when they lobby for more and better buses.

Efforts like these are multiplying as car-free advocacy groups grow in number and solidarity. The months-old WalkAmerica alliance already embraces more than 10 organizations. Advocates for greenways and bike routes, such as Transportation Alternatives, ally with environmental associations such as the 1000 Friends of Oregon, the Environmental Defense Fund, or the Sierra Club. Across the political spectrum, trolley and train fans are uniting with opponents of highway boondoggles. Many activists are engaged in the fight to retain the nation's six-year-old Intermodal Surface Transportation Efficiency Act (ISTEA). The act, which directs 50 percent of federal transportation funds to nonhighway uses, comes up for renewal this fall. 35

Perhaps the broadest front on which to combat car dependency is economic policy. Automobile travel is heavily subsidized by local governments' underwriting of streets and roads, federal funding of oil wars (Desert Storm), and the hidden costs of the car-generated infrastructure that breeds sprawl. Hence there are many opportunities to curtail car use through the cash register. Our artificially low gas price of $1.25 or so is a quarter of Japan's or Europe's $4 to $5, which includes taxes to cover social and environmental costs. By paying the true cost of petroleum, other countries spend half the 20 percent of GDP[2] that Americans spend on the

[2]GDP, Gross Domestic Product.

private car (according to the Institute for Transportation and Development Policy in New York City) and can thus afford decent public transportation.

Stop subsidizing cars, and solo driving will go down while carpooling, cycling, and mass transit will rise, enhancing the car-free life. We can pay at the pump or pay in excise taxes or registration fees. Congestion pricing — charging more on roads and bridges during peak periods, as is done in Norway and Singapore — works well. So would a carbon, horsepower, or gas-guzzling tax: a nickel-a-mile surcharge would cut car travel (and hence automotive smog) 10 percent while reducing congestion 30 percent, according to research by economist Komanoff.

These are the choices our society must make collectively. If our culture rejects automobility, or hypermobility, as its Manifest Destiny, the car will be a servant, not a master. We have alternatives to a carbound existence. People can live in places not encrusted with asphalt, improve their daily existence, establish a stronger sense of community, and know that they are advancing global well-being. For me, the long journey began with the footsteps toward a car-free life.

Responding as a Reader

1. Each car costs the public $4,000–$5,000 per year, according to Kay (para. 2) — and these costs do not include the personal costs associated with owning a car. What are these "invisible" costs?

2. How did selling her car change Kay's life? What kinds of sacrifices did she have to make? What kinds of sacrifices would she have to make if she lived in the country, or the suburbs? If her children were still small?

3. Rather than suggesting that we do away with cars altogether, Kay proposes a number of strategies for cutting down on car use. How practicable are these suggestions? Can you think of others?

Responding as a Writer

1. Do you own a car? If you do, imagine what your life would be like without one. If you don't, imagine what your life would be like if you had a car. In an essay, describe what a typical day or week would be like and speculate about whether your overall quality of life would improve or diminish.

2. What if everyone did what Kay did? In an essay, speculate how life in the United States would change, in the long term. How could cities, suburbs, towns, and countrysides be affected? Which industries would benefit? Which would suffer? What effect would these changes have on the economy?

3. The automobile is one of many expensive, conveniences that many Americans have come to rely on. What other such devices can you think of? In an essay, argue that Americans should reduce their use of one such convenience. Try to anticipate unfavorable effects as well as favorable ones.

JAMES Q. WILSON

Cars and Their Enemies

[COMMENTARY/July 1997]

Imagine the country we now inhabit — big, urban, prosperous — with one exception: The automobile has not been invented. We have trains and bicycles, and some kind of self-powered buses and trucks, but no private cars driven by their owners for business or pleasure. Of late, let us suppose, someone has come forward with the idea of creating the personal automobile. Consider how we would react to such news.

Libertarians might support the idea, but hardly anyone else. Engineers would point out that such cars, if produced in any significant number, would zip along roads just a few feet — perhaps even a few inches — from one another; the chance of accidents would not simply be high, it would be certain. Public-health specialists would estimate that many of these accidents would lead to serious injuries and deaths. No one could say in advance how common they would be, but the best experts might guess that the number of people killed by cars would easily exceed the number killed by murderers. Psychologists would point out that if any young person were allowed to operate a car, the death rate would be even higher, as young-

JAMES Q. WILSON (b. 1931) was Henry Lee Shattuck Professor of Government at Harvard for fourteen years and is now a Collins professor of management and public policy at UCLA. He remains one of the leading experts on crime and bureaucracy. His previous books include Crime *(1996) and* The Moral Sense *(1997). His most recent book is* Moral Judgment: Does the Abuse Excuse Threaten Our Legal System?, *which was published in May 1997.*

sters — those between the ages of sixteen and twenty-four — are much more likely than older persons to be impulsive risk-takers who find pleasure in reckless bravado. Educators would explain that, though they might try by training to reduce this youthful death rate, they could not be optimistic they would succeed.

Environmentalists would react in horror to the idea of automobiles powered by the internal combustion engine, apparently the most inexpensive method. Such devices, because they burn fuel incompletely, would eject large amounts of unpleasant gases into the air, such as carbon monoxide, nitrogen oxide, and sulfur dioxide. Other organic compounds, as well as clouds of particles, would also enter the atmosphere to produce unknown but probably harmful effects. Joining in this objection would be people who would not want their view spoiled by the creation of a network of roads.

Big-city mayors would add their own objections, though these would reflect their self-interest as much as their wisdom. If people could drive anywhere from anywhere, they would be able to live wherever they wished. This would produce a vast exodus from the large cities, led in all likelihood by the most prosperous — and thus the most tax-productive — citizens. Behind would remain people who, being poorer, were less mobile. Money would depart but problems remain.

Governors, pressed to keep taxes down and still fund costly health, welfare, educational, and criminal-justice programs, would wonder who would pay for the vast networks of roads that would be needed to carry automobiles. Their skepticism would be reinforced by the worries of police officials fearful of motorized thieves evading apprehension and by the opposition of railroad executives foreseeing the collapse of their passenger business as people abandoned trains for cars.   5

Energy experts would react in horror at the prospect of supplying the gasoline stations and the vast quantities of petroleum necessary to fuel automobiles that, unlike buses and trucks, would be stored at home and not at a central depot and would burn much more fuel per person carried than some of their mass-transit alternatives.

In short, the automobile, the device on which most Americans rely for not only transportation but mobility, privacy, and fun would not exist if it had to be created today. Of course, the car does exist and has powerfully affected the living, working, and social spaces of America. But the argument against it persists. That argument dominates the thinking of academic experts on urban transportation and much of city planning. It can be found in countless books complaining of dreary suburban architecture, endless trips to and from work, the social isolation produced by solo auto trips, and the harmful effects of the car on air quality, noise levels, petroleum consumption, and road congestion.

In her recent book, *Asphalt Nation: How the Automobile Took Over America and How We Can Take It Back*, Jane Holtz Kay, the architecture critic for the *Nation,* assails the car unmercifully. It has, she writes, "strangled" our lives and landscape, imposing on us "the costs of sprawl, of pollution, of congestion, of commuting." For this damage to be undone, the massively subsidized automobile will have to be sharply curtailed by investing heavily in public transportation and imposing European-like taxes on gasoline. (According to Kay, if we cut highway spending by a mere $10 million, we could buy bicycles for all 93,000 residents of Eugene, Oregon, over the age of eleven.) What is more, people ought to live in cities with high population densities, since "for mass transit," as Kay notes, "you need mass." Housing should be built within a short walk of the corner store and industries moved back downtown.

In Kay's book, hostility to the car is linked inextricably to hostility to the low-density suburb. Her view is by no means one that is confined to the political Left. Thus, Karl Zinsmeister, a conservative, has argued in the *American Enterprise* that we have become "slaves to our cars" and that, by using them to live in suburbs, we have created "inhospitable places for individualism and community life." Suburbs, says Zinsmeister, encourage "rootlessness" and are the enemy of the "traditional neighborhood" with its "easy daily interactions."

The same theme has been taken up by Mark Gauvreau Judge in the *Weekly Standard.* Emerging from his home after a heavy snowfall, Judge, realizing that the nearest tavern was four miles away, concluded that he had to leave the suburbs. He repeats Zinsmeister's global complaint. Suburbanization, he writes, has fed, and sometimes caused,

> hurried life, the disappearance of family time, the weakening of generational links, our ignorance of history, our lack of local ties, an exaggerated focus on money, the anonymity of community life, the rise of radical feminism, the decline of civic action, the tyrannical dominance of TV and pop culture over leisure time.

Wow.

These people must live in or near very odd suburbs. The one in which I lived while my children were growing up, and the different ones in which my married daughter and married son now live, are not inhospitable, rootless, isolated, untraditional, or lacking in daily interactions. The towns are small. Life is organized around the family, for which there is a lot of time. Money goes farther for us than for Manhattanites struggling to get their children into the nursery school with the best link to Harvard. Television is less important than in big cities, where the streets are far less safe and TV becomes a major indoor activity. In most cases you can walk to a store. You know your neighbors. There is a Memorial Day parade. People care passionately and argue intensely about school policies and land-use controls. Of course, these are only my personal experiences — but unlike the critics, I find it hard to convert personal beliefs into cosmic generalizations.

Now I live in a suburb more remote from a big city than the one where my children were raised. Because population density is much lower, my wife and I walk less and drive more. But as I write this, my wife is at a neighborhood meeting where she will be joined by a travel agent, a retired firefighter, a hospital manager, and two housewives who are trying to decide how best to get the city to fix up a road intersection, prevent a nearby land development, and induce our neighbors to prepare for the fire season. On the way back, she will stop at the neighborhood mail station where she may talk to other friends and then go on to the market where she will deal with people she has known for many years. She will do so by car.

And so back to our theme. Despite the criticisms of Kay and others, the use of the automobile has grown. In 1960, one-fifth of all households owned no car and only one-fifth owned two; by 1990, only one-tenth owned no car and over one-third owned two. In 1969, 80 percent of all urban trips involved a car and only one-twentieth involved public transport; by 1990, car use had risen to 84 percent and public transit had fallen to less than 3 percent. In 1990, three-fourths or more of the trips to and from work in nineteen out of our twenty largest metropolitan areas were by a single person in an automobile. The exception was the New York metropolitan region, but even there — with an elaborate mass-transit system and a residential concentration high enough to make it possible for some people to walk to work — solo car use made up over half of all trips to work.

Some critics explain this American fascination with the car as the unhappy consequence of public policies that make auto use more attractive than the alternatives. To Jane Holtz Kay, if only we taxed gasoline at a high enough rate to repay society for the social costs of automobiles, if only we had an elaborate mass-transit system that linked our cities, if only we placed major restraints on building suburbs on open land, if only we placed heavy restrictions on downtown parking, then things would be better.

Would they? Charles Lave, an economist at the University of California at Irvine, has pointed out that most of Western Europe has long had just these sorts of antiauto policies in effect. The result? Between 1965 and 1987, the growth in the number of autos per capita has been three times faster in Western Europe than in the United States. Part of the reason for the discrepancy is that the American auto market is approaching saturation: We now have roughly one car in existence for every person of driving age. But if this fact helps explain why the car market here is not growing rapidly, it does not explain the growth in Europe, which is the real story. Despite policies that penalize car use, make travel very expensive, and restrict parking spaces, Europeans, once they can afford to do so, buy cars and drive them; according to Lave, the average European car is driven

15

about two-thirds as many miles per year as the average American car. One result is obvious: The heavily subsidized trains in Europe are losing business to cars, and governments there must pay an even larger share of the running cost to keep the trains moving.

In fact, the United States *has* tried to copy the European investment in mass transit. Relentlessly, transportation planners have struggled to find ways of getting people out of their cars and into buses, trains, and subways (and car pools). Relentlessly, and unsuccessfully. Despite spending about $100 billion, Washington has yet to figure out how to do it.

New subway systems have been built, such as the BART system in San Francisco and the Metro system in Washington, D.C. But BART, in the words of the transportation economist Charles L. Wright, "connects almost nothing to little else." The Metro is still growing and provides a fine (albeit expensive) route for people moving about the city, but only 7 percent of all residential land area in Washington is within a mile of a Metro station, which means that people must either walk a long way to get to a stop or continue to travel by car. Between 1980 and 1990, while the Washington Metrorail system grew from thirty to seventy-three miles of line and opened an additional thirty stations, the number of people driving to work increased from 980,000 to 1,394,000, and the transit share of all commutes declined.

The European experience should explain why this is so: If people can afford it, they will want to purchase convenience, flexibility, and privacy. These facts are as close to a Law of Nature as one can get in the transportation business. When the industrial world became prosperous, people bought cars. It is unstoppable.

Suppose, however, that the anti-car writers were to win over the vastly more numerous pro-car drivers. Let us imagine what life would be like in a carless nation. People would have to live very close together so they could walk or, for healthy people living in sunny climes, bicycle to mass-transit stops. Living in close quarters would mean life as it is now lived in Manhattan. There would be few freestanding homes, many row houses, and lots of apartment buildings. There would be few private gardens except for flowerpots on balconies. The streets would be congested by pedestrians, trucks, and buses, as they were at the turn of the century before automobiles became common.

Moving about outside the larger cities would be difficult. People would   20 be able to take trains to distant sites, but when they arrived at some attractive locale it would turn out to be another city. They could visit the beach but only (of necessity) crowded parts of it. They could go to a national park but only the built-up section of it. They could see the countryside but (mostly) through a train window. More isolated or remote locations would be accessible, but since public transit would provide the only way of getting there, the departures would be infrequent and the transfers frequent.

In other words, you could see the United States much as most Europeans saw their countryside before the automobile became an important means of locomotion. A train from London or Paris would take you to "the country" by way of a long journey through ugly industrial areas to those rural parts where either you had a home (and the means to ferry yourself to it) or there was a resort (that would be crowded enough to support a nearby train stop).

All this is a way of saying that the debate between car defenders and car haters is a debate between private benefits and public goods. List the characteristics of travel that impose few costs on society and, in general, walking, cycling, and some forms of public transit will be seen to be superior. Noncar methods generate less pollution, use energy a bit more efficiently, produce less noise, and (with some exceptions) are safer. But list the characteristics of travel that are desired by individuals, and (with some exceptions) the car is clearly superior. The automobile is more flexible, more punctual, supplies greater comfort, provides for carrying more parcels, creates more privacy, enables one to select fellow passengers, and, for distances over a mile or more, requires less travel time.

As a practical matter, of course, the debate between those who value private benefits and those who insist on their social costs is no real debate at all, since people select modes of travel based on individual, not social, preferences. That is why in almost every country in the world, the automobile has triumphed, and much of public policy has been devoted to the somewhat inconsistent task of subsidizing individual choices while attempting to reduce the costs attached to them. In the case of the automobile, governments have attempted to reduce exhaust pollution, make roadways safer, and restrict use (by tolls, speed bumps, pedestrian-only streets, and parking restrictions) in neighborhoods that attach a high value to pedestrian passage. Yet none of these efforts can alter the central fact that people have found cars to be the best means for getting about.

Take traffic congestion. Television loves to focus on grim scenes of gridlocked highways and angry motorists, but in fact people still get to work faster by car than by public transit. And the reason is not that car drivers live close to work and transit users travel a greater distance. According to the best estimates, cars outperform public transit in getting people quickly from their front doors to their work places. This fact is sometimes lost on car critics. Kay, for example, writes that "the same number of people who spend an hour driving sixteen lanes of highway can travel on a two-track train line." Wrong. Train travel is efficient *over a fixed, permanent route,* but people have to find some way to get to where the train starts and get to their final destination after the train stops. The *full* cost of moving people from home to work and back to the home is lower for cars than for trains. Moreover, cars are not subject to union strikes. The Long Island railroad or the bus system may shut down when workers walk off the job; cars do not.

The transportation argument rarely seems to take cognizance of the su-   29
periority of cars with respect to individual wants. Whenever there is a discussion about how best to move people about, mass-transit supporters typically overestimate, usually by a wide margin, how many people will leave
their cars and happily hop onto trains or buses. According to one study, by
Don Pickerell, the vast majority of American rail-transportation proposals
greatly exaggerate the number of riders to be attracted; the actual ridership
turns out to be about a third of the predicted level. For this reason, urban
public transport almost never recovers from the fare box more than a fraction of the actual cost of moving people. Osaka, Japan, seems to be the
only large city in the world that gets back from passengers what it spends;
in Atlanta, Detroit, and Houston, public transit gets from passengers no
more than a third of their cost.

So the real debate ought not be one between car enthusiasts and mass-
transit advocates, but about ways of moderating the inevitable use of cars
in order to minimize their deleterious effects.

One such discussion has already had substantial effects. Auto-exhaust
pollution has been dramatically reduced in this country by redesigning en-
gines, changing fuels (largely by removing lead), and imposing inspection
requirements.

Since the mid-1960s, auto emissions have been reduced by about 95
percent. Just since 1982, ten years after the Clean Air Act was passed,
carbon-monoxide levels have fallen by 40 percent and nitrogen-oxide levels
by 25 percent. I live in the Los Angeles area and know from personal experience how irritating smog was in the 1950s. I also know that smog has decreased dramatically for most (but not all) of the region. The number of
"smog alert" days called by the South Coast Air Quality Management District (AQMD) declined from 121 in the mid-1970s to seven in 1996.
AQMD now predicts that by the year 2000 the number may fall to zero.

Nationally, very little of this improvement has come about from moving people from solo cars into car pools or onto mass transit. What experts
call "Transportation Control Measures" (TCMs) — the combined effect of
mass transit, car pools, telecommuting, and the like — have produced
small reductions in smog levels. Transit expansion has decreased carbon
monoxide by six-tenths of 1 percent and car pools by another seven-tenths
of 1 percent. Adding BART to San Francisco has had only trivial effects on
pollution. The Environmental Protection Agency (in the Clinton administration) has issued a report that puts it bluntly: "Efforts to reduce emissions through traditional TCMs have not generated significant air-quality
benefits." The methods that *have* reduced pollution significantly are based
on markets, not capital investments, and include smog fees, congestion
pricing, gas taxes, and higher parking charges.

There is still more pollution to eliminate, but the anticar enthusiasts   30
rarely approach the task rationally. General Motors now leases electric

cars, but they are very expensive and require frequent recharging from scarce power outlets. The electric car is an impressive engineering achievement, but not if you want to travel very far.

We could pass laws that would drive down even further the pollution output of cars, but this would impose huge costs on manufacturers and buyers without addressing the real source of auto pollution — a small percentage of older or modified cars that generate huge amounts of exhaust. Devices now exist for measuring the pollution of cars as they move on highways and then ticketing the offenders, but only recently has there been a large-scale trial of this method, and the results are not yet in. The method has the virtue of targeting enforcement on real culprits but the defect (for car critics) of not requiring a "tough new law" aimed at every auto owner.

As for traffic congestion, that has indeed become worse — because highway construction has not kept pace with the growth of automobile use. But it is not as bad as some imagine — the average commuting time was the same in 1990 as in 1980 — and it is not bad where it is often assumed to be bad. A road is officially called "congested" if its traffic volume exceeds 80 percent of its designed capacity. By this measure, the most congested highways are in and around Washington, D.C., and San Francisco. But if you drive these roads during rush hour, as I have, you will acquire a very different sense of things. The highways into Washington and San Francisco do produce blockages, usually at familiar intersections, bridges, or merges. They rarely last very long and, on most days, one can plan around them.

Indeed, the fact and consequences of auto congestion are greatly exaggerated in most large cities. During rush hour, I have driven into and out of Dallas, Kansas City, Phoenix, St. Louis, and San Diego without much more than an occasional slowdown. Moreover, despite the massive reliance on cars and a short-term decline in the economic vitality of their downtown areas, most of these cities have restored their central areas. Kansas City is bleak in the old downtown, but the shopping area (built 75 years ago!), called Country Club Plaza, is filled with people, stores, and restaurants. San Diego and San Francisco have lively downtowns. Los Angeles even managed to acquire a downtown (actually, several downtowns) after it grew up without much of one — and this in a city allegedly "built around the car." Phoenix is restoring its downtown and San Diego never really lost its center.

Real congestion, by contrast, is found in New York City, Chicago, and Boston, where almost any movement on any downtown street is extremely difficult. From the moment you enter a car or taxi, you are in a traffic jam. Getting to the airport by car from Manhattan or Boston is vastly more difficult than getting there from San Francisco, Los Angeles, or Washington.

But the lesson in this should be disturbing to car critics: *Car travel is most congested in cities that have the oldest and most highly developed* 35 *rail-based transit systems.* One reason is historical: Having subways from their early days, these cities built up to high levels of residential and commercial concentration. A car added to this mix has to navigate through streets surrounded by high office buildings and tall apartment towers. When many people in those buildings take cars or taxis, the congestion can be phenomenal.

But there is another reason as well. Even where rail transportation exists, people will not use it enough to relieve congestion. There is, for example, an excellent rail line from O'Hare Airport to downtown Chicago, and some people use it. But it has done little or nothing to alleviate congestion on the parallel highway. People do not like dragging suitcases on and off trains. And the train does not stop where people want to go — namely, where they live. It stops at busy street corners, sometimes in dangerous neighborhoods. If you take the train, you still must shift to a car at the end, and finding one is not always easy. This is why taking a car from the Los Angeles airport, though it will place you in a few pockets of congestion, gets you to your home faster (and with all of your belongings) than taking a train and taxi a comparable distance from O'Hare.

A great deal can still be done to moderate the social costs of automobile traffic. More toll roads can be built with variable rates that will allow people to drive — at different prices, depending on the level of congestion — to and from cities. Bridges into cities can charge tolls to ensure that only highly motivated people consume scarce downtown road space. (A friend of mine, a distinguished economist, was once asked, in derision, whether he would buy the Brooklyn Bridge. "I would if I could charge tolls on it," he replied.) Cars can be banned from streets that are capable of being pedestrian malls — though there are not many such places. (A number of such malls were created for the purpose of keeping people downtown who did not want to be downtown and were doomed to failure from the start.)

Other measures are also possible. More bicycle pathways can be created, though these are rarely alternatives to auto transportation; some people do ride a bike to work, but few do so often. Street patterns in residential areas can be arranged to minimize the amount of through-road traffic they must endure. Gasoline taxes can be set high enough to recover more of the social costs of operating automobiles. (This will not happen in a society as democratic as ours, but it is a good idea, and maybe someday a crisis will create an opportunity.)

Portland, Oregon, has become well-known among American cities for having adopted a law — the Urban Growth Boundary — that denies people the right to build almost any new structure in a green belt starting about twenty minutes from downtown. This means that new subdivisions to which one must travel by car cannot be created outside the line. The nice result is that outside the city, you can drive through unspoiled farm land.

The mayor and downtown business leaders like what they have cre-   40
ated. So do environmentalists, social-service organizations, and many ordinary citizens. The policy, described in a recent issue of *Governing* magazine, is called the New Urbanism and has attracted interest from all over
the country. But the policy also has its costs. As the city's population
grows, more people must be squeezed into less space. Housing density is
up. Before the Urban Growth Boundary, the average Portland house was
built on a lot about 13,000 feet square and row houses made up only 3
percent of all dwelling units. Now, the average lot size has fallen to 8,700
square feet and row houses make up 12 percent of the total. And housing
prices are also up. Six years ago, Portland was the nation's 55th most affordable city; today, it is the 165th.

As density goes up in Portland, so will the problems associated with
density, such as crime. Reserving land out of a city for scenic value is an
important goal, but it must be balanced with supplying affordable housing.
Portland will work out the balance once people begin to yearn for lower
density.

But even if we do all the things that can be done to limit the social
costs of cars, the campaign against them will not stop. It will not stop because so many of the critics dislike everything the car stands for and everything that society constructs to serve the needs of its occupants.

Cars are about privacy; critics say privacy is bad and prefer group effort. (Of course, one rarely meets these critics in groups. They seem to be
too busy rushing about being critics.) Cars are about autonomy; critics say
that the pursuit of autonomy destroys community. (Actually, cars allow
people to select the kind of community in which they want to live.) Cars
are about speed; critics abhor the fatalities they think speed causes. (In fact,
auto fatalities have been declining for decades, including after the 55-mile-
per-hour national speed limit was repealed. Charles Lave suggests that this
is because higher speed limits reduce the variance among cars in their rates
of travel, thereby producing less passing and overtaking, two dangerous
highway maneuvers.) Cars are about the joyous sensation of driving on
beautiful country roads; critics take their joy from politics. (A great failing
of the intellectual life of this country is that so much of it is centered in
Manhattan, where one finds the highest concentration of nondrivers in the
country.) Cars make possible Wal-Mart, Home Depot, the Price Club, and
other ways of allowing people to shop for rock-bottom prices; critics want
people to spend their time gathering food at downtown shops (and paying
the much higher prices that small stores occupying expensive land must
charge). Cars make California possible; critics loathe California. (But they
loathe it for the wrong reason. The state is not the car capital of the nation;
thirty-six states have more cars per capita, and their residents drive more
miles.)

Life in California would be very difficult without cars. This is not because the commute to work is so long; in Los Angeles, according to Charles Lave, the average trip to work in 1994 was twenty-six minutes, five minutes *shorter* than in New York City. Rather, a carless state could not be enjoyed. You could not see the vast areas of farm land, the huge tracts of empty mountains and deserts, the miles of deserted beaches and forests.

No one who visits Los Angeles or San Francisco can imagine how   45
much of California is, in effect, empty, unsettled. It is an empire of lightly used roads, splendid vistas, and small towns, intersected by a highway system that, should you be busy or foolish enough to use it, will speed you from San Francisco to Los Angeles or San Diego. Off the interstate, it is a kaleidoscope of charming places to be alone.

Getting there in order to be alone is best done in one of the remarkably engineered, breathtakingly fast, modern cars that give to the driver the deepest sense of what the road can offer: the beauty of its views, the excitement of command, the passion of engagement.

I know the way. If you are a friend, you need only ask.

Responding as a Reader

1. Reread Wilson's opening paragraphs (to para. 8). What expectations does this opening set up for the rest of the essay? Why do you think Wilson chose to begin this way? Is the opening effective?

2. Convert the statistics in paragraphs 13, 15, and 17 to a format that makes them easier to compare. You could make a table, a bar graph, or a line graph, and you'll probably want to convert all the fractions to percentages. The goal is to get a clear picture of the increase in the number of cars per household and in amount of driving (measured in either time or distance).

3. What specific reasons does Wilson offer for the car's superiority over other modes of transportation? Can you think of other modes of transportation that offer the same benefits?

4. Find all the references to "car critics," "anticar enthusiasts," and "car haters" in this essay. What are the characteristics of these critics? What do they stand for? Do they seem to bear any resemblance to the other writers in this unit?

Responding as a Writer

1. At several points Wilson quotes Jane Holtz Kay who is represented by another selection in this book (p. 78). Read Holtz Kay's article and review Wilson's criticisms of her. Then try writing a response to Wilson's criticisms from Holtz Kay's perspective.

2. Wilson focuses on two modes of transportation: the car and public transit (subways and buses). What other alternatives exist? What other alternatives can you imagine? Consider one problem with public transit and propose a mode of transportation (real or imagined, but not the car) that would solve this problem.

3. Wilson reduces the debate over cars to "a debate between private benefits and public goods" (para. 22). One function of government is to mediate this debate, to attempt to balance personal and public good. In an essay, argue for legislation that would balance the public problems with automobiles that Wilson mentions in his opening paragraphs with the personal rights that he holds dear.

In the News

Car Ads Sell the Fantasy, Not Facts

Selling cars these days is often less about what's under the hood than it is about how the vehicle reflects on the driver. Car makers spend $3 billion a year on advertisements that promise not only good brakes and a dependable engine but, more prominently, excitement, freedom, and sex.

Pontiac now builds "excitement." Mazda has a "passion for the road."

"The car is sold as more than just practical transportation," said Dartmouth College history professor Ron Edsforth, an expert on cars in American culture. "The car has always had this character as an object that is just as important for its symbolic value. . . . The car enables you to project yourself as something you may think you're not."

In other words, you're delusional if you think you bought that red convertible with the shoebox-size trunk just because it gets great mileage and is easy to park. Cars create instant public images, read in a flash at sixty-five mph: I'm hip. I'm rugged. I love my kids. I read Consumer Reports. I question my manhood. You may have seen me on *Cops*.

"It's been proven in psychological studies that the car is often an extension of the self," said Eugene Fram, the J. Warren McClure research professor of marketing at Rochester Institute of Technology. "When you see a sixty-year-old man driving a souped-up car, they are clearly making a statement that they don't want to be sixty. They want to be twenty-five."

Advertisers know this — and prey on it as they try to make their pitch stand out in the 600 to 1,200 messages the average American is bombarded with every day.

Hart points out that some of the most successful ads never mention anything about the car's features.

continued on next page

continued from previous page

Part of this is a function of the car market itself. As quality improves and features are standardized, buyers expect vehicles to last longer than 50,000 miles, start reliably, and not rattle and squeak within weeks of driving off the lot.

Sometimes, attitude is all that distinguishes cars within the same class from one another. In many ways, it has always been like this. From the first days of driving, fantasy was as much a part of car buying as function.

— From Stephanie Simon, "Car Ads Sell the Fantasy, Not Facts" (*Los Angeles Times*, April 26, 1996, pp. B–2).

WILLIAM HAMILTON

Automotivational Counseling

[BUZZ/June–July, 1996]

Driving is emotional. Vile epithets spew in cars the way they do in torture chambers. Outbursts that would normally require falling, scalding, breaking, or losing explode like popcorn. Judgmental, descriptive, hateful imprecations made up of body parts and functions, of racial, gender, sexual, occupational, and religious slurs, as well as anatomically impossible suggestions, regularly interrupt the vehicle's digitally enhanced sound system with descriptive imagery as horrible as medieval visions of damnation.

WILLIAM HAMILTON *(b. 1939) graduated from Yale in 1962 and has since written many novels including* The Love of Rich Women, The Charlatan, *and* The Lap of Luxury. *He is currently working on a production of a new play entitled* She's Here, *and has been a cartoonist with the* New Yorker *since 1965.*

Yes, I saw her. Yes, I could have let this desperate woman out of her traffic trap. But I also had a right to the opening she needed. And pretending not to have noticed her, I took it. Unfortunately for me, this gap closed with me in it, stuck right in front of her, with my top down, encircled by rings of other cars enjoying her forthcoming speech:

"Oh, brother. You get the prize. You take the cake. Yes, you. Nice going. Good job. Are you happy now? Great move. What a gentleman. Your mother must be proud. Great work. Thanks a million. Congratulations. . . ."

Her diatribe was all the worse for its relentless civility. If only her language had been foul, it might have besmirched her position a little with the smiling witnesses rolling down their windows all around me. At least if she'd cursed, I might have been left with some dignity, some defense of my disproven honor and worth.

Instead, like a former official paraded in a pointed hat through a pelting   5
public by the Red Guard, I could only endure her increasing delight in the unfortunately just humiliation chance had allowed her to stage so spectacularly.

Normally, I wouldn't have heard her. I would have cut her off and been on my way. Further along, possibly in subconscious penance for this by now officially forgotten refusal of courtesy, I might have joined a line of cars squeezing left to make an exit or detour a little earlier than I had to, playing the good citizen, the knight of the road. Awaiting my turn in such a queue, I would inevitably marvel with outrage at the cars passing on the right, intending to cut in up at the top, pretending they hadn't noticed our long line until they were at its end. As a recently exposed villain myself, I'd know intimately how these opportunists were intoxicated with the happy effect of outstripping the stalled, elephantine processional on their left. We were dull, common oafs. They were self-appointed wild and crazy exceptions to the rule. I'd be hoping that when one of these falsely oblivious line breakers tried to blend back into decency in front of me, I could keep the miscreant motorist out of the righteous lane for at least the length of my car — even if it resulted in some body work.

Such behavior illustrates the unreasoningly weird emotionality of the traffic experience. How could the mere length of a car be worth committing mayhem to win? Yes these minute advantages are sought at great risk all the time. Seething just below the orderly surface of traffic is a force overlooked by driving schools and departments of motor vehicles — an inchoate subconscious energy, a car id only civilized by the ego of social reason and the superego of the highway patrol.[1]

How do a thousand birds at full flight suddenly change direction without a single collision? How do those flocks function as a spectacularly co-

---

[1]The founder of psychoanalysis, Sigmund Freud (1856–1939) divided the human psyche into three processes: roughly, the id (which seeks instinctual gratification), the ego (which aims at rational behavior and socialization), and the superego (which represents the constraints of conscience).

ordinated whole without any apparent leader or signal? By subconsciously tuning into the government of an overall pattern, a social order. On the road our mad diversity of personalities, intelligences, personal needs, and emotional states somehow weaves into a similar consciousness, allowing any two of us, exaggerated by our vehicles into tons of metal and glass, to pass in opposite directions a few feet apart at a combined speed of over a hundred miles an hour without even thinking about it.

It is this overmind — the same sort of thing that marches the ants and flocks the birds and schools the fish — that makes road behavior such a social phenomenon, which explains why it's not rage but outrage that we feel in cars: slights to our social, not personal, being; insults to our rights; affronts to our dignity. Road anger is righteous indignation. It's not our personal but our public selves out there strutting in the mighty metal and velocity of traffic. Unlike the arts, traffic is not a place where those marching to a different drummer will find any more admiration, affection, and understanding than a rogue sparrow ruining the trip to Capistrano for the rest.[2]

[2]At Capistrano, twenty-five miles from Los Angeles, flocks of swallows punctually fly south every October and return just as punctually every March.

Responding as a Reader

1. Why do you think Hamilton called his essay, "Automotivational Counseling"? As you read, how does he expand on the meaning of the title? (To answer, you may want to consider all of Hamilton's references to psychology.)

2. Why does Hamilton wish that the woman he refused to let into traffic had used foul and abusive language to complain (para. 4)? What advantage would that have given him? How does she make him feel?

3. Read Hamilton's concluding paragraphs carefully. What point is he making about our identities as drivers? Why does he say that what we feel in traffic is not "rage" but "outrage"? Why is that distinction central to his main point?

Responding as a Writer

1. Try explaining Hamilton's final point about the "overmind" in your own words. Then, discuss whether you believe his explanation can help people overcome their anger in traffic.

2. What counseling can you offer readers to help them cope with traffic anger? In a short essay, offer several practical suggestions that you believe can relieve some of the emotional stress of being stuck in traffic.

3. Traffic jams bring out the worst in people. In a short essay, try to explain why traffic has this effect. Is it because of impatience? Has it anything to do with being in an automobile? Do the drivers usually seem more frustrated than the passengers? Do people experience the same emotions while waiting on any line — at banks, supermarkets, amusement parks, for example? Discuss any differences you see between human traffic and automobile traffic.

Advertisement

— From *Life* (Fall 1997).

Discussing the Unit

Suggested Topic for Discussion

What role *should* cars play in our society? Can we continue to use cars as much as we have and to let car use continue to grow? If so, should we be taking measures to address the problems that cars cause, and what should those measures be? If we need to curtail our use of cars, what modes of transportation should take their place?

Preparing for Class Discussion

1. Draw a line down the middle of a piece of paper and list arguments FOR cars on one side and AGAINST on the other. Consider public pros and cons as well as personal ones.

2. Interview a few people who do not have cars. If possible, talk to people of different ages, lifestyles, and socioeconomic groups. How do they get around? How do they feel about it? Do they wish they did have cars?

3. Cars cost a lot of money; and car companies spend a lot to promote their products. Look at the ad for the Oldsmobile Intrigue on page 101 and read the copy carefully. What exactly is being sold here? What is the significance of the woman, the lipstick and compact, the car parked in front of a hotel? Spend some time studying other car ads — on TV, in magazines, on billboards. Can you make any generalizations about how cars are marketed?

4. *Prewriting Assignment:* Write down all the modes of transportation that you use and all the additional modes of transportation that are available to you. For each, write a sentence or a paragraph on the pros and cons of this method of transportation.

From Discussion to Writing

Make a plan for using the automobile in a way that works for your life and supports your values. In an essay, describe that plan in detail and explain its benefits. Try to anticipate criticisms of your plan (possibly from the writers represented in this unit) and address them fully and respectfully. How would you sell your plan to others?

6

Gender Differences:
How Real Are They?

Most people will acknowledge some real differences between men and women: We have different hormones and body parts. But just how these physiological differences affect our social roles and psychological profiles remains unclear. Although numerous scientific studies have begun to show the presence of greater genetic and neurological differences than had previously been assumed, most writers and scholars believe that the overwhelming reason for most gender differences is cultural: Girls and boys are treated differently in families, schools, and other institutions, girls "sugar and spice," boys "snakes and snails."

Is that why men find it so much harder than women to apologize? asks one of the nation's leading experts on gender differences, Deborah Tannen, in "I'm Sorry, I Won't Apologize." Or — as a *New York Times* front page news item suggests — is it really biology that allows women to say "I'm sorry"? Biology may explain some physical differences, but, according to media analyst James Fallows, gender doesn't determine pitching styles. In "Throwing Like a Girl," Fallows claims that men and women aren't "hinged" differently and shows how anyone — with enough practice — can learn to throw like an athlete.

Throwing like an athlete, although it might help women compete with men on the playing field, may not be of much help in the more violent battles between the sexes. In her essay "In the Combat Zone," the Native American novelist Leslie Marmon Silko considers a notable gender difference that is rarely discussed: the greater degree of public safety enjoyed by

103

men. Women are targets of violence, forced to spend their lives taking pre-cautions, and not because of "height or weight or strength": "From in-fancy women are taught to be self-sacrificing, passive victims." Yet where does the combat zone begin and end? What are its social and geographi-cal boundaries?

How real are the differences between male and female college stu-dents? The selected survey results for the Class of 2000 show that there *are* real differences, at least in opinion.

Selected Survey Results

Gender Differences

- Men who rate themselves above average or highest 10% in leader-ship ability: 58.6%
- Women who do: 49.6%
- Men who rate themselves above average in popularity: 46.0%
- Women who do: 31.3%
- Men who rate themselves above average in self-confidence (intellec-tual): 62.4%
- Women who do: 46.6%
- Men who rate themselves above average in understanding of others: 60.2%
- Women who do: 66.9%
- Men who rate themselves above average in cooperativeness: 67.8%
- Women who do: 70.4%
- Freshmen women who agree that sex is OK if two people like each other: 31.9%
- Men who do: 53.8%

— From *The American Freshman: National Norms For Fall 1996.*

I'm Sorry, I Won't Apologize

[THE NEW YORK TIMES MAGAZINE/July 21, 1996]

Almost daily, news reports include accounts of public figures or heads of companies being forced to say they're sorry. In a recent case, Marge Schott, managing partner of the Cincinnati Reds, at first did not want to apologize for her remark that Hitler "was good at the beginning but he just went too far." Under pressure, she finally said that she regretted her remarks "offended many people." Predictably — and especially given her history with such comments — many were not satisfied with this response and successfully lobbied for her resignation.

This particular use of "I'm sorry" has a familiar ring. The other day my husband said to me, "I'm sorry I hurt your feelings." I knew he was really trying. He has learned, through our years together, that apologies are important to me. But he was grinning, because he also knew that "I'm sorry I hurt your feelings" left open the possibility — indeed, strongly suggested — that he regretted not what he did but my emotional reaction. It sometimes seems that he thinks the earth will open up and swallow him if he admits fault.

It may appear that insisting someone admit fault is like wanting him to humiliate himself. But I don't see it that way, since it's no big deal for me to say I made a mistake and apologize. The problem is that it becomes a big deal when he won't.

This turns out to be similar to the Japanese view. Following a fender bender, according to a *Times* article, the Japanese typically get out of their cars and bow, each claiming responsibility. In contrast, Americans are instructed by their insurance companies to avoid admitting fault. When an American living in Japan did just that — even though he knew he was to

DEBORAH TANNEN (b. 1945) is a University Professor at Georgetown University. Previously, she has taught linguistics and has written widely on how people talk to each other. Her best-selling book You Just Don't Understand: Women and Men in Conversation, was published in 1990 and was on the New York Times bestseller list for nearly four years. Her television appearances include 48 Hours, The Today Show, Donahue, Oprah, CBS This Morning, and The McLaughlin Show. Her two most recent publications are Gender and Discourse, published by Oxford University Press, and Talking From 9 to 5.

blame — the Japanese driver "was so incensed by the American's failure to show contrition that he took the highly unusual step of suing him."

The Japanese driver and I are not the only ones who are offended   5 when someone obviously at fault doesn't just fess up and apologize. A woman who lives in the country told me of a similar reaction. One day she gave her husband something to mail when he went into town. She stressed that it was essential the letter be mailed that day, and he assured her it would. But the next day, when they left the house together, she found her unmailed letter in the car. He said, "Oh, I forgot to mail your letter." She was furious — not because he had forgotten, but because he didn't apologize. "If I had done that," she said, "I would have fallen all over myself saying how sorry I was. And if he had said he was sorry, I would have been upset about the letter, but I would have forgiven him. After all, anyone can forget something. But I couldn't stop being angry, because he didn't seem to care that much that he'd let me down. I know he felt bad about it, but he wouldn't say so. Is that just him," she asked, "or is it something about men?"

I think it's something about men — not all men, of course. There are plenty of men who apologize easily and often and plenty of women who — like Marge Schott — avoid it at all costs. But there are many women, seemingly more than men, who easily say they're sorry and can't understand why it's such a big deal for others. Indeed, many women say "I'm sorry" as a conversational ritual — an automatic tip of the verbal hat to acknowledge that something regrettable happened. And others sometimes take this too literally.

One woman, for example, was talking on the phone when she got an interrupting call that she had to take immediately. When she rang the first caller back, she began by acknowledging that she had inconvenienced him and possibly been rude. "This is Sharon," she said. "I'm sorry." He responded, "You're sorry you're Sharon?" He may well have intended this retort as a good-natured tease, but it irritated her because it implied there was something odd about what she had said, while she felt it was run-of-the-mill, even required. I suspect it struck him as odd because he would avoid saying "sorry" if he could. One C.E.O. found that he could avoid it entirely: His deputy told me that part of his job was to make the rounds after the boss had lost his temper and apologize for him.

It's as if there's a tenet that real men don't say they're sorry. Take the closing scene in "Crimson Tide." Gene Hackman plays an unyieldingly authoritarian Navy captain in charge of a submarine carrying nuclear warheads. When he gets an unconfirmed order to launch, he is determined to comply but is thwarted by his lieutenant commander, played by Denzel Washington, who defies his commanding officer, sparks a mutiny, and averts nuclear war. The order to launch turns out to have been an error. The final scene is one of those exhilarating, dramatic moments when justice is served. Standing at attention before a panel that has investigated the mutiny without hearing his side, the lieutenant commander expects to be court-martialed. Instead he is promoted — on the recommendation of his captain. As the film ends, the captain turns to his deputy and says, "You were right and I was wrong. . . ." The audience gasps: This icon of authoritarian rigidity is admitting error. Then he grins mischievously and finishes the sentence, ". . . about the horses — the Lipizzaners. They *are* from Spain, not Portugal." Never mind that they're really from Austria; the two men exchange a look of intense rapport, and the audience heaves a sigh of satisfying relief.

Not me. I felt frustrated. Why couldn't he just say it? "I made a mistake. You were right. I was wrong about starting that nuclear war."

And saying you're sorry isn't enough in itself. You have to seem sorry: 10 Your face should look dejected, your voice should sound apologetic. Describing how bad you feel is also a plus. Furthermore, the depth of remorse should be commensurate with the significance of the offense. An offhand "Sorry about that" might be fine for an insignificant error like dropping a piece of paper, but if you drop a glass of red wine on your host's brand new white couch, a fleeting "Sorry about that" will not suffice.

The same people who resist displaying contrition may be eager to see it in others. Nowhere is this more evident than in court. Judges and juries are widely believed to give milder sentences to defendants who seem contrite. Prisons used to be called "penitentiaries" because inmates were expected not only to serve their time but also to repent. Nowadays many offenders seem to regard prison sentences as contractual: I served my time, I paid my debt. No apologies.

Apologies seem to come most easily from those who know their error was not intentional. The Japanese Government, for example, quickly apologized for the obviously accidental downing of an American plane during joint military exercises. But they have been much more reluctant to apologize for offenses committed during World War II, like forcing Korean, Chinese, and Filipina girls to serve as "comfort women" to Japanese soldiers.

Sometimes, though, people react negatively to an apology from a public figure. The First Lady discovered this last year when she met with a group of female columnists — off the record, she thought — and talked about how she had been portrayed in the press. "I regret very much that the efforts on health care were badly misunderstood, taken out of context, and used politically against the Administration. I take responsibility for that, and I'm very sorry for that," she said.

The first part of this quote clearly indicates that the fault was not with her actions —"the efforts on health care"— but rather with the way they were received and distorted by others. But because she went on to say the big, bad "S" word, all hell broke loose. One newspaper article quoted a political scientist as saying, "To apologize for substantive things you've

In the News

Is Sugar and Spice in Genes of Girls?

Scientists have found that a gene on a chromosome that girls receive from their fathers may give girls greater social skills and fewer behavioral and learning disorders when compared with boys.

In a study of children with an unusual hereditary condition called Turner's syndrome, researchers found preliminary evidence of a gene or genes on the X chromosome that might account for the differences.

The study being published today in the journal *Nature* found significantly different social behavior between two groups of girls with Turner's, a condition in which a child inherits a single X chromosome rather than the matched set of X chromosomes they normally receive.

The researchers determined that if a Turner girl inherited her lone X chromosome from her father, she displayed far greater social skills than if her one X chromosome was bequeathed by her mother.

— From the *New York Times*, June 12, 1997.

done raises the white flag. There's a school of thought in politics that you never say you're sorry. The best defense is a good offense." A Republican woman in the Florida state cabinet was quoted as saying: "I've seen women who overapologize, but I don't do that. I believe you negotiate through strength."

And there's the rub — apologizing is seen as a sign of weakness. This explains why more men than women might resist apologizing, since most boys learn early on that their peers will take advantage of them if they appear weak. Girls, in contrast, tend to reward other girls who talk in ways that show they don't think they're better than their peers.

Hillary Clinton's experience also explains why those who resist saying "I apologize" may find it more palatable to say "I'm sorry," because I'm sorry is not necessarily an apology. It can be — and in the First Lady's statement it clearly was — an expression of regret. It means "I'm sorry that happened." Her experience shows how easily this expression of regret can be mistaken for an apology.

Given this ambiguity, shouldn't we all strike the phrase "I'm sorry" from our vocabularies? Not necessarily. I think we'd do better as a society if more people said "I'm sorry" rather than fewer. Instead of all the railing against Hillary Clinton for apologizing when she expressed regret, how come no one thought that either Newt Gingrich or his mother should apologize when the latter quoted her son as uttering an irrefutable insult against the

First Lady? The problem seems to be not a surfeit of apologies but a dearth of them. One business manager told me he has discovered that apologies can be a powerful tool: Subordinates so appreciate his admitting fault that they not only forgive his errors but also become ever more loyal employees.

History includes many examples of apologies that were not weak but highly potent. Following the calamitous Bay of Pigs invasion,[1] John F. Kennedy demonstrated the power not only of "taking responsibility" but also of actually taking blame. For someone that high up to admit fault was shocking — and effective. People forgave the President, and his Administration, for the colossal error.

I think those brave enough to admit fault would find a similar power at home: It's amazing how an apology, if it seems sincere, can dissipate another's anger, calm the roiling waters. Erich Segal[2] got it exactly wrong. Love doesn't mean never having to say you're sorry. Love means being able to say you're sorry — and, like J.F.K., being strong enough to admit you were at fault.

[1] On April 17, 1961, President Kennedy authorized U.S. troops to assist anti-Castro exiles in an unsuccessful invasion of Cuba at the Bay of Pigs.

[2] Erich Segal's 1970 novel, *Love Story*, opens with the now famous line, "Love means never having to say you're sorry."

Responding as a Reader

1. Tannen gives a number of examples of men or women who do or do not apologize. Make a list of these examples. Are there ways of classifying these people other than by gender?

2. According to Tannen, why is it that women apologize more often than men?

3. Tannen draws a distinction between saying "I'm sorry" and saying "I apologize." What is the difference between these two statements, in her view?

Responding as a Writer

1. Think of a particular instance when you realized that you were at fault. Did you apologize? Why or why not? Do you believe your gender influenced your willingness to apologize? In an essay, apply Tannen's theory to your circumstance.

2. Behaviorally, men and women differ in many ways. Choose one of these ways (other than willingness to apologize) and analyze it as Tannen does. What do you think accounts for this difference? Be sure to include plenty of examples.

3. In other works, Deborah Tannen has argued that men tend to view personal relationships in terms of power — someone must be up;

someone must be down. Women, on the other hand, see personal relationships as opportunities for closeness and belonging. Consider how
Tannen's arguments about apologizing fit into this larger theory. Then,
try to apply this theory to another context. How might it apply to the
willingness to ask for directions, for example?

JAMES FALLOWS

"Throwing Like a Girl"

[THE ATLANTIC MONTHLY/August 1996]

Most people remember the 1994 baseball season for the way it ended —
with a strike rather than a World Series. I keep thinking about the way it
began. On opening day, April 4, Bill Clinton went to Cleveland and, like
many Presidents before him, threw out a ceremonial first pitch. That same
day Hillary Rodham Clinton went to Chicago and, like no First Lady before
her, also threw out a first ball, at a Cubs game in Wrigley Field.

The next day photos of the Clintons in action appeared in newspapers
around the country. Many papers, including the *New York Times* and the
Washington Post, chose the same two photos to run. The one of Bill Clinton showed him wearing an Indians cap and warm-up jacket. The President, throwing lefty, had turned his shoulders sideways to the plate in
preparation for delivery. He was bringing the ball forward from behind his
head in a clean-looking throwing action as the photo was snapped. Hillary
Clinton was pictured wearing a dark jacket, a scarf, and an oversized Cubs

JAMES FALLOWS *(b. 1949) is a defense reporter, economic theorist, and
media critic. He attended Harvard University and received a diploma in
economic development from Queen's College, Oxford. He has been editor
of the* Washington Monthly, Texas Monthly, *and the* Atlantic Monthly.
He authored the book National Defense, *which won the National Book
Award. He also wrote* Looking at the Sun *(1995) and* Breaking the News:
How the Media Undermines American Democracy *(1996).*

hat. In preparation for her throw she was standing directly facing the plate. A right-hander, she had the elbow of her throwing arm pointed out in front of her. Her forearm was tilted back, toward her shoulder. The ball rested on her upturned palm. As the picture was taken, she was in the middle of an action that can only be described as throwing like a girl.

The phrase "throwing like a girl" has become an embattled and offensive one. Feminists smart at its implication that to do something "like a girl" is to do it the wrong way. Recently, on the heels of the O. J. Simpson case, a book appeared in which the phrase was used to help explain why male athletes, especially football players, were involved in so many assaults against women. Having been trained (like most American boys) to dread the accusation of doing anything "like a girl," athletes were said to grow into the assumption that women were valueless, and natural prey.

I grant the justice of such complaints. I am attuned to the hurt caused by similar broad-brush stereotypes when they apply to groups I belong to — "dancing like a white man," for instance, or "speaking foreign languages like an American," or "thinking like a Washingtonian."

Still, whatever we want to call it, the difference between the two Clintons in what they were doing that day is real, and it is instantly recognizable. And since seeing those photos I have been wondering, Why, exactly, do so many women throw "like a girl"? If the motion were easy to change, presumably a woman as motivated and self-possessed as Hillary Clinton would have changed it. (According to her press secretary, Lisa Caputo, Mrs. Clinton spent the weekend before opening day tossing a ball in the Rose Garden with her husband, for practice.) Presumably, too, the answer to the question cannot be anything quite as simple as, because they *are* girls.

A surprising number of people think that there is a structural difference between male and female arms or shoulders — in the famous "rotator cuff," perhaps — that dictates different throwing motions. "It's in the shoulder joint," a well-educated woman told me recently. "They're hinged differently." Someday researchers may find evidence to support a biological theory of throwing actions. For now, what you'll hear if you ask an orthopedist, an anatomist, or (especially) the coach of a women's softball team is that there is no structural reason why men and women should throw in different ways. This point will be obvious to any male who grew up around girls who liked to play baseball and became good at it. It should be obvious on a larger scale this summer, in broadcasts of the Olympic Games. This year, for the first time, women's fast-pitch softball teams will compete in the Olympics. Although the pitchers in these games will deliver the ball underhand, viewers will see female shortstops, center fielders, catchers, and so on pegging the ball to one another at speeds few male viewers could match.

Even women's tennis is a constant if indirect reminder that men's and women's shoulders are "hinged" the same way. The serving motion in tennis is like a throw — but more difficult, because it must be coordinated with the toss of the tennis ball. The men in professional tennis serve harder than the women, because they are bigger and stronger. But women pros serve harder than most male amateurs have ever done, and the service motion for good players is the same for men and women alike. There is no expectation in college or pro tennis that because of their anatomy female players must "serve like a girl." "I know many women who can throw a lot harder and better than the normal male," says Linda Wells, the coach of the highly successful women's softball team at Arizona State University. "It's not gender that makes the difference in how they throw."

So what is it, then? Since Hillary Clinton's ceremonial visit to Wrigley Field, I have asked men and women how they learned to throw, or didn't. Why did I care? My impetus was the knowledge that eventually my sons would be grown and gone. If my wife, in all other ways a talented athlete, could learn how to throw, I would still have someone to play catch with. My research left some women, including my wife, thinking that I am some kind of obsessed lout, but it has led me to the solution to the mystery. First let's be clear about what there is to be explained.

At a superficial level it's easy to tick off the traits of an awkward-looking throw. The fundamental mistake is the one Mrs. Clinton appeared to be making in the photo: trying to throw a ball with your body facing the target, rather than rotating your shoulders and hips ninety degrees away from the target and then swinging them around in order to accelerate the ball. A throw looks bad if your elbow is lower than your shoulder as your arm comes forward (unless you're throwing sidearm). A throw looks really bad if, as the ball leaves your hand, your wrist is "inside your elbow"— that is, your elbow joint is bent in such a way that your forearm angles back toward your body and your wrist is closer to your head than your elbow is. Slow-motion film of big-league pitchers shows that when they release the ball, the throwing arm is fully extended and straight from shoulder to wrist. The combination of these three elements — head-on stance, dropped elbow, and wrist inside the elbow — mechanically dictates a pushing rather than a hurling motion, creating the familiar pattern of "throwing like a girl."

It is surprisingly hard to find in the literature of baseball a deeper explanation of the mechanics of good and bad throws. Tom Seaver's pitching for the Mets and the White Sox got him into the Hall of Fame, but his book *The Art of Pitching* is full of bromides that hardly clarify the process of throwing, even if they might mean something to accomplished pitchers. His chapter "The Absolutes of Pitching Mechanics," for instance, lays out these four unhelpful principles: "Keep the Front Leg Flexible!" "Rub Up the Baseball." "Hide the Baseball!" "Get it Out, Get it Up!" (The fourth refers to the need to get the ball out of the glove and into the throwing hand in a quick motion.)

10

A variety of other instructional documents, from *Little League's Official How-to-Play Baseball Book* to *Softball for Girls & Women*, mainly reveal the difficulty of finding words to describe a simple motor activity that everyone can recognize. The challenge, I suppose, is like that of writing a manual on how to ride a bike, or how to kiss. Indeed, the most useful description I've found of the mechanics of throwing comes from a man whose specialty is another sport: Vic Braden made his name as a tennis coach, but he has attempted to analyze the physics of a wide variety of sports so that they all will be easier to teach.

Braden says that an effective throw involves connecting a series of links in a "kinetic chain." The kinetic chain, which is Braden's tool for analyzing most sporting activity, operates on a principle like that of crack-the-whip. Momentum builds up in one part of the body. When that part is suddenly stopped, as the end of the "whip" is stopped in crack-the-whip, the momentum is transferred to and concentrated in the next link in the chain. A good throw uses six links of chain, Braden says. The first two links involve the lower body, from feet to waist. The first motion of a throw (after the body has been rotated away from the target) is to rotate the legs and hips back in the direction of the throw, building up momentum as large muscles move body mass. Then those links stop — a pitcher stops turning his hips once they face the plate — and the momentum is transferred to the next link. This is the torso, from waist to shoulders, and since its mass is less than that of the legs, momentum makes it rotate faster than the hips and legs did. The torso stops when it is facing the plate, and the momentum is transferred to the next link — the upper arm. As the upper arm comes past the head, it stops moving forward, and the momentum goes into the final links — the forearm and wrist, which snap forward at tremendous speed.

This may sound arcane and jerkily mechanical, but it makes perfect sense when one sees Braden's slow-mo movies of pitchers in action. And it explains why people do, or don't, learn how to throw. The implication of Braden's analysis is that throwing is a perfectly natural action (millions and millions of people can do it) but not at all innate. A successful throw involves an intricate series of actions coordinated among muscle groups, as each link of the chain is timed to interact with the next. Like bike riding or skating, it can be learned by anyone — male or female. No one starts out knowing how to ride a bike or throw a ball. Everyone has to learn.

Readers who are happy with their throwing skills can prove this to themselves in about two seconds. If you are right-handed, pick up a ball with your left hand and throw it. Unless you are ambidextrous or have some other odd advantage, you will throw it "like a girl." The problem is not that your left shoulder is hinged strangely or that you don't know what a good throw looks like. It is that you have not spent time training your leg, hip, shoulder, and arm muscles on that side to work together as required for a throw. The actor John Goodman, who played football seriously and baseball casually when he was in high school, is right-handed. When cast in the 1992 movie *The Babe*, he had to learn to bat and throw left-handed, for realism in the role of Babe Ruth. For weeks before the filming began, he would arrive an hour early at the set of his TV show, *Roseanne*, so that he could practice throwing a tennis ball against a wall left-handed. "I made damn sure no one could see me," Goodman told me recently. "I'm hard enough on myself without the derisive laughter of my so-called friends." When *The Babe* was released, Goodman told a newspaper interviewer, "I'll never say something like 'He throws like a girl' again. It's not easy to learn how to throw."

What Goodman discovered is what most men have forgotten: that if they know how to throw now, it is because they spent time learning at some point long ago. (Goodman says that he can remember learning to ride a bicycle but not learning to throw with his right hand.) This brings us back to the roots of the "throwing like a girl" phenomenon. The crucial factor is not that males and females are put together differently but that they typically spend their early years in different ways. Little boys often learn how to throw without noticing that they are learning. Little girls are more rarely in environments that encourage them to learn in the same way. A boy who wonders why a girl throws the way she does is like a Frenchman who wonders why so many Americans speak French "with an accent."

"For young boys it is culturally acceptable and politically correct to develop these skills," says Linda Wells, of the Arizona State softball team. "They are mentored and networked. Usually girls are not coached at all, or are coached by Mom — or if it's by Dad, he may not be much of an athlete. Girls are often stuck with the bottom of the male talent pool as examples. I would argue that rather than learning to 'throw like a girl,' they learn to throw like poor male athletes. I say that a bad throw is 'throwing like an old man.' This is not gender, it's acculturation."

Almost any motor skill, from doing handstands to dribbling a basketball, is easier to learn if you start young, which is why John Goodman did not realize that learning to throw is difficult until he attempted it as an adult. Many girls reach adulthood having missed the chance to learn to throw when that would have been easiest to do. And as adults they have neither John Goodman's incentive to teach their muscles a new set of skills nor his confidence that the feat is possible. Five years ago, Joseph Russo, long a baseball coach at St. John's University, gave athletic-talent tests to actresses who were trying out for roles in *A League of Their Own,* a movie about women's baseball. Most of them were "well coordinated in general, like for dancing," he says. But those who had not happened to play baseball or softball when they were young had a problem: "It sounds silly to say it, but they kept throwing like girls." (The best ball-field talents, by the way, were Madonna, Demi Moore, and the rock singer Joan Jett, who according to Russo "can really hit it hard." Careful viewers of *A League of*

Their Own will note that only in a fleeting instant in one scene is the star, Geena Davis, shown actually throwing a ball.)

I'm not sure that I buy Linda Wells's theory that most boys are "mentored" or "networked" into developing ball skills. Those who make the baseball team, maybe. But for a far larger number the decisive ingredient seems to be the hundreds of idle hours spent throwing balls, sticks, rocks, and so on in the playground or the back yard. Children on the playground, I think, demonstrate the moment when the kinetic chain begins to work. It is when a little boy tries to throw a rock farther than his friend can or to throw a stick over a telephone wire thirty feet up. A toddler's first, instinctive throw is a push from the shoulder, showing the essential traits of "throwing like a girl." But when a child is really trying to put some oomph into the throw, his natural instinct is to wind up his body and let fly with the links of the chain. Little girls who do the same thing — compete with each other in distance throwing — learn the same way, but whereas many boys do this, few girls do. Tammy Richards, a woman who was raised on a farm in central California, says that she learned to throw by trying to heave dried cow chips farther than her brother could. It may have helped that her father, Bob Richards, was a former Olympic competitor in the decathlon (and two-time Olympic champion in the pole vault) and that he taught all his sons and daughters to throw not only the ball but also the discus, the shotput, and the javelin.

Is there a way to make up for lost time if you failed to invest those long hours on the playground years ago? Of course. Adults may not be able to learn to speak unaccented French, but they can learn to ride a bike, or skate, or throw. All that is required for developing any of these motor skills is time for practice — and spending that time requires overcoming the sense of embarrassment and futility that adults often have when attempting something new. Here are two tips that may help.

One is a surprisingly valuable drill suggested by the Little League's   20
How-to-Play handbook. Play catch with a partner who is ten or fifteen feet away — but do so while squatting with the knee of your throwing side touching the ground. When you start out this low, you have to keep the throw high to get the ball to your partner without bouncing it. This encourages a throw with the elbow held well above the shoulder, where it belongs.

The other is to play catch with a person who can throw like an athlete but is using his or her off hand. The typical adult woman hates to play catch with the typical adult man. She is well aware that she's not looking graceful and reacts murderously to the condescending tone in his voice ("That's more like it, honey!"). Forcing a right-handed man to throw left-handed is the great equalizer. He suddenly concentrates his attention on what it takes to get hips, shoulder, and elbow working together. He is suddenly aware of the strength of character needed to ignore the snickers of onlookers while learning new motor skills. He can no longer be condescending. He may even be nervous, wondering what he'll do if his partner makes the breakthrough first and he's the one still throwing like a girl.

Responding as a Reader

1. Try Fallows's recommendations. If you are happy with the way you throw, try throwing with the hand that you do not normally use. If you don't throw as well as you'd like, try it again using the guidelines from the Little League handbook. Do you understand Fallows's point differently after trying these exercises than after just reading about them?

2. In paragraph 18, Fallows argues that the typical American boy spends "hundreds of idle hours" learning to throw a ball "farther than his friend can" while "few girls do" this. What is he implying, here, about the difference between boys and girls?

3. Consider the implications of Fallows's main point. Is he arguing that males and females possess identical athletic abilities? Or is he only claiming that there is no difference in the mechanics (the "kinetic chain") between the sexes? Do you think he believes that women have the raw ability to pitch in the major leagues? If so, what has prevented them so far?

Responding as a Writer

1. Reread Fallows's description of Braden's "kinetic chain" explanation, in which he explains how a good throw works. Write a paragraph explaining how to perform a simple action that you do very well but have never really thought about — like walking or pronouncing your name. Try using an analogy, as Braden does.

2. Make a list of actions that are often said to be performed like a woman or a girl ("to cry like a woman," for example) and another list of actions that are often said to be performed like a man or a boy ("fight like a man"). Mark the positive actions with a "+" and the negative actions with a "–." Does each of your lists break down evenly between positive and negative? Try to account for the discrepancy — is it due to your gender, your culture, the English language?

3. What kinds of things are girls generally taught how to do in the culture in which you were brought up? What kinds of things are boys taught to do? In an essay, classify the kinds of things contemporary American parents teach their children, and compare boys' lessons to girls' lessons. What effect does this difference have on the next population of working (and child-rearing) adults?

In the Combat Zone

[HUNGRY MIND REVIEW/Fall 1995]

Women seldom discuss our wariness or the precautions we take after dark each time we leave the apartment, car, or office to go on the most brief errand. We take for granted that we are targeted as easy prey by muggers, rapists, and serial killers. This is our lot as women in the United States. We try to avoid going anywhere alone after dark, although economic necessity sends women out night after night. We do what must be done, but always we are alert, on guard, and ready. We have to be aware of persons walking on the sidewalk behind us; we have to pay attention to others who board an elevator we're on. We try to avoid all staircases and deserted parking garages when we are alone. Constant vigilance requires considerable energy and concentration seldom required of men.

I used to assume that most men were aware of this fact of women's lives, but I was wrong. They may notice our reluctance to drive at night to the convenience store alone, but they don't know or don't want to know the experience of a woman out alone at night. Men who have been in combat know the feeling of being a predator's target, but it is difficult for men to admit that we women live our entire lives in a combat zone. Men have the power to end violence against women in the home, but they feel helpless to protect women from violent strangers. Because men feel guilt and anger at their inability to shoulder responsibility for the safety of their wives, sisters, and daughters, we don't often discuss random acts of violence against women.

When we were children, my sisters and I used to go to Albuquerque with my father. Sometimes strangers would tell my father it was too bad that he had three girls and no sons. My father, who has always preferred

LESLIE MARMON SILKO (b. 1948) grew up at the Laguna Pueblo Reservation near her birthplace, Albuquerque, New Mexico. Winner of a prestigious MacArthur Foundation grant, Silko has published collections of poems as well as two highly regarded novels, Ceremony (1977) and Almanac of the Dead (1992). Her miscellany Storyteller combines poetry, family history, fiction, and photographs to reconstruct Native American myths and was published in 1981. Her most recent book, Yellow Woman and a Beauty of the Spirit was published in 1996 by Simon and Schuster.

the company of women, used to reply that he was glad to have girls and not boys, because he might not get along as well with boys. Furthermore, he'd say, "My girls can do anything your boys can do, and my girls can do it better." He had in mind, of course, shooting and hunting.

When I was six years old, my father took me along as he hunted deer; he showed me how to walk quietly, to move along, and then to stop and listen carefully before taking another step. A year later, he traded a pistol for a little single shot .22 rifle just my size.

He took me and my younger sisters down to the dump by the river and taught us how to shoot. We rummaged through the trash for bottles and glass jars; it was great fun to take aim at a pickle jar and watch it shatter. If the Rio San Jose had water running in it, we threw bottles for moving targets in the muddy current. My father told us that a .22 bullet can travel a mile, so we had to be careful where we aimed. The river was a good place because it was below the villages and away from the houses; the high clay riverbanks wouldn't let any bullets stray. Gun safety was drilled into us. We were cautioned about other children whose parents might not teach them properly; if we ever saw another child with a gun, we knew to get away. Guns were not toys. My father did not approve of BB guns because they were classified as toys. I had a .22 rifle when I was seven years old. If I felt like shooting, all I had to do was tell my parents where I was going, take my rifle and a box of .22 shells and go. I was never tempted to shoot at birds or animals because whatever was killed had to be eaten. Now, I realize how odd this must seem; a seven year old with a little .22 rifle and a box of ammunition, target shooting alone at the river. But that was how people lived at Laguna when I was growing up; children were given responsibilities from an early age.

Laguna Pueblo people hunted deer for winter meat. When I was thirteen, I carried George Pearl's saddle carbine, a .30–30, and hunted deer for the first time. When I was fourteen, I killed my first mule deer buck with one shot through the heart.

Guns were for target shooting and guns were for hunting, but also I knew that Grandma Lily carried a little purse gun with her whenever she drove alone to Albuquerque or Los Lunas. One night my mother and my grandmother were driving the fifty miles from Albuquerque to Laguna down Route 66 when three men in a car tried to force my grandmother's car off the highway. Route 66 was not so heavily traveled as Interstate 40 is now, and there were many long stretches of highway where no other car passed for minutes on end. Payrolls at the Jackpile Uranium Mine were large in the 1950s, and my mother or my grandmother had to bring home thousands from the bank in Albuquerque to cash the miners' checks on paydays.

After that night, my father bought my mother a pink nickel-plated snub-nose .22 revolver with a white bone grip. Grandma Lily carried a tiny

Beretta as black as her prayer book. As my sisters and I got older, my father taught us to handle and shoot handguns, revolvers mostly, because back then, semiautomatic pistols were not as reliable — they frequently jammed. I will never forget the day my father told us three girls that we never had to let a man hit us or terrorize us because no matter how big and strong the man was, a gun in our hand equalized all differences of size and strength.

Much has been written about violence in the home and spousal abuse. I wish to focus instead on violence from strangers toward women because this form of violence terrifies women more, despite the fact that most women are murdered by a spouse, relative, fellow employee, or next-door neighbor, not a stranger. Domestic violence kills many more women and children than strangers kill, but domestic violence also follows more predictable patterns and is more familiar: He comes home drunk and she knows what comes next. A good deal of the terror of a stranger's attack comes from its suddenness and unexpectedness. Attacks by strangers occur with enough frequency that battered women and children often cite their fears of such attacks as reasons for remaining in abusive domestic situations. They fear the violence they imagine strangers will inflict on them more than they fear the abusive home. More than one feminist has pointed out that rapists and serial killers help keep the patriarchy securely in place.

An individual woman may be terrorized by her spouse, but women are   10
not sufficiently terrorized that we avoid marriage. Yet many women I know, including myself, try to avoid going outside of their homes alone after dark. Big deal, you say; well, yes, it is a big deal since most lectures, performances, and films are presented at night; so are dinners and other social events. Women out alone at night who are assaulted by strangers are put on trial by public opinion: Any woman out alone after dark is asking for trouble. Presently, for millions of women of all socioeconomic backgrounds, sundown is lockdown. We are prisoners of violent strangers.

Daylight doesn't necessarily make the streets safe for women. In the early 1980s, a rapist operated in Tucson in the afternoon near the University of Arizona campus. He often accosted two women at once, forced them into residential alleys, then raped each one with a knife to her throat and forced the other to watch. Afterward the women said that part of the horror of their attack was that all around them, everything appeared normal. They could see people inside their houses and cars going down the street — all around them life was going on as usual while their lives were being changed forever.

The afternoon rapist was not the only rapist in Tucson at that time; there was the prime-time rapist, the potbellied rapist, and the apologetic rapist all operating in Tucson in the 1980s. The prime-time rapist was actually two men who invaded comfortable foothills homes during television prime time when residents were preoccupied with television and eating dinner. The prime-time rapists terrorized entire families; they raped the women and sometimes they raped the men. Family members were forced to go to automatic bank machines to bring back cash to end the ordeal. Potbelly rapist and apologetic rapist need little comment, except to note that the apologetic rapist was good looking, well educated, and smart enough to break out of jail for one last rape followed by profuse apologies and his capture in the University of Arizona library. Local papers recounted details about Tucson's last notorious rapist, the red bandanna rapist. In the late 1970s, this rapist attacked more than twenty women over a three-year period, and Tucson police were powerless to stop him. Then one night, the rapist broke into a midtown home where the lone resident, a woman, shot him four times in the chest with a .38 caliber revolver.

In midtown Tucson, on a weekday afternoon, I was driving down Campbell Avenue to the pet store. Suddenly the vehicle behind me began to weave into my lane, so I beeped the horn politely. The vehicle swerved back to its lane, but then in my rearview mirror I saw the small late-model truck change lanes and begin to follow my car very closely. I drove a few blocks without looking in the rearview mirror, but in my sideview mirror I saw the compact truck was right behind me. OK. Some motorists stay upset for two or three blocks, some require ten blocks or more to recover their senses. Stoplight after stoplight, when I glanced into the rearview mirror I saw the man — in his early thirties, tall, white, brown hair, and dark glasses. This guy must not have a job if he has the time to follow me for miles — oh, ohhh! No beast more dangerous in the U.S.A. than an unemployed white man.

At this point I had to make a decision: Do I forget about the trip to the pet store and head for the police station downtown, four miles away? Why should I have to let this stranger dictate my schedule for the afternoon? The man might dare to follow me to the police station, but by the time I reach the front door of the station, he'd be gone. No crime was committed; no Arizona law forbids tailgating someone for miles or for turning into a parking lot behind them. What could the police do? I had no license plate number to report because Arizona requires only one license plate, on the rear bumper of the vehicle. Anyway, I was within a block of the pet store where I knew I could get help from the pet store owners. I would feel better about this incident if it was not allowed to ruin my trip to the pet store.

The guy was right on my rear bumper; if I'd had to stop suddenly for any reason, there'd have been a collision. I decide I will not stop even if he does ram into the rear of my car. I study this guy's face in my rearview mirror; six feet two inches tall, 175 pounds, medium complexion, short hair, trimmed moustache. He thinks he can intimidate me because I am a woman, five feet five inches tall, 140 pounds. But I am not afraid, I am furious. I refuse to be intimidated. I won't play his game. I can tell by the face I see in the mirror this guy has done this before, he enjoys using his truck to menace lone women.

I keep thinking he will quit, or he will figure that he's scared me enough, but he seems to sense that I am not afraid. It's true. I am not afraid because years ago my father taught my sisters and me that we did not have to be afraid. He'll give up when I turn into the parking lot outside the pet store, I think. But I watch in my rearview mirror; he's right on my rear bumper. As his truck turns into the parking lot behind my car, I reach over and open the glove compartment. I take out the holster with my .38 special and lay it on the car seat beside me.

I turned my car into a parking spot so quickly that I was facing my stalker who had momentarily stopped his truck and was watching me. I slid the .38 out of its holster onto my lap. I watched the stranger's face, trying to determine whether he would jump out of his truck with a baseball bat or gun and come after me. I felt calm. No pounding heart or rapid breathing. My early experience deer hunting had prepared me well. I did not panic because I felt I could stop him if he tried to harm me. I was in no hurry. I sat in the car and waited to see what choice my stalker would make. I looked directly at him without fear because I had my .38 and I was ready to use it. The expression on my face must have been unfamiliar to him; he was used to seeing terror in the eyes of the women he followed. The expression on my face communicated a warning: If he approached the car window, I'd kill him.

He took a last look at me then sped away. I stayed in my car until his truck disappeared in the traffic of Campbell Avenue.

I walked into the pet store shaken. I had felt able to protect myself throughout the incident, but it left me emotionally drained and exhausted. The stranger had only pursued me — how much worse to be battered or raped.

Years before, I was unarmed the afternoon that two drunken deer   20
hunters threatened to shoot me off my horse with razor-edged hunting arrows from fiberglass crossbows. I was riding a colt on a national park trail near my home in the Tucson Mountains. These young white men in their late twenties were complete strangers who might have shot me if the colt had not galloped away erratically bucking and leaping — a moving target too difficult for the drunken bow hunters to aim at. The colt brought me to my ranch house where I called the county sheriff's office and the park ranger. I live in a sparsely populated area where my nearest neighbor is a quarter-mile away. I was afraid the men might have followed me back to my house so I took the .44 magnum out from under my pillow and strapped it around my waist until the sheriff or park ranger arrived. Forty-five minutes later, the park ranger arrived; the deputy sheriff arrived fifteen minutes after him. The drunken bow hunters were apprehended on the national park and arrested for illegally hunting; their bows and arrows were seized as evidence for the duration of bow hunting season. In southern Arizona that is enough punishment; I didn't want to take a chance of stirring up additional animosity with these men because I lived alone then; I chose

not to make a complaint about their threatening words and gestures. I did not feel that I backed away by not pressing charges; I feared that if I pressed assault charges against these men, they would feel that I was challenging them to all-out war. I did not want to have to kill either of them if they came after me, as I thought they might. With my marksmanship and my .243 caliber hunting rifle from the old days, I am confident that I could stop idiots like these. But to have to take the life of another person is a terrible experience I will always try to avoid.

It isn't height or weight or strength that make women easy targets; from infancy women are taught to be self-sacrificing, passive victims. I was taught differently. Women have the right to protect themselves from death or bodily harm. By becoming strong and potentially lethal individuals, women destroy the fantasy that we are sitting ducks for predatory strangers.

In a great many cultures, women are taught to depend on others, not themselves, for protection from bodily harm. Women are not taught to defend themselves from strangers because fathers and husbands fear the consequences themselves. In the United States, women depend on the courts and the police, but as many women have learned the hard way, the police cannot be outside your house twenty-four hours a day. I don't want more police. More police on the streets will not protect women. A few policemen are rapists and killers of women themselves; their uniforms and squad cars give them an advantage. No, I will be responsible for my own safety, thank you.

Women need to decide who has the primary responsibility for the health and safety of their bodies. We don't trust the State to manage our reproductive organs, yet most of us blindly trust that the State will protect us (and our reproductive organs) from predatory strangers. One look at the rape and murder statistics for women (excluding domestic incidents) and it is clear that the government FAILS to protect women from the violence of strangers. Some may cry out for a "stronger" State, more police, mandatory sentences, and swifter executions. Over the years we have seen the U.S. prison population become the largest in the world, executions take place every week now, inner-city communities are occupied by the National Guard, and people of color are harassed by police, but guess what? A woman out alone, night or day, is confronted with more danger of random violence from strangers than ever before. As the U.S. economy continues "to downsize," and the good jobs disappear forever, our urban and rural landscapes will include more desperate, angry men with nothing to lose.

Only women can put a stop to the "open season" on women by strangers. Women are TAUGHT to be easy targets by their mothers, aunts, and grandmothers, who themselves were taught that "a woman doesn't kill" or "a woman doesn't learn how to use a weapon." Women must learn how to take aggressive action individually, apart from the police and the courts.

Presently, twenty-one states issue permits to carry concealed weapons; most states require lengthy gun safety courses and a police security check before issuing a permit. Inexpensive but excellent gun safety and self-defense courses designed for women are also available from every quality gun dealer who hopes to sell you a handgun at the end of the course. Those who object to firearms need trained companion dogs or collectives of six or more women to escort one another day and night. We must destroy the myth that women are born to be easy targets.

25

Responding as a Reader

1. What is a "combat zone"? In what ways do women live in a combat zone, according to Silko?

2. What is the function of the passages on hunting? What skills did Silko learn from her childhood hunting experiences? What else do you think she might have learned from deer hunting and target shooting in the river?

3. Why does Silko tell the stories of violence — the rapes, and her grandmother's and her own highway threats, the deer hunters with their arrows? Do all these stories have a common point or function?

Responding as a Writer

1. "If he approached the car window, I'd kill him" (para. 17). Reread Silko's description of this incident, up to that sentence. If she did kill the stalker, would she be justified? Do you think she would have actually done it? Explain.

2. What specific changes is Silko arguing for? Imagine what the world would be like if Silko got her way. What would change for the better, and what for the worse? Would Silko's changes be beneficial, in the last analysis?

3. Do women need protection from violence more than men do? In an essay, explain why or why not and speculate about what can be done to reduce violent crime. Can we reduce violence by changing what we teach little girls and little boys? Would greater economic equity reduce the risks to women (and to men)? Or are these differences between the sexes innate?

Discussing the Unit

Suggested Topic for Discussion

The main selections in this unit argue that the behavioral differences between men and women are a result of our culture — social patterns of raising boys and girls rather than biology. Of all the differences between men and women, which do you think are biological and which cultural? Do we, as a society, have the power to eliminate the cultural differences in future generations? Should we?

Preparing for Class Discussion

1. List behavioral differences between men and women that you observe regularly. Which of the behaviors on your list are more likely to be the result of social constructs? Which are more likely to be based in biology? Which items on your list are you hesitant to commit to either category?

2. Arrange to observe a group of young children at play (perhaps you could visit a local day-care center, playground, or nursery school). Look for general differences between what the boys do and what the girls do. Also look for differences between how the adults interact with the boys and with the girls. Take notes.

3. *Prewriting Assignment:* Think of times when you have noticed an important behavioral difference between you and a person of the opposite sex. Select one instance and in a paragraph describe your experience. In a second paragraph, explain whether any of the views presented in this chapter have altered or confirmed your original perception.

4. Consider the ad for the Oldsmobile Intrigue (p. 101) in the context of the selections in this unit. The ad shows a woman touching up her lipstick, checking out the "muscular lines" of a sports sedan in her compact mirror. Whom is this ad targeted for — men or women? What is implied about gender differences?

From Discussion to Writing

What difference does it make whether we regard sex differences as biologically innate or socially constructed? Consider this question in a carefully thought-out essay. How could the answer to this question affect social, economic, political, and cultural attitudes? Choose one of these four perspectives in shaping your response.

7

"I'm a Feminist, But . . .": Where Is the Women's Movement Headed?

It has been some thirty-five years since the publication of Betty Friedan's feminist classic, *The Feminine Mystique,* a book many claim launched the modern women's movement. Since then, feminism has undergone a great many changes, in both style and substance. Today, one of the central feminist issues involves the vitality of the movement itself. Has feminism lost ground among current college women, many of whom take its hard-fought principles of social and economic equality for granted? Is feminism primarily an elitist enterprise driven by academia and publishing that has established little connection with the lives of poor, working women, wives, and mothers? For several decades these questions have been debated among feminists, but lately, as this chapter demonstrates, the philosophical differences and internal conflicts among feminist leaders themselves have grown more public and openly hostile. In "The Independent Woman (and Other Lies)," Katie Roiphe, a controversial young essayist, explores forbidden feminist territory when she asks: "Why shouldn't we find a man who will take care of us the way our fathers did?"

Husbands and traditional weddings are also at the center of Jenny McPhee's *New York Times* opinion piece that provoked a deluge of angry responses in an attempt to redefine the meaning of feminism for a younger generation. For many younger, articulate women, feminism's main culprit is no longer male oppression but, strangely enough, feminism itself.

In "Lipstick Liberation," Boston journalist Yvonne Abraham scrutinizes "third-wave" feminism: "By moving feminism's agenda from politics and economics to bedrooms and cosmetic counters," Abraham charges, "third-wave writers effectively sidestep many of the serious problems that still beset women and undermine attempts to fix them."

Yet "third-wave" feminist writers are not feminism's only female challengers. The "contemporary women's movement is obsessed with proving that our system is rigged against women," argues philosophy professor Christina Hoff Sommers. In "The 'Fragile American Girl' Myth," she vigorously disputes recent claims that the "American girl" represents a genuinely disadvantaged group. An advertisement for the American Indian College Fund vividly shows how feminism must compete with other claims on individual identity. Finally, an exchange of online messages between two notable feminist writers (Susan Faludi and Karen Lehrman, who exchanged six letters but came no closer to accord) reveals a serious intellectual rift that is currently splitting the women's movement into hostile camps.

As for the "fourth wave" of feminism, the survey results for the Class of 2000 suggest that all this ferment isn't converting most college men and women to the cause.

Selected Survey Results

Feminism

- Freshman women who agree that married women are best at home: 19%
- Men who agree: 30.8%
- Freshman women who agree that abortion should be legal: 56.7%
- Men who do: 55.7%

— From *The American Freshman: National Norms For Fall 1996.*

The Independent Woman
(and Other Lies)

[ESQUIRE / February 1997]

I was out to drinks with a man I'd recently met. "I'll take care of that," he said, sweeping up the check, and as he said it, I felt a warm glow of security, as if everything in my life was suddenly going to be taken care of. As the pink cosmopolitans glided smoothly across the bar, I thought for a moment of how nice it would be to live in an era when men *always* took care of the cosmopolitans. I pictured a lawyer with a creamy leather briefcase going off to work in the mornings and coming back home in the evenings to the townhouse he has bought for me, where I have been ordering flowers, soaking in the bath, reading a nineteenth-century novel, and working idly on my next book. This fantasy of a Man in a Gray Flannel Suit[1] is one that independent, strong-minded women of the nineties are distinctly not supposed to have, but I find myself having it all the same. And many of the women I know are having it also.

Seen from the outside, my life is the model of modern female independence: I live alone, pay my own bills, and fix my stereo when it breaks down. But it sometimes seems like my independence is in part an elaborately constructed facade that hides a more traditional feminine desire to be protected and provided for. I admitted this once to my mother, an ardent seventies feminist, over Caesar salads at lunch, and she was shocked. I saw it on her face: *How could a daughter of mine say something like this?* I rushed to reassure her that I wouldn't dream of giving up my career, and it's true that I wouldn't. But when I think about marriage, somewhere deep in the irrational layers of my psyche, I still think of the man as the breadwinner. I feel as though I am working for "fulfillment," for "reward," for the richness of life promised by feminism, and that mundane things such as

---

[1]Roiphe's fantasy has a literary source: Sloan Wilson's bestseller, *The Man in the Gray Flannel Suit*, was published in 1955 and the following year was made into a film with Gregory Peck.

KATIE ROIPHE (b. 1968) has contributed to the New York Times Magazine *and* Playboy. *She has published two books,* The Morning After: Sex, Fear, and Feminism on Campus *(1993), and most recently,* Last Night in Paradise: Sex and Morals at the Century's End *(1997).*

rent and mortgages and college tuitions are, ultimately, the man's responsibility — even though I know that they shouldn't be. "I just don't want to have to *think* about money," one of my most competent female friends said to me recently, and I knew exactly what she meant. Our liberated, postfeminist world seems to be filled with women who don't want to think about money and men who feel that they have to.

There are plenty of well-adjusted, independent women who never fantasize about the Man in the Gray Flannel suit, but there are also a surprising number who do. Of course, there is a well-established tradition of women looking for men to provide for them that spans from Edith Wharton's *The House of Mirth* to Helen Gurley Brown's *Sex and the Single Girl* to Mona Simpson's *A Regular Guy*. You could almost say that this is the American dream for women: Find a man who can lift you out of your circumstances, whisk you away to Venice, and give you a new life.

In my mother's generation, a woman felt she had to marry a man with a successful career, whereas today she is supposed to focus on her own. Consider that in 1990, women received 42 percent of law degrees (up from 2.5 percent in 1960) and that as of 1992, women held 47 percent of lucrative jobs in the professions and management. And now that American women are more economically independent than ever before, now that we don't *need* to attach ourselves to successful men, many of us still seem to want to. I don't think, in the end, that this attraction is about bank accounts or trips to Paris or hundred-dollar haircuts; I think it's about the reassuring feeling of being protected and provided for, a feeling that mingles with love and attraction on the deepest level. It's strange to think of professional women in the nineties drinking café lattes and talking about men in the same way as characters in Jane Austen novels, appraising their prospects and fortunes, but many of us actually do.

A friend of mine, an editor at a women's magazine, said about a recent   5
breakup, "I just hated having to say, 'My boyfriend is a dog walker.' I hated the fact that he didn't have a real job." And then immediately afterward, she said, "I feel really awful admitting all of this." It was as if she had just told me something shameful, as if she had confessed to some terrible perversion. And I understand why she felt guilty. She was admitting to a sort of 1950s worldview that seemed as odd and unfashionable as walking down the street in a poodle skirt. But she is struggling with what defines masculinity and femininity in a supposedly equal society, with what draws us to men, what attracts us, what keeps us interested. She has no more reason to feel guilty than a man who says he likes tall blonds.

I've heard many women say that they wouldn't want to go out with a man who is much less successful than they are because "he would feel uncomfortable." But, of course, *he's* not the only one who would feel uncomfortable. What most of these women are really saying is that they themselves would feel uncomfortable. But why? Why can't the magazine editor be happy with the dog walker? Why does the woman at Salomon Brothers feel unhappy with the banker who isn't doing as well as she is? Part of it may have to do with the way we were raised. Even though I grew up in a liberal household in the seventies, I perceived early on that my father was the one who actually paid for things. As a little girl, I watched my father put his credit card down in restaurants and write checks and go to work every morning in a suit and tie, and it may be that this model of masculinity is still imprinted in my mind. It may be that there is a picture of our fathers that many of us carry like silver lockets around our necks: Why shouldn't we find a man who will take care of us the way our fathers did?

I've seen the various destructive ways in which this expectation can affect people's lives. Sam and Anna met at Brown. After they graduated, Anna went to Hollywood and started making nearly a million dollars a year in television production and Sam became an aspiring novelist who has never even filed a tax return. At first, the disparity in their styles of life manifested itself in trivial ways. "She would want to go to an expensive bistro," Sam, who is now twenty-seven, remembers, "and I would want to get a burrito for $4.25. We would go to the bistro and either she'd pay, which was bad, or I'd just eat salad and lots of bread, which was also bad." In college, they had been the kind of couple who stayed up until three in the morning talking about art and beauty and *The Brothers Karamazov,* but now they seemed to be spending a lot of time arguing about money and burritos. One night, when they went out with some of Anna's Hollywood friends, she slipped him eighty dollars under the table so that he could pretend to pay for dinner. Anna felt guilty. Sam was confused. He had grown up with a feminist mother who'd drummed the ideal of strong, independent women into his head, but now that he'd fallen in love with Anna, probably the strongest and most independent woman he'd ever met, she wanted him to pay for her dinner so badly she gave him money to do it. Anna, I should say, is not a particularly materialistic person; she is not someone who cares about Chanel suits and Prada bags. It's just that to her, money had become a luminous symbol of functionality and power.

The five-year relationship began to fall apart. Sam was not fulfilling the role of romantic lead in the script Anna had in her head. In a moment of desperation, Sam blurted out that he had made a lot of money on the stock market. He hadn't. Shortly afterward, they broke up. Anna started dating her boss, and she and Sam had agonizing long-distance phone calls about what had happened. "She kept telling me that she wanted me to be more of a man," Sam says. "She kept saying that she wanted to be taken care of." There was a certain irony to this situation, to this woman who was making almost a million dollars a year, sitting in her Santa Monica house, looking out at the ocean, saying that she just wanted a man who could take care of her.

There is also something appalling in this story, something cruel and hard and infinitely understandable. The strain of Anna's success and Sam's as of yet unrewarded talent was too much for the relationship. When Anna told Sam that she wanted him to be more masculine, part of what she was saying was that she wanted to feel more feminine. It's like the plight of the too-tall teenage girl who's anxiously scanning the dance floor for a fifteen-year-old boy who is taller than she is. A romantic might say, What about love? Love isn't supposed to be about dollars and cents and who puts their Visa card down at an expensive Beverly Hills restaurant. But this is a story about love in its more tarnished, worldly forms; it's about the balance of power, what men and women really want from one another, and the hidden mechanics of romance and attraction. In a way, what happened between my friends Sam and Anna is a parable of the times, of a generation of strong women who are looking for even stronger men.

I've said the same thing as Anna — "I need a man who can take care of me" — to more than one boyfriend, and I hear how it sounds. I recognize how shallow and unreasonable it seems. But I say it anyway. And, even worse, I actually feel it.   10

The mood passes. I realize that I can take care of myself. The relationship returns to normal, the boyfriend jokes that I should go to the bar at the Plaza to meet bankers, and we both laugh because we know that I don't really want to, but there is an undercurrent of resentment, eddies of tension, and disappointment that remain between us. This is a secret refrain that runs through conversations in bedrooms late at night, through phone wires, and in restaurants over drinks. One has to wonder why, at a moment in history when women can so patently take care of themselves, do so many of us want so much to be taken care of?

The fantasy of a man who pays the bills, who works when you want to take time off to be with your kids or read *War and Peace,* who is in the end *responsible,* is one that many women have but fairly few admit to. It is one of those fantasies, like rape fantasies, that have been forbidden to us by our politics. But it's also deeply ingrained in our imaginations. All of girl culture tells us to find a man who will provide for us, a Prince Charming, a Mr. Rochester, a Mr. Darcy, and Rhett Butler.[2] These are the objects of our earliest romantic yearnings, the private desires of a whole country of little girls, the fairy tales that actually end up affecting our real lives. As the feminist film critic Molly Haskell says, "We never really escape the old-fashioned roles. They get inside our heads. Dependence has always been eroticized."

Many of the men I know seem understandably bewildered by the fact that women want to be independent only sometimes, only sort of, and only

[2] Mr. Rochester, Mr. Darcy, and Rhett Butler are the leading male characters in, respectively, Charlotte Brontë's *Jane Eyre* (1847), Jane Austen's *Pride and Prejudice* (1813), and Margaret Mitchell's *Gone with the Wind* (1936).

selectively. The same women who give eloquent speeches at dinner parties on the subject of "glass ceilings" still want men to pay for first dates, and this can be sort of perplexing for the men around them who are still trying to fit into the puzzle that the feminism of the seventies has created for them. For a long time, women have been saying that we don't want a double standard, but it sometimes seems that what many women want is simply a more subtle and refined version of a double standard: We want men to be the providers *and* to regard us as equals. This slightly unreasonable expectation is not exactly new. In 1963, a reporter asked Mary McCarthy[3] what women really wanted, and she answered, "They want everything. That's the trouble — they can't have everything. They can't possibly have all the prerogatives of being a woman and the privileges of being a man at the same time."

"We're spoiled," says Helen Gurley Brown, one of the world's foremost theorists on dating. "We just don't want to give up any of the good stuff." And she may have a point. In a world in which women compete with men, in which all of us are feeling the same drive to succeed, there is something reassuring about falling — if only for the length of a dinner — into traditional sex roles. You can just relax. You can take a rest from yourself. You can let the pressures and ambitions melt away and give in to the archaic fantasy: For just half an hour, you are just a pretty girl smiling at a man over a drink. I think that old-fashioned rituals, such as men paying for dates, endure precisely because of how much *has* actually changed; they cover up the fact that men and women *are* equal and that equality is not always, in all contexts and situations, comfortable or even desirable.

This may explain why I have been so ungratefully day-dreaming about   15
the Man in the Gray Flannel Suit thirty years after Betty Friedan published *The Feminine Mystique*. The truth is, the knowledge that I *can* take care of myself, that I don't really need a man, is not without its own accompanying terrors. The idea that I could make myself into a sleek, self-sufficient androgyne is not all that appealing. Now that we have all of the rooms of our own that we need, we begin to look for that shared and crowded space. And it is this fear of independence, this fear of *not* needing a man, that explains the voices of more competent, accomplished corporate types than me saying to the men around them, "Provide for me, protect me." It may be one of the bad jokes that history occasionally plays on us: that the independence my mother's generation wanted so much for their daughters was something we could not entirely appreciate or want. It was like a

---

[3] The American novelist and intellectual, Mary McCarthy (1912–1989) published *The Group*, a novel about young college women, in 1963, the same year that Betty Friedan came out with *The Feminine Mystique* and Sylvia Plath's *The Bell Jar* appeared in England.

birthday present from a distant relative — wrong size, wrong color, wrong style. And so women are left struggling with the desire to submit and not submit, to be dependent and independent, to take care of ourselves and be taken care of, and it's in the confusion of this struggle that most of us love and are loved.

For myself, I continue to go out with poets and novelists and writers, and with men who don't pay for dates or buy me dresses at Bergdorf's or go off to their offices in the morning, but the Man in the Gray Flannel Suit lives on in my imagination, perplexing, irrational, revealing of some dark and unsettling truth.

Responding as a Reader

1. This essay appeared in *Esquire,* which is subtitled "The Magazine for Men." Why do you think Roiphe sent this article to *Esquire?* How is this article supposed to make men feel?

2. Consider the story of Anna and Sam (paras. 7–9). What does Anna mean when she tells Sam that she wants him "to be more of a man"? What does Roiphe mean when she writes that Anna "wanted to be more feminine"? How do these definitions of gender roles influence the definition of feminism?

3. Why does Roiphe describe herself as "ungrateful" (para. 15). Ungrateful to whom? For what? Do you think she truly feels ungrateful? How can you tell?

4. How does Roiphe try to persuade her readers that the "Man in the Gray Flannel Suit" is not merely her own personal fantasy but represents a fantasy shared by many women of her generation? Does Roiphe convince you that her experiences and ideals represent those of many women her age? What aspects of her life do you personally find typical; what aspects do you find atypical?

Responding as a Writer

1. Why exactly is it that women of the nineties are *not supposed to* wish for a big strong man to take care of them? What *are* they supposed to wish for? And who says? In a few paragraphs, lay out the two schools of thought and explain the conflict between them. You might want to bring in the woman in the coffee shop in Jenny McPhee's editorial (p. 133) and the responses to the editorial.

2. Roiphe identifies "the American dream for women" as: "Find a man who can lift you out of your circumstances, whisk you away to Venice, and give you a new life" (para. 3). In an essay, explore the origins of

this dream and compare it to the "American dream for men." Are the two in conflict or compatible? You might also want to propose an alternate success fantasy for women, for men, or for both.

3. Consider Mary McCarthy's answer to the question "What do women want?" (para. 13) and Helen Gurley Brown's (para. 14). In your experience, what *do* women want? What do men want? What do *you* want (regardless of your gender) in the big picture? Do you believe these desires to be reasonable? Do you believe these desires to be in conflict with what members of the opposite sex want, or with what society says you should want, or with what is good for society? Attempt to answer these questions in an essay, exploring the connection between desire, expectation, and achievement.

Exchange

A Feminist Redefined, with Replies

The following editorial by Jenny McPhee ran on the March 4,1997, opinion page of the New York Times. *The paper received so many angry responses from readers arguing with McPhee's take on feminism that the letters ran over three separate days. We're reprinting McPhee's original piece and three of the letters to the editor.*

The other day, I was having lunch in a croissant shop in midtown Manhattan and eavesdropping on the people sitting at the next table. A twenty-something college-educated woman was describing her wedding plans in detail to a friend. Between discussing how much the caterer would cost and what color the bridesmaids' dresses would be, she said, with considerable embarrassment, "I can't believe I'm actually doing this, that I'm talking about me doing this. But if I don't get excited about it, who will?"

I find the subject of weddings fascinating, so I kept listening as she justified her choice of band and church, made clear why her ex-boyfriend was in the wedding party, and explained her decision not to use the designation "Ms." in addressing her invitations to women. "It just seems so, well, professional," she said, looking inside her sandwich. Then, with a bit of hesitation, she added, "I just don't want people to think that I'm, you know, a feminist or anything."

For a long time now, I've been trying to figure out what it is about that word that gives women so much trouble. The definition of feminism in my Webster's is the following: "1. Feminine character or characteristics; also, a feminine expression. 2. The theory, cult, or practice of those who advocate

continued on next page

continued from previous page

such legal and social changes as will establish political, economic, and social equality of the sexes; propaganda or activity favoring the emancipation of women." Given that definition, what woman in her right mind wouldn't be proud to call herself a feminist?

I have heard many blame the feminist movement itself for having alienated women from the cause. Feminism, they claim, has surrendered to the will of radicals and extremists, has become splintered and factious, does not have a unified and truly representative voice.

I don't buy it. All movements are fraught with extremism, infighting, and power struggles. The problem with feminism goes much deeper, and the woman in the croissant shop gave me a clue: shame.

Women are deeply ashamed of themselves for being women. At a moment that is clearly of utmost significance to this woman — her wedding — she is apologetic and ashamed of herself for taking center stage. Why isn't she saying, "This is important, this is about me"?

If a woman can't allow herself to feel proud and powerful at her own wedding — a traditional rite in which a woman is both central and celebrated — then how will she feel in situations where the circumstances aren't necessarily favorable, like applying for a job or running for office?

Which brings me to the dictionary's first definition of "feminism." The word "feminism" is rooted in the concept of the feminine, and women are as prejudiced as men against the feminine, especially where issues of power are concerned. In the public sphere (with the exception of Hollywood), most women do not find power in the so-called characteristics of our sex — from physical beauty to a reluctance to compete. We are afraid of being labeled bimbos or ineffective.

Traditionally, we have sought power through association with a male — usually father or husband. More recently, some women have gained power by assuming androgynous appearances and acting more aggressively. I do not mean that women (or men for that matter) should not exploit male characteristics. I'm just sorry that women don't see their identity as something to be proud of, as something that doesn't need to be modified.

As women, as feminists, one of our greatest challenges is to claim the power of our feminine character — whatever we choose it to be. As the woman in the croissant shop said to her friend, If we don't get excited about it, who will?

Replies

To the Editor:

How can Jenny McPhee (Op-Ed, March 4) write that Webster's definition of feminism would make any woman "in her right mind" proud of being a feminist?

In our culture, most people do not flock to movements that are associated with "cult" and "propaganda." One reason women feel the "shame" that Ms. McPhee refers to is the notion her article seems to support: that women (and apparently only they) should be exclusively and exceptionally powerful, central, celebrated, and proud on their wedding day.

What about all the other days in their lives?

Alex Bergier
Brooklyn, NY, March 6, 1997

To the Editor:

Re "A Feminist Redefined" (Op-Ed, March 4): Like many women I know, I am tired of talking about feminism and whether I am one or should be one. It irks me that overhearing a conversation in a croissant shop leads to a sweeping statement like "women are deeply ashamed of themselves for being women."

The same conversation could lead one to think that the young woman Jenny McPhee overhead is confused by the message that society and the media send her: that being married is not compatible with being a feminist. One might also conjecture that she is confused not just by her wedding logistics but by the prospect of adding the titles of wife and mother to her job description, roles that have been labeled incompatible with feminism.

Sarah T. Connell Campbell
Groton, Mass., March 4, 1997

To the Editor:

Jenny McPhee (Op-Ed, March 4) asserts that women who don't want to be identified with feminism must be ashamed of being women. She subtly attempts to shift the blame for feminism's unpopularity to men, for it is men who must make women ashamed to be women.

For Ms. McPhee, this is just another way in which women are victimized. But for women who don't want to be identified as victims, who believe in the community of men and women, who believe in something like a traditional family, feminism has made itself unattractive. The estrangement between radical feminists and our society has become worse even as women have made progress.

Roderic Fabian
Friendswood, Tex., March 4, 1997

— From the *New York Times* (March 4, 6, and 10, 1997).

Lipstick Liberation [THE BOSTON PHOENIX / May 30, 1997]

Dear Publisher,

Enough about you. Let's talk about me.

Me, me, me.

Childhood extraordinarily ordinary. Family abnormally normal. Adolescence momentously unmomentous. Life to date remarkably unremarkable.

Could pass for twentysomething. Could pass for writer. Took women's-studies courses in college. Feel guilty for skipping Take Back the Night march junior year. Feel guilty about spending $16 on Vamp. Don't want to feel guilty anymore. Will fess up, when pushed, to angst about place in universe. Will, if absolutely necessary, recount tragically horrifically embarrassingly ill-advised sexual encounters from pre-Vamp era.

Therefore, judging by current spate of books on market, am eminently qualified to write memoir or, better yet, memoir-ish postfeminist text (with portrait of brooding but attractive self on jacket, please?), drawing heavily on highly typical personal experience as proof of central arguments re: current state of women.

Thesis of book: oppression by men no longer main problem for feminists. New culprit? Feminism itself.

Please send contract.

Seems like only yesterday that traditional feminism was looking pretty darn healthy. In 1991, Susan Faludi's *Backlash: The Undeclared War Against American Women* and Naomi Wolf's *The Beauty Myth* were released, both challenging the Virginia Slims version of women's progress: *A long way, baby? Yeah, right.* Both books were hits, lingering on best-seller lists for months. And the 1991 Clarence Thomas confirmation hearings galvanized women into such a state of pissed-offedness that they swept unprecedented numbers into government in the 1992 election. Heady days for feminists.

But they didn't last long. Hot on the — one hesitates to say heels — of *Backlash* and *The Beauty Myth* have come a steady run of books and articles. Many of these are by women who were born with choices their mothers couldn't take for granted; all writers identify themselves as feminists; and all of the books take a dim view of traditional feminism. Among them

YVONNE ABRAHAM *(b. 1966) is a staff writer at the* Boston Phoenix, *where she covers city politics, race, and most anything else. She has also written for* George, Boston *magazine, and Australian magazines* HQ *and* Good Weekend.

are Katie Roiphe's *The Morning After: Sex, Fear, and Feminism on Campus*; Christina Hoff Sommers's *Who Stole Feminism? How Women Have Betrayed Women*; Rebecca Walker's *To Be Real: Telling the Truth and Changing the Face of Feminism*; and Rene Denfeld's *The New Victorians: A Young Woman's Challenge to the Old Feminist Order*. Even Naomi Wolf, herself a target of these critiques, has been inching closer to this group of late.

The books spawned talk-show appearances, articles, op-eds, and such, most notably a piece in *Esquire* about "do me" feminism, a piece in *Ms.* in which Faludi refers to Roiphe *et al.* as "pod feminists," an article in *Mother Jones* in which journalist Karen Lehrman says women's studies is a ludicrous crock, and another recent *Esquire* piece [see p. 127] in which Roiphe says she wants some big, protective guy to just come take care of her, please (and she knows that's what you want, too, deep down).

There are few signs that the stream of publications will let up anytime soon. This past month or two has seen new titles by Wolf, Denfeld, and Roiphe and a first book from Lehrman: *The Lipstick Proviso: Women, Sex and Power in the Real World*.

It's been referred to variously as postfeminism, revisionist feminism, 5 postideological feminism, and liberal feminism, but the label that's sticking best these days is "third-wave feminism." The first wave — the women's suffrage movement — began feminism by planting the idea that women deserve equal rights under the law. But it's the second wave that has defined modern feminism. "The personal is political" was the movement's classic slogan: All the extra burdens women are forced to bear privately — from harassment to domestic abuse — are social problems that demand public solutions.

The third wave defines itself primarily in contrast to the second. Despite these writers' many differences (most of them wouldn't be caught dead with the others), the upshot of their work is that traditional second-wave feminism has made women's lives more difficult than they should be. It has put more demands on them than they should have to handle, elided the personal in favor of the political, and relegated women to what Rebecca Walker calls "a feminist ghetto."

It's unlikely that third-wave feminists will be relegated to any kind of ghetto: They're too marketable. Unlike their second-wave forebears, they're completely in sync with their times and, more significant, with publishing trends. These days, sensational personal revelations get big-time attention and are sure ways to move books and boost TV ratings. These feminists wisely exploit that, many of them peppering their analysis with compelling personal details, or vice versa.

When they write about traditional feminism's underappreciation of the personal obstacles some women still battle, and the gains many of them have made, third wavers have something of a point. But they go too far.

Second-wave feminists, confronted with a world that revolved around men, wanted — and in some measure got — a world that also revolved around women. Third-wave feminists write as if the world revolved around *them:* not men, not women, but them. In so doing, they help shift debate about women's lives from larger — and still vital — political and economic questions to individual dilemmas over cosmetics, fetishes, and guilt. Like some kind of fantastic whirlybird, third-wave writers fly in smaller and smaller circles, zooming in on ever more personal issues, threatening finally to disappear up their own media-savvy behinds, taking feminism — and, most important, the causes of less lucky women — with them.

"Bell Hooks calls this the patriarchal pulpit," says Rebecca Walker, by   10
way of introduction, as she steps up to the lectern at the front of Faneuil Hall [in Boston] for a Ford Hall Forum in late March. "But I hope to create a more interactive experience. I hope we can have a real time of sharing together."

Walker, editor of an anthology of writing by young women and men called *To Be Real* (in its fourth printing) and head of the women's activist group Third Wave, is tall and hip, with curly hair cut close to her head. Her silver rings catch the lights whenever she moves her hands, which is often. She seems completely at ease before the hundred or so mostly young, mostly rapt women looking up at her. She sprinkles her speech with pop references only the younger folks in the audience would understand. They nod and laugh appreciatively.

At age 27, Walker is already a veteran of such appearances, one of *Time* magazine's 50 future leaders of America and a face of late-'90s feminism. "I want to tell you a bit about what was going on in my life when I put this book together," she continues, "I realized that not only would people in my generation have to redefine feminism, but I would, too. That terrified me."

Traditional feminism is mostly about women. Third-wave writing, by contrast, is mostly about feminism. As a critique of the second wave, the third wave makes enough sense to be appealing. And by repackaging it for younger women, third-wave writers give feminism serious style and accessibility points.

Which it apparently needs quite badly. A 1992 *Time* magazine survey found that although 57 percent of respondents believed there was still a need for a women's movement, only 29 percent thought of themselves as feminists. When Toni Troop, president of the Greater Boston branch of the National Organization for Women, talks to young women in high schools and colleges, "More than 80 percent of them come down unequivocally in favor of women's rights," she says. "But if you ask them if they're feminists, they're not so sure."

"It felt to me like younger women felt discomfort identifying with fem-   15
inism in general," says Walker. "And from the older women there was a lot of disdain and a real lack of understanding of the perspective of the younger women."

Walker is more respectful of the feminism of her mother, Alice Walker,[1] and of her godmother, Gloria Steinem, than some of her contemporaries are. Both she and Naomi Wolf hold more-traditional feminist positions than do Denfeld, Roiphe, and especially Lehrman. But they share a fundamental complaint: They feel oppressed, to varying degrees, by traditional feminism. Despite its many achievements, second-wave feminism has become a thorn in young women's sides. For some of Walker's contemporaries, it has even become the enemy.

Backlash, The Beauty Myth, feminist lawyer Catharine MacKinnon, antipornography activist Andrea Dworkin, NOW, *Ms.* magazine — they're all selling a brand of feminism, and a view of women, that doesn't quite fit anymore. Too political, overly pessimistic, stuck on conspiracy theories, not mindful enough of women's individual experiences. By contrast, third-wave writers put women's private lives — particularly their own — front and center.

"There's this continual need to overpoliticize many issues I now feel are personal issues," says *Lipstick Proviso* author Karen Lehrman. "That takes the responsibility off women and puts it on society and government, and I think women themselves need to do it."

Even Naomi Wolf, whose *The Beauty Myth* has been much criticized by third-wave writers, has modified her tune. "The thesis of books like *Backlash* and *The Beauty Myth* are true," she says, "but that's not the whole truth. The mindset of the second wave is far more primed to lead a young writer like me to do the conspiratorial analysis of how women are victimized rather than how we can end our victimization." Second-wave feminism's us-versus-them mentality, Wolf says, "is not very spiritually evolved."

Walker reads from *To Be Real,* from her own introduction: "A year   20
before I started this book, my life was like a feminist ghetto. Every decision I made, person I spent time with, word I uttered, had to measure up to an image I had in mind of what was morally and politically right according to my vision of female empowerment."

Then she reads from several essays, including one by a woman guilt-ridden about liking misogynist hip-hop and another by Naomi Wolf about her discomfort with her own white wedding. All of the essays are about their authors' struggles to apply feminism to their lives a generation after the women's movement as we know it began.

And they seem to agree that the struggle is harder than it should be — harder precisely because the previous generation of feminists achieved so much. Traditional feminism is still spouting fire and revolutionary zeal when — hello *Roe v. Wade,* Pat Schroeder, Hillary, family leave, soccer moms — lots of good stuff has already happened for women. Second-wave

---

[1] Rebecca Walker's mother, Alice Walker, one of America's highly esteemed writers, is the author of the novel *The Color Purple* and several major collections of essays.

feminism, they argue, needs to chill out and stop telling women what to do and how to act to qualify as good feminists.

Traditional feminism, says Roiphe, raised awareness of date rape, but it went too far — making all women into powerless victims, taking the fun out of sex. Feminism has rightly exposed the wrongs of men, says Denfeld, but now persecutes them, and relegates women to the quasi-Victorian status of long-suffering victims. Feminism has successfully introduced women's studies in colleges, but classes have turned into kooky, back-rubby, group-therapy victimhood sessions, says Lehrman, who also argues that feminism denies women their femininity. Feminism has put the kibosh on chivalry, a fact both Lehrman and Roiphe lament. And it has devalued motherhood, making women feel as if they *have* to combine high-powered careers and family even when they don't really want to.

For younger women who reaped the benefits of the women's movement, such criticisms make sense: Women's studies can be overly therapeutic; some feminists do see women as helpless victims and all men as potential rapists; and some traditional feminists do underestimate the gains women have made since the '60s and '70s. For those women, a feminism based on the assumption that women can't take personal responsibility for their own lives is mildly offensive.

And third-wave writers, eminently marketable in a publishing climate   25
where marketing is all, present women like themselves with an attractive, free-to-be-me alternative to traditional feminism. Mostly in their 20s or early 30s, stylish and cool, these writers stare out from moody black-and-whites on their book jackets. They infuse their work with pop-culture references, writing refreshingly, candidly, and optimistically about sex and clothes. They celebrate young women's freedom and are comfortable assuming they have plenty of choices.

What's not to like?

During question time, Rebecca Walker gets plenty of gushy softballs. A skinny young man from McGill reverently asks her, "Where are we supposed to come out of all this?"

"There's no rule book that tells you what it means to be a feminist," Walker replies. "I'm hoping that *To Be Real* gives people their own space, to dig around in their own psyches. I'm looking for a feminism that is decentralized."

Next, a young black woman, who looks to be about Walker's age, steps up to the microphone. "We've been passing your book around, the four of us," she says, pointing to her friends, "and we really love it. My question is, what do you think qualifies you to put this anthology together?"

Walker puts her hand to her chest, gives the woman a quizzical look,   30
recomposes herself. "That's an interesting question," she says. "I'll try to take that as a gentle question and not an antagonistic one. Um, that's pretty interesting. What makes you ask that question?"

It was simple enough, really, and innocently meant. But it requires a shift in thinking that many of Walker's contemporaries seem to have difficulty making. Third-wave writers are central to their own works; they're qualified to hold forth on the fallout from second-wave feminism, and on the situation of women, because they're living it. Period. No one, after all, would ask what qualifies someone to write a memoir — a form to which much third-wave writing comes very close.

"Well," Walker replies. "I've been thinking about this stuff for a long time, and I'm as entitled as any other artist or thinker."

As a critique of traditional feminism, third-wave writing makes sense for many women. But a critique of feminism does not a women's movement make. As much as they criticize second-wave feminists for being overly prescriptive and for failing to appreciate each woman's uniqueness, third-wave writers allow their own lives and experiences to determine their view of where feminism's priorities should be. And their own lives and experiences are vastly different from most women's.

To Be Real is composed almost entirely of first-person pieces by writers digging around in their own psyches, as Walker puts it. Roiphe's *The Morning After*, about date-rape hype on college campuses, also draws on her own experiences (of hype, not rape). Her *Last Night in Paradise* is about sexual repression, again drawing heavily on her life and on that of her HIV-positive sister. Naomi Wolf's latest, *Promiscuities: The Secret Struggle for Womanhood*, about the torture of girls' sexual awakening, goes into great detail about her own San Francisco adolescence. And Karen Lehrman, who in a March 30 [1997] *Washington Post* article derided the current memoir epidemic ("Gratuitous displays of a woman's sexual proclivities or emotional angst aren't necessarily empowering"), begins each of her chapters in *The Lipstick Proviso* with an episode from her personal life.

As the swarm of Prozac-, alcohol-, and incest-laden memoirs foisted on the American public lately shows only too well, that kind of thing sells — or at least gets airtime and ink. And these books are riding that trend. Those marketing folk don't get the big bucks for nothing.

Naomi Wolf, for one, maintains that personal details make feminist books more accessible to women. But there's a danger in it, too. Self-absorption in a memoir, tiresome or no, is kind of the point. In some of these feminist books, though, the writers use their own experiences to drive their arguments, drawing from them major conclusions about women and feminism, apparently believing their own experiences to be distillations of all women's.

To wit: in *The Morning After*, Katie Roiphe challenges the statistics for acquaintance rape on college campuses: If so many women are being raped, she asks, wouldn't she know some of them? In *The Lipstick Proviso*, one of Lehrman's main arguments is that sisterhood — the idea that women have common political interests, a linchpin of traditional feminism — is a myth

("I am a sister only to my brother," she writes). To start that chapter, Lehrman tells the story of her friend "Nena": "tall and thin with cool retro glasses," spouter of antipatriarchal proverbs, roommate of Lehrman's boyfriend. You can see where this is going: When Lehrman breaks up with her boyfriend, Nena promptly snatches him for herself. "Since then, I've been far more alert to women who treat other women with less than sisterly affection," Lehrman writes. "Artificial sisterhood is not only a crock, as Nena demonstrated," she concludes. "It is also not especially empowering."

Both Lehrman and Roiphe might have perfectly good points about date rape and sisterhood, but where they run aground is that having subjected the reader to their misty watercolors, they then take the next step and say, "As I go, so go all women."

But Katie Roiphe is not like all women. She grew up in an Upper West Side brownstone, with *Up the Sandbox* author Anne Roiphe for a mother; she had a Princeton education and a book contract before age 25. Rebecca Walker's mother is an even more famous writer; Naomi Wolf's parents were ultraliberal, and liberated, San Francisco academics. None of this means that their experiences are any less valid than other women's, but it does seem scary to suggest that conclusions about the lives of American women — the welfare mother in Lawrence or the housewife in Quincy — can be extrapolated from those of Roiphe *et al.* This is hardly a novel criticism. Second-wave feminists have been criticized for being similarly out of touch with ordinary women. But second- and third-wave feminists were born into very different worlds and are out of touch in very different ways. Second-wave feminists faced the same legislative and political obstacles to their rights as poorer or nonprofessional women did. Third-wave feminists, who reaped the benefits of the movement politically, do not face many of the problems their less lucky counterparts do. Before 1973, for example, no woman could get a legal abortion, whatever her economic situation. Now it's just poor women who can't get them. Before protections were in place against sexual harassment, all women had little choice but to put up with it. Now, that's true only of women who lack the resources and knowledge to pursue harassment claims. But from where your garden-variety postfeminist sits — *i.e.,* at the center of the universe — things are looking pretty good. "There will always be a need for vigilance," writes Karen Lehrman, "But many of the problems that plague most women (in the West) on a daily basis now fall in the personal realm; government can do little to solve them."

Unwittingly or not, third-wave writers give the strong impression that   40
the world is now kind to women, thereby ceding important ground to critics of feminism and to those who would undo the gains of the second wave. By moving feminism's agenda from politics and economics to bedrooms and cosmetics counters, third-wave writers effectively sidestep many of the serious problems that still beset women and undermine attempts to fix them.

There's no denying that women's lives have improved more in one generation than they did over the previous century. Nor is it unreasonable to expect those women who can take more responsibility for their own lives and happiness to do so. However, if second-wave feminists are overly pessimistic about women in the '90s, third-wave writers are overly optimistic.

If you were to take a snapshot of women in America even now, it wouldn't be a pretty picture. White women still earn only seventy-one cents for every dollar a white man earns. Over 95 percent of this country's top executives are still white men. Domestic abuse is the leading cause of injury for women between fifteen and forty-four, and 1.8 million women were seriously assaulted by men in the last twelve months. Over 90,000 rapes are reported each year. Many women still have inadequate access to birth control and face insurmountable obstacles to abortion. For some women, none of the old problems have gone away, despite feminism's huge victories.

Indeed, talk to any feminist activist and she'll tell you that things have actually been sliding for women lately: State legislatures all over the country have limited access to abortion for minors, setting parental consent and waiting-period rules. Welfare-reform legislation affects women far more than men, imposing family caps without adequately providing for good birth control and work requirements without child care for many women.

"Where is it that we've entered the promised land," Susan Faludi scoffs, "other than in our choice of lipstick?"

And, contrary to what their popular image suggests, most feminists do deal with those kinds of problems. NOW, that bulwark of second-wave feminism, and a favorite piñata of postideological feminists, spends much of its energies helping women for whom lingerie guilt is a long way off. The Boston office gets about twenty calls a week from women seeking counsel because they're being sexually harassed at work, or are losing too much in a divorce, or being paid too little compared to male equivalents. NOW's Toni Troop and her colleagues are also lobbying private companies to extend domestic-partner benefits to employees and to accommodate working mothers with flextime and other work arrangements.

And Emily's List, the political-action committee begun almost twelve years ago, is working to further enfranchise women, raising money — these days, lots of it — to get women elected to office. There are nine women in the U.S. Senate (and 91 men), and only 51 women in the 435-member House. "If we relied on the traditional structures in place," says Karin Johanson, communications director for the PAC [Political Action Committee], "we wouldn't even have *that* many women in office." Women senators and legislators have won increased funding for research into breast cancer, fought welfare-reform legislation, and opposed assaults on women's reproductive freedoms.

And both organizations are healthy. NOW's membership, which surged after the Anita Hill–Clarence Thomas controversy, has remained

45

steady at 200,000. Emily's List, which women joined in droves after those hearings, has grown to 66,000 members. Although the marginal extremes of traditional feminism may well bear little connection to real women's lives, the rest of the movement still plays an important role in them.

Yet many third-wave critiques of feminism remain fixated on those extremes. In other words, Roiphe, Lehrman, Denfeld, and company have taken the silly fringes, academic edges, and media stereotypes of the women's movement, balled them up into a big ol' hairy-legged straw woman, and are beating away. "Lehrman, like a lot of women her age, was raised on a particular brand of feminism, which wasn't really feminism but pop culture's version of feminism," says Faludi, who has gone head-to-head with Lehrman recently, most notably in the online magazine *Slate* [see p. 152]. "It's the consumer-culture idea that you can have it all. She feels feminism has cheated her because she can't be the Aviance woman, where you come home looking ravishing and fry up the bacon. There's this disconnect between what feminism is about and what it became once it was mediated through TV screens."

"I confess," writes Gloria Steinem in her foreword to *To Be Real*, "that there are moments in these pages when I — and perhaps other readers over thirty-five — feel like a sitting dog being told to sit." Motherhood, lipstick, and miniskirts have always been a part of the women's movement, she notes.

But since they've shifted their emphasis from the public world of politics and social problems and onto women's private lives, third-wave writers are predisposed to diminish, or overlook, the important political- and social-activism work feminists do and to concentrate instead on their intrusion into women's personal lives.

By painting traditional feminists as a kind of PC police force, they inadvertently perpetuate the stereotypes that continue to alienate women from feminism. And they provide extra ammunition for the Rush Limbaughs of the world, who don't discriminate between second- and third-wave feminists.

Certainly, there are third-wave writers who still see the political as vital to feminism. "In our personal lives, we're finding things are much more fuzzy and complicated," Rebecca Walker says, "but in the world, there's nothing fuzzy and complicated about the welfare bill." Walker's Third Wave activist group continues along the more traditional lines of a NOW or an Emily's List. "Thank God," says Walker. "Otherwise I'd be screwed — and skewered."

Ditto Naomi Wolf. Despite her shift from too-simple second-wave feminism, Wolf is more heavily involved politically now than ever, having advised White House policymakers on women's issues and worked to improve the situations of women refugees and prostitutes.

However, all of those are-men-really-that-bad-all-I-really-need-is-a-good-one *Esquire* stories add up to something, and, like it or not, third-wave feminists helped to put them there. The logical extension of even the most respectful third-wave writing is *The Lipstick Proviso,* in which Lehrman makes the mind-boggling observation that "The huge main problem with contemporary feminism is that it has attached itself to a political agenda." (She also gladly concedes that "Activism supporting abortion rights and battered women and rape-crisis work is incredibly important, and we need to do more of it." Go figure.)

Welfare reform, which affects so many more women than men, is   55 "outside the scope of feminism," she says. "The problem that poor women exist is not a problem of feminism," she continues, "it's a problem of class. The point of feminism is equality of opportunity for women, not equality of result."

But class problems and women's problems are inextricable. What to do when political acts affect women far more adversely than men? That welfare reform has effectively nixed equality of opportunity for some women recipients — by, say, relegating them to minimum-wage jobs indefinitely — has apparently not occurred to Lehrman.

Because it sucks the politics — and therefore women's most intractable problems — out of feminism, Lehrman's work dovetails perfectly with the current political climate in this country. "It's part of a larger dynamic in the culture," says Faludi, "in which people are urged to turn their eyes away from political concerns and inward, and not in a spiritual way, either. Forget about the political revolutionary pursuits: just have a revolution with your Nike sneakers. It takes all the language of political rhetoric and hollows it out."

It occurs to few in the third wave to see feminism's decline in the context of America's retreat from all kinds of labels and politics since the Republican landslide of 1994. It's not just feminism that's a dirty word these days. "Liberal" is having such a rough time of it that even our Democrat president has trouble saying the word, choosing instead wishy-washy, jello terms like "the politics of meaning" and various and sundry verses from Isaiah. Maybe it's not just feminism that's out of sync with today's world: It's the idea of holding any political philosophy at all.

What's left is Spice Girls feminism. As "Scary Spice" Mel B put it in a recent *Entertainment Weekly* interview: "You can wear your Wonderbra, you can wear your mascara, but you've got a bit of intelligence. . . . Don't rely on your sexuality, but don't be afraid of it."

"Just because you've got a short skirt on and a pair of tits, you can still   60 say what you want to say. We're still very strong," Baby Spice Emma chimes in. Heavy.

The Spice Girls have been anointed a feminist pop outfit by more than a few writers. The Spicies themselves prefer the term Girl Power: Personal, and especially sexual, empowerment is central to their act. And sexy feminism certainly works as a marketing approach (the fact that the quintet churning out the prefab Brit-pop also have good abs and producers helps, too). They take feminism's shell and fill it up with lip gloss, ribbed condoms, and girls-on-top innuendo. Nobody tells the Spice Girls what to do. They're young and stylish and sexy as they wannabe. And they chew men up and spit 'em out:

> I won't be hasty. I'll give you a try
> If you really bug me then I'll say goodbye.

It's balder and tackier, but it's very much like what many third-wave writers are saying: If every woman felt that free, we'd all be fine.

Feminism should now concern itself with "personal work," Karen Lehrman says. "Under real feminism," she writes, "women have ultimate responsibility for their problems, happiness, and lives.

"The personal, in other words, is no longer political." Instead of agitating on Capitol Hill, feminists would do better to revive consciousness-raising groups for poor women, says Lehrman: It's all about self-esteem now. Which is distressingly close to the touchy-feeliness she pillories in much of her work.

None of the other third-wave writers goes quite as far as Lehrman, but hers is the logical conclusion of feminism's retreat into the personal. Girl Power has its limits. Take away the sexual freedom and the guiltless push-up bras and you're not left with much.

"For so many of these women," says Faludi, "what they want to break off and call feminism is their own personal advancement, their own personal freedoms, their own personal choices, so feminism must be about what I want to wear, about fashion and beauty and flirting at the office. Here's our new brand of feminism. Tastes good, less filling."

Problem is, a lot of women need something more substantial.

> But enough about them. Let's talk about me.
> Me, me, me.
> Childhood extraordinarily ordinary . . .

Responding as a Reader

1. What is the function of the opening "Dear Publisher" letter? What is its tone? Is it written in Abraham's own voice or some other voice? What seems to be Abraham's attitude toward the writer of the letter? How does the letter relate to the rest of the article?

2. Abraham mentions a large number of women who call themselves feminists: Susan Faludi, Naomi Wolf, Katie Roiphe, Christina Hoff Sommers, Rebecca Walker, Alice Walker, Rene Denfield, Karen Lehrman, Catharine MacKinnon, Andrea Dworkin, Anne Roiphe, Toni Troop,

Karin Johanson, Gloria Steinem . . . and don't forget Abraham herself. How would you classify the different attitudes toward feminism represented by these women? Which person, for example, strikes you as most radical? Who seems to be most mainstream? Which remarks lead you to these impressions?

3. Read the exchange between Susan Faludi and Karen Lehrman that begins on page 144. After reading these writers' own words, do you feel that Abraham has represented their views fairly? Look also at the pieces by Katie Roiphe (p. 127) and Christina Hoff Sommers (p. 148). Do you agree with the way Abraham has characterized them?

Responding as a Writer

1. "It's been referred to variously as postfeminism, revisionist feminism, postideological feminism, and liberal feminism, but the label that's sticking best these days is 'third-wave feminism'" (para. 5). Which of these names for the current phase of feminism do you prefer and why? Can you think of a more appropriate name?

2. Consider the statistics in paragraph 14. What does being a feminist seem to mean to the young women who were polled? Why do you think most of these women choose not to identify themselves as feminists? List the measures that the Third Wave is taking to appeal to younger women and speculate about how effective these measures will be.

3. Who are these leaders of third-wave feminism? What constituency do they represent? Who exactly are they speaking for and who *aren't* they speaking for? In an essay, lay out the primary needs of American women and the changes that would be most beneficial to all American women. Is today's feminist movement addressing these needs?

The "Fragile American Girl" Myth

[AMERICAN ENTERPRISE / May–June 1997]

Did you know that the United States Congress now categorizes American girls as "a historical underserved population"? In a recent education statute, girls are classified with African Americans, native Americans, the physically handicapped, and other disadvantaged minorities as a group in need of special redress. Programs to help girls who have allegedly been silenced and demoralized in the nation's sexist classrooms are now receiving millions of federal dollars. At the United Nations women's conference in Beijing, the alleged silencing and short-changing of American schoolgirls was treated as a pressing human rights issue.

Several popular books have appeared in recent years to build up the notion that ours is a "girl-poisoning culture." That phrase is Dr. Mary Pipher's and her book, *Reviving Ophelia: Saving the Selves of Adolescent Girls,* has been at the top of the *New York Times* bestseller list. According to Pipher, "Something dramatic happens to girls in early adolescence. Just as planes and ships disappear mysteriously into the Bermuda Triangle, so do the selves of girls go down in droves. They crash and burn."

Where did she get this idea? Where did the United States Congress get the idea that girls are a victim group? How did the "silencing" of American schoolgirls become an international human rights issue?

To answer that, consider some highlights of what might be called the myth of the incredible shrinking girl. The story epitomizes what is wrong with the contemporary women's movement. First, a few facts.

The U.S. Department of Education keeps records of male and female 5 school achievement. They reveal that girls get better grades than boys. Boys are held back more often than girls. Significantly fewer boys than girls go on to college today. Girls are a few points behind in national tests of math

---

CHRISTINA HOFF SOMMERS *(b. 1950) is an associate professor of philosophy at Clark University who specializes in contemporary moral theory. Her articles have appeared in publications such as the* New Republic, *the* Wall Street Journal, *the* Chicago Tribune, *and the* New England Journal of Medicine, *among others. She has edited two ethics textbooks, published numerous professional papers, and is the author of* Who Stole Feminism? *published in 1994. This selection is adapted from her remarks at a December 1996 American Enterprise Institute conference.*

and science, but that gap is closing. Meanwhile, boys are *dramatically* behind in reading and writing. We never hear about that gap, which is not shrinking.

Many more boys than girls suffer from learning disabilities. In 1990, three times as many boys as girls were enrolled in special education programs. Of the 1.3 million American children taking Ritalin, the drug for hyperactivity, three-quarters are boys. More boys than girls are involved in crime, alcohol, drugs.

Mary Pipher talks about the "selves" of girls going down in flames. One effect of a crashing self is suicide. *Six times* as many boys as girls commit suicide. In 1992, fully 4,044 young males (ages fifteen to twenty-four) killed themselves. Among same-age females, there were 649 suicides. To the extent that there is a gender gap among youth, it is boys who turn out to be on the fragile side.

This is not to deny that some girls are in serious trouble or that we can't do better by girls, educationally and otherwise. What I am saying is, you cannot find any responsible research that shows that girls, as a group, are worse off than boys or that girls are an underprivileged class. So, where did that idea come from? Therein lies a tale.

The reality is, the contemporary women's movement is obsessed with proving that our system is rigged against women. No matter what record of success you show them, they can always come up with some example of oppression. Never is good news taken as real evidence that things have changed. The women's movement is still fixated on victimology. Where they can't prove discrimination, they invent it.

I, for one, do not believe American women are oppressed. It is simply irresponsible to argue that American women, as a gender, are worse off than American men.   10

More women than men now go to college. Women's life expectancy is seven years longer than men's. Many women now find they can choose between working full-time, part-time, flex-time, or staying home for a few years to raise their children. Men's choices are far more constricted. They can work full-time. They can work full-time. Or they can work full-time.

The reason we hear nothing about men being victims of society or boys suffering unduly from educational and psychological deficits is because the feminist establishment has the power to shape national discussion and determine national policy on gender issues.

Feminist research is advocacy research. When the American Association of University Women released a (badly distorted) survey in 1991 claiming that American girls suffer from a tragic lack of self-esteem, a *New York Times* reporter got AAUW President Sharon Shuster to admit that the organization commissioned the poll to get data into circulation that would support its officers' belief that schoolgirls were being short-changed. Usually, of course, belief comes after, not before, data gathering. But advocacy research doesn't work that way. With advocacy research, first you believe and then you gather figures you can use to convince people you are right.

The myth of the short-changed schoolgirl is a perfect example of everything that's gone wrong with contemporary feminism. It's all there: the mendacious advocacy research, the mean-spiritedness to men that extends even to little boys, the irresponsible victimology, the outcry against being "oppressed," coupled with massive lobbying for government action.

The truth is, American women are the freest in the world. Anyone who doesn't see this simply lacks common sense.

___

Responding as a Reader

1. What, according to Sommers, is wrong with the contemporary women's movement? What should the movement be focusing on?

2. Consider the quotation from Mary Pipher in paragraph 2 and the statistics that Sommers cites in paragraphs 5–7. What do you think Pipher means by "the selves of girls"? What do the statistics measure? What is the contradiction between the statistics and Pipher's thesis? What does Sommers leave unsaid?

3. What is the point of the story Sommers tells in paragraph 13? Do you agree with Sommers that "usually, of course, belief comes after, not before, data gathering"? If you have studied scientific and research methods in other courses, what do these methods tell you about the order of events?

Responding as a Writer

1. In paragraph 3, Sommers asks where Mary Pipher got the idea that "the selves of girls go down in droves" during early adolescence. Where do you suppose Pipher got that idea? Note a few stories you have heard that would support Pipher's thesis. Do these stories come from your direct observation or are they anecdotal? Do the statistics that Sommers quotes contradict these stories?

2. What changes for girls and for boys during adolescence? What psychological and sociological changes result? How do these factors affect the way girls mature into women? Should these factors be a concern for feminists? What, if anything, should feminists be doing about them? In an essay, attempt to define the most appropriate role for feminism in the lives of teenagers.

3. Is the feminist movement "mean-spirited to men" (para. 14)? Or do you agree with Susan Faludi that "issues of feminism are not a matter of the girls versus the guys" (p. 152)? In an essay, explore what feminism can do for men and what men can do for feminism.

Advertisement

The Navajo is a matriarchal society. It is the Navajo woman who owns the land and the houses, and she brings to her marriage a flock of sheep that she has tended since childhood, contributions which form the basis of the couple's wealth. When Navajos meet they introduce themselves by their mother's clan name first, and then their father's, and if a Navajo woman wants her husband to go away she has only to put his saddle in front of the door and he will do just that. Navajo women have always had at least as much power and respect as Navajo men; their folk tales abound with resourceful heroines, and so do their immediate families. Generation after generation of Navajo girls are brought up guided by strong, smart women who don't raise their voices because they don't need to, and who have never had to fight for equality because they have never been without it.

I'LL NEVER FIGHT FOR WOMEN'S RIGHTS.

AMERICAN
INDIAN
COLLEGE
FUND

Help save a culture that could save ours
by giving to the American Indian College Fund, Dept. PN,
21 West 68th St., New York, NY 10023. 1-800-776-FUND.
We would like to give a special thanks
to US West for all their concern and support.

Photo: Tina Bogay, Tribal College Student

— From American Indian College Fund's public-service advertising campaign.

Exchange

Susan Faludi and Karen Lehrman on Revisionist Feminism

The following letters mark the first exchange in a much longer dialogue be-tween two well-known feminist writers, Susan Faludi and Karen Lehrman, that appeared in the Webzine Slate *in May 1997. Susan Faludi is author of* Back-lash: The Undeclared War Against American Women. *Karen Lehrman is au-thor of* The Lipstick Proviso: Women, Sex & Power in the Real World, *re-leased May 1,1997.*

Message #1: April 28, 1997
From: Susan Faludi
To: Karen Lehrman

Dear Karen,

I enter into this conversation with you about feminism with some misgiv-ings. Not because I don't want to talk to you. It's just that I suspect it will be like a phone conversation where the connection's so bad neither party can hear the other through the static. I say this because in my experience, there's no getting through to the group of "feminists" (and I use that word with heavy quotation marks and highly arched brows) who are your sister travelers. I mean the group that maintains that an "orthodoxy" of "reigning feminists" (your terms) torments the American female population with its highhanded fiats, its litmus tests of "proper" feminist behavior, its regulatory whip seek-ing to slap the femininity out of the American girl. Christina Hoff Sommers, Katie Roiphe, Laura Ingraham, Danielle Crittenden, and the rest of the inside-the-Beltway "revisionist feminists" (as the media would have it) condemn feminism for its "excesses" over and over on the *New York Times* and *Wash-ington Post* op-ed pages and the major TV talk shows (while complaining they are viciously "silenced" by the "reigning" feminists, who hardly ever get an airing in the aforementioned forums).

And you, too, Karen. Your own book-length addition to this chorus re-peats the argument that feminism has turned women off by denying them the right to display and revel in their feminine beauty and sexuality. You then adorn that old can of "revisionist" contents with a fancy new label, *The Lipstick Proviso,* which you define as "women don't have to sacrifice their individuality, or even their femininity — whatever that means to each of them — in order to be equal."

For the longer version of my response to the "revisionists" and their charges against feminism, please see "I'm Not a Feminist But I Play One on TV." For the shorter version, to your book specifically, here 'tis:

Earth to Karen! Do you read me? . . . 'Cuz back on planet Earth, femi-nists don't "reign" and they certainly don't stop women at checkpoints to strip them of their "individuality" by impounding their lipstick (though what a pathetic "individuality" that must be if it depends on the application of Revlon to achieve it). Bulletin from the front: I wear lipstick, and I've spotted it on other feminists, too. I've watched, in fact, legions of "militant" feminists apply makeup brazenly in public ladies' rooms, and no femi-Nazi police swooped down and seized their compacts. And you know why? Because lipstick *is not what feminism is about.*

Message #2: May 7, 1997
From: Karen Lehrman
To: Susan Faludi

Dear Susan,

Well, I think there would be much less static between us if you had read my book more carefully, did not take my words out of context, and did not lump me in with women with whom I clearly have little in common. I also think we'd have a much better connection if you'd drop the sneery, condescending tone you always seem to adopt when writing about women with whom you disagree. I respect you; I'd probably even like you if we met under slightly less fraught circumstances. Yes, I disagree with some of your philosophical and political views. But those views don't make you any less of a feminist. As long as you believe that women should have the same rights, opportunities, and responsibilities as men, you can have whatever political agenda, lifestyle, or wardrobe you wish.

Unfortunately, you don't seem to feel the same way about me or millions of other women. You say that "feminism, real feminism, is about freeing women to be genuine individuals — and recognizing that such individuality doesn't come in one size only or out of a bottle." But much of what you've written on the subject — in your book, magazine articles, and already in this dialogue — would indicate that you don't really mean it. And the same, I'm afraid, is true about most of the other self-appointed spokeswomen for feminism.

You each appear to believe that to be allowed to use the term "feminist," a woman has to adhere to a well-defined leftist political agenda, consisting of, at the very least, affirmative action, nationally subsidized day care, and "pay equity" (formerly known as comparable worth). In your *Ms.* article, you call a handful of women who happen to disagree with you politically (myself included) "pod" or "pseudo" feminists. You say that we're right-wing misogynists or pawns of right-wing misogynists. Perhaps most curiously, you imply that we're also racist. In 1992, the National Organization for Women tried to start a "women's party," offering a distinctly leftist "women's agenda." During the last election, NOW president Patricia

continued on next page

continued from previous page

Ireland said women should vote only for "authentic" female candidates, Gloria Steinem called Texas Republican Sen. Kay Bailey Hutchinson a "female impersonator," and Naomi Wolf described the foreign-policy analysis of Jeane Kirkpatrick as being "uninflected by the experiences of the female body." The desire to enforce political conformity is even worse in academia. Many women's-studies professors regularly judge texts and opinions in terms of their agreement with the orthodox political agenda. (For an honest "insider" account, check out *Professing Feminism,* by Daphne Patai and Noretta Koertge.)

Fortunately, all women don't think alike, and as far as feminism is concerned they certainly don't have to. The only items on the real feminist agenda are equal rights and opportunities, a society capable of accepting the widest array of women's choices, and women strong and independent enough to make rational ones. This in no way means that feminists should "junk the politics." It means that feminism is a moral ideal; how women achieve it is a matter of political debate.

— From the Webzine *Slate* (see "compost" for the whole exchange), at http://www.slate.com.

Discussing the Unit

Suggested Topic for Discussion

As the selections in this unit demonstrate, there are a number of conflicts in feminism today. What are those conflicts? What are the differences between what older and younger women want, what professional and working-class women want, what conservative and liberal women want, what men and women want? Can one movement speak for all of these groups? If so, how? If not, what should be done? Or if you think feminism has become unnecessary or obsolete, why do you think so? Should a new, more vital, movement take the place of feminism?

Preparing for Class Discussion

1. Turn back to the Silver (p. 52) and Henig (p. 55) articles in the Self-Image unit and note any information and opinions relevant to a discussion of feminism. What's the relationship between the feminist move-

ment and the way women feel about themselves? Also look back at the articles in the Gender Differences unit (p. 103). How do the innate and cultural differences between women and men influence the way we talk about women's rights?

2. If by the next millennium women were earning equal pay for equal work, would the feminist movement come to an end? Would it have reached its primary economic goal and have no reason to continue? Jot down a few other inequalities or causes that you think the movement would still need to address. Arrange your list in order of priority. How does your list differ from the lists of your classmates? How does your list suggest your own feminist viewpoint? Are you closer to Roiphe, Sommers, Lehrman, Abraham, or Faludi?

3. Yvonne Abraham criticizes a number of recent feminist writers for their "self-absorption" and dependence on the personal memoir. In some of their books, she says, "the writers use their own experience to drive their arguments, drawing from them major conclusions about women and feminism, apparently believing their own experiences to be distillations of all women's." Consider Abraham's criticism in light of the selections in this chapter. Do you think her remark is just? What do you think of her criticism in general? Is it inappropriate to rely too much on personal experience to drive one's arguments? What are the advantages of relying on one's personal experience? What are the disadvantages?

4. *Prewriting Assignment:* Christina Hoff Sommers argues that school-age girls are much better off than school-age boys, and the advertisement on page 151 implies that women in certain cultures may not even need a women's movement. What can feminism offer the next generation of American women that it's not offering now? In a few paragraphs, explore what today's feminism is *not* doing for young women.

From Discussion to Writing

Do you consider yourself a feminist? Why or why not? In an essay that quotes the writers represented in this unit (and others, if you wish), position yourself among them. Do you, like Christina Hoff Sommers, believe that American women are not oppressed? Or do you agree with Yvonne Abraham that "for some women, none of the old problems have gone away" (p. 143)? Or do you define the problems differently? If you're a man (and even if you're not), you'll want to consider whether men can be feminists and why they might or might not want to be.

8

Immigration:
Can We Formulate a Policy?

America has always been a nation of immigrants, a country made up of people who have come from every part of the globe. A century ago we were proud of the way the nation functioned as a "melting pot," where cultural ingredients from many lands were stirred together to form a new identity — an American. Lately, however, the tide against immigrants has been rising. Many government and community leaders are calling for tight restrictions on legal immigration, beefed-up border patrols, severe reductions in benefits, and even deportation measures. Some of these tighter restrictions are reflected in the Illegal Immigration Reform and Immigrant Responsibility Act of 1996. As this law was in the process of being enacted, many writers, ethnic organizations, and policymakers were confronting the spectrum of issues brought on by current immigration policy and changing patterns of assimilation. The recent immigration law promises to be only the beginning of widespread reform of all areas affecting immigrants: border patrols, labor regulations, passports and visas, and citizenship.

What ever happened to the "melting pot"? Has it been replaced by the "rainbow coalition," the "salad bowl," or the "gorgeous mosaic"? In "Assimilation, American Style," Peter Salins, an expert on immigration policy, analyzes the various ways that over the years we have pictured the complex process of becoming an American. "As a first-generation South Asian immigrant," writes Trishala Deb in "The Alien Nation: Debunking the

Myth," "I have always known that citizenship was a political and social construction." The legislation Deb attacks in her essay was introduced by Texas Representative Lamar Smith, who successfully argued to the House that the failures of the "current immigration system to encourage self-reliance are numerous."

Whenever the topic of immigration surfaces, the experiences of California are bound to be introduced. In "Go North, Young Man," one of America's best known contemporary essayists has something philosophical to say to his fellow Californians: "Immigration is always illegal."

And how do freshmen feel about immigration? The following survey results show that more than half of all freshmen agree that undocumented aliens should not have the right to attend public school. What will that mean for future immigrants?

Selected Survey Results

Immigration

- Freshmen who agree that the United States should deny educational access to undocumented aliens: 55.5%
- Freshmen at all black colleges who agree: 37.2%
- Freshmen who are U. S. citizens: 96.4%

— From *The American Freshman: National Norms For Fall 1996.*

PETER SALINS

Assimilation, American Style

[REASON / February 1997]

> California Chinese, Boston Irish, Wisconsin Germans, yes, and Alabama
> Negroes, have more in common than they have apart. . . . It is a fact that
> Americans from all sections and of all racial extractions are more alike than
> the Welsh are like the English, the Lancashireman like the Cockney, or for
> that matter the Lowland Scot like the Highlander.
>
> — *John Steinbeck, 1962*

Most Americans, both those who favor and those who oppose assimilation, believe that for immigrants to assimilate, they must abandon their
original cultural attributes and conform entirely to the behaviors and customs of the majority of the native-born population. In the terminology of
the armed forces, this represents a model of "up or out": Either immigrants
bring themselves "up" to native cultural standards or they are doomed to
live "out" of the charmed circle of the national culture.

The notion is not entirely far-fetched because this is exactly what assimilation demands in other societies. North African immigrants to France
are, for example, expected to assimilate by abandoning their native folkways with alacrity. Official French policy has been zealous in making
North African and other Muslim women give up wearing their *chadors*[1]
and, in the schools, instilling a disdain for North African and Muslim culture in their children. To varying degrees, most European countries that
have had to absorb large numbers of immigrants since World War II interpret assimilation this way — an interpretation that has promoted national
and ethnic disunity.

---

[1] *Chadors* are the long black veils worn by Muslim women.

PETER SALINS *(b. 1938) is chairman of the department of urban affairs
and planning at Hunter College and a senior fellow at the Manhattan Institute for Policy Research. He is a frequent contributor to the* Public Interest,
the New Republic, *and* City Journal *and has just recently published* Assimilation, American Style *(1997). A longer version of this essay appeared in
the February 1997 issue of* Reason.

In America, however, assimilation has not meant repudiating immigrant culture. Assimilation, American style has always been much more flexible and accommodating and, consequently, much more effective in achieving its purpose — to allow the United States to preserve its "national unity in the face of the influx of hordes of persons of scores of different nationalities," in the words of the sociologist Henry Fairchild.

A popular way of getting hold of the assimilation idea has been to use a metaphor, and by far the most popular metaphor has been that of the "melting pot," a term introduced in Israel Zangwill's 1908 play of that name: "There she lies, the great Melting-Pot — Listen! Can't you hear the roaring and the bubbling? . . . Ah, what a stirring and a seething! Celt and Latin, Slav and Teuton, Greek and Syrian, black and yellow . . . Jew and Gentile. . . . East and West, and North and South, the palm and the pine, the pole and the equator, the crescent and the cross — how the great Alchemist melts and fuses them with his purifying flame! Here shall they all unite to build the Republic of Man and the Kingdom of God."

For all its somewhat ahistorical idealism, the melting-pot metaphor still represents the standard around which fervent proponents of assimilation have rallied over the years. According to the melting-pot metaphor, assimilation involved the fine-grained intermingling of diverse ethnicities and cultures into a single national "alloy." If taken literally, this metaphor implied two things. The point most commonly taken is that the new human products of the melting pot would, of necessity, be culturally indistinguishable. Presumably every piece of metal taken from a melting pot should have the same chemical composition. Less frequently understood is the metaphor's implication that natives and their indigenous cultural characteristics would also be irreversibly changed — blended beyond recognition — because they constituted the base material of the melting pot.

These two corollaries of the melting-pot metaphor have long invited criticism by those who thought they were inconsistent with the ethnic realities of American society. Critics of the metaphor have spanned the ideological spectrum and mounted several different lines of attack on it. Empiricists submitted evidence that the melting pot wasn't working as predicted and concluded, as did Nathan Glazer and Daniel Patrick Moynihan in *Beyond the Melting Pot* (1963), "The point about the melting pot — is that it did not happen." Other critics rejected the second corollary of the metaphor — that natives were changed by it, too — and saw no reason that native Americans should give up any part of their cultural attributes to "melt" into the alloy. If true assimilation were to occur, the criticism went, immigrants would have to abandon all their cultural baggage and conform to American ways. It is the immigrant, said Fairchild, representing the views of many Americans, "who must undergo the entire transformation; the true member of the American nationality is not called upon to change in the least."

5

A third strain of criticism was first voiced by sociologist Horace Kallen in the early part of this century. Among the most prolific American scholars of ethnicity, Kallen argued that it was not only unrealistic but cruel and harmful to force new immigrants to shed their familiar, lifelong cultural attributes as the price of admission to American society. In place of the melting pot, he called for "cultural pluralism." In Kallen's words, national policy should "seek to provide conditions under which each [group] might attain the cultural perfection that is proper to its kind."

Kallen introduced the concept in 1916, only eight years after publication of Zangwill's *The Melting Pot,* determined to challenge that work's premises. Cultural pluralism rejects melting-pot assimilationism not on empirical grounds but on ideological ones. Kallen and his followers believed that immigrants to the United States should not "melt" into a common national ethnic alloy but, rather, should steadfastly hang on to their cultural ethnicity and band together for social and political purposes even after generations of residence in the United States. As such, cultural pluralism is not an alternative theory of assimilation; it is a theory opposed to assimilation.

Cultural pluralism is, in fact, the philosophical antecedent of modern multiculturalism — what I call "ethnic federalism": official recognition of distinct, essentially fixed ethnic groups and the doling out of resources based on membership in an ethnic group. Ethnic federalism explicitly rejects the notion of a transcendent American identity, the old idea that out of ethnic diversity there would emerge a single, culturally unified people. Instead, the United States is to be viewed as a vast ethnic federation — Canada's Anglo-French arrangement, raised to the nth power. Viewing ethnic Americans as members of a federation rather than a union, ethnic federalism, a.k.a. multiculturalism, asserts that ethnic Americans have the right to proportional representation in matters of power and privilege, the right to demand that their "native" culture and putative ethnic ancestors be accorded recognition and respect, and the right to function in their "native" language (even if it is not the language of their birth or they never learned to speak it), not just at home but in the public realm.

Ethnic federalism is at all times an ideology of ethnic grievance and inevitably leads to and justifies ethnic conflict. All the nations that have ever embraced it, from Yugoslavia to Lebanon, from Belgium to Canada, have had to live with perpetual ethnic discord. 10

Kallen's views, however, stop significantly short of contemporary multiculturalism in their demands on the larger "native" American society. For Kallen, cultural pluralism was a defensive strategy for "unassimilable" immigrant ethnic groups that required no accommodation by the larger society. Contemporary multiculturalists, on the other hand, by making cultural pluralism the basis of ethnic federalism, demand certain ethnic rights and concessions. By emphasizing the failure of assimilation, multiculturalists hope to provide intellectual and political support for their policies.

The multiculturalists' rejection of the melting pot idea is seen in the metaphors they propose in its place. Civil rights activist Jesse Jackson suggested that Americans are members of a "rainbow coalition." Former New York Mayor David Dinkins saw his constituents constituting a "gorgeous mosaic." Former Congresswoman Shirley Chisholm characterized America's ethnic groups as being like ingredients in a "salad bowl." Barbara Jordan, recent chairperson of the U.S. Commission on Immigration Reform, said: "We are more than a melting-pot; we are a kaleidoscope."

These counter-metaphors all share a common premise: that ethnic groups in the United States may live side by side harmoniously, but on two conditions that overturn both assumptions of the melting-pot metaphor. First, immigrants (and black Americans) should never have to (or maybe should not even want to) give up any of their original cultural attributes. And second, there never can or will be a single unified national identity that all Americans can relate to. These two principles are the foundations of cultural pluralism, the antithesis of assimilationism.

While all these metaphors — including the melting pot — are colorful ways of representing assimilation, they don't go far in giving one an accurate understanding of what assimilation is really about. For example, across the ideological spectrum, they all invoke some external, impersonal assimilating agent. Who, exactly, is the "great alchemist" of the melting pot? What force tosses the salad or pieces together the mosaic? By picturing assimilation as an impersonal, automatic process and thus placing it beyond analysis, the metaphors fail to illuminate its most important secrets. Assimilation, if it is to succeed, must be a voluntary process, by both the assimilating immigrants and the assimilated-to natives. Assimilation is a human accommodation, not a mechanical production.

The metaphors also mislead as to the purposes of assimilation. The melting pot is supposed to turn out an undifferentiated alloy — a uniform, ethnically neutral, American protoperson. Critics have long pointed out that this idea is far-fetched. But is it even desirable? And if it is desirable, does it really foster a shared national identity? The greatest failing of the melting-pot metaphor is that it overreaches. It exaggerates the degree to which immigrants' ethnicity is likely to be extinguished by exposure to American society and it exaggerates the need to extinguish ethnicity. By being too compelling, too idealistic, the melting-pot idea has inadvertently helped to discredit the very assimilation paradigm it was meant to celebrate.

On the other hand, behind their unexceptionable blandness, the antithetical cultural pluralist metaphors are profoundly insidious. By suggesting that the product of assimilation is mere ethnic coexistence without integration, they undermine the objectives of assimilation, even if they appear more realistic. Is assimilation only about diverse ethnic groups sharing the same national space? That much can be said for any multiethnic society. If the eth-

15

nic greens of the salad or the fragments of the mosaic do not interact and identify with each other, no meaningful assimilation is taking place.

Perhaps a new assimilation metaphor should be introduced — one that depends not on a mechanical process like the melting pot but on human dynamics. Assimilation might be viewed as more akin to religious conversion than anything else. In the terms of this metaphor, the immigrant is the convert, American society is the religious order being joined, and assimilation is the process by which the conversion takes place. Just as there are many motives for people to immigrate, so are there many motives for them to change their religion: spiritual, practical (marrying a person of another faith), and materialistic (joining some churches can lead to jobs or subsidized housing). But whatever the motivation, conversion usually involves the consistent application of certain principles. Conversion is a mutual decision requiring affirmation by both the convert and the religious order he or she wishes to join. Converts are expected in most (but not all) cases to renounce their old religions. But converts do not have to change their behavior in any respects other than those that relate to the new religion. They are expected only to believe in its theological principles, observe its rituals and holidays, and live by its moral precepts. Beyond that, they can be rich or poor, practice any trade, pursue any avocational interests, and have any racial or other personal attributes. Once they undergo conversion, they are eagerly welcomed into the fellowship of believers. They have become part of "us" rather than "them." This is undoubtedly what writer G. K. Chesterton had in mind when he said: "America is a nation with the soul of a church."

Responding as a Reader

1. What is the function of the epigraph from John Steinbeck? How does it prepare you for Salins's article? What seems to be Salins's attitude toward Steinbeck's remarks? How do you think John Steinbeck would respond to Salins's definition of "ethnic federalism" (paras. 7–13)?

2. What distinction does Salins make between the older "cultural pluralism" and "modern multiculturalism"? Why is this distinction important to his argument? Why does modern multiculturalism reject the "melting-pot" metaphor?

3. Can you detect Salins's attitude toward "modern multiculturalism"? Why does Salins call it "ethnic federalism"? Does he give a positive or negative meaning to this term? How can you tell?

Responding as a Writer

1. Consider the various older metaphors for the assimilation process mentioned in this essay. Which do you find most appropriate? (If you

don't like any of the metaphors, try to come up with your own.) In a paragraph, explain why one metaphor works better than the others.

2. Consider carefully the new metaphor for assimilation that Salins proposes in the final paragraph. What limitations of the previous metaphors does it, according to Salins, improve on? What problems do you find with it? Do you think it would ever catch on with the public — like "melting pot" or "rainbow coalition"? Why or why not?

3. Write a response to Salins in the voice of a recent immigrant to the United States (if you happen to be a recent immigrant, then of course you should use your own voice and rely on your own experience). What assumptions is Salins making about you? How do these assumptions make you feel?

TRISHALA DEB

The Alien Nation: Debunking the Myth

[CONTRABAND / May 1997]

As we are led through the maze of confusing and misleading information about the "immigration crisis," it becomes increasingly important to separate reality from perception. In a recent *New York Times* article, Priscilla Labovitz combined statistics from the Census Bureau, the Immigration and Naturalization Service, the National Immigration Law Center, New York City Planning Commission, and the *Washington Post.* She found that white people's perceptions of racial diversity in the United States were misguided — overestimating the percentage of people of color and underestimating their own numbers.

The combination of this information and the recent immigration legislation makes it apparent that white people in the United States view large

---

TRISHALA DEB *(b. 1972) was born in Bombay, India. She is currently a case manager at a shelter for battered women in Douglasville, Georgia. She also works with an organization called Empty the Shelters — a group of students and young people who support the work of the Atlanta Union of the Homeless and the Atlanta Labor Pool Workers Union.*

numbers of immigrants as a cultural and fiscal threat. Given this startling measure of xenophobia and panic, it is clear that whether or not white U.S. citizens understand the true nature of immigration and cultural representation, laws, standards of acceptance, and societal norms are being set by their perceptions. The Immigration and National Interest Act of 1996 singles out legal and illegal aliens with new laws, standards of welfare entitlement, and eligibility for emergency and preventive health care.

Among the most important precedent-setting aspects of H.R. 2202 are:

- Legal immigrants who use more than twelve months of public assistance within seven years of entry will be eligible for deportation;
- U.S. citizen children with undocumented parents must have an appointed guardian to receive Aid to Families with Dependent Children or other forms of cash assistance;
- Legal immigrants as well as U.S. citizens will be banned from public housing if caught sharing living space with an undocumented immigrant.

[For more on this legislation, see p. 166.]

The concept of "deeming" was also introduced through this legislation. "Deeming" refers to the process of determining a person's eligibility for entrance. Basically, legal immigrants have to establish sponsorship (usually family-based) to enter the country. H.R. 2202 established that the sponsor has to make 200 percent of the poverty level for family members (140 percent for spouse or child) to be deemed eligible. When the newly immigrated family members attempt to qualify for public assistance, their sponsors' incomes will be taken into account, generally rendering them ineligible. Should the immigrant qualify, federal, state, and local agencies can hold the sponsor financially liable for up to ten years after the benefits are received.

Predictably, laws concerning illegal immigrants and refugees are considerably harsher. While the federal government inched closer to Proposi-   5

Racial Diversity in the United States*
(% of the U.S. population)

	What White Folks Think	REALITY
Asian	10.8%	3.1%
Black	23.8%	11.8%
Hispanic	14.4%	9.5%
White	49.9%	74.0%

*Labovitz did not include Native Americans in her data.

(*Source: New York Times,* 1996.)

tion 187-esque[1] limitations on access to public education and emergency health care, Congress instituted laws that severely limited numbers of incoming legal immigrants and refugees, tightened enforcement of border control policies, and instituted a national identification system for employers to verify a person's immigration status.

While some immigrants and nonimmigrants were startled at the speed at which anti-immigrant fervor manifested itself as anti-immigrant law, many were not. As a first-generation South Asian immigrant, I have always known that citizenship was a political and social construction. It has been used as a label to determine my political access and cultural value.

It is important to note that "immigration" has been racialized — so when U.S. citizens think of an immigrant they think of a person of color. The nature of this stigmatization is the differentiation between white and non-white. Therefore, we have to understand immigrant issues through the lens of white supremacy. Until white people in the United States, especially those who are creating immigration policy, can appreciate the distinctions of race, ethnicity, cultural and linguistic affiliation, and the diversity within these categories, citizenship will be used as a tool of white supremacy.

This country's confusion over racial/cultural definitions and meanings have been apparent to me for a long time. For example, consider the basic categories you are asked to check on any standard identification questionnaire (these were taken from a Blue Cross/Blue Shield health insurance application form) — "American Indian/Alaskan Native, Black/African American, Mexican/Mexican American, Asian/Asian American or Pacific Islander, Puerto Rican, Other Hispanic or Latin, White (non-Hispanic), and Other."

When did cultural and linguistic affiliation become so blurred with racial identity? Would a white South African count as an African American? What would a Spanish-speaking Caucasian be? Would a person from Peru who spoke one of many indigenous languages be Hispanic (which means Spanish-speaking)? Many non-white immigrants might not ponder these questions too hard, knowing that these categories have long been thinly veiled attempts to identify non-whites for unsuspecting white people.

This is an indicator of a lack of clarity over the issue of citizenship in general. In many ways, the North American Free Trade Agreement skewed the issue of citizenship permanently. Republicans and Democrats alike support the concept that the primary criteria for citizenship is that the applicant will be an asset and not a liability to the national economy.

Until 1952, whiteness (as it was defined by law) was a mandatory condition for naturalization. Given the white supremacist origins of citizenship policy and current economic debates, I wonder if policymakers are including

10

---

[1]Proposition 187 was a ballot referendum in California that limited access to public and emergency services including health care and education for illegal immigrants.

Comment

Lamar Smith on Immigration

The following excerpts are from a longer article by Texas Representative Lamar Smith, who is chairman of the Subcommittee on Immigration and Claims of the House Judiciary Committee and responsible for the H. R. 2202 bill (the Immigration in the National Interest Act of 1995).

As chairman of the House Subcommittee on Immigration and Claims, I introduced H. R. 2202, the Immigration in the National Interest Act of 1995, to reduce illegal immigration and ensure that new Americans are self-reliant and productive contributors to our society. The bill prevents illegal aliens from taking advantage of taxpayer-funded welfare programs and requires immigrants to have jobs or financial sponsors who are responsible for supporting them. H. R. 2202 passed the House of Representatives on a strong bipartisan vote of 333–87, and its Senate companion passed by a vote of 97–3.

Self-sufficiency has been a basic principle of U.S. immigration law from this country's earliest immigration statutes. Since 1882, aliens found likely to become public charges have been subject to exclusion from the United States. Since 1917, immigrants who become public charges after entry have been subject to deportation.

It continues to be the immigration policy of the United States that aliens within our borders should not depend on taxpayer-funded public resources to meet their needs but, rather, rely on their own capabilities and the resources of their families, their sponsors, and private charitable organizations. The availability of taxpayer-funded welfare programs should not be an incentive to come to America — legally or illegally.

Despite our historic principles of self-sufficiency, non-citizens have been receiving welfare checks from federal, state, and local taxpayers at increasing rates. Only a negligible number of immigrants who become public charges are deported because courts effectively have invalidated the public charge statute. Various state court decisions, including those by immigration courts, have held that affidavits of financial support do not impose a legal obligation on sponsors to live up to their agreements. As a result, these provisions have failed to prevent immigrants from taking advantage of the generosity of American taxpayers.

Examples of the failure of the current immigration system to encourage self-reliance are numerous. Perhaps the most notable scholar in the field of immigrants and welfare, George Borjas of Harvard University, has found that 21% of immigrants currently are receiving welfare payments, compared to 14% of citizens. Not only is there a higher percentage of immigrants on the welfare rolls, but they receive more welfare dollars per person than citizens. For example, the nine percent of our population residing in immigrant households has accounted for 14% of the costs of major welfare programs.

— From "Immigration and Welfare Reform: Finally, Taxpayers Are Being Considered." — *U.S.A. Today Magazine*, March 1997.

under their definition of citizenship maquiladora workers and Asian sweatshop workers. These are populations that work inside and out of the geographic boundaries of the country, but they contribute equally to corporate profits based here in the United States. Free trade has come to apply not only to goods and services but the people that produce them also. It is no secret that the greatest asset to U.S. corporations is a labor force that is not accountable to domestic work and wage standards.

So as immigrants around this country gear up to protect our rights — including HeadStart and treatment for HIV/AIDS — it becomes necessary to not push just for reform such as loosening regulations on legal immigrants and refugees. We must also attack the legitimacy of the U.S. government and corporate coalition in defining and enforcing citizenship laws. Increasingly, the environmental and labor regulations that are set in the United States have repercussions across the globe. The paradigm of citizenship must expand to enable people to directly influence the very forces that shape their standards of living, their wages and working conditions, the environment that they live in, and the possibilities in their futures.

As the train of economic globalization pushes inexorably forward, it is imperative that we not only understand the fluidity of cultural identities and the complexity of race and class conflict therein but that we embrace it. At this juncture, nationalism and protectionism come at a high price. If there is a national data base for immigrant employability this year, what information will the data base contain in ten years? It could be criminal records or medical and psychological profiles of the permanent workforce. If Texaco is willing to let children build its oil pipelines in Burma this year, whose children will make up the workforce in 20 years?

It is apparent that the greatest tool in a global economy would be the solidarity of that workforce. Only when we make political and identity-based connections across the same geographic boundaries that the corporations have been crossing for the last century will we be able to understand the true worth of national affiliation, citizenship, and democracy.

Sources

Haney Lopez, Ian. *White by Law.* New York: NYU Press, 1996.
"Immigration . . . Just the Facts." *New York Times* 25 Mar. 1996.

Responding as a Reader

1. Deb argues that the statistics she cites in paragraph 1, when considered with recent immigration legislation, show that "white people in the United States view large numbers of immigrants as a cultural and fiscal threat" (para. 2). How do the figures lead Deb to that conclusion? Might those same figures lead to other conclusions?

2. Reread the passage leading up to Deb's assertion that "we have to understand immigrant issues through the lens of white supremacy" (para.
   7). What does she mean by this statement? Do you find her argument
   logical? Can you think of examples that might support Deb's argument?

3. In paragraph 12, Deb writes that "we must also attack the legitimacy
   of the U.S. government and corporate coalition in defining and enforcing citizenship laws." Who should have the legitimate power to define
   and enforce citizenship laws according to Deb? Do you agree?

Responding as a Writer

1. Deb writes that "citizenship . . . has been used as a label to determine
   my political access and cultural value" (para. 6). In your own words,
   define citizenship. Is it appropriate to use citizenship to determine political access? What about cultural values?

2. Deb seems to imply that white America's overestimate of the percentages of "people of color" is based on racism. Can you think of other
   reasons why white Americans may have overestimated these percentages? For example, could they have received different figures from
   other sources? Has the media provided distorted impressions? What
   numbers would you personally have estimated? In an essay, explain to
   what extent you believe the "overestimates" are due to racism or to
   other factors. You might want to check her percentages against those
   you can find conveniently in such sources as almanacs or recent encyclopedias.

3. Make a list of rights that you believe immigrants should be granted
   under law. You can start by considering the rights that Deb cites and
   then expand the list if you wish. Would you make a different list for
   naturalized U.S. citizens and for immigrants who are not U.S. citizens?
   Why or why not?

RICHARD RODRIGUEZ

Go North, Young Man

[MOTHER JONES/August 1995]

Traditionally, America has been an east-west country. We have read our history right to left across the page. We were oblivious of Canada. We barely noticed Mexico, except when Mexico got in the way of our westward migration, which we interpreted as the will of God, "manifest destiny."

In a Protestant country that believed in rebirth (the Easter promise), land became our metaphor for possibility. As long as there was land ahead of us — Ohio, Illinois, Nebraska — we could believe in change; we could abandon our in-laws, leave disappointments behind, to start anew further west. California symbolized ultimate possibility, future-time, the end of the line, where loonies and prophets lived, where America's fads necessarily began.

Nineteenth-century real estate developers and twentieth-century Hollywood moguls may have advertised the futuristic myth of California to the rest of America. But the myth was one Americans were predisposed to believe. The idea of California was invented by Americans many miles away.

Only a few early voices from California ever warned against optimism. Two decades after California became American territory, the conservationist John Muir stood at the edge of California and realized that America is a finite idea: We need to preserve the land, if the dream of America is to survive. Word of Muir's discovery slowly traveled backward in time, from the barely populated West (the future) to the crowded brick cities of the East Coast (the past).

RICHARD RODRIGUEZ (b. 1944) is an editor with Pacific News Service in San Francisco. He has contributed to many magazines and newspapers, including Harper's, American Scholar, the Los Angeles Times, and the New York Times. In 1982, Rodriguez published an autobiography entitled Hunger of Memory: The Education of Richard Rodriguez. He is the author of Days of Obligation: An Argument with My Mexican Father (1992), which was nominated for the Pulitzer Prize in nonfiction. An earlier version of this essay was presented at an international gathering of writers, "A New Moment in the Americas," sponsored by the United States Information Service.

I grew up in the California of the 1950s, when the state was filling   5
with people from New York and Oklahoma. Everyone was busy losing
weight and changing hair color and becoming someone new. There was,
then, still plenty of cheap land for tract houses, under the cloudless sky.

The 1950s, the 1960s — those years were our golden age. Edmund G.
"Pat" Brown was governor of optimism. He created the University of California system, a decade before the children of the suburbs rebelled, por-
traying themselves as the "counterculture." Brown constructed freeways
that permitted Californians to move farther and farther away from anything resembling an urban center. He even made the water run up the side
of a mountain.

By the 1970s, optimism was running out of space. Los Angeles needed
to reinvent itself as Orange County. Then Orange County got too crowded
and had to reinvent itself as North County San Diego. Then Californians
started moving into the foothills or out to the desert, complaining all the
while of the traffic and of the soiled air. And the immigrants!

Suddenly, foreign immigrants were everywhere — Iranians were buy-
ing into Beverly Hills; the Vietnamese were moving into San Jose; the Chi-
nese were taking all the spaces in the biochemistry courses at UCLA. And
Mexicans, poor Mexicans, were making hotel beds, picking peaches in the
Central Valley, changing diapers, even impersonating Italian chefs at Santa
Monica restaurants.

The Mexicans and the Chinese had long inhabited California. But they
never resided within the golden myth of the state. Nineteenth-century California restricted the Chinese to Chinatowns or to a city's outskirts. Mexicans were neither here nor there. They were imported by California to perform cheap labor, and then deported in bad economic times.

The East Coast had incorporated Ellis Island in its myth. The West   10
Coast regarded the non-European immigrant as doubly foreign. Though
Spaniards may have colonized the place and though Mexico briefly
claimed it, California took its meaning from "internal immigrants" —
Americans from Minnesota or Brooklyn who came West to remake their
parents' version of America.

But sometime in the 1970s, it became clear to many Californians that the
famous blond myth of the state was in jeopardy. ("We are sorry to intrude,
señor, we are only looking for work.") Was L.A. "becoming" Mexican?

Latin Americans arrived, describing California as "el norte." The
"West Coast" was a finite idea; el norte in the Latin American lexicon
means wide open. Whose compass was right?

Meanwhile, with the lifting of anti-Asian immigration restrictions,
jumbo jets were arriving at LAX from Bangkok and Seoul. People getting
off the planes said about California, "This is where the United States begins." Californians objected, "No, no. California is where the United
States comes to an end — we don't have enough room for you." Whose
compass was truer?

It has taken two more decades for the East Coast to get the point. Magazines and television stories from New York today describe the golden state as "tarnished." The more interesting possibility is that California has become the intersection between comedy and tragedy. Foreign immigrants are replanting optimism on California soil; the native-born know the wisdom of finitude. Each side has a knowledge to give the other.

Already, everywhere in California, there is evidence of miscegenation —   15
Keanu Reeves, sushi tacos, blond Buddhists, Salvadoran Pentecostals. But the forces that could lead to marriage also create gridlock on the Santa Monica freeway. The native-born Californian sits disgruntled in traffic going nowhere. The flatbed truck in front of him is filled with Mexicans; in the Mercedes next to him is a Japanese businessman using a car phone.

There are signs of backlash. Pete Wilson has become the last east-west governor of California. In a state founded by people seeking a softer winter and famous internationally for being "laid back," Californians vote for Proposition 187, hoping that illegal immigrants will stay away if there are no welfare dollars.

But immigrants are most disconcerting to California because they are everywhere working, transforming the ethos of the state from leisure to labor. Los Angeles is becoming a vast working city, on the order of Hong Kong or Mexico City. Chinese kids are raising the admission standards to the University of California. Mexican immigrant kids are undercutting union wages, raising rents in once-black neighborhoods.

Californians used to resist any metaphor drawn from their state's perennial earthquakes and floods and fires. Now Californians take their meaning from natural calamity. People turn away from the sea, imagine the future as existing backward in time.

"I'm leaving California, I'm going to Colorado."

"I'm headed for Arizona."   20

After hitting the coastline like flies against glass, we look in new directions. Did Southern California's urban sprawl invent NAFTA [North American Free Trade Agreement]? For the first time, Californians now talk of the North and the South — new points on our national compass.

"I've just bought a condo in Baja."

"I'm leaving California for Seattle."

"I'm moving to Vancouver. I want someplace cleaner."

"Go North, young man."   25

Puerto Ricans, Mexicans: Early in this century we were immigrants. Or not immigrants exactly. Puerto Ricans had awakened one day to discover that they suddenly lived on U.S. territory. Mexicans had seen Mexico's northern territory annexed and renamed the southwestern United States.

We were people from the South in an east-west country. We were people of mixed blood in a black and white nation. We were Catholics in a

Protestant land. Many millions of us were Indians in an east-west country that imagined the Indian to be dead.

Today, Los Angeles is the largest Indian city in the United States, though Hollywood filmmakers persist in making movies about the dead Indian. (For seven bucks, you can see cowboys slaughter Indians in the Kevin Costner movie — and regret it from your comfortable chair.) On any day along Sunset Boulevard, you can see Toltecs and Aztecs and Mayans.

Puerto Ricans, Mexicans — we are the earliest Latin American immigrants to the United States. We have turned into fools. We argue among ourselves, criticize one another for becoming too much the gringo or maybe not gringo enough. We criticize each other for speaking too much Spanish or not enough Spanish. We demand that politicians provide us with bilingual voting ballots, but we do not trouble to vote.

Octavio Paz, the Mexican writer, has observed that the Mexican 30 American is caught between cultures, thus a victim of history — unwilling to become a Mexican again, unable to belong to the United States. Michael Novak, the U.S. writer, has observed that what unites people throughout the Americas is that we all have said goodbye to our motherland. To Europe. To Africa. To Asia. *Farewell!*

The only trouble is: Adios was never part of the Mexican American or Puerto Rican vocabulary. There was no need to turn one's back on the past. Many have traveled back and forth, between rivals, between past and future, commuters between the Third World and First. After a few months in New York or Los Angeles, it would be time to head "home." After a few months back in Mexico or Puerto Rico, it would be time to head "home" to the United States.

We were nothing like the famous Ellis Island immigrants who arrived in America with no expectation of return to the "old country." In a nation that believed in the future, we were a puzzle.

We were also a scandal to Puerto Rico and Mexico. Our Spanish turned bad. Our values were changing — though no one could say why or how exactly. "Abuelita" (grandmother) complained that we were growing more guarded. Alone.

There is a name that Mexico uses for children who have forgotten their true address: "pocho." The pocho is the child who wanders away, ends up in the United States, among the gringos, where he forgets his true home.

The Americas began with a confusion about maps and a joke about 35 our father's mistake. Columbus imagined himself in a part of the world where there were Indians.

We smile because our fifteenth-century "papi" thought he was in India. I'm not certain, however, that even today we know where in the world we live. We are only beginning to look at the map. We are only beginning to wonder what the map of the hemisphere might mean.

Latin Americans have long complained that the gringo, with character-istic arrogance, hijacked the word "American" and gave it all to himself — "the way he stole the land." I remember, years ago, my aunt in Mexico City scolding me when I told her I came from "America." Pocho! Didn't I realize that the entire hemisphere is America? "Listen," my Mexican aunt told me, "people who live in the United States are norteamericanos."

Well, I think to myself — my aunt is now dead, God rest her soul — I wonder what she would have thought a couple of years ago when the great leaders — the president of Mexico, the president of the United States, the Canadian prime minister — gathered to sign the North American Free Trade Agreement. Mexico signed a document acknowledging that she is a North American.

I predict that Mexico will suffer a nervous breakdown in the next ten years. She will have to check into the Betty Ford Clinic for a long rest. She will need to determine just what exactly it means that she is, with the dread gringo, a norteamericana.

Canada, meanwhile, worries about the impact of the Nashville music 40 channel on its cable TV; Pat Buchanan imagines a vast wall along our southern flank; and Mexican nationalists fear a Clinton bailout of the lowly peso.

We all speak of North America. But has anyone ever actually met a North American? Oh, there are Mexicans. And there are Canadians. And there are so-called Americans. But a North American?

I know one.

Let me tell you about him — this North American. He is a Mixteco In-dian who comes from the Mexican state of Oaxaca. He is trilingual. His primary language is the language of his tribe. His second language is Span-ish, the language of Cortés. Also, he has a working knowledge of U.S. En-glish, because, for several months of the year, he works near Stockton, Calif.

He commutes over thousands of miles of dirt roads and freeways, knows several centuries, two currencies, two sets of hypocrisy. He is a criminal in one country and an embarrassment to the other. He is pursued as an "illegal" by the U.S. border patrol. He is preyed on by Mexican officers who want to shake him down because he has hidden U.S. dollars in his shoes.

In Oaxaca, he lives in a sixteenth-century village, where his wife 45 watches blond Venezuelan soap operas. A picture of la Virgen de Guadalupe rests over his bed. In Stockton, there is no Virgin Mary, only the other Madonna — the material girl.

He is the first North American.

A journalist once asked Chou En-lai, the Chinese premier under Mao Zedong, what he thought of the French Revolution. Chou En-lai gave a wonderful Chinese reply: "It's too early to tell."

I think it may even be too early to tell what the story of Columbus means. The latest chapter of the Columbus saga may be taking place right now, as Latin American teenagers with Indian faces violate the U.S. border. The Mexican kids standing on the line tonight between Tijuana and San Diego — if you ask them why they are coming to the United States of America, they will not say anything about Thomas Jefferson or *The Federalist Papers*. They have only heard that there is a job in a Glendale dry cleaner's or that some farmer is hiring near Fresno.

They insist: They will be returning to Mexico in a few months. They are only going to the United States for the dollars. They certainly don't intend to become gringos. They don't want anything to do with the United States, except the dollars.

But the months will pass, and the teenagers will be changed in the   5(
United States. When they go back to their Mexican village, they will no longer be easy. They will expect an independence and an authority that the village cannot give them. Much to their surprise, they will have been Americanized by the job in Glendale.

For work in the United States is our primary source of identity. There is no more telling question we Americans ask one another than "What do you do?" We do not ask about family or village or religion. We ask about work.

The Mexican teenagers will return to Glendale.

Mexicans, Puerto Ricans — most of us end up in the United States, living in the city. Peasants end up in the middle of a vast modern metropolis, having known only the village, with its three blocks of familiar facades.

The arriving generation is always the bravest. New immigrants often change religion with their move to the city. They need to make their peace with isolation, so far from relatives. They learn subway and bus routes that take them far from home every day. Long before they can read English, they learn how to recognize danger and opportunity. Their lives are defined by change.

Their children or their grandchildren become, often, very different. The   55
best and the brightest, perhaps, will go off to college — become the first in their family — but they talk about "keeping" their culture. They start speaking Spanish, as a way of not changing; they eat in the cafeteria only with others who look like themselves. They talk incessantly about "culture" as though it were some little thing that can be preserved and kept in a box.

The unluckiest children of immigrants drop out of high school. They speak neither good English or Spanish. Some end up in gangs — family, man — "blood." They shoot other kids who look exactly like themselves. If they try to leave their gang, the gang will come after them for their act of betrayal. If they venture to some other part of the city, they might get shot or they might merely be unable to decipher the freeway exits that speed by.

They retreat to their "turf" — three blocks, just like in their grandmother's village, where the journey began.

One of the things that Mexico had never acknowledged about my father — I insist that you at least entertain this idea — is the possibility that my father and others like him were the great revolutionaries of Mexico. Pocho pioneers. They, not Pancho Villa, not Zapata, were heralds of the modern age in Mexico. They left for the United States and then they came back to Mexico. And they changed Mexico forever.

A childhood friend of my father's — he worked in Chicago in the 1920s, then returned one night to his village in Michoacán with appliances for mamasita and crisp dollars. The village gathered round him — this is a true story — and asked, "What is it like up there in Chicago?"

The man said, "It's OK." 60

That rumor of "OK" spread across Michoacán, down to Jalisco, all the way down to Oaxaca, from village to village to village.

Futurists and diplomats talk about a "new moment in the Americas." The Latin American elite have condos in Miami and send their children to Ivy League schools. U.S. and Canadian businessmen project the future on a north-south graph. But for many decades before any of this, Latin American peasants have been traveling back and forth, north and south.

Today, there are remote villages in Latin America that are among the most international places on earth. Tiny Peruvian villages know when farmers are picking pears in the Yakima valley in Washington state.

I am the son of a prophet. I am a fool. I am a victim of history. I am confused. I do not know whether I am coming or going. I speak bad Spanish. And yet I tell Latin America this: Because I grew up Hispanic in California, I know more Guatemalans than I would if I had grown up in Mexico, more Brazilians than if I lived in Peru. Because I live in California, it is routine for me to know Nicaraguans and Salvadorans and Cubans. As routine as knowing Chinese or Vietnamese.

My fellow Californians complain loudly about the uncouth southern 65 invasion. I say this to California: Immigration is always illegal. It is a rude act, the leaving of home. Immigration begins as a violation of custom, a youthful act of defiance, an insult to the village. I know a man from El Salvador who has not spoken to his father since the day he left his father's village. Immigrants horrify the grandmothers they leave behind.

Illegal immigrants trouble U.S. environmentalists and Mexican nationalists. Illegal immigrants must trouble anyone, on either side of the line, who imagines that the poor are under control.

But they have also been our civilization's prophets. They, long before the rest of us, saw the hemisphere whole.

Responding as a Reader

1. When Rodriguez writes, in the second sentence, that "we have read our history right to left across the page," what image is he invoking? Where does the standard story of U.S. history begin and end? Who is left out of this story?

2. What does Rodriguez mean in paragraph 36, when he writes "I'm not certain ... that even today we know where in the world we live"? Who is the "we" in this sentence? How do you interpret his use of the word "live"?

3. Consider the definition of the North American (paras. 43–46). What is it that makes this particular person "the first North American"? What does it take to be a real North American, in Rodriguez's view?

Responding as a Writer

1. What has the West symbolized, historically, in the American imagination? What does it seem to symbolize now? In a few paragraphs, trace the trajectory of the myth of the golden west. Then speculate about what effect this popular myth might have on immigrants who come to the United States from across the Pacific Ocean.

2. In paragraphs 15 and 17, Rodriguez gives some examples of ethnic stereotypes and miscegenation. Do these examples ring true to you? Do you think Americans have stereotypical views of immigrants? Consider a single depiction of immigrants in the media that has had an impact on you and in a paragraph or two describe the image of immigration you were left with.

3. "We were nothing like the famous Ellis Island immigrants who arrived in America with no expectation of return to the 'old country' " (para. 32). In an essay, lay out the differences between immigrants who come to the United States with no intention of returning to the old country, immigrants who travel back and forth between the two countries, and immigrants who come to the United States to make money and then move back home. Do native-born Americans view these three groups differently? Should the law treat them differently?

Discussing the Unit

Suggested Topic for Discussion

How should the United States treat its immigrants? What standards (if any) should we enforce as grounds for immigration, eligibility for public benefits, and naturalized citizenship? Is it right to expect assimilation and acculturation from those who immigrate to the United States? How does an ethnic or racial group's degree of assimilation into American society influence the way that group is perceived? As you form your opinions, consider the information provided by the authors in this unit.

Preparing for Class Discussion

1. When arguing about controversial legislation, it's important to know where that legislation stands right now. Do a little research into recent immigration legislation by searching for the topic on the World Wide Web or in a recent index to a major newspaper. What was the last major immigration law that was passed and what exactly does that law say?

2. What positive contributions do immigrants make to U.S. society? What are some of the skills, qualities, and lifestyles that come to the United States from Southeast Asia, for example? From Mexico? From the Caribbean? From Japan?

3. *Prewriting Assignment:* In a page or two, reflect on your own ethnic heritage. Is America today significantly different from what it was when your family or ancestors arrived here? Does your background affect your views of immigration?

From Discussion to Writing

This unit raises many complex issues surrounding immigration. Which solution to the current immigration debate do you think makes the most sense? In an essay, develop your solution by using information from the articles in the unit. You may want to propose a solution of your own, endorse and expand on a solution proposed by one of the writers, or propose a solution that combines the most persuasive aspects of several solutions.

9

America's Schools:
What's Wrong with Education?

Are some 45 million elementary, middle, and high-school students denied a better education because of an entrenched and out-dated educational philosophy? Are American public schools a losing cause? Or can we
meet the educational challenges, build a better system, and teach our children the academic and social lessons we think most important?

John Taylor Gatto, a former New York City educator and two-time
winner of the "Teacher of the Year" award — who quit — knows from
first-hand experience why our schools are dysfunctional. In "Why Schools
Don't Educate" he offers some unconventional solutions for creating a less
passive, dependent, cruel, and materialistic society. Other educators in the
past have tackled failing students and lower test scores with two opposing
"schools" of thought: the self-esteem movement and the "back to basics"
approach. Neither works, according to educator Richard Weissbourd, who
proposes in "The Feel-Good Trap" a way to get past both educational
dead ends. What earns an "A+" in "creative mathematics"? A cartoonist
shows us his version. In "Education for Intimacy," Amitai Etzioni, the
founder of the modern Communitarian movement, explains why — and
more importantly *how* — sex should be taught in our public schools.

The first selection is John Taylor Gatto's acceptance speech, which he
gave after being named New York City's "Teacher of the Year" for the
second time.

Every participant in the *American Freshman* survey obviously was pretty successful in school — they made it to college after all (even if 28.9 percent spent 0 to 2 hours a week their senior year studying or doing homework). Do their reasons for going to college suggest any specific wrongs or rights in America's schools?

Selected Survey Results

Education

- College freshmen who had an average high school grade of A– or better: 31.5%
- Freshmen who spent 0 to 2 hours a week during their last year of high school studying or doing homework: 28.9%
- Freshmen who have no concern about financing college: 31.1%
- Freshmen who have major concern about financing college: 18.0%

Reasons noted as Very Important in deciding to go to college
- Parents wanted me to go: 37.8%
- Could not find a job: 6.9%
- Wanted to get away from home: 17.4%
- Get a better job: 76.7%
- Gain general education: 62.1%
- Improve reading and study skills: 42.8%
- Nothing better to do: 3.4%
- Become a more cultured person: 38.0%
- Make more money: 72.4%
- Learn more about things: 74.3%
- Role model/mentor encouraged me: 14.3%

— From *The American Freshman: National Norms For Fall 1996.*

Why Schools Don't Educate

[HOPE / October 1996]

I accept this award on behalf of all the fine teachers I've known over the years who've struggled to make their transactions with children honorable ones: men and women who are never complacent, always questioning, always wrestling to define and redefine endlessly what the word "education" should mean. A "Teacher of the Year" is not the best teacher around — those people are too quiet to be easily uncovered — but a standard-bearer, symbolic of these private people who spend their lives gladly in the service of children. This is their award as well as mine.

We live in a time of great social crisis. Our children rank at the bottom of nineteen industrial nations in reading, writing, and arithmetic. The world's narcotic economy is based on our own consumption of this commodity. If we didn't buy so many powdered dreams the business would collapse — and schools are an important sales outlet. Our teenage suicide rate is the highest in the world — and suicidal kids are rich kids for the most part, not the poor. In Manhattan, 70 percent of all new marriages last less than five years.

Our school crisis is a reflection of this greater social crisis. We seem to have lost our identity: Children and old people are penned up and locked away from the business of the world without precedent; nobody talks to them anymore. Without children and old people mixing in daily life, a community has no future and no past; only a continuous present. In fact, the name "community" hardly applies to the way we interact with each other. We live in networks, not communities, and everyone I know is lonely because of that. In some strange way, a school is a major actor in this tragedy, just as it is a major actor in the widening gulf among social classes. Using school as a sorting mechanism, we appear to be on the way to creating a caste system, complete with untouchables who wander

JOHN TAYLOR GATTO was a New York City public school teacher for twenty-five years and was named New York City Teacher of the Year in 1989, 1990, and 1991 and New York State Teacher of the Year in 1990 and 1991. Since quitting his teaching career, he has spoken to the engineers at NASA-Goddard Space Center, at the White House, and to a variety of organizations around the country. He is the author of Dumbing Us Down *(1992),* The Exhausted School *(1993), and* The Empty Child *(1996).*

through subway trains begging and [who] sleep on the streets. I've noticed a fascinating phenomenon in my twenty-five years of teaching — that schools and schooling are increasingly irrelevant to the great enterprises of the planet. No one believes anymore that scientists are trained in science classes or politicians in civics classes or poets in English classes. The truth is that schools don't really teach anything except how to obey orders. This is a great mystery to me because thousands of humane, caring people work in schools as teachers and aides and administrators, but the abstract logic of the institution overwhelms their individual contributions. Although teachers do care and do work very, very hard, the institution is psychopathic; it has no conscience. It rings a bell, and the young man in the middle of writing a poem must close his notebook and move to a different cell, where he learns that man and monkeys derive from a common ancestor.

Our form of compulsory schooling is an invention of the State of Massachusetts around 1850. It was resisted — sometimes with guns — by an estimated 80 percent of the Massachusetts population, the last outpost in Barnstable on Cape Cod not surrendering its children until the 1880s when the area was seized by militia and children marched to school under guard. Now here is a curious idea to ponder: Senator Ted Kennedy's [D–Massachusetts] office released a paper not too long ago claiming that, prior to compulsory education, the state literacy rate was 98 percent, and after it, the figure never again reached above 91 percent, where it stands in 1990. I hope that interests you.

Here is another curiosity to think about. The home-schooling movement has quietly grown to a size where one and a half million young people are being educated entirely by their own parents. Last month the education press reported the amazing news that children schooled at home seem to be five or even ten years ahead of their formally trained peers in their ability to think.   5

I don't think we'll get rid of the schools anytime soon, certainly not in my lifetime, but if we're going to change what's rapidly becoming a disaster of ignorance, we need to realize that the school institution "schools" very well, but it does not "educate." That's inherent in the design of the thing. It's not the fault of bad teachers or too little money spent. It's just impossible for education and schooling ever to be the same thing.

Schools were designed by Horace Mann, Barnas Sears, and W. R. Harper of the University of Chicago; Thorndyke of Columbia Teachers College; and others to be instruments of the scientific management of a mass population. Schools are intended to produce, through the application of formulae, formulaic human beings whose behavior can be predicted and controlled.

To a very great extent schools succeed in doing this. But our society is disintegrating, and in such a society the only successful people are self-reliant, confident, and individualistic — because the community life that protects the dependent and the weak is dead. The products of schooling are, as I've said, irrelevant. Well-schooled people are irrelevant. They can sell film and razor blades, push paper and talk on telephones, or sit mindlessly before a flickering computer terminal, but as human beings they are useless — useless to others and useless to themselves.

The daily misery around us is, I think, in large measure caused by the fact that — as Paul Goodman[1] put it thirty years ago — we force children to "grow up absurd." Any reform in schooling has to deal with its absurdities.

It is absurd and anti-life to be part of a system that compels you to sit in confinement with people of exactly the same age and social class. That system effectively cuts you off from the immense diversity of life and the synergy of variety. It cuts you off from your own past and future, sealing you in a continuous present much the same way television does.

It is absurd and anti-life to be part of a system that compels you to listen to a stranger reading poetry when you want to learn to construct buildings or to sit with a stranger discussing the construction of buildings when you want to read poetry.

It is absurd and anti-life to move from cell to cell at the sound of a gong for every day of your youth in an institution that allows you no privacy and even follows you into the sanctuary of your home demanding that you do its "homework."

"How will they learn to read?!" you say, and my answer is "Remember the lessons of Massachusetts." When children are given whole lives instead of age-graded ones in cellblocks they learn to read, write, and do arithmetic with ease if those things make sense in the life that unfolds around them.

But keep in mind that in the United States almost nobody who reads, writes, or does arithmetic gets much respect. We are a land of talkers; we pay talkers the most and admire talkers the most and so our children talk constantly, following the public models of television and schoolteachers.[2] It is very difficult to teach the "basics" anymore because they really aren't basic to the society we've made.

Two institutions at present control our children's lives — television and schooling, in that order. Both of these reduce the real world of wisdom, fortitude, temperance, and justice to a never-ending, nonstop abstraction. In centuries past, the time of a child and adolescent would be occupied in real work, real charity, real adventures, and the real search for mentors who might teach what one really wanted to learn. A great deal of

[1]The American psychoanalyst, novelist, dramatist, poet, and social critic Paul Goodman (1911–1972) published his highly influential analysis of youth, *Growing Up Absurd,* in 1960. It became one of the leading books in the development of the '60s countercultural movement.
[2]For more on this topic, see "Blah, Blah, Blah: Is Anyone Listening?" (p. 367).

time was spent in community pursuits, practicing affection, meeting and studying every level of the community, learning how to make a home, and dozens of other tasks necessary to becoming a whole man or woman.

But here is the calculus of time the children I teach must deal with:

Out of the 168 hours in each week, my children must sleep fifty-six. That leaves them 112 hours a week out of which to fashion a self.

My children watch fifty-five hours of television a week, according to recent reports. That leaves them fifty-seven hours a week in which to grow up.

My children attend school thirty hours a week; use about eight hours getting ready, going, and coming home; and spend an average of seven hours a week in homework — a total of forty-five hours. During that time they are under constant surveillance, have no private time or private space, and are disciplined if they try to assert individuality in the use of time or space. That leaves twelve hours a week out of which to create a unique consciousness. Of course my kids eat, too, and that takes some time — not much, because we've lost the tradition of family dining. If we allot three hours a week to evening meals we arrive at a net amount of private time for each child of nine hours.

It's not enough. It's not enough, is it? The richer the kid, of course, the   20 less television he watches, but the rich kid's time is just as narrowly proscribed by a broader catalogue of commercial entertainments and his inevitable assignment to a series of private lessons in areas seldom of his choice.

And these things are, oddly enough, just a more cosmetic way to create dependent human beings, unable to fill their own hours, unable to initiate lines of meaning to give substance and pleasure to their existence. It's a national disease, this dependency and aimlessness, and I think schooling and television and lessons — the entire Chatauqua idea[3] — have a lot to do with it.

Think of the things that are killing us as a nation: drugs, brainless competition, recreational sex, the pornography of violence, gambling, alcohol, and the worst pornography of all — lives devoted to buying things — accumulation as a philosophy. All are addictions of dependent personalities and that is what our brand of schooling must inevitably produce.

I want to tell you what the effect is on children of taking all their time — time they need to grow up — and forcing them to spend it on abstractions. No reform that doesn't attack these specific pathologies will be anything more than a facade.

---

[3]Evolving from mid-nineteenth-century religious assemblies at Lake Chautauqua, New York, the Chatauqua (or Chautauqua) movement, with its emphasis on edifying lectures, played an important part in the early development of American public education.

1. The children I teach are indifferent to the adult world. This defies the experience of thousands of years. A close study of what big people were up to was always the most exciting occupation of youth, but nobody wants to grow up these days, and who can blame them. Toys are us.

2. The children I teach have almost no curiosity, and what little they do have is transitory; they cannot concentrate for very long, even on things they choose to do. Can you see a connection between the bells ringing again and again to change classes, and this phenomenon of evanescent attention?

3. The children I teach have a poor sense of the future, of how tomorrow is inextricably linked to today. They live in a continuous present; the exact moment they are in is the boundary of their consciousness.

4. The children I teach are ahistorical; they have no sense of how the past has predestined their own present, limiting their choices, shaping their values and lives.

5. The children I teach are cruel to each other; they lack compassion for misfortune, they laugh at weakness, they have contempt for people whose need for help shows too plainly.

6. The children I teach are uneasy with intimacy or candor. They cannot deal with genuine intimacy because of a lifelong habit of preserving a secret self inside an outer personality made up of artificial bits and pieces of behavior borrowed from television or acquired to manipulate teachers. Because they are not who they represent themselves to be, the disguise wears thin in the presence of intimacy, so intimate relationships have to be avoided.

7. The children I teach are materialistic, following the lead of schoolteachers who materialistically "grade" everything — and television mentors who offer everything in the world for sale.

8. The children I teach are dependent, passive, and timid in the presence of new challenges. This timidity is frequently masked by surface bravado or by anger or aggressiveness, but underneath is a vacuum without fortitude.

I could name a few other conditions that school reform will have to tackle if our national decline is to be arrested, but by now you will have grasped my thesis, whether you agree with it or not. Either schools, television, or both have caused these pathologies. It's a simple matter of arithmetic. Between schooling and television, all the time children have is eaten up. That's what has destroyed the American family; it no longer is a factor in the education of its own children.

What can be done? First, we need a ferocious national debate that doesn't quit, day after day, year after year; the kind of continuous emphasis that journalism finds boring. We need to scream and argue about this school thing until it is fixed or broken beyond repair, one or the other. If we can fix it, fine; if we cannot, then the success of home schooling shows a different road that has great promise. Pouring the money back into family education might kill two birds with one stone, repairing families as it repairs children.

Genuine reform is possible but it shouldn't cost anything. We need to rethink the fundamental premises of schooling and decide what it is we want all children to learn and why. For 140 years this nation has tried to impose objectives from a lofty command center made up of "experts," a central elite of social engineers. It hasn't worked. It won't work. It is a gross betrayal of the democratic promise that once made this nation a noble experiment. The Russian attempt to control Eastern Europe has exploded before our eyes. Our own attempt to impose the same sort of social orthodoxy, using the schools as an instrument, is also coming apart at the seams, albeit more slowly and painfully. It doesn't work because its fundamental premises are mechanical, anti-human, and hostile to family life. Lives can be controlled by machine education, but they will always fight back with weapons of social pathology — drugs, violence, self-destruction, indifference, and the symptoms I see in the children I teach.

It's high time we looked backward to regain an educational philosophy   35
that works. One I like particularly well has been a favorite of the ruling classes of Europe for thousands of years. I think it works just as well for poor children as for rich ones. I use as much of it as I can manage in my own teaching; as much, that is, as I can get away with, given the present institution of compulsory schooling.

At the core of this elite system of education is the belief that self-knowledge is the only basis of true knowledge. Everywhere in this system, at every age, you will find arrangements that place the child alone in an unguided setting with a problem to solve. Sometimes the problem is fraught with great risks, such as the problem of galloping a horse or making it jump, but that, of course, is a problem successfully solved by thousands of elite children before the age of ten. Can you imagine anyone who had mastered such a challenge ever lacking confidence in his ability to do anything? Sometimes the problem is that of mastering solitude, as Thoreau did at Walden Pond or Einstein did in the Swiss customs house.

One of my former students, Roland Legiardi-Laura, though both his parents were dead and he had no inheritance, took a bicycle across the United States alone when he was hardly out of boyhood. Is it any wonder that in manhood he made a film about Nicaragua, although he had no money and no prior experience with film-making and that it was an international award-winner — even though his regular work was as a carpenter?

Right now we are taking from our children the time they need to develop self-knowledge. That has to stop. We have to invent school experiences that give a lot of that time back. We need to trust children from a very early age with independent study, perhaps arranged in school, but which takes place away from the institutional setting. We need to invent a curriculum where each kid has a chance to develop uniqueness and self-reliance.

A short time ago, I took seventy dollars and sent a twelve-year-old girl with her non-English speaking mother on a bus down the New Jersey coast. She took the police chief of Sea Bright to lunch and apologized for polluting his beach with a discarded Gatorade bottle. In exchange for this public apology, I had arranged for the girl to have a one-day apprenticeship in small-town police procedures. A few days later, two more of my twelve-year-old kids traveled alone from Harlem to West 31st Street, where they began an apprenticeship with a newspaper editor. Next week, three of my kids will find themselves in the middle of the Jersey swamps at six in the morning studying the mind of a trucking company president as he dispatches eighteen-wheelers to Dallas, Chicago, and Los Angeles.

Are these "special" children in a "special" program? They're just nice   40
kids from Central Harlem, bright and alert but so badly schooled when they came to me that most of them couldn't add or subtract with any fluency. And not a single one knew the population of New York City or how far it is from New York to California.

Does that worry me? Of course. But I am confident that as they gain self-knowledge they'll also become self-teachers, and only self-teaching has any lasting value.

We've got to give the kids independent time right away because that is the key to self-knowledge, and we must reinvolve them with the real world as fast as possible so that the independent time can be spent on something other than more abstractions. This is an emergency. It requires drastic action to correct. Our children are dying like flies in our schools. Good schooling or bad schooling, it's all the same — irrelevant.

What else does a restructured school system need? It needs to stop being a parasite on the working community. I think we need to make community service a required part of schooling. It is the quickest way to give young children real responsibility.

For five years I ran a guerrilla school program where I had every kid, rich and poor, smart and dipsy, give 320 hours a year of hard community service. Dozens of those kids came back to me years later and told me that this one experience changed their lives, taught them to see in new ways, to rethink goals and values. It happened when they were thirteen in my Lab School program — only made possible because my rich school district was in chaos. When "stability" returned, the Lab closed. It was too successful, at too small a cost, to be allowed to continue. We made the expensive, elite programs look bad.

There is no shortage of real problems in this city. Kids can be asked to   45
help solve them in exchange for the respect and attention of the adult world. Good for kids, good for the rest of us.

Independent study, community service, adventures in experience, large doses of privacy and solitude, a thousand different apprenticeships — these are all powerful, cheap, and effective ways to start a real reform of schooling. But no large-scale reform is ever going to repair our damaged children and our damaged society until we force the idea of "school" open — to include family as the main engine of education. The Swedes realized this in 1976, when they effectively abandoned the [national system] of adopting unwanted children and instead spent national time and treasure on reinforcing the original family so that children born to Swedes were wanted. They reduced the number of unwanted Swedish children from 6,000 in 1976 to fifteen in 1986. So it can be done. The Swedes just got tired of paying for the social wreckage caused by [unwanted children] so they did something about it. We can, too.

Family is the main engine of education. If we use schooling to break children away from parents — and make no mistake, that has been the central function of schools since John Cotton announced it as the purpose of the Bay Colony Schools in 1650 and Horace Mann announced it as the purpose of Massachusetts schools in 1850 — we're going to continue to have the horror show we have right now.

The curriculum of family is at the heart of any good life. We've gotten away from that curriculum — it's time to return to it. The way to sanity in education is for our schools to take the lead in releasing the stranglehold of institutions on family life: to promote during school time confluences of parent and child that will strengthen family bonds. That was my real purpose in sending the girl and her mother down the Jersey coast to meet the police chief.

I have many ideas to make a family curriculum, and my guess is that a lot of you will have many ideas, too, once you begin to think about it. Our greatest problem in getting the kind of grassroots thinking going that could reform schooling is that we have large, vested interests profiting from schooling just exactly as it is, despite rhetoric to the contrary.

We have to demand that new voices and new ideas get a hearing, my ideas and yours. We've all had a bellyful of authorized voices on television and in the press. A decade-long free-for-all debate is called for now, not any more "expert" opinions. Experts in education have never been right; their "solutions" are expensive, self-serving, and always involve further centralization. Enough.

Time for a return to democracy, individuality, and family.

I've said my piece. Thank you.

A year and a half after I gave that speech, I quit teaching (on the Op-Ed page of the *Wall Street Journal,* July 25, 1991). A week later, I was asked to speak to the engineers at NASA-Goddard Space Center and a week after that I was at the White House. Then in rapid order I was invited to open the full season at the Nashville Center for the Arts, be the Keynote speaker for the Colorado Librarians Convention, and spend eight hours with the comptrollers of the thirty-two operating divisions of United Technologies Corp. in Hartford, CT. From there to The Farm commune in central Tennessee, an Indian reservation in New Mexico, and a Christian homeschool convention in Atlanta.

All in all, since I quit teaching five years ago, I've given 522 talks and workshops in forty-nine states (missed Oklahoma) and six foreign countries. I don't advertise, but I go anywhere I'm invited as long as my hosts don't tell me what I have to say.

Being in an airplane seat about one day in every two has added eighty-five pounds, so I expect to translate to the spirit world momentarily, if I don't come up with a strategy, but in the meantime, I've met an amazing cross-section of fine and courageous ordinary people from every point on the political/social spectrum — enough to convince me an American renaissance is latent in the common folk of this country if we can figure out a way to restore the democratic promise.

I think we will. I have faith, as well as hope, that we can do it.

Responding as a Reader

1. Gatto's article was originally a speech given at an educational conference. Can you tell that these remarks were written to be listened to, rather than read?

2. What is the difference between education and schooling, according to Gatto?

3. In the postscript, Gatto tells us that he has quit teaching and has taken up an international lecture circuit. Why do you think the magazine's editors close to give readers this information at the end of the article rather than the beginning? Does this information cause you to see Gatto's remarks in a different light?

Responding as a Writer

1. To be persuasive, Gatto makes a few sweeping generalizations about our educational system, our society, and family life. Select one generalization that you disagree with and support your case with specific examples that you think Gatto should consider.

2. Write a proposal for a new kind of school, one that answers Gatto's list of eight objections — and your own objections as well. How would you organize the school day (or the educational day) so that children learn what they need to learn to lead full, happy, and productive lives?

3. What, in your experience, does the American educational system do *right*? Answer Gatto's objections with a defense of American schools.

4. Recall Senator Kennedy's comment about compulsory schooling and the literacy rate of Massachusetts (para. 4). What causal relationship is implied? Do you think Kennedy opposes our system of compulsory education? What explanations can you offer for the statistic he uses?

RICHARD WEISSBOURD

The Feel-Good Trap

[THE NEW REPUBLIC / August 19 and 26, 1996]

In the last twenty-five years, self-esteem has become a watchword in American education. Some schools have set up self-esteem classes and days. Others tack posters to the walls that exhort and praise: "YOU CAN DO ANYTHING," "YOU ARE BEAUTIFUL." The manifest risibility of this trend has prompted a sneering backlash; *commentary* pages and Doonesbury panels alike have lampooned the self-esteem movement as a baleful confluence of 1960s liberal indulgence and soft psychology that distracts from schools' central mission of teaching the basics. Even Bob Dole exploited the issue as a 1996 campaign plank. He attacked the demise of old-fashioned pedagogical tools such as spelling bees, ridiculing the notion that "such competitions can only deal a blow to the self-esteem of those who don't win."

Plenty of liberals as well as conservatives agree that this attention to self-esteem is not just useless but dangerous. Yet the self-esteem movement has at least tried to deal with serious problems that its critics have ignored. Indeed, the critics' back-to-basics call to teach just reading and writing will also fail large numbers of children. Instead, educators need to embark on a third path: developing a wide range of intellectual and social skills in children and creating more sustained relationships between children and adults. Such a plan is ambitious, to be sure, but, unlike the current solutions, it at least stands a chance of helping more children prosper in adult life.

The self-esteem movement arose not only out of a national infatuation, beginning in the late 1960s, with the inner life but also as a way to solve a host of problems plaguing children in schools. Poor and black students lagged behind their non-poor and white peers, it was argued, because racism and classism eroded their self-worth. The issue was not their ability to learn but their *confidence* in their ability to learn. Raising their self-esteem would boost their achievement. The notion fast became a panacea in some quarters, and by 1990, a California state task force enshrined "the promotion of self-esteem" as a central goal of the curriculum, calling it a "social vaccine" that would inoculate children against academic failure,

RICHARD WEISSBOURD *is the author of* The Vulnerable Child: What Really Hurts America's Children and What We Can Do About It *(1996).*

drug use, welfare dependence, violence, and other ills. This task force has since become the whipping boy for the self-esteem critics.

For good reason. Thousands of studies on self-esteem have shown that the tenets of the movement just don't hold up. While there are different definitions of self-esteem and problems in measuring it, a multitude of studies reach the same conclusions. Programs to raise self-esteem — defined as a positive, global evaluation of the self — are not raising it. And the very premise that greater self-esteem will boost academic achievement is simply wrong. Self-esteem has little or no impact on academic achievement or on drug use, violence, or any other serious problems. Violent criminals, studies show, often have high self-esteem. And black children *already* have levels of self-esteem similar to white children; they take an equally positive view of themselves, but they're less likely to have a sense of efficacy: they see the outside world as placing obstacles in their path.

What's going on? For one thing, self-esteem doesn't lead to greater academic achievement unless a child values such achievement — high-school athletes may have high self-esteem but no interest in school — and it's no secret that large numbers of children don't. Nor should we expect self-esteem to reduce violence or encourage ethical self-conduct. Self-esteem comes in part from feeling powerful, and playground bullies, violent gang leaders, and all sorts of other nonacademic achievers can feel powerful. If children grow up in cultures that condone unethical conduct, they may end up feeling good about such conduct.

Further, there's a problem with the concept of self-esteem. Though some violent children have high self-esteem, the self that is being esteemed is immature, incapable of empathy, unaware of itself. Many violent children lash out not because of low self-worth but because they are highly prone to shame (that's why so much violence is triggered by acts of disrespect). Even if schools could jack up children's self-esteem, it might not affect their academic competence, their ability to manage humiliation, or their maturity. These are largely separate problems and require largely separate solutions.

Even more troubling, the self-esteem movement has often been harmful. Children know when they have really accomplished something and when they haven't, and too much unconditional praise produces not self-confidence but cynicism about adults and doubts about themselves. Talking about children's selves all the time can also teach them to make how they feel about themselves paramount. As developmental psychologist Robert Karen puts it, too much talk about the value of a child's entire being "trains children to think globally, to make their selves the issue in whatever they do, and thus to be prone to both grandiosity and self-contempt."

All this advertises for seriously rethinking the entire self-esteem movement. Some of this rethinking has argued that self-esteem is the *result* of academic achievement, not vice versa; others say academic achievement is important for its own sake, regardless of what it does for self-esteem. Both groups argue that schools should be dedicated to academic achievement — in some cases to rudimentary skills. As John Leo writes in *U.S. News and World Report,* "[U]ntil we grapple with the real agenda of the self-esteem movement — ersatz therapeutic massage instead of learning — there will probably be no reform at all."

There's no question schools should focus on academic achievement, both for its own sake and because it builds self-esteem in some (though not all) children. While children should be aware of racism and discrimination, no amount of talking about discrimination can substitute for raising non-white children's achievements. And the focus on self-esteem has sometimes, as critics contend, detracted from academics; teachers dumb down curricula, inflate grades, and avoid discussing real academic problems with parents. A special education teacher who works with almost all poor students told me the last thing she wanted was "for a child to fail," so she spent her time providing "a lot of hugs and kisses." It's hard to imagine a greater threat to poor children's learning than this kind of dismal assessment of their capacities.

Nonetheless, to harp on academic achievement is irrelevant and insulting to most educators. It simply doesn't answer the question they struggle with daily. Most teachers care deeply that children learn basic skills. The problem is how to overcome the hurdles that interfere with that learning. Educators know what self-esteem critics don't: Huge numbers of children suffer from social and emotional problems that both shrink their self-esteem and choke their ability to learn. Some children can't concentrate in class, for instance, because they have been abandoned by a parent, or because their violence-wracked neighborhoods deprive them of an elementary sense of control, or because they live with caregivers who are too depressed to be involved in their lives. For all its failings, the self-esteem movement has at least tried to deal with these problems. To talk of academic achievement without addressing these devastating troubles is fantasy for these children. 10

Further, academic achievement often doesn't boost self-esteem. Many children, girls especially, achieve at high levels yet have little self-esteem. And anyone who believes academic achievement is a royal road to self-esteem should spend time with first-year law students at Harvard, who are disgusted with themselves because they find themselves ranked not at the top but wallowing somewhere in the middle of their classes.

Finally, harping on achievement ignores the evidence that both effectiveness in adult life and self-esteem depend on a wide range of intellectual and social competencies. Harvard education professor Howard Gardner has documented many different types of intelligence, including interpersonal skills, that are crucial to success in adult life. Cultivating capacities such as self-awareness, control of one's impulses, and persistence needn't detract from teaching academics. Good teachers build these competencies in the course of academic instruction. Teaching literature can clearly impart all sorts of social and moral lessons.

Schools need to forget about self-esteem altogether as an explicit goal. They should instead set high expectations of children, cultivate in them a wide range of competencies, coping strategies, and ethical sensibilities and show them the value of these abilities. Nonwhite children need to be given tools for understanding and responding to discrimination while still meeting high academic expectations. If schools want children to be less violent and more ethical, they should, among other things, provide them with opportunities to give to others, help them to manage their frustration and shame when they feel disrespected, and enable them to see moral issues from multiple points of view. A teacher might, for example, ask a violent child to host a talk show on gun control or create a classroom city government and ask a scapegoated kid to be mayor.

Cartoon

A +

— By Don Wright of the *Palm Beach Post;* reprinted in the *Washington Post* (February 17, 1997).

To prepare children for adult life schools also need to focus on something else, which neither self-esteem proponents nor critics talk about. Critical qualities that children need to develop for adulthood — persistence, the capacity to handle shame and disappointment, the ability to recognize the needs of others, and to balance them with one's own — cannot be simply transmitted. They are the ingredients of maturity, and this kind of maturity typically develops when children have a certain kind of relationship with adults.

The psychoanalyst Heinz Kohut argues that a child's self matures in   15
two ways: by being mirrored by adults and by being esteemed by consistent, admired adults. By "mirroring," Kohut meant that all children need adults who listen to and understand them and regularly reflect their understanding; such reflections develop children's sense of coherence and rightness in the world. Kohut also recognized that at certain stages of development, every child needs adults whom he or she idealizes. Psychologists have long recognized that in adolescence, children get a second chance to internalize the confident expectations of esteemed adults. That chance should not be squandered.

To listen and reflect, adults need first to spend more time with children. The self-esteem movement's constant praising of children is a short cut, a desperate substitute for the inability of teachers and other adults to pay sufficient attention to any one child. But time and attention are real to a child in ways that praise is not. Parents, of course, best provide this time and attention, but when parents cannot or do not do so, other adults should. This doesn't entail "babysitting": It means spending a few (or more) hours a week listening to, challenging, and developing the strengths of a child.

Schools need to push beyond the academic achievement versus self-esteem debate and embark on a variety of strategies that involve adults more in children's lives. Class sizes need to come down. Schools need to work harder to involve parents, including absentee fathers, in their children's education. And schools need to keep trying to bring more adults into children's lives who are worthy of esteem by making teaching and other types of work with children more attractive, including through higher status and better pay. Granted, this all amounts to a tall order. Yet these steps, taken together, would be far more meaningful than focusing simply on a nostrum like returning to basics or on a spurious metasolution like self-esteem.

Responding as a Reader

1. What, specifically, is wrong with teaching self-esteem, according to Weissbourd? What's right about it?

2. How does Weissbourd define self-esteem? How does he define maturity? How do children acquire these qualities?

3. Weissbourd advocates a third way to teach kids, distinct from the self-esteem movement and the back-to-basics movement. How would Weissbourd's plan work? List the steps.

Responding as a Writer

1. Is self-esteem the result of achievement or the cause of it? Think of a time when you accomplished something that made you feel proud and write an essay analyzing the psychic causes and effects of that accomplishment. What was it that enabled you to accomplish that feat, and what doors did its accomplishment open for you?

2. Weissbourd relies on several abstract nouns referring to feelings and personal qualities — such as self-esteem, confidence, achievement, ethics, power, empathy, shame, maturity. Choose one of these terms and define it at length, considering how the quality is developed. Be sure to supply examples.

3. Choose one aspect of life that is especially important to you — basketball, politics, the clarinet, anything you like. Write an essay explaining what you need to do to succeed at this activity. Are any of these qualifications also necessary for academic success?

AMITAI ETZIONI

Education for Intimacy

[TIKKUN / March–April 1997]

Instead of approaching the discussion of sex in public schools as a matter of health and safety bereft of moral content or forbidding discussion of sex out of traditional moral concerns (seeking to rely exclusively on the family and religious institutions for this purpose), schools should develop a program of education that provides children with the facts they need to know, within the context of values that responsible and moral persons seek to affirm and embody in their lives. Sex education should not be taught as a chapter in human hygiene or human biology, akin to dental care or car mechanics. We can find better sources and role models for teaching this subject than what the birds and the bees do. Nor should sex education be treated as if it is, was, or could be, value-free.

Education for interpersonal relations, family life, and intimacy should occur in all public schools, at least in junior high schools (or middle schools) and high schools. The program should include discussion of human nature, an examination of human beings as social creatures who require one another; who find deep satisfaction, longer and healthier lives, when they are part of lasting social relations; and who have transcendental needs for meanings and moral values. The program should explore the responsibilities that we have for one another as members of a community and ways we can strengthen our relations with one another, as co-workers, neighbors, friends, and potential family members. This topic includes teaching ways to work out differences, by techniques such as improved communication skills and conflict resolution. Discussion of family life will explore matters such as the nature of the commitments involved in marriage; shar-

---

Amitai Etzioni (b. 1929) received his B.A. and M.A. from the Hebrew University of Jerusalem and his Ph.D. from the University of California, Berkeley. He has previously taught at Columbia University and Harvard and has edited numerous publications. In 1991 he received the Scientific Achievement Award and the Jeffrey Pressman Award. He has published essays in prominent journals and many books such as The Spirit of Community: Rights, Responsibilities and the Communitarian Agenda, *which was published in 1993. He is currently a university professor at George Washington University, founder and chair of* The Communitarian Network, *editor of* The Responsive Community, *and author of* The New Golden Rule *(1996).*

ing decision-making in such matters as relocation and forming and adhering to budget; and the issues raised by intimate relations, ranging from the avoidance of exploitative relations to the use of contraceptives.

Schools now cover a good portion of these topics in a variety of classes such as social studies and home economics, while ignoring other parts. Schools need to combine some of these elements already in place with new ones to provide a comprehensive and morally sound approach to interpersonal relations and to provide the needed context for teaching sex education.

Specifically, a public school program of sex education should be folded into a much more encompassing treatment of interpersonal relations, family life, and intimacy to be developed by taking into account the premises and principles here articulated.

Developing a strong character needs to be at the core of all education programs and particularly of programs dedicated to interpersonal relations, family life, and intimacy. Persons of weak character cannot take responsibility for their actions, abide by values they themselves believe in, be good partners in a relationship, or be upstanding members of a community. Character development is essential both because without it all other educational efforts will be undermined (as we see in disorderly classrooms) and whatever education is imparted will be woefully lacking.

Two personality capabilities stand out as leading the agenda of character building. First, a person of good character is able to restrain his or her raw impulses by channeling them into socially constructive and morally sound avenues rather than mindlessly yielding to them. Such a person can express affection and commitment in socially and morally appropriate manners. Second, a person of good character can empathize with the other person involved who may have different needs or be in a different stage of sexual and social development.

The underlying orientation of the intimacy program to sex is that sex is inherently neither good nor evil, neither pure nor sinful; the context makes all the difference. Sex is somewhat akin to nuclear energy: properly contained it is a boon to the world; let loose it can be a highly destructive force. As Kevin Ryan, professor at the School of Education at Boston University, put it:

"Sex is strong stuff. It is a powerful force in people's lives, and as such, it can be a strong force for individual happiness and family stability. On the other hand, selfish and uncontrolled sex can be a raging cyclone, making havoc of those in its path.

We find throughout history extreme attempts to control sex through barbaric acts such as genital mutilation, stoning of prostitutes, and summary executions of adulterous princesses. And we find cultures that seek to "free" sex from its moral and social context, tolerating forcing children to marry old men and accepting child prostitution. The facts that need to be shared with the young generation are, as we learn from both historical and contemporary experiences, that both attempts to repress sex as well as to let it roam freely cause much human misery.

Sexual exploitation, for example, is far from unknown, even in our society. A high proportion of teen pregnancies are caused by men who are not high-school boys but who are at least five years older than the girls they impregnate. Frequently, these are men who hang around the mothers of the girls involved and sex is nonconsensual. Seventy-five percent of teenage pregnancies and youth-affected STDs [sexually transmitted diseases] would still occur if all teenage boys refrained from having sex; fifty-one percent of pregnancies in junior high school would still occur if teenage boys refrained from having sex, according to one study. Incest is also all too common. Strategies for dealing with those who pressure children to have sex should be included in all intimacy programs.

Several studies and surveys of teenage girls have found that, more than information about contraception, STDs, HIV, and pregnancy, what girls seek most is information on how to refuse to engage in sexual acts without hurting someone's feelings. Better communication skills are also necessary for boys, particularly relating to rape and sexual harassment prevention and how to relate better to fellow human beings. These skills make people into better friends, employees, neighbors, and community members. They are particularly significant in the context of sex education.

Even much less severe expressions of sex are matters of serious concern. Making sexual advances to someone committed to one's friend is a quick way to lose that friendship and to offend one's community. The same holds for continuing to make sexual advances to those who indicate that they do not appreciate being approached.

In contrast, sex properly contextualized is a precondition of our future. Sex can be an appropriate way to cement relations that have properly matured, and it can be a source of much joy. In short, sex should always be viewed, treated, and taught within the context of values and relations.

Specifically, when the general orientation of the program is brought to bear on sex education, the program should stress that bringing children into the world is a moral act — one that entails a set of personal and social responsibilities. We all need to appreciate that sex is not a merely biological act; sex is much more than "recreational." It is an act that can carry with it serious consequences, including loss of life. Responsible persons weigh the moral issues involved; they take into account that yielding to impulse in this area can lead to dire consequences for the child to be born, restrict the life chances of the parents, and corrode the values of the communities in which we are all members.

Education for intimacy seeks to encourage children to refrain from having children. Children born to children often suffer considerably physiologically, psychologically, and otherwise. These babies are more prone to illnesses, anxieties, and other afflictions. They often become public charges in a society that is increasingly disinclined to attend to children properly.

Children who have babies often find their life opportunities seriously constricted. They are much less likely to complete their studies, find work, and otherwise develop their own life, economically, socially, and otherwise.

When educational programs favor that young people defer engaging in sex, the question is raised: Should sex be deferred until a person is eighteen? Twenty-one? Married? The question is often raised by those who argue that sex is only proper within marriage. While much is to be said for deferring sex until two people have made the kind of permanent commitment and mutual responsibility implied by marriage, marriage does not provide the only criterion. We would urge young teens to defer both sex and marriage on the grounds that they are likely not to be ready to make a responsible decision in either department. And we are less troubled by intimate relations between mature adults than between children. Maturity is measured by behavior rather than chronological age, but it is more common among those who are older than those who are younger.

Many discussions of sex education start with the question of which sex education methodology to follow. I deliberately delayed addressing this issue to emphasize that if proper values and interpersonal skill development are included in the intimacy education program, intercourse is no longer the only issue or main focus. At the same time we maintain that programs that deal only with values or relations but exclude specific sex education are insufficient for reasons that will become evident shortly.

The methodology I favor diverges from the notion that sex should be described simply as a natural, healthy act and that children should be taught how to proceed safely but not be discouraged otherwise. Statements such as "sexuality is a natural and healthy part of living" and "all persons are sexual" may be correct by some standards of psychiatry (which consider all erotic responses sexual) but are open to gross misinterpretation when given to children, especially without the proper normative context. To state that "the primary goal of sexuality education is the promotion of sexual health" is particularly unfortunate in this context. At the same time, approaches that treat sex not tied to procreation as sinful, shameful, or dirty should be avoided. To say, in this context, that "most merciful God, we confess we are in bondage to sin and cannot free ourselves," may speak to some people with religious commitments (but surely offends others), provided as a part of a statement about "human sexuality" it sends a rather different message than the one endorsed here.

Sex should be viewed originally as a primordial urge. Like all others, it cannot be ignored and should not be suppressed but its expressions must be subject to self-control. What is needed is that a person will form judgments before he or she acts and that a person will channel expression of this urge into morally and socially proper, responsible channels.

Narrow sex education programs that favor sharing full information about safe sex with young children are problematic. These programs tend to assume that the resulting effects of encouraging sexual activity are minimal. Also troublesome are programs that address contraception in what Jane Mauldon and Kristin Luker say is ". . . a tone of value neutrality, focusing on clinical information to the exclusion of social, emotional, and moral aspects of sex," as some do.

At the same time I am also concerned about programs that promote abstinence only and do not take sufficiently into account the moral issues that arise by the many (even those in highly religious groups) who do not adhere to the high standards involved by engaging in sex and hence risking exposure to AIDS and other STDs or experience unwanted pregnancies. These effects can be significantly reduced, albeit not eliminated, if students are taught about safer sex.

Educators, parents, community members, and policymakers need to understand that there are ways to strongly urge young people to defer sexual behavior and still provide information for those who proceed anyhow, without making these two messages cancel each other out or seem contradictory. Schools ought to employ programs that urge children to wait — at least until they are mature enough to deal with the consequences of their sexual acts — but also provide them with information on how to conduct themselves if they do not wait. Responsibility should include the notion of deferring sex and engaging in it in a responsible manner. This position is advocated by Bishop Albert Rouet, the chairman of the French Roman Catholic bishops' social committee, among others.

In dealing with other topics, divorce for instance, religious groups have found ways to extol the importance of preserving marriage and still counsel those who divorce. The same can be done for sex education. One can strongly advocate abstinence but also provide youngsters with age-appropriate sex information and ways to proceed responsibly and more safely, lest they rely on misconstrued notions provided by much less wholesome and irresponsible sources. (This approach is sometimes referred to as "abstinence, plus.")

Merely relying on willpower, "just say no," is psychologically naive   25 and unrealistic. Educators should point out that use of drugs and alcohol reduces our self-control and that other forms of intimacy than intercourse are also best deferred. Our grandparents had a point: Dressing eight-year-old girls with training bras, arranging "socials" with close dancing for nine-year-old children, and other such activities do not always lead to premature sexual experimentation but neither are they without any such effects.

Children need to be taught that the use of alcohol and drugs lowers a person's ability to deal with urges in ways that are socially constructive and morally responsible. They need to learn — and above all experience — the joy of living up to their moral values and social commitment by engaging in acts such as community service, peer mentoring, sports, successful completion of taxing assignments, and sharing in the household duties.

"Just say no" should be preceded, accompanied and followed by mores one finds reason or value for saying "yes" to. The sociological record shows that those positively engaged are most able to resist yielding to their raw impulses. There are so many other meaningful and enjoyable activities to cultivate.

The program envisioned should not be limited to lectures and reading material. Role playing, role modeling, peer mentoring, school assemblies, plays, tapes, and other educational techniques should be used. Acquiring communication skills allows people to fend off unwanted and premature sexual advances without feeling inadequate, guilty, or isolated. They enable youngsters to handle conflicts that arise when the pace of development of two or more young people varies. Assemblies, peer juries, and other such educational techniques help develop the moral voice of the school community.

Parents should be involved; they have both rights and responsibilities in this area. If parents would initiate, advance, and complete the education of their children in a socially and morally appropriate manner, there would be no need for schools to become involved in this subject. The fact, though, is that all too many parents are either unable to unwilling to dedicate themselves sufficiently to the education of their children. Indeed, throughout modern times, schools have supplemented parental education and stepped in where parents were not available or their contributions to character education were inadequate. Public education for intimacy is no different.

The fact, however, that some of the responsibility for sex education is delegated to schools does not mean that parents have lost their right and duty to be involved in decision-making concerning the education to which their children are subjected, especially with highly charged and normatively loaded issues. True, parents are not the only ones who have a say when it comes to education; the state, for instance, mandates both attendance and numerous subjects and other matters of education policy. The parents, though, should not be excluded both as a matter of right and because their involvement can greatly enhance the education provided in school.

Parents have a right to be informed and consulted about all school programs. Schools should actively reach out to the parents and keep them informed about their approach to teaching sex education and what issues they will discuss. The parents' right is accompanied by a responsibility of the parents to inform themselves on the issues at hand before they act to curtail a program or urge the adoption of another or seek to remove their children from a given course. 30

Parents should have the right — and be afforded the opportunity — to opt children out of classes on intimacy but not to block the whole program. This opting-out system requires notifying parents ahead of time about the material that is going to be covered in such classes, the methodology to be used, and other relevant matters. Children who are being opted out by their parents should be given some other assignments in the same period.

At the same time, an opt-in system, according to which a child would only be enrolled in a course if his or her parents provided prior written approval, is not called for. Children should not be denied education of any kind just because their parents are not available or are indifferent to the point that they neglect to act. They should be given full opportunity to act on their values but not to block education by inaction.

There is an exception to the above policy: The community may take the position that withholding certain kinds of information directly endangers lives. Similar to vaccines, the common good may take priority over parental objections under certain limited conditions. If schools have evidence that in their jurisdiction a significant number of children die from AIDS and they believe that there is no other way to prevent the spread of the disease among their students, they may require "inoculation" of youngsters against such dangers by sharing with them proper information and devices. This should be done only after the community discusses these matters with its elected bodies and following open hearings.

Schools are but one factor in the societal matrix that affects children's attitudes toward sex. The media, families, adult role models, socioeconomic forces, and numerous other factors affect young people. Educators should make it clear that they cannot single-handedly deliver all the desired outcomes. Educators need to act as agents who endeavor to activate other social agents, calling on them to discharge their responsibilities in this area, become partners of and with educators. For instance, educators should support efforts to improve the messages to which children are exposed on television. At the same time, these "other" forces should not be used as a rationale for families or educators to not do their part.

Responding as a Reader

1. Jot down the skills and lessons that Etzioni advocates teaching in schools. What kinds of skills are these? Try sorting them into different groups. Do you agree with Etzioni that school is the right place to teach all these lessons?

2. What, according to Etzioni, is a person of "strong character"? How can schools help students to build character?

3. Etzioni is a founder of the Communitarian political party. From the name of the party and from the argument Etzioni proposes here, can you infer what the Communitarians are about? After you have sketched out your own definition, look the word up in a good, current dictionary or search for it on the World Wide Web. How does understanding Etzioni's politics help you to understand this article?

Responding as a Writer

1. Starting with paragraph 19, Etzioni sets forth his proposal for teaching "education for intimacy." Choose one paragraph in this section and rewrite it to address an audience that is ideologically opposed to Etzioni — one that believes that such discussions should be conducted within the family, for example. Try to anticipate this audience's concerns and address them fairly and logically.

2. How was sex education taught in your school system? Did the schools address the issues that you considered important, in ways that you considered appropriate? Write a critique that you could share with the school board.

3. What values are especially important to you? What is the best way for children to learn these values? Propose a program for teaching children one skill that you consider essential for a good life. This program can be offered by schools or by some other organization.

Discussing the Unit

Suggested Topic for Discussion

What exactly should be taught in our schools? Are ethical, psychological, and social lessons just as important as academic ones? If public schools need to teach more than reading, writing, and arithmetic, how do you suggest they accomplish this? If teaching ethical, psychological, and social skills is not the responsibility of the schools, then whose responsibility is it? Can we as a nation afford to leave these skills untaught?

Preparing for Class Discussion

1. List the skills that Gatto, Etzioni, and Weissbourd believe should be taught in school. Which do you think are most important, which least important? Would you add any skills to the list? Arrange the skills in order of importance.

2. Think about your own education. What were your academic goals when you were in elementary school? When you were in high school? Did you get what you were looking for? If not, why not? What are your academic goals now? What do you need to do to achieve them?

3. *Prewriting Assignment:* Consider the point of view of adults who do not currently have school-age children. Should they care about public education? Why or why not? Think of a few ways in which public edu-

cation affects the general public. For each, write a paragraph that makes the connection between school-age children and adults without school-age children.

From Discussion to Writing

In an essay, describe the ideal school, one that accomplishes all the goals that you believe are important. What classes are taught? How are the classrooms set up? What homework is assigned? How are teachers trained?

10

English-Only Laws: Does America Need an Official Language?

In August 1996, the House of Representatives overwhelmingly approved a bill to make English the official language of the United States. Although many influential academics and policymakers, both conservative and liberal, oppose such a law and although the Supreme Court early in 1997 dismissed an Arizona case that was expected to have a broad legal impact, there is enough popular sentiment to turn the proposal into a serious and divisive future issue. While running for president in 1996, Bob Dole voiced his support for English-only legislation, and even Bill Clinton, while governor of Arkansas, supported an English-only law (though as President he opposes one). What are the chances that English will be established as the "official language"? How would such a law operate? And would it end up causing more harm than good?

In "Should English Be the Law?," Robert D. King, a University of Texas specialist in world linguistics, examines the destructiveness of various official language movements throughout the world and finds the healthiest societies are usually those that tolerate a multiplicity of languages. Although she acknowledges the cultural importance of a shared language in "Language and American Citizens," Jean Bethke Elshtain, one of the nation's leading political theorists, believes that legislation to dictate an official language would be a sure sign of fear and civil weakness. Speaking as a member of an immigrant group that would be seriously affected by

English-only legislation, Karen Narasaki, the head of an Asian American legal consortium, argues that "English-only bills are not only extremely divisive, they are absurd in light of the fact that English, like any other modern language, is an ever-evolving amalgamation of words from different languages." In "Double Talk," she reminds us of estimates that show three of every four words in our dictionary are "non-Anglo in origin." Finally, an advertisement for the organization "U.S. English" makes it clear that this issue will be around for quite some time.

Do *you* think America needs an official language? Whatever your answer, you've got company, as the following survey results prove.

Selected Survey Results

English-Only

- Freshmen at all institutions who agree that all official documents should be in English: 44.3%
- Men who do: 54.9%
- Women who do: 35.9%
- At all black colleges: 31.7%
- Freshmen who are native English speakers: 93.1%

— From *The American Freshman: National Norms For Fall 1996.*

ROBERT D. KING

Should English Be the Law?

[THE ATLANTIC MONTHLY/April 1997]

We have known race riots, draft riots, labor violence, secession, anti-war protests, and a whiskey rebellion, but one kind of trouble we've never had: a language riot. Language riot? It sounds like a joke. The very idea of language as a political force — as something that might threaten to split a country wide apart — is alien to our way of thinking and to our cultural traditions.

This may be changing. On August 1 of last year, the U.S. House of Representatives approved a bill that would make English the official language of the United States. The vote was 259 to 169, with 223 Republicans and thirty-six Democrats voting in favor and eight Republicans, 160 Democrats, and one independent voting against. The debate was intense, acrid, and partisan. On March 25 of last year, the Supreme Court agreed to review a case involving an Arizona law that would require public employees to conduct government business only in English.[1] Arizona is one of several states that have passed "Official English" or "English Only" laws. The appeal to the Supreme Court followed a 6-to-5 ruling, in October of 1995, by a federal appeals court striking down the Arizona law. These events suggest how divisive a public issue language could become in America — even if it has until now scarcely been taken seriously.

Traditionally, the American way has been to make English the national language — but to do so quietly, locally, without fuss. The Constitution is silent on language: The Founding Fathers had no need to legislate that English be the official language of the country. It has always been taken for granted that English *is* the national language and that one must learn English to make it in America.

To say that language has never been a major force in American history or politics, however, is not to say that politicians have always resisted linguistic jingoism. In 1753 Benjamin Franklin voiced his concern that Ger-

---

[1] In March 1997, the Supreme Court dismissed the complaint because the plaintiff no longer worked for the state of Arizona.

ROBERT D. KING (b. 1936) is the Audre and Bernard Rapoport Chair of Jewish Studies at the University of Texas at Austin. He is a professor and writer of linguistics, India, and the Yiddish language. His latest book, Nehru and the Politics of India, was published in 1996.

man immigrants were not learning English: "Those [Germans] who come hither are generally the most ignorant Stupid Sort of their own Nation. . . . they will soon so out number us, that all the advantages we have will not, in My Opinion, be able to preserve our language, and even our government will become precarious." Theodore Roosevelt articulated the unspoken American linguistic-melting-pot theory[2] when he boomed, "We have room for but one language here, and that is the English language, for we intend to see that the crucible turns our people out as Americans, of American nationality, and not as dwellers in a polyglot boarding house." And: "We must have but one flag. We must also have but one language. That must be the language of the Declaration of Independence, of Washington's Farewell address, of Lincoln's Gettysburg speech and second inaugural."

Teddy Roosevelt's linguistic tub-thumping long typified the tradition of American politics. That tradition began to change in the wake of the anything-goes attitudes and the celebration of cultural differences arising in the 1960s. A 1975 amendment to the Voting Rights Act of 1965 mandated the "bilingual ballot" under certain circumstances, notably when the voters of selected language groups reached 5 percent or more in a voting district. Bilingual education became a byword of educational thinking during the 1960s. By the 1970s, linguists had demonstrated convincingly — at least to other academics — that black English (today called African American vernacular English or Ebonics) was not "bad" English but a different kind of authentic English with its own rules. Predictably, there have been scattered demands that black English be included in bilingual-education programs.

It was against this background that the movement to make English the official language of the country arose. In 1981, Senator S. I. Hayakawa,[3] long a leading critic of bilingual education and bilingual ballots, introduced in the U.S. Senate a constitutional amendment that not only would have made English the official language but would have prohibited federal and state laws and regulations requiring the use of other languages. His English Language Amendment died in the Ninety-Seventh Congress.

In 1983, the organization called U.S. English was founded by Hayakawa and John Tanton, a Michigan ophthalmologist. The primary purpose of the organization was to promote English as the official language of the United States. (The best background readings on America's "neolinguisticism" are the books *Hold Your Tongue,* by James Crawford, and *Language Loyalties,* edited by Crawford, both published in 1992.) Of-

5

---

[2]For further discussion of the "melting pot" theory, see Peter Salins (p. 158).

[3]A prominent semanticist, the Canadian-born S[amuel] I[chiye] Hayakawa (1906–1992) authored several books on language. In the late '60s, while serving as president of San Francisco State College, he strenuously opposed student radicalism. He served one term in the U.S. Senate in the 1970s and was a leading spokesman for promoting English as an official language.

ficial English initiatives were passed by California in 1986; by Arkansas, Mississippi, North Carolina, North Dakota, and South Carolina in 1987; by Colorado, Florida, and Arizona in 1988; and by Alabama in 1990. The majorities voting for these initiatives were generally not insubstantial: California's, for example, passed by 73 percent.

It was probably inevitable that the Official English (or English Only — the two names are used almost interchangeably) movement would acquire a conservative, almost reactionary undertone in the 1990s. Official English is politically very incorrect. But its cofounder John Tanton brought with him strong liberal credentials. He had been active in the Sierra Club and Planned Parenthood and in the 1970s served as the national president of Zero Population Growth. Early advisers of U.S. English resist ideological pigeonholing: they included Walter Annenberg, Jacques Barzun, Bruno Bettelheim, Alistair Cooke, Denton Cooley, Walter Cronkite, Angier Biddle Duke, George Gilder, Sidney Hook, Norman Podhoretz, Arnold Schwarzenegger, and Karl Shapiro. In 1987, U.S. English installed as its president Linda Chávez,[4] a Hispanic who had been prominent in the Reagan Administration. A year later she resigned her position, citing "repugnant" and "anti-Hispanic" overtones in an internal memorandum written by Tanton. Tanton, too, resigned, and Walter Cronkite, describing the affair as "embarrassing," left the advisory board. One board member, Norman Cousins, defected in 1986, alluding to the "negative symbolic significance" of California's Official English initiative, Proposition 63. The current chairman of the board and CEO of U.S. English is Mauro E. Mujica [see Advertisement, p. 224], who claims that the organization has 650,000 members.

The popular wisdom is that conservatives are pro and liberals con. True, conservatives such as George Will and William F. Buckley Jr. have written columns supporting Official English. But would anyone characterize as conservatives the present and past U.S. English board members Alistair Cooke, Walter Cronkite, and Norman Cousins? One of the strongest opponents of bilingual education is the Mexican American writer Richard Rodriguez [see p. 169], best known for his eloquent autobiography, *Hunger of Memory* (1982). There is a strain of American liberalism that defines itself in nostalgic devotion to the melting pot.

For several years relevant bills awaited consideration in the U.S. House 10 of Representatives. The Emerson Bill (H.R. 123), passed by the House last August, specifies English as the official language of government and requires that the government "preserve and enhance" the official status of English. Exceptions are made for the teaching of foreign languages; for actions necessary for public health, international relations, foreign trade, and

---

[4]Linda Chávez writes a regular column for *USA Today*. The highest ranking woman in the Reagan administration, she ran unsuccessfully for the U.S. Senate in 1986.

the protection of the rights of criminal defendants; and for the use of "terms of art" from languages other than English. It would, for example, stop the Internal Revenue Service from sending out income-tax forms and instructions in languages other than English, but it would not ban the use of foreign languages in census materials or documents dealing with national security. "*E Pluribus Unum*" can still appear on American money. U.S. English supports the bill.

What are the chances that some version of Official English will become federal law? Any language bill will face tough odds in the Senate, because some western senators have opposed English-only measures in the past for various reasons, among them a desire by Republicans not to alienate the growing number of Hispanic Republicans, most of whom are uncomfortable with mandated monolingualism. Texas Governor George W. Bush, too, has forthrightly said that he would oppose any English-only proposals in his state. Several of the Republican candidates for President in 1996 (an interesting exception is Phil Gramm) endorsed versions of Official English, as has Newt Gingrich. While governor of Arkansas, Bill Clinton signed into law an English-only bill. As President, he has described his earlier action as a mistake.

Many issues intersect in the controversy over Official English: immigration (above all), the rights of minorities (Spanish-speaking minorities in particular), the pros and cons of bilingual education, tolerance, how best to educate the children of immigrants, and the place of cultural diversity in school curricula and in American society in general. The question that lies at the root of most of the uneasiness is this: Is America threatened by the preservation of languages other than English? Will America, if it continues on its traditional path of benign linguistic neglect, go the way of Belgium, Canada, and Sri Lanka — three countries among many whose unity is gravely imperiled by language and ethnic conflicts?

Language and nationalism were not always so intimately intertwined. Never in the heyday of rule by sovereign was it a condition of employment that the King be able to speak the language of his subjects. George I spoke no English and spent much of his time away from England, attempting to use the power of his kingship to shore up his German possessions. In the Middle Ages, nationalism was not even part of the picture: one owed loyalty to a lord, a prince, a ruler, a family, a tribe, a church, a piece of land but not to a nation and least of all to a nation as a language unit. The capital city of the Austrian Hapsburg empire was Vienna, its ruler a monarch with effective control of peoples of the most varied and incompatible ethnicities, and languages, throughout Central and Eastern Europe. The official language, and the lingua franca[5] as well, was German. While it stood — and it stood for

---

[5]A "lingua franca" is any language that is used as a common language by those who speak different languages; for example, English is becoming the lingua franca of airline pilots.

hundreds of years — the empire was an anachronistic relic of what for most of human history had been the normal relationship between country and language: none.

The marriage of language and nationalism goes back at least to Romanticism and specifically to Rousseau, who argued in his *Essay on the Origin of Languages* that language must develop before politics is possible and that language originally distinguished nations from one another. A little-remembered aim of the French Revolution — itself the legacy of Rousseau — was to impose a national language on France, where regional languages such as Provençal, Breton, and Basque were still strong competitors against standard French, the French of the Ile de France. As late as 1789, when the Revolution began, half the population of the south of France, which spoke Provençal, did not understand French. A century earlier the playwright Racine said that he had had to resort to Spanish and Italian to make himself understood in the southern French town of Uzès. After the Revolution, nationhood itself became aligned with language.

In 1846 Jacob Grimm, one of the Brothers Grimm of fairytale fame but better known in the linguistic establishment as a forerunner of modern comparative and historical linguists, said that "a nation is the totality of people who speak the same language." After midcentury, language was invoked more than any other single criterion to define nationality. Language as a political force helped to bring about the unification of Italy and of Germany and the secession of Norway from its union with Sweden in 1905. Arnold Toynbee[6] observed — unhappily — soon after the First World War that "the growing consciousness of Nationality had attached itself neither to traditional frontiers nor to new geographical associations but almost exclusively to mother tongues."

The crowning triumph of the new desideratum was the Treaty of Versailles, in 1919, when the allied victors of the First World War began redrawing the map of Central and Eastern Europe according to nationality as best they could. The magic word was "self-determination," and none of Woodrow Wilson's Fourteen Points mentioned the word "language" at all. Self-determination was thought of as being related to "nationality," which today we would be more likely to call "ethnicity"; but language was simpler to identify than nationality or ethnicity. When it came to drawing the boundary lines of various countries — Czechoslovakia, Yugoslavia, Romania, Hungary, Albania, Bulgaria, Poland — it was principally language that guided the draftsman's hand. (The main exceptions were Alsace-Lorraine, South Tyrol, and the German-speaking parts of Bohemia and Moravia.) Almost by default, language became the defining characteristic of nationality.

---

[6]Arnold Toynbee (1889–1975) was a preeminent English historian and the author of a highly popular study of world civilizations.

And so it remains today. In much of the world, ethnic unity and cultural identification are routinely defined by language. To be Arab is to speak Arabic. Bengali identity is based on language in spite of the division of Bengali-speakers between Hindu India and Muslim Bangladesh. When eastern Pakistan seceded from greater Pakistan in 1971, it named itself Bangladesh: *"desa"* means "country"; *"bangla"* means not the Bengali people or the Bengali territory but the Bengali language.

Scratch most nationalist movements and you find a linguistic grievance. The demands for independence of the Baltic states (Latvia, Lithuania, and Estonia) were intimately bound up with fears for the loss of their respective languages and cultures in a sea of Russianness. In Belgium, the war between French and Flemish threatens an already weakly fused country. The present atmosphere of Belgium is dark and anxious, costive; the metaphor of divorce is a staple of private and public discourse. The lines of terrorism in Sri Lanka are drawn between Tamil Hindus and Sinhalese Buddhists — and also between the Tamil and Sinhalese languages. Worship of the French language fortifies the movement for an independent Quebec. Whether a united Canada will survive into the twenty-first century is a question too close to call. Much of the anxiety about language in the United States is probably fueled by the "Quebec problem": Unlike Belgium, which is a small European country, or Sri Lanka, which is halfway around the world, Canada is our close neighbor.

Language is a convenient surrogate for nonlinguistic claims that are often awkward to articulate, for they amount to a demand for more political and economic power. Militant Sikhs in India call for a state of their own: Khalistan ("Land of the Pure" in Punjabi). They frequently couch this as a demand for a linguistic state, which has a certain simplicity about it, a clarity of motive — justice, even, because states in India are normally linguistic states. But the Sikh demands blend religion, economics, language, and retribution for sins both punished and unpunished in a country where old sins cast long shadows.

Language is an explosive issue in the countries of the former Soviet Union. The language conflict in Estonia has been especially bitter. Ethnic Russians make up almost a third of Estonia's population, and most of them do not speak or read Estonian, although Russians have lived in Estonia for more than a generation. Estonia has passed legislation requiring knowledge of the Estonian language as a condition of citizenship. Nationalist groups in independent Lithuania sought restrictions on the use of Polish — again, old sins, long shadows.

In 1995, protests erupted in Moldova, formerly the Moldavian Soviet Socialist Republic, over language and the teaching of Moldovan history. Was Moldovan history a part of Romanian history or of Soviet history? Was Moldova's language Romanian? Moldovan — earlier called Moldavian — *is* Romanian, just as American English and British English are both English. But in the days of the Moldavian SSR, Moscow insisted that the two languages were different and in a piece of linguistic nonsense required Moldavian to be written in the Cyrillic alphabet to strengthen the case that it was not Romanian.

The official language of Yugoslavia was Serbo-Croatian, which was never so much a language as a political accommodation. The Serbian and Croatian languages are mutually intelligible. Serbian is written in the Cyrillic alphabet, is identified with the Eastern Orthodox branch of the Catholic Church, and borrows its high-culture words from the east — from Russian and Old Church Slavic. Croatian is written in the Roman alphabet, is identified with Roman Catholicism, and borrows its high-culture words from the west — from German, for example, and Latin. One of the first things the newly autonomous Republic of Serbia did, in 1991, was to pass a law decreeing Serbian in the Cyrillic alphabet the official language of the country. With Croatia divorced from Serbia, the Croatian and Serbian languages are diverging more and more. Serbo-Croatian has now passed into history, a language-museum relic from the brief period when Serbs and Croats called themselves Yugoslavs and pretended to like each other.

Slovakia, relieved now of the need to accommodate to Czech cosmopolitan sensibilities, has passed a law making Slovak its official language. (Czech is to Slovak pretty much as Croatian is to Serbian.) Doctors in state hospitals must speak to patients in Slovak, even if another language would aid diagnosis and treatment. Some 600,000 Slovaks — more than 10 percent of the population — are ethnically Hungarian. Even staff meetings in Hungarian-language schools must be in Slovak. (The government dropped a stipulation that church weddings be conducted in Slovak after heavy opposition from the Roman Catholic Church.) Language inspectors are told to weed out "all sins perpetrated on the regular Slovak language." Tensions between Slovaks and Hungarians, who had been getting along, have begun to arise.

The twentieth century is ending as it began — with trouble in the Balkans and with nationalist tensions flaring up in other parts of the globe. (Toward the end of his life, Bismarck predicted that "some damn fool thing in the Balkans" would ignite the next war.) Language isn't always part of the problem. But it usually is.

Is there no hope for language tolerance? Some countries manage to maintain their unity in the face of multilingualism. Examples are Finland, with a Swedish minority, and a number of African and Southeast Asian countries. Two others could not be more unalike as countries go: Switzerland and India.

German, French, Italian, and Romansh are the languages of Switzerland. The first three can be and are used for official purposes; all four are designated "national" languages. Switzerland is politically almost hyperstable. It has language problems (Romansh is losing ground), but they are not major, and they are never allowed to threaten national unity.

Contrary to public perception, India gets along pretty well with a host of different languages. The Indian constitution officially recognizes nineteen languages, English among them. Hindi is specified in the constitution as the national language of India, but that is a pious postcolonial fiction: Outside the Hindi-speaking northern heartland of India, people don't want to learn it. English functions more nearly than Hindi as India's lingua franca.

From 1947, when India obtained its independence from the British, until the 1960s blood ran in the streets and people died because of language. Hindi absolutists wanted to force Hindi on the entire country, which would have split India between north and south and opened up other fracture lines as well. For as long as possible, Jawaharlal Nehru, independent India's first Prime Minister, resisted nationalist demands to redraw the capricious state boundaries of British India according to language. By the time he capitulated, the country had gained a precious decade to prove its viability as a union.

Why is it that India preserves its unity with not just two languages to contend with, as Belgium, Canada, and Sri Lanka have, but nineteen? The answer is that India, like Switzerland, has a strong national identity. The two countries share something big and almost mystical that holds each together in a union transcending language. That something I call "unique otherness."

The Swiss have what the political scientist Karl Deutsch called 30 "learned habits, preferences, symbols, memories, and patterns of landholding": customs, cultural traditions, and political institutions that bind them closer to one another than to people of France, Germany, or Italy living just across the border and speaking the same language. There is Switzerland's traditional neutrality, its system of universal military training (the "citizen army"), its consensual allegiance to a strong Swiss franc — and fondue, yodeling, skiing, and mountains. Set against all this, the fact that Switzerland has four languages doesn't even approach the threshold of becoming a threat.

As for India, what Vincent Smith, in the *Oxford History of India,* calls its "deep underlying fundamental unity" resides in institutions and beliefs such as caste, cow worship, sacred places, and much more. Consider *dharma, karma,* and *maya,* the three root convictions of Hinduism; India's historical epics; Gandhi; *ahimsa* (nonviolence); vegetarianism; a distinctive cuisine and way of eating; marriage customs; a shared past; and what the Indologist Ainslie Embree calls "Brahmanical ideology." In other words, "We are Indian; we are different."

Belgium and Canada have never managed to forge a stable national identity; Czechoslovakia and Yugoslavia never did either. Unique otherness immunizes countries against linguistic destabilization. Even Switzerland and especially India have problems; in any country with as many different languages as India has, language will never *not* be a problem. However, it is one thing to have a major illness with a bleak prognosis; it is another to have a condition that is irritating and occasionally painful but not life-threatening.

History teaches a plain lesson about language and governments: There is almost nothing the government of a free country can do to change language usage and practice significantly, to force its citizens to use certain languages in preference to others, and to discourage people from speaking a language they wish to continue to speak. (The rebirth of Hebrew in Palestine and Israel's successful mandate that Hebrew be spoken and written by Israelis is a unique event in the annals of language history.) Quebec has since the 1970s passed an array of laws giving French a virtual monopoly in the province. One consequence — unintended, one wishes to believe — of these laws is that last year kosher products imported for Passover were kept off the shelves, because the packages were not labeled in French. Wise governments keep their hands off language to the extent that it is politically possible to do so.

We like to believe that to pass a law is to change behavior, but passing laws about language, in a free society, almost never changes attitudes or behavior. Gaelic (Irish) is living out a slow, inexorable decline in Ireland despite enormous government support of every possible kind since Ireland gained its independence from Britain. The Welsh language, in contrast, is alive today in Wales in spite of heavy discrimination during its history. Three of four people in the northern and western counties of Gwynedd and Dyfed speak Welsh.

I said earlier that language is a convenient surrogate for other national 3 problems. Official English obviously has a lot to do with concern about immigration, perhaps especially Hispanic immigration. America may be threatened by immigration; I don't know. But America is not threatened by language.

The usual arguments made by academics against Official English are commonsensical. Who needs a law when, according to the 1990 census, 94 percent of American residents speak English anyway? (Mauro E. Mujica, the chairman of U.S. English, cites a higher figure: 97 percent.) Not many of today's immigrants will see their first language survive into the second generation. This is in fact the common lament of first-generation immigrants: Their children are not learning their language and are losing the culture of their parents. Spanish is hardly a threat to English, in spite of isolated (and easily visible) cases such as Miami, New York City, and pockets of the Southwest and southern California. The everyday language of south Texas is Spanish, and yet south Texas is not about to secede from America.

But empirical, calm arguments don't engage the real issue: Language is a symbol, an icon. Nobody who favors a constitutional ban against flag burning will ever be persuaded by the argument that the flag is, after all,

Comment

Robert Dole on English Only

"Alternative language education should stop and English should be acknowledged once and for all as the official language of the United States. Schools should provide the language classes our immigrants and their families need, as long as their purpose is the teaching of English ... But we must stop the practice of multilingual education as a means of instilling ethnic pride or as therapy for low self-esteem or out of elitist guilt over a culture built on the traditions of the West."

— From the National Education Association's Web site, "The Debate Over English Only," at http://www.nea.org/info/engonly.html.

just a "piece of cloth." A draft card in the 1960s was never merely a piece of paper. Neither is a marriage license.

Language, as one linguist has said, is "not primarily a means of communication but a means of communion." Romanticism exalted language, made it mystical, sublime — a bond of national identity. At the same time, Romanticism created a monster: It made of language a means for destroying a country.

America has that unique otherness of which I spoke. In spite of all our racial divisions and economic unfairness, we have the frontier tradition, respect for the individual, and opportunity; we have our love affair with the automobile; we have in our history a civil war that freed the slaves and was fought with valor; and we have sports, hot dogs, hamburgers, and milk shakes — things big and small, noble and petty, important and trifling. "We are Americans; we are different."

If I'm wrong, then the great American experiment will fail — not because of language but because it no longer means anything to be an American; because we have forfeited that "willingness of the heart" that F. Scott Fitzgerald wrote was America; because we are no longer joined by Lincoln's "mystic chords of memory."

We are not even close to the danger point. I suggest that we relax and luxuriate in our linguistic richness and our traditional tolerance of language differences. Language does not threaten American unity. Benign neglect is a good policy for any country when it comes to language, and it's a good policy for America.

Responding as a Reader

1. Why does King bother to assert, in paragraphs 8 and 9, that many of the advocates for English as the official language are politically liberal and that many are bilingual? What difference might this fact make to

conservative and liberal readers? Does it cause you to view the issue differently?

2. What is the effect of the historical overview in paragraphs 13–16? What is the point of this passage? How does the historical passage compare to the following passage, on language use in different countries today (paras. 17–41)? What does King seem to be saying, by extension, about making English the official language of the United States?

3. King argues that language is a symbol (para. 37). What, then, does it symbolize, according to King? What does your native language mean to you?

Responding as a Writer

1. Sketch a chronology of English-only legislation (including the proposals that did not pass) based on the information in this article. Then try to write one sentence for each item that puts it in historical context. For example, Franklin's remarks (para. 4) were made before the Revolutionary War, when Benjamin Franklin was a British subject and the colonies were struggling to construct their own identity.

2. Reread the section on language use in Switzerland, India, and other countries (paras. 26–41). Which of these countries do you think is most similar to the United States in its use of language? In a few paragraphs, compare the language situation in the United States to the language situation in one of the countries King mentions or in another country that you know about.

3. Consider King's definition of "unique otherness" (paras. 39–40). Do you agree with King that the United States possesses this quality? If not, explain why not. If so, what defines Americans' sense of unique otherness? What specific beliefs and qualities contribute to that sense, other than language? Write an essay defining what it means to be American.

JEAN BETHKE ELSHTAIN

Language and American Citizens

[DISSENT / Summer 1996]

In his classic *Democracy in America,* Alexis de Tocqueville[1] claimed, "Language is perhaps the strongest and most enduring link which unites men. All the immigrants spoke the same language and were children of the same people." These common points of origin, symbolized by language, helped to lay the basis of American democracy and made possible "true liberty." Even as Europe was riven by conflicts between dynasties and over religion, the Americans, exiles though they may have been, carried with them "that fertile germ of free institutions" that "had already taken deep root in English ways."

This is the sort of insight the most articulate "English-only" advocates point to when they insist that more is at stake than a common language for commerce or for everyday community. The fate of the republic, no less, lies in the balance. If we fail to teach newcomers the English language, if we fail to insist that all government business go forward in English, if we confuse helping non-English speakers to make their way to English with legitimating continued use of a "foreign tongue," we undermine the basis of our free institutions.

Is there a legitimate case to be made along these lines? My answer is a cautious "yes," but that case should not take the form of punitive English-only laws. With the Supreme Court poised to take up the question of Arizona's constitutional amendment[2] and with some twenty-two other states

---

[1] The French public official and sociologist Alexis de Tocqueville (1805–1859) published his monumental study of the young American democracy in 1835–1840.

[2] In March 1997, the Supreme Court dismissed the complaint for mootness because the plaintiff no longer worked for the state of Arizona.

JEAN BETHKE ELSHTAIN (b. 1941), political theorist and author, received her Ph.D. at Brandeis University. She taught at Vanderbilt, Yale, and Harvard before joining the faculty of the Divinity School at the University of Chicago, where she is a Laura Spelman Rockefeller Professor of Social and Political Ethics. Elshtain currently lectures the world over, including locations such as Argentina and the Czech Republic, where she addresses human rights issues. Her books include Public Man, Private Woman: Women in Social and Political Thought *(1981),* Women and War *(1987),* Democracy on Trial *(1995), and* Augustine and the Limits of Politics *(1996).*

having passed symbolic Official English laws, the question promises to become a hot topic during this fall's presidential campaign. The Arizona law
contains penalties for noncompliance and bars all official use of languages
other than English in all governmental forms (including voting ballots).
Support for English only is running high — around 70 percent to 80 percent. Senator Bob Dole supports English-only legislation now pending in
Congress; President Bill Clinton opposes it, although, as governor of
Arkansas, he signed a version of an English-only law.

Do we require the glue of language to hold us together? Yes, we do,
but a *common language* means having some widely shared understanding
of public speech. It doesn't require the force-feeding of English across the
board. Transition to English takes place rather quickly — in roughly three
generations. That is, immigrant parents will find it difficult to converse
with their grandchildren unless they have themselves picked up a generous
store of English words — and most do. In my own family the transition
happened much faster. My mother could speak only a German dialect
when she began first grade in a one-room school building in rural Colorado. When her youngest brother, Ted, began formal instruction some
twelve years later, he was already an English speaker, having been taught
English by my mother; two other sisters, Mary and Martha; and his older
brother, Bill. None of my grandparents' twenty grandchildren speaks a
German dialect. My grandparents learned enough English to say what they
wanted to say to us, although my grandfather fell silent a lot. He had a
huge incentive to learn enough English for public transactions, however,
and he could bargain with anyone at a farm sale in good commercial,
rough-and-ready English. My grandmother didn't bother to become a citizen until she was sixty-five or so — I helped to prepare her for her exam —
but that wasn't because of language skills. She just didn't see the point
until she heard so many of her children and grandchildren talking politics
that she decided maybe she should be able to vote.

Our family story is probably not that unusual. The English-only people
might argue that the reason it isn't unusual is that my mother and her sib-
lings grew up at a time when we had an English-only public sphere and
schools were dominated by English. This is only partly true. Many teachers
had to know enough of certain immigrant tongues to help lead children
into English. Nearly all immigrant communities read newspapers in their
"own" language. Some of these newspapers, like the Yiddish *Forward* in
New York City, have had great histories. The American union movement
was always a colorful mix of immigrant traditions and languages, although
some claim that is precisely why an indigenous labor-based party akin to
European social democratic parties never emerged on these shores — there
was no single tongue to help unify working men and women.

But tacit or informal English dominance is one thing. English-only legislation that goes beyond symbolic affirmation of the importance of a
shared language to embrace punitive measures is another. Such efforts

speak to our lack of confidence in our ability to transmit our culture. We are rightly concerned with what is happening to civic life in America. But we should demonstrate this concern in efforts to strengthen our public schools overall; to help rebuild our civic institutions, including our political parties; to revivify all the many associations that helped to shape our passions and interests, including the always difficult move from an immigrant past into an American present. If a political culture loses a sense of confidence and authority, draconian measures rush into the breach. We try to do by compulsion what we don't seem to be doing as part of a normal evolution. This is a mistake. But, then, so was much of the bilingual ideology that no doubt provoked English-only fervor.

What do I mean by bilingual ideology? I mean a stance that goes far beyond calling for transitional instruction to ease students over a four-to-six-year period into English. Instead, it is a dogma that proclaims indifference, at best, concerning public life and identity, that preaches the false but soothing notion that education should never change us in any fundamental way. But education always does. This is what it is meant to do. We do not emerge at the other end the same person — the same child — we were when we went in. The bilingual ideologists cling to the illusion that you can educate children into their "own" culture and help them to remain whatever their point of family origin suggests that they are. Schools, however, are not families. They are precisely the *un*-familiar. There is pathos, wrenching, sadness, separation in this story. There is also possibility, promise, enlargement, entry into a bigger story.

If a sin of the past was creating shame in children about their parents or grandparents' odd ways, a sin of the present is deluding ourselves that education should just deepen a preexisting identity — or even, in certain forms of Afrocentricity, for example, *invent* a past that has no historic warrant. But we are living in a certain time and place, in one society by contrast to some other. What does it mean to take our bearings in this time and place? How do we best serve our children? How can we guarantee a fair opportunity to all? You cannot do that through failure to transmit the promise of a culture — a democratic culture — to all citizens. And — in this Tocqueville was right — language is "perhaps the strongest and most enduring link." I oppose the Arizona law. The other more symbolic efforts are anemic. They may assuage a certain anxiety. But they also instill fear in the hearts of many of our fellow citizens and would-be citizens. For English-only legislation suggests that we do not trust the newcomers among us enough to find their way to us, to join us and to make their own contributions to our common life.

Another characteristic of our time and place is a generalized fearfulness and anxiety. I submit that the source of English-only militance is our collective failure to sustain and transmit a strong yet critical version of our own past and present. Therefore, such militance is a sign of civic weakness, not strength. Unfortunately, it seems easier nowadays to make the grand gesture than to do the hard work of rebuilding our civic institutions; to this latter task, the English-only movement contributes nothing.

Responding as Reader

1. What distinction is Elshtain making, in paragraph 4, between the use of common language in "public speech" and "the force-feeding of English across the board"? What policy is she arguing for in these two situations?

2. Reread paragraphs 7 and 8. What, according to Elshtain, is the purpose of education? How does this point support her argument about bilingual education?

3. When Elshtain writes "the other more symbolic efforts are anemic" (para. 8), what efforts is she referring to? In what sense is she using the word "anemic"?

Responding as a Writer

1. How quickly did the transition to English take place in your family (if you don't know, ask an older relative)? Do your parents speak English fluently? Did theirs (and so on)? Are you able to speak the language of your ancestors? If your ancestors came from an English-speaking country, did their accents cause them to be treated differently from native-born Americans? Write a short language history of your family, like Elshtain's in paragraph 4.

2. Elshtain ends her essay with a plea for "a strong yet critical version of our own past and present" and "the hard work of rebuilding our civic institutions" (para. 9). Would it solve any of the language problems of the United States if we regarded our past differently in some specific way or if our public institutions were structured differently in some specific way? Argue in favor of one change that we could make in the way we define citizenship, or what we teach our children, or what takes place in schools or government institutions.

3. Turn to the advertisement on page 224. On what points do you think Mujica would agree with Elshtain? On what points would he disagree? Write a response to Elshtain from Mujica's point of view.

KAREN NARASAKI

Double Talk

[A. MAGAZINE / February–March 1996]

A battered immigrant spouse is unable to get a restraining order to stop her citizen husband's abuse because she cannot speak English.

A victim of anti-Asian violence is unable to testify against his assailants because he does not speak English.

A refugee calls 911 when her husband has a heart attack, but the operator is not permitted to instruct her in her native tongue.

These are just some of the stories you can expect to hear if English-only legislation and their thinly disguised cousins, English as the Official Language, or English as the Language of Government, become law.

Although these proposals appear to be innocuous on their face, their 5 impact on the Asian Pacific American community and the general public would be devastating. Under most versions of these laws, government employees would be forbidden from speaking any language but English while on the job. Government documents and notices would only be printed in English, and government services would only be offered in English. Bilingual education, bilingual ballots, and other government-provided voter education materials would be outlawed.

English-only supporters claim that these laws only acknowledge English as the common language of the United States and argue that without this, immigrants will seek to abolish English in favor of Spanish, Chinese,

KAREN NARASAKI *is the executive director of the National Asian Pacific American Legal Consortium. The consortium is devoted to advance the legal and civil rights of Asian Pacific Americans through litigation, advocacy, public education, and public policy development. She also serves on the Executive Committee of the Leadership Conference on Civil Rights as the chairperson of its Compliance/Enforcement Committee and is chairperson of the National Network Against Anti-Asian Violence. A graduate of Yale University and the UCLA School of Law, she won an Asian American Bar Association of the Delaware Valley 1996 Community Service Award and in 1997 won an award from the Organization of Chinese Americans and the Asian American Bar Association of Houston, Texas, for her outstanding contributions in the advocacy of the legal and civil rights of Asian Pacific Americans. She has published op-ed pieces and journal articles for publications such as the* San Francisco Chronicle, Asian Week, *and* NEXUS.

or some other language. They argue that these laws are necessary to encourage non-English-speaking immigrants to learn English so they can successfully integrate economically and socially in the United States. They add that it is unfair to American tax payers to provide government information in more than one language.

Their assertions and perceptions are fatally flawed. The primacy of English in America has survived for over 200 years despite waves of immigration from different parts of the non-English-speaking world. According to the last census, 97 percent of Americans speak English well. Studies show that immigrants are assimilating even faster now than previous generations. With English rapidly becoming the language of international commerce, it is absurd to believe that English is threatened by extinction in the United States.

Immigrants already understand the importance of learning English. With only limited proficiency in English, even professionally trained immigrants have trouble finding appropriate jobs and find themselves working as convenience store owners, janitors, restaurant workers, garment workers, and gardeners. They are exploited by landlords, employers, and scam artists and are vulnerable targets for crime. That is why there are long waiting lists for English classes. In Washington, D.C., an estimated 5,000 immigrants were turned away from English as a Second Language classes last year. In New York, the schools now conduct a lottery system to determine enrollment in classes. In Los Angeles, forty to fifty thousand immigrants are on waiting lists for classes.

For those who are sincere in their desire for more immigrants to learn English, their energies would be put to much better use in supporting increased resources for English training. But, not surprisingly, most of the members of Congress who back English-only laws have also voted this year to slash the bilingual education budget in half and to drastically cut funding for community colleges, the major provider of English classes.

Rather than serving to integrate immigrants, the bills being proposed in Congress and in various states would foster a second class of Americans based on language proficiency. The bills would limit the ability of certain Americans to exercise their legal rights and to use the government services for which they pay taxes.

English-only supporters are fond of citing the popularity of these proposals. However, any of the laws and government actions that we condemn today as bigoted and heinous were also popular in their day. The Chinese Exclusion Act and the internment of Japanese Americans during World War II were wildly popular, as were the Alien Land laws that prohibited Japanese immigrant farmers from owning property in thirteen states. All of these laws were driven by the same forces that motivate the English-only movement: xenophobia, racism, and resentment. It is no accident that these laws will have a disproportionate impact on Asians and Latinos, who have constituted over 80 percent of this country's immigrants over the past two decades.

Ultimately, English-only bills are outlandishly myopic, for it is far more costly in the long run to deny adequate education and health care to immigrant children — and to deny their parents equal protection under the law or the ability to fully participate in the democratic process — than it is to accommodate Americans at *all* levels of English proficiency.

Imagine an America in which the use of languages other than English was penalized. Public school administrators, teachers, counselors, and nurses would be breaking the law if they provided information to students or parents in any language but English, even if they themselves were fluent in that student's or parent's primary language. At a time when educators are working to get parents more involved in their children's education, these laws would make it impossible for many Asian parents.

Immigrant Asian convenience store owners who have been robbed or assaulted would not be able to receive appropriate police protection, use 911 emergency services, or testify in court in criminal cases. Immigrant small business owners with contract disputes or conflicts with regulatory agencies would be hampered because courts would not be allowed to provide translators.

Moreover, doctors and nurses in public hospitals would be barred   15 from effectively communicating with their patients. Many public health hospitals and clinics already underserve the Asian Pacific American community. All too often, treatment is delayed or denied because a hospital tells the patient they must find their own translator. Immigrant rape victims are often too embarrassed to describe the incident or go through the required physical exam when forced to rely on a son or neighbor to translate for them. Illnesses can be misdiagnosed when doctors rely on translation by untrained friends or volunteers.

Immigrant workers subjected to discrimination, sexual harassment, unfair labor practices, or unsafe working conditions would be unable to report and assist in enforcement of the laws by agencies such as the Equal Employment Opportunity Commission, the Occupational Safety and Health Administration, or the Department of Labor.

Political candidates would be prohibited from greeting voters in other languages, much less engaging in substantive communications or debates. In addition, election debates and election materials cover complex issues and measures that even native-born English speakers find difficult to understand. In the November 1994 elections, 31 percent of Chinese American voters polled by the Asian American Legal Defense and Education Fund indicated they used election materials translated into Chinese and 14 percent of the Chinese American voters polled in San Francisco by the Asian Law Caucus indicated they used such materials. Voting is not only a right but a responsibility, yet these laws would severely inhibit participation by members of our communities.

English-only bills are not only extremely divisive, they are absurd in light of the fact that English, like any other modern language, is an ever-evolving amalgamation of words from different languages. (It is estimated that three out of four words in the English dictionary are non-Anglo in origin.) The government will have to set up a new bureaucracy and millions of dollars will be wasted in litigation over which words are English or whether a government official was allowed to use them.

Isolating those who cannot fluently speak English will not help to integrate immigrants into our society nor will it, as its proponents naively suggest, reduce ethnic and racial friction. English proficiency has certainly not

— From the *National Review* (June 16, 1997).

immunized Jewish Americans from religious bigotry or African Americans and whites from tension or misunderstanding.

What binds American people together is the shared quest for equality, justice, and freedom — including the freedom to be different. The absurdity of the English-only debate was best illustrated during Senate and House hearings, when both committee chairmen referred to the hope that English-only laws would finally make a reality of the national motto, *E Pluribus Unum*, a Latin phrase meaning "out of many, one." 20

Responding as a Reader

1. Who seems to be Narasaki's intended audience? How can you tell? Does she refer to one language group more often than others? Why do you think she does this?

2. How do "xenophobia, racism, and resentment" (para. 11) inspire the English-only movement, according to Narasaki? Why should Asians and Latinos be especially vulnerable to these feelings at this point in U.S. history?

3. Narasaki uses many imaginary scenarios, from the battered immigrant spouse in paragraph 1 to the Chinese American voters in paragraph 17. Which of these scenarios argue most strongly against English-only legislation? Which scenarios are unlikely to result from such legislation and why?

Responding as a Writer

1. Narasaki argues that most immigrants already speak English and that immigrants certainly understand the need to learn English (paras. 7–8). Given that, why is she against declaring English the official language of the United States? How could this same fact be used to argue in favor of declaring English the official language? Write two paragraphs, one using this fact to support the argument in favor of English only and one using it to support the argument against.

2. Imagine, as Narasaki asks you to in paragraph 13, "an America in which the use of languages other than English was penalized." In a page or two, describe an imaginary occurrence in a school, a hospital, a store, or some other public place where more than one language might be spoken. Would it make sense to require the use of English in this particular situation? Why or why not?

3. Read the advertisement on page 224 and write an imaginary dialogue between Narasaki and Mujica. Imagine how Mujica would respond to

each of Narasaki's main points and what Narasaki would say about the assertions in the advertisement.

Discussing the Unit

Suggested Topic for Discussion

Is it appropriate for the government to regulate the languages spoken in this country? What role should the government take? Should it lean toward "benign neglect," as King argues? Should it put the emphasis on "rebuilding civic institutions" and take it off language, as Elshtain argues? Should it facilitate bilingualism — for instance, by making ballots available in several languages, as Narasaki advocates — or should it stop offering services in languages other than English? What proportion of your tax dollar do you believe should go toward helping non-English speakers get by in the United States?

Preparing for Class Discussion

1. If it is true that 94–97% of Americans speak English fluently, then why does it matter if English is legally declared the official language of the United States? Isn't English already the language of this country? What difference would a law make?

2. What other issues are involved in the English-only controversy? How do immigration issues come into play? Do racism, xenophobia, and protectionism contribute to this movement? Are there economic issues at stake? What social and political issues relate most directly to the language issue?

3. *Prewriting Assignment:* All the articles in this unit are against declaring English the official language of the United States, for different reasons. Consider the arguments in favor of legislation that declares English the official language and list as many as you can. Which are the strongest arguments, in your opinion? Put the list in order of strongest to weakest.

From Discussion to Writing

Write an argument for or against legislating English as the official language of the United States. In your essay, use examples of various real or imaginary Americans to support your argument (and let your readers know if these people are real or invented). How would non-English-speaking immigrants be affected by the approach you advocate? How would their children be affected? How would English-speaking Americans be affected? How would tax payers be affected?

11

Class War:
Can the Poor Survive?

More and more social critics identify the growing gap between rich and poor as one of the nation's most pressing problems. Why is it, many ask, that in a booming economy so many Americans live in poverty and hopelessness? Has it become more difficult than ever to improve one's condition through discipline and hard work alone? In searching for reasons why ghettos have become virtually uninhabitable, William Julius Wilson, a prominent professor of social policy at Harvard University, finds the disappearance of work as pivotal. In "Work," he warns that if solutions aren't found for generating inner-city jobs, the problem will have "lasting and harmful consequences for the quality of life in the cities and, eventually, for the lives of all Americans."

One way to break out of poverty, of course, is not through hard work. It's to get rich quick. In "Lotteryville, USA," Kim Phillips takes a close look at the exploitative methods of state lotteries, duping one class as they enrich another: "The lottery is a painless, if extremely narrow, form of redistribution," she argues, adding that while it may be "rational for the individual, it is clearly irrational for the class." Do we really know what money is? asks Fran Lebowitz, one of our funniest contrarians, who patiently explains some of its secrets.

For John J. Sweeney, however, money is no mystery. It is exactly what workers are running out of, claims the new President of the AFL-CIO, who believes working people "want to live in a country where you can raise a family without having to hold down three jobs to do it." Poverty is not only a minority issue, *U.S. News and World Report* magazine reminds us in its report on the rapidly growing number of poor whites. One leader in a new war on poverty will certainly be Minnesota Senator Paul Wellstone. In "The Unfinished Agenda: Race, Poverty, and Gender in America," Wellstone promises to travel the length and breadth of the nation "to observe the face of poverty, not from behind a Senate desk, but in the streets, the villages, and neighborhoods of those in distress."

The survey results don't tell us what the Class of 2000 thinks about the face of poverty, or about class itself — but they do suggest that moving up in the world is a top priority, no matter how much one's parents make.

Selected Survey Results

Class

- Freshmen who note getting a better job as very important in deciding to go to college: 76.7%
- Freshmen at private universities whose parents make over $100,000: 35.8%
- Freshmen at public 2-year colleges whose parents make over $100,000: 7.3%

— From *The American Freshman: National Norms For Fall 1996.*

WILLIAM JULIUS WILSON

Work

[THE NEW YORK TIMES MAGAZINE / August 18, 1996]

The disappearance of work in the ghetto cannot be ignored, isolated, or played down. Employment in America is up. The economy has churned out tens of millions of new jobs in the last two decades. In that same period, joblessness among inner-city blacks has reached catastrophic proportions. Yet during the past Presidential election, the disappearance of work in the ghetto was not on either the Democratic or the Republican agenda. There was harsh talk about work instead of welfare but no talk of where to find it.

The current employment woes in the inner city continue to be narrowly defined in terms of race or lack of individual initiative. It is argued that jobs are widely available, that the extent of inner-city poverty is exaggerated. Optimistic policy analysts — and many African Americans — would prefer that more attention be devoted to the successes and struggles of the black working class and the expanding black middle class. This is understandable. These two groups, many of whom have recently escaped from the ghetto, represent a majority of the African American population. But ghetto joblessness still afflicts a substantial — and increasing — minority: It's a problem that won't go away on its own. If it is not addressed, it will have lasting and harmful consequences for the quality of life in the cities and, eventually, for the lives of all Americans. Solutions will have to be found — and those solutions are at hand.

WILLIAM JULIUS WILSON *(b. 1935), a member of the University of Chicago faculty for twenty-four years, is now the Malcolm Wiener Professor of Social Policy at Harvard University. Wilson was elected to the American Academy of Arts and Sciences in 1988 and the National Academy of Sciences in 1991. He is author of* Power, Racism, and Privilege: Race Relations in Theoretical and Sociohistorical Perspectives *(1973) and* The Truly Disadvantaged: The Inner City, The Underclass, and Public Policy *(1987). In addition to these books, Professor Wilson has authored and coauthored numerous articles in professional journals and books. He has been a member of many groups and associations, including William T. Grant Foundation's Commission on Youth and America's Future. His book,* When Work Disappears: the World of the New Urban Poor, *was published in 1996.*

For the first time in the twentieth century, a significant majority of adults in many inner-city neighborhoods are not working in a typical week. Inner cities have always featured high levels of poverty, but the current levels of joblessness in some neighborhoods are unprecedented. For example, in the famous black-belt neighborhood of Washington Park on Chicago's South Side, a majority of adults had jobs in 1950; by 1990, only one in three worked in a typical week. High neighborhood joblessness has a far more devastating effect than high neighborhood poverty. A neighborhood in which people are poor but employed is different from a neighborhood in which people are poor and jobless. Many of today's problems in the inner-city neighborhoods — crime, family dissolution, welfare — are fundamentally a consequence of the disappearance of work.

What causes the disappearance of work? There are several factors, including changes in the distribution and location of jobs and in the level of training and education required to obtain employment. Nor should we overlook the legacy of historic racial segregation. However, the public debate around this question is not productive because it seeks to assign blame rather than recognizing and dealing with the complex realities that have led to economic distress for many Americans. Explanations and proposed solutions to the problem are often ideologically driven.

Conservatives tend to stress the importance of values, attitudes, habits,   5
and styles. In this view, group differences are reflected in the culture. The truth is, cultural factors do play a role, but other, more important variables also have to be taken into account. Although race is clearly a significant variable in the social outcomes of inner-city blacks, it's not the *only* factor. The emphasis on racial differences has obscured the fact that African Americans, whites, and other ethnic groups have many common values, aspirations, and hopes.

An elderly woman who has lived in one inner-city neighborhood on the South Side of Chicago for more than forty years reflects: "I've been here since March 11, 1953. When I moved in, the neighborhood was intact. It was intact with homes, beautiful homes, minimansions, with stores, laundromats, with Chinese cleaners. We had drugstores. We had hotels. We had doctors over on 39th Street. We had doctors' offices in the neighborhood. We had the middle class and upper middle class. It has gone from affluent to where it is today. And I would like to see it come back, that we can have some of the things we had. Since I came in young and I'm a senior citizen now, I would like to see some of the things come back so I can enjoy them like we did when we first came in."

In the neighborhood of Woodlawn, on the South Side of Chicago, there were more than 800 commercial and industrial establishments in 1950. Today, it is estimated that only about 100 are left. In the words of Loïc Wacquant, a member of one of the research teams that worked with me over the last eight years: "The once-lively streets — residents remember a time, not so long ago, when crowds were so dense at rush hour that one had to elbow one's way to the train station — now have the appearance of an empty, bombed-out war zone. The commercial strip has been reduced to a long tunnel of charred stores, vacant lots littered with broken glass and garbage, and dilapidated buildings left to rot in the shadow of the elevated train line. At the corner of 63rd Street and Cottage Grove Avenue, the handful of remaining establishments that struggle to survive are huddled behind wrought-iron bars. . . . The only enterprises that seem to be thriving are liquor stores and currency exchanges, those 'banks of the poor' where one can cash checks, pay bills, and buy money orders for a fee."

The state of the inner-city public schools was another major concern expressed by our urban-poverty study respondents. The complaints ranged from overcrowded conditions to unqualified and uncaring teachers. Sharply voicing her views on these subjects, a twenty-five-year-old married mother of two children from a South Side census tract that just recently became poor stated: "My daughter ain't going to school here. She was going to a nursery school where I paid and of course they took the time and spent it with her, because they was getting the money. But the public schools, no! They are overcrowded and the teachers don't care."

A resident of Woodlawn who had left the neighborhood as a child described how she felt upon her return about the changes that had occurred: "I was really appalled. When I walked down 63rd Street when I was younger, everything you wanted was there. But now, coming back as an adult with my child, those resources are just gone, completely. . . . And housing, everybody has moved, there are vacant lots everywhere."

Neighborhoods plagued by high levels of joblessness are more likely to experience low levels of social organization: The two go hand in hand. High rates of joblessness trigger other neighborhood problems that undermine social organization, ranging from crime, gang violence, and drug trafficking to family breakups. And as these controls weaken, the social processes that regulate behavior change. 10

Industrial restructuring has further accelerated the deterioration of many inner-city neighborhoods. Consider the fate of the West Side black community of North Lawndale in Chicago: Since 1960, nearly half of its housing stock has disappeared; the remaining units are mostly run down or dilapidated. Two large factories anchored the economy of this neighborhood in its good days — the Hawthorne plant of Western Electric, which employed more than 43,000 workers, and an International Harvester plant with 14,000 workers. But conditions rapidly changed. Harvester closed its doors in the late 1960s. Sears moved most of its offices to the Loop in downtown Chicago in 1973. The Hawthorne plant gradually phased out its operations and finally shut down in 1984.

"Jobs were plentiful in the past," attested a twenty-nine-year-old unemployed black man who lives in one of the poorest neighborhoods on the

South Side. "You could walk out of the house and get a job. Maybe not what you want, but you could get a job. Now, you can't find anything. A lot of people in this neighborhood, they want to work but they can't get work. A few, but a very few, they just don't want to work."

The more rapid the neighborhood deterioration, the greater the institutional disinvestment. In the 1960s and 1970s, neighborhoods plagued by heavy abandonment were frequently redlined (identified as areas that should not receive or be recommended for mortgage loans or insurance); this paralyzed the housing market, lowered property values, and encouraged landlord abandonment.

As the neighborhood disintegrates, those who are able to leave depart in increasing numbers; among these are many working- and middle-class families. The lower population density in turn creates additional problems. Abandoned buildings increase and often serve as havens for crack use and other illegal enterprises that give criminals — mostly young blacks who are unemployed — footholds in the community. Precipitous declines in density also make it even more difficult to sustain or develop a sense of community. The feeling of safety in numbers is completely lacking in such neighborhoods.

Problems in the new poverty or high-jobless neighborhoods have also 15 created racial antagonism among some of the high-income groups in the city. The high joblessness in ghetto neighborhoods has sapped the vitality of local businesses and other institutions and has led to fewer and shabbier movie theaters, bowling alleys, restaurants, public parks and playgrounds, and other recreational facilities. When residents of inner-city neighborhoods venture out to other areas of the city in search of entertainment, they come into brief contact with citizens of markedly different racial or class backgrounds. Sharp differences in cultural style often lead to clashes.

Some behavior on the part of residents from socially isolated ghetto neighborhoods — for instance, the tendency to enjoy a movie in a communal spirit by carrying on a running conversation with friends and relatives or reacting in an unrestrained manner to what they see on the screen — is considered offensive by other groups, particularly black and white members of the middle class. Expressions of disapproval, either overt or with subtle hostile glances, tend to trigger belligerent responses from the ghetto residents, who then purposely intensify the behavior that is the source of irritation. The white and even the black middle-class moviegoers then exercise their option and exit, expressing resentment and experiencing intensified feelings of racial or class antagonism as they depart.

The areas surrendered in such a manner become the domain of the inner-city residents. Upscale businesses are replaced by fast-food chains and other local businesses that cater to the new clientele. White and black middle-class citizens complain bitterly about how certain areas of the central city have changed — and thus become "off limits" — following the influx of ghetto residents.

The negative consequences are clear: Where jobs are scarce, many people eventually lose their feeling of connectedness to work in the formal economy; they no longer expect work to be a regular, and regulating, force in their lives. In the case of young people, they may grow up in an environment that lacks the idea of work as a central experience of adult life — they have little or no labor-force attachment. These circumstances also increase the likelihood that the residents will rely on illegitimate sources of income, thereby further weakening their attachment to the legitimate labor market.

A twenty-five-year-old West Side father of two who works two jobs to make ends meet condemned the attitude toward work of some inner-city black males:

"They try to find easier routes and had been conditioned over a period   20
of time to just be lazy, so to speak. Motivation nonexistent, you know, and the society that they're affiliated with really don't advocate hard work and struggle to meet your goals such as education and stuff like that. And they see who's around them and they follow that same pattern, you know. . . . They don't see nobody getting up early in the morning, going to work, or going to school all the time. The guys they be with don't do that . . . because that's the crowd that you choose — well, that's been presented to you by your neighborhood."

Work is not simply a way to make a living and support one's family. It also constitutes a framework for daily behavior because it imposes discipline. Regular employment determines where you are going to be and when you are going to be there. In the absence of regular employment, life, including family life, becomes less coherent. Persistent unemployment and irregular employment hinder rational planning in daily life, the necessary condition of adaptation to an industrial economy.

It's a myth that people who don't work don't want to work. One mother in a new poverty neighborhood on the South Side explained her decision to remain on welfare even though she would like to get a job: "I was working and then I had two kids. And I'm struggling. I was making, like, close to $7 an hour. . . . I had to pay a baby-sitter. Then I had to deal with my kids when I got home. And I couldn't even afford medical insurance. . . . I was so scared, when my kids were sick or something, because I have been turned away from a hospital because I did not have a medical card. I don't like being on public aid and stuff right now. But what do I do with my kids when the kids get sick?"

Working mothers with comparable incomes face, in many cases, even greater difficulty. Why? Simply because many low-wage jobs do not provide health care benefits and most working mothers have to pay for transportation and spend more for child care. Working mothers also have to spend more for housing because it is more difficult for them to qualify for housing subsidies. It is not surprising, therefore, that many welfare-reliant mothers choose not to enter the formal labor market. It would not be in their best economic interest to do so. Given the economic realities, it is also not surprising that many who are working in these low-wage jobs decide to rely on or return to welfare, even though it's not a desirable alternative for many of the black single mothers. As one twenty-seven-year-old welfare mother of three children from an impoverished West Side neighborhood put it: "I want to work. I do not work but I want to work. I don't want to just be on public aid."

As the disappearance of work has become a characteristic feature of the inner-city ghetto, so too has the disappearance of the traditional married-couple family. Only one-quarter of the black families whose children live with them in inner-city neighborhoods in Chicago are husband-wife families today, compared with three-quarters of the inner-city Mexican families, more than one-half of the white families, and nearly one-half of the Puerto Rican families. And in census tracts with poverty rates of at least 40 percent, only 16.5 percent of the black families with children in the household are husband-wife families.

There are many factors involved in the precipitous decline in marriage rates and the sharp rise in single-parent families. The explanation most often heard in the public debate associates the increase of out-of-wedlock births and single-parent families with welfare. Indeed, it is widely assumed among the general public and reflected in the recent welfare reform that a direct connection exists between the level of welfare benefits and the likelihood that a young woman will bear a child outside marriage.

However, there is little evidence to support the claim that Aid to Families With Dependent Children (A.F.D.C.) plays a significant role in promoting out-of-wedlock births. Research examining the association between the generosity of welfare benefits and out-of-wedlock childbearing and teen-age pregnancy indicates that benefit levels have no significant effect on the likelihood that African American girls and women will have children outside marriage. Likewise, welfare rates have either no significant effect or only a small effect on the odds that whites will have children outside marriage. The rate of out-of-wedlock teenage childbearing has nearly doubled since 1975 — during years when the value of A.F.D.C., food stamps, and Medicaid fell, after adjusting for inflation. And the smallest increases in the number of out-of-wedlock births have not occurred in states that have had the largest declines in the inflation-adjusted value of A.F.D.C. benefits. Indeed, while the real value of cash welfare benefits has plummeted over the past twenty years, out-of-wedlock childbearing has increased, and postpartum marriages (marriages following the birth of a couple's child) have decreased as well.

It's instructive to consider the social differences between inner-city blacks and other groups, especially Mexicans. Mexicans come to the United States with a clear conception of a traditional family unit that features men as breadwinners. Although extramarital affairs by men are tolerated, unmarried pregnant women are "a source of opprobrium, anguish, or great concern," as Richard P. Taub, a member of one of our research teams, put it. Pressure is applied by the kin of both parents to enter into marriage.

The family norms and behavior in inner-city black neighborhoods stand in sharp contrast. The relationships between inner-city black men and women, whether in a marital or nonmarital situation, are often fractious and antagonistic. Inner-city black women routinely say that black men are hopeless as either husbands or fathers and that more of their time is spent on the streets than at home.

The men in the inner city generally feel that it is much better for all parties to remain in a nonmarital relationship until the relationship dissolves rather than to get married and then have to get a divorce. A twenty-five-year-old unmarried West Side resident, the father of one child, expressed this view:

"Well, most black men feel now, why get married when you got six to seven women to one guy, really. You know, because there's more women out here mostly than men. Because most dudes around here are killing each other like fools over drugs or all this other stuff." 30

The fact that blacks reside in neighborhoods and are engaged in social networks and households that are less conducive to employment than those of other ethnic and racial groups in the inner city clearly has a negative effect on their search for work. In the eyes of employers in metropolitan Chicago, these differences render inner-city blacks less desirable as workers, and therefore many are reluctant to hire them. The white chairman of a car transport company, when asked if there were differences in the work ethic of whites, blacks, and Hispanics, responded with great certainty:

"Definitely! I don't think, I know: I've seen it over a period of thirty years. Basically, the Oriental is much more aggressive and intelligent and studious than the Hispanic. The Hispanics, except Cubans of course, they have the work ethnic [sic]. The Hispanics are *mañana, mañana, mañana* — tomorrow, tomorrow, tomorrow." As for native-born blacks, they were deemed "the laziest of the bunch."

If some employers view the work ethic of inner-city poor blacks as problematic, many also express concerns about their honesty, cultural attitudes, and dependability — traits that are frequently associated with the neighborhoods in which they live. A white suburban retail drugstore manager expressed his reluctance to hire someone from a poor inner-city neighborhood. "You'd be afraid they're going to steal from you," he stated. "They grow up that way. They grow up dishonest and I guess you'd feel like, geez, how are they going to be honest here?"

In addition to qualms about the work ethic, character, family influences, cultural predispositions, and the neighborhood milieu of ghetto residents, the employers frequently mentioned concerns about applicants' language skills and educational training. They "just don't have the language skills," stated a suburban employer. The president of an inner-city advertising agency highlighted the problem of spelling:

"I needed a temporary a couple months ago, and they sent me a black [35] man. And I dictated a letter to him. He took shorthand, which was good. Something like 'Dear Mr. So-and-So, I am writing to ask about how your business is doing.' And then he typed the letter, and I read the letter, and it's 'I am writing to ax about your business.' Now you hear about them speaking a different language and all that, and they say 'ax' for 'ask.' Well, I don't care about that, but I didn't say 'ax,' I said 'ask.'"

Many inner-city residents have a strong sense of the negative attitudes that employers tend to have toward them. A thirty-three-year-old employed janitor from a poor South Side neighborhood had this observation: "I went to a couple jobs where a couple of the receptionists told me in confidence: 'You know what they do with these applications from blacks as soon as the day is over?' They say, 'We rip them and throw them in the garbage.'" In addition to concerns about being rejected because of race, the fears that some inner-city residents have of being denied employment simply because of their inner-city address or neighborhood are not unfounded. A welfare mother who lives in a large public housing project put it this way:

"Honestly, I believe they look at the address and the — your attitudes, your address, your surround — you know, your environment has a lot to do with your employment status. The people with the best addresses have the best chances. I feel so, I feel so."

It is instructive to study the fate of the disadvantaged in Europe. There, too, poverty and joblessness are on the increase, but individual deficiencies and behavior are not put forward as the culprits. Furthermore, welfare programs that benefit wide segments of the population like child care, children's allowances (an annual benefit per child), housing subsidies, education, medical care, and unemployment insurance have been firmly institutionalized in many Western European democracies. Efforts to cut back on these programs in the face of growing joblessness have met firm resistance from working- and middle-class citizens.

My own belief is that the growing assault on welfare mothers is part of a larger reaction to the mounting problems in our nation's inner cities. When many people think of welfare, they think of young, unmarried black mothers having babies. This image persists even though roughly equal numbers of black and white families received A.F.D.C. in 1994, and there were also a good many Hispanics on the welfare rolls. Nevertheless, the rise of black A.F.D.C. recipients was said to be symptomatic of such larger problems as the decline in family values and the dissolution of the family. In an article published in *Esquire,* Pete Hamill wrote:

"The heart of the matter is the continued existence and expansion of what has come to be called the Underclass. . . . trapped in cycles of welfare dependency, drugs, alcohol, crime, illiteracy, and disease, living in anarchic and murderous isolation in some of the richest cities on the earth. As a reporter, I've covered their miseries for more than a quarter of a century. . . . And in the last decade, I've watched this group of American citizens harden and condense, moving even further away from the basic requirements of a human life: work, family, safety, the law."

One has the urge to shout, "Enough is enough!" 40

What can be done? I believe that steps must be taken to galvanize Americans from all walks of life who are concerned about human suffering and the public policy direction in which we are now moving. We need to generate a public-private partnership to fight social inequality. The following policy frameworks provide a basis for further discussion and debate. Given the current political climate, these proposals might be dismissed as unrealistic. Nor am I suggesting that we can or should simply import the social policies of the Japanese, the Germans, or other Western Europeans. The question is how we Americans can address the problems of social inequality, including record levels of joblessness in the inner city, that threaten the very fabric of our society.

Create Standards for Schools

Ray Marshall, former Secretary of Labor, points out that Japan and Germany have developed policies designed to increase the number of workers with "higher-order thinking skills." These policies require young people to meet high performance standards before they can graduate from secondary schools, and they hold each school responsible for meeting these standards.

Students who meet high standards are not only prepared for work but they are also ready for technical training and other kinds of postsecondary education. Currently, there are no mandatory academic standards for secondary schools in the United States. Accordingly, students who are not in college-preparatory courses have severely limited options with respect to pursuing work after high school. A commitment to a system of performance standards for every public school in the United States would be an important first step in addressing the huge gap in educational performance between the schools in advantaged and disadvantaged neighborhoods.

A system of at least local performance standards should include the kind of support that would enable schools in disadvantaged neighborhoods to meet the standards that are set. State governments, with Federal support, not only would have to create equity in local school financing (through loans and scholarships to attract more high-quality teachers, increased support for teacher training, and reforms in teacher certification) but would also have to ensure that highly qualified teachers are more equitably distributed in local school districts.

Targeting education would be part of a national effort to raise the performance standards of all public schools in the United States to a desirable level, including schools in the inner city. The support of the private sector should be enlisted in this national effort. Corporations, local businesses, civic clubs, community centers, and churches should be encouraged to work with the schools to improve computer-competency training. 45

Improve Child Care

The French system of child welfare stands in sharp contrast to the American system. In France, children are supported by three interrelated government programs, as noted by Barbara R. Bergmann, a professor of economics at American University: child care, income support, and medical care. The child-care program includes establishments for infant care, high-quality nursery schools (*écoles maternelles*), and paid leave for parents of newborns. The income-support program includes child-support enforcement (so that the absent parent continues to contribute financially to his or her child's welfare), children's allowances, and welfare payments for low-income single mothers. Finally, medical care is provided through a universal system of national health care financed by social security, a preventive-care system for children and a group of public-health nurses who specialize in child welfare.

Establish City-Suburban Partnerships

If the other industrial democracies offer lessons for a long-term solution to the jobs problem involving relationships between employment, education, and family-support systems, they also offer another lesson: the importance of city-suburban integration and cooperation. None of the other industrialized democracies have allowed their city centers to deteriorate as has the United States.

It will be difficult to address growing racial tensions in American cities unless we tackle the problems of shrinking revenue and inadequate social services and the gradual disappearance of work in certain neighborhoods. The city has become a less desirable place in which to live, and the economic and social gap between the cities and suburbs is growing. The groups left behind compete, often along racial lines, for declining resources, including the remaining decent schools; housing; and neighborhoods. The rise of the new urban poverty neighborhoods has worsened these problems. Their high rates of joblessness and social disorganization have created problems that often spill over into other parts of the city. All of these factors aggravate race relations and elevate racial tensions.

Ideally, we would restore the Federal contribution to city revenues that existed in 1980 and sharply increase the employment base. Regardless of changes in Federal urban policy, however, the fiscal crisis in the cities would be significantly eased if the employment base could be substantially increased. Indeed, the social dislocations caused by the steady disappearance of work have led to a wide range of urban social problems, including racial tensions. Increased employment would help stabilize the new poverty neighborhoods, halt the precipitous decline in density, and ultimately enhance the quality of race relations in urban areas.

Reforms put forward to achieve the objective of city-suburban cooperation range from proposals to create metropolitan governments to proposals for metropolitan tax-base sharing (currently in effect in Minneapolis-St. Paul), collaborative metropolitan planning, and the creation of regional authorities to develop solutions to common problems if communities fail to reach agreement. Among the problems shared by many metropolises is a weak public transit system. A commitment to address this problem through a form of city-suburban collaboration would benefit residents of both the city and the suburbs.

The mismatch between residence and the location of jobs is a problem for some workers in America because, unlike the system in Europe, public transportation is weak and expensive. It's a particular problem for inner-city blacks because they have less access to private automobiles and, unlike Mexicans, do not have a network system that supports organized car pools. Accordingly, they depend heavily on public transportation and therefore have difficulty getting to the suburbs, where jobs are more plentiful. Until public transit systems are improved in metropolitan areas, the creation of privately subsidized car-pool and van-pool networks to carry inner-city residents to the areas of employment, especially suburban areas, would be a relatively inexpensive way to increase work opportunities.

The creation of for-profit information and placement centers in various parts of the inner city not only could significantly improve awareness of the availability of employment in the metropolitan area but could also serve to refer workers to employers. These centers would recruit or accept inner-city workers and try to place them in jobs. One of their main purposes would be to make persons who have been persistently unemployed or out of the labor force "job ready."

Reintroduce the Works Progress Administration

The final proposal under consideration here was advanced by the perceptive journalist Mickey Kaus of the *New Republic,* who has long been concerned about the growth in the number of welfare recipients. Kaus's proposal is modeled on the Works Progress Administration (W.P.A.), the large public-works program initiated in 1935 by President Franklin D. Roosevelt. The public-works jobs that Roosevelt had in mind included highway construction, slum clearance, housing construction, and rural electrification. As Kaus points out: "In its eight-year existence, according to official records, the W.P.A. built or improved 651,000 miles of roads, 953 airports, 124,000 bridges and viaducts, 1,178,000 culverts, 8,000 parks, 18,000 playgrounds and athletic fields, and 2,000 swimming pools. It constructed 40,000 build-ings (including 8,000 schools) and repaired 85,000 more. Much of New York City — including La Guardia Airport, F.D.R. Drive, plus hundreds of parks and libraries — was built by the W.P.A."

A neo-W.P.A. program of employment, for every American citizen over eighteen who wants it, would provide useful public jobs at wages slightly below the minimum wage. Like the work relief under Roosevelt's W.P.A., it would not carry the stigma of a cash dole. People would be earning their money. Although some workers in the W.P.A.-style jobs "could be promoted to higher paying public service positions," says Kaus, most of them would advance occupationally by moving to the private sec-tor. "If you have to work anyway," he says, "why do it for $4 an hour?"

Under Kaus's proposal, after a certain date, able-bodied recipients on welfare would no longer receive cash payments. However, unlike the wel-fare-reform bill that Clinton has agreed to sign,[1] Kaus's plan would make public jobs available to those who move off welfare. Also, Kaus argues that to allow poor mothers to work, government-financed day care must be provided for their children if needed. But this service has to be integrated into the larger system of child care for other families in the United States to avoid creating a "day-care ghetto" for low-income children.

A W.P.A.-style jobs program will not be cheap. In the short run, it is considerably cheaper to give people cash welfare than it is to create public jobs. Including the costs of supervisors and materials, each subminimum-wage W.P.A.-style job would cost an estimated $12,000, more than the public cost of staying on welfare. That would represent $12 billion for every one million jobs created.

The solutions I outlined were developed with the idea of providing a policy framework that could be easily adopted by a reform coalition. A broad range of groups would support the long-term solutions — the devel-opment of a system of national performance standards in public schools, family policies to reinforce the learning system in the schools, a national system of school-to-work transition, and the promotion of city-suburban integration and cooperation. The short-term solutions, which range from job information and placement centers to the creation of W.P.A.-style jobs, are more relevant to low-income people, but they are the kinds of opportu-nity-enhancing programs that Americans of all racial and class back-grounds tend to support.

Although my policy framework is designed to appeal to broad seg-ments of the population, I firmly believe that if adopted, it would alleviate a good deal of the economic and social distress currently plaguing the inner cities. The immediate problem of the disappearance of work in many inner-city neighborhoods would be confronted. The employment base in these

[1]To the dismay of many liberals in his cabinet, President Clinton signed the welfare reform bill in 1997.

neighborhoods would be increased immediately by the newly created jobs, and income levels would rise because of the expansion of the earned-income tax credit. Programs like universal health care and day care would increase the attractiveness of low-wage jobs and "make work pay."

Increasing the employment base would have an enormous positive impact on the social organization of ghetto neighborhoods. As more people became employed, crime and drug use would subside; families would be straightened and welfare receipt would decline significantly; ghetto-related culture and behavior, no longer sustained and nourished by persistent joblessness, would gradually fade. As more people became employed and gained work experience, they would have a better chance of finding jobs in the private sector when they became available. The attitudes of employers toward inner-city workers would change, partly because the employers would be dealing with job applicants who had steady work experience and would furnish references from their previous supervisors.

Responding as a Reader

1. How does Wilson define "ghetto"? Which of the neighborhoods discussed in this essay fit that definition and which do not?

2. How is "a neighborhood in which people are poor but employed . . . different from a neighborhood in which people are poor and jobless" (para. 3)? What does work do for a person, other than bring in money?

3. What is Wilson saying, in paragraph 10, about "the social processes that regulate behavior"? What are these processes? What kind of behavior do they regulate and how? How does this issue relate to the issue of joblessness?

4. What is the relationship, according to Wilson, between "the disappearance of work" and the "disappearance of the traditional married-couple family" (para. 24)? How are both these factors related to the level of welfare benefits? How are they related to culture?

Responding as a Writer

1. What causes jobs to disappear, according to this essay? List the steps or phases in chronological order or make a flow chart. Which of these factors do you consider most significant and why? Which does Wilson seem to think are most significant?

2. Choose one of the solutions that Wilson advocates (starting with "What can be done," para. 41) and analyze it in detail. What specifically would need to happen to accomplish this goal? Where would the

money come from? Who would do the work? What might be the short-term and long-term effects?

3. Imagine that you're opening your own business. Where would you like to locate this business and why? Make sure to consider factors such as the cost of renting space and hiring workers and the possible return on your investment, the presence or absence of competing businesses in the area, and the ability to attract clients who would be interested in your product and employees who would want to work there. In two or three pages, list the factors you would consider and describe the ideal location for your new business. Would you want to open your business in a run-down neighborhood? Why or why not?

4. As more inner-city people find jobs, Wilson contends, "ghetto-related culture and behavior, no longer sustained and nourished by persistent joblessness, would gradually fade" (para. 59). What sort of culture and behavior is Wilson thinking of? Are there others who might find the disappearance of this culture and behavior regrettable? Has "ghetto-related culture" made any contributions to American society as a whole? Respond to Wilson's point in an essay in which you make an attempt to distinguish between positive and negative elements of this culture.

KIM PHILLIPS

Lotteryville, USA

[BAFFLER #7 / 1995]

What would you do if you won a million dollars? Forget the revolution: this is your ticket to the Kingdom of Freedom. No matter how many hours you log in at a fast-food restaurant or behind a secretary's desk, it's unlikely you'll ever save enough to buy a house or take a decent vacation, let alone get your hair and thighs to look like those of the Aaron Spelling[1]

[1] Aaron Spelling is the Hollywood producer of *Beverly Hills, 90210,* among other popular shows.

KIM PHILLIPS (b. 1975) has published work in the Grey City Journal. *She currently resides in Chicago.*

actresses who tantalize you every Monday and Wednesday night. The classless society is happening right now, at a party at a mansion in Beverly Hills. And a lottery ticket might buy you an invitation.

In Grand Crossing, a neighborhood on the South Side of Chicago, the average monthly spending on the lottery is $60 per household. Grand Crossing lies just west of the South Shore neighborhood, home of the much-lauded community-development-oriented South Shore Bank. Jeffery Boulevard, the busy commercial thoroughfare where the Bank's headquarters are located, is lined with thriving small businesses — hair salons, pizzerias, black-owned clothing stores. But traveling from South Shore to Grand Crossing you pass a boarded-up apartment building, an abandoned grocery store, a deserted TV repair shop. A little bit further and you come to Stony Island Avenue. The businesses here are distinctly different than on Jeffery — there's a Checkers, a Church's Fried Chicken, a Burger King; a neighborhood has started to become a ghetto. Next to a shuttered bar there's an ad for a pawn shop — "Need Cash Fast? Top Dollar for Broken Gold." Beyond the highway that passes over the neighborhood is a sudden proliferation of storefront churches, one of which, the House of Deliverance, has obviously been abandoned. At Cottage Grove there's a currency exchange and a store that advertises itself as selling liquor — and, as an afterthought, food. Beyond, there's nothing but ramshackle buildings; no businesses as far as the eye can see. Only the passing of an occasional bus reminds you that you're connected to the rest of the city.

Compare Grand Crossing to Bronzeville, the famous *Black Metropolis* described in 1945 by St. Clare Drake and Horace Cayton, with its "continuous and colorful movement" among locally owned businesses. A neighborhood, a city, is a concentration of people, goods, money, drawn in from the hinterlands; if much of this abundance is collected only to be dispersed again, a sizable portion remains and circulates within the closed system of the city. Drake and Cayton describe the neighborhood's policy wheels, illegal private precursors to the lottery that were run primarily by black syndicates and helped to amass capital within the community, to make sure a few people would always have enough to support local businesses and even invest. As a way of redistributing money within the neighborhood, policy wheels didn't work too badly. It's not a coincidence that policy was replaced by the lottery just as the local department stores and restaurants have been replaced by Burger King.

Today a monthly average of $4.48 is spent on the lottery per household in Flossmoor, a wealthy Chicago suburb where the average income is $117,000 a year. In Posen, a poor suburb where average household income is $33,000, the monthly average is $91.82. Although people of all incomes play the lottery, it remains overwhelmingly true that lottery players, like the policy wheel players of the past, are overwhelmingly poor. But in every other way the lottery serves a wholly different function than its predecessor. On one hand, it scrapes up revenue for starved state coffers. On the other, it inoculates the urban poor with a stiff ideological dose of eternal possibility and personal mobility. The one thing it does *not* do is collect money for local investment. In an era when Enterprise Zones and tax cuts for businesses are all that is offered to heal the wounds of the cities, the lottery is America's perverse way of dealing with the plight of its urban poor.

Lotteries are part of a long and vigorous tradition in American life, going back to the colonial period when they were used to amass funds for the construction of many of the hallmarks of colonial architecture — the Harvard and Yale campuses, Faneuil Hall — and even for getting supplies to Revolutionary troops. During the nineteenth century, private lotteries took in millions of dollars; the last of these, a fabulously corrupt money-making machine in Louisiana, was shut down in 1896. Yet even after the last of the legal lotteries disappeared, policy rackets continued to turn great profits, and instant sweepstakes like that of Publisher's Clearinghouse took the place of the lottery among the law-abiding — especially when times got tough.

The lottery returned as a tool of public finance in the late sixties and early seventies. Today, thirty-nine states have lotteries. The Illinois operation is typical: After a few years of slow growth between 1975 and 1980, it exploded; ticket sales climbed from $98 million in 1980 to $1.5 billion in 1990. Your Illinois lottery dollar breaks down like this: About 50¢ goes back in payoffs, 40¢ goes to the Common School Fund, 5¢ goes to commissions for lottery vendors, and 5¢ goes to operating the lottery. The transfer to the school fund in 1994 was $552,111,416. An enormous sum, to be sure, but it's an accounting fiction to say that the lottery *made* half a billion dollars for the school fund — if the money hadn't come from the lottery, it would have to have come from somewhere else in the tax structure. A more accurate way to put it might be to say that the lottery saved local property owners half a billion dollars in taxes.

It's misleading to think of state revenues as absolute figures; the crucial question about state taxes isn't whether they're "high" or "low" but who pays them. Since every state gets its revenue from somewhere, what matters is which part of society is expected to foot the bill, a question not of bookkeeping but politics. Tax structures, as Orange County is reminding the world, are ways of distributing financial power. Sales taxes, for example, are regressive not only because they take a more sizable cut of a poor person's income than that of someone in the upper-middle class but because they reduce the cumulative purchasing power of working people and hence the bargaining power workers have over the economy as a whole. The lottery is perhaps unique in that it is one of the only methods of raising revenue that applies solely to poor and working people and doesn't affect business or property owners at all. In this it seems closer to pre-Revolutionary France, when peasants picked up the brunt of the Crown's bill, than to the United States before the progressive income tax. To a policy wonk it may seem absurd to bring up feudalism in a discussion of taxes, but the comparison is more appropriate than it might seem. "Regressivity" is usually used to describe a state revenue source that exacts a larger proportion of a poor person's income than that of a rich person. However, many common state revenue sources — like excise taxes on cigarettes and the lottery — go farther than this; they take a larger *absolute* amount from the poor than the well-off, while other kinds of tax relief programs give businesses industrial parks and factory buildings at outrageous discounts.

Despite Chicago's vast ghettos, the poor here are easy to forget. Wealth is everywhere, as immanent and unreachable as the spires of the Loop seem from the South Side — a fairy city, hovering forever out of reach. Money hangs over the city like an unfulfilled promise, beckoning in the department stores, the glass skyscrapers, the taxicabs, a whiff of expensive perfume. "Get from Grand Boulevard to Easy Street," read a lottery advertisement put up in one of Chicago's poorest neighborhoods a few years ago. "This could be your ticket out." Lottery stories sometimes eat up fifteen minutes of a half-hour news program; the ubiquitous pot of Illinois State Lottery gold at the end of a rainbow sits in the window of liquor stores all over the South Side. The message blares from the newspapers that print winning numbers, "hot" numbers, "overdue" numbers, from the hysterical screams of winners on TV. Anyone can be a millionaire. You gotta play to win. Everybody gets another chance.

A chance for what? Lottery marketing firms — which make millions from state contracts — devise scenes of wealth so surreal that they could be Donald Trump's nightmares. An ad on the New York City subway a couple of years ago showed a throne room in an island mansion, the turquoise waves of some tropical sea visible through a window behind a velvet throne; a middle-aged man in tattered bathrobe with glasses and slippers sat reading the paper while a small poodle stood at attention before him, a peculiar mixture of suburbia and imperial Russia. But at Chicago's Kimbark Liquors, a little Hyde Park establishment that sells 2,700 tickets the day before a $20 million drawing, the purchasers don't seem to be thinking about waiting poodles. "It's just a dream, something to think about before you fall asleep, something to take your mind off its everyday hassles," says Larry, a salesman at Kimbark. What people think of when they play the lottery doesn't seem to be the fancy cars, the racks of CDs, the fabulous new house, the private jet; not the freedom that comes with unlimited consumption, but instead the quieter comfort of financial security, a security that is no longer obtainable through work. A middle-aged man at Kimbark who plays twenty dollars worth of tickets every day says that if he wins he'll go to Georgia, where it's warm. An older woman tells me she'd just like to pay off her bills. Mike Lang, of the Illinois Lottery, says, "Winners often buy a new car, not a Ferrari but a Buick or Cadillac." It's not being a millionaire that people long for, it's simply not being poor any more.

Statistically speaking, nobody ever wins the lottery. The chance of picking six random numbers out of fifty-four is one in 12,913,582.

Philosophers of capitalism from Adam Smith to Milton Friedman have long been perturbed by the phenomenon of people playing a game they ought to know they can't win. But sneering at the lottery as "a tax on the ignorant," claiming that people who play the lottery are poor fools, deluded and uneducated, manipulated into buying false promises of wealth, fame, and glory, bypasses the possibility that maybe poor people actually have a good understanding of what their life chances are; maybe lottery players are *right*. At issue here is not the lottery *per se* but the chance of personal mobility, the question of how far you can get in life by working industriously; the lottery should make sense to anyone for whom the answer is nowhere. Lottery tickets aren't like investments in the stock market; they are tickets to a dramatically different kind of life, the kind of life you'll never be able to save up to just by working nine to five.

In fact, the lottery is a perfectly rational investment for a person facing a lifetime of drudgery and uncertainty. The dictums of the economists — that saving can ultimately buy you a better life, that accumulation towards reinvestment ought to be the practice of any rational utility-maximizer — fail to take into account that money means one thing for the rich and quite another for the poor. Poor people's money doesn't work right. It doesn't save, it doesn't accumulate, it doesn't invest. For most people, money is simply a means to an end, a way to get food, clothing, shelter, and a little TV on the side. It gets traded in, given away, stolen, lost. Elusive and slippery, you can't put it somewhere it will stay — like a house or a pension plan — until you can make the down payment. The working man's purchasing power is just the boss' variable capital, so the saying goes. Money, the form both take, is a neutral medium. To compare the cash hidden in the mattresses of the poor to the investments of the wealthy is to postulate a continuum where there is in fact a radical break.

As the historical progression from Bronzeville to Grand Crossing indicates, what makes a ghetto a ghetto is not so much a lack of money but the lack of institutions in which money can collect. With no local businesses through which to circulate, the green stuff disappears from poor neighborhoods into the cash registers of the few remaining chain supermarkets. It goes to the makers of Olde English 800, to the tobacco millionaires, the fast-food chain owners, the landlords in the suburbs, the currency exchanges. The lottery is hardly unique in siphoning money out of a poor community — compared with most businesses that "serve" the poor it looks almost innocuous. If the model for the lottery isn't Robin Hood, it's not quite Ronald Reagan either — it robs the poor to give to the school system. That it goes to the state is perhaps a sign of how desperate state governments are for revenue, but for the players it's no different than other systems that suck their money away. To refer to the lottery as a swindle or a cheat on the poor ignores the basic truth about being poor, which is that you get cheated all the time.

Yet there is a lucky winner. The lottery is a painless, if extremely narrow, form of redistribution, taking money from the poor to enrich one of their own. While the lottery may, in a sense, be rational for the individual, it is clearly irrational for the class. Rather than simply manipulating ignorance, the lottery teaches a sly lesson: For people in desperate situations, fantasy is the answer. Reinforcing the message of personal mobility, lottery playing teaches that you're on your own, that organization and politics are loser's games. Unlike the liquor salesmen or absentee landlords, the lottery sells a vision of the future — a future imagined in terms of an unchangeable class system. The poor donate money to make one of their number rich, at which point that person and their newfound wealth pack up and move out. And the rich pay nothing for this self-containing system of political quiescence — in fact, they get a tax cut.

When people are laid off, budgets are tight, crime is rampant, and social dislocation is the norm, a microeconomic model explaining why this is the best of all possible worlds can't be far behind. The early 1980s found a new theoretical model afoot in the antiseptic world of sociologists and political scientists that suggested a city is not an economic unit in its own right, much less a place where people work and live, but rather a "service provider" — a place offering skyscrapers, office buildings, three-martini lunches, shoeshine boys. The earliest theorizers applied rational choice theory to urban life: People shop for cities the way one might look at a J. Crew catalogue, ultimately selecting the town with the ideal mix of services and taxes for them. Later academics contented themselves with explaining the only important thing — why cities should be prostrate and powerless vassals before the lord of corporate money. Since attracting big business to the city, where it will create jobs and pay (some) taxes, is, by definition, good for all the members of the city, it follows that all responsible city policies aim to attract private capital, with tax breaks, infrastructure, and perks like free electricity. Cities should compete for the privilege of housing the headquarters of Sears, the factories of U.S. Steel. And any microeconomist can tell you what the result of all this competition is — a better deal for the consumer.

Debates in academia rage — do "incentives" actually attract business   15
to an area? How much do taxes matter? *What does business want?* — questions that business publications happily answer. The *Site Selector Handbook,* for example, is quite straightforward on this intricate and difficult subject; in a recent article called "Incentive Lures: Firmly Embedded in the Location Equation," the president of a Colorado economic development council says, "I'd have to say incentives are brought up in discussions of prospects virtually 100% of the time today." Voltaire is brought in to defend the practice: "A little evil is often necessary for obtaining a great good." And the states and localities whip themselves into masochis-

tic lathers to demonstrate that they provide a perfect setting for *your* company. "To say our state is 'pro-business' is a little like saying the Sistine Chapel is 'kinda pretty,'" reads an ad for North Carolina, touting the state's right-to-work law, its balanced budget, and its favorable bond rating. An ad for the "Gateway Area," towns in Northern Illinois, Southern Iowa, and Northern Missouri, goes even farther, advertising the "Nordic stock" of the locals — "A Work Force that Earns Its Pay" — who, despite their Old World work ethic of "not just accepting hard work, but taking pride in it," come for lower wages than any workers in the surrounding cities.

A state budget is a tricky thing to unpack, containing such oddities in its murky depths as a steep sales tax on illegal drugs so that drug dealers can be busted for tax evasion and sales tax exemptions for all kinds of goodies ranging from manufacturing equipment to semen used for the artificial insemination of livestock. But a number of things are unmistakably clear about the lottery and the Illinois tax structure: The state has one of the highest sales taxes in the nation (6.25%) and one of the lowest income taxes (a flat tax of 3%; of the seven states with flat taxes, only Pennsylvania's is lower). The lottery, which makes up 5% of total state revenue, grosses about fifteen times the tax on real estate transfers ($28 million a year), about five times the tax on corporate franchises ($93 million a year), and is gaining apace on the corporate income tax ($851 million a year). In fact, total state revenue from all forms of gambling — riverboats, the racetrack, Bingo, and the lottery — now exceeds the corporate income tax, at $864 million a year. ("A tantalizing source of revenue," reads a brochure from the Comptroller's office.) Considering the lottery and, additionally, the variety of other revenue sources that fall predominantly on the poor — steep taxes on cigarettes, on liquor, and sales tax — it seems evident that Illinois wants to increase taxes on working-class people while easing up on corporations and their rich employees. But what else can they do? Chicago can't move; capital can. Rather than enact new income taxes, Illinois's politicians have decided to soak the poor.

While urban governments kow-tow to capital, local property owners have staged semirevolts at any hint of increased property taxes, leaving cities and states with a vacuum where there should be revenue. Public goods and services are needed to attract businesses and investors, and cities compete to undercut each other, each offering a better deal, lower taxes, more freebies, more docile workers. The "populist"-conservative ethic of personal responsibility and lower welfare payments dovetails nicely with the businessman's dream of a "flexible" labor market and a proliferation of low-wage workers — workers whose pockets can also be picked, at least in the short run, to make up for dwindling state coffers. The only thing cities have plenty of these days is poor people. And the lottery is a way of exploiting that human resource, the one taxable group in a state that won't move out and whose numbers are growing.

A British academic named Barbara Goodwin has written extensively about an imaginary "just society" that is organized around a mechanism called the Total Social Lottery. The lottery, held every five years, will determine which job you have, where you live, who has children, who governs. Every citizen will receive a basic social minimum — food, health care, a place to live — and all other income will be randomly redistributed every five years in Lifestyle Packages, which include random amounts of cash. The first question my friends in the primitive 1990s have about this society is not about its instability or lack of flexibility but is whether they would have to be treated by an untrained dentist every five years. While it's similar to the kind of fantasy kids dream up in the backseat during a long car ride, Goodwin's utopia sheds a little light on our own "meritocratic" society and the dozens of belief systems, from Andrew Carnegie's benevolent social Darwinism to the ramblings of Murray and Hernnstein,[2] which it has spawned in self-defense. The basic assumptions Goodwin makes about the lack of connection between the social importance of work and the size of one's income may not be so far from the mark. After all, the function of many jobs may have more to do with discipline and profit-making than with the social importance of the work itself; people who work at McDonald's don't make hamburgers as much as they make money for the people who own the fast-food chain.

The social philosophy played out in the daily drama of the lottery maintains that nobody *deserves* to be a millionaire. As in Goodwin's imaginary system, lottery players demonstrate a cunning awareness that wealth is little more than the luck of the draw. There's a strong tendency among lottery players to use numbers that have personal or numerological meaning, which are invariably random numbers in genesis — birthdays, for example, are perhaps the most random numbers of all. Numbers can have occult meanings as well — for example, 769 equals death, which for some reason makes it a lucky number. Images in dreams have numerical meaning; "abdomen" is 28-33-54, according to some dream-book publications, and "accident" is 4-31-50 if you witness one, 1-37-50 if you're in one. Other players seek order in absolute randomness; thousands of Illinois players let the Quick-Pick random-number generator pick their numbers for them. The world is moved by strange forces, irrational passions, dreams, and the randomness of birth, and wealth is largely a matter of chance, luck, and the uncontrollable variable of life choices dictated by who your parents are. While this emphasis on the blind hand of fate that causes some people to be born rich and others poor may obscure the logic

---

[2]The American industrialist Andrew Carnegie (1835–1919) was one of the wealthiest men of his time. His book, *The Gospel of Wealth* (1900), relies on the doctrine that the economic order resembles the biological in that it naturally selects those best suited to survive. Richard J. Hernnstein and Charles Murray are the authors of the highly controversial 1994 bestseller, *The Bell Curve: Intelligence and Class Structure in American Life.*

Q & A

Fran Lebowitz on Money

The following questions and answers cull some tongue-in-cheek words of wisdom about cash and the lottery. They are taken from a longer interview between the celebrated humorist Fran Lebowitz and Vanity Fair *magazine.*

How do people get rich?

I started out in life asking this question. Whenever I saw a rich person I would ask where their money was from, and invariably, or should I say inevitably, the answer was a natural resource or else an unnatural resource. Oil would be a common answer, or real estate, or steel — this was before computers. The answer was never the answer you wanted to hear. The answer was never "Poetry — their money's from poetry, Fran." Or "That's one of the great essay fortunes in this country." Or "You know, he's the biggest epigram magnate in Europe." And so I learned that I was not in the money-making end of the money-making business.

Have you ever thought of what you'd need to live comfortably or even to live without having to worry about anything?

Yes. Hourly. First of all, I'm a buyer of lottery tickets. I mention this only so you understand what a recreational attitude I have toward money — how it is largely fictional and anticipatory. Although not as fictional as some people's. Once I was standing in a lottery line and the woman behind me, who was clearly a cleaning lady because she had all her stuff with her, said to the man in front of me, "It's a big lottery this week — $23 million." And the guy said, "No, it's not. It's $3 million." And she said, "No, it's $23 million." And they argued back and forth and finally he said, "Look up there." And he

of a social system that keeps them that way, it poses a direct challenge to any perceived link between wealth and morality, between intellect and income, between productive power and money.

The peasants pay taxes while the noblemen joust; the unproductive economy feeds off an abundance of frustrated hopes. Instead of coming to grips with the harsh realities of poverty and urban decay, our empty cities exist in a hazy dream of riches. The lottery doesn't solve the problems of the city or cure the plight of the poor, and the lottery's fog of fantastical riches can't survive forever in the harsh reality of ghetto life — which, if nothing else, may mean that someone else will have to subsidize the school system. The answer lies in the very bond the lottery tries hardest to break — the bond of solidar-

pointed to the sign where the amount was posted. And it was $3 million. And she picked up her cleaning stuff and said, "Well, forget it. I'm not waiting in line for *that.*" And she left. I mean, after all, her time is worth something. It is impossible for me to extricate the thinking about money from the way I live now. Because the way I live now is primarily about thinking about money.

Do you think men and women see money differently?

Well, first of all, they see different amounts of it. Let's face it, as a friend of mine always says, men own the joint. It is often said that the advantage men have in business is that they don't take it personally. This is true. They hardly take anything personally, including, for example, their own children. Also, when you have a success, the first thing that happens is that you experience the reaction of your friends and relatives. And an enormous part of that reaction is envy. Most women respond to that envy by being upset, by feeling guilty, by feeling that they've hurt people's feelings. Men recognize envy for what it is — a sign of success. And it spurs them on. They're delighted: losing their best friend because they're successful — nothing better could happen. Having their brother never speak to them again — perfect. This incites them to further success. Hoping that these traits are environmental, people now try to train their little girls into them. I think it's fairly useless to try to train people into testosterone, which is the key element in money making, and also money keeping, which is just as important. So I think it's basically a boys' game and they'll always win. Consequently, women will simply have to content themselves with not having to play football in high school — a more than fair trade.

— From "On Money," *Vanity Fair* (July 1997).

ity, whether of class, neighborhood, or, finally, among cities. Imagine a kind of union of cities, a political unit that refused to compete for corporate relocation, instead working as a group to lay down terms for business — adequate wages for workers, laws mandating that a company remain in a given location for a specified number of years, consideration for the urban environment — rather than allowing business to lay down terms for them. The ideology of the lottery is the ideology of competition, in which each man is for himself and only one wins. Yet the only way cities can hope to win in the future is through solidarity. To get from Grand Crossing to Easy Street, cities will have to do better than the lottery — it's a loaded gamble, a fixed game, a bet that only capital can win.

Responding as a Reader

1. Why do people buy lottery tickets, according to Phillips? Why does this mean that the lottery "is one of the only methods of raising revenue that applies solely to the poor and working people and doesn't affect business or property owners at all" (para. 7)? How does this relate to Fran Lebowitz's comment (p. 250) that "money . . . is largely fictional and anticipatory"?

2. Do you agree with Phillips that "poor people's money doesn't work right" (para. 11)? What is the "right" way for money to work? Who defines how money "should" work in our society? Are there economic avenues that are open to the rich but blocked for the poor?

3. Consider the statistics in paragraph 16 — the rates for sales tax, income tax, and corporate taxes and the annual sum brought in by the lottery. What exactly gets taxed in each of these instances? Who pays these taxes? What is Phillips's point?

Responding as a Writer

1. If you agree with Phillips that the lottery robs the poor, who do you think is guilty of this robbery? Is it the rich, the state, the poor themselves? Write a letter to the guilty parties, trying to convince them to do their share to help turn this situation around. If you do not think that the lottery poses a real problem, write a response to Phillips explaining why.

2. Describe your own ideal "just society," comparable with Barbara Goodwin's (para. 18). Where does wealth come from, in this society? How is it distributed? Begin by defining what "just" means to you, in this context.

3. "The world is moved by strange forces, irrational passions, dreams, and the randomness of birth, and wealth is largely a matter of chance, luck, and the uncontrollable variable of life choices dictated by who your parents are" (para. 19). Argue for or against this statement. If this statement is true, what would be a fair way to distribute wealth?

4. In a personal essay, answer Phillips's opening question: "What would you do if you won a million dollars?"

The Unfinished Agenda:
Race, Poverty, and Gender in America

[THE PROGRESSIVE POPULIST / March 1997]

I want to address a matter that was of great concern to President Kennedy and was of defining urgency to his brother Robert — the unacceptable level of poverty that still exists in the midst of the enormous wealth of this great country.

As we turn our thoughts to the new century, we can celebrate a great deal. The past hundred years have seen massive improvements in the quality of our national life, American leadership in getting the world past murderous global conflict, and successful transcendence of economic crisis. Our population is more diverse than ever, and at mid-century we dismantled the legal framework encasing our original sin of state-sanctioned racism. We are in many varied ways a model for much of the world.

But there is at least one way in which we are not a model, one area in which we have in recent times been moving in the wrong direction. That is in fulfilling our national vow of equal opportunity. We said in 1776 that every American should have the right to life, liberty, and the pursuit of happiness. In 1997 that national commitment is in need of refurbishing and renewal.

More than thirty-five million Americans, one out of every seven of our fellow citizens, officially are poor. More than one in five American children is poor. And the poor are getting poorer. In 1994, of the poor children under the age of six, nearly half lived in families with incomes below half

---

PAUL WELLSTONE (b. 1944) graduated with a B.A. in political science at the University of North Carolina in Chapel Hill. He taught at Carleton College in Northfield, Minnesota, for twenty-one years before being elected to the U.S. Senate. He is the author of Powerline: The First Battle of America's Energy War *(1981). In 1996 he was re-elected to a second six-year term in the Senate. He serves on the Labor and Human Resources Committee, the Foreign Affairs Committee, the Small Business Committee, the Indian Affairs Committee, the Veterans' Affairs Committee, and Subcommittees on Aging, Children and Families, and Education, among others. This excerpt was adapted from a speech given at the John F. Kennedy School of Public Affairs.*

the poverty line. That figure has doubled over the past twenty years. The number of people who work full-time and still are poor has risen dramatically as well. In 1975, 6 percent of young children who lived in families with at least one full-time worker were poor. By 1994, that figure had gone up to 15 percent.

Poor people are increasingly hemmed into poor neighborhoods, with everything that means in terms of poor schools, crime, violence, lack of accessible jobs, and all the rest. The number of people living in concentrations of poverty in neighborhoods of more than 40 percent poverty went up by 75 percent from 1970 to 1980 and then doubled between 1980 and 1990. Over ten million Americans now live in very high poverty neighborhoods.

Minorities are poorer than the rest of Americans: African Americans at 29.3 percent in 1995 and Hispanics at 30.3 percent. Female-headed households are even poorer — 44.6 percent of the children who lived in such families were poor in 1994 and almost half of all children who are poor live in female-headed households.

What does it mean to be poor in America? We can offer no single description of American poverty. But for many, perhaps most, it means homes with peeling paint, inadequate heating, uncertain plumbing. It means that only the very lucky among the children receive a decent education. It often means a home where some go to bed hungry and malnutrition is a frequent visitor. It means that the most elementary components of the good life in America — a vacation with the kids, an evening out, a comfortable home — are but distant and unreachable dreams — more likely to be seen on the television set than in the neighborhood. And for almost all of the poor, all 35 million — it means a life that is a constant struggle to obtain the merest necessities of existence, those things most of us take for granted. We can do better.

It is an old saw that the rich get richer and poor get poorer. For nearly two decades that cliché has been a painful fact. Nearly all of America's economic growth has benefited the wealthiest among us, and the tiny slice of the pie allotted to the poor has actually gotten smaller. From 1977 to 1992, the richest 1 percent of Americans gained 91 percent in after-tax income, while the poorest fifth actually lost 17 percent of their income. The top 1 percent's total income equals that of the entire bottom two-fifths of the population.

Why? One view is it's their fault. We have had too much welfare for too long and "they" have become dependent on welfare and "they" don't get off their couch and go out and get a job. We have just had a major national debate on this whole subject, and the proponents of the "blame the welfare, blame the welfare recipients, blame the poor" view won. For now.

But, there is another view. And it happens to be the one that fits the facts. That view is that there are some fundamental problems in our American economy, some fundamental problems posed by the widening gap between rich and poor in this nation, and some fundamental problems in the way we view women and minorities.

People with less education are poorer. White high-school dropouts were earning 33 percent less in 1994 than they were in 1972, and African American dropouts' earnings were cut in half. Young families have lost income, with entry level wages for male high-school graduates down 27 percent from 1979 to 1995 and down 10 percent for female high-school graduates.

I will be the first to say that adults in our society need to take responsibility for themselves if they possibly can. Personal responsibility is a part of my values and it should be part of everyone's values. I will be the first to say that there are some basic issues about values that we need to confront. But until we come to a real understanding of the structural problems in our economy and our society that are getting in our way, we will continue to legislate by bumper stickers and slogans.

We need to have an honest national conversation, and an honest conversation in every community, about what is really going on, about why we face the unacceptable level of poverty and near poverty, and about what we are going to do about it.

We must not let the current debate over welfare or the role of government be used to mask the grim realities of American poverty. Most poor people are not poor by choice. Most would prefer to work for a decent wage. Nor can we offer a justification for the children who are born into a poverty that they did not choose or deserve and whose conditions prevent them from gaining the skills and ambitions that would allow them to escape.

I have come here today to make a commitment. I am going to do everything I possibly can to start that national conversation. I am going to travel the length and breadth of this country, as Robert Kennedy did thirty years ago and as Eleanor Roosevelt did during the Depression, to observe the face of American poverty, not from behind a Senate desk, but in the streets, the villages, and neighborhoods of those in distress. And hopefully I also can help to dramatize their plight, to reveal for many of our fellow citizens the face of poverty as it exists at the end of the millennium.

And, I want to share with our nation not only the problem as it really exists but also some of the wonderful, promising, exciting things that people are doing in communities to tackle the problem. And I have to say, if it is not obvious, I do not know all the answers. I do not know most of the answers. No one does. If any one of your professors here tells you they do, run the other way. These are hard, tough issues. We have to work on them in an open and honest way.

Poverty has many faces. There are the elderly, now less poor than the rest of America because of the success of Social Security and Medicare and Supplemental Security Income, as well as our private pension system. But women and minorities among the elderly are disproportionately poor. Our challenge for the elderly is to find the right way to protect Social Security and preserve Medicare. There are the disabled, protected by the historic

Americans with Disabilities Act but experiencing a backlash in recent benefit cuts, and for those who are employable, still unemployed at very high
rates. There are dislocated workers forced out of jobs by downsizing and
plant relocation. There are women and children made poor by divorce or
abandonment. There are rural poor who live far from available work, and
farmers who work as hard as anyone could and can't make ends meet.

I will visit all of these and help to tell their stories. Their problems are
real and pressing and we are not doing enough about them. But there are
four groups — four overlapping groups — whom I want particularly to
discuss today, groups who tend even more to set off the bumper sticker
talk and the political hot buttons and the simple-minded solutions. H. L.
Mencken[1] once said, "For every problem there is a solution that is neat
and simple — and wrong."

These groups are the working poor, welfare recipients, the inner-city
and rural poor, and poor children and youth.

Our left hand does not know what our right hand is doing. Think   20
about those numbers I cited a moment ago about entry-level wages. We recite the mantra of good jobs being replaced by lousy jobs until our minds
are numb. How many times have we heard, from Bob Reich[2] and many
others, the numbers about the rich getting richer and the poor literally losing real income? There are real people behind those numbers, literally millions of people, and more every day, who are working as hard as they can
and still are poor. And if we had a more honest measure of poverty the
numbers would be even higher. We know the answer so well that we recite
it as a bumper sticker: Make work pay.

But talk is cheap and bumper sticker slogans are a particularly cheap
form of talk. We are a day late and a dollar short in doing what we should
be doing to help. If there is any group of deserving poor in the United
States — although that is a term I greatly dislike — it is the working poor.
We have raised the earned income tax credit substantially. That is good.
We now have raised the minimum wage a little. That is good. But both are
still too low, and we look the other way when the question is whether
lousy jobs that too many Americans have carry health coverage. We do a
little shuffle when the real cost of child care is mentioned, and a small cal-
culation on the back of an envelope would reveal that the parents with the
lousy jobs can't afford the child care, especially if it is only one parent with
one lousy job.

And now we are about to flood the labor market with a new supply of
low-wage workers, pushed out there by the bumper sticker command of

---

[1] H[enry] L[ouis] Mencken (1880–1956) was a lively and prolific essayist who loved to de-
nounce national pieties.

[2] Robert B. Reich was Clinton's secretary of labor during his first term of office; he now
teaches at Brandeis University.

Comment

David Whitman on Poor Whites

America has long been home to millions of poor whites, from the Okie migrants of the 1930s to the Appalachian families of the 1960s. Yet poor whites have usually not been crowded into impoverished neighborhoods that resemble well-publicized black ghettos. While the country has more poor whites than poor blacks, more blacks than whites live in city slums. The Urban Institute reports that in 1990, 4.2 million blacks lived in black ghettos, compared with 1.6 million whites in white slums. Nonetheless, in white slums, as in black ones, many residents have dropped out of school, given up looking for work, become dependent on public aid, and been stricken by violence.

These social ills reflect the loss of manufacturing jobs and migration of low-wage work out of inner cities as well as a surge in family breakdowns and out-of-wedlock births among whites. The national economy expanded after the 1990–91 recession, and last year poverty dropped among most groups, including the black inner-city poor. But the number of poor central-city whites rose by at least 183,000, according to the Center on Budget and Policy Priorities. In urban areas, the small white underclass appears to be growing.

— From "White-Style Urban Woes" (*U.S. News & World Report,* December 9, 1996).

our new welfare law to find a job, any job. The vast majority of them are women, who still earn less than men, and minority women at that, who earn less than white women, so these new workers are especially likely to end up in low-wage jobs. And elementary labor economics says they are — if anything — going to depress these wages further for everyone at the low-wage end of the labor market.

Simply put, there are not enough jobs available that are geographically accessible and sufficiently undemanding of technical skills for all the long-term welfare recipients who have now been told to enter the job market or else. In real life, people of color will encounter discrimination when they try to find a job. But for a huge proportion of those who do find work, there will be a different, serious issue — how do I make ends meet? To add to the problem, in the same welfare bill there are large food stamp cuts that by 2002 will reduce the benefits across the board by 20 percent, for everyone including the millions of working poor who get a little help from food stamps in their constant struggle to keep things together.

The left hand does not want to ask what the right hand is doing. The problem of low-wage work has been getting worse and worse for nearly twenty-five years. It is a problem of economics, compounded by issues of gender and race discrimination that permeate our society. We need to talk about it and we need to act.

If some people will leave welfare for low-wage jobs because they have   25
to, even though they end up worse off, others will fall prey to the single worst aspect of the welfare bill — the arbitrary, fall-off-the-cliff five-year time limit for federally financed cash assistance, which can be even shorter if the states choose, and many of the states are so choosing. People can play by all the rules and do everything that is asked of them, and if they still come to a point after five years or intermittent spells on assistance totaling five years and have no job, they are out.

O-u-t.

The welfare law does allow 20 percent of the caseload to be exempted from the time limit. I am sorry to say that I believe the number who do not find work, or cannot go to work because they have a chronically ill child or relative to care for, or cannot go to work because they face violent retaliation from a husband or boyfriend if they do, or are functionally disabled, is much higher than 20 percent.

This approach is not the answer. The answer is not ending welfare as we know it. It is not ending welfare by fiat. The answer is to deal honestly with the real causes of poverty. We have to do this by genuinely making work pay, including health care and the child care that go along with it. But we do have to do it in two other fundamental ways as well: by committing ourselves to a genuine, positive, realistic developmental and educational strategy for children and young people so that they reach adulthood with the tools and attitudes they need to be responsible, self-sufficient adult citizens and by reclaiming our neighborhoods of endemic poverty and helping the parents and the other decent people there to create a safe and healthy environment in which to raise children and bring them along the road to responsible adulthood.

These last challenges underscore the complexity of the tasks and the complexity of the list of those who have to take responsibility if serious change is going to occur. There is a lot of talk going around about devolution, another politicized oversimplification in my estimation. Most of those who talk devolution confine their reformism impulse to handing control to the states and at bargain-basement prices to boot. The governors, who salivate for control, are all too ready to strike Faustian bargains for control without the money to carry it off. I am an enthusiast of devolution, but only so long as the term is defined accurately and the recipients of the sharing of responsibility include people in neighborhoods, nonprofits, and mayors and county executives.

If we are going to be effective in ensuring that the primary responsibil-   30
ity for children is where it belongs, which is with their parents, we have to stop and ask whether we are helping them do their job or getting in their way. We have to get past this silly political debate about whether it takes a village or it takes a family. The point is, the idea of community is very real and critically important. The idea of community is far broader than gov-

ernment. It is far broader than any particular program. Families may need help with income or services. But they can also use support in the arrangement of hours they work or the options afforded by their employee-assistance plan. Schools that welcome parents and make themselves into neighborhood beacons by the hours they keep and their partnerships with community organizations can be a great help to parents struggling to keep their children from succumbing to the pull of the street.

We need to pay particular attention to young men. The welfare law focuses on women, although not exactly in a positive way. It focuses on men in its tough new provisions on child support. But we need to be promoting responsible fatherhood, and that means marriage and involvement with the children and two earners in the family. One reason marriages do not form is lack of opportunity. Communities need to work on strategies to help young women and young men both to make it successfully into the job market. We have had a strategy for young men, but it is the wrong strategy. It is called prison, and it is eating its way through higher education budgets and school budgets across America. We will only stop feeding the correctional appetite if we stop supplying new customers.

But if too many parents find it terribly hard to meet all of their responsibilities and too many young people are falling by the wayside, communities cannot do the job of helping all by themselves. We need government and we need the federal government now.

Because there are some steps we can take as a nation — right now — that would make an enormous difference in the lives of children. It is a scandal that ten million children in America do not have basic health care to help them grow healthy and ready to reach their full potential. It is scandal that despite irrefutable and irreducible evidence that the Women, Infants, and Children (WIC) program is successful at providing women and children a healthy and nutritious diet, we have yet to fully fund it. We know WIC works. Yet currently it only reaches 50 percent of the eligible population. We can and must do better. It is a scandal that while we know that Head Start is effective in helping children from diverse backgrounds and circumstances to prepare for school, we have yet to fully fund it. Currently, Head Start reaches only 17 percent of eligible 3 year olds and only 41 percent of eligible 4 year olds!

Just because children are not the heavy hitters with the high-powered Washington lobbyists does not mean Congress and the President should remain silent. There simply is no excuse for not fully funding WIC and Head Start or ensuring basic health care for children — now. As a U.S. Senator I intend to bring these issues to the floor and fight again and again to force votes. And I expect to win because these kinds of successful antipoverty programs command broad-based support among the American people.

We also need federal financial support for many of the things people need to be empowered to do locally. There is a difference between federal funding and federal administration or even detailed federal regulation, just as there is a difference between government funding and the question

Speech

John J. Sweeney on Working

This speech is excerpted from a longer one by John J. Sweeney, president of the AFL-CIO. Sweeney delivered the full speech at the Columbia University Teach-In with the Labor Movement on October 3, 1996.

American workers are running out of money, running out of options, and running out of hope. They've exhausted their savings and they are loaded with debt. They are frustrated and bitter, and their anger is exceeded only by anxiety over keeping their jobs. They see the stock market soaring and profits roaring and they wonder, "Who the hell is getting my share?"

Because of the wage and the wealth gap, America is becoming edgier, angrier, and meaner. Until we ease the growing gaps in work, wages, and wealth, we will be reading more dispatches from a wounded nation — more militia movements, more bombings, more hate crimes, and more of the quiet anguish of Americans losing their sense of a common destiny and a common purpose. America will become more like the trouble spots where we send our sons and daughters to keep peace.

So what can we do about it? Of course, American business must change and American government must change. But American labor must also change. That is why I ran for president of the AFL-CIO and that is why I won. Here's the truth: The weakness of labor encouraged employers to take the low road. And only by rebuilding our strength can we bring American business back to the high road of high wages. That is why I am challenging every union to put millions of dollars into organizing from the Sunbelt to the

---

of who carries out the activities with the public money. We have a large, vital nonprofit sector in America, but it is able to do its work only because it receives considerable public funding. There are some who choose not to know this and somehow think the federal money can be removed without negative effect. This is the financial version of the Immaculate Conception.

There are hundreds and thousands of marvelous initiatives occurring in so many ways all over this nation that are making a major difference in the lives of poor people. We do not lack ideas. We do not lack knowledge. We do not lack committed people. But we lack scale. We lack a national commitment. We lack the means and methodology to get the shoulders of enough Americans at the wheel, to push our vehicle of opportunity out of the rut in which it has become stuck. We lack a genuine national debate over the real underlying questions — the way our economy is structured

Rustbelt and from health care to high tech. That is why we are pouring money and people into rebuilding our grassroots political strength.

"More." That's what Samuel Gompers said when he was asked nearly a century ago, "What does labor want?" Many of you know his words well. "More schoolhouses and less jails," he said, "more books and less arsenals, more learning and less vice, more constant work and less crime, more leisure and less greed, more justice and less revenge." [Samuel Gompers (1850–1924) was president of the American Federation of Labor from 1886 to 1924.] It was an eloquent statement of values trade unionists still hold dear. And what do working Americans want as we draw close to a new century? What we want is to work together to build an America that holds true to the values we honor in our homes and in our houses of worship.

We want to live in a country where you can raise a family without having to hold down three jobs to do it. Where you don't have to spend so much time at work that you have no time left to go to a movie or a ball game with your kids or grandchildren. Where your lot in life is determined by what you do and not by the color of your skin or the accident of your birth. Where our children and grandchildren can look forward to pay raises instead of layoff notices; to going to college instead of into a dead-end job; to enjoying life more, not less, than we've been able to.

Our idea of a just society is one in which honest labor raises the standard of living for all rather than one with enormous wealth for a few. And our notion of a moral nation is one that cares for its young, its old, and its poor — and leaves the rich to fend for themselves.

— From "Time for a New Contract," *Dissent* (Winter 1997).

and the very real issues of race and gender that are so deeply infused in so much of what goes on.

It was a combination of the civil rights movement and the activist movements of the sixties that generated our last truly national attack on the problems of poverty. That effort expired in the conflagration of Vietnam. But the successes of the civil rights activists, of the women's movement, of the peace movement were a clear demonstration of the truism that in a democracy significant social change comes from the bottom up, from an aroused opinion that forces our ruling institutions to do the right thing.

Robert Kennedy was fond of a quote from Albert Camus[3] that we could use to start our journey today: "Perhaps we cannot make this a

[3] The Algerian-born French novelist and philosopher, Albert Camus (1913–1960) supported many left-wing causes; he received the Nobel Prize for Literature in 1957.

262   Class War: Can the Poor Survive?

world in which children are no longer tortured," Camus said. "But at least we can reduce the number of tortured children." Won't you join me in that effort?

Responding as a Reader

1. Wellstone begins with a reference to John and Robert Kennedy. Who is Wellstone's audience for this speech, and who is his indirect audience? What does Wellstone accomplish (with both groups) by aligning himself with the Kennedys?

2. Study the paragraphs in which Wellstone cites statistics. According to these statistics, what are the conditions that lead to poverty? Which of these are most likely to lead to poverty?

3. Whom is Wellstone quoting in paragraph 9? What is his attitude toward the phrases in quotation marks? How can you tell?

Responding as a Writer

1. Wellstone says that "the idea of community is very real and critically important" (para. 30). Write a paragraph that spells out what Wellstone means by "community." How does Wellstone's definition differ from a dictionary definition? How does it differ from your personal definition?

2. Consider the quote from Albert Camus with which Wellstone ends his speech. What are some ways to "reduce the number of tortured children"? Choose one of these ways and argue for its implementation. What can individuals do to support this goal?

3. What, specifically, is Wellstone promising to do to help decrease poverty? What is he asking his listeners to do? In an essay, speculate about the possible effects of Wellstone's promised actions.

Discussing the Unit

Suggested Topic for Discussion

What specific problems face the poor in America today? What should the rest of the citizenry — the working, middle, and upper classes — do to address these problems? What should the federal government do? What should businesses do? What should the poor themselves do? How practical are these solutions?

Preparing for Class Discussion

1. What do the wealthy owe to the poor in a capitalistic society? What does big business owe to its workers and to its community? (To read what the president of the AFL-CIO has to say, look at John Sweeney's speech on p. 253.) Should the haves share with the have-nots, and if so, why should they? What's in it for them?

2. Consider theories of the distribution of wealth that you have studied in economics or history classes. Adam Smith, for example, argued that government should not get involved in business and that markets will take care of themselves according to the laws of supply and demand. Marx and Engels, on the other hand, argued that the government should arrange for wealth to come from each according to his ability and should be given to each according to his need. What have you learned in your other classes that you can contribute to this discussion?

3. *Prewriting Assignment:* Consider the differences between a family that has "just enough" money and a family that lives in poverty. What necessities does the poor family have to do without? What kinds of things does the other family have to do without? How does the lack of wealth affect other areas of family life, in both cases?

From Discussion to Writing

If you were elected to Congress, what legislation would you propose to fight poverty? Would you argue for welfare reform? Tax breaks for businesses that moved into poor neighborhoods? Changes in the public school system? Would you urge private citizens to make small contributions in their own neighborhoods? Choose one problem related to poverty and either draft a proposal for Congress to debate or write a speech to give to your constituents.

12

Same Sex . . . Any Sex: Is Marriage Obsolete?

Is same-sex marriage the defining civil rights issue of the 1990s? Many think so, and the national debate that followed a Hawaii court decision supporting the right of gays and lesbians to marry was heated and at times vicious. For traditionalists, homosexual marriage is morally repellent; many politicians quickly tried to enact state laws to prevent its possibility. For others, the issue led instead to a debate about marriage itself. What's all the fuss about? they wondered. Given the nation's galloping divorce rate, the institution of marriage appears to be dying anyway. Of course gays and lesbians should be allowed to marry, they say, but why on earth would they want to?

The issue forced many gays and lesbians themselves to confront their attitudes toward the convention of marriage. In "For Better or Worse," the Washington political essayist Jonathan Rauch carefully constructs a pro-marriage argument in which he concludes that it is in society's best interest to "marry off homosexuals." The associate editor of *Progressive* magazine, Anne-Marie Cusac, applauds the Hawaii decision but still has misgivings about the age-old institution of marriage: "If marriage were a different thing," she writes, "maybe I would want it — if it meant things like equality, cooperation, respect." On a more practical level, however, as a statement put out by the Lambda Legal Defense and Education Fund reveals, legally sanctioned marriage can mean that gay and lesbian couples can finally enjoy legal, economic, and practical benefits that heterosexual married couples have always taken for granted.

But such benefits aside, why do young people today even want to be married, asks *New York* magazine staff writer Ariel Kaminer. In her satirical "Something Old, Something New," she skewers all sorts of matrimonially minded folks, from Hollywood celebrities to your avid reader of *Bride* magazine. As for gays and lesbians, she says, "Beyond the civil-rights angle, the theory goes that the right to marry will prove once and for all that queers aren't crazed, drug-addled sex fiends; they're really just as boring as everyone else."

The prominent economist and nationally known columnist, Thomas Sowell, however, doesn't take the matter so lightly. In "The Gay 'Marriage' Issue," he argues that it "is one thing to say all people have the same rights, as the 14th Amendment does, and something very different to say that all behavior has the same rights." In an impassioned speech to the House on same-sex marriage, Iowa representative Ed Fallon defends gay marriage and condemns the stereotyping of gays and lesbians that has seriously interfered with their civil rights.

And how do freshmen today feel about marriage — be it same sex or the traditional kind? The survey results suggest a complicated answer.

Selected Survey Results

Marriage

- Freshmen men who agree that homosexual relations should be prohibited: 45.2%
- Women who agree: 24.1%
- Freshmen whose parents live with each other: 69.8%
- Freshmen at all-black colleges whose parents live with each other: 42.8%
- College freshmen who consider it essential or very important to raise a family: 72.2%

— From *The American Freshman: National Norms For Fall 1996.*

JONATHAN RAUCH

For Better or Worse?

[THE NEW REPUBLIC / May 6, 1996]

Whatever else marriage may or may not be, it is certainly falling apart. Half of today's marriages end in divorce, and, far more costly, many never begin — leaving mothers poor, children fatherless, and neighborhoods chaotic. With timing worthy of Neville Chamberlain,[1] homosexuals have chosen this moment to press for the right to marry. What's more, Hawaii's courts are moving toward letting them do so.[2] I'll believe in gay marriage in America when I see it, but if Hawaii legalizes it, even temporarily, the uproar over this final insult to a besieged institution will be deafening.

Whether gay marriage makes sense — and whether straight marriage makes sense — depends on what marriage is actually for. Current secular thinking on this question is shockingly sketchy. Gay activists say marriage is for love, and we love each other; therefore we should be able to marry. Traditionalists say marriage is for children, and homosexuals do not (or should not) have children; therefore you should not be able to marry. That, unfortunately, pretty well covers the spectrum. I say "unfortunately" because both views are wrong. They misunderstand and impoverish the social meaning of marriage.

So what is marriage for? Modern marriage is, of course, based on traditions that religion helped to codify and enforce. But religious doctrine has no special standing in the world of secular law and policy (the "Christian nation" crowd notwithstanding). If we want to know what and whom marriage is for in modern America, we need a sensible secular doctrine.

---

[1] In his efforts to avoid a second world war, Neville Chamberlain (1869–1940), British prime minister during the Nazi conquest of Europe (1937–1940), pursued a policy of appeasement toward Hitler's Germany. (He was supported by the U.S. ambassador to Great Britain, Joseph P. Kennedy, JFK's father.) After Hitler violated the peace pacts and invaded Poland, Chamberlain, too late, realized his diplomatic error and was forced to resign, turning the office over to Winston Churchill.

[2] A Hawaii judge ruled in 1996 that he could find no compelling reason to bar same-sex marriages.

JONATHAN RAUCH (b. 1960) attended Yale University and is the author of Demosclerosis: The Silent Killer of American Government (1994). He has contributed to such periodicals as Atlantic Monthly, New Republic, Los Angeles Times, New York Times, and Washington Post Book World. He has appeared on CNN, CNBC, C-SPAN, and the Financial News Network.

At one point, marriage in secular society was largely a matter of business: cementing family ties, providing social status for men and economic support for women, conferring dowries, and so on. Marriages were typically arranged, and "love" in the modern sense was no prerequisite. In Japan, remnants of this system remain, and it works surprisingly well. Couples stay together because they view their marriage as a partnership: an investment in social stability for themselves and their children. Because Japanese couples don't expect as much emotional fulfillment as we do, they are less inclined to break up. They also take a somewhat more relaxed attitude toward adultery. What's a little extracurricular love provided that each partner is fulfilling his or her many other marital duties?

In the West, of course, love is a defining element. The notion of life-long love is charming, if ambitious, and certainly love is a desirable element of marriage. In society's eyes, however, it cannot be the defining element. You may or may not love your husband, but the two of you are just as married either way. You may love your mistress, but that certainly doesn't make her your spouse. Love helps make sense of marriage emotionally, but it is not terribly important in making sense of marriage from the point of view of social policy.

If love does not define the purpose of secular marriage, what does? Neither the law nor secular thinking provides a clear answer. Today marriage is almost entirely a voluntary arrangement whose contents are up to the people making the deal. There are few if any behaviors that automatically end a marriage. If a man beats his wife, which is about the worst thing he can do to her, he may be convicted of assault, but his marriage is not automatically dissolved. Couples can be adulterous ("open") yet remain married. They can be celibate, too; consummation is not required. All in all, it is an impressive and also rather astonishing victory for modern individualism that so important an institution should be so bereft of formal social instruction as to what should go on inside of it.

Secular society tells us only a few things about marriage. First, marriage depends on the consent of the parties. Second, the parties are not children. Third, the number of parties is two. Fourth, one is a man and the other a woman. Within those rules a marriage is whatever anyone says it is.

Perhaps it is enough simply to say that marriage is as it is and should not be tampered with. This sounds like a crudely reactionary position. In fact, however, of all the arguments against reforming marriage, it is probably the most powerful.

Call it a Hayekian argument, after the great libertarian economist F. A. von Hayek,[3] who developed this line of thinking in his book *The Fatal*

[3] The Austrian economist and Nobel Prize winner F[riedrich] A[ugust] von Hayek (1899–1992) taught at the University of Chicago for many years. In a number of influential books, such as *The Road to Serfdom* (1944), von Hayek argued that governments should avoid regulating economic affairs. His economic principles have endeared him to the neoconservative and libertarian movements.

Conceit. In a market system, the prices generated by impersonal forces may not make sense from any one person's point of view, but they encode far more information than even the cleverest person could ever gather. In a similar fashion, human societies evolve rich and complicated webs of non-legal rules in the form of customs, traditions, and institutions. Like prices, they may seem irrational or arbitrary. But the very fact that they are the customs that have evolved implies that they embody a practical logic that may not be apparent to even a sophisticated analyst. And the web of custom cannot be torn apart and reordered at will because once its internal logic is violated it falls apart. Intellectuals, such as Marxists or feminists, who seek to deconstruct and rationally rebuild social traditions, will produce not better order but chaos.

So the Hayekian view argues strongly against gay marriage. It says that the current rules may not be best and may even be unfair. But they are all we have, and, once you say that marriage need not be male–female, soon marriage will stop being anything at all. You can't mess with the formula without causing unforeseen consequences, possibly including the implosion of the institution of marriage itself.

However, there are problems with the Hayekian position. It is untenable in its extreme form and unhelpful in its milder version. In its extreme form, it implies that no social reforms should ever be undertaken. Indeed, no laws should be passed, because they interfere with the natural evolution of social mores. How could Hayekians abolish slavery? They would probably note that slavery violates fundamental moral principles. But in so doing they would establish a moral platform from which to judge social rules and thus acknowledge that abstracting social debate from moral concerns is not possible.

If the ban on gay marriage were only mildly unfair, and if the costs of changing it were certain to be enormous, then the ban could stand on Hayekian grounds. But, if there is any social policy today that has a fair claim to be scaldingly inhumane, it is the ban on gay marriage. As conservatives tirelessly and rightly point out, marriage is society's most fundamental institution. To bar any class of people from marrying as they choose is an extraordinary deprivation. When not so long ago it was illegal in parts of America for blacks to marry whites, no one could claim that this was a trivial disenfranchisement. Granted, gay marriage raises issues that interracial marriage does not, but no one can argue that the deprivation is a minor one.

To outweigh such a serious claim, it is not enough to say that gay marriage might lead to bad things. Bad things happened as a result of legalizing contraception, but that did not make it the wrong thing to do. Besides, it seems doubtful that extending marriage to, say, another 3 or 5 percent of the population would have anything like the effects that no-fault divorce has had, to say nothing of contraception. By now, the "traditional" understanding of marriage has been sullied in all kinds of ways. It is hard to think of a bigger affront to tradition, for instance, than allowing married women to own property independently of their husbands or allowing them to charge their husbands with rape. Surely it is unfair to say that marriage may be reformed for the sake of anyone and everyone except homosexuals, who must respect the dictates of tradition.

Faced with these problems, the milder version of the Hayekian argument says not that social traditions shouldn't be tampered with at all, but that they shouldn't be tampered with lightly. Fine. In this case, no one is talking about casual messing around; both sides have marshaled their arguments with deadly seriousness. Hayekians surely have to recognize that appeals to blind tradition and to the risks inherent in social change do not, a priori, settle anything in this instance. They merely warn against frivolous change.

So we turn to what has become the standard view of marriage's purpose. Its proponents would probably like to call it a child-centered view, but it is actually an antigay view, as will become clear. Whatever you call it, it is the view of marriage that is heard most often, and in the context of the debate over gay marriage it is heard almost exclusively. In its most straightforward form it goes as follows (I quote from James Q. Wilson's[4] fine book *The Moral Sense*):

> A family is not an association of independent people; it is a human commitment designed to make possible the rearing of moral and healthy children. Governments care — or ought to care — about families for this reason, and scarcely for any other.

Wilson speaks about "family" rather than "marriage" as such, but one may, I think, read him as speaking of marriage without doing any injustice to his meaning. The resulting proposition — government ought to care about marriage almost entirely because of children — seems reasonable. But there are problems. The first, obviously, is that gay couples may have children, whether through adoption, prior marriage, or (for lesbians) artificial insemination. Leaving aside the thorny issue of gay adoption, the point is that if the mere presence of children is the test, then homosexual relationships can certainly pass it.

You might note, correctly, that heterosexual marriages are more likely to produce children than homosexual ones. When granting marriage licenses to heterosexuals, however, we do not ask how likely the couple is to have children. We assume that they are entitled to get married whether or not they end up with children. Understanding this, conservatives often make an interesting move. In seeking to justify the state's interest in marriage, they shift from the actual presence of children to the anatomical pos-

[4]For more on James Q. Wilson, see page 86.

sibility of making them. Hadley Arkes, a political science professor and prominent opponent of homosexual marriage, makes the case this way:

> The traditional understanding of marriage is grounded in the "natural tele-ology of the body" — in the inescapable fact that only a man and a woman, and only two people, not three, can generate a child. Once marriage is de-tached from that natural teleology of the body, what ground of principle would thereafter confine marriage to two people rather than some larger grouping? That is, on what ground of principle would the law reject the claim of a gay couple that their love is not confined to a coupling of two, but that they are woven into a larger ensemble with yet another person or two?

What he seems to be saying is that where the possibility of natural children is nil, the meaning of marriage is nil. If marriage is allowed between members of the same sex, then the concept of marriage has been emptied of content except to ask whether the parties love each other. Then anything goes, including polygamy. This reasoning presumably is what those opposed to gay marriage have in mind when they claim that once gay marriage is legal, marriage to pets will follow close behind.

But Arkes and his sympathizers make two mistakes. To see them, break down the claim into two components: (1) Two-person marriage derives its special status from the anatomical possibility that the partners can create natural children and (2) apart from (1), two-person marriage has no purpose sufficiently strong to justify its special status. That is, absent justification (1), anything goes.

The first proposition is wholly at odds with the way society actually views marriage. Leave aside the insistence that natural, as opposed to adopted, children define the importance of marriage. The deeper problem, apparent right away, is the issue of sterile heterosexual couples. Here the "anatomical possibility" crowd has a problem, for a homosexual union is, anatomically speaking, nothing but one variety of sterile union and no different even in principle: A woman without a uterus has no more potential for giving birth than a man without a vagina.

It may sound like carping to stress the case of barren heterosexual marriage: The vast majority of newlywed heterosexual couples, after all, can have children and probably will. But the point here is fundamental. There are far more sterile heterosexual unions in America than homosexual ones. The anatomical possibility crowd cannot have it both ways. If the possibility of children is what gives meaning to marriage, then a post-menopausal woman who applies for a marriage license should be turned away at the courthouse door. What's more, she should be hooted at and condemned for stretching the meaning of marriage beyond its natural basis and so reducing the institution to frivolity. People at the Family Research Council or Concerned Women for America should point at her and say, "If she can marry, why not polygamy?"

20

Obviously, the "anatomical" conservatives do not say this, because they are sane. They instead flail around, saying that sterile men and women were at least born with the right-shaped parts for making children, and so on. Their position is really a nonposition. It says that the "natural children" rationale defines marriage when homosexuals are involved but not when heterosexuals are involved. When the parties to union are sterile heterosexuals, the justification for marriage must be something else. But what?

Now arises the oddest part of the anatomical argument. Look at proposition (2) above. It says that absent the anatomical justification for marriage, anything goes. In other words, it dismisses the idea that there might be other good reasons for society to sanctify marriage above other kinds of relationships. Why would anybody make this move? I'll hazard a guess: to exclude homosexuals. Any rationale that justifies sterile heterosexual marriages can also apply to homosexual ones. For instance, marriage makes women more financially secure. Very nice, say the conservatives. But that rationale could be applied to lesbians, so it's definitely out.

The end result of this stratagem is perverse to the point of being funny. The attempt to ground marriage in children (or the anatomical possibility thereof) falls flat. But, having lost that reason for marriage, the antigay people can offer no other. In their fixation on excluding homosexuals, they leave themselves no consistent justification for the privileged status of *heterosexual* marriage. They thus tear away any coherent foundation that secular marriage might have, which is precisely the opposite of what they claim they want to do. If they have to undercut marriage to save it from homosexuals, so be it!

For the record, I would be the last to deny that children are one central 25
reason for the privileged status of marriage. When men and women get together, children are a likely outcome; and, as we are learning in ever more unpleasant ways, when children grow up without two parents, trouble ensues. Children are not a trivial reason for marriage; they just cannot be the only reason.

What are the others? It seems to me that the two strongest candidates are these: domesticating men and providing reliable care-givers. Both purposes are critical to the functioning of a humane and stable society, and both are much better served by marriage — that is, by one-to-one lifelong commitment — than by any other institution.

Civilizing young males is one of any society's biggest problems. Wherever unattached males gather in packs, you see no end of trouble: wildings in Central Park, gangs in Los Angeles, soccer hooligans in Britain, skinheads in Germany, fraternity hazings in universities, grope-lines in the military, and, in a different but ultimately no less tragic way, the bathhouses and wanton sex of gay San Francisco or New York in the 1970s.

For taming men, marriage is unmatched. "Of all the institutions through which men may pass — schools, factories, the military — marriage has the largest effect," Wilson writes in *The Moral Sense*. (A token of the casualness of current thinking about marriage is that the man who wrote those words could, later in the very same book, say that government should care about fostering families for "scarcely any other" reason than children.) If marriage — that is, the binding of men into couples — did nothing else, its power to settle men, to keep them at home and out of trouble, would be ample justification for its special status.

Of course, women and older men don't generally travel in marauding or orgiastic packs. But in their case the second rationale comes into play. A second enormous problem for society is what to do when someone is beset by some sort of burdensome contingency. It could be cancer, a broken back, unemployment, or depression; it could be exhaustion from work or stress under pressure. If marriage has any meaning at all, it is that when you collapse from a stroke, there will be at least one other person whose "job" is to drop everything and come to your aid, or that when you come home after being fired by the postal service there will be someone to persuade you not to kill the supervisor.

Obviously, both rationales — the need to settle males and the need to have people looked after — apply to sterile people as well as fertile ones and apply to childless couples as well as to ones with children. The first explains why everybody feels relieved when the town delinquent gets married and the second explains why everybody feels happy when an aging widow takes a second husband. From a social point of view, it seems to me, both rationales are far more compelling as justifications of marriage's special status than, say, love. And both of them apply to homosexuals as well as to heterosexuals. 30

Take the matter of settling men. It is probably true that women and children, more than just the fact of marriage, help civilize men. But that hardly means that the settling effect of marriage on homosexual men is negligible. To the contrary, being tied to a committed relationship plainly helps stabilize gay men. Even without marriage, coupled gay men have steady sex partners and relationships that they value and therefore tend to be less wanton. Add marriage, and you bring a further array of stabilizing influences. One of the main benefits of publicly recognized marriage is that it binds couples together not only in their own eyes but also in the eyes of society at large. Around the partners is woven a web of expectations that they will spend nights together, go to parties together, take out mortgages together, buy furniture at Ikea together, and so on — all of which helps tie them together and keep them off the streets and at home. Surely that is a very good thing, especially as compared to the closet-gay culture of furtive sex with innumerable partners in parks and bathhouses.

The other benefit of marriage — care-taking — clearly applies to homosexuals. One of the first things many people worry about when coming to terms with their homosexuality is: Who will take care of me when I'm ailing or old? Society needs to care about this, too, as the AIDS crisis has made horribly clear. If that crisis has shown anything, it is that homosexuals can and will take care of each other, sometimes with breathtaking devotion — and that no institution can begin to match the care of a devoted partner. Legally speaking, marriage creates kin. Surely society's interest in kin creation is strongest of all for people who are unlikely to be supported by children in old age and who may well be rejected by their own parents in youth.

Gay marriage, then, is far from being a mere exercise in political point making or rights mongering. On the contrary, it serves two of the three social purposes that make marriage so indispensable and irreplaceable for heterosexuals. Two of three may not be the whole ball of wax, but it is more than enough to give society a compelling interest in marrying off homosexuals.

There is no substitute. Marriage is the *only* institution that adequately serves these purposes. The power of marriage is not just legal but social. It seals its promise with the smiles and tears of family, friends, and neighbors. It shrewdly exploits ceremony (big public weddings) and money (expensive gifts, dowries) to deter casual commitment and to make bailing out embarrassing. Stag parties and bridal showers signal that what is beginning is not just a legal arrangement but a whole new stage of life. "Domestic partner" laws do none of these things.

I'll go further: Far from being a substitute for the real thing, marriage-lite may undermine it. Marriage is a deal between a couple and society, not just between two people: Society recognizes the sanctity and autonomy of the pair bond and in exchange each spouse commits to being the other's nurse, social worker, and policeman of first resort. Each marriage is its own little society within society. Any step that weakens the deal by granting the legal benefits of marriage without also requiring the public commitment is begging for trouble.

So gay marriage makes sense for several of the same reasons that straight marriage makes sense. That would seem a natural place to stop. But the logic of the argument compels one to go a twist further. If it is good for society to have people attached, then it is not enough just to make marriage available. Marriage should also be *expected*. This, too, is just as true for homosexuals as for heterosexuals. So, if homosexuals are justified in expecting access to marriage, society is equally justified in expecting them to use it. I'm not saying that out-of-wedlock sex should be scandalous or that people should be coerced into marrying. The mechanisms of expectation are more subtle. When grandma cluck-clucks over a still-unmarried young man or when mom says she wishes her little girl would settle down, she is expressing a strong and well-justified preference: one that is quietly echoed in a thousand ways throughout society and that produces subtle but important pressure to form and sustain unions. This is a good and necessary thing, and it will be as nec-

35

Document

The Marriage Project

Prepared by the Lambda Legal Defense and Education Fund, a national orga-
nization "committed to achieving full recognition of the civil rights of lesbians, gay
men, and people with HIV," the following list outlines a few of the hundreds of
rights and benefits married couples enjoy but same-sex couples are denied. The
Marriage Project was initiated in 1994 following the landmark ruling in the
Hawaii marriage case.

Although many lesbian and gay couples are in long-term relationships
and undertake responsibilities toward one another just as married couples
do, they are denied the vast array of legal, economic, and practical benefits
that married couples enjoy. Among these are the rights to

- share such government benefits as Social Security and Medicare;
- file joint tax returns and get special marriage or family rates or exemptions;
- have joint parenting, adoption, foster care, custody, and visitation;
- obtain joint insurance policies for home and auto, as well as family
  health coverage;
- inherit automatically in the absence of a will;
- secure equitable division of property and determine child custody
  and support in case of divorce;
- obtain veterans' discounts on medical care, education, and housing
  loans;
- enter jointly into rental leases with automatic renewal rights;

essary for homosexuals as heterosexuals. If gay marriage is recognized, single gay people over a certain age should not be surprised when they are dis-
approved of or pitied. That is a vital part of what makes marriage work. It's
stigma as social policy.

If marriage is to work it cannot be merely a "lifestyle option." It must
be privileged. That is, it must be understood to be better, on average, than
other ways of living. Not mandatory, not good where everything else is
bad, but better: a general norm rather than a personal taste. The biggest
worry about gay marriage, I think, is that homosexuals might get it but
then mostly not use it. Gay neglect of marriage wouldn't greatly erode the
bonding power of heterosexual marriage (remember, homosexuals are only

- make medical decisions on a partner's behalf in the event of illness;
- choose a final resting place for a deceased partner;
- take bereavement or sick leave to care for partner or child;
- receive spousal exemptions to property tax increases upon the death of a partner;
- obtain wrongful death benefits for a surviving partner and children;
- apply for immigration and residency for partners from other countries;
- obtain domestic violence protection orders;
- visit a partner or child in the hospital and other public institutions.

In total, there are *hundreds* of legal rights and responsibilities that come with civil marriage. Most of these protections cannot be privately arranged or contracted through other means, even for those who can afford a lawyer. Furthermore, private employers, banks, and other businesses often extend important benefits and privileges — such as special rates or memberships — to married couples only.

Gay people are moved by the same mix of personal, economic, and practical reasons as nongay people, who take for granted the right to choose whether and whom to marry. Denying equal marriage rights not only deprives same-sex couples of the social and emotional significance that marriage holds for many, it also deprives them of essential legal and economic protections.

— From the Web site for Lambda Legal Defense and Education Fund, which can be found at: http://www.gaysource.com/gs/ht/oct95/lambda.html.

a tiny fraction of the population) — but it would certainly not help. And heterosexual society would rightly feel betrayed if, after legalization, homosexuals treated marriage as a minority taste rather than as a core institution of life. It is not enough, I think, for gay people to say we want the right to marry. If we do not use it, shame on us.

Responding as a Reader

1. What exactly is the purpose of marriage, according to Rauch?
2. Consider the institutions and practices that Rauch compares with gay marriage and with the ban on gay marriages. Are all of these comparisons appropriate, in your view? Why or why not?

3. Rauch waits until the final two sentences of his article to use the words "we" and "us" to refer to gay people. Why do you think he does this? Would you read his essay differently if he revealed this information up front?

Responding as a Writer .

1. In your own words, explain F. A. von Hayek's theory (para. 9). How does it apply to gay marriage? Does this theory support heterosexual marriages? Are there some kinds of heterosexual marriages that it does not support? Give examples.

2. Evaluate one type of personal relationship other than marriage — friends, cousins, or neighbors, for example. In an essay, discuss what this type of relationship is *for* in the way Rauch discusses what marriage is *for*.

3. Some states allow couples to register as domestic partners to be eligible for the legal benefits of marriage, and straight couples as well as gay couples have entered this institution. What is the difference between a domestic partnership and a marriage?

ANNE-MARIE CUSAC

Tying the Gordian Knot

[THE PROGRESSIVE / January 1997]

I met my friend Tandy two-and-a-half years ago at a small wedding. As two out lesbians at a mostly heterosexual event, Tandy and I sat and commiserated during the reception. Did this, she wanted to know — nodding toward our newly married buddy, the few close friends she had in-

---

ANNE-MARIE CUSAC (b. 1966) is the managing editor and occasional reporter for the Progressive. Cusac won a Wallace Stegner Fellowship for Poetry, a George Polk Award in 1996, and a 1996–1997 Wisconsin Arts Board Fellowship for Poetry.

vited, the piles of strawberries and pineapples, and the bowls of champagne punch — make me want a wedding?

"Not really," I stammered. I had been moved by the ceremony, but Tandy's question took me aback. I had defined myself as outside marriage for years, ever since I started to understand that I was gay and broke a heterosexual engagement because, as I explained to my parents, "It just doesn't feel right." And I found it difficult to think of my own hypothetical wedding to a woman. "Marriage" to me had meant obligatory heterosexuality, loss, and a threat to self-honesty. I had always thought that if I married, I would no longer know who I was.

Tandy told me the wedding was making her wistful. She envied the ritual; she would have valued the chance to celebrate her love with ceremony and a gathering of her friends and family.

Although some Unitarians and Quakers allow gay unions, general social recognition is something that lesbians and gay men in long-term commitments do not have. Some gay people are intent on changing that and are rejoicing at a decision by Kevin Chang, a circuit-court judge in Honolulu. Chang ruled that the state of Hawaii had failed to show any compelling reason for denying gays and lesbians the right to marry. Tandy sent me an e-mail. "Just in case you haven't heard," it began.

I had heard. Though I have my misgivings about marriage, the news   5
was exhilarating. The idea of full equality under the law gives me a thrill.

For the second time in a year, I found myself hopping in a circle in response to a news event. The other time was when the Supreme Court overturned Colorado's Amendment Two, which had attempted to deny civil-rights protections to gays and lesbians.

When remarkable things like these two court decisions happen, we gay people start buzzing. The once impossible starts to seem possible. One friend observed that although it was logical to her that a ban on same-sex marriage was discriminatory, it was hard to believe that the Hawaiian courts shared her logic.

By denying us the right to marry, the government effectively denies us a whole list of benefits: family-insurance coverage, tax breaks, special rates on joint credit and banking accounts, the ability to visit an ailing partner in the intensive-care ward or emergency room, child custody, and inheritance and immigration privileges — the kinds of rights many people take for granted. For gays and lesbians, this feels a lot like discrimination.

For gay people with children, the risks are great. Lesbian mother Mary Ward recently lost custody of her daughter to her former husband, a convicted murderer. The judge thought Ward's sexuality might damage her child. In other cases, judges have justified removing children from their gay parents' homes because the social stigma attached to homosexuality might hurt the children — thus perpetuating that stigma, not to mention causing permanent damage to the children involved.

Comment

Thomas Sowell on Gay Marriage

On an issue where misleading and dishonest statements have been the norm, it should hardly be surprising that the headline on the San Francisco Chronicle read "House Votes Against Gay Marriages." The story claimed that the bill passed by the House was "a bill to restrict gay marriage."

In reality, after this vote you can still have all the gay marriages you want and any state that wants to recognize these marriages remains free to do so. What Congress refused to do was to force all 50 states to accord same-sex relationships the whole sweeping range of legislation that has been passed over the centuries, based on the assumption that this legislation would apply to a union between a man and a woman, who have the prospect of producing children that would have to be taken care of by them or by the society.

Any state that wants to apply any or all of this legislation to homosexual unions remains free to do so after the House vote. What the gay activists and their allies in the liberal media wanted was for all states to be forced to do so, if any single state decided to recognize homosexual unions as marriages, superseding the previously defined sense of the term.

In other words, what they wanted was an end-run around the democratic process, so that they could piggy-back onto legislation passed with entirely different situations in mind.

This is what the House of Representatives rejected — and rightly so. If homosexuals want to participate in the democratic process and convince state legislatures to apply some or all of the laws that were passed for husband-wife unions and their offspring to same-sex relationships as well, they have every right to do so.

They do not have a right to sneak in through the back door, pretending to be somebody else, just by using a word.

The issue of gay marriages exposes the hypocrisy of what was once homosexuals' strongest argument — that what consenting adults do in private is nobody else's business. Now it is suddenly everybody else's business to recognize these liaisons and to confer on them all the legal prerogatives created for others.

Serious changes in the law and public policy should be discussed seriously, not evaded by the verbal sleight-of-hand of using the word "marriage." Marriage is more than a contract between two individuals. It is an assertion of an interest in those people's relationship, and its possible offspring, by the society at large.

Gay activists are trying to have it both ways. If it is none of my business what they do, then it is none of their business what I think about it. Nor should I be forced to recognize it in word or deed.

Emotional assertions of how much homosexual relationships mean to those involved are relevant only to those people themselves, who are free to make whatever contractual relationships they wish with one another and to solemnize their relationship in whatever ceremony they prefer. But that is very different from trying to drag the rest of us into this, willy-nilly, through laws that our elected representatives never agreed to apply to them.

In a sense, the gay marriage issue is only a further extension of the notion that a "family" means whatever anybody wants it to mean. But there would never have been such a word in the language in the first place if any group of people, with any kind of relationship to one another, was considered the same as any other.

Families are not baseball teams, corporations, marching bands, or computer clubs. What the law has evolved over centuries of experience with families need not apply to any other kind of association. Calling other kinds of relationships "families" is playing games with words, submerging the very concept in a sea of verbal mush.

What our laws, our values, and our analyses have said about families was not meant to apply to any old set of people that might later be fashionably analogized to families. Such word games may be very clever, but all that they boil down to is that all things are the same, except for the differences, and different except for the similarities.

Gay activists have also thrived on the confusion between homosexuals and members of racial or ethnic minorities. But you are black or white or Chinese or Cuban, regardless of how you behave. Homosexuality is defined by behavior.

It is one thing to say that all people have the same rights, as the 14th Amendment does, and something very different to say that all behavior has the same rights. There is no reason why the law should make all behavior equally acceptable to all people or surround all behavior with legal obligations on others. Once more the call for "equal rights" has masked an attempt to get special privileges, without having to play by the rules.

— From "The Gay 'Marriage' Issue," *The Town Hall Conservative Current* (July 18, 1996), a webzine that collects popular syndicated conservative columnists. It can be found at: http://www.empower.org/thcc.

In Hawaii, Chang's ruling was definitive on the subject of same-sex 10 parenting. Gays and lesbians are just as capable of being good parents as are heterosexuals, he said. And he pointed out that even one of the state's witnesses had acknowledged that lesbians and gays "are doing a good job" raising children and "the kids are turning out just fine." His decision may set a precedent for future custody disputes.

For me, the Hawaii decision has made the thought of legal marriage to a woman a little less hypothetical. So I have started to think about what same-sex marriage might mean. What is it that I could hope for from a ritual that is so wrapped in suffocating cultural meanings?

I have a pretty rich life without marriage. I am one of those proud lesbians who has no problem knowing that her love is legitimate. So I do not agree with the former *New Republic* editor, Andrew Sullivan, who sees marriage as a tool for assimilating gay people into a straight world.

Marriage still has a lot of unappealing connotations for me. For centuries, marriage was a means of securing property and legitimizing ownership. Women were considered property. Because of its history, and because in the United States marriage even today remains strongly identified with financial security, I am wary. Is it possible to have an equal relationship within a civil marriage? It's difficult enough without one.

But if marriage were a different thing, maybe I would want it — if it meant things like equality, cooperation, respect.

The politicians who sponsored the Defense of Marriage Act, and the assorted anti–same-sex-marriage laws at the state level, fear just this — that gay people will change what marriage means. However silly some of their fears, they are partly justified. Some of us do want to change marriage. We want to make it better.   1.

The tradition of marriage, in the United States at least, is not such a settled thing. My mother had a hope chest full of china when she married at age twenty-three — a desperate age to be single for many women in the 1950s. My twenty-eight-year-old heterosexual sister is financially independent, enthusiastically single, and under very little pressure to tie the knot.

But those who want to protect marriage from the likes of me say, "Marriage is an age-old institution between a man and a woman. It's been that way for 6,000 years."

Aren't we bored yet?

Of course, here on the mainland, the fight has hardly started, and even in Hawaii the decision is undergoing a predictable appeal. During the months before the November [1996 Presidential] election, politicians around the country did their best to grab votes by stirring public anxiety about the supposed herds of same-sex couples galloping toward the chapels of America. As a result, sixteen states now have laws that refuse to recognize same-sex marriages performed in other states. And the Defense of Marriage Act both gives the states permission to disregard same-sex marriages and denies all federal benefits to gay couples who do marry.

These laws are discriminatory and unconstitutional. It is going to take years, plus a lot of good energy, to prove this. But, right now at least, it is heartening to see that the courts are on Tandy's side.   2

Responding as a Reader

1. Who is Cusac's intended audience? How can you tell? You might want to find out what kind of magazine the *Progressive* is (you can start by consulting p. 430).

2. Cusac reveals her sexual orientation in the first paragraph of her article. How does her personal presence affect your interpretation of her argument?

3. Identify the paragraphs in which Cusac does not refer to herself. What is the tone of these paragraphs and what is the effect of that tone? What would Cusac sacrifice if she had written these paragraphs from a personal point of view?

Responding as a Writer

1. Try rewriting Cusac's more personal paragraphs in the third person (using "she"). Compare these paragraphs to the original text. What is gained? What is lost?

2. What is the significance of a big wedding? What happens at a big expensive wedding that does not happen at a small ceremony at city hall? What does each kind of ceremony imply about the marriage to follow?

3. Imagine what society would be like if gay couples were allowed to marry in the same way that straight couples are, with all the accompanying social support and responsibility. Describe what life would be like in your community if this were the case.

ARIEL KAMINER

Something Old, Something New

[MIGHT / March–April 1997]

In the back room of a too-swank-by-half San Francisco nightclub, Rita, a woman in her late twenties, stands on a small stage with a microphone and a guitar, singing funny but perhaps too-clever folks songs to a largely uninterested audience. Silicon Valley software engineers, wearing identical woven belts slipped through their prewashed jeans, play pool and shout in each other's ears, glancing periodically over to the singer, who strums loudly and glares back. She flicks her long, brown hair out of her eyes and sings about capitalism vis-à-vis God, about wanting to join a cult, and about the pleasures of going to the mall. In one corner sits a group of Rita's friends and friends of those friends, most of whom have known her for two or three years. After a few songs, she pauses to sip from her beer, and then sets up her next song: "This next one is about marriage and divorce, something I know a thing or two about, unfortunately." She takes another swig. "Yep, in a few weeks my divorce will be final. Congratulate me!" The crowd, or the portion thereof that's paying attention, cheers. Then she sings.

None of the assembled friends and acquaintances knew she was getting divorced. As a matter of fact, not one of them had even known she was married. After she's done, they approach her, dumbstruck, and demand an explanation. Green-card thing, she says. How long for? they ask. Four years, she says. Who was the guy? they ask. A guy I met in London. Long pause. And you never told us? She pushes a strand of hair away from her face and shrugs.

"What's the big deal?"

Indeed.

This Essay Is Long and Meandering and Is Mostly About Marriage. It Contains Discussion of, But Not Necessarily Answers For, the Following Questions:

1. Are humans "programmed" for monogamy?

2. How did members of the British royalty come to have such influence on the way American commoners get married?

ARIEL KAMINER (b. 1969) is a contributing editor at New York *magazine.*

3. What causes people — seemingly intelligent people with law degrees and jobs and monthly payments on their Acuras — to do things like walk down the aisle to a ballad by a '70s hard-rock supergroup?

4. What exactly is meant by the phrase "starter marriage"?

5. Why do "cool" people get married?

6. Does the complex drive to get married threaten old-growth timber in the Pacific Northwest?

7. Is the fact that more people got married last year than voted indicative of the lackluster state of the American political system or merely suggestive of the vast numbers of single folk who still feel that marriage is a good idea?

NOTE: *All of the anecdotes contained above and herein are, sadly, true.*

Opening Statement Presented in the Second Person

You start to really look at marriage when people you know — normal, regular people, people capable of original and critical thought — start getting married or, like Rita, turn out to have been married for quite some time. You start thinking about it because you grew up wondering about marriage, never taking it for granted, perhaps even swearing against it. Your parents weren't happy or they were divorced or you hated your step-dad. You made lists of requirements for your future spouse, impossible lists that would ensure that if you bothered to go through with it — if you succumbed — at least you wouldn't screw it up. Then, for a long time, you forgot about marriage as a concept. It never came up; no one thought about it; no one you knew was even dating seriously. Fine. But suddenly it's spring, and you're going to a wedding, and another one, and then one every month and you start wondering what, exactly, happened. And you wonder whether you really understand the people around you, the people you call your friends — their thoughts and motivations. It's like that terrible dream where all your friends have joined some terrible cult, and you can't figure out why they've all joined that terrible cult, but it's too late and they're already in and they've all shaved their heads and are wearing knickers. You ask them why they're in the cult, why they're blindly following this cult and what, exactly, is the appeal of the cult? (And why the knickers?) But they just laugh to each other and shake their heads and look at you with that expression of pity. You are baffled and they are beatific.

Then, some time later, during an otherwise normal long-distance conversation with an old college housemate, he tells you he just got engaged. And so you express your humble opinion, perhaps your ambivalence about the idea, and he asks why you're raising your voice, and you say you're not raising your voice, and then you say something about Moonies and lemmings and the dream about the cult, and then he's mad at you.

Of course you make up, you go to the wedding and throw rice and maybe even cry, just like you're supposed to, but on some level you just don't get the whole thing, and you wonder if the happy couple is really as unconflicted about it as they seem or if secretly, individually, they're questioning its meaning, too.

Defensive Marriage Acts

Among politicians and religious leaders — who've been in the marriage business from the beginning — and under the conveniently vague heading of Family Values, it's lately become good sport to warn that the declining sanctity of marital union has caused and will continue to encourage lawlessness and depravity. Only by defending the traditional concept of the family, they argue, can society prevent illegal behavior and "alternative lifestyles" from poisoning our children's futures. And so we get a recent spate of laws on the books making it easier to wed, harder to divorce, and more advantageous to reproduce (unless you're receiving public assistance, in which case marriage is still subject to financial sanction). Last year [1996], Congress even passed the strangely literal-minded Defense of Marriage Act, which basically defined marriage as the legal union between two people, husband and wife. It might seem a long way to go for a definition already widely available in dictionaries (and how much of a threat do three-person marriages pose, anyway?), but the real point, never explicitly mentioned in the legislation, was to underscore the part about the man and woman. One of each, got it?

As it turns out, however, all this defensive lexicography is entirely unnecessary. Far from dying off, marriage is acquiring new and vital functions that are so attractive, people are fighting for a piece of the action. And it's largely because two groups of people — homosexuals and illegal immigrants — have found clever ways to adopt the institution to meet their own needs. Which means that, in one of the most satisfying ironies of recent history, "alternative lifestyles" and criminality — precisely the hazards that marriage was supposed to ward off — have proved to be not only its fastest growing markets but also the saviors of the institution's modern relevance.

For illegal immigrants who find the political climate increasingly hostile and for whom the chances of winning the immigration lottery are about as good as the chances of, well, winning the lottery, the green-card marriage is becoming a standard weapon of defense. According to Immigration and Naturalization Services (INS), marriages between U.S. citizens and foreign nationals have been on the rise since the '70s, and now comprise nearly 8 percent of all marriages annually. (INS speculates that about half of such marriages are fraudulent.) If, over a long and intrusive series of interviews, the participants can lie well enough to convince an immigration official that a spouse-by-contract is really a partner-for-life, they are rewarded with the full faith and credit of the U.S. government. Not only is it expensive, however ($10,000 is the current market standard, according to some estimates), it's risky as well: If La Migra calls your bluff, it's five years or $250,000 for the resident and the same plus possible deportation for the noncitizen. Yet, despite the scary downside loss, so many foreign-born residents are so eager to become full-status Americans that they've turned the process into a minieconomy all its own.

(For her part, Rita did it for free, as a favor to the man she met in London, with whom she had a short affair. She got nothing from the whole arrangement, although her husband, who she calls "a total asshole," was nice enough to pay for the divorce.)

Then there's the idea of gay marriage. Politically active queers, as anyone who's switched on the evening news knows, have recently moved their fight for the right to marry out of the fine print of the so-called gay agenda and onto Page A1. Through the same kind of buy-low strategy that had them lobbying for military service as everyone else was trying to escape it, lesbians and gays decided to make good old-fashioned marriage a frontier in the crusade for justice, starting with a test case in Hawaii, the results of which remain to be seen. Beyond the civil-rights angle, the theory goes that the right to marry will prove once and for all that queers aren't crazed, drug-addled sex fiends; they're really just as boring as everyone else.

An Abbreviated History of Marriage

Some anthropologists speculate that the first proto-marriages were of the group sort — a pack of men and women who determined that they had the same turn-ons (say, moonlit nights and eating wild boar) and turn-offs (being eaten by wild boar, the end of their genetic line) and decided to form a posse. Sitting by the newly invented campfire, members would sniff around and head back to the cave with whomever smelled best.

But once people figured out how to plant things and started settling down at fixed addresses, faster than you could say "agricultural revolution" they were putting on all sorts of airs, inventing concepts like virginity and weddings. People began consecrating marriage with formal rituals, some of which now seem quaintly odd, like tying man and woman together with reeds. Other more recognizable concepts included the organized pillage, the sack-the-city-and-take-the-women, and the ever-popular you-break-it-you-buy-it shotgun wedding.

Then in the twelfth century, the Church, for reasons that had less to do with bigheartedness than the desire to contest the power of secular authorities, decreed that marriage by force could no longer be carried out. A century or so later, the French and English aristocracy, while prancing about the hothouse of court society, found itself with far too much time on its uncalloused hands and came up with the idea of romantic love. These two developments resonated well, and pretty soon the idea caught on that spouses should actually love each other, in something like the modern sense of the word.

15

Speech

Ed Fallon on Same-Sex Marriage

The following is excerpted from a longer speech made to the House by Iowa Representative Ed Fallon on February 20, 1996, in which he argued against a bill designed to "protect" the institution of marriage.

Well, I suppose this is as good a time as any for me to come out of the closet. I can't help the way I was born. It's just who I am. I've never announced this to a group publicly, but I guess it's about time. I am heterosexual. I am absolutely certain in my entire being that I could never be homosexual, no matter how hard I might try. I've never been attracted to another man in my life, and the idea of engaging in a homosexual act is foreign and distasteful to me. But just as I would hope that homosexual men and women could accept me for who I am, I promise to try to accept them for who they are. Why can't you do the same? Why can't we all do the same?

Hatred grows out of fear, and fear grows out of ignorance. Though I've never hated homosexuals, I used to fear them. When I was a kid growing up, the worst name you could call someone was a gay loser. And the stereotype that still pervades the minds of many in this chamber — that of the highly aggressive, promiscuous gay man seeking countless, anonymous relationships — is the stereotype that I grew up with, and the stereotype that contributes to volumes of ignorance and volumes of fear.

Over time, I've come to learn that this stereotype, like most stereotypes, is based on hearsay, not fact. The rogues who may fit the previous description are the exception to the rule, just as there are male heterosexual rogues who are aggressive, promiscuous, and constantly hitting on and harassing women.

In my evolving experience with homosexuals, familiarity has displaced ignorance and dispelled fear. I now count as friends and constituents many same-sex couples. Some have children. Most are in long-term, stable relationships. All are very decent, kind, and normal people. I make no effort to judge the integrity of what they do in their bedroom, and to their credit, they've never judged the integrity of what I do in mine.

— The full text of Fallon's speech can be found at: http://www.tactix.com/ ~terry/speech.html.

But the greatest moment in the alliance between marriage and organized religion came when the Catholic church declared the institution to be a holy sacrament and therefore worthy of the crowd-pleasing pageantry that's kept the church in business ever since: pointy-spired cathedrals and rich, silken vestments and celebratory feasts and the like. It was a crafty papal move, one that seemed to benefit everyone involved: The newlyweds kicked off their union with a spiritual shot in the arm, the church bolstered its relevance (not to mention its coffers), and the community leaders were assured of the continuance of the existing social order.

And so it went for quite some time. Then came the 1960s and the '70s. Suddenly holy matrimony — along with any other patriarchal institutions that interfered with the ability of middle-class college kids to prolong adolescence — became highly unfashionable. It was perfectly acceptable to decide that you weren't interested in permanent, monogamous union. And if you did feel like committing, you could consecrate it yourself, using any combination of the following:

- Some close friends
- A grassy hilltop
- One guitar
- One flute
- Two or three tambourines
- A basket of flowers
- Some home-grown drugs
- A Howard Nemerov poem

It was simple and meaningful for the participants, particularly because there was no need to get The Man involved. Of course, this hurt The Man's feelings. For the first time, well, almost ever, young men and women had, through the power of sheer collective impulse, blown off the societal imperative to wed, and they'd done it in a way that didn't seem to deprive themselves of marriage's main benefits: They could still have sex and raise families and even establish stable networks of kinship. For many couples, then, the only difference came when they broke up — instead of having a judge arbitrate the equitable division of CDs and bookshelves, they could just flip for it.

Now, twenty years later: In California, the state's social-welfare agency has rescinded its long-standing policy of advising teen mothers to marry, saying it is no longer tenable or uniformly prudent. The news that the California state government was reversing a millennia-long trend and pulling government out of the marriage business merited only a paragraph in the back pages of a few daily newspapers. No one, it seems, thought it was that big of a deal.

Breaking Up Is Hard To Do, But It's a Little Bit Easier When There's a Magazine About It

With marriage now largely stripped of its defining moral or spiritual   20
context and (apparently) no longer doing a satisfactory job of maintaining
civic order, its social function has expanded to fill the remaining vacuum.
There are lots of people, then, who get married because, simply, it's the
kind of thing other people do. It's a social thing, a way to connect with
other married people — like joining a club of similarly occupied people
that you can join just by saying "I do."

The social aspects of marriage have become so predominant, in fact,
that marriage itself is almost an afterthought, one of a number of equivalent activities in which members can interact with other members. One of
the most popular of such activities, of course, is divorce.

Thus, there now exists something called *Divorce* magazine, a quarterly
Canadian publication making its first foray into the American market this
February. A kind of *Brides* magazine for the back end of the process, *Divorce* looks just like any other lifestyle publication — full of trend pieces
(the latest in property division) and personal essays (difficulties of dating
after all these years) and fluffed out with ads for niche-market services such
as Swingles, a furniture company that can outfit your new studio apartment in a day. *Divorce* tries hard to present divorce not as a crushing de-
feat but a fun, new activity that lots and lots of regular people are getting
into. Divorce has become so commonplace — the rate has tripled in the
past twenty years — that the magazine's publishers believe they can sell
100,000 copies of each issue. And they probably will. Like marriage itself,
divorce has so thoroughly lost its moral basis that it's become, for many
people, nothing more than a lifestyle choice.

Divorce has even found a brilliant way to maintain readership: Rather
than encourage happy couples to trash the institution in pursuit of the single life, its publishers instead encourage them to marry and divorce and re-
marry and divorce, again and again, presumably buying a new issue or two
each time. They even subsidize the process — a secret revealed on the subscription card. "Divorce," it says. "Have the next one on us."

The Inexplicable and, At the Very Least, Contradictory Tendency To Marry Among Otherwise Progressive Social and Cultural Opinion Leaders

The slyly subversive appropriation of marriage by those traditionally
excluded is a clever move of course, but that doesn't explain why anybody
else still wants a piece of it, and it certainly doesn't shed any light on those
marriages involving people you'd always counted on to challenge societal
mores, not buy into them. Learning that Michael J. Fox walked down the
aisle in full body armor is one thing. (Didn't happen, but it's easy to picture, isn't it?) Finding out that Patti Smith got married and lives family-

style in a Detroit suburb is, well, quite another. Jeff Koons and Cicciolina, Richard Hell and Patti Smythe, Adam Yauch and Ione Skye, Kurt Cobain and Courtney Love. Lou Reed. Kathy Acker. Oscar Wilde. Even *John Lennon* got married.

Not only were they nonconforming, ostensibly enlightened people who   25
decided to get married, they were nonconforming, ostensibly enlightened, fabulously talented or famous or rich people who decided to get married. They were outside the food chain, unencumbered by petty financial worries, masters of their domain. The assumption was that they were beyond marriage, *over* it. But then they all let us down. And while they still went to great lengths to skirt social and/or artistic convention, they happily submitted to one of the longest-lasting and rigorously defined social practices in human history — and usually took pictures.

The Fetishization of Weddings as Symptomatic of Civilization in Decline

> The people that once bestowed commands, consulships, legions, and all else now concerns itself no more, and longs eagerly for just two things — bread and circuses!
>
> — *Decimus Junius Juvenalis, A.D. 122*

At 4 A.M. Central Standard Time on July 29, 1981, a nineteen-year-old college student home for summer vacation is awakened by an alarm clock in a small city in northern Indiana. She puts on a Laura Ashley bathrobe and shuffles into the TV room, stepping carefully in her slippers so as not to awaken the rest of the family. She settles into her stepfather's reading chair and flicks the remote to NBC. There, Tom Brokaw and a British commentator are describing the event of the decade in England — the marriage of Prince Charles to Lady Diana Spencer. Extravagant, spectacular, and still hopelessly romantic, the event was the last, best expression of wealth and style by an empire in decline. Never mind the dubious notion of British royalty or of the future of the union, that day everything was in the details. Spotting the Queen Mother in a parade to Westminster Abbey, the British journalist cranes to see whether she is wearing a hat. "Oh, she *is* wearing a hat," he says. "Sort of a lovely cantaloupe color."

Less than five years later, on her twenty-fourth birthday, the young woman walks down the aisle of a church on Manhattan's Upper West Side. Her mother wears cantaloupe.

A generation of young women had its dreamy notions of marriage and, more specifically, weddings, defined by the spectacular opulence of Di's betrothal. Weddings — the perfect one, at the perfect place, with the perfect decor and music and flowers and people and, *oh, everything*! — have grown into so enormous an obsession that they often seem to have dwarfed the institution they celebrate. And though often seen as trite and anti-quated, the usual stuff is still expected: Men are to make the proposal, the two-months'-salary ring is considered a necessity, the dress looks like this, the invitations are engraved like this, the honeymoon takes place some-where warm, etc. Parades, thankfully, are still discretionary.

Along with many of our social ills — Jane Austen novels, the girdle, gen-ital piercings — the obsessive fascination with royal weddings started with Queen Victoria. Homely and independent, she made an unlikely role model for romantic young girls, but she really poured it on for her wedding with Al-bert (to whom she herself had proposed). She adorned her hair with orange blossoms and diamonds and wore a huge white gown, which only thereafter became the ceremony's standard uniform. The press, unable to resist the op-portunity to give a left-handed compliment, called it "her hour of beauty."

From then on, the basic imperative behind wedding planning — notwithstanding the occasional trendy misstep — has been more is more. The aesthetic agenda is to make the wedding appear as lavish as possible, to flout all sumptuary laws without fear of retribution. More guests! Bigger flowers! Champagne and caviar and pipers piping and lords a-leaping and china and silver and crystal! The results frequently look more like a pot-latch than a commitment ceremony. 30

Never mind that we live in an age when people who've been divorced by thirty blithely refer to those aborted unions as their "starter marriages," that the percentage of the population that was married slid from 72 per-cent in 1970 to 61 percent in 1995, that the rate of divorce tripled dur-ing the same period, that a third of all babies today are born "out-of-wedlock." People still love a good party. And while the marriage industry grows fat off this mystifying trend, we're all invited to watch the gruesome spectacle and applaud.

Oh, and Diana? She's lying on a beach in Cyprus with her accoun-tant's lips wrapped around her toes.

Our Friends in the Animal Kingdom and What Can Be Learned From Them

"There's nothing to suggest that monogamy is the 'normal' mode for humans," says Steig Johnson, a Ph.D. candidate in physical anthropology at the University of Texas. "The vast majority of human societies practice polygyny [single male, multiple females], with monogamy a distant sec-ond," Johnson says. Don't look to our closest relatives for evidence that we're not obeying our DNA, either: Among chimps, orangutans, and go-rillas, Johnson says, "monogamy may be absent. Chimps don't have nu-clear families or anything." Nor do the lesser apes (such as gibbons) mate for life. Johnson provides the caveat that "human social systems are highly flexible and variable — monogamous marriage is certainly not 'un-natural' or impossible for humans. But, obviously, neither is it *the* 'nat-ural' system."

Different Equals More Personal, More Meaningful, More Better

For whatever complicated reasons, whether psychological or social or spiritual, the public recognition of private commitment still seems to register deeply with people across the lines of culture and time. But with the relevance of organized religion fading for many (church attendance has slid by almost 18 percent in the past 12 years), those who are about to undergo a ritual inescapably inscribed in a specific historical tradition are left to grasp at *any* available tradition, in the interest of legitimizing their union. The wedding day has become a kind of crazy-quilt affair that includes recognizable elements of traditions stripped of their defining religious context, such as the once-Jewish glass stomp or the Quaker-inspired service without a minister. Beyond the liturgy, look for the now-*de rigueur* recitation by friends of appropriate poems or song lyrics or international flourishes such as jumping a broom (points awarded only if you're white). Self-penned vows are also a must, especially for those who ordinarily don't write anything. And if there's any way to show how much cooler you are than the institution into which you're entering — giving your dog a role or walking down the aisle in a gorilla mask while playing "Here Comes the Bride" on an electric guitar (as one bride did recently) — by all means, go for it.

Sometimes, in the Attempt To Make One's Wedding Unique, Things Get a Little Bit Out of Hand

After three months of dating and three more of living together, Beth and John knew it was forever. So, on a spectacular August day in a small beach town on the Pacific coast, they gathered their families and friends for a wedding of their own making. It would be, in every way, *unique*. Beth did most of the planning and had a long list of dos and don'ts that she had accumulated over the years:

1. No priest. She had been brought up Lutheran, but there wouldn't be any of that archaic language and patriarchal bullshit here. Whoever presided would be a minister of some sort — not simply a justice of the peace — but definitely nonsectarian. She wasn't religious, but spirituality is important, right?
2. The ceremony would take place on the beach.
3. She would be barefoot, wearing a simple, white dress.
4. John could wear shoes if he wanted.
5. She would be given away by her two brothers. (She was no longer in contact with her parents.)
6. There would be a reggae band.
7. She and John would walk down the aisle not to "The Wedding March" but to a more beautiful song, one that held particular meaning to her and her betrothed. Their favorite song — "their" song — was

that slow one by Bush, "Come Down" — but would that be too trendy?

8. Afterward, there would be an outdoor luncheon and then dancing.

When the day finally came, everything was set, but there had been some changes:

1. Beth couldn't figure out a way to have the ceremony on the beach; instead, it took place a hundred feet up, on a small outdoor platform on a bluff overlooking the Pacific.

2. Though there was no sand, she was barefoot anyway. The white dress became off-white and drapy — a Greek goddess sort of look.

3. John wore shoes.

4. She came to her senses in time to scratch the being-given-away-by-her-brothers part. What does that imply? she thought. Being "given away?" No way. She walked down the aisle herself (with John, of course).

5. The reggae band wanted $2,000; they got a DJ instead. Same dif.

6. They found the perfect song, one that had been her favorite since she was little. It was older than the Bush song; it seemed more appropriate to have a classic. She got goose bumps when the first chords tinkled out of the speakers and drifted over the forty or so people assembled and out over the ocean. It was Kiss. It was "Beth."

The Job's Okay, But the Benefits Are Great

Still, you can't argue with some of the perks. The financial and legal benefits to marriage are among the primary reasons that gays and lesbians and immigrants are so zealously seeking state recognition of their unions. For the straight and American-born, the bonuses can be just as inviting (and easier to obtain). Employee health insurance usually covers a spouse, cutting in half what is often a couple's no. 2 expense after housing. There are tax breaks, such as Clinton's much-vaunted $500-per-child credit, for raising a child in a married family. Housing costs would be split for any couple, but it's often easier to get a mortgage if a couple is married. Marriage permits the transfer of property, IRAs, and other specialized bank accounts to a widowed spouse, and studies show that married men earn about 25 percent more than single men.

Advice From the Experts, and the Death of Trees

The ever-growing industry that serves the ever-growing subculture addicted to ritual coupling currently pulls in $32 billion a year in this country alone. Bridal magazines are as thick as phone books and have been selling so well that mainstream, nonbridal magazines such as *People, In Style, Star,* and *Town & Country,* eager to cash in, now publish their own annual wedding issues. Not to be outmaneuvered, book publishers have joined the fray and now make bushels of money on wedding and marriage guides of every conceivable stripe, from *Emily Post's Complete Book of Wedding Etiquette* to *The Cheapskate's Guide to Weddings and Honeymoons* to *There Must Be Something For the Groom To Do.* And that's just "old media." Wedding-planning CD-ROMs and marriage-coping software cost money, too. Web sites, praise the Lord, are still free.

These, of course, are all peripheral expenses, compared with the costs of the actual ceremonies and receptions. The paradigm of the nouveau understated — though never underbudgeted — chic was the tantalizingly off-limits and consciously quaint wedding of John Kennedy Jr. and Carolyn Bessette in a Georgia slave church. Knockoffs of Bessette's clingy Narciso Rodriguez dress are already flying off the racks at malls across the country, and it's probably only a matter of time before some enterprising publisher commissions *The Slave Church Wedding Guide.*

Act of Generosity or Path of Least Resistance?

At age fifteen, Lisa Benton had tormented her strict Catholic parents   40
with various prominently displayed tattoos and had prematurely ended more than one family dinner with a loud rebuke of their conservative values. At eighteen, she'd gone to live with a boyfriend, which resulted in a two-year estrangement from her family. At twenty-one, she'd moved to New York City to pursue a career making documentary films. As recently as a year ago, she had fallen into the habit of telling people she wasn't the marrying type. Now twenty-five, Lisa and her new boyfriend of six months are making plans to head back to Waukesha, Wisconsin this summer to get married in a country church, because, as she says, "We decided that marriage is the last thing you do for your parents."

"I shocked my family for so long," she says. "Now I want the dress, flowers in my hair, everything to be perfect." Her family, meanwhile, remains stunned, not only by Lisa's unexpected turnaround but also by that of a close cousin. The cousin, who was always obedient and "perfect," is pregnant and refuses to marry her boyfriend.

Getting married, like a U.N. peacekeeping mission, is often an exercise in exacerbating existing tensions by way of simply meaning well. But Lisa's grudging sentiment — that, in the end, it is something one does for someone else — is common. After all, a wedding is a public expression of a very private act. While many people may question the necessity of winning external approval for intimate relations — be it from the church, the state, a relative — the truth is that they just don't care enough about marriage, one way or another, to break their mother's heart. They're more concerned with finding someone worthy of raising the question. Everyone likes to see Mom smile, right?

Fear and Other Improbably Motivating Factors

Among those who choose not to marry, it's common to dismiss the entire enterprise as a mere symptom of fear — the province of the stupid, the last resort of the insecure. And by any perspective, fear does play a role in commending people to the altar. The prospect of ending life alone strikes such genuine terror in so many young hearts that legally sane people break up with someone they love in favor of someone who'll marry them, even though they haven't yet met that person. Or the opposite: They hit some preordained birthday or anniversary and decide it's time to settle down, no matter who happens to be in their bed that month — a kind of marital musical chairs.

But fear *of* marriage is as important a motivating factor as fear of missing out on it. Even the distant specter of marriage can put a serious damper on otherwise happy pairings, forcing countless dating relationships to a decision that neither partner may be ready to make. The secondary symptom of this process, second-guessing one's partner's declared marital agenda (does he really want to marry me or is he just doing it as a favor, is she really okay about just living together, or am I depriving her of her dream?), has proven as difficult for those who undertake it as it is tedious for those to whom they narrate it.

The Suprisingly Tidy Conclusion

It's no mere coincidence that weddings are getting so extravagantly   45
mannerist, so preciously unique, just as the institution they're meant to celebrate ceases to perform and withers away to irrelevance. As the specific arrangement we know as Western marriage ceases to signify, and until an official replacement comes down the pike, those who still feel inclined to make their union official are left to mine the available traditions, picking up what bits and pieces appeal to them and cobbling together their own odd pastiche in a desperate search for meaning that basic institution can no longer offer. Like Laura, who buried microscopic clues in her wedding to link it to a recognizable historical tradition, one in which weddings and marriages are important acts of state. Or Rita, whose marriage was a tool of friendship — something vitally important to her husband but which meant nothing to her. Or Beth, for whom the details of personalizing her wedding were a subject of more years of careful thought than that of finding the person with whom to share it. Considering the odds against any marriage succeeding, the strange adaptations people come up with — no matter how haphazard — to distance their marriage from the doomed majority don't seem so strange, after all.

In defiant refusal of its declining significance, people in the mainstream of society are trying to retrofit the creaky old institution, to make it worthy of the feelings and importance with which they imbue it. It's kind of poignant, really, but these tape-and-bailing-wire solutions can only hold it together for so long. A much better hope for the institution's survival comes not from the crumbling center, but from its periphery, where people are so hell-bent on the idea of marriage that they're literally taking to the streets to fight for it. To some civil rights diehards, it may seem like a frivolous detour on the road to equality. But hey, everyone likes a wedding.

Responding as a Reader

1. How would you characterize Kaminer's tone? What is the effect of this tone?

2. What is the purpose of the subheadings ("Defensive Marriage Acts," for example)? What do all these headings have in common? How do they influence your reading?

3. Kaminer calls gays' desire to marry and to join the military a "buy-low strategy" (para. 12). What comparison is she making here? What is she implying about the desires of gay people?

4. Scan the essay and identify the cultural references (the San Francisco nightclub, old-growth timber, La Migra, the Kiss song). Get together with a group of classmates and help each other identify the familiar and unfamiliar references. What do these references add to the essay?

Responding as a Writer

1. For each section of this article, identify Kaminer's main point. (You will have to translate humorous anecdotes into straightforward, declarative sentences.) Consider the article's organization — which points she makes at the beginning, the middle, and the end of the article. Why do you think she organized the article this way?

2. Kaminer compares gay marriage to marriage between a U.S. citizen and an immigrant, for the sole purpose of allowing the immigrant to stay in the United States. In an essay, analyze this comparison. What do these two situations have in common? How are they different? How does this comparison support Kaminer's argument?

3. Is the institution of marriage old-fashioned, silly, obsolete? Using Kaminer's examples, examples from other articles in this unit, and/or examples from your own experience, argue for or against the institution's current relevance.

Discussing the Unit

Suggested Topic for Discussion

Should homosexuals be allowed to marry, under law? Why or why not? If gay marriage were legalized, how would gay people be affected (including those who might not wish to get married)? How would straight people be affected? How would other social institutions be affected? What would be gained by this change and what would be lost?

Preparing for Class Discussion

1. Why do people get married? Consider social and legal reasons, as well as personal reasons. Which of these reasons do you think are most important?

2. How does gay marriage compare to straight marriage? Is the bond between spouses exactly the same? Is the bond perceived to be the same by those outside the marriage? What effects might external stresses have on a gay marriage? Are these stresses comparable with those on a straight marriage?

3. *Prewriting Assignment:* In your own words, define marriage. What are the elements of a good marriage? Of a lasting marriage? Of a legal marriage?

From Discussion to Writing

Argue for or against the legalization of gay marriage. Try to anticipate any opposing arguments and address them in a logical way. Also try to anticipate the results of legalizing gay marriage and of not legalizing it. Why would one set of results be preferable to the other?

13

Affirmative Action: Do We Still Need It?

Affirmative action policies originated in the Civil Rights Act of 1964 and dominated public attention in the '70s, as American courts implemented legislation and supported college admission policies that would redress the effects of past discrimination. The '90s, however, have suddenly reversed this trend, as campus after campus experiences a backlash against what many now regard as "preferential treatment" or "reverse racism." Given this dramatic change in national attitude, many supporters of the policy worry about what can be done to prevent a drastic underenrollment of minority groups and to maintain the academic diversity they fought so hard to initiate.

One of the academics most committed to sustaining these programs is the noted professor of English and law, Stanley Fish. In "When Principles Get in the Way," Fish argues that by resorting to the language of principles instead of policy, opponents of affirmative action lose sight of the "actual historical circumstances" that make the policy morally necessary. But what are those historical circumstances? In "Whose Affirmative Action?" the distinguished sociologist, Raymond W. Mack takes a close look at the relevant language of the 1964 Civil Rights Act and shows that it says nothing at all about goals, quotas, preferences, or timetables. For Mack, recent history shows that the public now defines affirmative action very differently from how it was originally defined in 1964.

The modern, expanded definition of affirmative action, however, was clearly what the California Board of Regents had in mind when they passed "SP-1: Resolution of the University of California Board of Regents Adopting a Policy 'Ensuring Equal Treatment' of Admissions, 20 July 1995." Among its several resolutions, this landmark document states "Effective January 1, 1997, the University of California shall not use race, religion, sex, color, ethnicity, or national origin as criteria for admission to the University or to any program of study." Blaming the Regent's decision on California Governor Pete Wilson's strong-arming tactics, Jesse Jackson enumerates for the *Nation* precisely how the end of affirmative action is affecting minority students.

Though Jackson is careful to include Hispanics among his percentages, that isn't often the case, argues Rachel F. Moran, a prominent Berkeley law professor and expert on Chicano/Latino policy. In "Unrepresented," she explains why Latinos, though they far outnumber other disadvantaged minorities in California, have remained absent from the affirmative action debate.

And what about the freshmen around whom all this debate is swirling; how do *they* feel? The survey results suggest that there's no more consensus in the classroom than there is in the community at large.

Selected Survey Results

Affirmative Action

- Freshmen at all institutions who agree that affirmative action should be abolished as a factor in university admission: 54%
- Freshmen at all black colleges who agree: 25.2%
- Freshmen at all institutions who agree that racial discrimination is no longer a problem: 16.3%
- Freshmen at all black colleges who agree: 11.9%

— From *The American Freshman: National Norms For Fall 1996.*

When Principles Get in the Way

[THE NEW YORK TIMES / December 26, 1996]

Suppose you were arguing for something but were told that you would have to make your case without the facts that supported it. This is the situation proponents of affirmative action face when they find themselves defending their position in terms of principle rather than policy.

A policy is a response to actual historical circumstances; it is directed at achieving a measurable result — like an increase in the representation of minorities in business and education. A principle scorns actual historical circumstances and moves quickly to a level of generalization and abstraction so high that the facts of history can no longer be seen.

Affirmative action is an attempt to deal with a real-world problem. If that problem is recharacterized in the language of principle — if you stop asking, "What's wrong and how can we fix it?" and ask instead, "Is it fair?" — the real world fades away and is replaced by the arid world of philosophical puzzles.

The recipe for making real-world problems disappear behind a smokescreen of philosophizing was given to us years ago by the legal scholar Herbert Wechsler in his enormously influential 1959 *Harvard Law Review* article "Toward Neutral Principles." Wechsler was trying to justify the Supreme Court's decision in *Brown* v. *Board of Education,* which declared segregated schools unconstitutional. What troubled Wechsler about *Brown* was that the Justices, in reaching their decision, seemed moved by a practical desire to secure a result they favored (integrated schools) rather than by some general principle whose application would yield that result independently.

Unable to find any such principle spelled out in the Court's arguments, Wechsler was driven to provide one himself: the "right of freedom of association." But in attempting to make this case, he soon realized that the principle of freedom of association turned out not to justify *Brown* but to make it even more of a puzzle. "If the freedom of association is denied by segregation, integration forces an association upon those for whom it is . . . repugnant,"

STANLEY FISH *(b. 1938) received his B.A. at the University of Pennsylvania and his M.A. and Ph.D. at Yale, which published his dissertation on the English poet John Skelton. Fish has taught at Berkeley, Johns Hopkins, and Duke University, where he is a professor of English and law. He is also the author of* Professional Correctness: Literary Studies and Political Change *(1995).*

he wrote. And "given a choice between denying the association to those . . . who wish it and imposing it on those who would avoid it," he was unable to find a principle that would justify either the one or the other.

Here in as naked a form as one might like (or not like) is the logic of neutral principle. When Wechsler characterizes the choice as being between the rights of those who wish to associate and the rights of those who wish not to, these two wishes have lost all contact with the issue that made their opposition meaningful — whether the schoolhouse door should be open or shut. Once the historical specificity of that issue is lost, there no longer seems to be any moral difference between the two sides, although the difference was perfectly clear before Wechsler began his tortured analysis.

In other words, the puzzle of *Brown* is only a puzzle if you forget everything that made the case urgent in the first place — the long history of racism and its effects. You have substituted philosophical urgencies for social urgencies. This is what the demand for principle does and what opponents of affirmative action intend it to do. After all, isn't it convenient to be able to deny a remedy for longstanding injustices by invoking the higher name of principle?

It is a very bad game, but it is alive and well in the phrase *reverse racism,* which does in an instant what Wechsler needed an entire essay to do. The phrase makes the actions of college admissions officers who give preference to minority candidates equivalent to the hate crimes of the Ku Klux Klan. It does so by claiming that each is motivated by race consciousness, an argument that makes sense only if the very thought of race, no matter the content or context, is considered the sin. Like the freedom of association in Wechsler's argument, race consciousness invoked as an abstraction rides roughshod over history while laying claim to the noblest of motives.

That is in effect what Justice Clarence Thomas did in his concurring opinion in *Adarand* v. *Pena,* in which the Court struck down the policy of giving incentives to Federal contractors who hired minority subcontractors. "It is irrelevant," he wrote, "whether a government's racial classifications are drawn by those who wish to oppress a race or by those who have a sincere desire to help those thought to be disadvantaged. In each instance, it is racial discrimination, plain and simple."

But both the plainness and the simplicity are apparent only if the complex facts of history have been suppressed or declared out of bounds. In his dissent, Justice John Paul Stevens returned to history to make the *truly* plain and simple point: "There is no moral or Constitutional equivalence between a policy that is designed to perpetuate a caste system and one that seeks to eradicate racial subordination."

The important word in Justice Stevens's statement is "moral," for it shows that the choice here is not between the principled and the nonprincipled. It is between neutral principles, which refuse to acknowledge the dilemmas we face as a society, and moral principles, which begin with an awareness of those dilemmas and demand that we address them.

Those who favor affirmative action are moved by moral principles — principles that recognize the reality and persistence of historical inequities. And yet those who favor affirmative action are often maneuvered into using a vocabulary designed to remove from sight the very realities on which their case depends.

Of course, you could also try to work within that vocabulary and fight over its terms, arguing that "fairness," "equality," and "color blindness" really belong on your side. But even if you got good at the game, you would be playing on your opponent's field and thus buying into his position, and why would you want to do that?

It would be far wiser to refuse the lure of "fairness," "merit," and "equality," now code words for ignoring the effects of the long history of racial oppression. Let's be done with code words and concentrate on the problems we face and on possible ways of solving them. Those who support affirmative action should give up searching for theoretical consistency — a goal at once impossible and unworthy — and instead seek strategies with the hope of relieving the pain of people who live in the world and not in the never-never land of theory.

Let's stop asking "Is it fair or is it reverse racism?" and start asking   15
"Does it work and are there better ways of doing what needs to be done?" Merely asking these questions does not guarantee that affirmative action will be embraced, but it does guarantee that the shell game of the search for neutral principle will no longer stand between us and doing the right thing.

Responding as a Reader

1. What is evoked by the phrase *reverse racism* (para. 8). How does it do "in an instant what Wechsler needed an entire essay to do"?

2. Consider the principles of "freedom of association" (para. 5) and of "race consciousness" (para. 8). What do these two principles have in common? How does fairness or morality come into play in the exercise of these principles?

3. In the final paragraph, Fish compares "the search for neutral principle" to a "shell game." What is a shell game? In what ways is the search for neutral principle like a shell game?

Responding as a Writer

1. In your own words, define "neutral principle" (para. 6) and "moral principle" (para. 11). How does the story of Herbert Wechsler illustrate the distinction between the two? How do the quotations from Justices Thomas and Stevens illustrate it?

2. Is Fish arguing that it is never appropriate to question the fairness of an effective policy? Would he agree with Machiavelli that the ends justify the means, that unjust measures are permissible as long as the result is desirable? Where does morality come in, for Fish? Using evidence from the essay, argue that Fish's stance is or is not Machiavellian.

3. Think of a time when you had to choose between the theoretically "right" way to do something and the way that worked — anything from fixing a car to disciplining a child. How did you choose which way to follow? Would you do it the same way next time? In an essay, describe the predicament and explain how you handled it, and why.

RAYMOND W. MACK

Whose Affirmative Action?

[SOCIETY / March–April 1996]

Once upon a time, it was considered an effective put down to tell someone "You don't know what you're talking about!" Nowadays, when you hear someone lamenting the harm that affirmative action is inflicting on the country, this old saw is likely to be an accurate (if unappreciated) assessment.

Just what *are* we talking about here, anyway?

RAYMOND W. MACK (b. 1927) is professor emeritus of sociology at Northwestern University, where he has been provost since 1974. He has been the founding director of the Center for Urban Affairs and Policy Research and also the vice president and dean of faculties at Northwestern. Mack was associate editor of Trans-Action *and editor of* The American Sociologist. *He is the author and editor of numerous books, including* Transforming America: Patterns of Social Change *(1967),* Race, Class, and Power *(1968),* Our Children's Burden: Studies of Desegregation in Nine American Communities *(1968), and* The Changing South *(1970). His articles on social class, race relations, industrial conflict, and urbanization have appeared in* The American Sociological Review, Social Forces, Saturday Review, Trans-Action, *and other journals. Mack received an honorary Doctor of Humane Letters degree from DePaul University in 1990.*

Roots

When Congress passed the Civil Rights Act of 1964, it was not starting a social movement but, rather, recognizing one. Twenty-one years earlier, in 1943, legally enforced segregation had been dealt a mortal blow by the invention of the cotton-picking machine. The bell tolled again with the industrial job opportunities (and the military travel opportunities) afforded by World War II — and then the doors to higher education were opened by the G.I. Bill.

During the twenty-five years after the invention of a workable cotton-picking machine, nearly five million African Americans left a life of rural serfdom to seek a better life in urban-industrial society. Paralleling these years of demographic change were years of drastic social change. In 1954, the Supreme Court declared that "separate educational facilities are inherently unequal" — a decision calling for change so alarming to some that federal troops had to be called in to implement it.

But during the ensuing decade, as the resistance to desegregation made racial injustice a recurring national news story, the nation became aware of the unfair treatment accorded to descendants of slaves. Whites marched with blacks, and the civil rights movement became a nationwide event. Peaceful sit-ins and Freedom Riders helped to define a national climate of opinion opposing legalized discrimination. In 1964, Martin Luther King, Jr., won the Nobel Peace Prize. And in 1964, the Congress of the United States acted.

The Civil Rights Act of 1964 mandates an end to discrimination in employment. Title VII, Section 703(a) forbade any employer "to fail or refuse to hire or to discharge any individual, or otherwise discriminate against any individual with respect to his compensation, terms, conditions, or privileges of employment, because of such individual's race, color, religion, sex, or national origin."

The term "affirmative action" appears once in Title VII:

> If the court finds that the respondent has intentionally engaged in or is intentionally engaging in an unlawful employment practice . . . the court may . . . order such affirmative action as may be appropriate, which may include, but is not limited to, reinstatement or hiring of employees, with or without back pay . . . or any other equitable relief as the court deems appropriate.

Note that this does not call for quotas, percentages, or timetables. It is a statement allowing for redress of grievances.

The phrase appears one other time in U.S. law, in President Lyndon Johnson's Executive Order 11246, which prohibits discrimination by federal contractors. The order reads "The contractor will take affirmative action to ensure that applicants are employed and that employees are treated during employment, without regard to their race, color, religion, sex, or national origin." Like Title VII, this order does not call for preferential treatment.

The evidence shows that most Americans agree with the sentiments expressed in the Civil Rights Act of 1964 and in Executive Order 11246. Why, then, all the ruckus about affirmative action?

Practices

This brief historical summary does not describe what is meant by "affirmative action" today.   10

In 1969, the Department of Labor informed government contractors in Philadelphia that their bids would not be considered unless they contained minority-hiring goals. This was the beginning of a series of federal regulations that, in the name of affirmative action, effectively overturned the Civil Rights Act of 1964. Title VII, Section 703(a) forbade discrimination on the basis of race. Less frequently invoked is Title VII, Section 703(j):

> Nothing in this title shall be interpreted to require any employer . . . to grant preferential treatment to any individual or to any group because of the race, color, religion, sex, or national origin of such individual or group on account of an imbalance which may exist with respect to the total number of percentage of persons of any race, color, religion, sex, or national origin.

The Nixon administration began systematically violating this section of the act with the Philadelphia plan, and all succeeding administrations have joined with the courts in effectively overturning the stated intent of the Congress. The Equal Employment Opportunity Commission and the Office of Federal Compliance Programs have caused goals that include timetables and quotas to become standard methods of resolving disputes about affirmative action in employment.

In education, the courts have effected judicially what in the area of employment was accomplished administratively. The Supreme Court ruled that racial segregation, legally enforced, in public schools was unconstitutional. Justice Clarence Thomas argued that "the theory that black students suffer an unspecified psychological harm from segregation that retards their mental and educational development . . . not only relies upon questionable social science research rather than constitutional principle but also rests on an assumption of black inferiority." Not so. When members of a set of less powerful people are not permitted to mingle with the members of a set of more powerful people and the more powerful people think that the difference between the two is important enough to be mandated and enforced by law, then it does not take a terribly sophisticated social science to rightly conclude that those separate facilities are inherently unequal.

Unfortunately, the facts of residential segregation in the United States have made it difficult to act on the implications of the Supreme Court's ruling. Although we did away with de jure segregated public schools, most black students in large U.S. cities are still attending de facto segregated schools in their racially concentrated neighborhoods.[1] Most of our metropolitan areas have artificial city limits; that is, a significant proportion of their population lives outside the legal city limits, in suburbs. The resulting neighborhoods, both within the city limits and in the suburbs, are characterized not only by racial segregation but by class segregation as well. Changing the residential patterns of the cities would be a daunting challenge; therefore, the only way to keep neighborhood schools, and to desegregate them, would be to transport students. Court-ordered busing became the standard treatment for this problem.

Thirty years ago, "affirmative action" meant keeping a keen eye on   15
want ads and promotion policies. It meant assuring that opportunities were made known to all and that promotions depended not on old boy networks but on merit. It meant equality of access to opportunity — the dismantling of discrimination, the doing away with race as a factor in the market. Today, "affirmative action" means goals, timetables, quotas, busing, and preferential treatment.

Prospects

Justice Thomas wrote that "if separation itself is a harm, and if integration therefore is the only way that blacks can receive a proper education, then there must be something inferior about blacks." There is indeed something inferior about many blacks, but it is not genetic inferiority; rather, it is status inferiority resulting from de jure segregation. It will not be overcome by voluntary segregation and continuing isolation from mainstream U.S. culture.

Professor Alex M. Johnson, Jr., states that the Supreme Court's decision in *Brown* v. *Board of Education of Topeka* "failed because it did not acknowledge the prior development of a unique African American community with its own cultures, languages, religions, and territories." This is not just wrong; it is seriously wrong. The road to full equality in U.S. society is integration.

Professor Harold Cruse, whom David J. Garrow rightly identifies as "a black intellectual," has asserted that "separateness has the potential of achieving equality in its own right." But separateness denies access to open competition for the most desirable positions. To achieve equality of opportunity in U.S. society, one must be integrated into the culture as well as the social structure. Patricia Schroeder, Franklin Roosevelt, Arthur Ashe, Diane Feinstein, Pierre De Pont, Jessye Norman, and Kimball Young did

---

[1] In law, *de jure* (according to the law) is often distinguished from *de facto* (in fact, or reality). In other words, though we legally did away with segregation, it still in fact exists, Mack claims.

Document

SP-1: Resolution of the University of California Board of Regents Adopting a Policy "Ensuring Equal Treatment" of Admissions, 20 July 1995

Whereas, Governor Pete Wilson, on June 1, 1995, issued Executive Order W-124-95 to "End Preferential Treatment and to Promote Individual Opportunity Based on Merit"; and

Whereas, paragraph seven of that order requests the University of California to "take all necessary action to comply with the intent and the requirements of this executive order"; and

Whereas, in January 1995, the University initiated a review of its policies and practices, the results of which support many of the findings and conclusions of Governor Wilson; and

Whereas, the University of California Board of Regents believes that it is in the best interest of the University to take relevant actions to develop and support programs that will have the effect of increasing the eligibility rate of groups that are "underrepresented" in the University's pool of applicants as compared to their percentages in California's graduating high-school classes and to which reference is made in Section 4;

Now, Therefore, Be It Resolved As Follows:

Section 1. The Chairman of the Board, with the consultation of the President, shall appoint a task force representative of the business community, students, the University, other segments of education, and organizations currently engaged in academic "outreach." The responsibility of this group shall be to develop proposals for new directions and increased funding for the Board of Regents to increase the eligibility rate of those currently identified in Section 4. The final report of this task force shall be presented to the Board of Regents within six months after its creation.

Section 2. Effective January 1, 1997, the University of California shall not use race, religion, sex, color, ethnicity, or national origin as criteria for admission to the University or to any program of study.

Section 3. Effective January 1, 1997, the University of California shall not use race, religion, sex, color, ethnicity, or national origin as criteria for "admissions in exception" to UC eligibility requirements.

Section 4. The President shall confer with the Academic Senate of the University of California to develop supplemental criteria for consideration by the Board of Regents which shall be consistent with Section 2. In developing such criteria, which shall provide reasonable assurances that the applicant will successfully complete his or her course of study, consideration shall be given to individuals who, despite having suffered disadvantage economically or in terms of their social environment (such as an abusive or otherwise dysfunctional home or a neighborhood of unwholesome or anti-social influences), have nonetheless demonstrated sufficient character and determination in overcoming obstacles to warrant confidence that the applicant can pursue a course of study to successful completion, provided that any student admitted under this section must be academically eligible for admission.

Section 5. Effective January 1, 1997, not less than fifty (50) percent and not more than seventy-five (75) percent of any entering class on any campus shall be admitted solely on the basis of academic achievement.

Section 6. Nothing in Section 2 shall prohibit any action that is strictly necessary to establish or maintain eligibility for any federal or state program, where ineligibility would result in a loss of federal or state funds to the University.

Section 7. Nothing in Section 2 shall prohibit the University from taking appropriate action to remedy specific, documented cases of discrimination by the University, provided that such actions are expressly and specifically approved by the Board of Regents or taken pursuant to a final order of a court or administrative agency of competent jurisdiction. Nothing in this section shall interfere with the customary practices of the University with regard to the settlement of claims against the University relating to discrimination.

Section 8. The President of the University shall periodically report to the Board of Regents detailing progress to implement the provisions of this resolution.

Section 9. Believing California's diversity to be an asset, we adopt this statement: Because individual members of all of California's diverse races have the intelligence and capacity to succeed at the University of California, this policy will achieve a UC population that reflects this state's diversity through the preparation and empowerment of all students in this state to succeed rather than through a system of artificial preferences.

— From *Representations*, Summer 1996.

not make their contributions to U.S. society by following the path to "separate but equal."

Opponents of affirmative action generally take two positions: Affirmative action has not really accomplished anything, and white males are furious about its accomplishments. The idea that U.S. society is suffering from its policy of discriminating in favor of blacks would be ludicrous if it were not so injurious. Playing off the black middle class against the white middle class is an even more vicious political tactic now that we finally have a substantial black middle class.

Our success at middle-class racial integration has resulted in a damaging isolation of lower-class de facto segregation. The children of poorly educated, economically deprived, racially segregated parents are isolated in schools with other children of poorly educated, economically deprived, racially segregated parents. They grow up in neighborhoods and attend schools and churches and play on streets in lower-class ghettos, cut off from and insulated from mainstream educational values, job expectations, and standard American English.

The way to move people up from these degrading circumstances is not to acknowledge "a unique African American community with its own cultures, languages, religions, and territories." The way out is to practice affirmative action on the basis of class, not race. It is not all black Americans who need help; it is all desperately poor Americans.

The question is: Whose affirmative action?

Do we want the equality of access to opportunity guaranteed by the Civil Rights Act of 1964 or the expanded definition implemented by agencies and courts that includes goals, timetables, quotas, and preferences?

Comment

Jesse Jackson on Civil Rights

[Governor Pete] Wilson has strong armed the University of California into ending affirmative action admission and employment programs. He pushed the state's passage of Proposition 209, which prohibits the taking of affirmative steps to remedy discrimination. (Wilson argues that discrimination is no longer a problem.) The measure of his defiance can be seen in California law schools where affirmative action measures have been scotched. This year, offers of admission to African Americans at Boalt Hall, UC Berkeley's law school, are down 81 percent; to Hispanics, down 50 percent; and to Native Americans, down 78 percent. At UCLA's law school, offers to African Americans are down 80 percent, to Hispanics 32 percent. Law school officials acknowledge that the drop off in students actually admitted will be even worse, as talented minority candidates are likely to go where they are more welcome. Next year, the same decline will play itself out at the undergraduate level across the state as those schools abandon the law.

— From "Civil Rights Gone Wrong" (*The Nation*, June 9, 1997). The full text can be found on the Web at http://www.thenation.com/issue/970609/0609jack.htm.

Whatever definition of affirmative action we choose, I am convinced that most African Americans would see it as a great stride forward if we were simply to deliver on the promise of Title VII: equality of opportunity.

Most Americans, I think, would find a program extending a helping hand to the disadvantaged more acceptable than a program of reverse racial discrimination. "All men are created equal" does not imply that they shall remain equal. The U.S. work ethic offers equality of opportunity, not equality of outcome. In a democratic United States, every citizen is entitled to life, liberty, the pursuit of happiness, and the ballot. No one is entitled to anything on account of gender, religion, ethnicity, or race.

Responding as a Reader

1. Consider Mack's three sections: Roots, Practices, and Prospects. What is the purpose of each of these sections? Why do you think Mack has chosen to organize his essay this way?

2. What is the difference between *de jure* segregation and *de facto* segregation (para. 14)? What measures have been taken to mitigate de facto segregation? How effective were these measures?

3. What is Mack implying when he refers to Professor Harold Cruse as "a black intellectual" (para. 18)? What is the difference between an intellectual, an intellectual who happens to be black, and a black intellectual? How does Mack's use of this label relate to his stand on voluntary segregation?

4. Evaluate Mack's final paragraph from Stanley Fish's point of view in the preceding selection. Which argument do you agree with more?

Responding as a Writer

1. Reread sections 703(a) and 703(j) of Title VII of the 1964 Civil Rights Act, quoted in this article, and rephrase them in your own words. What sorts of affirmative action does this law provide for? What sorts does it not provide for?

2. Analyze the quotation from Justice Clarence Thomas in paragraph 13. Do you agree that "the theory that black students suffer . . . from segregation . . . rests on an assumption of black inferiority"? Write one paragraph that unpacks the Thomas quotation, explaining its logic. Then write a second paragraph that points out other reasons why segregation is harmful to black students (and other students, if you like).

3. Argue for or against Mack's assertion that "It is not all black Americans who need help; it is all desperately poor Americans" (para. 21). Whichever stand you take, make sure to specify what kind of help you are talking about.

RACHEL F. MORAN

Unrepresented

[REPRESENTATIONS / Summer 1996]

In the face of growing racial and ethnic controversy, California has become the first state to take serious steps to eliminate preferential programs for particular minority groups. My central question in this essay is, why has the affirmative action debate been framed in black–white terms, especially in a state like California where Latinos represent the single largest racial or ethnic minority — one that is rapidly expanding? I argue that Latinos have been unrepresented in the controversy because their identity and entitlements have been undercut by two competing policy models: civil rights and immigration. I demonstrate how Latinos' immigration status has eroded their claims for civil rights protection and how fears stemming from their special treatment under civil rights law have undermined their demands for inclusion as immigrants. I conclude by describing the challenges that Latinos face in merging these models in ways that mutually reinforce the definition of their unique identity and history, rather than mutually destroy their life chances.

The Affirmative Action Debate in California Higher Education

The nationwide debate over affirmative action is lively, but in California, the controversy has become particularly intense. On 20 July 1995, the Regents of the University of California voted to prohibit the use of "race, religion, sex, color, ethnicity, or national origin" in admissions, hiring, and contracting at the University's nine campuses [see p. 306].[1] In adopting the resolutions, the Regents disregarded the opposition of the President of the University, the Council of Chancellors, the Academic Council, and the Student Association. Despite calls by faculty, students, and staff to reconsider

---

RACHEL F. MORAN (b. 1956) is professor of law at Boalt Hall School of Law, University of California at Berkeley. She served as chair of the Chicano/ Latino Policy Project at the Institute for the Study of Social Change from 1993 to 1996. Currently, she is working on a book on interracial intimacy and a case study of a lawsuit involving bilingual education and desegregation in the Denver public schools. The text reprinted here omits a few passages referring to specific articles and books.

the abolition of affirmative action policies, the Regents to date have stead-fastly refused to revisit the issues.[2]

Although the Regents' resolutions eliminate racial, ethnic, and gender preferences in admissions, hiring, and contracting, the new policy explicitly embraces outreach programs to increase the pool of qualified candidates from underrepresented groups. Even with aggressive outreach initiatives, however, it seems likely that the numbers of black and Latino students at the University of California will decline; moreover, the drop will be partic-ularly striking at the most competitive campuses: Berkeley and Los Ange-les. The Regents' resolution on admissions provides that admissions poli-cies may take into account economic and social disadvantage, and as a result, some have argued that the resolution will not seriously undermine racial and ethnic diversity at the University.[3] Projections for enrollment based on grade point average, standardized test scores, and income indi-cate, however, that blacks and Latinos would still suffer a significant drop in numbers at the campuses even if socioeconomic status were considered; in fact, the primary beneficiaries of an income-based approach appear to be Asian Americans, whose grades and test scores are higher than those of other racial and ethnic groups when socioeconomic status is held constant.[4]

Measuring social disadvantage by other means, furthermore, remains an untested strategy. The University so far has provided only general guid-ance on how to implement this portion of the Regents' policy.[5] Campus ef-forts to evaluate social disadvantage are complicated by concern that the use of some factors, such as distinctive linguistic or cultural background, could be challenged on the ground that they are illicit proxies for race and ethnicity.

The flurry of activity in response to the Regents' resolutions will seem modest in comparison to the adjustments in statewide operations that will be required if the California Civil Rights Initiative* is placed on the No-vember 1996 ballot and passes.[6] Under the initiative, all institutions of higher education in California, including the California State University system, its community college, and the University of California, will be covered. Because the state universities and community colleges serve a large number of black and Latino students, these students' access to higher education in California will be restricted by the initiative. Moreover, out-reach programs that receive state funds will be prevented from remaining racially or ethnically specific and, arguably, an individual would even have the right to sue under the state constitution if a university program used proxies that allegedly tracked race or ethnicity too closely. The initiative thus would sweep far more broadly and deeply than do the Regents' reso-lutions.

5

*The Initiative passed.

The Unrepresented: The Absence of Latinos
from the Affirmative Action Debate

Most of the coverage of these changes in California's affirmative action policy has been framed in black–white terms. For instance, when I am contacted by reporters, they typically ask whether the time to rectify past discrimination against blacks is over and whether affirmative action programs now engender more unfairness than they eliminate. Media representatives often highlight the dangers of reverse discrimination by questioning preferential treatment for the black bourgeoisie, wondering why the son of a black surgeon or black banker should get special consideration. Latinos are nearly completely omitted from the discussion. This oversight is particularly baffling in California, where Latinos will constitute 36 percent of public high school graduates by the year 2000; this percentage is second only to whites at 41 percent and represents six times the number of blacks at 6 percent and slightly over twice the 17 percent of Asian Americans. Moreover, the salience of Latinos is growing nationwide: By 2010, Latinos are projected to become the largest minority group in the United States.[7]

In earlier skirmishes related to the demographic transformation of California, Latinos occupied a prominent place. For example, when Proposition 63, an initiative to make English the state's official language, was placed on the ballot and passed by an overwhelming margin, commentators focused on the Spanish-speaking population and the prevailing sense that Latinos were not assimilating as earlier generations of immigrants had. When Proposition 187 — designed to curtail illegal immigration by cutting off education, health, and social services to the undocumented — was adopted by a wide margin, the dominant images in the press were of Mexicans surreptitiously crossing the border at night or of pregnant Mexican women entering the country so that their American-born offspring could command the privileges of citizenship.

Now Latinos face a new challenge to their sense of belonging in the California polity: The assault on affirmative action threatens to limit their upward mobility as English speakers legally present in the state. Indeed, the size of the Latino population, its low levels of education and income, and its persistent underrepresentation in positions of leadership suggest that this group will be seriously affected by a declining commitment to affirmative action in California. Nevertheless, in describing the sequence of recent political events in California, one *Los Angeles Times* article began with and developed this observation by an attorney at the National Association for the Advancement of Colored People: "First the Latinos. Now the blacks. It is getting ugly."[8] This framing of the story suggests that, while earlier efforts to declare English the official language and cut off benefits to undocumented immigrants affected Latinos, the antiaffirmative action movement in California is "getting ugly" by undermining civil rights in a way that would primarily harm blacks. Like blacks, Latinos will be significantly affected by a retrenchment in affirmative action, but they have become "the disappeared" in this public policy debate.

The Paradigmatic Apostrophe: Why Latinos Find No Space in the Affirmative Action Debate

I believe that the presence of Latinos in the affirmative action debate has been elided because the two key models used to define their identity and entitlements have required them to conform to the experiences of other racial and ethnic groups. The mixed message of the civil rights paradigm, which is rooted in the black experience, is that Latinos have been treated similarly to blacks, but in reality they are more like white ethnic immigrants. The second model, the immigration paradigm, undercuts Latinos' claims to identity and entitlement because recent Latino immigrants are alleged to be different from earlier generations of ethnic immigrants. Latinos' shortcomings in assimilating American values have been substantiated, ironically, by invoking the same history of exclusion that they themselves invoke under the civil rights model. Here, the shorthand message is that Latinos should assimilate as white ethnics do, but in reality they will remain isolated and unassimilable as have blacks.

Civil Rights: You're Supposed to Be Black, But You're Really White Immigrants

The civil rights model in the United States is clearly based on the   10
African American experience. Modern civil rights protections arose primarily as a response to the persistence of a caste system rooted in slavery. The civil rights movement aimed to dismantle official segregative practices and to promote equal opportunity without regard to race. Early supporters of civil rights reform learned that individual antidiscrimination principles were insufficient to overcome a lengthy history of segregation and inequality. First, these individualized remedies placed the burden on victims to come forward to demand legal redress, yet, precisely because of their oppressed status, these individuals were often least able to muster the resources to advance their claims. Second, an individual rights model was ill equipped to address those systemic forms of discrimination without clearly identifiable victims. If, for example, an employer failed to recruit broadly and equitably for a job, those who never received word of the opening would be largely unaware of the harm they had suffered.

For these reasons, the federal government adopted proactive programs, like affirmative action, designed as temporary measures to undo the lingering effects of past discrimination. As the federal presence in the civil rights arena grew during the 1960s and 1970s, so did the number of groups (other than African Americans) that asserted an entitlement to special protection. Among those groups was the Latino population, which cited its own history of segregation and discrimination as a justification for inclusion in remedial programs including affirmative action. Eventually, Latinos gained recognition from Congress, the Supreme Court, and civil rights agencies as an ethnic group that should enjoy protections comparable to those available for blacks.[9]

Although Latinos earned formal recognition, informal doubts about the propriety of their inclusion in a civil rights model remained. First, Latinos are not a monolithic racial group: Their ancestors may be white, black, or indigenous peoples. Indeed, because the U.S. Census requires respondents to identify themselves as a single race, Latinos often mark "other" and then must be reclassified. To accommodate the ambiguities surrounding Latinos' racial identity, the Census identifies them separately as an *ethnic* group.[10]

This shift from a racial to an ethnic categorization calls into question Latinos' entitlements under a civil rights model. African American advocates of civil rights emphasize race as a central feature of disadvantage. Judges and legislators often lament that individuals are judged by the color of their skin rather than the content of their character; the Supreme Court has applied a stringent standard of review, "strict scrutiny," for racial classifications in part because it views race as an immutable characteristic.[11]

These depictions of race emphasize its links to biological expression through phenotype. The only relevant social correlate of race in this model is subordination. Ethnic categories, on the other hand, turn on ancestry but are typically associated with malleable social traits, such as language and culture: One can learn a new language or adopt new cultural practices. Precisely because ethnic classifications appear more mutable than racial ones, policymakers often are tempted to conclude that Latinos can escape the strictures of ethnicity by assimilating to dominant norms, but blacks are not similarly able to free themselves from racial prejudice. The perception that many Latinos have arrived in the United States as voluntary immigrants and, like earlier waves of newcomers, should be able to adapt themselves to an American way of life has only reinforced this view.

The black civil rights movement was rooted in the hardships of slavery. The small numbers of African immigrants from Haiti, Jamaica, and African nations represent such a tiny portion of the African American population that their presence does not significantly dilute blacks' demands for corrective justice.[12] By contrast, Latinos have diverse histories: Some are the descendants of Mexicans or Puerto Ricans whose lands were conquered by the United States. Others from Mexico and Central or South America arrived as immigrants, both legal and illegal, searching for a brighter economic future than their home countries could offer. Finally, many Cubans and Central Americans came as refugees seeking asylum from repressive political regimes. Because Latinos reflect such a wide-ranging mix of experiences, policymakers question their treatment as a collective group entitled to rectification of past discrimination. Latinos often find, therefore, that current patterns of segregation and inequality are an insufficient basis for relief because they are not necessarily an artifact of past governmental discrimination. . . .

Immigration: You're Supposed to Assimilate Like Whites But You'll End Up a Minority Like Blacks

The immigration model is rooted in the white ethnic experience. The traditional recounting of the immigrant experience is arguably a nostalgic exercise that omits the harsher aspects of newcomers' treatment.[13] Whatever the historical inaccuracies,[14] this account holds considerable sway over popular perceptions of current immigrants and the legitimacy of their demands for inclusion in the American polity.

According to the traditional immigration story, immigrants arrive in the United States by invitation only. Immigrants who accept the invitation are expected to make a permanent commitment to their new country; most become citizens through the naturalization process. By undergoing naturalization, immigrants forswear allegiance to their homelands and ally themselves exclusively with the United States. Through this commitment, newcomers can expect to traverse a steady path of upward mobility; whatever sacrifices they make will redound to the benefit of their children and grandchildren.[15]

This story is seriously incomplete, particularly insofar as it omits the instances of racial intolerance that have marred immigration policy. Due to concerns that some newcomers would be incapable of assimilating to an American way of life, the federal government has at various times restricted immigration from particular areas of the world. The Chinese Exclusion Act of 1882, for instance, prohibited Chinese from emigrating to the United States and becoming citizens.[16] In addition, state governments often adopted Americanization programs in public schools to ensure that immigrant populations assimilated to dominant norms and values. These federal and state initiatives punished certain newcomers for their perceived inability to conform to dominant norms.[17]

Latinos have similarly faced doubts about whether they legitimately belong to the American polity, especially since their experience does not jibe with that of earlier white ethnic immigrants. First, the terms of the invitation to come to the United States sometimes have been ambiguous. In contrast to an offer to join the polity on a permanent basis, Latinos have regularly received quite different signals: They have been offered the opportunity to work on a temporary basis with every expectation that they will return to their home countries. Sometimes this approach has been formalized through *bracero* programs.* At other times, the approach has been informal; the federal government is lax in policing its borders against illegal immigration so long as low-wage jobs are plentiful in the United States. In either case, these sojourners can be promptly dispatched to their countries of origin through termination of temporary work programs or deportation when labor cycles change.

Bracero programs in the 1940s and 1950s allowed Mexican farm workers to enter the United States on a temporary basis for seasonal labor.

Second, the close proximity of many Latinos to their homelands has   20
made it more difficult to sever ties to their original language and culture
than may have been true for earlier generations of immigrants. The steady
influx of new immigrants, the continuing ties with friends and relatives in
other countries, and the rise of transnational communities that challenge
the neat lines drawn by official borders — all of these contribute to a sense
that Latinos are not assimilating on the same terms as earlier generations
of immigrants. Indeed, dual loyalties to the home country and the United
States are proffered as the reason for low rates of naturalization among
Latino immigrants.[18]

Finally, Latino immigrants have found the path to upward mobility for
their children and grandchildren rocky and unsure. Although numerous
commentators have suggested that Latinos will pursue the same patterns of
success as earlier immigrants, others have argued that racial stratification
and subordination will impede Latinos' access to educational and economic opportunities. In the field of public health, for instance, recent studies suggest that second- and third-generation Latinos have poorer health
than do first-generation Latinos. Analysts have hypothesized that, among
other things, blocked acculturation has damaging effects on the progeny of
immigrants. In particular, first-generation Latinos compare their standing
to that of others in the home country and consider themselves successful;
by contrast, their children and grandchildren compare themselves to others
in the United States and conclude that they are less successful than their
peers. Moreover, second- and third-generation Latinos may doubt that
they can overcome systemic prejudice and therefore turn to self-destructive,
risk-taking behaviors like drug use and unsafe sex.[19]

Just as Latinos' claims to civil rights protections are undercut by referring to their immigrant status, their status as immigrants is undermined by
alluding to their potential claims under a civil rights model. The immigration model requires Latinos to conform to the experience of white ethnics,
but they cannot; in fact, Latinos' difficulties stem to a substantial extent
from a fear that they are unassimilable because of their distinctive ethnic
identity. In brief, Latinos are expected to acculturate as white ethnics do,
but at the same time there is a strong suspicion that, like blacks, they will
constitute a permanent minority. . . .

The Latino Challenge

Because Latinos are asked to conform to a black experience under the
civil rights model and a white experience under the immigration model,
they never succeed in fully establishing the legitimacy of their claims under
either approach. The first step that Latinos must take to avoid being whip-
sawed by civil rights and immigration models is to establish the ways in
which each paradigm accentuates the need for a heightened commitment to
fairness and equity under the other. Under the civil rights model, it is essential that Latinos demonstrate that the recent influx of immigrants in-

creases, rather than diminishes, the likelihood of discriminatory treatment. The growing visibility of Latino immigrant populations may reinforce stereotypical beliefs that Latinos are foreign and unwilling to assimilate. These stereotypes in turn are rooted in those historical practices that degraded Latinos out of fear that they would be less trustworthy Americans than other groups.

Under the immigration model, it is key that Latino advocates demonstrate that the failure to regularize the inevitable flow of cheap labor across a semipermeable border creates vulnerable populations trapped in poverty and ignorance. As the Supreme Court wrote in *Plyler* v. *Doe:*

> Sheer incapability or lax enforcement of the laws barring entry into this country, coupled with the failure to establish an effective bar to employment of undocumented aliens, has resulted in the creation of a substantial "shadow population" of illegal immigrants — numbering in the millions — within our borders. This situation raises the specter of a permanent caste of undocumented resident aliens, encouraged by some to remain here as a source of cheap labor, but nevertheless denied the benefits that our society makes available to citizens and lawful residents. The existence of such an underclass presents most difficult problems for a nation that prides itself on adherence to principles of equality under law.[20]

Recent proposals to eliminate benefits not only for undocumented persons but also for permanent resident aliens aggravate the dangers of creating hierarchical tiers of belonging and entitlement in a society committed to civil rights for all.[21] The destruction of the dignity and humanity of one segment of the population cannot easily be confined; tolerating the creation of a permanent underclass and then of a class of semilegitimate resident aliens makes it all too easy to retreat wholesale from a general commitment to equal treatment. Latinos must make clear that intelligent and humane immigration policy is integrally related to preserving the civil rights of all Americans.

Although I think that it is critical in the short run to contest the application of the civil rights and immigration models to Latinos, in the long run I hope that the Latino experience will challenge scholars and policymakers to reconsider the conventional parameters of each paradigm. The civil rights model is rooted in a black–white experience, but with the growth of Latino and Asian populations, this bilateral approach to race relations must be reconsidered. As was true in the 1930s, Latinos today do not fit either a black or a white typology, but instead of forcing them into a procrustean bed, it may be useful to analyze how this black–white vision has blinkered America's understanding of race. Perhaps race has been cast in excessively biological terms, when its correlation to social characteristics, such as religion, language, and culture, is critical; race may be wrongly treated as monolithic when race mixing has been a long-standing, if largely undiscussed, feature of American life. As Latinos gain prominence, their

25

experience may facilitate a thorough reexamination of America's out-moded conceptualization of race.[22]

Similarly, the Latino experience could alert us to the limitations of tra-ditional accounts of immigration. The rise of transnational communities may be the first harbinger of the global economy's impact on personal and national identity. As labor and capital flow across international borders, traditional boundaries may be less effective in marking and preserving an American way of life. Although the rise of immigrant populations is the most immediate and concrete evidence of these changes, the restructuring of the U.S. economy may have other serious long-term implications for tra-ditional conceptions of American customs and values. As capital is ex-ported abroad to draw on cheap labor supplies, Americans confront a growing inequality of opportunity between the highly skilled on the one hand and the semiskilled or unskilled on the other. Many Americans now find that instead of high-wage manufacturing jobs with benefits, they must settle for part-time work without benefits or security of employment in the service sector.

At some point, this rise in economic inequality may threaten the predi-cates of political equality so critical to the democratic process. The well-to-do will increasingly require that the political process insulate them from the discomfort and dangers associated with a class of unfortunates with lit-tle hope for personal advancement. By demonstrating how global flows of labor and capital affect a range of domestic traditions, scholarship on Lati-nos may alert the United States to the perils of failing to place immigration policy in the context of larger international economic imperatives. At a minimum, this work is likely to demonstrate that cracking down on immi-gration is by no means a complete answer to the larger challenges facing this country — now part of an international community with a range of political, social, and economic traditions.[23]

The transformation of popular thinking about civil rights and immi-gration is a tall order for Latinos. To accomplish this goal, government of-ficials, foundations, think tanks, and universities must support scholarly work on the burgeoning Latino population. Generating a substantial body of research on this group is a first step, but these findings then must reach policymakers and the media in accessible forms. To facilitate this dissemi-nation, at least some Latinos must assume the role of public intellectuals, providing commentary for newspapers, magazines, and television. Only in this manner can the conventional wisdom about Latinos be challenged. To maximize the impact of these commentators, Latinos should organize media watchdogs to ensure fairness, accuracy, and balance in the coverage of Latino concerns.[24]

Latinos need to show how the civil rights and immigration models in-teract in forming their identity and forging their life chances. Ultimately, though, the greatest contribution that Latinos may make is to alert Ameri-cans to the ways in which each paradigm has become obsolete. Latinos may not fit the models because the models just don't fit the complications of a multiracial, multiethnic, multicultural, multilingual America.

Notes

1. Regents of the University of California, *SP-1: Policy Ensuring Equal Treatment — Admissions,* 20 July 1995; Regents of the University of California. *SP-2: Policy Ensuring Equal Treatment — Employment and Contracting,* 20 July 1995.

2. Edward Epstein, "Faculty Opposes Gutting Affirmative Action at UC; They Want Share in Decision-Making," *San Francisco Chronicle,* 21 October 1995, A13.

3. Regents, *SP-1,* §4.

4. Gale Holland and Maria Goodavage, "California's Asian Students Face Quandary," *USA Today,* 23 August 1995, A1; Howard Witt, "At University of California, A New Set of Rules; With Affirmative Action Out, Racial Mix Could Change," *Chicago Tribune,* 30 July 1995, 13; B. Drummond Ayres, "Affirmative Action's End? Now, It's Not That Simple," *New York Times,* 24 July 1995, A1.

5. Pamela Burdman, "UC Officials Roll Out Plans on Preferences," *San Francisco Chronicle,* 14 December 1995, A19. When the President of the University of California asked for additional time to implement the resolution on student admissions, he met with a stinging rebuke from the Regents. "University's Leaders Are Torn by Affirmative-Action Ban," *New York Times,* 28 January 1996, A1; Pamela Burdman, "Regents Let UC Chief Off Hook: Conciliatory Letters Appease Critics,"*San Francisco Chronicle,* 30 January 1996, A1.

6. Gayle M. B. Hanson, "Color-Blind Initiative Makes Foes See Red," *Washington Times,* 20 February 1995, 6.

7. Jorge Chapa and Richard R. Valencia, "Latino Population Growth, Demographic Characteristics, and Educational Stagnation: An Examination of Recent Trends," *Hispanic Journal of Behavioral Science* 15 (1993): 165, 167; Bureau of the Census, *Current Population Reports: Population Projections for States, by Age, Sex, Race, and Hispanic Origin: 1993 to 2020,* prepared by the Population Division, Bureau of the Census (Washington, D.C., 1994), 21; Bureau of the Census, *Current Population Reports: Population Projections of the United States by Age, Sex, Race, and Hispanic Origin: 1993 to 2050,* prepared by the Population Division, Bureau of the Census (Washington, D.C., 1993), xxii; Jean Suhr Ludwig and Judy Kowarsky, "Eligibility of California's 1990 High School Graduates for Admission to the State's Public Universities," in Aida Hurtado and Eugene Garcia eds., *The Educational Achievement of Latinos: Barriers and Successes* (Santa Cruz, Calif., 1994), 259, 263.

8. Cathleen Decker, "Affirmative Action: Why Battle Erupted," *Los Angeles Times,* 19 February 1995, A1.

9. See, e.g., *Keyes v. School District No. 1,* 413 U.S. 189, 197–98 (1973) (noting that Latinos, like blacks, had suffered a history of discrimination and were entitled to special protection); *Hernandez v. Texas,* 347 U.S. 475, 478–80 (1954). For a general discussion of how civil rights statutes have been expanded to cover a range of minority groups, including Latinos, and the problems this expansion has posed, see Deborah Ramirez, "Multicultural Empowerment: It's Not Just Black and White Anymore," *Stanford Law Review* 47 (1995): 957.

10. Office of Management and Budget, "Race and Ethnic Standards for Federal Statistics and Administrative Reporting, Directive no. 15," *Federal Register* 43, no. 19 (1978): 260, 269; House Committee on Post Office and Civil Service, Subcommittee on Census, Statistics, and Postal Personnel, *Review of Federal Measurements of Race and Ethnicity,* 103d Cong., 1st Sess., 14 April 1993, 50 (remarks of Reynolds Farley, Research Scientist, Population Studies Center, University of Michigan).

11. See, e.g., *McLaughlin v. Florida,* 379 U.S. 184 (1964) (establishing strict scrutiny for racial classifications); *Frontiero v. Richardson,* 411 U.S. 677 (1973) (plurality opinion; explaining relevance of immutability to heightened scrutiny under equal protection law).

12. However, African Americans themselves are well aware of these differences, which often lead to hostility between native-born and immigrant blacks. See Sam Fulwood III, "U.S. Blacks: A Divided Experience," *Los Angeles Times,* 25 November 1995, A1.

13. Kevin R. Johnson, "Los Olvidados: Images of the Immigrant, Political Power of Non-citizens, and Immigration Law Enforcement," *Brigham Young University Law Review* (1993): 1139, 1150. See, generally, Nathan Glazer and Daniel P. Moynihan, *Beyond the Melting Pot: The Negroes, Puerto Ricans, Jews, Italians, and Irish of New York City* (Cambridge, Mass., 1970); Pastora S. J. Cafferty et al., *The Dilemma of American Immigration: Beyond the Golden Door* (New Brunswick, N.J., 1983).

14. Assimilation was not a straightforward proposition for earlier generations of immigrants. According to David Hollinger, of those immigrants who came to the United States during the great migration of 1880 to 1924, about one-third returned to their country of origin. David A. Hollinger, *Postethnic America: Beyond Multiculturalism* (New York, 1995).

15. See Milton M. Gordon, *Assimilation in American Life: The Role of Race, Religion, and National Origins* (New York, 1964), 107–8.

16. *Chae Chan Ping v. United States* (The Chinese Exclusion Case), 130 U.S. 581, 595 (1889).

17. See, generally, Heinz Kloss, *The American Bilingual Tradition* (Rowley, Mass., 1977), 45, 46–47, 52–53, 60–61, 67–74; Shirley Brice Heath, "English in Our Language Heritage," in Charles A. Ferguson and Shirley Brice, eds., *Language in the USA* (New York, 1981), 14–17.

18. See Johnson, "Los Olvidados," 1223 (the naturalization rate for Latinos was less than half the average for all immigrants); see also Sam Dillon, "Mexico Woos U.S. Mexicans, Proposing Dual Nationality," *New York Times,* 10 December 1995, A10.

19. See Elizabeth Hervey Stephen et al., "Health of the Foreign-Born Population: United States, 1989–90," *Advance Data* 74 (1994): 1, 4; Paul D. Sorlie et al., "Mortality by Hispanic Status in the United States," *Journal of the American Medical Association* 70 (1993): 2464, 2468; Jacqueline M. Golding and M. Audrey Burnam, "Immigration, Stress, and Depressive Symptoms in a Mexican-American Community," *Journal of Nervous and Mental Disease* 178 (1990): 161, 169.

20. *Plyler v. Doe,* 457 U.S. 202, 218–19 (1982). The insularity of this class of persons would be further entrenched by proposals to deny citizenship to children born to undocumented persons residing in the United States. See Neil A. Lewis, "Bill Seeks to End Citizenship as Birthright for Everyone," *New York Times,* 14 December 1995, A20.

21. See Robert Pear, "The Nation: Deciding Who Gets What in America," *New York Times,* 27 November 1994, A5.

22. There is evidence that these developments are already unfolding. See Luis Angel Toro, "'A People Distinct from Others': Race and Identity in Federal Indian Law and the Hispanic Classification in OMB Directive No. 15," *Texas Tech Law Review* 26 (1995): 1219, 1221–22. See generally Ian Haney-Lopez, "The Social Construction of Race," *Harvard Civil Rights — Civil Liberties Law Review* 29 (1994): 1.

23. For preliminary scholarship on how a global economy will affect social and political as well as economic conditions in the United States, see M. Patricia Fernandez Kelly, "Underclass and Immigrant Women as Economic Actors: Rethinking Citizenship in a Changing Global Economy," *American University Journal of International Law and Policy* 9 (1993): 151; Michael S. Knoll, "Perchance to Dream: The Global Economy and the American Dream," *Southern California Law Review* 66 (1993): 1599.

24. Latinos are seriously underrepresented in the media, accounting for only 2 percent of all prime-time television roles, although they currently comprise 10 percent of the nation's population. Blacks, by contrast, play 18 percent of all roles, even though they represent 13 percent of the population. Mark A. Perigard, "Alien Nation: How Well Does Prime-Time TV Match the Makeup of Society?" *Boston Herald,*

5 November 1995, 1. See also Valerie Menard, "The Latino Angle; Latino Community Journalists," *Hispanic* 8 (September 1995): 14; Mary Anne Perez, "Community News: East: Eastside: Media Watchdog Committee Formed," *Los Angeles Times,* 12 February 1995, 9.

Responding as a Reader

1. Moran argues that Latinos are caught between the civil rights paradigm and the immigration paradigm (para. 9). What is a paradigm, and what are the elements of each of these paradigms? How is it that Latinos do not fit into either?

2. Look over the notes on pages 319–322. What sources has Moran consulted in her research? What does Moran's use of these sources say about her and her article? Do they influence your interpretation of her arguments?

3. After reading the resolution of the University of California Board of Regents (reprinted on p. 306), reread the passages in which Moran quotes from this document or invokes it. Do you believe she is reading the document correctly, in all cases?

Responding as a Writer

1. Moran is using the University of California resolution as a microcosm for national affirmative action legislation. In what ways can a resolution passed in one state represent the attitudes of all the states? In what ways does this resolution apply only to California? Does it make a difference that *Representations* (in which this article appeared) is a publication of the University of California? Argue for or against the national relevance of this particular example.

2. List the arguments in favor of affirmative action for African Americans. Do these arguments also apply to Latinos? Explain why or why not. Also consider whether there are reasons to apply affirmative action to Latinos that do not apply to African Americans (such as language). What does Moran say on this subject?

3. Do the special problems of Latinos in the United States (the problems that Moran points out) fall under the umbrella of affirmative action, civil rights, immigration, or something else? Define the concerns of each of these categories and then argue that the issues raised in this article are or are not affirmative action issues.

Discussing the Unit

Suggested Topic for Discussion

Should affirmative action continue in its current form? Or should it return to the spirit of the 1964 Civil Rights Act, or be extended to include other groups, or be curtailed, or be abolished altogether? What are the benefits of affirmative action to all Americans? What are its drawbacks? What are the historical issues involved? The moral issues?

Preparing for Class Discussion

1. Make sure you know what the law says right now — in the nation, your state, and your school. Has any recent legislation been passed on this issue? Search for affirmative action on the World Wide Web or talk to a law professor, an American government professor, or an historian who specializes in the Constitution. You could also visit the personnel office at your school to find out about their hiring practices.

2. The articles in this unit (even Moran's) assume that when we're talking about affirmative action, we're talking about African Americans. What other groups are given preference for jobs and acceptance to college? What other groups should be given preference?

3. *Prewriting Assignment:* What might happen if affirmative action ended? List some probable results — favorable, unfavorable, or both. Think about long-term and short-term effects.

From Discussion to Writing

Using all the evidence in this unit (and any additional evidence that you care to gather), argue for or against affirmative action as it is now practiced. If you believe that affirmative action should continue as it has been, make sure to address the criticisms raised by Clarence Thomas, the University of California, Rachel Moran, and others. If you believe that the U.S. policy toward affirmative action must change, outline a better policy and argue for that.

14

CONFERENCE CHAPTER

Understanding Multiracialism: Are Labels Important?

Is race a meaningless and obsolete category? A growing number of social scientists are beginning to think so, as the nation rapidly evolves into an astonishingly diverse society. Yet race is not a category easily dismissed, either by racists intent on claiming a superiority or by ethnocentrists intent on claiming an identity. In fact, given the enormous influence today of identity politics, one might even argue that race is more politically significant than it ever was. In an interview on the meaning of race, Ann Laurer Stoler, a University of Michigan anthropology professor, discusses the social construction of racial categories and explains why she believes "there is absolutely no such thing as biological race." When the golf champion Tiger Woods described himself as a "Cablinasian," referring to his Caucasian, black, Thai, Chinese, and American Indian mix, he delighted those who hope to transcend racial labels but offended those who hoped to claim him exclusively as one of their own. More than any celebrity in our era, as *Time* magazine suggests in "I'm Just Who I Am," Woods has focused the nation on the complex issue of multiracial identity.

Woods, of course, would not find "Cablinasian" as a choice on any government or student form. Which box would he check? What do most multiracial individuals do when they are forced to make a choice? Although the *New York Times* reports that a poll reveals that "few people would opt to describe themselves as multiracial if given the chance on the census form," there nevertheless appears to be a growing number of Americans — especially young Americans — who dislike and distrust the conventional categories. Two such individuals are Sunil Garg and Lylah M. Alphonse. In "Under My Skin," Garg, an Indian American, objects to being called a "person of color." In "Race Needs 'Other' Option," Alphonse, a young woman tired of being asked what she is, finds it hard to believe that our institutions haven't come up with a different method of classifying people by now. Another antagonist to the conventional categories is one of America's most controversial authors. In her online advice column for the "culturally disgruntled," Camille Paglia asserts that "racial classification of any kind is poisoned at its source."

Yet, despite all of its opponents, racial classification surfaces everywhere. Even the racial identity of a 9,000-year-old skeleton can become the subject of intense dispute, as *New Yorker* reporter Douglas Preston finds as he covers a hard-fought battle between two opposing groups — scientifically minded physical anthropologists who want to study recently discovered prehistoric bones and Native American tribes who want to rebury them. What may be at issue could be of first-order importance: the possibility that Caucasian groups had arrived in the New World before Native Americans. That possibility, however, is to Native Americans a meaningless query of western science: "From our oral histories," says Armand Minthorn in a 1997 position paper for the Confederated Tribes, "we know that our people have been part of this land since the beginning of time."

It's one thing to say we should transcend race, but will white people transcend theirs? That question is posed in "The Unbearable Being of Whiteness," by the Chinese American essayist and commentator Eric Liu, who argues that in the final analysis "it is whiteness — not blackness — that is the original sin of identity politics."

And how do today's freshmen feel about racial classification? The survey results show that perhaps "multiracial" should have been an option; the total of the following categories comes to 104.6 percent, suggesting that some freshmen checked more than one box.

Selected Survey Results

Racial Profile of the Class of 2000

- White/Caucasian: 80.4%
- African American/black: 9.7%
- American Indian: 2.3%
- Asian American/Asian: 4.3%
- Mexican American/Chicano: 3.0%
- Puerto Rican: 0.9%
- Other Latino: 1.6%
- Other: 2.4%

— From *The American Freshman: National Norms For Fall 1996.*

Q&A

Ann Laurer Stoler on the Construction of Race

The following questions and answers are taken from a longer interview between the Detroit Free Press *and Ann Laurer Stoler, a University of Michigan anthropology professor.*

What do you do?

For twenty years, basically, I've worked on different ways of getting at how social inequalities come to seem as natural. How we come to see them as common sense. How we come to believe that we can't do much about them. Why they look as if they've always been there.

Can you give me an example?

When you go to Indonesia, you see people are poor. Many children are malnourished; few people have electricity. Yet people seem very happy and they deal well with it. And foreigners say, "Well, you know, this is just the way it is. I mean, in Java, they didn't develop the way we did."

But as a young researcher in Java in the early 1970s, I said, "Wait a minute: Isn't it possible that the rapid development of the United States and Europe is the reason there's been so little development here?" And I found, for example, that huge foreign-owned plantations made land unavailable for local farmers. So these landless workers had to work for foreigners at low wages because there were no other choices. Just as Uniroyal took advantage of that on its huge rubber plantations in the 1920s, now Nike does it today.

I guess I'm always interested in how what seems natural has come to be, and that's one of the reasons the categories of gender and race are so interesting. Because we all take those to be intuitively so visual, so common sense. We always know someone black and we always know someone white when we see them. But is that really the case? Have the divisions that we take to be the divisions always been like that?

Well? Have they?

No. One of the strongest turns in the last twenty years in my field is to look at the changes in these categories of humankind that we've taken to be so clear and unchanging. Once you start questioning whether race is a real, scientifically valid category — once you start asking questions about the way in which racial types, racial classifications, are something that we construct for political ends — you have to start asking, "Well, who gets placed where? Who's considered 'we,' who's considered 'they'?"

You can go across the world and see a range of rules. In the United States, it's the one-drop rule. The one-drop rule is if you have one traceable ancestor who is black and twenty who are white, you're black.

That's not a fact of race. That doesn't tell us that this person is black. That's only a social construction of how we've decided to define black and white. So whenever you ask a question about race, you have to ask about who is making up those categories — how people come to be in a category.

Are you saying there is absolutely no such thing as biological race?

I'm saying there is absolutely no such thing as biological race.

How do you explain this to people who have believed in race all their lives?

The fact is that the genetic variations within each racial group are greater than the variations between racial groups. Whatever index you take — skin color, head size, brain size, pigmentation, nose size, or whatever you want to take — it doesn't match up with what we socially define as race.

How have you used this information in your work?

Lots of people have talked about sexuality and lots of people have talked about race, but very few people looked at the way in which sexual arrangements — domestic arrangements — actually construct the category of race. And when I say construct, I mean the category is not there until you go and make the category.

For example, you have a child that's born of a Javanese woman and a Dutch man. OK? Well, how are you going to decide where that child belongs? Is the child Dutch? Is the child Javanese?

In some societies, the child always follows what the mother is. But then you start getting into questions of citizenship. Is the child going to be considered European because Dutch colonial law allowed fathers to legitimate their children, but not mothers? So the question of where you belong — what race you belong to — often got very, very tied up with the conditions under which the parents had sex.

European nations' citizenship laws also ended up being very crucial in deciding whether you were considered a European or not — whether you were considered really white or not. So one of the interesting historical questions to ask is about the ways in which the making of nation-states and the making of race have depended on one another.

In the Dutch East Indies at the turn of the century, they used to say any mixed-blood kid can have access to the Dutch schools. Fine. Anybody can go. But you have to be fluent in Dutch by the age of 7 to get in. Well, how do you get fluent in Dutch by the age of 7 in Java — unless you live in a household where everybody speaks Dutch fluently? By setting up that rule, you've already ensured racial discrimination. You never call it race. You say you believe in racial equality. But you have ensured discrimination

continued on next page

continued from previous page

based on color that's not about color — that's about having abilities, competencies.

If race is not about what we think of as race but is about what we think of as social skills and areas of knowledge . . .

It's not that it has nothing to do with biology. I think that biology and the physical becomes a powerful way of making these categories seem natural, of affirming that these categories are common sense. We draw on biology as a way of saying, "Yes, these differences are real."

The fact that human differences are claimed to be due to biology is something that has been there for a long time. If you look at the nineteenth century, what's so interesting is the number of scientific efforts to try to find the exact measurements that would show racial type. Phrenology — measure skull form and you can know race. Or genital size — measure that and you know race. Or measure the kinkiness of hair and you know.

Each time, it was debunked. The correlations didn't work. So, was race discredited as a category? No. The only thing those failures did was intensify the discussion around the fact that there are racial differences, but the failed scientists said, "We just haven't been able to find exactly the measure for them yet." It didn't ever undermine the credibility of racist beliefs.

There's been a lot written about what it means to be black or brown or red today. But you've also tried to define whiteness. What's that about?

Whiteness has always been the unmarked category. You don't study whiteness. You study what everybody else is. You study people who have different cultural customs, people of different color.

I've been reading colonial documents for the last ten years in which Dutch authorities in the 1880s, in what is now Indonesia, were trying to decide who should be considered European. The very fact that they needed to debate it so much made it painfully clear how arbitrary and unclear the category European was. For instance, they could never decide whether poor whites were real Europeans or not. And that made them very uncomfortable. Because this thing that's supposed to be so natural and is supposed to be in your blood could not be easily quantified or calculated — could not be decided sight unseen and, even seen could not be decided.

So I asked, instead of studying the "other," why don't we study what makes whiteness seem immune to investigation? Why don't we ever turn the mirror around?

Are we turning it around now?

Well, I think we are turning it around. Turning it around, when I began this research ten years ago, felt like a very subversive act. Turning it around said "Aha! If we can show that whiteness is so variable and changeable, the whole thing can be undone."

But racism is still alive and well because social systems based on race are resilient enough to withstand constant changes in the definitions of racial categories.

So we have a set of real physical variations, but then we have a set of made-up stories about what those variations tell us?

We have these stories because they work for certain kinds of purposes. They work for ensuring that certain people have access to certain resources and others don't. I guess the harder question is why do people who are subordinate buy into this system?

You can't just say that racism was put together by — constructed by — an elite. That's too easy. The rich aren't that smart and the poor are not that stupid.

There's a common sense power to racism that comes from the ways in which we as humans classify things in the world. This is something we all share — knowing who's "we" and who's "they." We're constantly making those distinctions.

How would a group that comes out on the short end of the stick gain by buying into these stories about what race means?

It depends on what historical moment you're talking about. If you look at the Negritude Movement in Africa in this century, it takes the racial categories of European colonialism and turns them back on themselves and says, "We have a distinctive identity as Africans. There is a 'we' that is African-ness." You can see the same kind of thing here in the United States, from black power movements in the '60s to identity politics today.

How do you feel about all the attention race is getting these days?

There's a nervousness today among people who are writing about race and racism. People are wondering how much are we contributing to making these categories more and more important.

It's like when the KKK came to Ann Arbor recently. To try to counter them, one could either pretend they didn't exist or confront them. Well, some young people chose to confront them, but they couldn't because there were 200 police protecting the KKK. So they started throwing bricks at the police. The KKK loved it and said, "We're coming back again. We haven't had this much attention in ages."

continued on next page

continued from previous page

And I think that's a microcosm of the much larger problem of how we deal with race today. Do we say, "Yes! We have these races. I'm going to enjoy my heritage and celebrate it." How do you do that without also saying that those are the most important ways in which human beings should be seen and evaluated, and make their affinities and affiliations, and create their desires and their communities?

— From "Race: What Does It Mean?" (*Detroit Free Press,* July 7, 1996). The full text of this interview can also be found at http://newslibrary.infi.net/freep.

JACK E. WHITE

"I'm Just Who I Am" (Tiger Woods and the Melding of America)

[TIME / May 5, 1997]

His nickname notwithstanding, professional golfer Frank ("Fuzzy") Zoeller saw Tiger Woods quite clearly. He gazed on the new king of professional golf, through whose veins runs the blood of four continents, and beheld neither a one-man melting pot nor even a golfing prodigy but a fried-chicken-and-collard-greens-eating Sambo. Zoeller saw Woods, in short, as just another stereotype, condemned by his blackness to the perpetual status of "little boy."

Zoeller soon paid a price for saying openly what many others were thinking secretly. K Mart, the discount chain with a big African American clientele, unceremoniously dumped him as the sponsor of a line of golf clothing and equipment, and he abjectly withdrew from the Greater Greensboro Open tournament. "People who know me know I'm a jokester. I just didn't deliver the line well," Zoeller tearfully explained. But his real crime was not, as he and his defenders seem to think, merely a distasteful breach of racial etiquette or an inept attempt at humor. The real crime was falling behind the times. The old black–white stereotypes are out of date, and Zoeller is just the latest casualty of America's failure to come to grips with the perplexing and rapidly evolving significance of racial identity in what is fast becoming the most polyglot society in history.

If current demographic trends persist, midway through the twenty-first century, whites will no longer make up a majority of the U.S. population. Blacks will have been overtaken as the largest minority group by Hispanics. Asians and Pacific Islanders will more than double their number of 9.3 million in 1995 to 19.6 million by 2020. An explosion of interracial, interethnic, and interreligious marriages will swell the ranks of children

JACK E. WHITE *is a national correspondent for* Time *magazine. He is the author of the column* Dividing Line *and has previously served as* Time's *Nation Editor. He has been a senior producer for domestic news for* ABC World News Tonight *and is also the first black journalist to become a columnist for* Time. *In 1995, White was assigned to organize a project to recruit minority journalists for all of Time Inc.'s magazines. White was a Nieman Fellow at Harvard and studied African affairs and American ethnic politics. He is a correspondent for NBC News.*

whose mere existence makes a mockery of age-old racial categories and attitudes. Since 1970, the number of multiracial children has quadrupled to more than two million, according to the Bureau of the Census. The color line once drawn between blacks and whites — or more precisely between whites and nonwhites — is breaking into a polygon of dueling ethnicities, each fighting for its place in the sun.

For many citizens, the "browning of America" means a disorienting plunge into an uncharted sea of identity. Zoeller is far from alone in being confused about the complex tangle of genotypes and phenotypes and cultures that now undercut centuries-old verities about race and race relations in the United States. Like many others, he hasn't got a clue about what to call the growing ranks of people like Woods who inconveniently refuse to be pigeonholed into one of the neat, oversimplified racial classifications used by government agencies — and, let's face it, most people. Are they people of color? Mixed race? Biracial? Whatever they like?

And if we don't know what to call them, how are we supposed to cope   5
with them? Are they a new and distinct category of "real" Americans, due the same respectful recognition — and governmental protections — as more familiar groups? Or should they be lumped into the demeaning catchall category of "minorities" or "other"? How we eventually answer these questions will affect everything from the first census forms of the twenty-first century, which will be issued a mere three years from now, to university admissions policies to the way civil rights laws are enforced. Even more important, it may ultimately transform the way Americans identify themselves and the tribe or tribes they belong to. In one grandiose vision, shared by conservative analyst Douglas Besharov of the American Enterprise Institute and communitarian sociologist Amitai Etzioni[1] of American University, the ambiguous racial identity of mixed-race children may be "the best hope for the future of American race relations," as Besharov puts it. Letting people define themselves as multiracial, Etzioni argues, "has the potential to soften the racial lines that now divide America by rendering them more like economic differences and less like harsh, almost immutable, caste lines." Those who blend many streams of ethnicity within their own bodies, the argument goes, will render race a meaningless concept, providing a biological solution to the problem of racial justice. This idea reflects a deeply pessimistic view of human nature. It suggests that people can get along with each other only if they are all the same, instead of learning to accept and respect differences.

In any event, the way Americans think and talk about race will have to catch up with the new reality. Just how anachronistic our racial vocabulary has become was made clear by Woods in an appearance last week [April 1997] on *The Oprah Winfrey Show*. When asked if it bothered him, the only

---

[1] For more on Etzioni, see page 195.

child of a black American father and a Thai mother, to be called an African American, he replied, "It does. Growing up, I came up with this name: I'm a 'Cablinasian,'" which he explained is a self-crafted acronym that reflects his one-eighth Caucasian, one-fourth black, one-eighth American Indian, one-fourth Thai, and one-fourth Chinese roots with a precision that a racial-classifications expert under South African apartheid would admire. He said that when he was asked to check a box for racial background, he couldn't settle on just one. "I checked off 'African American' and 'Asian.' Those are the two I was raised under, and the only two I know."

Kerboom! A miniracial fire storm erupted. Woods's remarks infuriated many African Americans who hailed his record-setting triumph at the Masters as a symbol of racial progress but see him as a traitor. To them Woods appeared to be running away from being an African American — a condition, they were quick to point out, that he himself had emphasized when he paid tribute to black golf pioneers Teddy Rhoades, Charlie Sifford, and Lee Elder in his graceful victory speech. In a mirror image of Zoeller's constricted views, some blacks saw Woods's assertion of a multiracial identity as a sellout that could touch off an epidemic of "passing." Arthur Fletcher, a black member of the U.S. Commission on Civil Rights, testified at a 1993 congressional hearing devoted to whether a new "multiracial" category should be added to U.S. Census forms that "I can see a whole host of light-skinned black Americans running for the door the minute they have another choice. All of a sudden they have a way of saying, 'In this discriminatory culture of ours, I am something other than black.'"

In their rush to judgment, the fearful apparently never stopped to consider that Woods was not turning his back on any part of his identity but instead was embracing every aspect of it. As he put it, "I'm just who I am, whoever you see in front of you" — and that includes his Asian side. "The influence of Tiger's mother Kultida in his life is very important," declares a family friend. "He goes to the temple with her occasionally. She's a devout Buddhist. He wears a family heirloom Buddha around his neck. He's a hybrid of a lot of things, and that's how he sees himself. He honestly sees himself as a somewhat separate person from the norm — not in terms of talent but in terms of his makeup."

Woods grew up in a suburb of Los Angeles with mostly white friends. But over the years he has made four visits to Thailand, where locals like to say he's "Asian from the eyes up," and he has also embraced the role model of his father Earl, who was the first black to play baseball in the Big Eight (for Kansas State). Now Tiger seems to be saying that if acknowledging the totality of his genetic and cultural makeup is difficult for many Americans, they will just have to try harder.

If history is any guide, a lot of them won't try at all. "It's very hard for other folks to embrace our philosophy without thinking we are being racist or trying to create a new race," says Nancy G. Brown, a Jewish woman

10

who is married to a black man and is a past president of the ten-year-old advocacy group Multiracial Americans of Southern California. "It's hard for people to believe we are just looking for equality and that we are able to live with the concept of duality. Constantly calling Tiger Woods black is a good example of what we are talking about."

Groups like Brown's have lobbied for a multiracial category on government forms, but they also point out that recognizing multiracialism is more than just a matter of "psychic comfort." There are important health issues, for example, such as bone-marrow matching and how such race-specific syndromes as Tay-Sachs manifest themselves and get treated in biracial individuals. And most multiracial Americans have had the experience of being arbitrarily assigned an ethnic identity by a school principal, a caseworker, or an employer that may differ from other family members' — or from one form to the next.

The noxious practice of pigeonholing people in narrow racial classifications is a deeply ingrained American habit that predates independence. It began with a desire to enforce firm distinctions between free citizens and slaves. In 1661, for example, Virginia decreed that the legal status of the mother would determine whether a black child was a slave or free. Three years later, Maryland went a step further, declaring that if either of a child's parents was a slave, the child would also be. The purpose of this law, its authors said, was to deter "divers freeborn English women" from marrying black slaves. But it did nothing to deter white male slave owners from trying to expand their human holdings by impregnating black female slaves.

Eventually, these pioneering efforts at codifying racial distinctions hardened into so-called miscegenation laws, which aimed to preserve the "purity" of the white race by making interracial sex a crime. Though upholding such laws required ever more tortured legal definitions of who was black and who wasn't, sixteen states continued to ban interracial marriages until 1967, when the U.S. Supreme Court struck down such laws. In what was perhaps the most ridiculous example of racial pigeonholing, Louisiana ordained that anyone with a "trace" of black ancestry would be classified as black. Then, in an ostensibly "humane" 1970 reform, it enacted the "one thirty-second rule," by which anyone with a single black great-great-great-great-grandparent and thirty-one white great-great-great-great-grandparents was legally black. That regulation went unchallenged until Susie Guillory Phipps, the wife of a wealthy seafood importer who had always considered herself white, got a look at her birth certificate when applying for a passport and discovered that according to the state, she was black. In 1982 she sued the state, which hired a genealogist to delve into Phipps' ancestry. He dug up, among other ancestors, Phipps' great-great-great-great-grandmother — the black mistress of an Alabama plantation owner back in 1760 — and concluded that Phipps was precisely three thirty-seconds black. The preposterous law stayed on the books until 1983.

For many decades, people on all sides of the color line chafed at these legal restraints on their ability to love and procreate. Even where black–

In the News

Poll Finds Few Support Label of Multiracial

A new Census Bureau study released today has again determined that few people would opt to describe themselves as multiracial if given the chance on the census form. And, with the exception of Asian Americans, few racial groups would see their numbers significantly diminished if such a category were added to the census.

The study, the first specifically conducted among predominantly black, Hispanic, American Indian, Alaskan native, and Asian American populations, found that the number of people who thought of themselves as being of more than one race was relatively small among all groups. For example, among blacks, no more than 2.7 percent and as few as 0.7 percent of those surveyed considered themselves anything but African American, depending on how the question was asked.

Among Asian Americans in the study, as many as 11.8 percent considered themselves as belonging to more than one racial category and as many as 3.1 percent of these respondents would opt to describe themselves as multiracial.

According to the 1990 census, of 1.5 million interracial couples, 31 percent had a spouse who was an Asian American or Pacific Islander. That compares with 22 percent in which one spouse was American Indian or Alaskan native and 14 percent in which one was African American.

Advocates for the inclusion of a multiracial category said they were hopeful that the study's findings might help assuage the concerns of some civil rights organizations that say a multiracial category would diminish the official count of the country's black population.

Lawsuits asserting job discrimination often use statistical evidence from the census to compare the proportion of a particular racial group in a job category with the percentage of that group in a relevant labor pool. Should the use of the multiracial label become in vogue, the number of Asian Americans could be reduced, making it more difficult to win some job discrimination cases.

The study was part of a three-year effort to determine whether the Office of Management and Budget should change the official racial categories that are used in Federal data collection, including the census.

— From the *New York Times,* May 16, 1997.

white marriages were legal, these couples had to seek refuge in more tolerant black neighborhoods and raise their children as African Americans. But
in the past twenty years, as the number of mixed-race marriages has increased dramatically, to more than three million by some estimates, attitudes among all racial groups have evolved. Tracey Mandell, twenty-six, is
an English instructor at Loyola Marymount University. Her partner
Michael Bartley is a black man from Jamaica, and their son Noah is coming up on his first birthday. Mandell remembers last March, when she and
members of her family were taking a get-acquainted tour of the maternity
ward at Santa Monica Hospital. "There were about fifty couples on the
tour," she says. "At least half of them were multiracial. My cousin, who
lives in Minnesota, pointed it out to me. I hadn't even noticed. I think in
L.A. there are so many multiracial people you don't even pay attention.
But it's different when you leave Los Angeles."

It is precisely because they feel under attack and in need of solidarity   15
that many American minorities fear the blurring of racial lines. Congressional black leaders argue that adding a multiracial category to census
forms, which the Office of Management and Budget will be considering
through June of this year, would make it much harder to detect and combat racial discrimination. For example, according to a recent article in
Emerge, the black news magazine, in 1991 some 35,000 people chose
"other" on Home Mortgage Disclosure Act papers meant to track bias in
lending. Allowing people to opt out of traditional race categories, says
Congressional Black Caucus chairwoman Maxine Waters, a California Democrat, "just blurs everything. [People pushing for a multiracial category]
want to be seen for all they are, but I don't think they're making the connection about how it could affect how they're represented or who's being
an advocate for them when they get mistreated." Among the many programs administered on the basis of racial tallies: minority employment on
government contracts, court-ordered school desegregation plans, and protection of minority voting rights. All would have to be retooled, at great
cost, if the categories change.

In the end, however, the impact of multiracialism will be decided not
by the content of a census form but in the hearts of Americans. Tiger
Woods can proclaim his personal diversity, but if most people, like Zoeller,
just see a "boy," it won't make much difference. Multiracial Americans
will not get the right to define themselves as they choose without a fight.

Responding as a Reader

1. In the first paragraph, White writes that Zoeller saw Woods as a
   "Sambo" and a "boy." What is the root of these references? How do
   these labels symbolize prejudice against black people?

2. Why do you think White relates the story of Woods's appearance on *The Oprah Winfrey Show* (para. 6)? What is the irony in the label Woods invented for himself? Does Woods seem to feel differently about that label, now that he's older?

3. Why are some African Americans against creating a "multiracial" category on the census? What do African Americans, as a group, stand to lose from the creation of this category? Is there any way in which they might benefit from it?

Responding as a Writer

1. Most Americans descend from more than one nationality, and all people have felt conflicting loyalties at one time or another. Do you understand how it feels to be both *this* and *that*, when society seems to want you to be one or the other? In an essay, describe a time when you felt pressured to choose between different aspects of yourself. How did you deal with it? How is this situation similar to, and different from, Tiger Woods's situation?

2. Consider Maxine Waters's comment that people who want to be classified as multiracial aren't thinking "about how it could affect how they're represented" (para. 15). In an essay, speculate about the possible effects of adding the designation "multiracial" to the government's racial classification system. Try to come up with both positive and negative possibilities.

3. Read the interview with anthropologist Ann Laurer Stoler on page 326. What do you suppose Stoler would say about the American public's response to Tiger Woods's mixed ethnicity? Try writing an analysis of White's article from Stoler's point of view.

SUNIL GARG

Under My Skin ("Don't Call Me a Person of Color")

[THE NEW YORK TIMES / September 7, 1996]

I am a person of color — or at least that is how people often categorize me. Yet what do they mean by that?

Certainly, I am brown. My parents emigrated from India in the early 1960s, and I have always thought of myself as Indian American. But I have never seriously thought of myself as a brown man or as a person of color.

I was first confronted with the term when I was accepted to the John F. Kennedy School of Government at Harvard University a few years ago. I received an invitation from the school to attend a special orientation for "students of color." Suddenly, the color of my skin qualified me for special attention.

What was the purpose of separating the student body into two groups, whites and those with "color"? Students had not even had the opportunity to introduce themselves on their own terms. By allowing a separate orientation in addition to the general one, the school sent a message to students that color was the one way it had chosen to define the student body.

Other students at the Kennedy School explained to me that the term 5 "people of color" includes those who have historically been alienated or oppressed by the Western white world and whose perspectives and cultures have not been properly heard or appreciated.

Yet this explanation creates a false relationship between color and culture. Having color does not give anyone a particular culture, nor does having color mean that one's culture or perspective differs from that of whites. I, for instance, identify almost exclusively with Western culture.

People can also become disaffected from American culture because of their religious beliefs, their class, sex, or even their weight. Yet the term

Public policy analyst SUNIL GARG *(b. 1966) now serves as assistant to Chicago Mayor Richard Daley and has developed studies on inner-city revitalization and initiatives to combat poverty for the Chapin Hall Center for Children at the University of Chicago. He has contributed articles on the challenges for long-term community change in* Vision: Harvard Students Look Ahead, *and in* Urban Affairs Review. Garg *is currently working on a book about his parents' immigration to the United States while finishing his M.B.A. at the University of Chicago.*

"people of color" implies that only skin color separates and alienates individuals from society.

The term also lumps together the different experiences and challenges facing racial and ethnic groups in the United States. Many times, "people of color" will be used when discussing discrimination, when in fact different groups feel different degrees of discrimination. For instance, a black youth in Harlem has a different experience with racism than does a middle-class Indian American like myself.

By creating this false union among most of the world's population, the term "people of color" also promotes the idea that Western culture and whites are the exercisers of all power and the perpetrators of all evil. One need not be a student of history, however, to understand that racism and oppression are known in almost every nation and that factors beyond color lead men and women to oppress their brethren.

I am not denying the existence of racism in America or the importance   10
of skin color in our society. But my fear is that the term "people of color" creates an environment not where cultural diversity is increased, but where alternative perspectives are reduced to tales of racism and victimization.

As the ethnic and racial composition of our nation changes substantially, we need to understand and relate to one another, regardless of the color of our skin.

We need to find ways to appreciate our country's true diverse perspectives, cultures, knowledge, and experiences. This is a far greater challenge, but a necessary one.

Responding as a Reader

1. Garg tells us that his parents emigrated from India in the early 1960s (para. 2), but that he "identifies almost exclusively with Western culture" (para. 6). What other details does Garg give us to support this argument? What might this imply about the way Garg was raised and what attitudes about race his parents might have brought from India?

2. What does Garg mean when he writes that although his skin is brown, he has never thought of himself "as a brown man" (para. 2)? What is the difference between being brown, as he puts it, and being "a brown man"? Why do you suppose he says brown instead of black?

3. What is the significance, in this piece, of the JFK School of Government?

Responding as a Writer

1. Consider the distinction between "color" and "culture" that Garg makes in paragraph 6. How is Garg defining each? In an essay, exam-

ine how the two areas overlap, and try to identify where they diverge. Do you think both qualities are equally meaningful? Does Garg?

2. Although Garg's classmates told him that the label "people of color" refers to "those who have historically been alienated or oppressed by the Western white world" (para. 5), he points out that people can also be alienated "because of their religious beliefs, their class, sex, or even their weight" (para. 7). In an essay, compare the discrimination that comes with one of these nonracial factors to racial discrimination.

3. Write an extended definition of the term "people of color." What does the term mean and to whom does it apply? What does the term imply? Do you agree with Garg's analysis of the term's implications, in the last third of this piece? Can you suggest a more appropriate term to take its place — or should the practice of grouping all nonwhite people together come to an end? Why or why not?

LYLAH M. ALPHONSE

Race Needs "Other" Option

[THE BOSTON GLOBE / October 5, 1996]

This is me: caramel-colored skin, light-brown eyes, brown-black hair with a few silver threads just to the right of my temple. I have a few freckles, like cocoa powder dusted under my right eye. I'm 5 foot 3, 115 pounds, was a field hockey goalie, still am a fencer.

This is me: I have my mother's Persian features, my father's Haitian coloring, and curly hair that's somewhere in between. When I was little, I desperately wanted my younger brother's graceful hands and my youngest brother's huge green eyes.

LYLAH M. ALPHONSE (b. 1972) is an editor at the Boston Globe. Her articles have appeared in the Princeton Packet, the Post Standard (Syracuse), as well as in the Boston Globe where they have been featured in a column dedicated to writers under thirty. Alphonse currently lives in Brookline, Massachusetts.

This is me: On census forms, aptitude tests, and applications, whenever possible I check the box for "other" after the question about race. When there's no "other" option, I check four boxes: white (German and French on my father's side), Asian (Persian Indian on my mother's side), Native peoples (Arawak Indian on my father's side), and black (an African great-grandfather on my father's side). If the instructions limit me to only one box, I skip it entirely.

One would think that institutions could have come up with a different method of classifying people by now. According to 1990 census information, the number of "other" people has grown to 9.8 million — a 45 percent increase since 1980 — and it's still on the rise. "Mixed" marriages doubled between 1980 and 1992, when 1.2 million were reported. And "mixed" is more than just black and white, though those unions have increased also — by 50 percent, to 250,000, since 1980.

"Mixed" relationships are nothing new, even though the media still sometimes treats them as though they are. My family's been doing it for four generations. Five, if you count me and my blond-haired, blue-eyed boyfriend.

There's a massive push to include a "mixed-race" box on the census for the year 2000, but SATs, GREs, and other aptitude tests can surely rethink their designations more than once a decade. Why isn't there a "mixed" box on all those other forms yet? Or instructions that tell us to "check all that apply?" Or, better still, a new question: "What group do you identify with?"

Natives of Zimbabwe, which used to be Rhodesia, who are descended from that country's British settlers are just as African as natives of Ethiopia, but in the United States we wouldn't call them African Americans. Yet we would give that label to the child of a Caucasian woman and a man from the West Indies, even though the child's connection to the African continent is distant, if it exists at all.

Why do we call mixed marriages "interracial"? Isn't it your ethnicity — the culture in which you are raised — that defines who you are more so than your race? Race is part of the equation, of course, but the color of your skin doesn't necessarily dictate the culture and traditions that surround you while you're growing up.

I grew up in Princeton, N.J. It was very sheltered — kind of like growing up wrapped in cotton, which I think was a good thing. When I left Princeton to go to college in Syracuse, N.Y., I was naive about racial matters. I still think I am. I was surprised by the looks I'd get when I walked around on campus at night with my friends and by the fliers I got year after year inviting me to attend the "African American Orientation" at the student center. I didn't understand why, when I was reporting a stalker, the campus police officer told me that I spoke English very well.

Then I realized that people were looking at my skin and deciding that I was African American; or looking at my features and deciding I was Indian; or listening to me talk and not being able to place me at all.

Q&A

Camille Paglia on the Tyranny of Racial Categories

The following question and answer is taken from the Webzine Salon's "advice column for the culturally disgruntled," where readers get advice on current issues from the outspoken cultural commentator Camille Paglia.

Dear Camille:
Would it not be useful for all levels of government to prohibit describing people, individually and in groups, by racial classifications?
— **Color-blind**

Dear Color-blind:
I completely agree with you. Racial classification was born in the era of slavery, whose fascist assumptions are simply perpetuated in the government's clumsy attempts to repair injustices. As a libertarian, I am suspicious of all government intrusion; however, it is indisputable that without federal action, African Americans would still be waiting for their civil rights in the South, where terror and intimidation were once a fact of life.

For all its noble aims, liberalism was asleep at the wheel in the 1960s, when it failed to see that progressive goals cannot be won by authoritarian means. Federal legislation and surveillance became liberals' quick-fix ticket to utopia now. Busing and affirmative action — neither one carefully considered — were overoptimistically hailed as the solution to racism by white upper-middle-class technocrats, few of whom had to suffer the consequences of their plans.

Court-ordered busing destroyed neighborhood schools and created a firestorm of racial hostility in white working-class neighborhoods that will take several generations to subside. The money and time wasted on shipping students around like color-coded parcels would have been far better spent on massively upgrading the schools themselves. Affirmative action (which has primarily benefited white middle-class women instead of the disadvantaged blacks for whom it was intended) is directly responsible for the present, nightmarishly hyperacute race-consciousness in the United States.

My blood boils every time I see a government form demanding to know my racial identity. It's appalling that biracial citizens are forced to artificially choose one lineage over another. Or that Chicanos, Puerto Ricans, and Portuguese-speaking Brazilians — with their hugely different cultures — are all lumped together as "Hispanics." Or that Italian immigrants and Jewish refugees are consigned to the same homogenized "White" category as the privileged WASP elite who came over on the Mayflower or fanned out from Virginia to create the slave-holding plantation system in the first place.

Racial classification of any kind is poisoned at its source. Genuine affirmative action begins at the bottom, not at the top. Strong, well-funded public education (without the cop-out of vouchers) is the only way to guarantee equal opportunity and job training to citizens of every race and ethnicity. But right now, inner-city schools are in a scandalous state of disorder and neglect. This is a national emergency. Not one more penny of taxpayers' dollars should be spent on foreign aid or peacekeeping junkets by our troops until American public education is restored to its former high standard.

— From "Ask Camille" (*Salon,* March 18, 1997). The current issue of *Salon* can be found at http://www.salon1999.com.

People still try to figure out my background. But now, instead of just looking at me and wondering, they ask me questions like "So, were you born here?" Or "Where in India are your parents from?" And "What do you consider yourself?" A friend's father once asked, point-blank, "What exactly *is* Lylah?" ("Female," my friend replied.)

These are the answers I give them: I was born and raised in Princeton, N.J. My mother is from India. My father is from Haiti. As for what I consider myself . . .

I'm just me.

Responding as a Reader

1. As Alphonse points out, American descendants of British settlers in Zimbabwe are not labeled African American (para. 7). For that matter, American descendants of light-skinned Egyptians probably wouldn't be called African American, either. Why is this? Does this inconsistency grow out of African racial politics, or American racial politics, or the very nature of labeling?

2. What distinction is Alphonse making between ethnicity and race (para. 8)? How does this distinction relate to her main argument?

3. Alphonse tells us that she grew up in Princeton, N.J., which was "kind of like growing up wrapped in cotton" (para. 9). Other multiracial subjects represented in this unit include Tiger Woods, who became fa-

mous after winning the Masters; Sunil Garg, a Harvard graduate; and Eric Liu, self-described "child of the suburbs." What do these writers have in common? How might their backgrounds influence their attitudes about race?

Responding as a Writer

1. Imitate Alphonse's "this is me" paragraphs (1–3). How do you appear to strangers? How does your appearance reflect your ethnic background? What else does your appearance reflect?

2. Jot down the various conflicts that Alphonse raises. Would a mixed-race category on the census address all of these conflicts? Which would it not address? In an essay, try to propose a solution to one of these.

3. Why does Alphonse believe it would be better to ask people "What group do you identify with?" than to ask them to identify the racial group or groups to which they belong (para. 6)? Do you agree with her? Would such a question work well on a simple form? Answer the question for yourself in three different ways; in a sentence, in a paragraph, and in an essay.

DOUGLAS PRESTON

The Lost Man

[THE NEW YORKER / June 16, 1997]

On Sunday, July 28, 1996, in the middle of the afternoon, two college students who were watching a hydroplane race on the Columbia River in Kennewick, Washington decided to take a shortcut along the river's edge. While wading through the shallows, one of them stubbed his toe on a human skull partly buried in the sand. The students picked it up and, thinking it might be that of a murder victim, hid it in some bushes and called the police.

Floyd Johnson, the Benton County coroner, was called in, and the police gave him the skull in a plastic bucket. Late in the afternoon, Johnson called James Chatters, a forensic anthropologist and the owner of a local consulting firm called Applied Paleoscience. "Hey, buddy, I got a skull for you to look at," Johnson said. Chatters had often helped the police identify skeletons and distinguish between those of murder victims and those found in Indian burial sites. He is a small, determined, physically powerful man of forty-eight who used to be a gymnast and a wrestler. His work occasionally involves him in grisly or spectacular murders, where the victims are difficult to identify, such as burnings and dismemberments.

"When I looked down at the skull," Chatters told me, "right off the bat I saw it had a very large number of Caucasoid features" — in particular, a long, narrow braincase, a narrow face, and a slightly projecting upper jaw. But when Chatters took it out of the bucket and laid it on his worktable he began to see some unusual traits. The crowns of the teeth were worn flat, a common characteristic of prehistoric Indian skulls, and

---

DOUGLAS PRESTON (b. 1956) is the author of nonfiction books such as Dinosaurs in the Attic: An Excursion into the American Museum of Natural History *(1986),* Cities of Gold: A Journey Across the American Southwest in Pursuit of Coronado *(1992), and* Talking to the Ground: One Family's Journey on Horseback Across the Sacred Land of the Navajo *(1995). He has written a novel entitled* Jennie *(1994) and has co-written the suspense thrillers* Relic *(1995),* Mount Dragon *(1996), and the sequel to* Relic, Reliquary *(1997). He was a columnist for* Natural History *and has also contributed regularly to periodicals such as* Audubon *and the* New Yorker. *The text reprinted here has been edited; a section dealing with the evidence of stone tools and technology has been omitted.*

the color of the bone indicated that it was fairly old. The skull sutures had fused, indicating that the individual was past middle age. And, for a prehistoric Indian of what was then an advanced age, he or she was in exceptional health; the skull had, for example, all its teeth and no cavities.

As dusk fell, Chatters and Johnson went out to the site to see if they could find the rest of the skeleton. There, working in the dying light, they found more bones, lying around on sand and mud in about two feet of water. The remains were remarkably complete: Only the sternum, a few rib fragments, and some tiny hand, wrist, and foot bones were missing. The bones had evidently fallen out of a bank during recent flooding of the Columbia River.

The following day, Chatters and Johnson spread the bones out in Chatters's laboratory. In forensic anthropology, the first order of business is to determine sex, age, and race. Determining race was particularly important, because if the skeleton turned out to be Native American it fell under a federal law called the Native American Graves Protection and Repatriation Act, or NAGPRA. Passed in 1990, NAGPRA requires the government — in this case, the Army Corps of Engineers, which controls the stretch of the Columbia River where the bones were found — to ascertain if human remains found on federal lands are Native American and, if they are, to "repatriate" them to the appropriate Indian tribe.

Chatters determined that the skeleton was male, Caucasoid, from an individual between forty and fifty-five years old, and about five feet nine inches tall — much taller than most prehistoric Native Americans in the Northwest. In physical anthropology, the term "Caucasoid" does not necessarily mean "white" or "European"; it is a descriptive term applied to certain biological features of a diverse category that includes, for example, some south Asian groups as well as Europeans. (In contrast, the term "Caucasian" is a culturally defined racial category.) "I thought maybe we had an early pioneer or fur trapper," he said. As he was cleaning the pelvis, he noticed a gray object embedded in the bone, which had partly healed and fused around it. He took the bone to be x-rayed, but the object did not show up, meaning that it was not made of metal. So he requested a CAT scan. To his surprise, the scan revealed the object to be part of a willow-leaf-shaped spear point, which had been thrust into the bone and broken off. It strongly resembled a Cascade projectile point — an Archaic Indian style in wide use from around nine thousand to forty-five hundred years ago.

The Army Corps of Engineers asked Chatters to get a second opinion. He put the skeleton into his car and drove it a hundred miles to Ellensburg, Washington, where an anthropologist named Catherine J. MacMillan ran a forensic consulting business called the Bone-Apart Agency. "He didn't say anything," MacMillan told me. "I examined the bones, and I said 'Male, Caucasian.' He said 'Are you sure?' and I said 'Yeah.' And then he handed me the pelvis and showed me the ancient point embedded in it, and he said, 'What do you think now?' And I said, 'That's extremely interesting, but it still looks Caucasian to me.'" In her report to the Benton County coroner's office, she wrote that in her opinion the skeleton was "Caucasian male."

Toward the end of the week, Chatters told Floyd Johnson and the Army Corps of Engineers that he thought they needed to get a radiocarbon date on Kennewick Man. The two parties agreed, so Chatters sent the left fifth metacarpal bone — a tiny bone in the hand — to the University of California at Riverside.

On Friday, August 23rd, Jim Chatters received a telephone call from the radiocarbon lab. The bone was between ninety-three hundred and ninety-six hundred years old. He was astounded. "It was just a phone call," he said. "I thought, maybe there's been a mistake. I had to see the report with my own eyes." The report came on Monday, in the form of a fax. "I got very nervous then," Chatters said. He knew that, because of their age, the bones on his worktable had to be one of the most important archeological finds of the decade. "It was just a tremendous responsibility." The following Tuesday, the coroner's office issued a press release on the find, and it was reported in the Seattle *Times* and other local papers.

Chatters called in a third physical anthropologist, Grover S. Krantz, a professor at Washington State University. Krantz looked at the bones on Friday, August 30th. His report noted some characteristics common to both Europeans and Plains Indians but concluded that "this skeleton cannot be racially or culturally associated with any existing American Indian group." He also wrote, "The Native Repatriation Act has no more applicability to this skeleton than it would if an early Chinese expedition had left one of its members there."

Fifteen minutes after Krantz finished looking at the bones, Chatters received a call from Johnson. Apologetically, the coroner said, "I'm going to have to come over and get the bones." The Army Corps of Engineers had demanded that all study of the bones cease and had required him to put the skeleton in the county sheriff's evidence locker. On the basis of the carbon date, the Corps had evidently decided that the skeleton was Native American and that it fell under NAGPRA.

"When I heard this, I panicked," Chatters said. "I was the only one who'd recorded any information on it. There were all these things I should have done. I didn't even have photographs of the postcranial skeleton. I thought, am I going to be the last scientist to see these bones?"

On September 9th, the Umatilla Indians, leading a coalition of five tribes and bands of the Columbia River basin, formally claimed the skeleton under NAGPRA, and the Corps quickly made a preliminary decision to "repatriate" it. The Umatilla Indian Reservation lies just over the border, in northeastern Oregon, and the other tribes live in Washington and Idaho; all consider the Kennewick area part of their traditional territories. The Umatillas announced that they were going to bury the skeleton in a secret site, where it would never again be available to science.

Three weeks later, the *New York Times* picked up the story, and from there it went to *Time* and on around the world. Television crews from as far away as France and Korea descended on Kennewick. The Corps received more than a dozen other claims for the skeleton, including one from a group known as the Asatru Folk Assembly, the California-based followers of an Old Norse religion, who wanted the bones for their own religious purposes.

On September 2nd, the Corps had directed that the bones be placed in   15 a secure vault at the Pacific Northwest National Laboratory in Richland, Washington. Nobody outside of the Corps has seen them since. They are now at the center of a legal controversy that will likely determine the course of American archeology.

What was a Caucasoid man doing in the New World more than ninety-three centuries ago? In the reams of press reports last fall, that question never seemed to be dealt with. I called up Douglas Owsley, who is the Division Head for Physical Anthropology at the National Museum of Natural History, Smithsonian Institution, in Washington, D.C. and an expert on Paleo-American remains. I asked him how many well-preserved skeletons that old had been found in North America.

He replied, "Including Kennewick, about seven."

Then I asked if any others had Caucasoid features, and there was a silence that gave me the sense that I was venturing onto controversial ground.

He guardedly replied, "Yes."

"How many?"   20

"Well," he said, "in varying degrees, all of them."

Kennewick Man's bones are part of a growing quantity of evidence that the earliest inhabitants of the New World may have been a Caucasoid people. Other, tentative evidence suggests that these people may have originally come from Europe. The new evidence is fragmentary, contradictory, and controversial. Critical research remains to be done, and many studies are still unpublished. At the least, the new evidence calls into question the standard Beringian Walk theory, which holds that the first human beings to reach the New World were Asians of Mongoloid stock, who crossed from Siberia to Alaska over a land bridge. The new evidence involves three basic questions. Who were the original Americans? Where did they come from? And what happened to them?

"You're dealing with such a black hole," Owsley told me. "It's hard to draw any firm conclusions from such a small sample of skeletons, and there is more than one group represented. That's why Kennewick is so important."

Kennewick man made his appearance at the dawn of a new age in physical anthropology. Scientists are now able to extract traces of organic material from a person's bone and perform a succession of powerful biochemical assays that can reveal an astonishing amount of information about the person. In March, for example, scientists at Oxford University announced that they had compared DNA extracted from the molar cavity of a nine-thousand-year-old skeleton known as Cheddar Man to DNA collected from fifteen pupils and five adults from old families in the village of Cheddar, in Somersetshire. They had established a blood tie between Cheddar Man and a schoolteacher who lived just half a mile from the cave where the bones were found.

In the few weeks that Kennewick Man was in the hands of scientists, they discovered a great deal about him. Isotopic-carbon studies of the bones indicate that he had a diet high in marine food — that he may have been a fisherman who ate a lot of salmon. He seems to have been a tall, good-looking man, slender and well proportioned. (Studies have shown that "handsomeness" is largely the result of symmetrical features and good health, both of which Kennewick Man had.) Archeological finds of similar age in the area suggest that he was part of a small band of people who moved about, hunting, fishing, and gathering wild plants. He may have lived in a simple sewn tent or mat hut that could be disassembled and carried. Some nearby sites contain large numbers of fine bone needles, indicating that a lot of delicate sewing was going on: Kennewick Man may have worn tailored clothing. For a person at that time to live so long in relatively good health indicates that he was clever or lucky, or both, or had family and close friends around him.

He appears to have perished from recurring infections caused by the stone point in his hip. Because of the way his bones were found, and the layer of soil from which they presumably emerged, it may be that he was not deliberately buried but died near the river and was swept away and covered up in a flood. He may have perished alone on a fishing trip, far from his family.

Chatters made a cast of the skull before the skeleton was taken from his office. In the months since, he has been examining it to figure out how Kennewick Man may have looked. He plans to work with physical anthropologists and a forensic sculptor to make a facial reconstruction. "On the physical characteristics alone, he could fit on the streets of Stockholm without causing any kind of notice," Chatters told me. "Or on the streets of Jerusalem or New Delhi, for that matter. I've been looking around for someone who matches this Kennewick gentleman, looking for weeks and weeks at people on the street, thinking, This one's got a little bit here, that one a little bit there. And then, one evening, I turned on the TV, and there was Patrick Stewart" — Captain Picard, of *Star Trek* — "and I said, 'My God, there he is! Kennewick Man!'"

In September, following the requirements of NAGPRA, the Corps advertised in a local paper its intention of repatriating the skeleton secreted in the laboratory vault. The law mandated a thirty-day waiting period after the advertisements before the Corps could give a skeleton to a tribe.

Physical anthropologists and archeologists around the country were horrified by the seizure of the skeleton. They protested that it was not possible to demonstrate a relationship between nine-thousand-year-old remains and any modern tribe of the area. "Those tribes are relatively new," says Dennis Stanford, the chairman of the Department of Anthropology at the Smithsonian's National Museum of Natural History. "They pushed out other tribes that were there." Both Owsley and Richard L. Jantz, a biological anthropologist at the University of Tennessee, wrote letters to the Army Corps of Engineers in late September saying that the loss to science would be incalculable if Kennewick Man were to be reburied before being studied. They received no response. Robson Bonnichsen, the director of the Center for the Study of the First Americans, at Oregon State University, also wrote to the Corps and received no reply. Three representatives and a United States senator from the state of Washington got in touch with the Corps, pleading that it allow the skeleton to be studied before reburial or, at least, refrain from repatriating the skeleton until Congress could take up the issue. The Corps rebuffed them.

The Umatillas themselves issued a statement, which was written by Armand Minthorn [see following selection], a tribal religious leader. Minthorn, a small, well-spoken young man with long braids, is a member of a new generation of Native American activists, who see religious fundamentalism — in this case, the Washat religion — as a road back to Native American traditions and values:

> Our elders have taught us that once a body goes into the ground, it is meant to stay there until the end of time. . . . If this individual is truly over 9,000 years old, that only substantiates our belief that he is Native American. From our oral histories, we know that our people have been part of this land since the beginning of time. We do not believe that our people migrated here from another continent, as the scientists do. . . . Scientists believe that because the individual's head measurement does not match ours, he is not Native American. Our elders have told us that Indian people did not always look the way we look today. Some scientists say that if this individual is not studied further, we, as Indians, will be destroying evidence of our history. We already know our history. It is passed on to us through our elders and through our religious practices.

Despite the mounting protests, the Corps refused to reconsider its decision to ban scientific study of the Kennewick skeleton. As the thirty-day waiting period came to a close, anthropologists around the country panicked. Just a week before it ended, on October 23rd, a group of eight anthropologists filed suit against the Corps. The plaintiffs included Douglas Owsley, Robson Bonnichsen, and also Dennis Stanford. Stanford, one of the country's top Paleo-Indian experts, is a formidable opponent. While attending graduate school in New Mexico, he roped in local rodeos and helped support his family by leasing an alfalfa farm. There's still a kind of laconic, frontier toughness about him. "Kennewick Man has the potential to change the way we view the entire peopling of the Americas," he said to me. "We had to act. Otherwise, I might as well retire."

The eight are pursuing the suit as individuals. Their academic institutions are reluctant to get involved in a lawsuit as controversial as this, particularly at a time when most of them are negotiating with tribes over their own collections.

In the suit, the scientists have argued that Kennewick Man may not meet the NAGPRA definition of "Native American" as being "of, or relating to, a tribe, people, or culture that is indigenous to the United States." The judge trying the case has asked both sides to be prepared to define the word "indigenous" as it is used in NAGPRA. This will be an interesting exercise, since no human beings are indigenous to the New World: We are all immigrants.

The scientists have also argued that the Corps had had no evidence to support its claim that the skeleton had a connection to the Umatillas. Alan Schneider, the scientists' attorney, says, "Our analysis of NAGPRA is that first you have to make a determination if the human remains are Native American. And then you get to the question of cultural affiliation. The Army Corps assumed that anyone who died in the continental United States prior to a certain date is automatically Native American."

The NAGPRA law appears to support the scientists' point of view. It says that when there are no known lineal descendants, "cultural affiliation" should be determined using "geographical, kinship, biological, archeological, anthropological, linguistic, folkloric, oral traditional, historical," or other "relevant information or expert opinion" before human remains are repatriated. In other words, human remains must often be studied before anyone can say whom they are related to.

The Corps, represented by the Justice Department, has refused to comment on most aspects of the case. "It's really as if the government didn't want to know the truth about Kennewick Man," Alan Schneider told me in late April. "It seems clear that the government will *never* allow this skeleton to be studied, for any reason, unless it is forced to by the courts."

Preliminary oral arguments in the case were heard on June 2nd in the United States District Court for the District of Oregon. The scientists asked for immediate access to study the bones, and the Corps asked for summary judgment. Judge John Jelderks denied both motions and said that he would have a list of questions for the Corps that it is to answer within a reasonable time. With the likelihood of appeals, the case could last a couple of years longer and could ultimately go to the Supreme Court.

Schneider was not surprised that the Corps had sided with the Indians. "It constantly has a variety of issues it has to negotiate with Native American tribes," he told me, and he specified, among others, land issues, water rights, dams, salmon fishing, hydroelectric projects, and toxic-waste dumps. The Corps apparently decided, Schneider speculated, that in this case its political interests would be better served by supporting the tribes than by supporting a disgruntled group of anthropologists with no institutional backing, no money, and no political power. There are large constituencies for the Indians' point of view: fundamentalist Christians and liberal supporters of Indian rights. Fundamentalists of all varieties tend to object to scientific research into the origins of humankind, because the results usually contradict their various creation myths. A novel coalition of conservative Christians and liberal activists was important in getting NAGPRA through Congress.

Kennewick Man, early as he is, was not one of the first Americans. But he could be their descendant. There is evidence that those mysterious first Americans were a Caucasoid people. They may have come from Europe and may be connected to the Clovis people of America. Kennewick may provide evidence of a connection between the Old World and the New.

The Clovis mammoth hunters were the earliest widespread culture that we know of in the Americas. They appeared abruptly, seemingly out of nowhere, all over North and South America about eleven thousand five hundred years ago — two thousand years before Kennewick. (They were called Clovis after a town in New Mexico near an early site — a campground beside an ancient spring that is littered with projectile points, tools, and the remains of fires.) We have only a few fragments of human bone from the Clovis people and their immediate descendants, the Folsom, and these remains are so damaged that nothing can be learned from them at present.

The oldest bones that scientists have been able to study are the less than a dozen human remains that are contemporaneous with Kennewick. They date from between eight thousand and nearly eleven thousand years ago — the transition period between the Paleo-Indian and the Archaic Indian traditions. Most of the skeletons have been uncovered accidentally in recent years, primarily because of the building boom in the west. (Bones do not survive well in the east: The soil is too wet and acidic.) Some other ancient skeletons, though, have been discovered gathering dust in museum drawers. Among these oldest remains are the Spirit Cave mummy and Wizard's Beach Willie, both from Nevada; the Hourglass Cave and Gordon's Creek skeletons, from Colorado; the Buhl Burial, from Idaho; and remains from Texas, California, and Minnesota.

Douglas Owsley and Richard Jantz made a special study of several of these ancient remains. The best-preserved specimen they looked at was a partial mummy from Spirit Cave, Nevada, which is more than nine thousand years old. Owsley and Jantz compared the Spirit Cave skull with thirty-four population samples from around the world, including ten Native American groups. In an as yet unpublished letter to the Nevada State Museum, they concluded that the Spirit Cave skull was "very different" from any historic-period Native American groups. They wrote, "In terms of its closest classification, it does have a 'European' or 'Archaic Caucasoid' look, because morphometrically it is most similar to the Ainu from Japan and a Medieval period Norse population." Additional early skeletons that they and others have looked at also show Caucasoid-like traits that, in varying degrees, resemble Kennewick Man's. Among these early skeletons, there are no close resemblances to modern Native Americans.

But, even though the skeletons do look Caucasoid, other evidence indicates that the concept of "race" may not be applicable to human beings of ten or fifteen thousand years ago. Recent studies have discovered that all Eurasians may have looked Caucasoid-like in varying degrees. In addition, some researchers believe that the Caucasoid type first emerged in Western Asia or the Middle East rather than in Europe. The racial differences we see today may be a late (and trivial) development in human evolution. If this is the case, then Kennewick may indeed be a direct ancestor of today's Native Americans — an idea that some preliminary DNA and dental studies seem to support.

Owsley and other physical anthropologists who have studied the skulls of the earliest Americans say that the living population they most closely match is the mysterious Ainu, the aboriginal inhabitants of the Japanese islands. Called the Hairy People by the Japanese, the Ainu are considered by some researchers to be a Causasoid group who, before mixing with the Japanese, in the late nineteenth and twentieth centuries, had European faces, wavy hair, thick beards, and a European-type distribution of body hair. Early travellers reported that some also had blue eyes. Linguists have not been able to connect the Ainu language with any other on earth. The American Museum of Natural History, in New York, has a collection of nineteenth-century photographs of pure-blood Ainu, which I have examined: They stare from the glass plates like fierce, black-bearded Norwegians.

Historically, the Ainu have been the "Indians" of Japan. After the ancestors of the Japanese migrated from the mainland a couple of thousand years ago, they fought the Ainu and pushed them into the northernmost islands of the Japanese archipelago. The Japanese later discriminated against the Ainu, forcing their children to attend Japanese schools and suppressing their religion and their language. Today, most Ainu have lost their language and many of their distinct physical characteristics, although there has recently been a movement among them to recapture their traditions, their religion, their language, and their songs. Like the American Indians, the Ainu suffer high rates of alcoholism. The final irony is that the Ainu, like the American Indians for Americans, have become a popular Japanese tourist attraction. Many Ainu now make a living doing traditional dances and selling handicrafts to Japanese tourists. The Japanese are as fascinated

45

by the Ainu as we are by the Indians. The stories are mirror images of each other, with only the races changed.

If the Ainu are a remnant population of those people who crossed into America thirteen or more millennia ago, then they are right where one might expect to find them, in the extreme eastern part of Asia. Stanford says, "That racial type goes all the way to Europe, and I suspect that originally they were the same racial group at both ends. At that point in time, this racial diversification hadn't developed. They could have come into the New World from two directions at once, east and west."

There is a suspicion among anthropologists that some of the people behind the effort to rebury Kennewick and other ancient skeletons are afraid that the bones could show that the earliest Americans were Caucasoid. I asked Armand Minthorn about this. "We're not afraid of the truth," he said calmly. "We already know our truth. We're not telling the scientists what *their* truth is."

The Umatillas were infuriated by the research that Chatters did on the skeleton before it was seized by the Corps. "Scientists have dug up and studied Native Americans for decades," Minthorn wrote. "We view this practice as desecration of the body and a violation of our most deeply held religious beliefs." Chatters told me that he had received "vitriolic" and "abusive" telephone calls from tribe members, accusing him of illegalities and racism. (The latter was an odd charge, since Chatters's wife is of Native American descent.) A client of his, he said, received an unsigned letter from one of the tribes, telling the client not to work with Chatters anymore. "They're going to ruin my livelihood," the forensic consultant said.

In a larger sense, the anger of the Umatillas and other Native American tribes is understandable, and even justified. If you look into the acquisition records of most large, old natural-history museums, you will see a history of unethical, and even grisly, collecting practices. Fresh graves were dug up and looted, sometimes in the dead of night. "It is most unpleasant to steal bones from a grave," the eminent anthropologist Franz Boas[1] wrote in his diary just around the turn of the century, "but what is the use, someone has to do it." Indian skulls were bought and sold among collectors like arrowheads and pots. Skeletons were exhibited with no regard for tribal sensitivities. During the Indian wars, warriors who had been killed on the battlefield were sometimes decapitated by Army doctors so that scientists back in the East could study their heads. The American Museum of Natural History "collected" six live Inuits in Greenland and brought them to New York to study; four of them died of respiratory diseases, whereupon the

---

[1]The German-born Franz Boas (1858–1942) was a prominent anthropologist at Columbia University and author of many ethnological studies of Native Americans and of books such as *The Mind of Primitive Man* (1911).

museum macerated their corpses and installed the bones in its collection. When I worked at the museum, in the 1980s, entire hallways were lined with glass cases containing Indian bones and mummified body parts — a small fraction of the museum's collection, which includes an estimated twenty thousand or more human remains, of all races. Before NAGPRA, the Smithsonian had some thirty-five thousand sets of human remains in storage; around eighteen thousand of them were Native American.

Now angry Native Americans, armed with NAGPRA and various state   50 reburial laws, are emptying such museums of bones and grave goods. Although most anthropologists agree that burials identified with particular tribes should be returned, many have been horrified to discover that some tribes are trying to get everything — even skeletons and priceless funerary objects that are thousands of years old.

An amendment that was introduced in Congress last January would tighten NAGPRA further. The amended law could have the effect of hindering much archeology in the United States involving human remains and add to the cost of construction projects that inadvertently uncover human bones. (Or perhaps the law would merely guarantee that such remains would be quietly destroyed.)

Native Americans have already claimed and reburied two of the earliest skeletons, the Buhl Burial and the Hourglass Cave skeleton, both of which apparently had some Caucasoid characteristics. The loss of the Buhl Burial was particularly significant to anthropologists, because it was more than ten thousand years old — a thousand years older than Kennewick Man — and had been found buried with its grave goods. The skeleton, of a woman between eighteen and twenty years old, received, in the opinion of some anthropologists, inadequate study before it was turned over to the Shoshone-Bannock tribe. The Northern Paiute have asked that the Spirit Cave mummy be reburied. If these early skeletons are all put back in the ground, anthropologists say, much of the history of the peopling of the Americas will be lost.

When Darwin proposed his theory of natural selection, it was seized upon and distorted by economists, social engineers, and politicians, particularly in England: They used it to justify all sorts of vicious social and economic policies. The scientific argument about the original peopling of the Americas threatens to be distorted in a similar way. Some tabloids and radio talk shows have referred to Kennewick as a "white man" and have suggested that his discovery changes everything with respect to the rights of Native Americans in this country. James Chatters said to me, "There are some less racially enlightened folks in the neighborhood who are saying, 'Hey, our ancestors were here first, so we don't owe the Indians anything.' "

This is clearly racist nonsense: These new theories cannot erase or negate the existing history of genocide, broken treaties, and repression. But

Document

Human Remains Should Be Reburied

The following position paper was written by Armand Minthorn, Board of Trustees member and religious leader with the Confederated Tribes of the Umatilla Indian Reservation. On behalf of the Confederated Tribes, Minthorn claims the 9,000-year-old man as Native American, along with the right to rebury him.

This summer a human burial, believed to be about 9,000 years old, was discovered near Columbia Park in Kennewick, Washington. Scientists and others want to study this individual. They believe that he should be further desecrated for the sake of science and for their own personal gain. The people of my tribe, and four other affected tribes, strongly believe that the individual must be reburied as soon as possible.

My tribe has ties to this individual because he was uncovered in our traditional homeland — a homeland where we still retain fishing, hunting, gathering, and other rights under our 1855 Treaty with the U.S. Government.

Like any inadvertent discovery of ancestral human remains, this is a very sensitive issue for me and my tribe. Our religious beliefs, culture, and our adopted policies and procedures tell us that this individual must be reburied as soon as possible. Our elders have taught us that once a body goes into the ground, it is meant to stay there until the end of time.

It is not our practice to publicize these types of discoveries, both for the protection of the individual as well as sensitivity to our tribal members. In this case, however, we must take the opportunity this incident has created to help educate the general public about the laws governing these discoveries and what these discoveries mean to us, as Indians. We also hope to give people a better understanding of why this is such a sensitive issue.

The *Native American Graves Protection and Repatriation Act* (NAGPRA) and Archaeological Resources Protection Act (ARPA), as well as other federal and state laws, are in place to prevent the destruction of, and to protect, human burials and cultural resources. The laws also say that authorities must notify affected tribes and consult with tribal officials on how to handle the discovery, as well as protection and preservation. Out tribe was not properly notified and if we had been, this difficult situation might have been avoided.

Under NAGPRA, tribes are allowed to file a claim to have ancestral human remains reburied. My tribe has filed a claim for this individual, and when it is approved, we will rebury him and put him back to rest.

In filing this claim, we have the support of the four other tribes who potentially have ties to this individual. These tribes are the Yakama, Nez

Perce, Colville, and Wanapum. We share the same religious belief, traditional practices, as well as oral histories that go back 10,000 years.

If this individual is truly over 9,000 years old, that only substantiates our belief that he is Native American. From our oral histories, we know that our people have been part of this land since the beginning of time. We do not believe that our people migrated here from another continent, as the scientists do.

We also do not agree with the notion that this individual is Caucasian. Scientists say that because the individual's head measurement does not match ours, he is not Native American. We believe that humans and animals change over time to adapt to their environment. And, our elders have told us that Indian people did not always look the way we look today.

Some scientists say that if this individual is not studied further, we, as Indians, will be destroying evidence of our own history. We already know our history. It is passed on to us through our elders and through our religious practices.

Scientists have dug up and studied Native Americans for decades. We view this practice as desecration of the body and a violation of our most deeply held religious beliefs. Today thousands of native human remains sit on the shelves of museums and institutions, waiting for the day when they can return to the earth, and waiting for the day that scientists and others pay them the respect they are due.

Our tribal policies and procedures, and our own religious beliefs, prohibit scientific testing on human remains. Our beliefs and policies also tell us that this individual must be reburied as soon as possible.

Our religion and our elders have taught us that we have an inherent responsibility to care for those who are no longer with us. We have a responsibility to protect all human burials, regardless of race. We are taught to treat them all with the same respect.

Many people are asking if there's any chance for a compromise in this issue. We remind them that not only has this individual already been compromised, but our religious beliefs have once again been compromised. Many non-Indians are looking for a compromise — a compromise that fits their desires.

And, many non-Indians are trying to bend the laws to fit their desires. NAGPRA was passed by Congress in 1990 to protect Native American burials and set in place a mechanism to have human remains and artifacts returned to the tribes.

We are trying to ensure that the federal government lives up to its own laws, as well as honoring our policies, procedures, and religious beliefs. We understand that non-Indian cultures have different values and be-

continued on next page

continued from previous page

liefs than us, but I ask the American people to please understand our stance on this issue. We are not trying to be troublemakers, we are doing what our elders have taught us — to respect people, while they're with us and after they've become part of the earth.

> — From Web site containing history, culture, tribal issues, and news of the Confederated Tribes of the Umatilla Indian Reservation, which can be found at http://www.ucinet.com/~umatribe/main.html#menu.

it does raise an interesting question: If the original inhabitants of the New World were Europeans who were pushed out by Indians, would it change the Indians' position in the great moral landscape?

"No," Stanford said in reply to this question. "Whose ancestors are the people who were pushed out? And who did the pushing? The answer is that we're all the descendants of those folks. If you go back far enough, eventually we all have a common ancestor — *we're all the same*. When the story is finally written, the peopling of the Americas will turn out to be far more complicated than anyone imagined. There have been a lot of people who came here, at many different times. Some stayed and some left, some made it and some didn't, some got pushed out and some did the pushing. It's the history of humankind: The tough guy gets the ground."

Chatters put it another way. "We didn't go digging for this man. He fell out — he was actually a volunteer. I think it would be wrong to stick him back in the ground without waiting to hear the story he has to tell. We need to look at things as human beings, not as one race or another. The message this man brings to us is one of unification: There may be some commonality in our past that will bring us together."

Responding as a Reader

1. Could the anthropologists have other than objective, scientific interest in the human remains? Why would it be more advantageous for them to identify the skeleton as Caucasoid? How does self-interest also motivate all the other parties in the dispute, including the government?

2. Whose side do you think the author is on, if any? Can you point to any features of his writing (Choice of detail? Quotations? Word selection?) that indicate his position? Do you find him neutral?

3. Read the full text of Armand Minthorn's paper (p. 356). Does Minthorn's argument cause you to see the issue differently? Why or why not?

Responding as a Writer

1. Is a compromise possible — say, one that would allow the scientists to study the bones for a specified period of time and then have them turned over to the tribes for reburial? What interferes with such a compromise? In an essay, suggest a way of resolving the issue in which each group obtains some satisfaction. Make sure you indicate the reasons why you believe your terms would be mutually acceptable.

2. Consider how Preston tells his story — the article's pacing and the order in which he gives readers the details. Does this style remind you of any fictional form? What is the advantage of telling a story in this way? Go back to an essay that you wrote earlier in the semester and try rewriting it in this form. What does the essay gain? What does it lose?

3. Analyze Alan Schneider's comment, "It's really as if the government didn't want to know the truth about Kennewick Man" (para. 36). Why would the government want to keep this discovery quiet? Using evidence from the essay, argue that this is or is not the story of a government coverup.

ERIC LIU

The Unbearable Being of Whiteness

[SLATE / June 13, 1997]

What would it be like to be white?

It's a question I've never really considered, but pondering it now, I find the answer unsettling: It wouldn't be all that different. Yes, of course it would mean unstitching from my soul that thread of thoughts and habits one might call "Chinese" — and who knows just how unraveled I'd be-

---

ERIC LIU (b. 1968) is founder and editor of The Next Progressive, *a Washington, D.C.-based journal produced by writers in their twenties. Liu has served as a speech writer for President Clinton and currently attends Harvard Law School.*

come without that thread? But as far as how the world would treat me — ignoring me or not, abusing me or not, redeeming me or not — I can't say I would be much better off for being white.

For although I am Chinese American and thus a "person of color," I am also this: child of the suburbs, product of mostly white schools, junior officer of the overclass, skeptic of hard-core multiculturalism, friendly with many minorities but friends with few, never once the victim of blatant discrimination, husband now of a woman named Haymon. I am, by the reasoning of racial ascription, already quite white.

What that says about me I'll leave for those who know me to assess. What it says about our idea of whiteness, though, is for all of us to contemplate. In the cosmology of race, whiteness is something like a black hole — a crushingly dense complex of myth and rumor that pulls us, invisibly and irresistibly, into its hold. We move according to its properties, yet we know not why we move.

But whiteness studies have also been mightily, and deliberately, misun-   5 derstood. It is not the self-adulation of an already dominant class or a crusade by the oppressed to demonize The Man. It is simply an attempt to identify the ways that whites remain blind to, and blinded by, an unspoken faith in race — and to expose the means by which white skin and "white attitudes" still confer social advantage.

It seems to me that we could all use some of that schooling. For it is whiteness — not blackness — that is the original sin of identity politics. And it falls on all our shoulders — not just colored ones — to rid the country of its viral color consciousness. What would it be like to be white? One day, perhaps, there will be a better way to measure the blessings and burdens of American life.

But alas, we've hit a sure conversation-stopper now: the question of white power. No one, really, wants to talk about that. Perhaps it's because "white power" sounds too much like an accusation. Perhaps it's because "white power" brings to mind those neo-Nazi supremacists, those hateful extremists who, most white folks will say, "aren't like us" — and who, truly, *aren't* like most white folks. But whatever the reason, we have an almost allergic reaction to any serious consideration of the ideology of privilege we call "whiteness."

How else to explain the reaction to "whiteness studies," an academic discipline that has emerged in the last few years? Sure, whiteness studies, which might include everything from the history of Irish laborers to the folkways of suburban mallrats, is open to abuse and therefore to ridicule. It appears, at a glance, like ethnic studies gone fatuously awry — and some of it is indeed loopy.

The spectacle of the Left-Behind White tells us again that many whites who complain about black obsessions with blackness are themselves obsessed with whiteness. What they are obsessed with in this case, though, is the cultural emptiness of whiteness. In a cruel reversal, it is the white guy, with no tradition to call his own, no history but one laden with guilt and apology, who is "truly disadvantaged."

Just desserts, you might say, for those minority multiculturalists who pretended that equality of cultural recognition was as good as equality of actual power: Now whites want to play the same game, recounting to us the sufferings of the Celts, the indignities borne by the Welsh, yet still retaining the power premium they've long enjoyed — as whites.   10

The second variety of white race-consciousness — whiteness-as-burden — is no less tangled up in hypocrisy. But while whiteness-as-blessing expresses the arrogance of privilege, whiteness-as-burden reveals the willful ignorance of privilege. Nowhere is that more clear than in the periodic appearance of what I call the Left-Behind White.

In the '70s, the Left-Behind White appeared in the form of the "unmeltable ethnic," that long-assimilated Italian or Irish or Polish American who, in the wake of the Black Power movement, felt it necessary to dust off and revive the ways of the Old Country. He re-materialized in the late '80s, this time in the guise of the Angry White Male, the forgotten victim of minority preferences and "reverse discrimination." A decade later, he has entered the scene again, dressed now in the finery of the Euro-American, a pitiable white who can't find his heritage but doesn't want to get left behind in the parade of affirming identities.

It used to be, of course, that "becoming white" was an option open only to European immigrants. But over the last generation, high-achieving Asian Americans have been anointed "honorary" whites, usually so ordained by conservatives wary of black militancy. By striving and succeeding without complaint, Asian immigrants have become, in the words of Irving Kristol,[1] "just another 'European' ethnic group."

Ah, I see: Some are born white, others achieve whiteness, still others have whiteness thrust upon them. This is sheer narcissism, the notion that "making it" means whitening. And when it comes from the white right, it's narcissism in the service of hypocrisy. For some of the very guardians of America's alabaster template — Pat Buchanan, Peter Brimelow,[2] and their ilk — are the same ideologues who reflexively rebuke blacks for any show of ethnocentrism.

White race consciousness manifests itself in two forms: as blessing and as burden. In both cases, it exists mainly by negation; it nourishes itself upon all that it excludes. Thus it is that whites don't generally think of themselves as having a race at all. To be white, really, is *not* to be many   15

---

[1]The prominent neoconservative intellectual Irving Kristol is publisher of an influential periodical, *The National Interest.*

[2]A former speech writer, the conservative columnist Pat Buchanan ran for president in 1996; Peter Brimelow is senior editor at *Forbes* magazine and *National Review,* and is the author of *Alien Nation: Common Sense About America's Immigration Disaster* (1995).

things — most notably, black — and to derive both security and standing from the absence of the stigma.

It is precisely this sense of "anti-race" — this affectation of colorless neutrality — that has allowed whiteness to insinuate itself as the social norm. This is whiteness-as-blessing: the knowledge whites have that in law, in literature, in politics, and in a hundred other realms, "a regular person" is, by default, a white person. Our vocabulary for assimilation makes the point. How do we describe the method by which nonwhites enter the mainstream and climb the class ladder? We say, or at least think, that they're "becoming white."

Consider, for instance, the now-standard formulation that *if blacks would only surrender their race consciousness, we could all ascend to a color-blind nirvana.* You hear this line from plenty of well-meaning whites. But you also find it embedded in nasty right-wing polemics against diversity and affirmative action. The idea is simple: Given "the end of racism," or at least the end of "irrational" discrimination, minority bellyaching only upsets what would otherwise be the proper social equilibrium.

I'm the first to concede the awful, balkanizing folly of many left-liberals on race. And to be sure, we've stockpiled so much "difference" over the years that a round of identity disarmament would be welcome. But we should first acknowledge that it is *white* race consciousness — never quite named as such in our popular discourse — that begets the compensatory identities of nonwhite Americans. And it is *whiteness* that must first be revealed and surrendered before we can ever hope to transcend race.

Responding as a Reader

1. Why does Liu describe himself as "already quite white" (para. 3)? How is he defining whiteness? Why does Liu distinguish between what this comment says about him and what it says about our culture?

2. What is "balkanizing" (para. 18)? What do the views of "left-liberals" have in common with the situation in the Balkans after the break up of the Soviet Union?

3. Why does Liu call whiteness "the original sin of identity politics" (para. 6)? What is identity politics, and what is original sin? Analyze this metaphor and evaluate its effectiveness.

Responding as a Writer

1. In his opening paragraph, Liu asks "What would it be like to be white?" Try to imagine what it would be like to belong to a different

racial group. Choose one or two aspects of your life that you believe would be different (for the better or for the worse) and, in an essay, explain how and why.

2. What, ethnically speaking, is "whiteness"? Is whiteness "culturally empty," as Liu argues in paragraph 9? In a paragraph, define whiteness as a cultural or ethnic category. Do white people in the United States have a particular, unified culture?

3. Liu's article appeared in *Slate,* an online magazine. At the end of the article, *Slate* lists three links: to the *Center for the Study of White American Culture Inc., 5 White Guys Sitting Around Talking,* and *Race Traitor* magazine. Go to one of these sites and analyze it using the points that Liu raises.

Discussing the Unit

Suggested Topic for Discussion

What is race? Is it determined by physical features alone? What does it mean to be multiracial? What do the experiences of the writers represented in this unit say about the utility of the concept of race? What would have to change in American society for multiracial people to feel recognized and comfortable? If American society ever reached that point, how would that affect our concept of race?

Preparing for Class Discussion

1. In the interview with the anthropologist Ann Laurer Stoler on page 326, Stoler says that "whiteness has always been the unmarked category. . . . Why don't we study what makes whiteness seem immune to investigation?" Why don't we? What are the characteristics of whiteness?

2. A number of essays in this unit are concerned with whether a "multiracial" category should be added to government forms. Consider the arguments against the creation of such a category (including the statistics in the *New York Times* article on p. 335). What are the practical objections? Can you think of broader, more philosophical objections?

3. *Prewriting Assignment:* Consider the differences between race, ethnicity, culture, and class. Write a paragraph defining each. Do you consider one of these terms more meaningful than the others? Why?

From Discussion to Writing

Why do we classify people according to race, and should the practice continue? Begin by explaining what race is, drawing on the readings in this unit, class discussion, and your own experience. What does this classification system allow us to do? What does it prevent us from doing? Would life in the United States (and the world) flow more smoothly if people were indifferent to what we call *race*? Do you believe such a state is possible?

15

CONFERENCE CHAPTER

American Mass Media and Popular Culture: How Does It Influence Us?

Does America's mass culture cater to the population's worst taste and the lowest common denominator? Is our society, as former Senator Bob Dole and other political figures (on both the right and left) have charged, morally endangered by movies and television shows that regularly trade on "gratuitous" sex and violence? Are we being continually dumbed down by mindless news programs, talk shows, and infotainment? Or are these elitist and narrow views that miss the way an audience interacts with and dialogically reshapes the products of popular culture?

The chapter's first three selections cover two of the mass media's most popular formats: television talk shows and talk radio. In "Blah, Blah, Blah: Is Anyone Listening?," Cynthia Crossen discusses the ways talk shows in general have affected the patterns of everyday conversation. Have all the outlets for talk, she wonders, turned us into a nation of blabbermouths who have sorely lost the capacity to listen? Yet someone must be listening to the talk shows themselves. One careful listener is Jill Nelson, who spent several months analyzing dozens of popular daytime television programs. "Watching TV talk shows," she writes, in "Talk is Cheap," "was like being caught in a daylong downpour of fear, hostility, and paranoia." This experience is shared by a leading African American legal scholar, Patricia J. Williams, who can hardly believe the anger and outrage she hears on popular call-in radio shows. In "Hate Radio," she asks "what does it mean that a manic, adolescent Howard Stern is so popular among radio listeners, that Rush Limbaugh's wittily smooth sadism has gone the way of prime-time television, and that both vie for the number one slot on all the best-selling book lists?"

Talk used to be a staple of another important television program: the news. But in recent years, informed talk has given way to "action news," as pictures — preferably of damage, destruction, and death — dominate the screen. In "Local News: The Biggest Scandal on TV," Steven D. Stark laments the fact that "the local newscast has replaced the network evening news and the newspaper alike as the average American's main source of news." ABC turns Stark's critique into a positive feature in their ad titled, "T.V. is good," inviting us all to "celebrate our cerebral-free non-activity."

Is there a line to be drawn between news and entertainment? As radio celebrity Don Imus put it recently: "The news isn't sacred to me. It's entertainment. The show is an entertainment device designed to revel in the agony of others." If that's so, then perhaps audiences are finding out as much about society from sitcoms as from news shows. In "Sein of the Times," Geoffrey O'Brien examines the reasons behind the enormous popularity of *Seinfeld,* which *Entertainment Weekly* called "the defining sitcom of our age."

In "But First, A Word From Our Sponsor," James Twitchell asserts that "human beings like things," and that simple fact drives our consumer-oriented society: "The culture we live in is carried on the back of advertising." If you think the media culture is responsible for the "dumbing down" of America, Twitchell argues, then your only hope is to resist the commercials by buying a "different brand" each time you shop. There's not much more that can be done. Nick Gillespie, in "View Masters: The Audience's Power over Media's Message," takes a more positive attitude toward the American audience. He sees audiences not as passive recipients of the media but as active, engaged, and discriminatory individuals who play a distinct role in constructing meaning and reshaping the media's messages. "The audience has a mind of its own," Gillespie writes, and our dynamic pop culture will never be kept in line.

The American freshman should be an expert on the media: As the survey results show, 80 percent of freshmen spend an hour or more "studying" TV.

Selected Survey Results

Media

- Freshmen who spend less than an hour a week watching TV: 19.7%
- Freshmen who spend less than an hour a week reading for pleasure: 51.9%

— From *The American Freshman: National Norms For Fall 1996.*

CYNTHIA CROSSEN

Blah, Blah, Blah: Is Anyone Listening?

[THE WALL STREET JOURNAL / July 10, 1997]

America has become a nation of blabbermouths. Too bad nobody's listening.

From television talk shows to on-line chat, call-in radio to support groups, hot lines to electronic mail, Americans today have more outlets for expressing themselves than ever before. Ordinary people can publicly opine on every conceivable topic from the heartbreak of eczema to whether the squad car on *The Andy Griffith Show* was a Ford Galaxie (it was). Americans have something to say about everything — and plenty of places to say it.

Unfortunately, human physiology notwithstanding, many more mouths are operating today than ears.

Overwhelmed by the incessant, intrusive babble of the modern world, the skill of listening has fallen on hard times. People say they are constantly repeating orders, directions, and questions. The word "What?" rings through the halls of commerce. In fact, studies show that people recall only about 25 percent of what they have heard in the past few days.

Hurried Living

Why have Americans become so hard of hearing? "It's because of our fast-paced world," says Kathy Thompson, who teaches courses on conversation at Alverno College in Milwaukee. "We're always in a hurry. Mentally we're saying, get to the point, we don't have time to hear the whole story. We're busy running from house to job to store to church. Good listening takes time." 5

That's part of it, agrees Wicke Chambers, a partner in Speechworks, an Atlanta communications-training firm. "But also, people think listening is boring; it's more fun to talk," she says. In late twentieth-century America, talking is seen as active and dominant, listening as passive and deferential. "There's the old joke, the opposite of talking isn't listening, it's wait-

CYNTHIA CROSSEN *(b. 1951) has been a reporter and an editor of the* Wall Street Journal *for thirteen years and now holds the title of Senior Editor. An author and a free-lancer, Crossen is most interested in covering stories on how our culture has changed in the past millennium. She wrote* Tainted Truth, *which was published in 1994. A new novel is currently in the works.*

ing to talk," Ms. Chambers says. "That's what a lot of people do, they just wait to talk."

Still others blame TV and radio, which allow people to combine listening with so many other activities that simply listening to music seems like a waste of time. Television also encourages passive, rather than active, listening. "When you watch television, you're listening in a way that doesn't require you to retain anything and doesn't object if you leave the room," says Sheila Bentley, a Memphis, Tenn., communications consultant who does listening training. "And because it's interrupted by commercials, you don't have to develop sustained attending skills. With people spending six hours a day doing that kind of listening, it's no wonder there's concern that we're becoming a nation of poor listeners."

Word Game

If all this weren't bad enough, biology also works against attentive listening. Most people speak at a rate of 120 to 150 words a minute, but the human brain can easily process more than 500 words a minute, leaving plenty of time for mental fidgeting. If the speaker also happens to be slow, monotonal, and wordy, it requires a heroic effort to stay tuned instead of simply faking it.

Poor listening can cause disasters, as it did in the 1977 runway collision at Tenerife Airport in the Canary Islands, when misunderstood instructions caused 583 deaths. But more often, poor listening results in millions of little time-wasting mistakes a day — the wrong coffee order, credit card or telephone number, or fact in a newspaper story. Ms. Bentley does seminars with medical managers because of the massive liability awards doctors and hospitals can pay because of poor listening. "People are realizing that a lot of mistakes we attributed to other things are actually listening problems," she says.

Coffee Formula

At Starbucks Coffee Co. stores, where a customer can order a "double-shot decaf grande iced half-skim vanilla dry cappucino," employees are taught a procedure for hearing and calling orders developed by the company four years ago. It systematizes the sequence of words describing the drink — size, flavoring, milk, decaf — with automatic defaults. Then the person making the drink echoes the order aloud.

"We expect our employees to listen," says Alan Gulick, a Starbucks spokesman. "It's an important component of customer service."

In today's service economy, it also makes financial sense. If every worker in America makes one $10 mistake a year because of poor listening, "that adds up to more than a billion dollars a year," says Lyman Steil, president of a St. Paul, Minn., consulting firm, Communication Development, which specializes in listening. Mr. Steil was also a founder of the International Listening Association in 1979, an eclectic group that promotes better listening. "We're drowning in a sea of noise," Mr. Steil says. "The listener of today has to make more careful choices about who, what, and when they listen."

Yesteryear's listeners were drowning in a sea of quiet, and they did the opposite of filtering out sound: They needed and welcomed it. Most of their days were spent in the isolation of a home or field without television, telephone, radio, or even neighbors. The sound of distant horses' hooves could mean mortal danger, and a snappy harmonica offered the audio pleasure of a symphony orchestra. When listening was a matter of survival, there were few more comforting sounds than human voices. With little visual entertainment, people would patiently listen to itinerant lecturers, politicians, or preachers deliver three- or four-hour perorations. Because there was no way of replaying speech, if people didn't hear it when spoken, they would never hear it.

Perhaps the fact that listening was once a matter of life and death explains why the educational establishment teaches students to read, write, and speak but rarely to listen. "We think listening is innate, but it's not, it's a skill," says Kathryn Dindia, a professor in the department of communication at the University of Wisconsin in Milwaukee. "We spend a huge amount of our waking hours listening, but we aren't taught how to do it." In fact, children's listening skills actually decline as they grow older.

Listening can be taught, experts agree, but it isn't as easy as it looks.   15
For one thing, good listening requires that people banish their own prejudices and try to see the world through the speaker's eye. "Whenever we listen thoroughly to another person's ideas, we open ourselves up to the possibility that some of our own ideas are wrong," wrote R.G. Nichols and L.A. Stevens in their 1957 book, *Are You Listening?*

"To be a good listener," Ms. Thompson says, "you have to forgo your own ego and put the other person first. You have to shut off the talking inside your own head." That concept is completely foreign to many people, particularly those who are constantly surrounded by sycophantic listeners.

"Dialogues of the Deaf"

Yet wanting to be listened to is a universal desire. "It is impossible to overemphasize the immense need humans have to be really listened to, to be taken seriously, to be understood," wrote the Swiss psychiatrist Paul Tournier. "Listen to all the conversations of our world, between nations as well as those between couples. They are for the most part dialogues of the deaf."

The shortage of listeners means "crowded appointment books for therapists, psychologists, and support groups," says Carolyn Gwynn Coakley, co-author of the book *Listening,* who teaches seminars on listening. "People are going elsewhere to get the listeners they should have with their families or friends." They are paying for something that was once free.

The deterioration in listening skills also creates a deadly downward spiral with the art of speaking. Conversations become dueling or intersecting monologues or monologues in the presence of a witness. Long-winded speakers turn thousands of business meetings a day into tests of mental endurance. "Sometimes people don't listen well because it's boring," says Spring Asher, a partner of Speechworks. "Someone says, 'Good afternoon, I'm glad to be here today,' they're just doing this blah, blah, blah. You could die. Start with a story or grab them with a 'gee whiz' fact. You have to be a storyteller." . . .

One of the obvious byproducts of the imbalance between talkers and listeners is interruption, with three or four people talking and no one listening. Tune in to any number of television talk shows and notice how frequently the participants' voices "overlap," as linguists describe interrupting. (Obnoxious interrupting is called "uncooperative overlap.") "The idea is to be aggressive and competitive," says Sam Nelson, director of debate at the University of Rochester in New York. "If it's more like a fight, it's more like a sporting event, and as spectators we enjoy it more. It's more exciting."

Talk-Show Strategy

Rick Davis, senior executive producer of the Washington talk show *Crossfire,* has a different analogy. If four friends go out to dinner, and they have differing views on a topic they all know something about, there will naturally be times when everyone's talking, he says. "Most people aren't used to seeing that on television, but they're used to seeing it in real life. We don't totally discourage interruption because it's natural, but we know viewers don't like it when everyone is talking at the same time." Adds Amy Rosenblum, coproducer of the *Sally Jessy Raphael Show,* "A guest who can't interrupt isn't a good guest for a talk show. We only try to stop it when there's cross-talk, when guest one is talking about his infidelity while guest two is talking about his mother-in-law."

Mr. Davis is absolutely correct that there is a lot of interrupting going on around the nation's dinner tables. "We have become a nation of interrupters," says Ms. Thompson of Alverno College. "At our house we warn new friends to be careful because we treat conversation like a competitive sport. The first one to take a breath is considered the listener."

That's true in many business meetings, too, when several people may be vying for the boss's attention, and none much cares what his or her competitors are saying. "People want to take credit for things," Mr. Nelson says. "If you're the first person to get it out, it's yours. So you go into the meeting thinking, 'I'm going to get this out if it kills me.'" That also helps explain the disappearance of the pause from many people's speech. "A pause signals that you have a sense of confidence," Ms. Chambers says. "I hear women say they're scared to pause because people will jump in and they'll lose control."

Gender differences in speaking and listening have been a popular topic of research in recent years, with the consensus generally being that women are more sympathetic listeners than men and their interruptions more supportive than intrusive. Men's conversation tends to be an exchange of information, and they reach their point more quickly. In male–female conversations, men tend to dominate by speaking more. But, writes Deborah Tannen,[1] author of *You Just Don't Understand,* men dominating conversations "is not always the result of an intention to dominate."

Becoming a good listener carries some risks. Talkers attach themselves to listeners like barnacles to boats, and detaching them isn't easy. How do the experts handle the predatory prattler? Mr. Steil advocates a polite but firm, "I'm sorry, I'd love to talk more, but I have work to do." Other people carry headsets, often attached to nothing, as a defensive weapon. Ms. Coakley, the author, suggests something like, "At this point, I really can't be the listener I want to be and feel you need." To a nonstop talker on the telephone, Ms. Bentley recommends, "I know you're busy, so I won't keep you any longer." Depending on your relationship with the speaker, say all the experts, at some point it may be appropriate to say, "Get to the point."

The point is this: The world needs more good listeners, people like the   25
world-famous listener Jacqueline Onassis. And like the Bill Clinton character in Joe Klein's *Primary Colors,*[2] whose "big ears" listened so aggressively it was as if "he were hearing quicker than you can get the words out, as if he were sucking the information out of you." A good listener has an animated face, makes eye contact, and pays attention to the hundreds of nonverbal cues that orchestrate the typical discussion.

"Think about keeping the tennis ball in play," Ms. Chambers says. "You're not trying to lob it over the other one's head, and you're not trying to kill it. But you're also not trying to keep it going so long that no one gets the point. Each side gives something, each side gets something."

---

[1]For more on Deborah Tannen and the influence of gender on conversation, see page 105.

[2]One of the bestselling novels of 1995, *Primary Colors,* a fictional account of the Clinton White House, was published anonymously. Only afterward did it surface that the author was the political journalist Joe Klein.

Responding as a Reader

1. Crossen includes a lot of quotations. Whom does she quote? Are all of her points supported by quotations? What do all the quotations have in common?

2. What is Crossen implying in paragraphs 8 and 19 about the relationship between speaker and listener and the responsibility of each for effective communication?

3. This article appeared in the *Wall Street Journal*, a New York newspaper devoted to business coverage. Why would business people be especially interested in the topic of listening? What elements of Crossen's article are most directly applicable to this audience?

4. How do you think the author researched her article? Go back through the selection and identify the various kinds of information: What information came from interviews? What from reading? What sources seem to be most important to the author? How does that affect the overall selection?

Responding as a Writer

1. Look through the article again and note all the possible explanations for the decline in listening that Crossen cites. Put the list in order from the most persuasive reason to the least persuasive. If you can think of other possible reasons, add them to the list.

2. For one day (or even half a day), observe your own listening behavior. Which are the sounds you *hear* and what are the sounds you *listen to*? How often do you miss something that you wanted to hear? Do you "wait to talk" (para. 6) instead of listening? How much of what you hear do you remember? After paying some attention to your own behavior, define *hearing* and *listening*, give examples of each, and explain the difference between them.

3. To what extent are the mass media responsible for the decline of listening? Which media, or which kinds of programming, are most responsible? Is this a problem that needs to be fixed? In an essay, define the problem, gauge its seriousness, and suggest one action that the mass media (and consumers of mass media) can take to fix it.

4. Consider the ways conversation is learned. How do you know when to talk and when to listen? Are there cultural norms? What etiquette is involved? How does gender influence conversation? How do peer groups play an influence? What conversational styles do we pick up from radio and television? Write an essay in which you discuss and analyze what you believe is the most significant influence on the development of an individual's conversational style.

JILL NELSON

Talk Is Cheap

[THE NATION / June 5, 1995]

On a plane headed to New York, my seatmate is a young woman who confides that she is on her way to be a guest on *Rolonda,* one of dozens of syndicated talk shows currently on television. "What's the topic?" I ask.

"Secret crushes."

"Do you have one?" I wonder. By the time we land in New York, I find out she doesn't, though she's told the producers she does and given them the name of a man she vaguely knows. It turns out that she and her girlfriends were sitting around watching *Rolonda* and when the call for guests with secret crushes came up during a break, complete with an 800 number, she picked up the phone as a goof. Except *Rolonda's* producers didn't know it was a joke, or didn't care. She says they called her more than ten times, and in exchange for airfare, a hotel room, and a limo, she's agreed to risk public humiliation. The producers even suggested she bring a pair of panties as a gift for her crush, but she drew the line. She did agree to lug a suitcase full of local gourmet specialties for them.

Over the past few months I've spent several hours a day, five days a week, watching talk shows. From *Rolonda* to *Geraldo* to *Jenny Jones* to *Richard Bey* to *Donahue* to *Ricki Lake* to *Gordon Elliott* to *Jerry Springer* to *Sally Jessy Raphael* to *Maury Povich* to *Montel Williams* to *Oprah.* I've watched shows on mate swapping, men who beat women, fat women who are porno stars, the superiority in size of black men's penises, transvestites, men who don't support their children, bisexuality, people who love to have unprotected sex, women who love murderers, children who are out of control, white women who love black men, strippers, black women who love white men. You name it, I've probably seen it; I've seen it all.

JILL NELSON (b. 1952) is the author of Volunteer Slavery: My Authentic Negro Experience *(1993). She studied at the City University of New York and at Columbia University and became a radical journalist. In 1986 she accepted a position at the prestigious* Washington Post's Sunday Magazine, *becoming the news magazine's first black and first female writer. After a brief period with the* Post, *she quit her job because of the bias of the paper's managerial and editorial policies. Her work has appeared in numerous publications, including* Essence, Ms., USA Weekend, *and the* Village Voice.

In 1986, when *The Oprah Winfrey Show* went national, media atten-   5
tion focused on what impact Winfrey's personal, emotional style would
have on the ratings of the long-time king of serious daytime talk, Phil Donahue. Television critics grumbled that her confessional approach — and
soaring ratings — would force the news-oriented Donahue to abandon his
format. Almost a decade later, it's clear that Winfrey's success influenced a
lot more than Phil Donahue. Imitators have taken the cornerstones of Winfrey's success — guests who confess their victimization, confront their victimizer, and through public confession hope for some sort of healing —
and reduced it to its lowest common denominator. They've taken Winfrey's formula to its most hideous extreme, leaving Winfrey, who is appalled by what she created (last year [1994] she announced she would
change her format), and Donahue, who always seemed uncomfortable with
the role of priest in TV's confessional, seeming to be above it all. Today's
talk shows celebrate victim and victimizer equally; they draw no lines and
have no values except the almighty dollar. And, cheap as they are to produce, they pay: Over the past decade, television talk shows have prolifer-
ated like roaches in the walls of a New York City apartment building.

In a fundamental way, the success of these shows is based on external
economic, social, and political factors: the disappearance of entry-level
employment for young high school graduates, the disintegration of communities, the elimination of government support programs for young
people and families — from school loans to daycare centers to community-
based health facilities — and the resulting despair and rage that pervade
many people's lives. Like the woman on the airplane, they crave their fifteen minutes of fame, with its illusion of success and importance. An appearance on television, even if it is based on a lie and depends on making
themselves and others look ridiculous, is their best chance of attaining it.
The audience too, both in the studio and at home, feeds off the misery and
humiliation of others. Less obvious is the price we all pay for those fifteen
minutes in increased alienation, contempt, and hatred.

The current crop of talk shows exists solely as entertainment based on
the humiliation, or potential humiliation, of their guests. Much has been
made of the murder of a gay man, Scott Amedure. Jonathan Schmitz, apparently unable to stand the thought of being desired by another man, shot
and killed Amedure several days after he confessed at a taping of the *Jenny
Jones* show that Schmitz was his "secret crush." But as frightening as that
was, I'm more terrified by the daily killing off of any sense of understanding, connectedness, collective responsibility, and the potential for redemption that these talk shows foster.

The effect is subtle, cumulative, and wholly negative. With the frequent exception of Donahue, and occasionally Oprah, I cannot say that I
learned one useful thing, gained any understanding, or was ever informed
or enriched after months of watching Ricki, Montel, Richard Bey, and the
rest of the crew. For the first few days I found the programs amusing, in a

snide way. It was initially fascinating to watch people spill the most intimate details about their sex lives, lack of value systems, antisocial activities, and absence of a connection to a community greater than the self. But after the first week, I was embarrassed, sickened, and enraged by what I heard.

I found myself yearning for the good old days of talk shows hosted by the likes of Joe Pyne, Alan Burke, and Morton Downey Jr., who made their own prejudices and politics so clear that they provided a contrast to their guests, a line of demarcation around which sides could be taken. Today's talk-show hosts are slick media creations masquerading as people like us: hip Ricki; macho ex-Marine Montel; middle-aged, clean-cut suburban types à la Jenny Jones, Jerry Springer, and Maury Povich. Where Pyne, Burke, and Downey were full of opinions and vitriol, these hosts pose as facilitators, egging their guests on to greater revelation and humiliation while they remain above the fray, inquiring minds who want to know.

But their mission is not to get beneath our assumptions and stereotypes   10 but to exploit and solidify them. The guests are overwhelmingly young, mostly black and Latino, apparently poor, and often unemployed. Their personalities and behaviors are cast as representative. Young black men become walking penises. Young women of all colors are victims, or stupid, sex-addicted, dependent baby-makers, with an occasional castrating bitch thrown in. Young white males are either nerds or, to the extent they are able to mimic the antisocial, highly sexualized behavior of the black males, equally obnoxious, dick-identified studs.

In the world of talk, young black men are portrayed as arrogant, amoral, violent predators out to get you with their penis, their gun, or both. A few pathological individuals are presented as representatives of the group, and there's seldom any discussion of the economic, social, and political conditions that produce antisocial behavior. It's hard to recall seeing any young black man on TV representing the majority: decent guys struggling to get a foothold in a society that provides scant support and expects the worst. You'd think that when the first-grade teacher asked the class what they wanted to do when they grew up, all the black boys raised their hands and said, "Deal crack, decimate my community, and do drive-bys."

This representation of black men as dicks is the dominant motif of many of the shows: "I wouldn't sleep with him so he dumped me," "My man's a dog and you can have him," "Confronting the person who dumped you," "Women who let their men have sex with other women," "I'd do anything for my man," and endless variations of "secret crush," "dating game," and "he has to choose between me and her."

Whatever the topic, the format is as follows: One person — usually a woman, since women are most frequently cast in the role of stupid, powerless victim — comes out and tells all the couple's business to the apparently sympathetic host and a leering, jeering, cheering audience of her peers. This done, the other person — usually a man — is brought onstage, where he is confronted by his woman/women, booed or cheered by the audience, and gleefully encouraged by the host to confirm our worst suspicions. It was initially interesting to see that a significant number of these couples are interracial, but the subtext quickly became clear: Penis-waving black men prey not only on black women, who deserve/are used to it, but on WHITE WOMEN. Thus the shows confirm the popular political line that black men are to be feared — not only in the street but in the bedroom. Violence, teenage pregnancy, poverty, spousal abuse, the spread of AIDS and other STDs, AFDC[1] — you name it and Mandingo's behind it.

Unfortunately, TV's Mandingo seldom disappoints. Neither does young Mr. Charlie. This is not surprising, since the desperate desire to be seen, recognized, and on TV appears to have overridden 95 percent of whatever common sense exists. Almost daily, I witnessed a man attacked for his sexual promiscuity stand up and proudly gyrate or clutch his penis for the camera. I began to wonder if talk-show producers' preinterview of prospective guests consists of anything more than asking them to execute a bump and grind.

It's rare that guests are given any advice, analysis, or support. There is almost never a psychologist, counselor, or even a writer hawking a book on the topic to listen, place in context, or advise remedial action. A few talk shows use audience members as counselors or judges, but this is solely for entertainment value. The guests have gotten their fifteen minutes of fame, but leave essentially as they came: alienated, angry, and, most important, jobless. The hosts leave with a fat paycheck.

All this has a profound political effect; daytime talk shows, intentionally or not, have become storm troopers for the right. Both the talk shows and the right wing erase the line between the anecdotal and the factual. Both focus attention on the individual, aberrant behavior of a small number of citizens and declare them representative of a group. So the black woman labeled a "welfare cheat" by elected officials comes to represent *most* women receiving Aid to Families With Dependent Children, when the overwhelming majority of women receiving AFDC do not "cheat" the system and would like nothing better than to get a job with benefits greater than those provided by welfare. Rather than present an honest look at what life on welfare's really like and initiating a discussion of positive "welfare reform," most talk shows seek out the exception who appears to prove the right-wing rule: a poor, uneducated, 21-year-old woman on welfare with four children. Why bother to have a serious discussion about education, unemployment, or building community when it's so much easier to demonize poor black women?

---

[1]STD = sexually transmitted disease; AFDC = Aid to Families with Dependent Children; i.e., welfare.

Watching TV talk shows was like being caught in a daylong downpour of fear, hostility, and paranoia. I found myself feeling mean spirited and snarling by the time the news came on at 6 o'clock and full of lust for revenge. In that mood it was almost possible to entertain the notion that old Newt [Gingrich] might have some good ideas. Maybe we ought to take out a Contract With America and punish the young, poor, female, black, Latino, and gay — those troublemakers we've watched swagger through talk shows all day.

While the pundits and the President discuss the negative impact of right-wing radio talk shows in the wake of the Oklahoma bombing, TV talk continues unnoticed and unanalyzed. But television reaches a much broader audience than the already converted who tune in to talk radio. Television gives not only a voice but a face to our fear and rage, enables us to point the finger of blame at the tube — at "them" — and roar for punishment. Isn't that what the Contract on [sic] America is all about?

Responding as a Reader

1. What practice is Nelson comparing talk shows to in paragraph 5? In what ways are these two formats truly similar? How are they different?

2. How, according to Nelson, do talk shows help to kill off "any sense of understanding, connectedness, collective responsibility, and . . . potential for redemption" (para. 7)? How do the hosts and/or the guests on the shows achieve this?

3. What argument is Nelson making, in the final section of her essay, about the connection between talk shows and right-wing politics? What is the most dangerous result of this type of entertainment, according to her? Do you agree?

Responding as a Writer

1. Nelson lists a number of possible causes for the success of talk shows (para. 6), but she does not explain how these social factors could have led to the proliferation of this type of entertainment. In an essay, choose one or two of the social problems Nelson lists (or choose one of your own) and explain, step by step, how it could have helped make talk shows popular.

2. Watch one or two of the shows that Nelson watched. Do you agree with her assessment of them? Or do you find them to be harmless, or actually to have some redeeming qualities? In an essay, give your own examples to prove or disprove her points.

3. Is television a reflection of society or an agent for social change (for good or bad)? Or is it, somehow, both? In an essay, try to define the relationship between television and society. Support your argument with evidence from this article, from the news, or from your own experience.

PATRICIA J. WILLIAMS

Hate Radio [MS. / 1994]

Three years ago [1991] I stood at my sink, washing the dishes and listening to the radio. I was tuned to rock and roll so I could avoid thinking about the big news from the day before — George Bush had just nominated Clarence Thomas to replace Thurgood Marshall on the Supreme Court. I was squeezing a dot of lemon Joy into each of the wine glasses when I realized that two smoothly radiocultured voices, a man's and a woman's, had replaced the music.

"I think it's a stroke of genius on the president's part," said the female voice.

"Yeah," said the male voice. "Then those blacks, those African Americans, those Negroes — hey 'Negro' is good enough for Thurgood Marshall — whatever, they can't make up their minds [what] they want to be called. I'm gonna call them Blafricans. Black Africans. Yeah, I like it. Blafricans. Then they can get all upset because now the president appointed a Blafrican."

"Yeah, well, that's the way those liberals think. It's just crazy."

PATRICIA J. WILLIAMS *(b. 1951) is a law professor at Columbia University. She was an undergraduate at Wellesley College, received her J.D. from Harvard University, and was a fellow in the prestigious School of Criticism and Theory at Dartmouth College. She is a contributing editor to* The Nation, *a popular political magazine, and has also written for publications such as* Ms. *She has published* The Alchemy of Race and Rights *(1990) and more recently,* The Rooster's Egg: On the Persistence of Prejudice *(1995).*

"And then after they turn down his nomination the president can say   5
he tried to please 'em, and then he can appoint someone with some intelligence."

Back then, this conversation seemed so horrendously unusual, so sin-
gularly hateful, that I picked up a pencil and wrote it down. I was certain
that a firestorm of protest was going to engulf the station and purge those
foul radio mouths with the good clean soap of social outrage.

I am so naive. When I finally turned on the radio and rolled my dial to
where everyone else had been tuned while I was busy watching Cosby reruns, it took me a while to understand that there's a firestorm all right, but
not of protest. In the two and a half years since Thomas has assumed his
post on the Supreme Court, the underlying assumptions of the conversation I heard as uniquely outrageous have become commonplace, popularly
expressed, and louder in volume. I hear the style of that snide polemicism
everywhere, among acquaintances, on the street, on television in toned-
down versions. It is a crude demagoguery that makes me heartsick. I feel
more and more surrounded by that point of view, the assumptions of being
without intelligence, the coded epithets, the "Blafrican"-like stand-ins for
"nigger," the mocking angry glee, the endless tirades filled with nonspe-
cific, nonempirically based slurs against "these people" or "those minorities" or "feminazis" or "liberals" or "scumbags" or "pansies" or "jerks"
or "sleazeballs" or "loonies" or "animals" or "foreigners."

At the same time I am not so naive as to suppose that this is something
new. In clearheaded moments I realize I am not listening to the radio anymore, I am listening to a large segment of white America think aloud in ever
louder resurgent thoughts that have generations of historical precedent. It's
as though the radio has split open like an egg, Morton Downey, Jr.'s[1] clones
and Joe McCarthy's[2] ghost spilling out, broken yolks, a great collective of
sometimes clever, sometimes small, but uniformly threatened brains — they
have all come gushing out. Just as they were about to pass into oblivion, Jack
Benny and his humble black side-kick Rochester get resurrected in the un-
gainly bodies of Howard Stern and his faithful black henchwoman, Robin
Quivers. The culture of Amos and Andy has been revived and reassembled in
Bob Grant's radio minstrelry and radio newcomer Darryl Gates's[3] sanctimo-
nious imprecations on behalf of decent white people. And in striking imitation of Jesse Helm's nearly forgotten days as a radio host, the far Right has
found its undisputed king in the personage of Rush Limbaugh — a polished

[1]Morton Downey, Jr. was a talk-show host of the 1980s who often ridiculed his guests and
took up controversial topics.

[2]U.S. Senator Joseph R. McCarthy (1909–1957), chair of the House Un-American Activities
Committee, hunted and prosecuted suspected Communists and Communist sympathizers in
the 1950s.

[3]Darryl Gates was Los Angeles police commissioner during the Rodney King beating affair of
the early 1990s.

demagogue with a weekly radio audience of at least twenty million, a television show that vies for ratings with the likes of Jay Leno, a newsletter with a circulation of 380,000, and two best-selling books whose combined sales are closing in on six million copies.

From Churchill to Hitler to the old Soviet Union, it's clear that radio and television have the power to change the course of history, to proselytize, and to coalesce not merely the good and the noble but the very worst in human nature as well. Likewise, when Orson Welles made his famous radio broadcast "witnessing" the landing of a spaceship full of hostile Martians, the United States ought to have learned a lesson about the power of radio to appeal to mass instincts and incite mass hysteria. Radio remains a peculiarly powerful medium even today, its visual emptiness in a world of six trillion flashing images allowing one of the few remaining playgrounds for the aural subconscious. Perhaps its power is attributable to our need for an oral tradition after all, some conveying of stories, feelings, myths of ancestors, epics of alienation, and the need to rejoin ancestral roots, even ignorant bigoted roots. Perhaps the visual quiescence of radio is related to the popularity of E-mail or electronic networking. Only the voice is made manifest, unmasking worlds that cannot — or dare not? — be seen. Just yet. Nostalgia crystallizing into a dangerous future. The preconscious voice erupting into the expressed, the prime time.

What comes out of the modern radio mouth could be the *Iliad,* the   1
Rubaiyat, the griot's song of our times. If indeed radio is a vessel for the American "Song of Songs," then what does it mean that a manic, adolescent Howard Stern is so popular among radio listeners, that Rush Limbaugh's wittily smooth sadism has gone the way of prime-time television, and that both vie for the number one slot on all the best-selling book lists? What to make of the stories being told by our modern radio evangelists and their tragic unloved chorus of callers? Is it really just a collapsing economy that spawns this drama of grown people sitting around scaring themselves to death with fantasies of black feminist Mexican able-bodied gay soldiers earning $100,000 a year on welfare who are so criminally depraved that Hillary Clinton or the Antichrist-of-the-moment had no choice but to invite them onto the government payroll so they can run the country? The panicky exaggeration reminds me of a child's fear. . . . *And then, and then, a huge lion jumped out of the shadows and was about to gobble me up, and I can't ever sleep again for a whole week.*

As I spin the dial on my radio, I can't help thinking that this stuff must be related to that most poignant of fiber-optic phenomena, phone sex. Aural Sex. Radio Racism with a touch of S & M. High-priest hosts with the power and run-amok ego to discipline listeners, to smack with the verbal back of the hand, to smash the button that shuts you up once and for all. "Idiot!" shouts New York City radio demagogue Bob Grant and then the sound of droning telephone emptiness, the voice of dissent dumped out some trapdoor in aural space.

As I listened to a range of such programs what struck me as the most unifying theme was not merely the specific intolerance on such hot topics as race and gender but a much more general contempt for the world, a verbal stoning of anything different. It is like some unusually violent game of "Simon Says," this mockery and shouting down of callers, this roar of incantations, the insistence on agreement.

But, ah, if you *will* but only agree, what sweet and safe reward, what soft enfolding by a stern and angry radio god. And as an added bonus, the invisible shield of an AM community of fans who are Exactly Like You, to whom you can express, in anonymity, all the filthy stuff you imagine "them" doing to you. The comfort and relief of being able to ejaculate, to those who understand, about the dark imagined excess overtaking, robbing, needing to be held down and taught a good lesson, needing to put it in its place before the ravenous demon enervates all that is true and good and pure in this life.

The audience for this genre of radio flagellation is mostly young, white, and male. Two thirds of Rush Limbaugh's audience is male. According to *Time* magazine, 75 percent of Howard Stern's listeners are white men. Most of the callers have spent their lives walling themselves off from any real experience with blacks, feminists, lesbians, or gays. In this regard, it is probably true, as former Secretary of Education William Bennett says, that Rush Limbaugh "tells his audience that what you believe inside, you can talk about in the marketplace." Unfortunately, what's "inside" is then mistaken for what's outside, treated as empirical and political reality. The *National Review* extols Limbaugh's conservative leadership as no less than that of Ronald Reagan, and the Republican party provides Limbaugh with books to discuss, stories, angles, and public support. "People were afraid of censure by gay activists, feminists, environmentalists — now they are not because Rush takes them on," says Bennett.

U.S. history has been marked by cycles in which brands of this or that   15
hatred come into fashion and go out, are unleashed, and then restrained. If racism, homophobia, jingoism, and woman-hating have been features of national life in pretty much all of modern history, it rather begs the question to spend a lot of time wondering if right-wing radio is a symptom or a cause. For at least 400 years, prevailing attitudes in the West have considered African Americans less intelligent. Recent statistics show that 53 percent of people in the United States agree that blacks and Latinos are less intelligent than whites, and a majority believe that blacks are lazy, violent, welfare-dependent, and unpatriotic.

I think that what has made life more or less tolerable for "out" groups have been those moments in history when those "inside" feelings were relatively restrained. In fact, if I could believe that right-wing radio were only about idiosyncratic, singular, rough-hewn individuals thinking those inside thoughts, I'd be much more inclined to agree with Columbia University media expert Everette Dennis, who says that Stern's and Limbaugh's popularity represents the "triumph of the individual," or with *Time* magazine's bottom line that "the fact that either is seriously considered a threat . . . is more worrisome than Stern or Limbaugh will ever be." If what I was hearing had even a tad more to do with real oppressions, with real white *and* black levels of joblessness and homelessness, or with the real problems of real white men, then I wouldn't have bothered to slog my way through hours of Howard Stern's miserable obsessions.

Yet at the heart of my anxiety is the worry that Stern, Limbaugh, Grant, et al. represent the very antithesis of individualism's triumph. As the *National Review* said of Limbaugh's ascent, "It was a feat not only of the loudest voice but also of a keen political brain to round up, as Rush did, the media herd and drive them into the conservative corral." When asked about his political aspirations, Bob Grant gloated to the *Washington Post,* "I think I would make rather a good dictator."

The polemics of right-wing radio are putting nothing less than hate onto the airwaves, into the marketplace, electing it to office, teaching it in schools, and exalting it as freedom. What worries me is the increasing-to-constant commerce of retribution, control, and lashing out, fed not by fact but fantasy. What worries me is the re-emergence, more powerfully than at any time since the institution of Jim Crow, of a sociocentered self that excludes "the likes of," well, me for example, from the civic circle and that would rob me of my worth and claim and identity as a citizen. As the *Economist* rightly observes, "Mr. Limbaugh takes a mass market — white, mainly male, middle-class, ordinary America — and talks to it as an endangered minority."

I worry about this identity whose external reference is a set of beliefs, ethics, and practices that excludes, restricts, and acts in the world on me, or mine, as the perceived if not real enemy. I am acutely aware of losing *my* mythic individualism to the surface shapes of my mythic group fearsomeness as black, as female, as left wing. "I" merge not fluidly but irretrievably into a category of "them." I become a suspect self, a moving target of loathsome properties, not merely different but dangerous. And that worries me a lot.

What happens in my life with all this translated license, this permission   20 to be uncivil? What happens to the social space that was supposedly at the sweet mountaintop of the civil rights movement's trail? Can I get a seat on the bus without having to be reminded that I *should* be standing? Did the civil rights movement guarantee us nothing more than to use public accommodations while surrounded by raving lunatic bigots? "They didn't beat this idiot [Rodney King] enough," says Howard Stern.

Not long ago I had the misfortune to hail a taxicab in which the driver was listening to Howard Stern undress some woman. After some blocks, I had to get out. I was, frankly, afraid to ask the driver to turn it off — not because I was afraid of "censoring" him, which seems to be the only thing people will talk about anymore, but because the driver was stripping me too, as he leered through the rearview mirror. "Something the matter?" he demanded, as I asked him to pull over and let me out well short of my destination. (I'll spare you the full story of what happened from there — trying to get another cab, as the cabbies stopped for all the white businessmen who so much as scratched their heads near the curb; a nice young white man, seeing my plight, giving me his cab, having to thank him, he hero, me saved-but-humiliated, cabdriver pissed and surly. I fight my way to my destination, finally arriving in bad mood, militant black woman, cranky feminazi.)

When Yeltsin blared rock music at his opponents holed up in the parliament building in Moscow, in imitation of the U.S. Marines trying to torture Manuel Noriega in Panama, all I could think of was that it must be like being trapped in a crowded subway car when all the portable stereos are tuned to Bob Grant or Howard Stern. With Howard Stern's voice a tinny, screeching backdrop, with all the faces growing dreamily mean as though some soporifically evil hallucinogen were gushing into their bloodstreams, I'd start begging to surrender.

Surrender to what? Surrender to the laissez-faire resegregation that is the metaphoric significance of the hundreds of "Rush rooms" that have cropped up in restaurants around the country; rooms broadcasting Limbaugh's words, rooms for your listening pleasure, rooms where bigots can capture the purity of a Rush-only lunch counter, rooms where all those unpleasant others just "choose" not to eat? Surrender to the naughty luxury of a room in which a Ku Klux Klan meeting could take place in orderly, First Amendment fashion? Everyone's "free" to come in (and a few of you outsiders do), but mostly the undesirable nonconformists are gently repulsed away. It's a high-tech world of enhanced choice. Whites choose mostly to sit in the Rush room. Feminists, blacks, lesbians, and gays "choose" to sit elsewhere. No need to buy black votes, you just pay them not to vote; no need to insist on white-only schools, you just sell the desirability of black-only schools. Just sit back and watch it work, like those invisible shock shields that keep dogs cowering in their own backyards.

How real is the driving perception behind all the Sturm und Drang of this genre of radio-harangue — the perception that white men are an oppressed minority, with no power and no opportunity in the land that they made great? While it is true that power and opportunity are shrinking for all but the very wealthy in this country (and would that Limbaugh would take that issue on), the fact remains that white men are still this country's most privileged citizens and market actors. To give just a small example, according to the *Wall Street Journal*, blacks were the only racial group to suffer a net job loss during the 1990–91 economic downturn at the companies reporting to the Equal Employment Opportunity Commission. Whites, Latinos, and Asians, meanwhile, gained thousands of jobs. While whites gained 71,144 jobs at these companies, Latinos gained 60,040, Asians gained 55,104, and blacks lost 59,479. If every black were hired in the

United States tomorrow, the numbers would not be sufficient to account for white men's expanding balloon of fear that they have been specifically dispossessed by African Americans.

Given deep patterns of social segregation and general ignorance of his-   25
tory, particularly racial history, media remain the principal source of most Americans' knowledge of each other. Media can provoke violence or induce passivity. In San Francisco, for example, a radio show on KMEL called *Street Soldiers* has taken this power as a responsibility with great consequence: "Unquestionably," writes Ken Auletta in *The New Yorker,* "the show has helped avert violence. When a Samoan teenager was slain, apparently by Filipino gang members, in a drive-by shooting, the phones lit up with calls from Samoans wanting to tell [the hosts] they would not rest until they had exacted revenge. Threats filled the air for a couple of weeks. Then the dead Samoan's father called in, and, in a poignant exchange, the father said he couldn't tolerate the thought of more young men senselessly slaughtered. There would be no retaliation, he vowed. And there was none." In contrast, we must wonder at the phenomenon of the very powerful leadership of the Republican party, from Ronald Reagan to Robert Dole to William Bennett, giving advice, counsel, and friendship to Rush Limbaugh's passionate divisiveness.

The outright denial of the material crisis at every level of U.S. society, most urgently in black inner-city neighborhoods but facing us all, is a kind of political circus, dissembling as it feeds the frustrations of the moment. We as a nation can no longer afford to deal with such crises by *imagining* an excess of bodies, of babies, of job-stealers, of welfare mothers, of overreaching immigrants, of too-powerful (Jewish, in whispers) liberal Hollywood, of lesbians and gays, of gang members ("gangsters" remain white, and no matter what the atrocity, less vilified than "gang members," who are black), of Arab terrorists, and uppity women. The reality of our social poverty far exceeds these scapegoats. This right-wing backlash resembles, in form if not substance, phenomena like anti-Semitism in Poland: There aren't but a handful of Jews left in that whole country, but the giant balloon of heated anti-Semitism flourishes apace, Jews blamed for the world's evils.

The overwhelming response to right-wing excesses in the United States has been to seek an odd sort of comfort in the fact that the First Amendment is working so well that you can't suppress this sort of thing. Look what's happened in Eastern Europe. Granted. So let's not talk about censorship or the First Amendment for the next ten minutes. But in Western Europe, where fascism is rising at an appalling rate, suppression is hardly the problem. In Eastern and Western Europe as well as the United States, we must begin to think just a little bit about the fiercely coalescing power of media to spark mistrust, to fan it into forest fires of fear, and revenge. We must begin to think about the levels of national and social complacence in the face of such resolute ignorance. We must ask ourselves what the expected result is, not of censorship or suppression but of so much encouragement, so much support, so much investment in the fashionability of hate. What future is it that we are designing with the devotion of such tremendous resources to the disgraceful propaganda of bigotry?

Responding as a Reader

1. Reread Williams's opening paragraph. Why do you think she begins her essay this way? What does the paragraph tell you about her? How does it prepare you for the rest of the essay?

2. What gives the medium of radio its special power, according to Williams? How is this power connected to human physiology, and history, and psychology?

3. According to Williams, is "hate radio" a symptom of racism or a cause? What is the real danger of this format, in her view?

Responding as a Writer

1. Take an informal poll of the people you know. How many of them listen to call-in shows on the radio? Which shows do they listen to? Why do they listen to them? Write up your results and speculate about whether the people you spoke to are representative of the general public or merely representative of a small group with specialized interests.

2. Analyze the radio conversation in paragraphs 2–5. What are the implications of this conversation? In a few paragraphs, spell out what these two voices are saying about liberals, African Americans, the president, the Supreme Court, and themselves.

3. Tune in to Rush Limbaugh or Howard Stern. Do you agree with Williams's analysis? Summarize the content of the show you listened to, characterize its tone, and give examples to prove or disprove Williams's points.

STEVEN D. STARK

Local News: The Biggest Scandal on TV

[THE WASHINGTON MONTHLY / June 1997]

Turn on the television set at 5 P.M. or 6 P.M. in any part of America, or do the same at 10 o'clock or 11 o'clock, and you are likely to encounter one of the oddest, if not most pernicious, phenomenons on television: the local newscast. What makes these programs so strange is that they are so eerily alike from Maine to Mississippi, no matter the network affiliation. There are always the breathless promos ("Nude man found at mall: Film at 11!"). There are always the two amiable chatting anchors, usually a middle-aged man and a somewhat younger woman. There are the younger roving reporters, featured live at various points around the community or nation, where they chat up the anchors. ("Do you know why the man was wearing no clothes, Jim?" "We're working on that, Susan.") There's the joking weatherman, the jock sportscaster, and, more recently, the health editor and the lifestyle reporter. In a nation of enormous diversity, there's something both comforting and appalling in knowing that no matter where you are, the local news — like the local McDonalds — is always the same.

What makes most of these newscasts pernicious is that they are at the same time so influential and so awful — at least in journalistic terms. In recent years, the local newscast has replaced the network evening news and the newspaper alike as the average American's main source of news: A study by the Pew Research Center for the People and the Press in 1996 found that 65 percent of all adults said they regularly watched the local TV news; only 42 percent reported that they did the same with a network newscast. In about two-thirds of all markets, according to another study, the early-evening local news shows attracted better ratings than the network newscast that followed them — and the local news is on for a longer time. Though local newscasts have been studied far less systematically than the national news, nearly everyone who has examined their content has come away with the same conclusion. For example:

STEVEN D. STARK, *author of* Glued to the Set *(1997), is a pop culture commentator for* National Public Radio *and the* Voice of America *and has written extensively for the* New York Times, *the* Boston Globe, *the* Los Angeles Times, *and the* Atlantic Monthly.

- A 1995 study of the local news in fifty major markets by the Rocky Mountain Media Watch found that crime and disaster news make up about 53 percent of the news on local newscasts — the grislier the crime, the better. ("Son shoots mother five times with bow and arrow.") Fluff — defined by the study as "soft news, anchor chatter, teases, and celebrity items" — takes up about 31 percent of the whole newscast, on average (items such as "Girl reunited with dog" or "How to tango").

- An informal 1993 survey by the *Washington Post* of local newscasts on stations in five big cities found the percentage of stories involving crime, sex, disasters, accidents, or public fears running at anywhere from 46 to 74. In its survey, the *Post* found local newscasts obsessed with murders, serial killers, snakebites, spider bites, tornadoes, mudslides, explosions, and satanic activity.

- A 1990 study published by the *Columbia Journalism Review* found that eighteen of thirty-two stories analyzed on local newscasts were inaccurate or misleading, and the station usually made no attempt to correct the mistakes. A report published the same year in the *L.A. Reader,* following examination of a week's worth of stories in that market, found stations routinely airing PR [public relations] footage provided by companies with no acknowledgment that this was what was going on.

- In a 1991 book examining the local news, *Making Local News,* Phyllis Kaniss found, among other things, that local TV news reporters are more likely to accept their sources' viewpoints than are print reporters.

- A Chicago reporter looking at "sweeps week" on Los Angeles television found heavily promoted news stories on lesbian nuns, Geraldo Rivera's love life, and sex after sixty.

As a critic once put it: The worst scandal the local news could ever uncover is itself.

Local news didn't start out this way. Until about 1970, local news — with its mix of local stories, weather, and sports delivered in a low-key broadcast — was an insignificant part of the television day. In the late '60s and early '70s, however, stations began to recognize the economic values of these newscasts. A news program is often less expensive than a dramatic show to produce, and, unlike national programming, the local station can retain the profits. Once they commenced in earnest, these newscasts began generating about one-third to half of the profits of local stations. Thus, in many markets, the local newscast started to expand — to a half-hour before the evening network news, then an hour, and in many markets to ninety minutes in the early evening and several other times throughout the day.

National network news had grown from radio, along with a concomi-   5
tant duty recognized by the networks to deliver information responsibly to
their viewers. Run by journalists, it was assumed these broadcasts would
be loss leaders. By contrast, the local news arose because there was money
to be made; the notion of what could possibly fill these hours came later,
and in many cases the shows were run by television people with no use for
traditional, pavement-pounding journalism.

Like the tabloid press at the turn of the century — faced with a similar
dilemma about how to bring a larger audience to news — the locals frequently turned to such sensationalistic topics as crime. They also turned to
the same small group of media consultants, who in turn tended to give
them the same instructions whether they were in Laredo or Los Angeles.
That explains the subsequent uniformity. In fact, anyone watching prime-
time television knew how the medium worked in the '70s and could have
guessed the advice: Crime shows like *Kojak* attract the largest audience.
Viewers respond to likable characters. All sitcoms revolve around families.
It was the "genius" of these marketers to take the principles of prime-time
fictional television and bring them to every local newscast in the nation,
where they still remain in force. As one consultant's report put it

> It is not surprising that research indicates ratings rise when the broadcast is
> successful in exposing the listener to what he wants to hear, in the very per-
> sonal way he wants to hear it. In terms of news, this means ratings are im-
> proved not when listeners are told what they should know, but what they
> want to hear.

In other words, news would become a form of entertainment.

The whole style had begun, of all places, on public television in the late
1960s, when KQED in San Francisco had experimented with a daily newscast for nine weeks during a local newspaper strike. For this newscast the
reporters gathered at a long table, where they discussed the stories they
presented in depth with an anchor. The first commercial station to adopt
the practice — beginning with the local San Francisco ABC affiliate — borrowed KQED's style, not its substance. Thus, "happy talk" became an
early feature of the local newscast, not to highlight the news but rather the
news*casters*.

According to Ron Powers, who chronicled the rise of local news in his
book *The Newscasters,* this style then became the signature of many ABC-
owned stations around the country, and others soon followed. One station
had a typical ad campaign that went, "So good news or bad, laugh a little
with your News-4 favorites: You'll feel better." The industry trotted forth
the usual analysts to explain its decision. "Audiences," said one, "have dia-
metrically opposed needs: The desire to know, and a tremendous fear of
finding out what happened. The communicator has to be someone they
like if he is to put the whole frightening world together for them." By

1971, *Time* was already complaining. "What counts is not how the banana men relate the news," it wrote, "but how they relate to each other."

The main competitor to happy news on the local newscircuit was the closely related concept of "action news," dubbed in many places "Eyewitness News." Also developed by consulting firms, its signature was a high story count, an increasing number of striking visuals, and exciting upbeat music. Typical consultant recommendations called for "simplifying and limiting treatment of complex news, and elimination of 'upper-class English.'" Key to all this was the presence of a personable male anchor — although if things went wrong in the ratings, he was usually the guy blamed. That may explain why New York's WNBC in its formative period for local news went through a half-dozen or so anchormen — including Jim Hartz, Gabe Pressman, John Palmer, and Frank McGee — in a search for the holy ratings grail. It wasn't long, of course, before the two styles merged, so that virtually every station was using "happy talk" along with the impressionistic, tabloid approach of "action news." "You must have action in the first 12 seconds," Don Hewitt, the producer of *60 Minutes,* would say one day. "It doesn't matter what the action is."

Over the years, these approaches have continued to dominate the style of local TV news, though improvements in technology have affected the mix. The use of satellites allowed stations to send more reporters "live" into the field, with the result that most newscasts eventually featured the daily obligatory story or two of reporters wandering around the crime scene with little to report but their own presence.   10

By the 1980s, the technology had also improved enough that many local stations could send reporters to both national and international events, to report back live. They usually managed to do that even before the network news had come on the air. In the past, the networks had restricted to their own national shows both the national and international footage they obtained — if not to preserve the quality of the reporting, then to maintain their exclusive franchise and keep ratings high. At the same time that local stations began traveling around, however, CNN broke the networks' monopoly on world and national footage by offering such feeds to the locals.

The result was that local stations began to become the average viewer's window on the whole world rather than just the local area. The same sketchy, tabloid coverage that had characterized local events now became the trademark of national and international coverage. "Can you imagine how the civil-rights movement would have been affected if only local stations handled it?" former CBS News President Richard Salant once asked a reporter. Actually, the question might have been *if* they had covered it at all, since local stations always seemed to prefer stories like plane crashes or hurricanes, which allowed them to fly their reporters somewhere, put them on a beach in rain gear, and encourage them to babble and act fearful.

Ironically, national feeds of all sorts became so easy for local stations to pick up that they stopped doing some of the harder work of local reporting. "Why have a reporter hang around City Hall when he or she can sit in your tape room in Des Moines or wherever, monitor an incoming feed on, say, Michael Jackson leaving a New York hospital, and then report 'live from the newsroom' on the story?" a former network news executive questioningly complained to former *New York Times* editor and current magazine columnist Max Frankel.

A similar inclination to laziness and self-promotion increasingly led the locals to use "news stories" to promote entertainment shows on their own network. "Meet *The Beast* at 9, then meet the man who created it at 11!" screamed one NBC promo in New York in the '90s (*The Beast* was a made-for-TV movie). In Washington, D.C., it was "The author of *The Beast* tells you what to fear right here in D.C.!" "You saw *Law and Order*," asked another, "but can it really happen?"

The effect of all this was to change the content of the national network newscasts themselves — which saw their ratings beginning to tumble as they faced this local threat. "After you have watched an hour of local news," Tom Bettag, an executive producer of the *CBS Evening News* asked in 1990, "why would you watch another half-hour of network?" So national anchors like Dan Rather hit the road, and the networks began becoming more tabloid themselves in an attempt to win back the audience they had lost to the locals.

By the '90s, the tail was wagging the dog: Now, local news was setting the journalistic standard for the networks. The result was that tabloid-like stories about Michael Jackson or Tonya Harding and Nancy Kerrigan also became the province of national newscasts — as did the perennial local obsession with crime. Even excluding the O.J. Simpson case, the three network newscasts spent four times as many hours covering murder cases in 1994 as they had only four years earlier. In 1995, the three network newscasts broadcast 2,574 crime stories — nearly one of every five stories run. That was four times the number of crime stories they had run as late as 1991, even though crime had actually declined in this later period.

With local stations providing an alternative to national broadcasts, newsmakers also had the option of going to them to make their case. During his presidency, George Bush often used local media to get his message across, knowing that local anchors — awed by the presidency and their own lack of national experience — would ask less-threatening questions than the network reporters. The practice continued in earnest throughout the 1992 campaign, when Bill Clinton did the same thing — beginning in the New Hampshire primary, as he circumvented national reporters who seemed to want to talk only about Gennifer Flowers.

On the one hand, these local stations do provide a venue for national figures to talk about issues when the national press tends to get bogged down talking about "insider" strategy rather than substance. On the other hand, such reports often provide virtually no critical analysis; many congressmen have been known to get their canned "news feeds" directly on

15

the air, particularly in smaller markets. Communication it is, but journalism it isn't.

Improved technology also gave greater prominence on the local newscast to the weather — for very practical reasons often the heart of the show. Weather is only a small part of newspaper journalism, but it has been an integral part of local TV news since its inception in the 1950s. After all, the introduction of weather news permitted another commercial between segments — and, with news in those primitive days consisting entirely of a sober anchor reading a script at a desk, it allowed local news shows to introduce their first nonhard-news personalities. Joining the early ranks were New York's Tex Antoine with Uncle Weatherbee and Washington's Willard Scott, who occasionally would dress up as Robin Hood, George Washington, or whomever, and once said, "A trained gorilla could do what I do." In the 1950s some stations even turned to attractive "weather girls," one of whom once said, "The temperature in New York is 46 — and me, I'm 36-26-36."

With the development of weather satellites in the '70s and '80s, however, the visuals improved greatly — allowing viewers to observe the process of weather formation in ways they couldn't before. In fact, with the hiring of meteorologists as weather forecasters, weather reporting became so good on TV that once the cable industry was up and running, one of its more successful stations proved to be the Weather Channel. In late summer, Americans would begin tracking every tropical storm, hour by hour, and in the winter they did the same with snow. "The news media, particularly if there are no other big events, tend to overhype the storms compared to what storms actually do," Bill Gray, a professor of atmospheric science at Colorado State University once told a reporter. "You have a lot of these beautiful satellite pictures that create a lot of interest. And people have a natural interest in damage and other people's problems. It makes your own problems seem a little less." 20

Yet on the local news, weather would always take a back seat to crime. And studies showed that an overload of crime news tends to make viewers ever more fearful and increasingly likely to support ever more radical measures designed to curb disorder. "What I object to is the lack of context," a local TV news reporter once said. "It all goes hurtling by, and the world is a frightening and inexplicable place."

Moreover, what gets ignored gets forgotten. "[C]overage of the environment, education, the economy, science, the arts, children, civil rights, parenting, conflict resolution, and homelessness didn't make the news today on most stations," stated the aforementioned Rocky Mountain Media Watch study, reporting on the results of its survey of a day in the life of local news. "And if it's not in the news, it's not on our public agenda."

In his book *The Newscasters,* Ron Powers suggested twenty years ago that local TV news had an obligation to sacrifice some of its profits to give

Advertisement

— From *People* (September 15, 1997).

its community better-informed newscasts. Yet, better-informed citizens now know to avoid local TV news for much of anything but weather and sports. In an atomized market, where wealthier viewers can turn to computers or cable (including around-the-clock local cable news in many areas), local TV news is increasingly left with a downscale audience that doesn't think that "journalism" as practiced in the *National Enquirer* or the tabloids is all that terrible. The producers of these newscasts are right when they proclaim that local TV news gives viewers what they want. It just doesn't give them what they need.

Responding as a Reader

1. Look at the passages in which Stark cites the subjects of news stories and explains what takes place on the local TV news. What is the tone of these passages? What is Stark's attitude toward his readers? Who is his intended audience?

2. "Communication it is," writes Stark, "but journalism it isn't" (para. 18). What is Stark's definition of journalism? Why doesn't local news fit this definition?

3. What is Stark saying, in the final paragraph, about the American public? What distinction is he making between what viewers want and what they need? Do viewers know the difference between what kind of news they want and what kind of news they need? Who should be the judge of that, according to Stark? What do you think?

Responding as a Writer

1. Watch your local news for at least a few nights. Does it fit Stark's description? What percentage of time is dedicated to each type of coverage? What features of the news remain the same from one day to the next? Write a report on your findings.

2. Compare one day's coverage of a major local news story on the TV news and in the newspaper. How much time does the TV news dedicate to the story? How much space does the newspaper dedicate? What pictures are shown in each medium? What authorities are quoted? What evidence and details are given? Which medium do you think covers the story more effectively and why?

3. Consider the quotation from Don Imus on page 366. Who is Don Imus? Do you consider his view of the news to be typical of radio and television personalities? In an essay, apply Imus's perspective to one medium that covers the news — AM or FM radio, local or national TV news, newspapers or magazines.

Sein of the Times

[THE NEW YORK REVIEW OF BOOKS / August 14, 1997]

It is just another day in the Republic of Entertainment, and as always a major story is taking shape. DANGER SEIN, reads the headline of the *Daily News* for May 9, 1997, over a photograph of the stars of NBC's phenomenally popular sitcom *Seinfeld:* Jerry Seinfeld, Julia Louis-Dreyfus, Jason Alexander, and Michael Richards. They are clearly out of character, huddling cozily together and beaming with an appearance of warm feeling entirely inappropriate to the needling and conniving personae they embody on TV. The issue in the story is money, specifically the one million dollars per episode that each of Jerry Seinfeld's co-stars is demanding for the impending ninth season of what the *News* reporter describes as "television's first billion-dollar sitcom." THREE STARS HOLD OUT IN HIGH-STAKES BATTLE OVER NBC MEGAHIT: Only the language of hostage-taking and terrorist attack (the actors "imperil" the series with their "hard-line demands" and "it is essential that the impasse be resolved soon") can do justice to the drama of the event. (The impasse was resolved a few days later for roughly $600,000 per episode.)

A few days later, a counterattack of sorts takes place, in the form of a *New York Times* Op-Ed piece in which Maureen Dowd professes shock at the "breathtaking" salaries demanded by the "surreally greedy" actors and proceeds to a ringing denunciation of the "ever more self-referential and self-regarding" *Seinfeld:* "The show is our Dorian Gray[1] portrait, a reflection of the what's-in-it-for-me times that allowed Dick Morris and Bill Clinton to triumph." For backup she cites Leon Wieseltier of the *New Republic,* who describes the show as "the worst, last gasp of Reaganite, grasping, materialistic, narcissistic, banal self-absorption." (Neither addresses the question of why it is greedy for veteran actors who are indis-

---

[1]The 1891 novel by Oscar Wilde, *The Picture of Dorian Gray* concerns a beautiful young man whose portrait continually mirrors his moral degeneration.

GEOFFREY O'BRIEN *(b. 1948) is executive editor of the Library of America and the author of* Dream Time: Chapters From the Sixties *(1988),* The Phantom Empire *(1993), and* Hardboiled America *(1981), of which a new edition was just recently published. O'Brien is a frequent contributor to the* New York Review of Books.

pensable to the most successful show on television — and who cannot reasonably expect another comparable windfall — to insist on a fair chunk of the money that would otherwise flow into the NBC kitty.)

In any event, the diatribe scarcely registers, crowded out by celebratory cover stories in *TV Guide* ("Michael Richards: Still Kramer After All These Years . . . Seinfelds' slapstick sidekick strikes it rich!"); *Business Week* ("*Seinfeld:* The Economics of a TV Supershow, and What It Means for NBC and the Industry"); and an encyclopedic special issue of *Entertainment Weekly* — "The Ultimate *Seinfeld* Viewer's Guide" — including a plot summary of the series' 148 episodes to date (an admirably meticulous piece of scholarship, by the way).

The ramifications extend: A franchising company will turn a soup restaurant called Soup Nutsy (inspired by the *Seinfeld* episode about the Soup Nazi, itself inspired by the allegedly intimidating proprietor of Soup Kitchen International on West 55th Street) into a name-brand chain, that is if it is not outflanked by another chain, Soup Man Enterprises, which (according to another story) has struck a deal with the man from Soup Kitchen International (although the latter is duly appalled by " 'the hateful name' . . . he had been given on *Seinfeld*"); the *New York Times* interviews Canadian comic Mike Myers about *Seinfeld* as emblem of American comedic values ("that observational comedy — observing the everyday minutiae and creating a glossary of terms"); the *New York Post* reports that a Miller Brewing Company manager has been fired for talking in the office about a *Seinfeld* episode (the one about the woman whose name rhymes with a female body part) — SEINFELD RHYME IS REASON BEER EXEC GOT CANNED — and the ensuing trial is covered by Court TV; in *Vanity Fair, The New Yorker,* and elsewhere, Jerry Seinfeld himself poses with shoe polisher, goldfish bowl, and boxes of cereal as an advertising representative for the American Express Card; a discussion in *New York* about the erosion of Jewish identity cites *Seinfeld* as a supreme and troubling example of the assimilation of Jewish cultural style into the mainstream; and *TV Guide* enshrines two *Seinfeld* episodes in its special issue of the "100 Greatest Episodes of All Time" (an issue produced in conjunction with the cable channel Nickelodeon to promote a "Greatest Episodes of All Time Week," which will promote, in turn, a spinoff channel called TV Land, which is lobbying to be added to the roster of Time Warner's New York cable).

In exposure it doesn't get any better in this republic, all to make people even more conscious of a show they would probably have been watching anyway, since, quite aside from the hype, it happens to be inventive and suggestive and consistently funny in ways that television rarely permits. How weirdly, in fact, the speed and rigor of the show contrast with the elephantine and intrinsically humorless mechanisms of publicity and subsidiary marketing that accrue around it. My feelings about *Seinfeld* — a show I had long since gotten into the habit of watching in reruns, as a welcome respite from the execrable local news at eleven — might have been different had I known I was watching (in the words of a spokesman for what *Business Week* calls a "top media buyer") not merely a funny show but "one of the most important shows in history."

Once there wasn't anything that seemed quite so overpoweringly important, at least not anything short of World War II or space travel. I can remember, barely, what it was like when television was still a distinctive and somewhat raggedy presence in a world to which it was foreign. The memories have a pastoral quality, mixing in bushes from the other side of the window, perhaps, or a vase of flowers adjacent to the TV cabinet. Into that world of rich colors and complex textures emanated — from the squat monolithic box in the corner — a vague and grayish mass of moving figures, characters in a story line that often (given the vagaries of reception, the inadequacy of early TV amplification, and the clatter of household interruptions which people had not yet learned to tune out) had to be deduced from partial evidence.

The memories are imbued as well with a flavor of voluptuous indolence — an indolence associated with sofas, pillows, bowls of candy or popcorn, and apparently endless stretches of disposable time — which only at later ages would come to seem more like the flavor of weakness or compulsion or simple lack of anything better to do. (It took about a generation for the culture to acquire the absolute sense of the TV watcher's ennui that provides a major subtext for *Seinfeld*, which often ends as the characters are just clicking the set on as if in resignation to their fate.)

It doesn't seem to matter particularly what programs were on. Between the ages of five and ten, for instance, I absorbed any number of installments of a stream of television comedies, including *The Abbott and Costello Show, Amos and Andy, You Bet Your Life, The Jack Benny Program, Private Secretary, Mr. Peepers, The George Burns and Gracie Allen Show, Make Room for Daddy, My Little Margie, The Adventures of Ozzie and Harriet, The Life of Riley, Ethel and Albert, Father Knows Best, December Bride, Mama, The Bob Cummings Show,* and *Bachelor Father*. Of all these, barely a single specific episode has engraved itself in memory, although each left behind a vivid impression of its essential nature, a sort of Platonic episode embodying all possible variants.

The plots, as I recall, tended to revolve around failed practical jokes, embarrassing household mishaps, doomed get-rich-quick schemes, ceaseless unsuccessful attempts to get the better of one's next-door neighbor, misinterpreted telephone calls, misdirected packages. A well-meaning husband would sell his wife's heirloom to the junkman by mistake or invest his savings in a con man's Florida real estate scam; a household pet would knock Aunt Flora's elderberry wine into the punch bowl; Junior would go to elaborate lengths to lie about the window he knocked out playing softball; a secretary would mix up the dunning letters and the party invitations, or uproariously blow off her boss's toupee by turning up the air conditioner full blast.

There were also other and better comedies — *The Phil Silvers Show,*   10
The Honeymooners, I Love Lucy — of which, with the reinforcement of endless reruns, I retain a much sharper recollection. But the overall effect was of an ill-defined, continually shifting flow not altogether unlike the movement of fishes in an aquarium, soothing, diverting, and (with the exception of certain programs — such as *The Web* or *Danger* — given over to tales of the eerie and uncanny) incapable of causing upset. It was stuff that danced before one's eyes and then never came back; that was its charm and its limitation.

The sheer quantity of programming was already impressive in the '50s. In retrospect — as I scan complete schedules of network shows and realize just how many of them I watched — it seems unaccountable that there was ever time for other important cultural activities like going to the movies, reading comic books, listening to LPs of Broadway show tunes, collecting bubble gum cards, or studying with the utmost seriousness each new issue of *Life* and *Children's Digest* and, of course, *TV Guide.* Yet the evidence is inescapable as my eye runs down the listings and recognizes one forgotten companion after another, *The Court of Last Resort, The Millionaire, Mark Saber of London, Sergeant Preston of the Yukon, Name That Tune, To Tell the Truth,* not to mention *Schlitz Playhouse* and *The Gisele MacKenzie Show.*

Of course nothing was ever as unconscious as early television programming appears in hindsight. In fact, we thought television was a big deal then too; we just didn't have any idea what "big deal" really meant. Only by comparison with the present day do those rudimentary efforts take on the improvisational air of a reign of accident, where words and images washed up — anything to fill ten minutes here, twenty minutes there — as if their purveyors had given only the faintest glimmer of a thought to the overall design they formed.

The big deal that is *Seinfeld* is also just a quick little thing, a concentrated dose of farcical invention that seems to be watched by just about everybody. People watch it for reasons as varied as its uncannily precise analysis of miserable but inescapable relationships, its evocation of the bizarre randomness of urban life, its pratfalls and grimaces, its original contributions to the language (the "glossary of terms" to which Mike Meyers refers, evolving out of an almost Elizabethan fondness for protracted quibbles), its affinity with the fantastically mutating formalism of Edmund Spenser,[2] or the platform it provides for the fantastically mutating eyes and eyebrows and mouth of Julia Louis-Dreyfus. It is a brief and reliable pleasure.

---

[2] The English poet Edmund Spenser (c. 1552–1599) is the author of *The Faerie Queene,* a major literary epic; mutability is one of its central themes.

The most obvious source for this pleasure is a cast capable of unusual refinements of ensemble playing. Seinfeld himself (originally a stand-up comic whose routines revolved around rather mild evocations of life's minor absurdities) is the indispensable straight man, the perfect stand-in for anybody, just a guy in sneakers who lives alone on the Upper West Side of Manhattan, watches television, hangs out with his friends, and only gradually reveals himself as the *homme moyen obsessionel*,[3] whose mania for neatness keeps incipient panic at bay. Seinfeld's manner, so understated as to make his lines seem thrown away, works beautifully against the relentlessly goading, operatically whining style of Jason Alexander's George (a character apparently modeled on the series' co-creator, Larry David), in whom the classic Woody Allen neurotic persona is cranked to a far more grating level of cringing self-abasement and equally monstrous self-serving. Alexander is the real workhorse of the series and inhabits the role so thoroughly that he can get away, for instance, with an episode in which he knocks over small children in an effort to escape from a smoke-filled building.

The blank zone inhabited by Jerry and George — their trademark   15 ennui punctuated by ricocheting gags — is made richer and stranger by Julia Louis-Dreyfus as Jerry's ex-girlfriend Elaine and Michael Richards as the perpetually mooching across-the-hall neighbor Kramer. Less striking in the earliest episodes, Louis-Dreyfus's brand of facial comedy has evolved into a distinct art form. Analyzed in slow motion, her shifts of expression are revealed as a complex ballet in which eyes, nose, mouth, neck, and shoulder negotiate hairpin turns or spiral into free fall. The smirk, the self-satisfied grin, the effusion of faked warmth, the grimace of barely concealed revulsion: each is delineated with razor precision before it slides into a slightly different shading.

As for Richards's Kramer, it seems hardly necessary at this point to praise what has become probably the most familiar comic turn in recent memory. Kramer as a character embodies all the expansive and ecstatic impulses that are severely curtailed in the others, creating an opportunity for the mercurial transformations in which Richards adopts by rapid turns the masks of Machiavellian intrigue, righteous anger, infant rapture, jaded worldliness, Buddhistic detachment, down-home bonhomie. Richards practices a refinement of the school of manic role-shifting of which Robin Williams and the Michael Keaton of *Beetlejuice* were earlier exemplars and seals his performance with pratfalls which by now are legendary.

Seinfeld's singular intensity has everything to do with its brevity, the twenty-two minutes of programming paid for by eight minutes of commercials. (In this case it works out to more than a million dollars a minute.) By

[3]*Homme moyen obsessionel* (French) means "the obsessive average man."

straining at the limits of what can fit into a twenty-two-minute slot (rather than visibly struggling to fill it, like most shows), *Seinfeld* distends time. Its best episodes feel like feature films and indeed have busier narratives than most features. (The periodic one-hour episodes, by contrast, sometimes go weirdly slack.) There is no padding; plot exposition is relayed in telegraphic jolts. An episode normally encompasses three separate plots that must converge in some fashion at the end, and the management of these crisscrossing storylines, the elisions and internal rhymes and abrupt interlacements, is one of the show's delights.

The sheer quantity of matter to be wrapped up enforces an exhilarating narrative shorthand. Comic opportunities that most shows would milk are tossed off in a line or two. The tension and density of working against the time constraint is a reminder of how fruitful such constraints can be. If Count Basie had not been limited to the duration of a 78 rpm record, would we have the astonishing compression of "Every Tub" (three minutes, fourteen seconds) or "Jumpin' at the Woodside" (three minutes, eight seconds)?

The enormous budget, of course, makes possible frequent and elaborate scene changes that would be prohibitive for most shows. (It also makes possible a brilliant and constantly shifting supporting cast of taxi drivers, doormen, liquor store owners, television executives, German tourists, midwestern neo-Nazis, and hundreds more.) We are far from the primal simplicity of *The Honeymooners,* whose aura owed much to the rudimentary and unchanging space of Ralph and Alice Kramden's impoverished kitchen. *Seinfeld* — despite the recurrent settings of Jerry's apartment and Monk's Café — is not about space in the same way, only about the psychic space of the characters and the catch phrases and body language that translate it. They carry their world with them into elevators and waiting rooms, gyms and airplanes and Chinese restaurants.

It is a world in sharp focus (rendered with an obsessive concern for surface realism of speech and clothing and furniture) in which everyone, friend and stranger alike, undergoes permanent uncomfortable scrutiny. The prevailing mood of *Seinfeld*'s protagonists is hypercritical irritation. Deeply annoyed by others most of the time, the four leads are only erratically conscious of how much annoyance they generate in turn. The spectrum of self-awareness ranges from George's abject self-loathing ("People like me shouldn't be allowed to live!") to the blissed-out self-approbation of Kramer, with a special place reserved for the scene where subtitles translate the comments of the Korean manicurists on whom Elaine is bestowing what she imagines to be a friendly smile while she waits impatiently to have her nails done: "Princess wants a manicure. . . . Mustn't keep Princess waiting."

The mutual kvetching of Jerry and George — of which we're given just enough to know how unbearable continuous exposure would be — serves as the ground bass over which Kramer, Elaine, and the expanding circle of subsidiary characters weave endless comic variations. The relationship of Jerry and George is much like that of talk show host and sidekick, marked by constant obligatory banter indistinguishable from nagging. In short, a comfortable level of hostility and mistrust is maintained, upheld by everyone's fundamental desire not to get too closely involved with other people.

Seinfeld is defined by a series of refusals. Romantic love is not even a possibility, although deceptive or obsessive forms of it occasionally surface. Sex figures merely as a relentless necessity and an endless source of complications, and the intrigues that surround it have a detached, businesslike tone. (*Seinfeld* succeeds in making a joke not only out of sex but, more scandalously, out of sexual attractiveness, the "telegenic" currency of the medium.) Nor does the show succumb to the feel-good impulses that are the last resort of American movies and TV shows; it remains blessedly free of that simulation of human warmth evident in everything from weather reports to commercials for investment banking. There is a tacit contract that at no point will Seinfeld and friends break down and testify to how much they really like one another. It's clear that each thinks he really could have done better in the way of friends but happens to be stuck with these ones and can't imagine how to survive without them.

The emotional tone is a throwback to the frank mutual aggressiveness of Laurel and Hardy or Abbott and Costello (the latter frequently acknowledged by Seinfeld as a prime influence), who never made the error of thinking their characters lovable. *Seinfeld* likewise keeps in sight the comic importance of subjecting its characters to cruelty and humiliation, of forcing them constantly to squirm and lie and accept disgrace before disappearing into the ether until next week. (The humiliations in question are often physical; the show has tirelessly enlisted body parts, bodily fluids, disgusting personal habits, diseases, and medical operations into its scenarios, as if the comedy of the lower body were necessary to keep in balance all that disembodied verbal riffing.)

What a relief to encounter comedy that does not mistake itself for anything else. Its characters are free to start from zero each time, free to indulge the marvelous shallowness that is the privilege of the creatures of farce. Nothing counts here, nothing has consequences; as one of the show's writers (Larry Charles, in *Entertainment Weekly*) has observed, the crucial guideline is that the characters do not learn from experience and never move beyond what they intrinsically and eternally are.

They cannot better themselves: a condition with positively subversive   25
implications in a culture of self-help and self-aggrandizement where has-beens no longer attempt comebacks but rather "reinvent themselves" and where a manual for would-be best-selling autobiographers advises how to "turn your memories into memoirs." There is a wonderful moment when Kramer, swelling with indignation at some petty trespass of Jerry's, asks

him: "What kind of person *are* you?" and he replies in squeaky desperation, "I don't know!" The characters can only play at self-knowledge; any real consciousness of who they are — unless in some alternate world, along the lines of the celebrated "Bizarro Jerry" episode, in which the leads are stalked by uncanny near-copies of themselves — would be like the cartoon moment when Bugs Bunny looks down and realizes he's walking on air.

Although they cannot evolve, they do change form ceaselessly. The fact of not really being people gives them an ideal flexibility. If Kramer is convinced in one episode that Jerry has been a secret Nazi all along, or if sexual abstinence enables George to become an absurd polymath effortlessly soaking up Portuguese and advanced physics, it will leave no aftertaste the next time around.

If *Seinfeld* is indeed, in the words of *Entertainment Weekly,* "the defining sitcom of our age" (one wonders how many such ages, each defined by its own sitcom, have already elapsed), the question remains what exactly it defines. Deliberate satire is alien to the spirit of the enterprise. *Seinfeld* has perfected a form in which anything can be invoked — masturbation, Jon Voight, death, kasha, deafness, faked orgasms, Salman Rushdie, Pez dispensers — without assuming the burden of saying anything about it (thereby avoiding the "social message" trap of programs like Norman Lear's *All in the Family* or *Maude*).

The show does not comment on anything except, famously, itself, in the series of episodes where Jerry and George create a pilot for a sitcom "about nothing," a sitcom identical to the one we are watching. This ploy — which ultimately necessitates a whole set of look-alikes to impersonate the cast of the show-within-a-show *Jerry* — ties in with the recursive, alternate-universe mode of such comedies as *The Purple Rose of Cairo* and *Groundhog Day,* while holding back just this side of the paranormal. If conspiracy theories surface from time to time, it is purely for amusement value, as in the episode where a spitting incident at the ballpark becomes the occasion for an elaborate parody — complete with Zapruder-like home movie[4] — of the Single Bullet Theory (figuring in this context as the ultimate joke on the idea of explanation).

The result is a vastly entertaining mosaic of observed bits and traits and frames. Imagine some future researcher trying to annotate any one of these episodes, like a Shakespearean scholar dutifully noting that "tapsters were proverbially poor at arithmetic." It would not merely be a matter of explaining jokes and cultural references and curt showbiz locutions — "He does fifteen minutes on Ovaltine" or "They cancelled Rick James" — but of explicating (always assuming that they were detected in the first place) each shrug and curtailed expostulation and deftly averted glance.

---

[4]Zapruder-like home movie is a reference to the Dallas bystander who caught John F. Kennedy's assassination on film.

Where it might once have been asked if *Seinfeld* was a commentary on   30
society, the question now should probably be whether society has not been
reconfigured as a milieu for commenting on *Seinfeld*. If the craziness enacted on the show is nothing more than the usual business of comedy, the
craziness that swirls around it in the outside world is of a less hilarious
order. Comedy and money have always been around, but not always in
such intimate linkage, and certainly not on so grandiose a scale. In the fifteenth century, the fate of Tudor commerce was not perceived to hinge on
the traveling English players who wowed foreign audiences as far afield as
Denmark.

The information-age money culture for which *Seinfeld* is only another,
fatter, bargaining chip clearly lost its sense of humor a long time ago, a fact
that becomes ever more apparent as we move into an economy where sitcoms replace iron and steel as principal products and where fun is not
merely big business but seemingly the only business. The once-endearing
razzmatazz of showbiz hype warps into a perceptible desperation that registers all too plainly how much is at stake for the merchandisers. One becomes uncomfortably aware of them looming behind the audience, running
electronic analyses of the giggles, and nervously watching for the dreaded
moment when the laughter begins to dry up. It all begins to seem too much
like work even for the audience, who may well begin to wonder why they
should be expected to care about precisely how much their amusement is
worth to the ticket-sellers.

As for the actual creators of the fun, I would imagine that — allowing
for difference of scale and pressure — they go about their work pretty
much the same way regardless of the going price for a good laugh. Some
years ago, in a dusty corner of Languedoc,[5] I watched a dented circus truck
pull up unannounced along the roadside. The family of performers who
clambered out proceeded to set up a makeshift stage, which in a few hours
time was ready for their show: a display of tumbling and magic that could
have been presented without significant difference in the fifteenth century.
After two hours of sublime entertainment, they passed the hat around and
drove away toward the next bend in the road. It is strange to think of the
fate of empires, even entertainment empires, hinging on such things.

---

[5] Languedoc is a region in southern France.

Responding as a Reader

1. Go over the "ramifications" O'Brien lists in paragraph 4. What do
   these examples imply about *Seinfeld*'s influence? About television in
   general? About viewers?

2. Consider O'Brien's claims that "we thought television was a big deal [in the early days] too; we just didn't have any idea what 'big deal' really meant" (para. 12) and that "the big deal that is *Seinfeld* is also just a quick little thing" (para. 13). What is the big deal here? What is O'Brien saying about the aspects of television that have changed and those that have stayed the same?

3. Of all the *Seinfeld* episodes that O'Brien mentions, how many have you seen? Do you agree with what he says about the show? If somehow you have managed to avoid seeing *Seinfeld*, watch a few episodes (it's also in syndication) and test O'Brien's critique against your own experience.

Responding as a Writer

1. Choose a television program that you enjoy and analyze it as O'Brien does *Seinfeld*. Consider any or all of the following elements: the acting, the writing, the jokes, the pace, the sets and locations, the similarity to real life, and its overall entertainment value.

2. "If *Seinfeld* is indeed . . . the defining sitcom of our age . . . the question remains what exactly it defines" (para. 27). Explore this question in an essay. Is it possible for a time period (say the last ten years) to be defined, or summed up, by a sitcom? If not, why not, and if so, how? In what ways does *Seinfeld* seem to capture the spirit of its time? Are there aspects of life at the end of the twentieth century (or, to be fair, middle-class Manhattan life) that *Seinfeld* does not touch on?

3. Much of this article pertains to money and how much *Seinfeld* brings in. Does *Seinfeld* deserve a million dollars a minute and do Louis-Dreyfus, Richards, and Alexander deserve $600,000 an episode? Why or why not? How do these salaries compare to those of big-draw professional athletes or movie stars? Where does the money come from?

JAMES B. TWITCHELL

But First, A Word From Our Sponsor

[THE WILSON QUARTERLY / Summer 1996]

Whenever a member of my paunchy fiftysomething set pulls me aside and complains of the dumbing down of American culture, I tell him that if he doesn't like it, he should quit moaning and go buy a lot of Fast-Moving Consumer Goods. And every time he buys soap, toothpaste, beer, gasoline, bread, aspirin, and the like, he should make it a point to buy a different brand. He should implore his friends to do likewise. At the same time, he should quit giving so much money to his kids. That, I'm sorry to say, is his only hope.

Here's why. The culture we live in is carried on the back of advertising. Now I mean that literally. If you cannot find commercial support for what you have to say, it will not be transported. Much of what we share, and what we know, and even what we treasure, is carried to us each second in a plasma of electrons, pixels, and ink, underwritten by multinational advertising agencies dedicated to attracting our attention for entirely non-altruistic reasons. These agencies, gathered up inside worldwide conglomerates with weird, sci-fi names like WPP, Omnicom, Saatchi & Saatchi, Dentsu, and Euro RSCG, are usually collections of established shops linked together to provide "full service" to their global clients. Their service is not moving information or creating entertainment, but buying space and inserting advertising. They essentially rent our concentration to other companies — sponsors — for the dubious purpose of informing us of something that we've longed for all our lives even though we've never heard of it before. Modern selling is not about trading information, as it was in the nineteenth century, as much as about creating an infotainment culture with sufficient allure to enable other messages — commercials — to get through. In the spirit of the enterprise, I call this new culture Adcult.

JAMES B. TWITCHELL (b. 1943) has taught at Duke University and California State College and has been nominated for the National Book Award and the National Book Critic's Circle Award. He is the author of Carnival Culture: The Trashing of Taste in America *(1992) and most recently,* Adcult USA: The Triumph of Advertising in American Culture *(1995). He is currently a professor of English at the University of Florida in Gainesville. The text reprinted here is taken from the opening section of a longer essay that details the history of advertising in the various media.*

Adcult is there when we blink, it's there when we listen, it's there when we touch, it's even there to be smelled in scent strips when we open a magazine. There is barely a space in our culture not already carrying commercial messages. Look anywhere: in schools there is Channel One; in movies there is product placement; ads are in urinals, played on telephone hold, in alphanumeric displays in taxis, sent unannounced to fax machines, inside catalogs, on the video in front of the Stairmaster at the gym, on T-shirts, at the doctor's office, on grocery carts, on parking meters, on tees at golf holes, on inner-city basketball backboards, piped in along with Muzak . . . ad nauseam (and yes, even on airline vomit bags). We have to shake magazines like rag dolls to free up their pages from the "blow-in" inserts and then wrestle out the stapled- or glued-in ones before reading can begin. We now have to fast-forward through some five minutes of advertising that opens rental videotapes. President Bill Clinton's second inaugural parade featured a Budweiser float. At the Smithsonian, the Orkin Pest Control Company sponsored an exhibit on exactly what it advertises it kills: insects. No venue is safe. Is there a blockbuster museum show not decorated with corporate logos? The Public Broadcasting Service is littered with "underwriting announcements" that look and sound almost exactly like what PBS claims they are not: commercials.

Okay, you get the point. Commercial speech is so powerful that it drowns out all other sounds. But sounds are always conveyed in a medium. The media of modern culture are these: print, sound, pictures, or some combination of each. Invariably, conversations about dumbing down focus on the supposed corruption of these media, as demonstrated by the sophomoric quality of most movies, the fall from the golden age of television, the mindlessness of most best-sellers, and the tarting-up of the news, be it in or on *USA Today, Time,* ABC, or *Inside Edition.* The media make especially convenient whipping boys because they are now all conglomerated into huge worldwide organizations such as Time Warner, General Electric, Viacom, Bertelsmann, and Sony. But, alas, as much fun as it is to blame the media, they have very little to do with the explanation for whatever dumbing down has occurred.

The explanation is, I think, more fundamental, more economic in nature. These media are delivered for a price. We have to pay for them, either by spending money or by spending time. Given a choice, we prefer to spend time. We spend our time paying attention to ads, and in exchange we are given infotainment. This trade is central to Adcult. Economists call this "cost externalization." If you want to see it at work, go to McDonald's. You order. You carry your food to the table. You clean up. You pay less. Want to see it elsewhere? Buy gas. Just as the "work" you do at the self-service gas station lowers the price of gas, so consuming ads is the "work" you do that lowers the price of delivering the infotainment. In Adcult, the trade is more complex. True, you are entertained at lower cost, but you are also encultured in the process.

Infotainment Culture

So far, so good. The quid pro quo of modern infotainment culture is that if you want it, you'll get it — no matter what it is — as long as there are enough of you who (1) are willing to spend some energy along the way hearing "a word from our sponsor" and (2) have sufficient disposable income possibly to buy some of the advertised goods. In Adcult you pay twice: once with the ad and once with the product. So let's look back a step to examine these products because — strange as it may seem — they are at the center of the dumbing down of American culture.

Before all else we must realize that modern advertising is tied primarily to things and only secondarily to services. Manufacturing both things and their meanings is what American culture is all about. If Greece gave the world philosophy, Britain drama, Austria music, Germany politics, and Italy art, then America gave mass-produced objects. "We bring good things to life" is no offhand claim. Most of these "good things" are machine made and hence interchangeable. Such objects, called parity items, constitute most of the stuff that surrounds us, from bottled water to toothpaste to beer to cars. There is really no great difference between Evian and Mountain Spring, Colgate and Crest, Miller and Budweiser, Ford and Chevrolet. Often, the only difference is in the advertising. Advertising is how we talk about these fungible things, how we know their supposed differences, how we recognize them. We don't consume the products as much as we consume the advertising.

For some reason, we like it this way. Logically, we should all read Consumer Reports and then all buy the most sensible product. But we don't. So why do we waste our energy (and billions of dollars) entertaining fraudulent choice? I don't know. Perhaps just as we drink the advertising, not the beer, we prefer the illusion of choice to the reality of decision. How else to explain the appearance of so much superfluous choice? A decade ago, grocery stores carried about 9,000 items; they now stock about 24,000. Revlon makes 158 shades of lipstick. Crest toothpaste comes in thirty-six sizes and shapes and flavors. We are even eager to be offered choice where there is none to speak of. AT&T offers "the right choice"; Wendy's asserts that "there is no better choice"; Pepsi is "the choice of a new generation"; Taster's Choice is "the choice for taste." Even advertisers don't understand the phenomenon. Is there a relationship between the number of soft drinks and television channels — about twenty-seven? What's going to happen when the information pipe carries 500?

Things

I have no idea. But I do know this: Human beings like things. We buy things. We like to exchange things. We steal things. We donate things. We live through things. We call these things "goods," as in "goods and services." We do not call them "bads." This sounds simplistic, but it is crucial to understanding the power of Adcult. The still-going-strong Industrial Revolution produces more and more things, not because production is what machines do and not because nasty capitalists twist their handlebar mustaches and mutter, "More slop for the pigs," but because we are powerfully attracted to the world of things. Advertising, when it's lucky, supercharges some of this attraction.

This attraction to the inanimate happens all over the world. Berlin   10 Walls fall because people want things, and they want the culture created by things. China opens its doors not so much because it wants to get out, but because it wants to get things in. We were not suddenly transformed from customers to consumers by wily manufacturers eager to unload a surplus of products. We have created a surfeit of things because we enjoy the process of "getting and spending." The consumption ethic may have started in the early 1900s, but the desire is ancient. Kings and princes once thought they could solve problems by amassing things. We now join them.

The Marxist balderdash of cloistered academics aside, human beings did not suddenly become materialistic. We have always been desirous of things. We have just not had many of them until quite recently, and, in a few generations, we may return to having fewer and fewer. Still, while they last, we enjoy shopping for things and see both the humor and the truth reflected in the aphoristic "born to shop," "shop 'til you drop," and "when the going gets tough, the tough go shopping." Department store windows, whether on the city street or inside a mall, did not appear by magic. We enjoy looking through them to another world. It is voyeurism for capitalists. Our love of things is the cause of the Industrial Revolution, not the consequence. We are not only homo sapiens, or homo ludens, or homo faber, but also homo emptor.[1]

Mid-twentieth-century American culture is often criticized for being too materialistic. Ironically, we are not too materialistic. We are not materialistic enough. If we craved objects and knew what they meant, there would be no need to add meaning through advertising. We would gather, use, toss out, or hoard based on some inner sense of value. But we don't. We don't know what to gather, we like to trade what we have gathered, and we need to know how to evaluate objects of little practical use. What is clear is that most things in and of themselves simply do not mean enough. In fact, what we crave may not be objects at all but their meaning. For whatever else advertising "does," one thing is certain: By adding value to material, by adding meaning to objects, by branding things, advertising performs a role historically associated with religion. The Great Chain of Being, which for centuries located value above the horizon in the world Beyond, has been reforged to settle value into the objects of the Here and Now.

---

[1]Latin expressions for man (homo) as rational (sapiens), as playful (ludens), as builder (faber), and as buyer (emptor).

Consumption

I wax a little impatient here because most of the literature on modern culture is downright supercilious about consumption. What do you expect? Most of it comes from a culture professionally hostile to materialism, albeit secretly envious. From Thorstein Veblen[2] on there has been a palpable sense of disapproval as the hubbub of commerce is viewed from the groves of academe. The current hand-wringing over dumbing down is not new. It used to be Bread and Circuses. Modern concepts of bandwagon consumption, conspicuous consumption, keeping-up-with-the-Joneses, the culture of narcissism, and all the other barely veiled reproofs have limited our serious consideration of Adcult to such relatively minor issues as manipulation and exploitation. People surely can't want, uhh!, things. Or, if they really do want them, they must want them for all the wrong reasons. The idea that advertising creates artificial desires rests on a profound ignorance of human nature, on the hazy feeling that there existed some halcyon era of noble savages with purely natural needs, on romantic claptrap first promulgated by Rousseau[3] and kept alive in institutions well isolated from the marketplace.

We are now closing in on why the dumbing down of American culture has occurred with such startling suddenness in the last 30 years. We are also closing in on why the big complainers about dumbing down are me and my paunchy pals. The people who want things the most and have the best chance to acquire them are the young. They are also the ones who have not yet decided which brands of objects they wish to consume. In addition, they have a surplus of two commodities, time and money, especially the former. If you can make a sale to these twentysomethings, if you can "brand" them with your product, you may have them for life. But to do this you have to be able to speak to them, and to do that you have to go to where you will be heard.

The history of mass media can be summarized in a few words: If it   15 can't carry advertising, it won't survive.

---

[2]One of the most original and influential economists, Thorstein Veblen (1857–1929) wrote some of the earliest studies of consumption and advertising; in his classic *Theory of the Leisure Class* (1899), he examined the process of "conspicuous consumption."

[3]The French philosopher and social reformer Jean Jacques Rousseau (1712–1778) is thought by many to have inspired the Romantic movement in Europe.

Responding as a Reader

1. What is the nature of Twitchell's "Adcult" (introduced in para. 2)? What are the rules and the features of this culture?

2. What is the meaning of the final sentence in paragraph 11? How much can you figure out from context? Why do you think Twitchell put it in Latin?

3. How do we pay, according to Twitchell, for the media that we consume? How, exactly, does money flow from the consumers of media to its producers?

Responding as a Writer

1. Explain Twitchell's assertion that "we are not too materialistic. We are not materialistic enough" (para. 12). What does it mean to be materialistic? How can materialism be positive?

2. Evaluate the advertisement for the Oldsmobile Intrigue that appears on page 101. How does it conform to Twitchell's observations? What value does the ad give to the product? What connection is made between the advertised product and the scene depicted? In an essay, discuss this advertisement in the context of Twitchell's article.

3. For one day, take note of all the advertising around you. Notice billboards, newspaper ads, radio ads, TV commercials, and so on. Choose one of these advertisements and explain, in an essay, how it attempts to appeal to the people who will see it. For example, you might explain why a commercial that airs during the Superbowl appeals to sports fans, or an ad on a matchbook appeals to people who go to bars, or a billboard appeals to people who drive in that part of town.

NICK GILLESPIE

View Masters: The Audience's Power over Media's Message

[REASON / February 1996]

Sad but true story: When I was in the fourth grade, some well-meaning teachers arranged a special viewing of the movie *Charly*, which had been released a few years earlier. Based on the novella *Flowers for Algernon,* the film tells the story of a mildly retarded man named Charly Gordon who, through an experimental surgical procedure, becomes a prodigious intellect. The beneficial effects, however, turn out to be temporary and Charly eventually reverts back to his original level of intelligence — tragically conscious of the enfeebling of his own mind. It's a good story, well told and well acted (Cliff Robertson won an Academy Award for the title role).

Although my teachers had no reason to believe we were a particularly mean-spirited crew to begin with, they figured, I assume, that the movie would inculcate a sense of sympathy so that we would be more sensitive to mentally impaired individuals. We walked away from the theater having learned quite a different lesson, though.

During the film, whenever Charly's co-workers (who *are* a mean-spirited crew) make a mistake, they inevitably quip, "I pulled a Charly Gordon." The day after we saw the movie, a student knocked over a display in the back of a classroom and, as the teacher began to upbraid him, he turned his palms outward and shrugged. "I pulled a Charly Gordon," he explained as the class erupted into laughter. By the end of the day, the phrase had become a ubiquitous defense for any and all manner of goof-up, mistake, or academic error. And for weeks after, kids — boys and girls, teachers' pets, and class cutups — hurled the epithet *"Charly Gordon"* as

---

NICK GILLESPIE *(b. 1963) is a senior editor of* Reason. *He has written and spoken extensively on a wide variety of cultural and public policy issues, including mass media, popular culture, immigration, criminal justice, drug legalization, and the political process. He has written a number of articles and features for the* Washington Post, *the* Los Angeles Times, *the* Utne Reader, *and the* National Review, *among others. He is an occasional book reviewer for the* Los Angeles Daily News *and is a regular contributor to* Bridge News Service. *Gillespie has taught writing and literature and received his doctorate in American Literature from the State University of New York at Buffalo.*

an all-purpose invective. Every time the teachers heard the phrase, you could see them grit their teeth and shake their heads — they had no one to blame but themselves.

Besides the self-evident truth that children like to disappoint their elders, there's a larger point to this story, one that bears on the recent and seemingly endless attempts to police popular culture: *The audience has a mind of its own.* Individuals sitting in a theater, or watching television, or listening to a CD don't always see and hear things the way they're "supposed" to.

Consider TV, for instance. "People talk at it, through it, and around it," observes Constance Penley, a professor of film and women's studies at the University of California, Santa Barbara, who has extensively studied "fan" communities. The one thing they *don't* do is merely absorb it, notes Penley, one of a growing number of scholars who stress the audience's role in constructing meaning and value in popular culture. Such media analysts say that consumers of popular culture are not that different from consumers of, say, food and clothing — that is, they are engaged, knowledgeable, discriminating, and self-interested.

That would be news to most participants in the public debate over depictions of sex and violence in movies, TV, and music. Liberals and conservatives are as tight as Beavis and Butt-head in agreeing that consumers of popular culture — the very people who make it popular — are little more than tools of the trade. Joe Sixpack and Sally Baglunch — you and I — aren't characters in this script. Just like TV sets or radios, we are dumb receivers that simply transmit whatever is broadcast to us. We do not look at movie screens; we *are* movie screens, and Hollywood merely projects morality — good, bad, or indifferent — onto us.

"We have reached the point where our popular culture threatens to undermine our character as a nation," Bob Dole thundered last summer in denouncing "nightmares of depravity" and calling for movies that promote "family values." "Bob Dole is a dope," responded actor-director Rob Reiner, a self-described liberal activist. Fair enough, but it apparently takes one to know one: "Hollywood should not be making exploitive violent and exploitive sex films. I think we have a responsibility [to viewers] not to poison their souls," continued Reiner, who rose to prominence playing the role of Meathead on *All in the Family.*

Token antagonism, then, belies fundamental agreement: Pop culture can undermine (or, implicitly, ennoble) our character; movies can poison (or save) our souls. There is no sense that the ticket-buying public might have a say in the matter, that we might be responsible for our own damnation. Indeed, one of the most striking characteristics of the continuing public discussion regarding popular culture is the eerie sense of solidarity between feuding politicians and players. Scratch the surface and everyone from Bill Clinton to Charlton Heston, Newt Gingrich to Chevy Chase,

5

Janet Reno to Sally Field, agrees: Movies, music, and TV should be the moral equivalent of a high colonic, Sunday school every damn day of the week.

This isn't to suggest that popular culture has no effect on how we think, feel, or act, that we exist somehow forever and apart from what we watch and listen to. But the interplay between pop and its audience is far more complicated than most of its critics acknowledge. It's not just that people such as Bob Dole, who admitted that he hadn't even seen the movies he criticized, and William Bennett,[1] who has most recently lambasted daytime talk shows, don't have a solid working knowledge of popular culture. Even more important, they don't understand the *experience* of interacting with pop culture, of how individuals react, respond, and revise what they see and hear.

Of course, it is hardly surprising that denizens of Washington and Tinseltown frame the debate so that all interpretive power resides with would-be government regulators and entertainment industry types. Clearly, it makes sense for them to conceptualize popular culture as a top-down affair, one best dealt with by broadcasters and bureaucrats. This consensus, however, has implications far beyond the well-worn notion that entertainment should be properly didactic.

Because it assumes that the viewer, the listener, or the audience member is a passive receiver of popular culture, this consensus must inevitably result in calls for regulation by the government (such as the V-chip, which is part of both the House and Senate telecommunications bills) or paternalism by producers ("More and more we're tending toward all-audience films . . . that have civic values in them," Motion Picture Association of America head Jack Valenti told the *Lost Angeles Times*). The viewer simply can't be trusted to handle difficult, sensitive, ironic material — or to bring his own interpretation to bear on what he sees.

Hence the focus on "context," which inevitably refers to the narrative context of a given work. Pop culture regulators assume that if sex and violence are shown within a "moral" framework, the viewer will absorb that framework and, presumably, act accordingly.

In a symposium on media violence in *Time* magazine, Sen. Bill Bradley (D-New Jersey) noted, "Violence without context and sex without attachment come into our homes too frequently in ways that we cannot control unless we are monitoring the television constantly." Bradley didn't, however, discuss the contexts and attachments *into* which shows are broadcast. This includes not only how we view TV but, for example, family structure. Now more than ever, technologies such as VCRs and remote controls

[1]William Bennett, a former secretary of education in the Reagan administration, is the author of the 1994 bestseller, *The Book of Virtues*.

allow individuals to create their own viewing contexts: We channel-surf, flicking between dozens of stations, switching between a ball game and a performance of *Oedipus Rex*. We fastforward through commercials and coming attractions, or stop the tape altogether. Simultaneously, paradoxically, we are both bombarded with more and more media signals and have more and more control over what we watch and when we watch it.

What is on the screen or on the stereo is not irrelevant, of course. But it matters far less than one might suppose. Individuals interpret and reconstruct what they see and hear the way they want to. In a classroom, interpretations can be graded as better or worse, depending on the instructor's criteria. But there is no analogous oversight in the real world and people are free to spin out their own interpretations and cross-references. *Reductio ad absurdum*[2]: Mark David Chapman read *The Catcher in the Rye* as legitimizing his murder of John Lennon. Clearly, this is not an A+ interpretation of the novel, but it is an interpretation nonetheless. And it points to a simple truth: The most relevant interpretive context is not the producer's but the consumer's.

A similar fixation on and extremely limited definition of context infuses the recently released *UCLA Television Monitoring Report*. The study, underwritten by the broadcast networks after Sen. Paul Simon (D-Illinois) threatened them with governmental action in 1993, charts "violence" in the 1994–95 TV season, including prime-time series, made-for-TV movies and miniseries, theatrical films shown on TV, on-air promotions for network shows, and Saturday morning children's programming. The authors go to great pains to distinguish between "appropriate" and "inappropriate" violence, stressing, "Context is the key to the determination of whether or not the use of violence is appropriate." In determining whether violence is objectionable, they rely on a series of questions — "Is the violence integral to the story?," "Is the violence glorified?," "Is the violence intentional or reactional?," etc. — that speaks only to authorial intentions. While such distinctions may allow for a moral (and aesthetic) judgment of a particular program, they don't speak to the viewer's experience. If a viewer, for instance, tunes into or out of a show midway through, he may have no idea of whether violence is integral to the story.

When viewers are mentioned in the UCLA study, they are typically characterized as unwitting dupes. In a discussion of "Misleading Titles," for instance, the report focuses on two made-for-TV movies, *Falling For You* and *Gramps*. *Falling For You* featured a serial killer with a taste for defenestration, while *Gramps* told the story of "an outwardly charming but psychotic grandfather" who murders his daughter-in-law and tries to kill a number of children.

15

---

[2]In an argument, *reductio ad absurdum* (Latin) is a strategy for showing that the logical conclusion of an opponent's statement would be absurd.

"Ironically, while some films with violent titles were relatively non-violent, two of the most violent television movies of the season had seriously misleading titles promising innocent family fare," says the report. "*Falling For You* and *Gramps* promised content very different from what was delivered. This is a particular problem given the fact that these shows lacked advisories. Had there been advisories, viewers would have learned that the misleadingly titled movies . . . contained intense acts of violence. Starring likable celebrities Jenny Garth and Andy Griffith and lacking advisories, these stories appear to be about falling in love and a kindly old grandfather."

One wonders what the authors would make of, say, *Of Mice and Men* ("Contrary to the title, rodents were of minimal importance to the plot, which contained a good deal of sex and violence . . . ") or *The Neverending Story* ("Oddly, the film's running time was only two hours and ten minutes . . . "). They dismiss out of hand the idea that viewers would understand, let alone enjoy, the irony inherent in titles like *Falling For You* and *Gramps*. Would it be better if *Gramps* had been called something like *My Old Man Is An Outwardly Charming But Psychotic Grandfather*? (Curiously, the authors criticize "ominous and threatening titles that imply the show will be violent," such as *Bonanza: Under Attack, Deadline for Murder, Dangerous Intentions,* and *With Hostile Intent,* even when such titles are accurate.)

The authors imply viewers lack virtually any critical faculties or knowledge independent of what program producers feed them. For starters, they assume we determine what we watch based solely — or largely, at least — on titles. In fact, that decision is based on a variety of information — promos, capsule summaries, reviews — some within industry control, some not. And when a performer steps out of character, that very fact is usually stressed in the publicity build-up as a marketing point. Similarly, although certain stars are identified with certain types of characters (Andy Griffith = Sheriff Andy Taylor = Matlock = Good Family Fun), few people respond with Pavlovian certainty to any given actor or actress's efforts — the nature of the particular product matters greatly.

The notion of TV viewers and consumers of pop culture as intellectual   20 couch potatoes closely parallels longstanding conventional scholarly analyses of how popular culture works. As with the political consensus, the intellectual indictment crosses traditional right/left boundaries. Critics usually charge that pop culture, in seeking the broadest audience possible, appeals to the lowest common denominator and thereby cheapens and coarsens society. Most critics take the argument a step further and claim that, even as pop culture gives the people what they want, it destroys consumers' critical faculties, effectively infantilizing them.

Consider, for instance, conservative Allan Bloom's commentary on rock music. In *The Closing of the American Mind* (1987), Bloom writes,

"[R]ock music has one appeal only, a barbaric appeal, to sexual desire — not love, not eros, but sexual desire undeveloped and untutored. . . . My concern here is not with the moral effects of this music — whether it leads to sex, violence, or drugs. The issue here is its effect on education, and I believe it ruins the imagination of young people and makes it very difficult for them to have a passionate relationship to the art and thought that are the substance of liberal education."

Television can lay claim to the status of most-favored punching bag and academic attacks on the small screen are representative of broader indictments of pop culture. Watching the idiot box, goes the argument, turns viewers into idiots. As their titles suggest, books such as *The Plug-In Drug, Media: The Second God, The Glass Teat* (and its sequel, *The Other Glass Teat*), and *Telegarbage* attempt to detail just how horrible and intellectually enervating the medium actually is.

Boxed In: The Culture of TV (1988), by Mark Crispin Miller, a left-leaning media critic and professor at Johns Hopkins University, provides a good example. "Those who have grown up watching television are not, because of all that gaping, now automatically adept at visual interpretation. That spectatorial 'experience' is passive, mesmeric, undiscriminating, and therefore not conducive to the refinement of the critical faculties," writes Miller.

From politicians and intellectuals alike, mass culture stands charged with and convicted of sexing us up, predisposing us toward violence, and dumbing us down.

But if we are neither robotic stooges programmed by the shows we   25
watch nor trained dogs drooling every time certain bells are rung, just how do we interact with popular culture? Not surprisingly, most regulation-minded pols and intellectual critics discuss pop in terms that mirror what they know best: A podium from which a leader or professor lectures to audiences who (they assume) pay rapt attention to every uttered pearl of wisdom. But the operative principle in popular culture (as in the best politics and teaching) is dialogue, as opposed to monologue.

Newer models of the consumption of popular culture have a lot in common with a show such as Comedy Central's *Mystery Science Theatre 3000,* in which wise-cracking characters watch B movies and provide running commentary. The characters in *MST3K* represent what's known in literary studies as "resisting readers." They don't merely soak up what they see, they actively process information, spin it to their own purposes, and critique it. The same goes for Beavis and Butt-head, the animated whipping boys of would-be censors. Even they don't watch videos the way they're "supposed" to.

Think of the choices you make — consciously — while, say, watching TV. You turn it on, you change the channels. Maybe you talk back to the screen (not quite the sign of insanity it once was). If you are with friends, you explicate what's on screen, hash out interpretations, or perhaps start talking about something completely unrelated. Maybe you call someone to discuss what you're watching. If you're on-line, you might post your comments on an appropriate bulletin board. But the point is that you react, and not always in ways the producer wants (sometimes you turn off the set altogether). In this sense, media have always been interactive.

Such critical engagement with pop culture texts is perhaps most clearly visible in the various fan "communities" that spring up around TV shows, film stars, and bands. "Fan critics pull characters and narrative issues from the margins; they focus on details that are excessive or peripheral to the primary plots but gain significance within the fans' own conceptions," writes Henry Jenkins, a professor of literature at Massachusetts Institute of Technology, in *Textual Poachers: Television Fans & Participatory Culture* (1992).

Jenkins has studied fan communities based around TV shows such as *Star Trek, Twin Peaks, Beauty and the Beast, The Avengers, Remington Steele,* and *Dr. Who.* (Although fan communities have developed around any and all manner of shows, Jenkins notes that science fiction–oriented groups seem to predominate. He chalks this up to "the utopian possibilities always embedded within" the genre; that is, science fiction explicitly attempts to create and explore new worlds and social possibilities.) Some of these groups are quite formal, holding regular meetings, circulating newsletters, and staging conventions, while others are less structured.

Central to Jenkins's "reading" of fan activity are notions of rereading and appropriation. Among other fan-generated artifacts, Jenkins describes fans who create music videos by splicing together shots from their favorite shows in new sequences and adding a soundtrack. Sometimes, the process is quite simple and humorous, as in a video that weds the song "Bad, Bad Leroy Brown" with footage from the *Star Wars* movies. Others are more ambitious: Using "Hungarian Rhapsody" for music, a video art group known as "the California Crew" created a 189-shot montage that included footage from *Remington Steele, Magnum P.I., Riptide, Moonlighting, Hunter, Simon and Simon,* and other shows. The video's "plot" is itself a sly commentary on intertextuality: The various characters assemble at the Universal Sheraton Hotel, a location at which each series had filmed, to attend a detectives convention and then try to solve the "murder" of TV producer Stephen J. Cannell (who once had a cameo on a *Magnum, P.I.* episode). "Working entirely from 'found footage,' California Crew constructs a compelling and coherent crossover," writes Jenkins.

Other fan-generated texts are decidedly more outrageous. In an essay included in *Technoculture,* a 1991 collection she coedited, Constance Penley, the UC-Santa Barbara professor, analyzed the phenomenon of *Star Trek* "K/S" or "slash" fandom. "Slash" revolves around the creation of fan-generated homosexual pornography involving the characters of Capt. Kirk and Mr. Spock. (The term *slash* refers to the slash between K and S and serves as a code to those purchasing fanzines through the mail.)

30

While slash fandom — largely made up of heterosexual women — may strike even diehard Trekkies as strange, Penley convincingly argues that the phenomenon demonstrates how people interact with popular culture "texts." Slash fans, says Penley, also use *Star Trek* as a way of creating a community of like-minded people. More important, writes Penley, "Slash fans do more than 'make do'; they make. Not only have they remade the *Star Trek* fictional universe to their own desiring ends, they have achieved it by enthusiastically mimicking the technologies of mass-market cultural production, and by constantly debating their own relation, as women, to those technologies."

Although Penley refrains from generalizing from the activity of slash fans — for one thing, they actually produce literal texts of their own — she says that "slash is suggestive of various ways people react to mass or popular culture." And, especially in light of the current debate over popular culture, says Penley, it is important to realize all viewers or consumers have "agency": They *process* what they see or hear — they do not merely lap it up. On the other hand, Penley says, "Politicians, producers, and advertisers want to believe that everything they say is accepted as intended."

MIT's Jenkins agrees that producers and regulators of popular culture share a common goal: control of an audience that is inherently beyond control. Although they obviously benefit from pleasing consumers, producers of popular culture have an ambivalent relationship with their audience, says Jenkins. That's because fans don't merely accept what they are given — they actively appropriate or reshape things to their own liking. Such activity can take any number of forms, from letter-writing campaigns, to producing "unauthorized" novels, stories, and song cycles, to recutting videotaped footage into "new" episodes. In an age where photocopying, audio sampling, videotaping, and computer technology make it ever easier for fans to cut and paste their own versions of pop culture, it is increasingly difficult for original producers to control all representations of their product, says Jenkins, who notes that *Star Trek* distributor Viacom has cracked down on fan clubs in Australia over fan-generated materials.

Moral regulators face a more daunting task. "A top-down conception 35 of culture goes back to the very roots of the concept of *culture*," says Jenkins. "Educational, intellectual, or political elites assume that the mass has no taste or culture of its own, that culture can be used by elites to refine the tastes of the mass." As a result, says Jenkins, reformers have an uneasy relationship to popular culture: They like it because it can be used to push certain types of "good" beliefs. But that also means that pop can be used to present competing messages. "For the Clintons and the Doles," says Jenkins, "it's an either/or proposition. Either movies, TV, and music teach good behavior or else they're teaching bad behavior."

But that dichotomy runs up a blind alley, says Jenkins. There is simply no way to effectively police popular culture because that would mean controlling every individual exposed to it. "Culture is something we all participate in," says Jenkins. "We're all in dialogue with the cultural materials that come out there."

The dialogue Jenkins mentions extends beyond media-related culture as well. Consider two examples that range far beyond the unholy trinity of TV, movies, and music, and that point out just as strongly the fallacy of reining in pop culture: pogs and the use of "blunt" cigars for smoking pot.

Pogs, hailed and bemoaned as "the marbles of the '90s," are colorfully decorated, silver-dollar-sized cardboard circles that kids play with. Costing anywhere from a dime up to a couple of dollars, pogs are currently a multi-million-dollar-a-year industry, complete with "official" world championships and trademark disputes galore. A number of schools across the country have banned pogs, which they blame for inciting fights, theft, student inattentiveness, and generally bad behavior.

In a game of pogs, kids stack a number of the circles and then "slam" them with a heavy plastic or metal piece, the winner keeping any pogs that have flipped over. The craze started a few years ago on Oahu, when an elementary school teacher showed her students a Depression-era game played with milk bottle caps. The current incarnation of the game gets its name from the lids of a local juice drink called POG, which stands for passion fruit-orange-guava juice. The game of pogs migrated from Hawaii to the West Coast and then headed eastward. Along the way, a California businessman bought the POG trademark and various companies started making intricately designed pogs bearing images of celebrities.

The POG phenomenon is an unpredictable mix of ground up and top-down forces, of accident and design, impossible to predict and, according to most industry observers, already in decline. Teachers can breathe easy — until the next fad shows up on the playground.

The use of "blunt" cigars, particularly the brand Phillies Blunt, is an example of pop culture appropriation. A few years ago — like many pop phenomena, the origins are hazy — teenage boys started buying blunts — cheap, medium thickness cigars — cutting them open, hollowing them out, and replacing most of the tobacco with marijuana (girls apparently enjoy Tiparillos). After the rap groups Cypress Hill and Beastie Boys started sporting Phillies Blunts T-shirts and hats in concert, wearing Phillies Blunts paraphernalia became something of a fashion statement as well.

The makers of Phillies Blunts, Hav-A-Tampa Inc., have seen sales jump, an increase largely attributed to the unintended and unauthorized use of the product. Some tobacco stores have stopped selling the brand because of its new connotations, but the trend continues. It will no doubt pass out of favor at some point, only to be replaced by another equally unforeseeable object.

As with all market-based exchanges, knowledge, value, and power in popular culture are dispersed. And reining in popular culture — or, more precisely, the meaning of a particular piece of pop culture — is like trying to nail Jell-O to the wall. It's messy, difficult, and doesn't make a whole lot of sense. Regulators and paternalists are in the difficult position of stanching the dynamic flow of culture. They can outlaw "gratuitous" violence in movies, censor inflammatory lyrics in rock and rap, plant a V-chip in every television in the country. But they will still be frustrated in their attempts to keep pop culture — and its creators — in line. In that sense, they are like Canute attempting to hold back the waves, Gatsby[3] striving to relive the past, or perhaps more appropriately, the castaways forever trying to get off *Gilligan's Island:* It just can't be done.

[3]Canute was the eleventh century Danish king of England, Denmark, and Norway; Gatsby is the mysterious and romantic gangster at the center of F. Scott Fitzgerald's 1925 novel, *The Great Gatsby.*

Responding as a Reader

1. What is the point of the Charly Gordon story, which opens the essay? How do the other examples and arguments in this essay support that point?

2. What is meant by presenting sex and violence with "a 'moral' framework" (para. 12)? Why would the head of the Motion Picture Association want to make the effort to do this? What is gained by this approach? What is lost?

3. What is going on in the fan communities that Henry Jenkins and Constance Penley study (paras. 27–33)? How are these fans different from other consumers of popular culture? How does their experience contribute to Gillespie's point?

Responding as a Writer

1. For one week, observe the behavior of television viewers. How often do they carry on conversations during a program, talk back to the TV, make fun of what's on TV, ignore the TV, flip from one channel to the next, walk away, fall asleep? Organize your findings in a small report.

2. Consider the examples of blunt cigars and pogs, in the last section of the essay. What do these examples illustrate? Can you think of other such examples? Choose one and describe the phenomenon in an essay, explaining what the example shows us about human nature.

3. "The most relevant interpretive context is not the producer's but the consumer's" (para. 14). Using evidence from this essay, other essays in

this unit, and your own experience, argue for or against this statement. You might want to compare the products of the media to other kinds of products — like sneakers or cars.

Discussing the Unit

Suggested Topic for Discussion

What is the relationship between mass media and society? Do the media simply reflect the values and conditions of society? Or do they have the power to change it, to raise or lower expectations, educate or stupefy, do real and lasting good or harm? Do consumers determine what products the media will offer? Or do the mass media shape and create their own audiences? Who are the makers of mass culture? Who has the real power in this scenario?

Preparing for Class Discussion

1. Consider all the media that are discussed in this unit — TV talk shows, radio call-in shows, local TV news, sitcoms, movies, newspapers, magazines, books, advertising of all kinds. Which of these media do you consider most powerful, most influential? Why?

2. Make a list of other factors that influence society, and the choices that people make (including family, religion, and school) — list as many factors as you can think of. Put these items in order of importance in your life. Where do media influences (including all the ads and programs you see on TV and read in the papers) fit on that list?

3. *Prewriting Assignment:* Consider one media product that is not addressed in the articles in this unit — such as soap operas, hospital dramas, game shows, sports broadcasts, or tabloids. How does this product influence society and how is it influenced by society? Make some notes and be prepared to discuss your example in class.

From Discussion to Writing

Choose one medium — television, radio, newspapers, magazines, or movies — and explain its role in society. What does this medium do for us? What doesn't it do? What should we not expect it to do? What is the most effective way for this medium to function within our day-to-day lives? What would daily life be like without it?

Alternate Tables of Contents:
Rhetorical Patterns,
Integrating Information, and
Motivations for Writing

The selections in the fifth edition of *Our Times* can be arranged in a variety of ways, depending on the instructor's or the writing program's compositional agenda. The following three organizations suggest some popular, alternative ways to introduce the topical readings. These arrangements can be easily coordinated with most composition textbooks and handbooks.

First, with its heavy emphasis on expository and argumentative writing, the collection easily covers the popular rhetorical patterns. Second, instructors who want to cover the research process will find numerous selections that demonstrate the integration of information and the use of various types of resources. And third, the collection's wide range of compositional purposes will assist those who want their students to understand some of the fundamental reasons for writing.

I. Rhetorical Patterns

NARRATION

DESCRIPTION

EXEMPLIFICATION

II. Integrating Information

FROM PERSONAL EXPERIENCE

FROM CAREFUL OBSERVATION

FROM READING AND RESEARCH

FROM INTERVIEWS

III. Motivations for Writing

The Periodicals:
Information for Subscription

A. *Magazine: Inside Asian America:* bimonthly. $2.95/issue, $15/yr. A "national consumer magazine, by, for, and about Asian Americans, covering personalities, events, and experiences that shape the Asian-American community." Subscription address: *A. Magazine,* 131 West 1st St., Duluth, MN 55802-2065; or call (800)346-0085, ext. 4077; Web site: http://www.amagazine.com.

Adbusters: Journal of the Mental Environment: quarterly. $5.75/issue, $20/yr. "A magazine that brings together artists, activists, educators, and entrepreneurs who want to build a new social activist movement of the information age." Subscription address: *Adbusters,* 1243 West 7th Ave., Vancouver, B.C., Canada, V6H 1B7; or call (800)663-1243; Web site: http://www.adbusters.org.

American Enterprise: bimonthly. $5/issue, $28/yr. "A national magazine of politics, business, and culture." Subscription address: *The American Enterprise,* P.O. Box 2014, Marion, OH 43306; or call (800)269-6267; Web site: http://www.aei.org/taesub.htm.

The Atlantic Monthly: monthly. $2.95/issue, $17.94/yr.; students ask for "educator rate," $9/9 mos., $9.95/yr. A magazine of public affairs and the arts, addressing contemporary issues through journalism, commentary, criticism, humor, fiction, and poetry. Subscription address: Atlantic Subscription Processing Center, Box 52661, Boulder, CO 80322; or call (800)234-2411; Web site: http://www.theatlantic.com.

The Baffler: quarterly. $6/issue, $20/yr. "A critical review of American culture and literature." Subscription address: *The Baffler,* P.O. Box 378293, Chicago, IL 60637; or call (773)493-0413.

The Boston Globe: daily, with Sunday edition. Rates vary according to area; New England 50¢/issue, $2/Sunday ed., $35/wk.; outside New England $45/wk. Focuses on regional and national news, with some international news; sections include metro/region, business, living arts, sports, and editorial. Subscription address: *The Boston Globe,* Subscription Dept., P.O. Box 2378, Boston, MA 02107; or call (617)929-2215; Web site: http://www.boston.com/globe.

The Boston Phoenix: weekly. $1.50/issue, $80/yr., 3rd class mail, $200/yr., 1st class mail. Features articles on the arts and politics in and around the Boston area. Subscription address: *The Boston Phoenix,* 126 Brookline Ave., Boston, MA 02215; or call (617)859-3340; Web site: http://www.bostonphoenix.com.

Buzz: 10 issues/yr. $7/issue, $15/yr. A Los Angeles general interest magazine with articles on theater and nightlife; featuring photography. Subscription address: *Buzz,* P.O. Box 56797, Boulder, CO 80322; or call (800)876-7884; Web site: http://www.buzzonline.com.

Civilization: bimonthly. $4.50/issue, $20/yr. The magazine of the Library of Congress, with articles on current events, politics, and the arts, featuring visual art and printed materials from the library's collection. Subscription address: *Civilization* Membership, P.O. Box 420235, Palm Coast, FL 32142-0235; or call (800)829-0427; Web site: http://www.loc.gov.

Commentary: monthly. $3.75/issue, $39/yr.; students, $19.95/yr. Analyses of current events in politics, social sciences, and culture. Special focus on Jewish affairs. Subscription address: *Commentary,* 165 East 56th St., New York, NY 10022; or call (800)829-6270; Web site: http://www.commentarymagazine.com.

Contraband (formerly *L'Ouverture*): quarterly. $4/issue, $12/yr. "A magazine of general fugitive thought." Features left-perspective essays and satire, as well as short stories, poetry, and art. Subscription address: *Contraband,* P.O. Box 8565, Atlanta, GA 31106; or call (404)572-9141.

The Detroit Free Press: daily, with Sunday edition. 35¢/daily, $1.50/Sunday ed. Covers Detroit regional news with national and international news. Subscription address: *The Detroit Free Press,* 615 West LaFayette St., Detroit, MI 48226; or call (800)395-3300; Web site: http://www.freep.com.

Dissent: quarterly. $7.50/issue, $22/yr.; students, $15/yr. "A journal of liberal and radical political and cultural commentary." Subscription address: *Dissent,* 521 Fifth Ave., Suite 1700, New York, NY 10017; or call (212)595-3084; Web site: http://www.igc.apc.org/dissent.

Esquire: monthly. $3/issue, $15.94/yr. Male audience; subjects include business, sports, fashion, the arts, interviews, and fiction. Subscription address: *Esquire,* P.O. Box 7146, Red Oak, IA 51591; or call (800)888-5400; Web site: http://www.esquireb2b.com.

Glamour: monthly. $2.50/issue, $16/yr.; students, $11.97/yr. Articles on fashion, makeup, lifestyle. Primarily for young women. Subscription address: *Glamour,* P.O. Box 53716, Boulder, CO 80322; or call (800)274-7410; Web site: http://www.glamour.com.

Harper's: monthly. $3.95/issue, $21/yr. Articles by prominent writers on contemporary issues, including politics, the arts, entertainment, and business. Subscription address: *Harper's,* P.O. Box 7511, Red Oak, IA 51591-0511; or call (800)444-4653; Web site: http://www.harpers.org.

Hope: bimonthly. $4.15/issue, $24.95/yr. "A broad, social issues magazine," featuring "solutions journalism," stories of human interest, articles on community activism, personal essays, book reviews. Subscription address: *Hope,* P.O. Box 52241, Boulder, CO 80322; or call (800)513-0869; Web site: http://www.hopemag.com.

Hungry Mind Review: quarterly. $3/issue, $14/yr. Features reviews of poetry, literary fiction, and literary nonfiction. Subscription address: *Hungry Mind Review,* 1648 Grand Ave., St. Paul, MN 55105; or call (612)699-2610; Web site: http://www.bookwire.com/hmr.

Life: monthly. $3.95/issue, $35/14 issues. A general interest magazine featuring photo-essays and articles. Subscription address: *Life,* Time & Life Building, Rockefeller Center, New York, NY 10020; or call (800)621-6000; Web site: http://lifemag.com.

Los Angeles Times: daily, with large Sunday edition. Rates vary according to area. Articles on current events, national and international news, arts and entertainment, business. For subscription information call (800)252-9141; Web site: http://www.latimes.com.

Los Angeles Times Magazine: Sunday supplement to the *Los Angeles Times,* a daily newspaper. Rates vary according to area. Articles and features on current events, the arts, and entertainment. For subscription information call (800)252-9141; Web site: http://www.latimes.com.

Mademoiselle: monthly. $2.50/issue, $16/yr. Young women's fashion magazine. Subscription address: *Mademoiselle,* P.O. Box 54348, Boulder, CO 80322; or call (800)274-4750; Web site: http://www.mademoiselle.com.

Might: no longer publishing, but back issues available, ranging from $6–$35/issue. "*Might* was a current events magazine of marginal culture, media criticism, and satire." For back issues, call (415)896-1528.

Mother Jones: bimonthly. $3.95/issue, $18/yr.; order online for student discount. "A publication of investigative reporting that challenges conventional wisdom, exposes abuses of power, and offers fresh solutions for positive social change." Subscription address: *Mother Jones,* P.O. Box 469024, Escondido, CA 92046; or call (800)334-8152; Web site: http://www.motherjones.com.

Ms.: bimonthly. $5.95/issue, $45/yr. Articles on feminist issues, personalities, health, and politics. Subscription address: *Ms.,* P.O. Box 5299, Harlan, IA 51537; or call (800)234-4486; Web site: http://www.womweb.com.

The Nation: weekly. $2.75/issue, $52/yr. "A liberal journal of critical opinion, committed to racial justice, anti-imperialism, civil liberties, and social equality," with commentary on politics, culture, books, and the arts. Subscription address: *The Nation,* P.O. Box 37072, Boone, IA 50037; or call (800)333-8536; Web site: http://www.thenation.com.

National Review: biweekly. $3.50/issue, $57/yr. for 25 issues; students, $21.95/yr. for 18 issues. A conservative journal of news and opinion with analyses on national and international trends in culture, economics, and politics. Subscription address: *National Review,* P.O. Box 668, Mount Morris, IL 61054; or call (815)734-1232; Web site: http://www.nationalreview.com.

The New Republic: weekly. $3.50/issue, $69.97/yr.; students and educators, $39.99/yr. A mix of liberal and conservative articles and commentary on American politics, foreign policy, literature, and the arts. Subscription address: *The New Republic,* P.O. Box 602, Mount Morris, IL 61054; or call (800)827-1289; Web site: http://www.enews.com/magazines/tnr.

Newsweek: weekly. $2.95/issue, $41.34/yr. News and commentary on the week's events in national and international affairs. Subscription address: The Newsweek Building, Livingston, NJ 07039-1666; or call (800)631-1040; Web site: http://www.politicsnow.com.

The New Yorker: weekly. $2.95/issue, $39.95/yr.; students, $19.98/yr. Current events, cartoons, criticism, biographical profiles, short fiction, and poetry. Subscription address: *The New Yorker*, Box 56447, Boulder, CO 80322; or call (800)825-2510; Web site: http://www.enews. com/magazines/new_yorker.

The New York Review of Books: biweekly. $3.50/issue, $55/yr.; students, $29.64/yr. Book reviews, essays, and current events articles by contemporary writers. Subscription address: *The New York Review of Books*, P.O. Box 420384, Palm Coast, FL 32142-0384; or call (800)829-5088; Web site: http://www.nybooks.com/nyrev.

The New York Times: daily, with large Sunday edition that contains *The New York Times Magazine* and *The New York Times Book Review*, as well as other supplements. Considered the definitive source for current events, daily, national, and international news, business, and arts reporting. Rates vary according to location and frequency of delivery. Subscription address: *The New York Times*, 229 West 43rd St., New York, NY 10036; or call (800)631-2500; Web site: http://www. nytimes.com.

People: weekly. $2.69/issue, $98.28/yr.; students, $83.38/yr. "Personality journalism." Articles on people in the news, television, and film. Subscription address: *People*, Box 61390, Tampa, FL 33661-1390; or call (800)541-9000; Web site (Time Warner's home page): http://www. pathfinder.com.

The Progressive: monthly. $3.50/issue, $30/yr.; students, $19.97/yr. "A journal of cultural and political opinion from a left/progressive perspective." Subscription address: *The Progressive*, 409 East Main St., Madison, WI 53703; or call (800)827-0555; Web site: http://www. progressive.org.

The Progressive Populist: monthly. $2/issue, $18/yr.; see Web site for special discounts. "Reports from the heartland of America on issues of interest to workers, small business owners, family farmers, and ranchers. A monthly journal of the American way." Subscription address: *The Progressive Populist*, P.O. Box 150517, Austin, TX 78715-0517; or call (800)732-4992; Web site: http://www.eden.com/~reporter.

Reason: monthly. $2.95/issue, $19.95/yr. A libertarian journal of current events, public policy, arts, and leisure. Subscription address: *Reason*, P.O. Box 526, Mount Morris, IL 61054; or call (800)998-8989; Web site: http://www.reasonmag.com.

Representations: quarterly. $9.50/issue, $36/yr.; students, $24/yr. A publication of the Regents of the University of California. An interdisciplinary journal with articles on literature, history, anthropology, and social history. Subscription address: University of California Press

Journals, 2120 Berkeley Way, #5812, Berkeley, CA 94720-5812; call (510)642-3907, or fax (510)642-9917; Web site: http://www. ucpress.berkeley.edu/journals.

Salon: daily Webzine. Available on the World Wide Web, free of charge; no print version to date. "An original content Internet magazine covering books, arts, and ideas." Articles on the media and entertainment industry, interviews with cultural personalities, daily news commentary, technology news and analysis, travel pieces, book reviews, reader forum. Information: *Salon,* 706 Mission St., Second Fl., San Francisco, CA 94103; or call (415)882-8720; Web site: http://www. salonmagazine.com.

Slate: weekly Webzine. Available on the World Wide Web free of charge; weekly print version is $70/yr. "A weekly online magazine of news, politics, and culture." Subscription address: *Slate,* 1 Microsoft Way, Redmond, WA 98052; or call (800)555-4995; Web site: http://www. slate.com.

Society: monthly, $8/issue, $54/yr.; students, $20. "The periodical of record in social science and public policy." Subscription address: *Society,* c/o Transaction Publishers, Rutgers University, 35 Berrue Circle, Piscataway, NJ 08854; or call (888)999-6778; Web site: http://www. transactionpub.com.

Technology Review: bimonthly. $3.95/issue, $21/yr.; see Web site for special discounts. A publication of the Massachusetts Institute of Technology Alumni Association. "Ideas and innovations from the world of technology." Subscription address: *Technology Review,* 201 Vassar Street, MIT, W59-200, Cambridge, MA 02139; or call (617)253-8292; Web site: http://web.mit.edu/techreview.

Tikkun: bimonthly. $6/issue, $31/yr. "A bimonthly Jewish critique of politics, culture, and society." Subscription address: *Tikkun,* 26 Fell St., San Francisco, CA 94102; or call (800)395-7753; Web site: http://members.aol.com/einsof.

Time: weekly. $2.95/issue, $51.48/yr.; students, $29.97/yr. National and international news, reporting on education, religion, law, entertainment, and the arts. Published by Time Inc., Time & Life Building, Rockefeller Center, New York, NY 10020-1393. To subscribe, call (800)843-TIME; Web site: http://www.time.com.

The Town Hall Conservative Current: daily online newspaper. $25/6 mos., $40/yr. Print version, *The Conservative Current,* available at $24/yr. "Conservative commentary and analysis of current events with an online forum for conservative opinion." Features daily articles by syndicated columnists. Subscription address: *The Town Hall Conservative Current,* 214 Massachusetts Ave., N.E., Washington, D.C. 20002; or call (800)441-4142; Web site: http://www.townhall.com.

U.S.A. Today Magazine (not affiliated with the newspaper, *U.S.A. Today*): monthly. Available only by subscription, at $225/yr. Coverage of national and international affairs, with articles on economics, business, health, science, technology, religion, education, mass media, new products, and books. Subscription address: *U.S.A. Today Magazine,* 99 West Hawthorne Avenue, Valley Stream, NY 11580; or call (516)568-9191.

U.S. News & World Report: weekly. $2.95/issue, $44.75/yr.; students, $22.50/yr. National and international news. Subscription address: *U.S. News & World Report,* P.O. Box 55929, Boulder, CO 80322; or call (800)523-5940; Web site: http://www.usnews.com.

Utne Reader: bimonthly. $4/issue, $19.97/yr. Presents articles and reviews selected from independently published newsletters, magazines, and journals. Subscription address: *Utne Reader,* P.O. Box 7460, Red Oak, IA 51591; or call (800)736-UTNE; Web site: http://www.utne.com.

Vanity Fair: monthly. $3.50/issue, $18/yr.; students, $15/yr. "Devoted to readers with an interest in contemporary society." Features include photoessays and interviews with leaders in the entertainment industry, reviews of books, film, and music. Subscription address: *Vanity Fair,* P.O. Box 53516, Boulder, CO 80322; or call (800)365-0635.

The Wall Street Journal: print edition available Monday through Friday. 75¢ issue, $175/yr.; students, $93/yr. or $34/15 wks. Interactive Edition available online at $49/yr. Articles, features, and commentary on national and international business and current events. Subscription address for print version: *The Wall Street Journal,* 84 Second Ave., Chicopee, MA 01020; or call (800)JOURNAL; Interactive Edition customer service (800)369-2834; Interactive Edition subscription address: http://www.wsj.com.

The Washington Monthly: monthly. $3.95/issue, $29.95/yr.; see Web site for discounts. Focuses on government affairs of national interest, current public affairs issues, reviews of political books. Subscription address: *The Washington Monthly,* P.O. Box 587, Mount Morris, IL 61054-7928; or call (202)462-0128; Web site: http://www.enews. com/magazines/wash_month.

The Washington Post: daily, with Sunday edition. Rates vary according to area. Covers Washington D.C. regional news, with national and international news; reporting on business, sports, travel, and lifestyles. Subscription address: *The Washington Post,* Mail Subscriptions Dept., 1150 15th St., N.W., Washington, D.C. 20071; or call (800)446-4418; Web site: http://www.washingtonpost.com.

The Washington Post National Weekly Edition: weekly. $1.95/issue, $48/yr.; students, 75¢/issue, $19.59/6 mos., $38/yr. National publication of *The Washington Post* summarizing the week's news, with additional feature articles. Subscription address: *The Washington Post National Weekly Edition,* P.O. Box 37168, Boone, IA 50036; or call (800)333-3889.

The Weekly Standard: weekly. $2.95/issue, $59.96/yr.; students, $47.96/yr. "A forum for the expression of conservative political opinion." Analyses of issues including taxes, welfare reform, crime, drugs, health care, and the national budget. Subscription address: *The Weekly Standard,* Customer Service Dept., P.O. Box 710, Radnor, PA 19088-0710; or call (800)677-8600; Web site: http://www. weeklystandard.com.

The Wilson Quarterly: quarterly. $6/issue, $24/yr. A publication of The Woodrow Wilson International Center for Scholars. A general interest magazine with essays on education, reviews of books, poetry, and periodicals. Subscription address: *The Wilson Quarterly,* P.O. Box 420235, Palm Coast, FL 32142-0235; or call (800)829-5108.

(continued from page ii)

Tim Appelo, "The Millennium Looms: Do You Know What to Call the New Century?" *Los Angeles Times Magazine,* June 23, 1996. Reprinted by permission of the author.

Cartoon: "A+", by Don Wright, *Washington Post,* February 17, 1997; originally appeared in the *Palm Beach Post.* Reprinted by permission of the artist.

Comment: "Robert Dole on English Only," from "The Debate over English Only." Used by permission of the National Education Association.

Comment: "Jesse Jackson on Civil Rights," from "Civil Rights Gone Wrong," *The Nation,* June 9, 1997. Reprinted with permission from *The Nation* magazine.

Comment: "Lamar Smith on Immigration," from "Immigration and Welfare Reform: Finally, Taxpayers Are Being Considered," *USA Today Magazine,* March 1997. Reprinted by permission of the author.

Comment: "Thomas Sowell on Gay Marriage," from "The Gay 'Marriage' Issue," *Town Hall Conservative Current,* July 18, 1996. Reprinted by permission of the author.

Comment: "David Whitman on Poor Whites," from "White-Style Urban Woes," *U.S. News & World Report,* December 9, 1996. Copyright © 1996, *U.S. News & World Report.*

Cynthia Crossen, "Blah, Blah, Blah: Is Anyone Listening?"; originally published as "Blah, Blah, Blah: The Crucial Question for These Noisy Times May Just Be: Huh?" *Wall Street Journal,* July 10, 1997. Reprinted by permission of *The Wall Street Journal.* Copyright © 1997 Dow Jones & Company, Inc. All Rights Reserved Worldwide.

Anne-Marie Cusac, "Tying the Gordian Knot," *The Progressive,* January 1997. Reprinted by permission of *The Progressive.*

Trishala Deb, "The Alien Nation: Debunking the Myth," *Contraband,* May 1997. Reprinted by permission of the author.

Document: "Linguistics Society of America (LSA) Resolution on the Oakland 'Ebonics' Issue." Unanimously adopted at the Annual Meeting of the Linguistics Society of America, Chicago, Illinois, 3 January 1997. Reprinted by permission of the Linguistics Society of America.

Document: "The Marriage Project," Reprinted by permission of the Lambda Legal Defense and Education Fund, Inc., The Marriage Project.

Document: "Human Remains Should Be Reburied," by Armand Minthorn, Confederated Tribes of the Umatilla Indian Reservation, 1997. Reprinted by permission of the author.

Richard Dooling, "Unspeakable Names," *New York Times,* September 6, 1996. Copyright ©1996 by The New York Times Co. Reprinted by permission.

M. P. Dunleavey, "'Guy' Envy," *Glamour,* May 1996. Courtesy *Glamour.* Copyright © 1996 by The Condé Nast Publications, Inc.

Jean Bethke Elshtain, "Language and American Citizens," *Dissent,* Summer 1996. Reprinted by permission of the author.

Amitai Etzioni, "Education for Intimacy," *Tikkun,* March/April 1997. Reprinted from *Tikkun Magazine,* with permission.

Exchange: "A Feminist Redefined," by Jenny McPhee, *New York Times,* March 4, 1996. Copyright © 1996 by The New York Times Co., reprinted by permission. With replies by Alex Bergier, Sarah Campbell, and Roderic Fabian, *New York Times,* March 6 and 10, 1996; reprinted by permission of the authors.

Exchange: "Susan Faludi and Karen Lehrman on Feminist Revisionism," *Slate,* www.slate.com, April 28 and May 7, 1997. Reprinted by permission. Copyright © 1997 Microsoft Corporation. Copyright © 1997 Susan Faludi.

James Fallows, "Throwing Like a Girl," *The Atlantic Monthly,* August 1996. Reprinted by permission of the author.

Stanley Fish, "When Principles Get in the Way," *New York Times,* December 26, 1996. Copyright © 1996 by The New York Times Co. Reprinted by permission.

Sunil Garg, "Under My Skin," *New York Times,* September 7, 1996. Copyright © 1996 by The New York Times Co. Reprinted by permission.

John Taylor Gatto, "Why Schools Don't Educate," *Hope,* October 1996. Reproduced by permission of the author.

Nick Gillespie, "View Masters: The Audience's Power over Media's Message," *Reason,* February 1996. Reprinted with permission from *Reason* magazine. Copyright © February 1996.

Meg Greenfield, "Back to the Future," *Newsweek,* January 27, 1997. Copyright © Meg Greenfield. Reprinted by permission of the author.

William Hamilton, "Automotivational Counseling," *Buzz,* June/July 1996. Reprinted by permission of the author.

Robin Marantz Henig, "The Price of Perfection," *Civilization,* May/June 1996. Copyright © Robin Marantz Henig. Used with permission.

In the News: "Car Ads Sell the Fantasy, Not Facts," by Stephanie Simon, *Los Angeles Times,* April 26, 1996. Copyright © 1996, *Los Angeles Times.* Reprinted by permission.

In the News: "Is Sugar and Spice in Genes of Girls?" *New York Times,* June 12, 1997. Copyright © 1997 by The New York Times Co. Reprinted by permission.

In the News: "Poll Finds Few Support Label of Multiracial," by Steven A. Holmes, *New York Times,* May 16, 1997. Copyright © 1997 by The New York Times Co. Reprinted by permission.

In the News: "The Pending Millennium," *Harper's,* August 1997. Copyright © 1997 by *Harper's.* All rights reserved. Reproduced from the August issue by special permission.

In the News: "Survey Finds '90s College Freshmen More Conservative Than Predecessors," by Someni Sengupta, *New York Times,* January 13, 1997. Copyright © by The New York Times Co. Reprinted by permission.

Ariel Kaminer, "Something Old, Something New," *Might,* March/April 1997. Reprinted by permission of the author.

Jane Holtz Kay, "Without a Car in the World," *Technology Review,* July 1997. Reprinted with permission from *MIT's Technology Review Magazine,* copyright © 1997.

Robert D. King, "Should English Be the Law?" *The Atlantic Monthly,* April 1997. Copyright © 1997 Robert D. King.

Eric Liu, "The Unbearable Being of Whiteness," *Slate,* www.slate.com, June 13, 1997. Reprinted by permission. Copyright © 1997 Microsoft Corporation.

Raymond W. Mack, "Whose Affirmative Action?" *Society,* March/April 1996. Copyright © 1996 by Transaction Publishers; all rights reserved. Reprinted by permission.

Rachel F. Moran, "Unrepresented," *Representations,* Summer 1996. Copyright © 1996 by Rachel Moran. Reprinted from *Representations,* vol. 55, Summer Issue, pp. 139–154.

Karen Narasaki, "Double Talk," *A. Magazine,* February/March 1997. Reprinted by permission.

Jill Nelson, "Talk Is Cheap," *The Nation,* June 5, 1995. Reprinted with permission from *The Nation* magazine.

Geoffrey O'Brien, "Sein of the Times," *New York Review of Books,* August 14, 1997. Copyright © 1997 Nyrev, Inc.

Oldsmobile advertisement: "Intrigue: A Sophisticated Twist on a Sports Sedan," *Life,* Fall 1997. By permission of Oldsmobile Division, General Motors Corporation.

Stephen D. O'Leary, "Heaven's Gate and the Culture of Popular Millennialism," Center for Millennial Studies, April 1997. Reprinted by permission of the author.

"An Overview of the Class of 2000," from L. J. Sax, A. W. Astin, W. S. Korn, and K. M. Mahoney, *The American Freshman: National Norms For Fall 1996.* Los Angeles: Higher Education Research Institute, UCLA. Reprinted by permission of the Higher Education Research Institute, UCLA.

Kim Phillips, "Lotteryville, USA." *The Baffler* #7, 1995. Reprinted by permission.

Douglas Preston, "The Lost Man," *The New Yorker,* June 16, 1997. Copyright © 1997 Douglas Preston. Reprinted by permission of the author.

Q & A: "Richard Landes on the Millennium," from "Countdown," *People,* June 9, 1997. As told to Tom Duffy/*People Weekly.* Copyright © 1997 Time Inc.

Q & A: "Fran Lebowitz on Money," *Vanity Fair,* July 1997. Copyright © 1997 by Fran Lebowitz. Reprinted by permission of William Morris Agency, Inc., on behalf of the author.

Q & A: "Camille Paglia on the Tyranny of Racial Categories," from "Ask Camille," *Salon,* March 1997. Reprinted by permission of the publisher and the author.

Q & A: "Ann Lauer Stoler on Race," from "Shedding Light on Race, a U-M Professor Insists That Despite What You May Think, Neatly Defining Racial Groups Is Impossible," by Kirk Cheyfitz, *Detroit Free Press,* July 7, 1996. Reprinted by permission of the *Detroit Free Press.*

William Raspberry, "To Throw in a Lot of 'Bes,' or Not?" *Washington Post National Edition,* January 6, 1997. Copyright © 1997, Washington Post Writers Group. Reprinted with permission.

Jonathan Rauch, "For Better or Worse," *The New Republic,* June 17, 1996. Copyright © 1996 Jonathan Rauch. Reprinted by permission of the author.

Richard Rodriguez, "Go North, Young Man," *Mother Jones,* August 1995. Copyright © 1995 by Richard Rodriguez. Reprinted by permission of Georges Borchardt, Inc.

Katie Roiphe, "The Independent Woman (and Other Lies)," *Esquire,* February 1997. Reprinted by permission of International Creative Management, Inc. Copyright © Katie Roiphe.

Peter Salins, "Assimilation, American Style," *Reason,* February 1997. Reprinted with permission from *Reason* magazine. Copyright © February 1997.

"Selected 1996 Survey Results," from L. J. Sax, A. W. Astin, W. S. Korn, and K. M. Mahoney, *The American Freshman: National Norms For Fall 1996.* Los Angeles: Higher Education Research Institute, UCLA. Reprinted by permission of the Higher Education Research Institute, UCLA.

Leslie Marmon Silko, "In the Combat Zone," *Hungry Mind Review,* Fall 1995. Copyright © 1995 Leslie Marmon Silko, reprinted with the permission of the Wylie Agency, Inc.

Jennifer Silver, "Caught with a Centerfold," *Mademoiselle,* January 1997. Courtesy *Mademoiselle.* Copyright © 1997 by The Condé Nast Publications, Inc.

Christina Hoff Sommers, "The 'Fragile American Girl' Myth," *The American Enterprise,* May/June 1997. Reprinted by permission of the author and the publisher.

Speech: "Ed Fallon on Same-Sex Marriage," from a speech to the Iowa House of Representatives, February 20, 1996. Used by permission of Iowa Representative Ed Fallon from 70th District in Des Moines.

Speech: "John J. Sweeney on Working Americans," from "Time for a New Contract" [excerpted from a speech given at the Columbia University Teach-In with the Labor Movement, October 3, 1996], *Dissent,* Summer 1996. Reprinted by permission of John J. Sweeney.

Steven D. Stark, "Local News: The Biggest Scandal on TV," *The Washington Monthly,* June 1997. Reprinted with permission of *The Washington Monthly.* Copyright © by The Washington Monthly Company.

"Student Information Form," (Higher Education Research Institute), from L. J. Sax, A. W. Astin, W. S. Korn, and K. M. Mahoney, *The American Freshman: National Norms For Fall 1996.* Los Angeles: Higher Education Research Institute, UCLA. Reprinted by permission of the Higher Education Research Institute, UCLA.

Deborah Tannen, "I'm Sorry, I Won't Apologize," *New York Times Magazine,* July 21, 1996. Copyright © 1996 Deborah Tannen. Portions of this article appear in the author's book *Talking from 9 to 5: Women and Men in the Workplace: Language, Sex and Power* (Avon, 1995). Reprinted by permission.

Garry Trudeau, "My Inner Shrimp," *New York Times Magazine,* March 31, 1997. Copyright © 1996 by The New York Times Co. Reprinted by permission.

James B. Twitchell, "But First, a Word from Our Sponsors," *The Wilson Quarterly,* Summer 1996. Reprinted by permission of the author.

U.S. English advertisement: "Why an Immigrant Heads an Organization Called U.S. English." Copyright © 1997 by U.S. English.

Richard Weissbourd, "The Feel-Good Trap," *The New Republic,* August 19 and 26, 1996. Reprinted by permission of *The New Republic.*

U.S. Senator Paul Wellstone, "The Unfinished Agenda: Race, Poverty, and Gender in America," *The Progressive Populist,* March 1997. Reprinted by permission of Senator Wellstone.

Jack E. White, "I'm Just Who I Am," *Time,* May 5, 1997. Copyright © 1997 Time Inc. Reprinted by permission.

Patricia J. Williams, "Hate Radio," *Ms.,* March/April 1994. Reprinted by permission of *Ms.* Magazine. Copyright © 1994.

James Q. Wilson, "Cars and Their Enemies," *Commentary,* July 1997. Reprinted by permission; all rights reserved.

William Julius Wilson, "Work," *New York Times Magazine,* August 18, 1996. Copyright © 1996 by The New York Times Co. Reprinted by permission.

Index of Authors and Titles